P9-BVH-377

OBSESSIVE–COMPULSIVE DISORDER

Obsessive–Compulsive Disorder

Theory, Research, and Treatment

EDITED BY

Richard P. Swinson
Martin M. Antony
S. Rachman
Margaret A. Richter

THE GUILFORD PRESS
New York   London

© 1998 The Guilford Press
A Division of Guilford Publications, Inc.
72 Spring Street, New York, NY 10012
http://www.guilford.com

Printed in the United States of America

This book is printed on acid-free paper.

Last digit is print number: 9 8 7 6 5 4 3 2 1

Library of Congress Cataloging-in-Publication Data

Obsessive-compulsive disorder : theory, research, and treatment /
    edited by Richard P. Swinson . . . [et al.].
        p.   cm.
    Includes bibliographical references and index.
    ISBN 1-57230-335-2 (hard cover : alk. paper)
    1. Obsessive-compulsive disorder.   I. Swinson, Richard P.
    [DNLM: 1. Obsessive-Compulsive Disorder.   WM 176 01457 1998]
RC533.0274   1998
616.85'227—dc21
DNLM/DLC
for Library of Congress   98-14388
                                                             CIP

ABOUT THE EDITORS

Richard P. Swinson, MD, is Professor and Chair of the Department of Psychiatry, Faculty of Health Sciences, McMaster University. He is also Professor in the Department of Psychiatry at the University of Toronto, and Psychiatrist in Chief at St. Joseph's Hospital and Hamilton Psychiatric Hospital in Hamilton, Ontario. Previously, he held several appointments at the Clarke Institute of Psychiatry, including Vice President Medical Affairs, Chief of Medical Staff, and Head of the Anxiety Disorders Clinic. Dr. Swinson is currently Chair of the Examination Board in Psychiatry for the Royal College of Physicians and Surgeons in Canada. He has published approximately 200 scientific papers, book chapters, and reports, mostly on anxiety disorders and related conditions. In addition, he was a member of the DSM-IV subcommittees for obsessive–compulsive disorder and for panic disorder and agoraphobia.

Martin M. Antony, PhD, is Chief Psychologist and Director of the Centre for the Study of Anxiety at St. Joseph's Hospital in Hamilton, Ontario. He is also on faculty in the Department of Psychiatry at McMaster University. Previously, Dr. Antony was Assistant Professor in the Department of Psychiatry, University of Toronto, and staff psychologist in the Anxiety Disorders Clinic, Clarke Institute of Psychiatry. He received his Ph.D. in clinical psychology from the State University of New York at Albany in 1994 and completed his predoctoral internship training at the University of Mississippi Medical Center in Jackson. Dr. Antony has written several books, including *Mastery of Your Specific Phobia* (and the accompanying therapist manual) with Drs. Michelle G. Craske and David H. Barlow, as well as numerous research papers and book chapters in the areas of obsessive–compulsive disorder, panic disorder, social phobia, and specific phobias. He is actively involved in clinical research in the area of anxiety disorders, teaching and education, and maintains a clinical practice.

94744

S. Rachman, PhD, is currently Professor of Psychology at the University of British Columbia in Vancouver, British Columbia, and was formerly Professor of Abnormal Psychology at the Institute of Psychiatry, University of London. He is an active clinician and researcher and has published extensively on the subjects of fear, anxiety, anxiety disorders, and obsessive–compulsive disorder. He has written or edited more than 15 books and monographs and many additional journal articles and book chapters. In 1980, along with R. Hodgson, Dr. Rachman published *Obsessions and Compulsions.* In 1992, he published a guide for patients and their families called *Obsessive Compulsive Disorders* with P. de Silva. His book, *Fear and Courage,* was published in a second edition in 1990. Dr. Rachman received a Distinguished Scientist Award from the American Psychological Association (Division 12) in 1984 and was made a fellow of the Royal Society of Canada in 1989.

Margaret A. Richter, MD, received her M.D. from the University of Ottawa and completed her psychiatric training at the University of Toronto. She was named the *Mary Early Fellow* by the Canadian Psychiatric Research Foundation from 1990–1992 for her work on the familial nature of OCD. Currently, she is Assistant Professor in the Department of Psychiatry, University of Toronto, and Staff Psychiatrist in the Anxiety Disorders Clinic, Clarke Institute of Psychiatry. She continues to be actively involved as a clinician and researcher in the area of OCD, particularly with respect to the genetic basis of OCD and the relationship between OCD and spectrum disorders.

CONTRIBUTORS

Martin M. Antony, PhD, Department of Psychology, St. Joseph's Hospital and Department of Psychiatry, McMaster University, Hamilton, Ontario, Canada

Patricia M. Averill, PhD, Department of Psychiatry and Behavioral Sciences, University of Texas Health Sciences Center at Houston, Houston, Texas

Elizabeth A. Billett, BSc, Neurogenetics Section, Clarke Institute of Psychiatry, Toronto, Ontario, Canada

Donald W. Black, MD, Department of Psychiatry, University of Iowa College of Medicine, Iowa City, Iowa

Timothy A. Brown, PsyD, Center for Anxiety and Related Disorders, Boston University, Boston, Massachusetts

Miriam Chopra, BA, Division of Psychiatry, Chaim Sheba Medical Center, Tel-Hashomer, Israel

Jean Cottraux, MD, Anxiety Disorder Unit, Department of Psychiatry, Hôpital Neurologique and University Lyon, Lyon, France

Fiona Downie, BA, Department of Counseling Psychology, Ontario Institute for Studies in Education, University of Toronto, Toronto, Canada

Edna B. Foa, PhD, Center for the Treatment and Study of Anxiety, Department of Psychiatry, Allegheny University of the Health Sciences, Philadelphia, Pennsylvania

Martin E. Franklin, PhD, Center for the Treatment and Study of Anxiety, Department of Psychiatry, Allegheny University of the Health Sciences, Philadelphia, Pennsylvania

Daniel Gérard, MD, Centre d'Exploration et de Recherche Médicales par Emissions de Positrons (CERMEP), Hôpital Neurologique, Lyon, France

Toby Goldsmith, MD, Biological Psychiatry Program, University of Cincinnati College of Medicine, Cincinnati, Ohio

Raz Gross, MD, Division of Psychiatry, Chaim Sheba Medical Center and Tel Aviv University, Sackler School of Medicine, Tel-Hashomer, Israel

Susan A. Gunn, RN, MSN, Buffalo General Hospital, Community Mental Health Center, Buffalo, New York

Veronika Huta, BSc, Department of Psychology, McGill University, Montreal, Quebec, Canada

James L. Kennedy, MD, PhD, Neurogenetics Section, Clarke Institute of Psychiatry and Department of Psychiatry, University of Toronto, Toronto, Ontario, Canada

Michael J. Kozak, PhD, Center for the Treatment and Study of Anxiety, Department of Psychiatry, Allegheny University of the Health Sciences, Philadelphia, Pennsylvania

Henrietta L. Leonard, MD, Brown University Programs in Child Psychiatry and Rhode Island Hospital, Providence, Rhode Island

John S. March, MD, MPH, Program in Child and Adolescent Anxiety Disorders, Departments of Psychiatry and Psychology: Social and Health Sciences, Duke University Medical Center, Durham, North Carolina

Susan L. McElroy, MD, Biological Psychiatry Program, University of Cincinnati College of Medicine, Cincinnati, Ohio

Carlos N. Pato, MD, Department of Psychiatry, University of Buffalo, State University of New York, Buffalo, New York

Michele T. Pato, MD, Department of Psychiatry, University of Buffalo, State University of New York, Buffalo, New York

Katharine A. Phillips, MD, Butler Hospital and the Department of Psychiatry and Human Behavior, Brown University School of Medicine, Providence, Rhode Island

Teresa A. Pigott, MD, Department of Psychiatry and Behavioral Sciences, Department of Pharmacology and Toxicology, University of Texas Medical Branch, Galveston, Texas

Nina A. Pruyn, MSW, Boston University School of Social Work, Boston, Massachusetts

S. Rachman, PhD, Department of Psychology, University of British Columbia, Vancouver, British Columbia, Canada

Margaret A. Richter, MD, Anxiety Disorders Clinic, Clarke Institute of Psychiatry and Department of Psychiatry, University of Toronto, Toronto, Ontario, Canada

Karen Rowa, BA, Department of Psychology, Simon Fraser University, Burnaby, British Columbia, Canada

Paul M. Salkovskis, PhD, University of Oxford, Department of Psychiatry and Warneford Hospital, Oxford, England

Yehuda Sasson, MD, Division of Psychiatry, Chaim Sheba Medical Center and Tel Aviv University, Sackler School of Medicine, Tel-Hashomer, Israel

Sheila Seay, MA, University Psychiatric Center, Houston, Texas

Roz Shafran, PhD, Department of Psychology, University of British Columbia, Vancouver, British Columbia, Canada

Nathan A. Shapira, MD, Biological Psychiatry Program, University of Cincinnati College of Medicine, Cincinnati, Ohio

Melinda A. Stanley, PhD, Department of Psychiatry and Behavioral Sciences, University of Texas Health Sciences Center at Houston, Houston, Texas

Gail Steketee, PhD, Boston University School of Social Work, Boston, Massachusetts

Laura J. Summerfeldt, MA, Anxiety Disorders Clinic, Clarke Institute of Psychiatry, Toronto, Ontario, Canada

Richard P. Swinson, MD, Department of Psychiatry, McMaster University, Hamilton, Ontario, Canada

Steven Taylor, PhD, Department of Psychiatry, University of British Columbia, Vancouver, British Columbia, Canada

Anton J. L. M. van Balkom, MD, PhD, Department of Psychiatry and Institute for Research in Extramural Medicine, Vrije Universiteit Amsterdam, and Outpatient Clinic for Anxiety Disorders, Psychiatric Centre Amsterdam, The Netherlands

Richard van Dyck, MD, PhD, Department of Psychiatry and Institute for Research in Extramural Medicine, Vrije Universiteit Amsterdam, and Outpatient Clinic for Anxiety Disorders, Psychiatric Centre Amsterdam, The Netherlands

Joseph Zohar, MD, Division of Psychiatry, Chaim Sheba Medical Center and Tel Aviv University, Sackler School of Medicine, Tel-Hashomer, Israel

PREFACE

Most people experience occasional intrusive thoughts or engage in repetitive compulsive rituals from time to time (Rachman & De Silva, 1978; Salkovskis & Harrison, 1984). However, for the majority of individuals, intrusive thoughts and compulsive behaviors do not pose a significant problem. In contrast, people suffering from obsessive–compulsive disorder (OCD) have obsessions and compulsions that are of an intensity and frequency sufficient enough to cause serious distress and interference across many life domains (Antony, Roth, Swinson, Huta, & Devins, 1998). In fact, individuals with severe OCD are among the most impaired of all anxiety disorder patients, often reporting chronic underemployment, relationship problems, and difficulty completing simple day-to-day tasks that most people take for granted.

Although OCD has been recognized by mental health practitioners for some time, psychodynamically oriented writings dominated the literature on OCD for many years, despite the lack of empirical support for viewing OCD from this perspective. For a long time, OCD was seen as a treatment refractory condition. In the past few years, we have seen great advances in the area of OCD and its treatment. Investigators have now established that OCD is a multifaceted problem, involving factors from areas as diverse as genetics, serotonin function, neuroanatomical functioning, family variables, learning experiences, and cognition. In addition, a variety of treatments including behavior therapy and pharmacotherapy have been shown to reduce obsessions and compulsions in the majority of individuals who are treated by these methods.

This volume is organized into four main sections. The first section consists of chapters addressing theory and research on OCD, from both psychological and biological perspectives. Antony, Downie, and Swinson discuss diagnostic issues and review the literature pertaining to demographics and epidemiology. Salkovskis presents his cognitive model of OCD and contrasts it with other cognitive and behavioral views. Rachman and Shafran review the literature on cognitive and behavioral features of OCD including research on information processing in OCD and their own work on "thought-action fusion." Summerfeldt, Huta, and Swinson provide an in-depth review of the role of personality in OCD and the relationship between OCD and personality disorders. Steketee and Pruyn provide a detailed chapter on the role of the family for people suffering from OCD. Gross, Sasson, Chopra, and Zohar review studies pertaining to the serotonin hypothesis of OCD, from their own research center and from other research centers around the world. Cottraux and Gérard provide a detailed summary of research on structural and functional imaging in OCD and provide a new model, based on their research, suggesting that, for some people, OCD may be related to what they have termed "perceived impulsivity." Billett, Richter, and Kennedy discuss the literature on the role of genetics in OCD including a summary of some of their own new, still unpublished findings. Finally, Brown discusses the relationship between OCD and the other anxiety disorders.

The second section covers topics related to the assessment and treatment of OCD. Taylor provides a critical review of the most commonly used self-report, interview, and behavioral assessments for OCD. In addition to providing a thorough review of the literature, this chapter also contains helpful practical suggestions for the clinician. Foa, Franklin, and Kozak discuss the latest developments in the literature on psychosocial treatments of OCD. In a chapter written primarily for professionals working with OCD patients, Stanley and Averill discuss practical issues in treating OCD using behavior therapy. Pigott and Seay review the literature on biological treatments of OCD, including serotonin reuptake inhibitors, pharmacotherapy augmenting strategies, and psychosurgery. Pato, Pato, and Gunn provide an overview of the practical aspects of providing biological treatment, including how to choose among medications and issues related to side effects. This chapter also includes case histories illustrating the use of pharmacotherapy with patients suffering from OCD. Van Balkom and van Dyck review the literature and provide practical suggestions regarding the treatment of OCD by combining cognitive-behavioral and pharmacological interventions. Finally, March and Leonard provide a detailed overview of OCD in children and adolescents, including the nature, assessment, and treatment of the disorder in young people.

The final section of this volume contains two chapters on disorders often considered to be part of the OCD spectrum, including trichotillomania and impulse control disorders, Tourette's disorder and other tic disorders, somatoform disorders, and eating disorders. Goldsmith, Shapira, Phillips, and McElroy review the conceptual foundations and research literature pertaining to the OCD spectrum. Black complements this with his chapter on the assessment and treatment of disorders in the OCD spectrum.

We have also included an appendix at the back of the book, including resources on OCD and OCD spectrum disorders that might be helpful for clinicians and their patients. These include lists of organizations that deal with OCD, self-help books, academically oriented books, treatment manuals, and resources on the internet.

We would like to thank the authors of each chapter for their contributions as well as the staff at Guilford Press for their support and hard work throughout the process of putting together this book. Finally, we would like to thank Andrea Liss, Shitij Kapur, and Laura Rocca for providing comments and assisting with the editorial process for several of the chapters.

RICHARD P. SWINSON
MARTIN M. ANTONY
S. RACHMAN
MARGARET A. RICHTER

REFERENCES

Antony, M. M., Roth, D., Swinson, R. P., Huta, V., & Devins, G. M. (1998). Illness intrusiveness in individuals with panic disorder, obsessive compulsive disorder, or social phobia. *Journal of Nervous and Mental Disease, 186,* 193–197.

Rachman, S., & De Silva, P. (1978). Abnormal and normal obsessions. *Behaviour Research and Therapy, 16,* 233–248.

Salkovskis, P.M., & Harrison, J. (1984). Abnormal and normal obsessions: A replication. *Behaviour Research and Therapy, 22,* 549–552.

CONTENTS

OBSESSIVE–COMPULSIVE DISORDER

Part I

PSYCHOPATHOLOGY AND THEORETICAL PERSPECTIVES

Chapter 1

DIAGNOSTIC ISSUES AND EPIDEMIOLOGY IN OBSESSIVE–COMPULSIVE DISORDER

Martin M. Antony
Fiona Downie
Richard P. Swinson

Obsessive–compulsive disorder (OCD) is an anxiety disorder characterized by intrusive and distressing thoughts, urges, and images as well as repetitive behaviors aimed at decreasing the discomfort caused by these obsessive thoughts. Although clinicians have long been interested in the features of OCD, knowledge stemming from OCD has increased exponentially over the past two decades. This chapter provides an overview of the nature of OCD in adults, including definitions of relevant term(s), diagnostic criteria, reviews of comorbid conditions, epidemiology, and demographics. A review of OCD in children is provided in Chapter 16 of this volume.

Where relevant, we provide recent findings from our own database at the Anxiety Disorders Clinic of the Clarke Institute of Psychiatry in Toronto. All patients in our database were diagnosed using the Structured Clinical Interview for DSM-IV (SCID-IV; First, Spitzer, Gibbon, & Williams, 1996). Patients who currently met DSM-IV criteria for substance abuse or dependence, bipolar disorder, or a psychotic disorder were excluded from our database. For some variables, we compare findings for OCD patients ($n = 87$) to those for individuals with other anxiety disorders, including panic disorder with or without agoraphobia (PD; $n = 88$), social phobia ($n = 98$), and specific phobia ($n = 20$).

DEFINITIONS

In DSM-IV (American Psychiatric Association, 1994), the hallmark of OCD is the presence of obsessions or compulsions. Obsessions are defined as persistent thoughts, impulses, or images that occur repeatedly and are experienced as intrusive, inappropriate, and distressing. Common examples include fears of contamination, doubts about one's actions, and aggressive impulses. Because obsessions are anxiety provoking, individuals with OCD attempt to ignore or suppress the obsessions or to neutralize them with another thought or action (i.e., a compulsion). According to DSM-IV, obsessions are not simply worries about real-life problems. In addition, individuals with OCD recognize that their obsessions are products of their own mind.

Compulsions are repetitive behaviors (e.g., washing, cleaning, repeating actions) or mental acts (e.g., thinking certain words, counting, checking) that an individual feels compelled to perform in response to an obsession or according to certain rigid rules (e.g., having to complete tasks in a particular order). Although compulsions are carried out to reduce discomfort or to prevent some dreaded event, they are clearly excessive or are unconnected in a realistic way to the event they are aimed to prevent.

To meet criteria for OCD, an individual must recognize *at some point* during the course of the disturbance that the obsessions or compulsions are excessive or unreasonable. Individuals with OCD who do not view their symptoms as excessive most of the time are said to have OCD *with poor insight*. This distinction is similar to the definition for "overvalued ideation" in the DSM-III-R criteria for OCD (American Psychiatric Association, 1987). As with the other anxiety disorders, the OCD criteria require that symptoms cause significant distress or functional impairment, are not better accounted for by another Axis I disorder, and are not due to a substance or general medical condition.

DIAGNOSTIC CONSIDERATIONS

In DSM-IV, OCD is included with the anxiety disorders, where it has been categorized since publication of DSM-III. The relationship between obsessional thoughts and compulsive actions is explicitly seen as being related to behavioral (motor or cognitive) responses to the anxiety created by the recurrent and persistent thoughts, which are in turn described as causing marked anxiety or distress. In ICD-10, OCD is categorized separately from the anxiety disorders in keeping with long-established European views (Montgomery, 1992). The essential element of OCD from this viewpoint is the occurrence of a repetitive thought or act, recognized as pathological by the sufferer, but accompanied by a sense of compulsion and an inability to resist (Freeman, 1992). Lewis (1936) drew attention to the distinction between focusing on the disorder of affect and the disorder of formal thought that has been present in the debates about the essential nature of OCD since the writings of St. Ignatius of Loyola.

Whether OCD is considered to be primarily an anxiety disorder or not, the major features of the condition are essentially the same—the presence of repeated, unwanted thoughts, images or impulses, and the feeling of compulsion to carry out repetitive acts in response to the obsessions. In addition, some people with OCD experience a drive to carry out actions perfectly—sometimes in a repetitive manner and sometimes only once, but very carefully and very slowly.

In addition to the primary symptoms of OCD, there are commonly other affective symptoms of fear, anxiety, chronic worry, and depression. The secondary effects of OCD can be marked if the disorder occupies many hours of activity each day. At times, anger and irritability are prominent and may seriously affect relationships and family functioning. Also, individuals with OCD may make extreme demands on others (e.g., for conformity to the patient's needs for cleanliness). Persons may be unable to prepare food, to attend to their hygiene, to leave the house, or to change their clothes.

The diagnosis of OCD is usually fairly straightforward provided that the interviewer is careful to ask for the appropriate information. However, the range of possible differential diagnoses is extensive. For example, there is now growing recognition of symptom overlap between OCD and a variety of disorders, including tic disorders (e.g., Tourette's disorder), impulse control disorders (e.g., trichotillomania), somatoform disorders (e.g., body dysmorphic disorder), and eating disorders (e.g., bulimia nervosa). Collectively, these disorders have come to be known as the OCD spectrum disorders (see Chapters 17 and 18 of this volume for a review). It is important to distinguish between OCD, other anxiety disorders, and OCD spectrum disorders). In addition, when the patients symptoms appear to fit more than one diagnostic category, the clinician must decide whether to focus on differential diagnosis (deciding between two or more diagnoses) or to assign two or more comorbid diagnoses.

Organic conditions (categorized in DSM-IV as "anxiety disorders due to general medical condition) that affect the basal ganglia may present with repetitive, compulsive activity. We recently saw a 64-year-old man who had no history of OCD or perfectionism, who developed checking compulsions, without prominent anxiety, after he developed multivascular occlusive phenomena including transient ischemic attacks, coronary artery occlusion, and sudden-onset impotence of vascular origin. Interestingly, he responded well to behavior therapy including exposure and response prevention. Substance-induced anxiety disorders causing repetitive behaviors may be a consideration, particularly if stimulant use such as cocaine or amphetamine precede the onset of the compulsive behaviors. Usually, these syndromes resolve when the substance use is discontinued.

Major depression may present with obsessional ruminations and minor checking rituals. A clear history of the onset of the apparent OCD in the setting of a mood change may be sufficient to rule out the diagnosis of OCD, particularly if the onset is later in life and if the condition resolves completely when the depression recovers. A woman in her 50s from our clinic, who suffers from recurrent major depressive episodes, is able to predict the onset of the next episode because she develops checking rituals regarding changing money a few weeks before the mood change is obvious. As her mood improves, the rituals and the worry resolve completely.

Generalized anxiety disorder (GAD) is similar to OCD in that it is often associated with prominent ruminations, anxiety, a lack of control over worry, and sometimes checking rituals (usually related to safety or illness). In contrast to individuals with OCD, people suffering from GAD typically experience worries about more ordinary life circumstances, including finances, work, and minor matters. However, for certain types of worries (e.g., health-related fears), the boundaries can be more blurred. Also, when repetitive behaviors are present in GAD, they are frequently cognitive and usually do not involve the common OCD rituals of washing, checking, or counting. Despite overlap in the features of OCD and GAD, these disorders typically do not occur together and are usually easy to distinguish from one another (see Chapter 9 in this volume for a review).

Hypochondriacal fears may be prominent in OCD and cause people to check for signs of ill health frequently. A 32-year-old nurse developed fears that she might develop breast cancer after two friends developed the disease. In order to be sure that she was not developing cancer, she would examine her breasts each morning and night then ask her physician husband to check her daily. She was not reassured by the frequent reassurance seeking at the time she presented for treatment, and she also engaged in a number of other rituals, including checking her underwear at least hourly for signs of discharge from her nipples, checking her 8-year-old daughter's underwear each day, washing to remove contamination from germs, and moving back and forth from one floor surface to another as a ritual to protect others in her extended family from developing illness.

Delusional disorder and psychotic disorder not otherwise specified each may share features with OCD. The question of what degree of insight must be maintained for the diagnosis of OCD to be made has been the subject of much research. Foa and Kozak (1995) examined the strength of obsessive belief in 431 patients as part of the DSM-IV field trial. Of the total sample, 250 subjects had primary obsessions involving fear of some potential consequence. Only 13% were assessed as being certain that their feared consequence would *not* (original emphasis) occur; 30% were either mostly certain or completely certain that it would not occur. In addition, clinicians rated 8% as currently not having insight into their beliefs and 5% as never having had insight.

A 29-year-old man who had had classical contamination fears, together with washing rituals, developed the idea that sunlight would possibly harm him even when he was inside the house, and that shaking hands with someone would harm him by crushing his bones. Although he had insight into the excessive nature of the contamination fears, he was utterly convinced that the newly arising ideas were reasonable. He refused to leave the house unless covered totally (particularly in bright, hot weather) and would not sit where he could see a window, so that his eyes would not be damaged. In order to protect his bones, he refused to shake hands with anyone or to attempt to lift heavy objects. Although he had initially done well in treatment with exposure plus ritual prevention and selective serotonin reuptake inhibitors, he refused further treatment and was lost to follow-up.

Many behaviors that are repetitive and excessive are not compulsive or driven by obsessional ideas. The rituals seen in eating disorders, the repetitions in pervasive developmental delay, and the uncontrollable urges in gambling or sexual sadism are not considered part of OCD. These issues are considered in Chapters 17 and 18 of this volume.

OCD SYMPTOMS AND SUBTYPES

Although there appear to be distinct dimensions in OCD, it should be noted that most patients report multiple symptoms that cut across dimensions. For example, individuals who are concerned about contamination will often wash a particular number of times or check their surroundings for contaminants. Rasmussen and Tsuang (1986) reported on the prevalence of particular types of obsessions and compulsions in 44 individuals diagnosed with OCD. In their sample, 59% of patients reported more than one type of obsession, and 41% reported more than one type of ritual. Only 4.5% of individuals had obsessions in the absence of compulsions. The percentage of patients with compulsions in the absence of obsessions was 2.0%. The most common obsessions reported in this group were related to contamination (55%), aggressive thoughts (50%), need for symmetry or exactness (36%), somatic fears (34%), and sexual thoughts (32%). Eighty-three percent of those with contamination obsessions also engaged in cleaning rituals, whereas 82% of those with aggressive obsessions (e.g., thoughts of hurting one's baby) engaged in checking rituals. The most common compulsive rituals were checking (80%), cleaning (46%), and counting (21%). Findings were similar in a larger study ($n = 200$) reviewed by the same group of investigators (Rasmussen & Eisen, 1992).

Using a sample of 182 individuals with OCD from our own clinic, Summerfeldt, Antony, Downie, Richter, and Swinson (1997) examined the prevalence of various obsessions and compulsions based on the symptom checklist from the Yale–Brown Obsessive–Compulsive Scale (YBOCS; Goodman et al., 1989a, 1989b). These findings are summarized in Table 1.1.

Although the prevalence of these various obsessions and compulsions varies from study to study, most investigators have tended to accept the symptoms listed on the YBOCS as representing the main OCD symptom types. The distinction between washers and checkers (Rachman & Hodgson, 1980) in particular has been supported in several studies (Khanna & Mukherjee, 1992; Steketee, Grayson, & Foa, 1985). Furthermore, although studies using factor and cluster analyses of OCD symptoms have yielded inconsistent results overall, one consistent finding is the tendency for washing and checking be categorized on different dimensions (Khanna, Kaliaperumal, & Channabasavanna, 1990; van Oppen, Hoekstra, & Emmelkamp, 1995).

TABLE 1.1. Current Symptoms as Reported
by 182 Patients with OCD on the YBOCS
Symptom Checklist

Symptom	n^a	% of sample
Obsessions		
Aggressive	125	68.7
Contamination	105	57.7
Symmetry/exactness	97	53.2
Somatic	62	34.1
Hoarding/saving	55	30.2
Religious	44	24.2
Sexual	36	19.8
Miscellaneous	101	55.5
Compulsions		
Checking	147	80.7
Washing	116	63.7
Repeating	101	55.5
Ordering/arranging	73	40.1
Counting	64	35.2
Hoarding	51	28.0
Miscellaneous	108	59.3

Note. YBOCS, Yale–Brown Obsessive–Compulsive Scale. From
Summerfeldt, Antony, Downie, Richter, & Swinson (1997).
[a]This represents the total number of individuals reporting at least
one current symptom from this category.

The largest factor-analytic study of OCD symptoms to data was reported
by Leckman et al. (1997). The relationship among 13 categories used to group
symptoms in the YBOCS was examined in two independent samples ($n = 208$,
$n = 98$). Both samples yielded exactly the same four symptom factors: (1) obsessions and checking—including aggressive obsessions, sexual obsessions, religious
obsessions, somatic obsessions, and checking compulsions, (2) symmetry and ordering—including obsessions of symmetry, (3) cleanliness and washing—including contamination obsessions and cleaning compulsions, and (4) hoarding—including hoarding obsessions. These four factors accounted for more than 60% of
the variance in each data set.

PATTERNS OF SYNDROME AND
SYMPTOM COMORBIDITY

Although several studies have examined comorbidity among OCD and other diagnostic categories, we could find no published studies that were based on DSM-
IV criteria. However, from our own clinic, we present recent data on the frequency of various current additional diagnoses among 87 individuals with a DSM-IV

principal diagnosis of OCD. In this data set, the principal diagnosis was the disorder causing the most distress or functional impairment. Additional diagnoses were those that were clinically significant but judged to be of a lesser severity than the principal diagnosis. All participants were patients presenting for assessment and treatment in the Anxiety Disorders Clinic at the Clarke Institute of Psychiatry in Toronto. Patients were excluded if there was evidence that they met current diagnostic criteria for substance abuse/dependence or a psychotic disorder. All diagnoses were based on the SCID-IV (First et al., 1995).

Nearly 36% of 87 OCD patients from our clinic met criteria for OCD only, whereas 28.7% of patients met criteria for one additional diagnosis, 17.2% met criteria for two additional diagnoses, and 18.4% met criteria for three or more diagnoses. The most common additional diagnosis was social phobia, for which 41.4% of patients currently met criteria. For the other diagnostic categories examined, percentages of patients meeting diagnostic criteria were 24.1% for major depressive disorder, 20.7% for specific phobia, 13.8% for dysthymic disorder, 11.5% for PD, 11.5% for GAD, 8.0% for tic disorder, and 4.6% for trichotillomania. No patients met current criteria for posttraumatic stress disorder or agoraphobia without a history of panic disorder.

We also examined the frequency of OCD additional diagnoses among individuals with principal diagnoses of PD ($n = 88$), social phobia ($n = 98$), and specific phobia ($n = 20$). The percentages of these patients that met criteria for OCD as an additional diagnosis were 5.6% for PD, 6.1% for social phobia, and 0% for specific phobia. In summary, we found that OCD was more likely to be the principal diagnoses when it co-occurred with other anxiety disorders.

The findings from our sample confirm findings from previous studies (based primarily on DSM-III-R diagnostic criteria), suggesting that OCD is often associated with various other conditions. In a large sample of patients with OCD ($n = 391$), Yaryura-Tobias et al. (1996) found that 42.2% of individuals had at least one other DSM-III-R condition. The most common comorbid diagnoses were major mood disorder (29.1%), specific phobia (27.9%), substance dependence (14.5%), schizophrenia (11%), body dysmorphic disorder (9.7%), hypochondriasis (9.7%), Tourette's disorder (7.2%), anorexia nervosa (7.2%), social phobia (5.5%), impulse control disorder (5.5%), agoraphobia (4.8%), and attention-deficit/hyperactivity disorder (ADHD; 4.8%). Whereas ADHD, Tourette's disorder, impulse control disorder, social phobia, and anorexia nervosa tended to have earlier onsets than OCD among individuals with comorbid conditions, specific phobias, schizophrenia, agoraphobia, substance dependence, hypochondriasis, and major mood disorders tended to begin after the OCD in patients who had OCD and one or more of these conditions.

Sanderson, Di Nardo, Rapee, and Barlow (1990) found that 10 out of 12 patients with OCD had one or more additional DSM-III-R diagnoses, the most common of which were major depression (4 individuals), dysthymia (4 individuals), and simple phobia (3 individuals). One person received an additional diagnosis of PD and another met criteria for social phobia. In a larger study from the same center ($n = 25$ OCD patients), Moras, Di Nardo, Brown, and Barlow

(1994), found that 56% of OCD patients met criteria for at least one additional diagnosis, and the mean number of additional diagnoses was one. The most common additional diagnoses included dysthymia (28%), social phobia (24%), major depressive disorder (12%), PD (12%), GAD (4%), and simple phobia (4%). For both of these studies, diagnoses were determined by the Anxiety Disorders Interview Schedule—Revised (Di Nardo & Barlow, 1988).

In a study of lifetime comorbidity in 108 patients with OCD (Crino & Andrews, 1996), rates of co-occurrence were considerably higher for most disorders compared to previous studies. Rates of comorbidity were higher in OCD than for other anxiety disorders, and OCD occurred relatively infrequently as an additional diagnosis when another disorder was the principal diagnosis. Eighty-six percent of patients met DSM-III-R criteria for more than one additional diagnosis, the most common of which were PD (54%), major depressive disorder (50%), social phobia (42%), GAD (31%), and dysthymia (19%). These findings were similar to those reported in another study from the same group (Hunt & Andrews, 1995), showing higher rates of comorbidity than in previous studies. The elevated rates of comorbidity observed in these two studies are most likely related to the examination of comorbidity for lifetime diagnoses, which are generally more prevalent than current diagnoses. Additionally, diagnoses were based on a self-administered, computerized structured interview (C-DIS, CIDI Auto V1.0), which has been shown in other research to overdiagnose disorders by a factor of two, compared to a clinician-administered structured interview (Ross, Swinson, Larkin, & Doumani, 1994).

One consistent finding across most studies is that OCD commonly co-occurs with a mood disorder. Bellodi, Sciuto, Diaferia, Ronchi, and Smeraldi (1992) found that among the 35.9% of OCD patients who also met criteria for a mood disorder, only 15% reported that the depression predated the OCD, suggesting that the depression may have occurred in response to the OCD. Demal, Lenz, Mayrhofer, Zapotoczky, and Zitterl (1993) found that 79% of OCD patients had clinical levels of depression (based on a clinician-administered severity measure). Of the patients who were depressed, the depression began first in 36% of individuals, the OCD began first in 47% of individuals, and both conditions began concurrently for the remaining 17% of individuals. According to a study by Ricciardi and McNally (1995), presence of comorbid depression seems to be related to more severe obsessions but is not related to the severity of compulsive behaviors.

Several additional studies have examined the relationship between OCD symptoms and specific psychological problems. With respect to eating disorders, most studies have shown a consistent relationship between eating disorders symptoms and OCD. Thiel, Broocks, Ohlmeier, Jacoby, and Schüssler (1995) found that 37% of patients with anorexia nervosa or bulimia nervosa also met criteria for OCD. Similarly, Schwalberg, Barlow, Alger, and Howard (1992) found that 15% of bulimic individuals had a lifetime diagnosis of OCD. OCD diagnoses were assigned in 5% of individuals (or fewer) for each other group (social phobia,

PD, obese binge eaters). In a group of 62 OCD patients, 12.9% met criteria for an eating disorder.

Panic disorder is also associated with OCD symptoms in about 27% of cases (Mellman & Uhde, 1987), and the presence of OCD symptoms in this group appears to be related to poorer outcome, earlier age of onset, and increased comorbidity with depression and substance abuse. Interestingly, behavioral treatment of agoraphobia appears to decrease OCD symptoms in PD patients with obsessions or compulsive behaviors (Fava, Zielezny, Luria, & Canestrari, 1988).

Studies have also shown that OCD symptoms are sometimes associated with alcohol/substance abuse (Eisen & Rasmussen, 1989; Fals-Stewart & Angarano, 1994; Riemann, McNally, & Cox, 1992), hypochondriacal concerns (Savron et al., 1996), mental retardation (Vitiello, Spreat, & Behar, 1989), schizophrenia (Berman, Kalinowski, Berman, Lengua, & Green, 1995), and GAD (Schut, Castonguay, Plummer, & Borkovec, 1995). Among patients with GAD, compulsive checking appears to be more prevalent than obsessional symptoms (Schut et al., 1995).

PREVALENCE OF OCD

The true prevalence of OCD has been a source of controversy in the literature. Until the 1980s, OCD was believed to be an extremely rare disorder, with community prevalence estimates as low as 0.05% (Rudin, 1953). Even in psychiatric populations, OCD was diagnosed infrequently. For example, Coryell (1981) reported the prevalence of OCD among psychiatric inpatients to be 0.5%. More recently, findings from clinical samples, as well as community samples, have begun to challenge the assumption that OCD is a rare disorder.

In our own Anxiety Disorders Clinic, 24.3% of 304 anxiety disorder patients who completed our clinic evaluation (including a semistructured diagnostic interview) between 1995 and 1996 received a principal DSM-IV diagnosis of OCD. Among those who received a different principal diagnosis, 3.6% met criteria for OCD as an additional diagnosis. The fact that our clinic has a reputation in the community for treating OCD (few other specialty clinics exist in the Toronto area) may be partially responsible for the high frequency of this diagnosis in our sample. However, these data are also consistent with the hypothesis that OCD is more common than previously believed.

With respect to occurrence in the general population, six major studies have recently examined the prevalence of OCD in adult community samples, all using DSM-III diagnostic criteria (American Psychiatric Association, 1980). To date, the largest epidemiological study that included questions about OCD is the Epidemiologic Catchment Area (ECA) Study (Regier et al., 1988; Robins et al., 1984). In this study, about 20,000 adults from five locations across the United States (New Haven, Baltimore, St. Louis, Durham, Los Angeles) were assessed by trained lay interviewers. The lifetime prevalence (ignoring the hierarchical exclusion criteria in DSM-III) for OCD was 2.5%. Prevalence rates for 2 weeks, 1 month, 6 months, and 1 year were 1.2%, 1.3%, 1.5%, and 1.6%, respectively (Karno & Golding, 1991; Karno, Golding, Sorenson, & Burnam, 1988). These findings were confirmed in the Munich Follow-Up Study (MFS; Wittchen, 1988), in which a community sample from Munich, Germany, was interviewed. In the MFS, the 6-month and lifetime prevalence of OCD were 1.79% and 2.03%, respectively. In both the ECA and MFS studies, diagnoses were determined by the Diagnostic Interview Schedule (DIS), a structured interview designed to be administered by lay interviewers.

In Canada, Bland and colleagues (Bland, Orn, & Newman, 1988; Kolada, Bland, & Newman, 1994) studied the prevalence of major DSM-III disorders in a sample of 3,258 individuals living in Edmonton. Six-month and lifetime prevalence estimates, based on DIS interviews, were similar to those in the ECA and MFS studies, at 1.6% and 2.9%, respectively.

Henderson and Pollard (1988) examined the point prevalence of OCD in a sample of 497 individuals from St. Louis. Unlike previous studies, interviews were conducted by lay interviewers over the telephone. In addition, this study used a different diagnostic instrument (Anxiety Symptom Interview) than did other studies. OCD symptoms were categorized into three groups: (1) washing, (2) checking, and (3) repeating/counting/collecting. Overall, the prevalence of OCD was 2.8%. Prevalence estimates for each of the three subtypes were 0.8% for washing, 1.6% for checking, and 1.0% for repeating/counting/collecting.

Finally, two studies found relatively low prevalence rates for OCD in community samples. Faravelli, Degl'Innocenti, and Giardinelli (1989) interviewed 1,110 individuals living in Florence, Italy. Interviews were conducted by general practitioners and psychiatric residents. Overall, the lifetime and point prevalence estimates for OCD were 0.72% and 0.63%, respectively. Although these estimates are lower than those in other studies, this study found relatively low estimates of prevalence for other DSM-III anxiety disorders as well. Nestadt, Samuels, Romanoski, Folstein, and McHugh (1994) used the Standard Psychiatric Examination to interview 810 adults in Baltimore. Only 0.3% met diagnostic criteria for OCD, although 1.5% of the sample reported having obsessions and/or compulsions.

A Critical Analysis of OCD Prevalence Studies

The tendency for several OCD prevalence estimates to be relatively high has led many investigators to conclude that OCD is far more common than previously believed. Assuming that early data reflected underestimates of the true prevalence of OCD, investigators have speculated about why this might be the case. Rasmussen and Eisen (1990) suggested three possible reasons: (1) Clinicians have tended not to ask appropriate screening questions for OCD, focusing instead on the associated symptoms of depression or anxiety; (2) individuals with OCD are reluctant to talk about their symptoms, because they might be seen as crazy or bizarre; and (3) OCD symptoms are often difficult to differentiate from symptoms of related disorders, such as impulse control problems, depressive ruminations, and somatoform disorders.

Unfortunately, there is little data available to assess the validity of these post hoc explanations. It is possible that earlier prevalence estimates are lower than more recent estimates because clinicians are now more likely to ask about OCD symptoms than in the past. This possibility warrants investigation. However, it is unlikely that the other two hypotheses can account for the recent increase in prevalence estimates. Presumably, if OCD symptoms were once difficult to distinguish from other disorders, and difficult for patients to discuss, this would still be the case. In other words, although it is possible that past estimates of OCD prevalence are too low, it is equally possible that recent OCD prevalence rates are an overestimation of the true frequency with which OCD occurs.

Recently, researchers have provided documentation to support the observation that OCD is diagnosed more frequently today than in past years. In a review of hospital charts from 1969 to 1990, Stoll, Tohen, and Baldessarini (1992) found that the relative frequency of OCD discharge diagnoses rose dramatically, especially in the 1980s. This rise in OCD was highly correlated with a relative increase in publications on the treatment of OCD. The authors concluded that the recent increase in prevalence seen for OCD may reflect a bias of clinicians to more readily consider diagnostic categories for which innovative and effective treatments exist. Ricciardi (1993) added that there is an increased public awareness of the disorder due to frequent coverage in the media, outreach by such organizations as the Obsessive–Compulsive Foundation, and a relative increase in available treatments. He suggests that the increased awareness of OCD may have led to higher rates of self-diagnosis and self-referral for treatment.

Overall, it appears that OCD may in fact be diagnosed more frequently in recent years than in the past. However, there is still reason to question the high prevalence rates in some of the most influential studies published recently. Of the studies reviewed earlier, those in which diagnoses were determined by lay interviewers based on the DIS (i.e., ECA study, MFS study, Edmonton study) or the Anxiety Symptom Interview (Henderson & Pollard, 1988) have tended to find higher prevalence estimates than studies based other diagnostic instruments, administered by clinicians (e.g., Faravelli et al. 1989; Nestadt et al., 1994). The utility of the DIS for estimating the prevalence of other conditions (e.g., panic disorder, agoraphobia) has been questioned in recent years (McNally, 1994, pp. 26–42). Furthermore, there is reason to believe that the DIS (1) leads to overdiagnosis of anxiety disorders and (2) is neither a reliable nor valid method of diagnosing OCD.

With respect to the issue of overdiagnosis, Ross et al. (1994) found that a computerized version of the DIS overdiagnosed psychiatric disorders by a factor of two, compared to a clinician-administered semistructured interview. Although this tendency to overdiagnose may be limited to the computerized DIS and not applicable to the interviewer-administered DIS, it is also possible that this is not the case. The DIS is a *structured* interview, in which questions are administered in a particular way and responses are recorded exactly as they are spoken. Administration of the DIS does not permit the interviewer to ask additional questions to clarify information provided by the interviewee. In contrast, *semistructured* interviews such as the SCID-IV (First et al., 1996) allow the clinician to ask for clarifying information after the required questions have been asked. Although other explanations can explain these data, the findings from by Ross et al. (1994) are consistent with the possibility that structured interviews lead to more false positives than clinician-administered, semistructured interviews.

More troubling for DIS estimates of OCD prevalence is a recent report by Nelson and Rice (1997) on the 1-year stability of OCD lifetime diagnoses in the ECA study. In the ECA study, a subset of participants was reassessed as part of a second wave of interviews, 12 months after the initial assessment. Excluding data from the New Haven site due to methodological differences (at this site, questions regarding occurrence of symptoms *at any time in the past* were replaced with questions regarding symptom occurrence *since the last interview*), stability of OCD diagnoses across the remaining four sites (as reflected by the kappa statistic) ranged from 0.16 in Durham to 0.25 in Los Angeles. These very low stability estimates suggest that the DIS is neither a reliable nor valid method of determining a diagnosis of OCD. In fact, of the 291 patients who met criteria for OCD at Time 1, only 19.2% reported at Time 2 that they experienced symptoms meeting criteria for OCD *at any time in their life*. Diagnoses were especially unstable for older and less-educated participants. Because most estimates of OCD prevalence have been based on the DIS, Nelson and Rice conclude that the true prevalence of OCD remains unknown. The Nelson and Rice study confirms earlier findings that the DIS, when administered by lay interviewers, has a bias to overdiagnose OCD, compared to interviews by trained psychiatrists (Helzer et al., 1985).

In another study to question the validity of the ECA prevalence estimates for OCD, Stein, Forde, Anderson, and Walker (1997) examined the prevalence of DSM-IV OCD in a survey of 2,261 adults in four regions of Canada. Assessments were based on structured interviews (a modified version of the Comprehensive International Diagnostic Interview) conducted over the telephone by lay interviewers. Using this method, the 1-month prevalence rate of OCD was 3.1%. However, when participants were reinterviewed by trained clinicians using the SCID-IV, the 1-month prevalence estimate dropped to 0.6%. The most common reasons for the overdiagnosis of OCD by the lay interviewers were (1) a tendency to mislabel "worries" as obsessions, and (2) a tendency to overestimate the degree of distress and impairment related to the OCD symptoms.

Taken together, these findings suggest that OCD is probably not as prevalent as has been reported in recent years. Discrepancies across studies are likely due to differences in diagnostic instruments and interviewer expertise, although they could be due to other variables as well (e.g., differences in sampling methods, interviewer biases). Furthermore, with the exception of the Stein et al. (1997) study, the most recent prevalence estimates for OCD are all based on data collected in the 1970s and early 1980s, all based on DSM-III criteria. Despite the fact that several recent epidemiological studies have used DSM-III-R criteria (e.g., Kessler et al., 1994), they have tended not to include data on OCD. Clearly, new epidemiological data for OCD are needed, based on the most recent diagnostic criteria.

Obsessions and Compulsions in Nonclinical Samples

It appears that most of us engage in obsessive thinking and compulsive rituals at one time or another. As many as 80% of people in nonclinical groups experience unpleasant intrusions that are similar in content to clinical obsessions, although these normal obsessions are experienced less frequently, less intensely, and for a shorter duration relative to those in clinical OCD patients (Rachman & De Silva, 1978; Salkovskis & Harrison, 1984). With respect to compulsions, about 55% of people in nonclinical groups report engaging in compulsive rituals (Muris, Merckelbach, & Clavan, 1997). As with obsessions, compulsions in nonclinical groups tend to be less frequent, less distressing, less intense, and are not resisted as intensely, compared to those in OCD patients. However, the content of compulsive rituals appears to be similar in clinical and nonclinical groups (Muris et al., 1997).

DEMOGRAPHIC FEATURES OF OCD

Gender and Prevalence

FREQUENCY OF PARTICULAR OCD SYMPTOMS

A number of studies have examined gender differences in the prevalence rates for particular types of obsessions and compulsions (Castle, Deale, & Marks, 1995; Hanna, 1995; Khanna & Mukherjee, 1992; Lensi et al., 1996; Noshirvani, Kasvikis, Marks, Tsakiris, & Monteiro, 1991). Overall, there appears to be a great deal of symptom overlap for men and women, with a few exceptions. Lensi et al. (1996) found that men, compared to women, reported more sexual obsessions (27% vs. 12.7%), obsessions concerning symmetry and exactness (28.6% vs. 8%), and more odd rituals (34.8% vs. 22.1%). Women reported more aggressive obsessions (26.2% vs. 15.3%) and cleaning rituals (59.6% vs. 43.7%) than did men. The finding that women are more likely to engage in washing and cleaning rituals than men is supported by other research as well (Castle et al., 1995; Drummond, 1993; Khanna & Mukherjee, 1992; Noshirvani et al., 1991; Rachman & Hodgson, 1980). Given the findings that men tend to experience more sexual obsessions and women display more washing and cleaning rituals, some authors have suggested that the content and clinical expression of OCD symptoms may be influenced by sociocultural factors (Lensi et al., 1996; Khanna & Mukherjee, 1992).

GENDER AND THE PREVALENCE OF OCD

A summary of findings on sex and prevalence from several major *epidemiological studies* is presented in Table 1.2. As shown in Table 1.2, there is a tendency across studies for OCD to be slightly more prevalent among women than men in most studies, although some estimates fail to show differences. In the ECA study (Karno et al., 1988), sex differences were no longer significant when other demographic variables (e.g., employment status) were controlled statistically. Several studies did not provide prevalence estimates separately for males and females and therefore were not included in Table 1.2. Among these studies not included, Faravelli et al. (1989) reported a 1:1 ratio for the prevalence of OCD among men and women. Similarly, Nestadt et al. (1994) reported that obsessions and compulsions were equally common among men and women in their sample, although they did not report data on the relationship between sex and the prevalence of OCD. The tendency for OCD to be more prevalent among women than men, or equally common across the sexes, has been replicated across a number of different countries (see section on Geographical Location). In a study by Weissman et al. (1994), the female–male ratio varied across sites from 0.8 in Munich to 3.8 in Germany.

In most studies of *clinical samples*, the ratio of females to males is approximately equal, at least among adult patients. In a review of 11 studies of obsessional neurosis, Black (1974) concluded that of a total of 1,386 inpatients and outpatients with OCD, 51.4% were female. Similarly, Rasmussen and Eisen (1992) reported that of 560 patients meeting DSM-III-R criteria for OCD, 53.8% were female. However, in our own clinical sample of patients meeting DSM-IV criteria for OCD, 46.0% were female. In our sample, the sex ratio for OCD was similar to that for social phobia but significantly different than those for PD or specific phobia, which tended to be primarily female.

Our findings regarding sex ratio in OCD are similar to findings for children and adolescents, which tend to show a higher percentage of males in clinical samples (Rapoport, 1989). However, epidemiological studies of children and

TABLE 1.2. Sex and the Prevalence of OCD in Selected Epidemiological Studies

Study	Type of estimate	Prevalence estimates (%)	
		Females	Males
ECA (Karno, Golding, Sorenson, & Burnam, 1988)	Lifetime prevalence	2.9	2.0
ECA (Regier et al., 1988)	1-month prevalence	1.5	1.1
Henderson & Pollard (1988)	Point prevalence	3.2	2.4
Kolada, Bland, & Newman (1994)	Lifetime prevalence	3.1	2.8
	6-month prevalence	1.6	1.6

Note. ECA, Epidemiologic Catchment Area study.

adolescents have yielded mixed findings, and sex differences tend to be small, when they are present. For example, Flament et al. (1988) found that 55% of high school students with OCD are male. In contrast, Douglass, Moffitt, Dar, McGee, and Silva (1995) found that the majority of 18-year-olds with OCD are female (59.5%). Finally, in a study of 12- to 14-year-old students, Valleni-Basile et al. (1994) found that the prevalence of OCD in males and females is equal. Although studies provide mixed findings on this issue, the extent to which OCD is more common in male children than female children may be related to the relatively consistent finding that OCD begins earlier in males than females, as reviewed later in this chapter.

Ethnicity

In our Anxiety Disorders Clinic, 83.5% of individuals with a principal diagnosis of OCD described themselves as white, 3.5% as Hispanic, 3.5% as Asian, 1.2% as black, none as Native Canadian, and 8.2% as "other." These percentages did not differ significantly from those of other diagnostic categories (e.g., PD, social phobia, specific phobia).

In epidemiological samples, there appear to be consistent differences in the prevalence of OCD in different ethnic groups. In a community sample of 810 individuals in Baltimore, Nestadt et al. (1994) found the prevalence of obsessions and compulsions (not necessarily of clinical severity) to be 2.1% among whites and 0.5% among nonwhites. These findings were consistent with those in the ECA study (Karno et al., 1988; Karno & Golding, 1991), indicating that OCD tends to be relatively rare in Hispanic and African American individuals relative to Caucasian individuals.

Although researchers have recently begun to study the nature and prevalence of anxiety disorders across ethnic groups (e.g., Karno et al., 1989; Neal & Turner, 1991), relatively little is known about the impact of ethnicity on the expression of OCD. More studies are needed to better understand the ways in which ethnic diversity relates to the types of obsessions and compulsions expressed, as well as the usefulness of established assessment and treatment methods in ethnically diverse groups.

Religious Background

In our own clinic sample, OCD patients did not differ from patients with PD, social phobia, or specific phobia with respect to religious background. Of the OCD patients who provided data on religion, 30.1% were Roman Catholic, 24.1% were Protestant, 18.1% were Jewish, 3.6% were Muslim, 1.2% were Buddhist, 1.2% were Hindu, and 21.7% were of another religion. This finding is consistent with previous studies showing that the religious backgrounds of people with OCD are not significantly different from those of other anxiety disorder patients or individuals in the general population (Raphael, Rani, Bale, & Drummond, 1996; Rasmussen & Eisen, 1992; Steketee, Grayson, & Foa, 1987).

However, there is reason to believe that religion may play a role in the severity and content of OCD symptoms for some individuals. It appears that OCD patients are more likely to identify themselves as being affiliated with a religious group than are other psychiatric outpatients (Raphael et al., 1996). Although OCD patients tend not to be more religious than people with other anxiety disorders, OCD severity (but not mood) is correlated with religiosity within OCD patients (Steketee, Quay, & White, 1991). Furthermore, the content of OCD symptoms is more likely to be related to religion in individuals with OCD who are more religious (Greenberg & Witztum, 1994; Steketee et al., 1991). In fact, studies of OCD patients who live in countries where conservative religious upbringings predominate, such as Saudi Arabia (Mahgoub & Abdel-Hafeiz, 1991) and Egypt (Okasha, Saad, Khalil, Seif El Dawla, & Yehia, 1994), have found that religious themes dominate the content of obsessions and compulsions. In other studies, religiosity is correlated with guilt in people with OCD, but not people with other anxiety disorders (Steketee et al., 1991). In addition, OCD patients tend to report more religious conflict, relative to PD patients, and people with other (nonanxiety) psychiatric disorders (Higgins, Pollard, & Merkel, 1992).

Geographic Location

Weissman et al. (1994) reported on the 1-year and lifetime prevalence of OCD (based on DSM-III criteria, diagnosed using the DIS) in community samples in seven different locations across the world (United States, Edmonton, Puerto Rico, Munich, Taiwan, Korea, and New Zealand). At all sites, except Taiwan, lifetime prevalence estimates for OCD were similar (ranging from 1.9% to 2.5%), as were 1-year prevalence estimates (ranging from 1.1% to 1.8%). In contrast, OCD was diagnosed infrequently in Taiwan, where the lifetime and 1-year prevalence estimates were 0.7% and 0.4% respectively. Prevalence estimates for other psychiatric disorders were also lower in Taiwan than in other sites.

Blazer and colleagues (Blazer et al., 1985; George, Hughes, & Blazer, 1986) examined differences in the prevalence of OCD and other disorders among individuals living in urban versus rural settings. Findings were based on 3,648 adults living in the Piedmont region of North Carolina, who participated in the ECA study. Overall, the prevalence of OCD was similar in rural (2.07%) and urban (2.00%) settings. However, within certain age groups, significant differences between urban and rural settings emerged. Among individuals between the ages of 18 and 24, OCD was significantly more prevalent in urban households (5.03%) than rural households (0.95%). This pattern was reversed for individuals over 65 years old, for which OCD was significantly more prevalent in rural homes (2.62%) than urban homes (0.24%). For individuals between ages 25 and 64, differences in prevalence for urban and rural settings were not significant. Among African Americans, individuals living in a rural setting (2.37%) were more likely to be diagnosed with OCD than those living in an urban setting (0.86%). For Caucasians, geographic setting did not affect prevalence rates. Also, neither sex nor education level were predictive of geographical differences in the prevalence of OCD.

In a related study, Henderson and Pollard (1988) found that OCD was more prevalent among those living in the city than those living outside the city. Effects of the interaction between geographic location and other variables on OCD prevalence were not reported in this study.

Education, Employment Status, and Income

Epidemiological data from the ECA study suggest that the lifetime prevalence of OCD differs depending on the level of education, although the pattern of findings is difficult to interpret. Karno and Golding (1991) reported that the prevalence of OCD among people who completed some high school was 3.4%, whereas among those who graduated from high school, the prevalence was 1.9%. For college/university education, the pattern was reversed, such that the prevalence of OCD among those with some college education and those who graduated from college was 2.4% and 3.1%, respectively.

In our Anxiety Disorders Clinic sample, the proportion of OCD patients who completed high school was 90.7%. College/university was completed by 53.5% of individuals, and 10.4% completed a graduate degree. Education level did not differ among patients with OCD, PD, social phobia, and specific phobia.

Data regarding employment status and income are inconsistent. In the ECA study (Karno et al., 1988; Karno & Golding, 1991), there was no relationship between OCD and current unemployment, although OCD was more common among "underemployed" individuals (i.e., individuals who had been out of work for at least 6 months of the last 5 years). This finding was not unique to OCD, however, as a range of other psychiatric disorders were also associated with underemployment. In the ECA study, there was no relationship between income and OCD.

The pattern of findings in clinical samples is mixed. Steketee et al. (1987) compared a sample of OCD patients to a group of patients with a variety of other anxiety disorders. Whereas 68.3% of the individuals in the anxiety disorder group were currently employed, only 30.7% of the OCD patients were employed. In addition, a higher percentage of people in the OCD group (24%) were receiving welfare or family support, relative to the mixed anxiety disorder group (10%). Income was significantly lower in the OCD group than in the comparison group. In contrast, in our own clinic patients, we found no significant income differences among patients with OCD, PD, social phobia, and specific phobia.

Marital Status

Eighty-seven individuals with OCD from our clinic provided information regarding marital status. Fifty-four percent reported being single, whereas 41% were married (or cohabiting), and 4.6% were separated, divorced, or widowed. Although group differences were not significant, OCD patients were less likely to be single than social phobia patients (60.2%), and more likely to be single than individuals with PD (39.1%) and individuals with specific phobias (25%). Previously, Steketee et al. (1987) found that individuals with OCD and other anxiety disorders do not differ significantly with respect to marital status.

Data from epidemiological samples have shown a relationship between OCD and marital status, but, unfortunately, findings have been contradictory. Two studies suggest that OCD is more common among separated and divorced individuals than among people who are married or have never married (Bland et al., 1988; Karno et al., 1988). In contrast, Nestadt et al. (1994) found that obsessions and compulsions (not necessarily of clinical severity) were about twice as prevalent among people who are married or widowed than among people who are single or separated/divorced.

A fairly consistent finding is that females with OCD are more likely than males to be married or in stable cohabitation (Castle et al., 1995; Noshirvani et al., 1991) and to have children (Noshirvani et al., 1991). As reviewed later in this chapter, OCD tends to begin earlier in males than females, which may account for these gender differences. In addition, society may be more accepting of women having an anxiety disorder, compared to men, which might lead to greater social impairment (e.g., tendency not to marry) for men than women.

OCD in the Elderly

Although a great deal of research has been conducted on obsessive compulsive disorder (OCD), very little is known about this disorder in the elderly (Calamari, Faber, Hitsman, & Poppe, 1994; Jenike, 1991; Richardson & Bell, 1989). Only recently has research begun to focus on the occurrence and nature of OCD in older groups. For example, Jenike (1991) reported that until very recently this topic was rarely included in textbooks of geriatric psychiatric disorders. Furthermore, much more attention has been given to depression or dementia in the elderly than anxiety disorders in general (Flint, 1994).

Once thought to be uncommon among older people (Myers, Weissman, & Tischler, 1984), recent research has suggested that OCD may be as common among the elderly as in younger groups (Calamari et al., 1994; Flint, 1994). Studies examining the 6-month prevalence rate of the population over 65 years of age have ranged from 0.2% to 2.5% (Bland et al., 1988; Kolada et al., 1994), with lifetime rates for individuals 60 years or older ranging from 1.9% to 3.3% (Calamari et al., 1994). In the ECA study (Regier et al., 1988), the 1-month prevalence rate for OCD in individuals 65 years of age or older was 0.7% for men and 0.9% for women. In a Canadian epidemiological sample (Bland et al., 1988), the 6-month prevalence rates for OCD were 3.4% for individuals 45–54 years of age, 1.4% for individuals 55–64 years of age, and 2.5% for those age 65 years and older. This was somewhat higher then the findings reported by Copeland et al. (1987), which reported a 1-month prevalence of 1.7% for individuals in Liverpool and 0.7% for New York.

A number of studies have noted that the rate of OCD tends to decline somewhat as individuals age (Brickman & Eisdorfer, 1989; Regier et al., 1988). In a study of 6-month prevalence rates, Brickman and Eisdorfer (1989) reported that OCD occurred in 2.2% of those younger than 64 and in 1.3% of individuals between the ages of 65 and 74 years. In the oldest group (75 years or older), less than 1% reported OCD. Two other studies have noted that the rate of OCD tends to decline somewhat among individuals over age 65, while remaining consistent for the younger groups (e.g., middle-aged individuals) (Bland et al., 1988; Kramer, German, Anthony, Von Korff, & Skinner, 1985).

The reason for this decrease is not entirely clear. One possibility may be related to the increased likelihood of institutionalization, particularly for those with age-related physical health problems (Bland et al., 1988). To date, very few studies have examined the rates of OCD in institutionalized elderly samples. Karno et al. (1991) noted that in the ECA study, institutionalized individuals (e.g., people living in prisons, psychiatric hospitals, etc.) had prevalence rates of OCD three times higher than individuals living in households (4.9% vs. 1.6%), although this finding was not specifically related to the elderly. Furthermore, Bland et al. (1988) reported that OCD was more prevalent in institutionalized elderly women and men compared to their cohort in the community.

Brickman and Eisdorfer (1989) suggested that the decrease in OCD in the elderly may be due to the existence of a differential mortality rate for those with psychiatric conditions. Specifically, the association between chronic stress, anxiety, and cardiovascular disease may lead to earlier mortality than for individuals who have not suffered from any anxiety disorders. Finally, a third explanation for decreased prevalence rates in the elderly is related to the possibility of a cohort effect, whereby people currently being studied in elderly samples might actually have lower lifetime rates of OCD than individuals born more recently (Brickman & Eisdorfer, 1989).

There have been a number of difficulties with research related to the elderly. Studies have found that the elderly infrequently seek help for mental health problems and many have avoided psychiatric care for many years (Shapiro et al., 1984; Speer, Williams, West, & Dupree, 1991). Furthermore, when these patients do seek help, they are most likely a to consult their family physician (Waxman, Carner, & Klein, 1984; Yates, 1986). Older patients may also minimize or not remember symptoms (Karno & Golding, 1991), particularly if they are experiencing an increase in cognitive difficulties or organic brain syndromes (e.g., dementia) associated with advanced age (Nilsson & Persson, 1984). For these reasons, it may be more difficult to obtain information on the elderly.

When patients do receive specialized consultation, the diagnostic criteria for OCD in the elderly are the same as those applied to other age groups. However, the diagnosis may be complicated by comorbid depression, cognitive changes, or physical difficulties associated with advanced age. For example, Lindesay (1993) noted that the development of obsessional orderliness and the need for routines may be also be associated with the onset of dementia.

Few studies have examined the symptom presentation in the elderly, but Jenike (1991) has reported it to be similar to younger patients. One symptom noted for a few patients with an onset in old age included obsessions/compulsions related to recalling names. When a name was mentioned, it was reported that patients would begin a search of their memory for anyone they might have known with the name (Jenike, 1991).

A few studies have also reported that the type of treatment a patient receives may be affected by his or her age. Richardson and Bell (1989) found that younger people were more likely to be referred for psychotherapy for anxiety disorders than older people. Also, a greater number of elderly people are prescribed anxiolytic medication compared to younger anxiety sufferers (Thompson, Moran, & Nies, 1983). This may in part be due to the erroneously held belief by some practitioners that the elderly are less likely to benefit from psychotherapy (Richardson & Bell, 1989). Jenike (1991) also reported that most of the patients referred to his clinic had never received trials of behavior therapy, and approximately 50% had not been treated with medication. This finding is surprising given the well-documented success of behavior therapy in younger groups (Chapter 11, this volume). To date, there is little systematic research on the generalizability of behavior therapy to the geriatric population. However, it has been found that among the elderly who are referred for treatment consisting of behavior therapy and psychotropic medication, many show marked improvement (Jenike, 1991). Furthermore, Jenike suggests that elderly patients who initially appear treatment resistant simply may not have received the appropriate treatment.

AGE OF ONSET AND COURSE OF OCD

Age of Onset

Findings from research examining the age of onset for OCD have been surprisingly consistent despite the fact that studies have differed with respect to the diagnostic criteria used (DSM-III through DSM-IV) and the types of individuals studied (e.g., clinical vs. epidemiological samples). In our own clinic, we examined the age of onset among 56 individuals with a DSM-IV principal diagnosis of OCD, based on a structured interview. Means (Ms) and standard deviations (SDs) for age of onset were as follows: total sample ($n = 56$; $M = 21.12$, $SD = 10.15$); males ($n = 33$, $M = 19.56$, $SD = 8.70$); females ($n = 23$, $M = 23.54$, $SD = 11.75$) (Antony, Downie, & Swinson, 1997). Although differences between males and females were not significant in our sample, t (54) $= -1.46$, ns., most other studies have tended to find that OCD begins earlier in males than females (e.g., Burke, Burke, Regier, & Rae, 1990; Castle et al., 1995; Khanna, Rajendra, & Channabasavanna, 1988; Lensi et al., 1996; Minichiello, Baer, Jenike, & Holland, 1990; Noshirvani et al., 1991; Rasmussen & Tsuang, 1986; Thyer, Parrish, Curtis, Nesse, & Cameron, 1985). Table 1.3 summarizes findings from previously published studies on age of onset in adults with OCD. Overall, the means are similar to findings from our own sample.

A number of studies have investigated factors that may influence the discrepant ages of onset for men and women with OCD. Neziroglu, Anemone, and

TABLE 1.3. Age of Onset in OCD

Study	Type of sample (and n)	Age of onset		
		Overall	Females	Males
Burke, Burke, Regier, & Rae (1990)	Epidemiological sample (n = 585 people with OCD)	23	24	21
Castle, Deale, & Marks (1995)	Clinical sample (n = 219)	24.3	26.0	22.0
Lensi et al. (1996)	Clinical sample (n = 263)	22.9	24.3	21.1
Minichiello, Baer, Jenike, & Holland (1990)	Clinical sample (n = 138)	22.3	24.6	19.8
Noshirvani, Kasvikis, Marks, Tsakiris, & Montiero (1991)	Clinical sample (n = 307)	22.7	24.0	21.0
Rasmussen & Tsuang (1986)	Clinical sample (n = 44)	19.8	22.9	15.5
Thyer, Parrish, Curtis, Nesse, & Cameron (1985)	Clinical sample (n = 27)	25.6	—	—

Note. Data provided are mean ages of onset, except for Burke et al. (1990), for which the estimate is the median age of onset.

Yaryura-Tobias (1992) reported that the age of onset appears to differ for women with and without children. In their sample, women without children tended to have earlier ages of onset, with 28.6% experiencing onset between ages 13 and 15. In addition, there were two peaks for mean age of onset among women, the first between ages 22 and 24, and the second between ages 29 and 31.

Some authors have suggested that age of onset may be related to etiology, and that the gender differences associated with age of onset may be reflective of different etiological factors for men and women (Noshirvani et al., 1991). A childhood onset is often associated with greater severity, particularly in males (De Silva, Rachman, & Seligman, 1977; Flament et al., 1988; Hanna, 1995), a higher frequency of prenatal trauma (Flament & Rapoport, 1984; Lensi et al., 1996), and a poorer prognosis (Rasmussen & Tsuang, 1986).

Furthermore, Minichiello et al. (1990) found that age of onset differed among subtypes of OCD, with individuals suffering from obsessions only or from cleaning rituals having the highest age of onset, and those who primarily engage in checking rituals or mixed rituals having the lowest age of onset. In addition, Rasmussen and Tsuang (1986) reported a bimodal distribution for age of onset, with one peak at ages 12–14 and another peak between ages 20 and 22.

Hanna (1995) reported the ages of onset for 31 children and adolescents suffering from OCD. Percentages of individuals reporting onsets during particular age ranges were as follows: age 7 or less = 29%; ages 8–12 = 52%; age 13 and above = 19%. Although age of onset did not differ across sexes in this study, males were overrepresented in this sample of children and adolescents (61% male). The fact that most of the children presenting for treatment in this study were male is consistent with the view that OCD begins earlier in males than females.

A number of studies have reported that symptom onset after the age of 50 is rare (Ingram, 1961; Jenike, 1991; Kolada et al., 1994). In a group of 89 hospital inpatients, Ingram (1961) noted that only 3 patients experienced symptom onset between 55 and 65 years of age, and no patients reported onset at or after 65. Karno and Golding (1991) reported that in the ECA study, only 1 in 12 OCD sufferers developed symptoms after age 50.

Course

Demal et al. (1993) identified five major courses for OCD in a retrospective study of 62 patients meeting ICD 8 or ICD 9 criteria for OCD. These included (1) continuous and unchanging (27.4%), (2) continuous with deterioration (9.7%), (3) continuous with improvement (24.4%), (4) episodic with partial remission (24.4%), and (5) episodic with full remission (11.3%). In cases in which depression and OCD were comorbid, the course of OCD was not affected by the temporal relationship between the OCD and depression.

In contrast, Rasmussen and Tsuang (1986) identified three courses for OCD. In their sample of 44 patients, 84% of individuals had a continuous course, 14% had a deteriorating course, and 2% had an episodic course. All patients reported having substantial obsessive traits before the onset of OCD, and the mean time between OCD onset and first seeking treatment was 7.6 years. In this study, 25% reported an environmental trigger for the onset of their OCD, and 75% did not report a trigger. Typical triggers included an increase in responsibility (e.g., a new baby, a promotion at work) or a loss of some kind (e.g., death of a loved one, loss of employment). For almost all patients, stress often led to an increase in OCD symptoms.

The stress of pregnancy may be a trigger for OCD symptoms for some women (Neziroglu et al., 1992). In a group of 59 mothers with OCD, 39% reported that the onset of their OCD was during pregnancy. Among 5 OCD patients who had abortions, 4 reported an OCD onset during pregnancy.

Unfortunately, few prospective follow-up studies on OCD have been published. In one such study (Rettew, Swedo, Leonard, Lenane, & Rapoport, 1992), 79 children and adolescents with severe OCD were followed up for a mean of 7.9 years. Although OCD continued to be a problem for many of the patients, no individuals maintained the same constellation of symptoms from their original presentation to follow-up. Thomsen (1995) followed 47 children with OCD into adulthood. Although age of onset did not predict the course of OCD, the severity of symptoms in childhood was predictive of OCD severity in adulthood. In addition, females were more likely than males to have an episodic course.

IMPACT OF OCD

A number of studies have shown that anxiety disorders, including OCD, are associated with high health care costs (Simon, Ormel, VonKorff, & Barlow, 1995) and other direct and indirect economic costs (DuPont et al., 1996). As discussed earlier, individuals with OCD are more likely than others to be chronically unemployed. In addition, data from the ECA study suggest that people with OCD are more likely to receive welfare or disability payments (Leon, Portera, & Weissman, 1995) than others in the general population.

In the ECA sample, individuals with OCD were also more likely to receive mental health services from general medical practitioners and mental health specialists than those with phobic disorders and nonanxiety disorders. In contrast, individuals with OCD were less likely to seek these services than were people with PD (Karno et al., 1988). It should be noted that the majority of individuals with OCD do not seek help. Pollard, Henderson, Frank, and Margolis (1989) found that only 28% of individuals with OCD in the general population had sought help for their OCD. Furthermore, almost half of those who had sought help approached a nonpsychiatric physician or member of the clergy rather than a mental health professional.

OCD leads to significant impairment in quality of life. Koran, Thienemann, and Davenport (1996) examined health-related quality of life in 60 outpatients with OCD. Quality of life was impaired in OCD patients to the same degree as in patients suffering from depression. Instrumental functioning (e.g., at work, home, school) and social functioning were impaired relative to those in the general population and individuals with diabetes. Impairment in social functioning was correlated with the severity of OCD symptoms. These findings are consistent with previous studies showing impaired quality of life (Elizondo, Calamari, & Janeck, 1996) and impaired social adjustment (Khanna et al., 1988), and impaired family functioning (e.g., Calvocoressi et al., 1995).

Recent data from our own clinic confirm these findings. Antony, Roth, Swinson, Huta, and Devins (1998) investigated the extent to which OCD ($n = 46$), PD ($n = 32$), and social phobia ($n = 42$) impact on 13 different domains of functioning (e.g., interpersonal relationships, work, health). All three anxiety disorders were associated with high levels of illness intrusiveness relative to norms for a variety of chronic physical conditions. In addition, although there were no differences in overall levels of illness intrusiveness among the three groups, OCD patients were more impaired than social phobia patients on two domains of functioning: religious expression and passive recreation (e.g., reading).

SUMMARY AND CONCLUSIONS

Despite inconclusive evidence, OCD is now believed to be more prevalent than was once thought. It appears to be equally common across religious groups and around the world, although there is evidence that OCD is less prevalent in Taiwan than in other places. Although obsessions and compulsions are very common in the general population, individuals with OCD tend to experience these symptoms more frequently, more intensely, and with greater distress relative to people without OCD. OCD tends to begin in early adulthood or in childhood and usually has a chronic course. Data regarding OCD and other demographic variables (e.g., sex, marital status, ethnicity) have been inconsistent.

In closing, OCD is often associated with impairment in many domains of functional impairment. Furthermore, it often co-occurs with other psychological disorders, most often depression, social phobia, and specific phobias. Fortunately, as reviewed throughout this volume, our understanding of the nature of OCD has increased exponentially over the past two decades, and effective psychological and pharmacological treatments have been developed.

REFERENCES

American Psychiatric Association. (1980). *Diagnostic and statistical manual of mental disorders* (3rd ed.). Washington, DC: Author.

American Psychiatric Association. (1987). *Diagnostic and statistical manual of mental disorders* (3rd ed., rev.). Washington, DC: Author.

American Psychiatric Association. (1994). *Diagnostic and statistical manual of mental disorders* (4th ed.). Washington, DC: Author.

Antony, M. M., Downie, F., & Swinson, R. P. (1997). *Age of onset for individuals with obsessive–compulsive disorder.* Unpublished data.

Antony, M. M., Roth, D., Swinson, R. P., Huta, V., & Devins, G. M. (1998). Illness intrusiveness in individuals with panic disorder, obsessive compulsive disorder, or social phobia. *Journal of Nervous and Mental Disease, 186,* 193–197.

Bellodi, L., Sciuto, G., Diaferia, G., Ronchi, P., & Smeraldi, E. (1992). Psychiatric disorders in the families of patients with obsessive–compulsive disorder. *Psychiatry Research, 42,* 111–120.

Berman, I., Kalinowski, A., Berman, S. M., Lengua, J., & Green, A. I. (1995). Obsessive and compulsive symptoms in chronic schizophrenia. *Comprehensive Psychiatry, 36,* 6–10.

Black, A. (1974). The natural history of obsessional neurosis. In H. R. Beech (Ed.), *Obsessional states* (pp. 19–54). London: Methuen.

Bland, R. C., Orn, H., & Newman, S. C. (1988). Lifetime prevalence of psychiatric disorders in Edmonton. *Acta Psychiatrica Scandinavica, 77*(Suppl. 338), 24–32.

Blazer, D., George, L. K., Landerman, R., Pennybacker, M., Melville, M. L., Woodbury, M., Manton, K. G., Jordan, K., & Locke, B. (1985). Psychiatric disorders: Rural/urban comparisons. *Archives of General Psychiatry, 42,* 651–656.

Brickman, A. L., & Eisdorfer, C. (1989). Anxiety in the elderly. In E. W. Busse & D. G. Blazer (Eds.), *Geriatric psychiatry* (pp. 415–427). Washington, DC: American Psychiatric Press.

Burke, K. C., Burke, J. D., Regier, D. A., & Rae, D. S. (1990). Age of onset of selected mental disorders in five community populations. *Archives of General Psychiatry, 47,* 511–518.

Calamari, J. E., Faber, S. D., Hitsman, B. L., & Poppe, C. J. (1994). Treatment of obsessive compulsive disorder in the elderly: A review and case example. *Journal of Behavior Therapy, 25,* 95–104.

Calvocoressi, L., Lewis, B., Harris, M., Trufan, S. J., Goodman, W. K., McDougle, C. J., & Price, L. H. (1995). Family accommodation in obsessive compulsive disorder. *American Journal of Psychiatry, 152,* 441–443.

Castle, D. J., Deale, A., & Marks, I. M. (1995). Gender differences in obsessive compulsive disorder. *Australian and New Zealand Journal of Psychiatry, 29,* 114–117.

Copeland, J. R. M., Dewey, M. E., Wood, N., Searle, R., Davidson, I. A., & McWilliam, C. (1987). Range of mental illness among the elderly in the community prevalence in Liverpool using the GMS-AGECAT package. *British Journal of Psychiatry, 150,* 815–823.

Coryell, W. (1981). Obsessive compulsive disorder and primary unipolar depression: Comparisons of background, family history, course, and mortality. *Journal of Nervous and Mental Disease, 169,* 220–224.

Crino, R. D., & Andrews, G. (1996). Obsessive–compulsive disorder and Axis I comorbidity. *Journal of Anxiety Disorders, 10,* 37–46.

Demal, U., Lenz, G., Mayrhofer, A., Zapotoczky, H.-G., & Zitterl, W. (1993). Obsessive–compulsive disorder and depression: A retrospective study on course and interaction. *Psychopathology, 26,* 145–150.

De Silva, P., Rachman, S., & Seligman, M.E.P. (1977). Prepared phobias and obsessions: Therapeutic outcome. *Behaviour Research and Therapy, 15,* 65–77.

Di Nardo, P. A., & Barlow, D. H. (1988). *Anxiety Disorders Interview Schedule—Revised* (ADIS-R). Albany, NY: Graywind Publications.

Douglass, H. M., Moffitt, T. E., Dar, R., McGee, R., & Silva, P. (1995). Obsessive–compulsive disorder in a birth cohort of 18-year-olds: Prevalence and predictors. *Journal of the American Academy of Child and Adolescent Psychiatry, 34,* 1424–1431.

Drummond, L. M. (1993). The treatment of severe, chronic, resistant, obsessive–compulsive disorder. An evaluation of an in-patient programme using behavioural psychotherapy in combination with other treatments. *British Journal of Psychiatry, 163,* 223–229.

DuPont, R. L., Rice, D. P., Miller, L. S., Shiraki, S. S., Rowland, C. R., & Harwood, H. J. (1996). Economic costs of anxiety disorders. *Anxiety, 2,* 167–172.

Eisen, J. L., & Rasmussen, S. A. (1989). Coexisting obsessive compulsive disorder and alcoholism. *Journal of Clinical Psychiatry, 50,* 96–98.

Elizondo, D. M., Calamari, J. E., & Janeck, A. S. (1996, November). *Quality of life in obsessive-compulsive disorder.* Paper presented at the meeting of the Association for Advancement of Behavior Therapy, New York, NY.

Fals-Stewart, W., & Angarano, K. (1994). Obsessive–compulsive disorder among patients entering substance abuse treatment: Prevalence and accuracy of diagnosis. *Journal of Nervous and Mental Disease, 182,* 715–719.

Faravelli, C., Degl'Innocenti, B. G., & Giardinelli, L. (1989). Epidemiology of anxiety disorders in Florence. *Acta Psychiatrica Scandinavica, 79,* 308–312.

Fava, G. A., Zielezny, M., Luria, E., & Canestrari, R. (1988). Obsessive–compulsive symptoms in agoraphobia: Changes with treatment. *Psychiatry Research, 23,* 57–63.

First, M. B., Spitzer, R. L., Gibbon, M., & Williams, J. B. W. (1996). *Structured Clinical Interview for DSM-IV Axis I Disorders—Patient Edition (SCID-I/P, Version 2.0).* New York: Biometrics Research Department, New York State Psychiatric Institute.

Flament, M., & Rapoport, J. (1984). Childhood obsessive–compulsive disorder. In T. Insel (Ed.), *Obsessive–compulsive disorder* (pp. 24–43). Washington, DC: American Psychiatric Press.

Flament, M. F., Whitaker, A., Rapoport, J. L., Davies, M., Berg, C. Z., Kalikow, K., Sceery, W., & Shaffer, D. (1988). Obsessive compulsive disorder in adolescence: An epidemiological study. *Journal of the American Academy of Child and Adolescent Psychiatry, 27,* 764–771.

Flint, A. J. (1994). Epidemiology and comorbidity of anxiety disorders in the elderly. *American Journal of Psychiatry, 151,* 640–649.

Foa, E. B., & Kozak, M. J. (1995). DSM-IV field trial: Obsessive–compulsive disorder. *American Journal of Psychiatry, 152,* 90–96.

Freeman, C. P. (1992). What is obsessive compulsive disorder?: The clinical syndrome and its boundaries. *International Clinical Psychopharmacology, 7*(Suppl. 1), 11–17.

George, L. K., Hughes, D. C., & Blazer, D. G. (1986). Urban/rural differences in the prevalence of anxiety disorders. *American Journal of Social Psychiatry, 6,* 249–258.

Goodman, W. K., Price, L. H., Rasmussen, S. A., Mazure, D., Delgado, P., Heninger, G. R., & Charney, D. S. (1989a). The Yale–Brown Obsessive–Compulsive Scale: Part II. Validity. *Archives of General Psychiatry, 46,* 1012–1016.

Goodman, W. K., Price, L. H., Rasmussen, S. A., Mazure, D., Fleischmann, R. L., Hill, C. L., Heninger, G. R., & Charney, D. S. (1989b). The Yale–Brown Obsessive–Compulsive Scale: Part I. Development, use and reliability. *Archives of General Psychiatry, 46,* 1006–1011.

Greenberg, D., & Witztum, E. (1994). The influence of cultural factors on obsessive compulsive disorder: Religious symptoms in a religious society. *Israeli Journal of Psychiatry and Related Sciences, 31,* 211–220.

Hanna, G. L. (1995). Demographic and clinical features of obsessive–compulsive disorder in children and adolescents. *Journal of the American Academy of Child and Adolescent Psychiatry, 34,* 19–27.

Henderson, J. G., & Pollard, C. A. (1988). Three types of obsessive compulsive disorder in a community sample. *Journal of Clinical Psychology, 44,* 747–752.

Higgins, N. C., Pollard, C. A., & Merkel, W. T. (1992). Relationship between religion-related factors and obsessive compulsive disorders. *Current Psychology: Research and Reviews, 11,* 79–85.

Hunt, C., & Andrews, G. (1995). Comorbidity in the anxiety disorders: The use of a life-chart approach. *Journal of Psychiatric Research, 29,* 467–480.

Ingram, I. M. (1961). Obsessional illness in mental hospital patients. *Journal of Medical Science, 107,* 382–402.

Jenike, M. A. (1991). Geriatric obsessive–compulsive disorder. *Journal of Geriatric Psychiatry and Neurology, 4,* 34–39.

Karno, M., & Golding, J. M. (1991). Obsessive compulsive disorder. In L. N. Robins & D. A. Regier (Eds.), *Psychiatric disorders in America: The Epidemiologic Catchment Area Study* (pp. 204–219). New York: Free Press.

Karno, M., Golding, J. M., Burnam, M. A., Hough, R. L., Escobar, J. I., Wells, K. M., & Boyer, R. (1989). Anxiety disorders among Mexican Americans and non-Hispanic whites in Los Angeles. *Journal of Nervous and Mental Disease, 177,* 202–209.

Karno, M., Golding, J. M., Sorenson, S. B., & Burnam, A. (1988). The epidemiology of obsessive–compulsive disorder in five US communities. *Archives of General Psychiatry, 45,* 1094–1099.

Kessler, R. C., McGonagle, K. A., Zhao, S., Nelson, C. B., Hughes, M., Eshleman, S., Wittchen H.-U., & Kendler, K. S. (1994). Lifetime and 12-month prevalence of DSM-III-R psychiatric disorders in the United States: Results from the National Comorbidity Survey. *Archives of General Psychiatry, 51,* 8–19.

Khanna, S., & Mukherjee, D. (1992). Checkers and washers: Valid subtypes of obsessive compulsive disorder. *Psychopathology, 25,* 283–288.

Khanna, S., Rajendra, P. N., & Channabasavanna, S. M. (1988). Social adjustment in obsessive compulsive disorder. *International Journal of Social Psychiatry, 34,* 118–122.

Khanna, S., Kaliaperumal, V. G., & Channabasavanna, S. M. (1990). Clusters of obsessive–compulsive phenomena in obsessive–compulsive disorder. *British Journal of Psychiatry, 156,* 51–54.

Kolada, J. L., Bland, R. C., & Newman, S. C. (1994). Obsessive–compulsive disorder. *Acta Psychiatrica Scandinavica* (Suppl. 376), 24–35.

Koran, L. M., Thienemann, M. L., & Davenport, R. (1996). Quality of life for patients with obsessive–compulsive disorder. *American Journal of Psychiatry, 153,* 783–788.

Kramer, M., German, P. S., Anthony, J. C., Von Korff, M., & Skinner, E. A. (1985). Patterns of mental disorders among the elderly residents of eastern Baltimore. *Journal of the American Geriatric Society, 33,* 236–245.

Leckman, J. F., Grice, D. E., Boardman, J., Zhang, H., Vitale, A., Bondi, C., Alsobrook, J., Peterson, B. S., Cohen, D. J., Rasmussen, S. A., Goodman, W. K., McDougle, C. J., & Pauls, D. L. (1997). Symptoms of obsessive compulsive disorder. *American Journal of Psychiatry, 154,* 911–917.

Lensi, P., Cassano, G. B., Correddu, G., Ravagli, S., Kunovac, J. L., & Akiskal, H. S. (1996). Familial-developmental history, symptomatology, comorbidity, and course with special reference to gender-related differences. *British Journal of Psychiatry, 169,* 101–107.

Leon, A. C., Portera, L., & Weissman, M. M. (1995). The social costs of anxiety disorders. *British Journal of Psychiatry, 166*(Suppl. 27), 19–22.

Lewis, A. (1936). Problems of obsessional illness. *Proceedings of the Royal Society of Medicine, 29,* 325–336.

Lindesay, J. (1993). Neurotic disorders in the elderly. *International Review of Psychiatry, 5,* 461–467.

Mahgoub, O. M., & Abdel-Hafeiz, H. B. (1991). Pattern of obsessive–compulsive disorder in Eastern Saudi Arabia. *British Journal of Psychiatry, 158,* 840–842.

McNally, R. J. (1994). *Panic disorder: A critical analysis.* New York: Guilford Press.

Mellman, T. A., & Uhde, T. W. (1987). Obsessive–compulsive symptoms in panic disorder. *American Journal of Psychiatry, 144,* 1573–1576.

Minichiello, W. E., Baer, L., Jenike, M. A., & Holland, A. (1990). Age of onset of major subtypes of obsessive–compulsive disorder. *Journal of Anxiety Disorders, 4,* 147–150.

Montgomery, S. A. (1992). The place of obsessive compulsive disorder in the diagnostic hierarchy. *International Clinical Psychopharmacology, 7*(Suppl. 1), 19–23.

Moras, K., Di Nardo, P. A., Brown, T. A., & Barlow, D. H. (1994). *Comorbidity, functional impairment, and depression among the DSM-III-R anxiety disorders.* Unpublished manuscript.

Muris, P., Merckelbach, H., & Clavan, M. (1997). Abnormal and normal compulsions. *Behaviour Research and Therapy, 35,* 249–252.

Myers, J. K., Weissman, M. M., & Tischler, G. (1984). Six-month prevalence of psychiatric disorders in three communities: 1980–1982. *Archives of General Psychiatry, 41,* 959–967.

Neal, A. M., & Turner, S. M. (1991). Anxiety disorders research with African Americans: Current Status. *Psychological Bulletin, 109,* 400–410.

Nelson, E., & Rice, J. (1997). Stability of diagnosis of obsessive–compulsive disorder in the Epidemiologic Catchment Area Study. *American Journal of Psychiatry, 154,* 826–831.

Nestadt, G., Samuels, J. F., Romanoski, A. J., Folstein, M. F., & McHugh, P. R. (1994). Obsessions and compulsions in the community. *Acta Psychiatrica Scandinavica, 89,* 219–224.

Neziroglu, F., Anemone, R., & Yaryura-Tobias, J.A. (1992). Onset of obsessive–compulsive disorder in pregnancy. *American Journal of Psychiatry, 149,* 947–950.

Nilsson, L. V., & Persson, G. (1984). Prevalence of mental disorders in an urban sample examined at 70, 75 and 79 years of age. *Acta Psychiatrica Scandinavica* (Suppl. 69), 519–527.

Noshirvani, H. F., Kasvikis, Y., Marks, I. M., Tsakiris, F., & Monteiro, W. O. (1991). Gender-divergent aetiological factors in obsessive–compulsive disorder. *British Journal of Psychiatry, 158,* 260–263.

Okasha, A., Saad, A., Khalil, A. H., Seif El Dawla, A., & Yehia, N. (1994). Phenomenology of obsessive–compulsive disorder: A transcultural study. *Comprehensive Psychiatry, 35,* 191–197.

Pollard, C. A., Henderson, J. G., Frank, M., & Margolis, R. B. (1989). Help-seeking patterns of anxiety-disordered individuals in the general population. *Journal of Anxiety Disorders, 3,* 131–138.

Rachman, S., & De Silva, P. (1978). Abnormal and normal obsessions. *Behaviour Research and Therapy, 16,* 233–248.

Rachman, S., & Hodgson, R. (1980). *Obsessions and compulsions.* Englewood Cliffs, NJ: Prentice-Hall.

Raphael, F. J., Rani, S., Bale, R., & Drummond, L. M. (1996). Religion, ethnicity, and obsessive compulsive disorder. *International Journal of Social Psychiatry, 42,* 38–44.

Rapoport, J. L. (Ed.). (1989). *Obsessive compulsive disorder in children and adolescents.* Washington, DC: American Psychiatric Association.

Rasmussen, S. A., & Eisen, J. L. (1990). Epidemiology of obsessive compulsive disorder. *Journal of Clinical Psychiatry, 51*(Suppl.), 10–13.

Rasmussen, S. A., & Eisen, J. L. (1992). The epidemiology and clinical features of obsessive compulsive disorder. *Psychiatric Clinics of North America, 15,* 743–758.

Rasmussen, S. A., & Tsuang, M. T. (1986). Clinical characteristics and family history in DSM-III obsessive–compulsive disorder. *American Journal of Psychiatry, 143,* 317–322.

Regier, D. A., Boyd, J. H., Burke, J. D. Jr., Rae, D. S., Myers, J. K., Kramer, M., Robins, L. N., George, L. K., Karno, M., & Locke, B. Z. (1988). One-month prevalence of mental disorders in the United States: Based on five Epidemiologic Catchment Area sites. *Archives of General Psychiatry, 45,* 977–986.

Rettew, D. C., Swedo, S. E., Leonard, H. L., Lenane, M. C., & Rapoport, J. L. (1992). Obsessions and compulsions across time in 79 children and adolescents with obsessive–compulsive disorder. *Journal of the American Academy of Child and Adolescent Psychiatry, 31,* 1050–1056.

Ricciardi, J. N. (1993). Frequency of diagnosis of obsessive compulsive disorder [letter]. *American Journal of Psychiatry, 150,* 682.

Ricciardi, J. N., & McNally, R. J. (1995). Depressed mood is related to obsessions, but not to compulsions, in obsessive compulsive disorder. *Journal of Anxiety Disorders, 9,* 249–256.

Richardson, R. M., & Bell, J. A. (1989). Anxiety disorders in the elderly: An update on diagnosis and treatment. *Postgraduate Medicine, 85,* 67–80.

Riemann, B. C., McNally, R. J., & Cox, W. M. (1992). The comorbidity of obsessive compulsive disorder and alcoholism. *Journal of Anxiety Disorders, 6,* 105–110.

Robins, L. N., Helzer, J. E., Weissman, M. M., Orvaschel, H., Gruenberg, E., Burke, J. D., & Regier, D. A. (1984). Lifetime prevalence of specific psychiatric disorders in three sites. *Archives of General Psychiatry, 41,* 949–958.

Ross, H. E., Swinson, R., Larkin, E. J., & Doumani, S. (1994). Diagnosing comorbidity in substance abusers: Computer assessment and clinical validation. *Journal of Nervous and Mental Disease, 182,* 556–563.

Rudin, E. (1953). Ein beitrag zur frage der zwangskranheit insebesondere ihrere hereditaren beziehungen. *Archiv für Psychiatrie und Nervenkrankheiten, 191,* 14–54.

Salkovskis, P. M., & Harrison, J. (1984). Abnormal and normal obsessions: A replication. *Behaviour Research and Therapy, 22,* 549–552.

Sanderson, W. C., Di Nardo, P. A., Rapee, R. M., & Barlow, D. H. (1990). Syndrome comorbidity in patients diagnosed with a DSM-III-R anxiety disorder. *Journal of Abnormal Psychology, 99,* 308–312.

Savron, G., Fava, G. A., Grandi, S., Rafanelli, C., Raffi, A. R., & Belluardo, P. (1996). Hypochondriacal fears and beliefs in obsessive–compulsive disorder. *Acta Psychiatrica Scandinavica, 93,* 345–348.

Schut, A. J., Castonguay, L. G., Plummer, K., & Borkovec, T. D. (1995, November). *Compulsive checking behaviors in generalized anxiety disorder.* Paper presented at the meeting of the Association for Advancement of Behavior Therapy, Washington, DC.

Schwalberg, M. D., Barlow, D. H., Alger, S. A., & Howard, L. J. (1992). Comparison of bulimics, obese binge eaters, social phobics, and individuals with panic disorder on comorbidity across DSM-III-R anxiety disorders. *Journal of Abnormal Psychology, 101,* 675–681.

Shapiro, S., Skinner, E. A., Kessler, L. G., Von Korff, M., German, P. S., Tischler, G. L., Leaf, P. J., Benham, L., Cottler, L., & Regier, D. A. (1984). Utilization of health and mental services: Three epidemiological area sites. *Archives of General Psychiatry, 41,* 971–978.

Simon, G., Ormel, J., VonKorff, M., & Barlow, W. (1995). Health care costs associated with depressive and anxiety disorders in primary care. *American Journal of Psychiatry, 152,* 352–357.

Speer, D. C., Williams, J., West, H., & Dupree, L. (1991). Older adult users of outpatient mental health services. *Community Mental Health Journal, 27,* 69–76.

Steketee, G. S., Grayson, J. B., & Foa, E. B. (1985). Obsessive compulsive disorder: Differences between washers and checkers. *Behaviour Research and Therapy, 23,* 197–201.

Steketee, G., Grayson, J. B., & Foa, E. B. (1987). A comparison of characteristics of obsessive–compulsive disorder and other anxiety disorders. *Journal of Anxiety Disorders, 1,* 325–335.

Steketee, G., Quay, S., & White, K. (1991). Religion and guilt in OCD patients. *Journal of Anxiety Disorders, 5,* 359–367.

Stoll, A. L., Tohen, M., & Baldessarini, R. J. (1992). Increasing frequency of the diagnosis of obsessive–compulsive disorder. *American Journal of Psychiatry, 149,* 638–640.

Summerfeldt, L., Antony, M. M., Downie, F., Richter, M. A., & Swinson, R. P. (1997). *Prevalence of particular obsessions and compulsions in a clinic sample.* Unpublished manuscript.

Thiel, A., Broocks, A., Ohlmeier, M., Jacoby, G. E., & Schüssler, G. (1995). Obsessive–compulsive disorder among patients with anorexia nervosa and bulimia nervosa. *American Journal of Psychiatry, 152,* 72–75.

Thompson, T. L., Moran, M. G., & Nies, A. S. (1983). Psychotropic drug use in the elderly. *New England Journal of Medicine, 308,* 134–138, 194–199.

Thomsen, P. H. (1995). Obsessive–compulsive disorder in children and adolescents: Predictors in childhood for long-term phenomenological course. *Acta Psychiatrica Scandinavica, 92,* 255–259.

Thyer, B. A., Parrish, R. T., Curtis, G. C., Nesse, R. M., & Cameron, O. G. (1985).

Ages of onset of DSM-III anxiety disorders. *Comprehensive Psychiatry, 26,* 113–122.

Valleni-Basile, L. A., Garrison, C. Z., Jackson, K. L., Waller, J. L., McKeown, R. E., Addy, C. L., & Cuffe, S. P. (1994). Frequency of obsessive–compulsive disorder in a community sample of young adolescents. *Journal of the American Academy of Child and Adolescent Psychiatry, 33,* 782–791.

van Oppen, P., Hoekstra, R. J., & Emmelkamp, P. M. G. (1995). The structure of obsessive–compulsive symptoms. *Behaviour Research and Therapy, 33,* 15–23.

Vitiello, B., Spreat, S., & Behar, D. (1989). Obsessive–compulsive disorder in mentally retarded patients. *Journal of Nervous and Mental Disease, 177,* 232–236.

Waxman, H. M., Carner, E. A., & Klein, M. (1984). Underutilization of mental health professionals by community elderly. *Gerontologist, 24,* 23–30.

Weissman, M. M., Bland, R. C., Canino, G. J., Greenwald, S., Hwu, H.-G., Lee, C. K., Newman, S. C., Oakley-Brown, M. A., Rubio-Stipec, M., Wickramaratne, P. J., Wittchen, H.-U., & Yeh, E.-K. (1994). The cross national epidemiology of obsessive compulsive disorder. *Journal of Clinical Psychiatry, 55*(Suppl.), 5–10.

Wittchen, H.-U. (1988). 1. Natural course and spontaneous remissions of untreated anxiety disorders: Results of the Munich Follow-Up Study (MFS). In I. Hand & H.-U. Wittchen (Eds.), *Panic and phobias 2: Treatment and variables affecting course and outcome* (pp. 3–17). New York: Springer-Verlag.

Yaryura-Tobias, J., Todaro, J., Grunes, M. S., McKay, D., Stockman, R., & Neziroglu, F. A. (1996, November). *Comorbidity versus continuum of Axis I disorders in OCD.* Paper presented at the meeting of the Association for Advancement of Behavior Therapy, New York, NY.

Yates, W. R. (1986). The National Institute of Mental Health Epidemiologic study: Implications for family practice. *Journal of Family Practice, 22,* 251–255.

Chapter 2

PSYCHOLOGICAL APPROACHES TO THE UNDERSTANDING OF OBSESSIONAL PROBLEMS

Paul M. Salkovskis

The key to current psychological approaches to obsessional problems lies in the observation made by Rachman and De Silva (1978), who found that intrusive thoughts, indistinguishable from obsessional thoughts in terms of their content, were reported by almost 90% of a nonclinical sample. This robust and frequently replicated finding (e.g., Freeston, Ladouceur, Thibodeau, & Gagnon, 1991; Freeston, Ladouceur, Thibodeau, & Gagnon, 1992; Parkinson & Rachman, 1981; Salkovskis & Harrison, 1984) has more recently been supplemented by work indicating that "normal compulsions" are also common in nonclinical subjects. Earlier behavioral and more recent cognitive-behavioral theories have as their starting point the hypothesis that the origins of obsessional problems are to be found in such normal intrusive cognitions, and that the key to understanding obsessional disorders is to be found in the way in which intrusions come to be associated with mood disturbance and compulsive behaviors.

BEHAVIORAL APPROACHES

The origins of current cognitive-behavioral treatment are to be found in learning theory, which also provided the impetus for the development of behavior therapy. Mowrer (1947, 1960) described a two-factor model of fear and avoidance behavior in anxiety disorders. He suggested that fear of specific stimuli is *acquired* through *classical* conditioning and *maintained* by *operant* conditioning processes as the organism learns to reduce aversive stimuli initially by escaping, and later by avoiding, the fear-associated conditioned stimuli. Solomon and Wynne (1954) made the further important observation in animal experiments that if stimuli had become classically conditioned by previous association with strongly aversive stimuli, then avoidance responses to the conditioned stimuli were extremely resistant to extinction; that is, they demonstrated that avoidance responses continued unabated long after any pairing of conditioned stimuli with aversive consequences had ceased. The avoidance behavior observed under these circumstances tended to become stereotyped in a fashion analogous to the behavior of obsessional patients. Only when the avoidance behavior was blocked did high levels of anxiety reappear; these animals would persistently attempt to continue the avoidance/escape behavior for a considerable time after the behavior was blocked, although these efforts eventually ceased.

In the first application of learning theory approaches to obsessional problems, Meyer (1966) reported the successful behavioral treatment of two cases of chronic obsessional neurosis, followed by a series of successful case reports. Meyer's work heralded the application of psychological models to obsessions and the development of effective behavioral treatments. Meyer seems to have drawn the idea from animal models of compulsive behavior such as that of Metzner (1963). It is notable that attempts to generalize systematic desensitization (as used by Wolpe in the treatment of phobias) to obsessional rituals had been unsuccessful. Meyer argued that it was necessary to tackle avoidance behavior directly by ensuring that rituals did not take place within or between treatment sessions. He emphasized the role of expectations of harm in obsessions and the importance of invalidating these expectations during treatment in a way reminiscent of current cognitive-behavioral approaches to anxiety in general (e.g., Salkovskis, 1991). Rachman, Hodgson, and Marks (1971) adapted and developed this treatment method, combining specific *in vivo* exposure to feared situations with response prevention.

In its most mature form, behavioral theory of obsessive–compulsive disorder (OCD) hypothesizes that normal intrusive thoughts, images, and impulses become associated, through classical conditioning processes, with anxiety that has subsequently failed to extinguish. The failure to extinguish is said to occur because sufferers develop escape and avoidance behaviors (such as obsessional checking and washing) that have the effect of preventing extinction of the anxiety (Rachman & Hodgson, 1980). The behavioral treatment known as exposure and response prevention (ERP) flows directly from this hypothesis; the person is (1) exposed to stimuli that provoke the obsessional response and (2) helped to desist from avoidance and escape (compulsive) responses (Salkovskis & Kirk, 1989).

In a crucial series of experiments, Rachman and his colleagues found (1) that elicitation of the obsession was associated with increased anxiety and discomfort; (2) that if the patient was then allowed to ritualize then anxiety and discomfort almost immediately decreased; (3) that if the ritualizing was delayed, anxiety and discomfort decreased ("spontaneously decayed") over a somewhat longer period (up to 1 hour); and (4) when the patient refrained from ritualizing, the anxiety level on the next trial was relatively lower, and this did not occur if the ritualizing took place (see Rachman & Hodgson, 1980).

Behavioral theory stipulates that compulsive behaviors are crucial to the *maintenance* of obsessional problems. Obsessional ruminations are, by definition, obsessions in which there is no *overt* compulsive behavior. Salkovskis and Westbrook (1989) highlighted the prevalence and importance of covert compulsive behavior, which appears to be invariably present in some form in obsessional rumination. Obsessions without overt compulsions can be considered as a type of OCD in which avoidance and compulsive activity are almost totally *covert* and are therefore especially difficult to gain access to and control. The term "obsessional ruminations" is confusing, because it has been used indiscriminately to describe both obsessions and mental neutralizing. For example, a patient reported that she had thoughts and images about her family dying; she would ruminate about these thoughts for periods of up to 3 hours at a time. Careful questioning elicited two functionally different types of thoughts: first, she had intrusive thoughts such as, "My son is dead." If she had a thought like this, she would neutralize it by making herself have the second thought, "My son is NOT dead" and by forming a clear image of her son carrying out normal activities.

Obsessions and neutralizing thoughts are mixed together in the cognitive domain, and discriminating between them is crucial to treatment. *Intrusive, involuntary* thoughts that produce anxiety must be differentiated from thoughts that the patient *deliberately initiates by voluntary effort* and that are intended to reduce anxiety or risk. There may also be covert avoidance behaviors, such as attempts *not* to think particular thoughts. Avoidance is not defined in terms of how successful it is in preventing anxiety, but rather in terms of what the behavior is intended to do. Covert avoidance and neutralizing are assessed by asking the patient about any mental efforts that are made because of the problem. For example, a patient felt compelled to think every "bad" thought an even number of times. He spent much of his day trying not to have "bad" thoughts (avoidance); these efforts were frequently followed by thoughts such as, "I never liked my father" (obsession). He would then have to think "I never liked my father" again (neutralizing) and try to stop (avoidance); this cycle then repeated. The obsessional thought can become a neutralizing thought if there is voluntary effort (e.g., the patient who makes himself think particular thoughts before they occur on their own).

THE NEED FOR COGNITIVE APPROACHES

While it was undoubtedly true that the development of two-process theory and its application to treatment in exposure and response prevention revolutionized the psychological treatment of obsessional problems (including ruminations), it was also clear in the early 1980s that something more was required. There were two main indicators of the need for further theoretical development: (1) the limitations of exposure and response prevention, and (2) the need to incorporate experimental and phenomenological observations not accounted for by behavioral theories.

Treatment refusals and dropouts are common in behavioral therapy for OCD. Where treatment was taken to its conclusion, success in the treatment usually meant that the patients were "much improved" or "improved"; the proportion of patients fully relieved of their obsessional problem was considerably less. When allowances are made for treatment refusal and early dropout, the proportion showing 30% improvement or better appeared to be 50% or less of those suitable for inclusion and seeking treatment in clinical trials. The significant residual levels of social and occupational impairment at the end of treatment persist to longer-term follow-up, with little sign of further improvement (Kasvikis & Marks, 1988). This is true of programs involving high levels of exposure with continuous response prevention. Thus, even when conditions are set to maximize the impact of ERP, there is considerable room for improvement both in the response rate for those offered treatment and the extent to which patients are completely better at the end of treatment.

The greatest limitation of the behavioral theory was its failure to differentiate between the theoretical conceptualization of different anxiety disorders. The two-process theory can be applied equally to specific phobia, agoraphobia, and OCD. It was suggested that the focus of anxiety was a result of random superstitious learning, with the an aversive unconditioned stimulus (UCS) coinciding with a neutral conditioned stimulus (CS) such as a spider or a locked door. Thus, any object could become the focus of anxiety. This "equipotentiality premise" was clearly not justified by the nonrandom distribution of fears. Seligman (1971) pointed out that human fears are seldom associated with those objects that are most likely to have been associated with painful experiences (such as cars and electrical sockets). He proposed the notion of "preparedness" to deal with this problem. It was argued that fear can be conditioned particularly easily to stimuli where such ease of acquisition is likely to have had adaptive consequences in evolutionary terms. Although there has now been some validation of a version of this hypothesis (taking into account developmental factors and "vicarious" conditioning experiences), it does not provide a satisfactory explanation of why some people become obsessional and others phobic. In fact, some of the stimuli feared by obsessionals seem to contradict the preparedness view. Thus, obsessional fears tend to reflect the concerns of the time rather than of the last 100,000 years (e.g., the distribution of the most contamination fears have tended to evolve rapidly over the last century from tuberculosis disease to radiation to HIV and, recently, in the United Kingdom, Creutzfeldt–Jakob disease). It is not uncommon for the fears of obsessionals to focus on their house, gas, electricity, cars, and other more "modern" objects.

Rachman and his colleagues observed in the course of their experiments on checking that the presence of the therapist or other trusted person blocked obsessional anxiety. The link between obsessions and reassurance seeking also appeared puzzling. Although anxiety reduction was clearly the most common consequence of obsessional rituals, there were individuals in whom anxiety increments consistently occurred in a way that defied explanation on the basis of two-process theory, even when schedules of reinforcement were considered. The behavior of checkers, where at least superficially the problem appeared to be one of memory, was also difficult to account for (leading some to suggest mnestic deficits; discussed later).

Thus, both the obvious and considerable strengths of the behavioral approach and its limitations suggested the need for an alternative approach to the conceptualization and therapy of OCD while retaining the best features of behavioral theory and therapy. Given that obsessional problems are, by definition, driven by unusual and distorted patterns of thinking, a cognitive approach seemed attractive. The late development of an effective cognitive approach was almost certainly due to the fact that, as part of a three-systems conceptualization of obsessions, the primary cognitive focus tended to be on obsessional thoughts (i.e., intrusive cognitions). By contrast, Salkovskis (1985, 1989a, 1989b) took as his starting point Rachman's (1971) conceptualization of obsessional thoughts stimuli that had become associated with negative affect. He reasoned that the crucial cognitive element was not the intrusions (which were in any case a universal phenomenon) but rather the meaning that the person attached to such intrusions. This way of conceptualizing obsessions has similar features to cognitive approaches to other anxiety problems, with the key differences arising from the consequences of the specific beliefs of the person concerned. Before considering this cognitive approach in greater detail, psychological deficit models (where a general impairment of cognitive functioning is hypothesized) will be evaluated. These approaches do not concern themselves with the content of cognition, hypothesizing instead that obsessions result from the failure of normal cognitive functioning, presumably based in neurological problems.

SPECIFIC VERSUS GENERAL THEORIES OF OCD

OCD readily lends itself to deficit-based theorizing. Thoughts intrude uncontrollably, suggesting a failure of inhibition; repetitive, stereotyped, and sometimes bizarre behavior is prominent and pervasive; patients report problems with their memory (and behave in ways that agree with this judgment), and difficulties with decision making are manifest. It is therefore not surprising that several writers and researchers have proposed that there may be a general cognitive deficit, possibly related to structural/and or neurochemical disturbances. Such deficit theories have been based on one of two main views: (1) that obsessional patients have a poor general memory and decision-making abilities or (2) that obsessional patients are experiencing a general failure in cognitive control.

No attempt has thus far been made to use these views to account for the effectiveness of cognitive-behavioral treatments, which does not seek to improve the patients memory or ability to inhibit thoughts. Another problem for general deficit theories is their inability to account for key aspects of the phenomenology of OCD. OCD sufferers do appear to have memory and decision-making problems. However, these are highly specific. Although they will check the door of their house many times, the same patients seldom have problems locking a broom cupboard door. As described earlier, the presence of a trusted other (e.g., therapist or spouse) also removes the urge to check (Rachman, 1993). Similarly, with contamination, there is a degree of specificity involved in the experience of an object as contaminating (e.g., by particular people or classes of people) that is difficult to account for as a general problem of deciding what is clean and what is contaminated.

The evidence for memory deficits in clinical OCD is slender. The main evidence for memory problems has come from the work of Sher and colleagues (Sher, Frost, Kushner, Crews, & Alexander, 1989), who have correlated Mandsley Obsessional–Compulsive Inventory (MOCI) checking scores with the Weschler Memory Scale, and report that both nonclinical and clinical "checkers" have lower WMS scores than subjects scoring low on the checking scale. Curiously, obsessional patients do not have such memory impairment, nor indeed do such patients show any signs of problems with their memory *outside areas directly linked to their obsessional problems.* However, if someone is *concerned* about his or her memory, he or she may check because of this concern. This means that at least two types of people will report checking: those who have a memory problem and make attempts to compensate for it, and those who are *unduly* concerned about their memory and attempt similar compensation. The possible explanation of the Sher et al. (1989) findings is therefore that people who actually have general problems with poor memory tend to check more than those who do not. The evidence from clinical obsessional checkers indicates that there is not a generalized memory deficit; the cognitive-behavioral hypothesis suggests that in these instances, checking may arise from undue and highly focused concern about memory for particular things. Some recent research provides support for this view; for example, Maki, O'Neill, and O'Neill (1994) found that (nonclinical) checkers performed similarly to noncheckers on tests of inhibitory control of cognition. However, checkers *perceived themselves* to be more prone to failures of cognitive control, consistent with the hypothesis that even in the absence of actual failures of control, these people will try to exert control over their perceived shortcomings in this area. Checking may also develop in other people who *know* that they tend to have a poor memory; these probably constitute Sher's "non-obsessional clinical checkers."

A number of studies have investigated neuropsychological functioning and "neurological soft signs" in obsessional patients. There are two main problems in the interpretation of these studies. First, none have compared obsessional patients with other patients suffering from anxiety. This means that it is not clear whether findings arise from the diagnosis of OCD or result from being a patient suffering from anxiety. Second, such studies have failed to deal with the issue of tests being affected by obsessional symptoms. For example, tests involving prolonged concentration are likely to be disrupted by obsessional thinking.

A more recent suggestion has been that obsessional patients show similar cognitive deficits to those found in schizophrenic patients. Enright (1996) suggests that obsessional problems are a result of a centrally determined failure in the mechanism that is usually involved in the inhibition of unwanted thoughts, and that as a result, OCD patients suffer from what amounts to a mild form of schizophrenia. Crucial to this hypothesis is the debatable assumption that schizotypy is a measure of vulnerability to schizophrenia. However, there is no evidence of an increased prevalence of schizophrenia among OCD patients. This may be less of a problem for this theory than is immediately apparent, given the puzzling finding that schizophrenics score lower on schizotypy than high schizotypes who are not schizophrenic.

That obsessional patients score relatively higher on schizotypy questionnaires may be accounted for by some specific items used in the scales, such as "No matter how hard I try to concentrate, unrelated thoughts always creep into my mind" and "I often have difficulty in controlling my thoughts when I am thinking."

Potentially more interesting is the suggestion that obsessional patients may have a deficit in negative priming (i.e., the tendency to continue to inhibit a previously inhibited response). The lack of such a tendency might account for the relative ease with which cognitive intrusions would occur. Enright (1996) reports data showing that OCD patients' scores were "closer to those exhibited by high schizotypal and schizophrenic subjects," and that anxious controls showed similar negative priming to normal subjects (low schizotypes). However, recalculation of *mean normal* scores (i.e., combining high and low schizotypy subjects) indicates that obsessional patients (and schizophrenics!) are more similar to nonclinical subjects than anxious controls.

The cognitive-behavioral hypothesis described next in greater detail does not necessarily rule out the possibility that general deficits may be involved in the vulnerability to obsessional problems, and that the experience of obsessional problems may give rise to relatively generalized information-processing problems. It is argued that such deficits are neither necessary nor sufficient for the development and maintenance of OCD, but that interference with information processing may worsen and therefore maintain some obsessional difficulties.

THE COGNITIVE-BEHAVIORAL HYPOTHESIS

Both behavioral and cognitive-behavioral theories starts with the proposition that obsessional thinking has its origins in normal intrusive thoughts rather than being qualitatively different. Intrusive thoughts occur in almost 90% of the general population yet are indistinguishable in terms of content from clinical obsessions (Rachman & De Silva, 1978; Salkovskis & Harrison, 1984). Normal intrusive thoughts and obsessions differ not in the occurrence or controllability of these thoughts but in the way in which obsessional patients *interpret* intrusions as an indication that they may be responsible for harm or its prevention. The concept is comparable to the cognitive hypothesis of panic (Clark, 1986; Salkovskis, 1988), in which panic attacks are said to occur as a result of the misinterpretation of normal bodily sensations, particularly the sensations of normal anxiety. Most normal people experience such sensations, but only people who have an enduring tendency to interpret them in a catastrophic fashion will experience repeated panic attacks. By the same token, intrusive thoughts, impulses, images, and doubts are normal, but only people who have an enduring tendency to misinterpret their own mental activity as indicating personal "responsibility" will experience the pattern of discomfort and neutralizing characteristic of OCD.

For example, an obsessional patient may believe that the occurrence of a thought such as "I will kill my baby" means that there is a risk that she will succumb to the action unless she does something to prevent it, such as avoiding being left alone with her child or by seeking reassurance from people around her, by trying to think positive thoughts to balance the negative ones, and so on. Thus, the *interpretation* of obsessional thoughts as indicating increased responsibility has a number of important effects in people suffering from OCD: (1) increased discomfort, anxiety, and depression; (2) greater accessibility of the original thought and other related ideas; (3) behavioral "neutralising" responses that constitute attempts to escape or avoid responsibility. These may include compulsive behavior, avoidance of situations related to the obsessional thought, seeking reassurance (thus diluting or sharing responsibility), and attempts to get rid of or exclude the thought from his or her mind. Each of these effects contributes not only to the maintenance of anxiety but also to a worsening spiral of intrusive thoughts leading to maladaptive affective, cognitive, and behavioral reactions.

This cognitive hypothesis may account for those observations that suggest cognitive deficits and poor mental control in OCD. If obsessional patients misinterpret aspects of their own mental functioning (including memory for actions and their ability to inhibit intrusive thoughts and doubts), a likely response would be to increase deliberate efforts to exert control. However, in doing so, they attempt to monitor closely and take control over processes that would otherwise operate in automatic and well-practiced ways. In many situations this would result in poorer perceived performance, which would sometimes be accompanied by actual performance impairments as well as increased preoccupation.

The use of the word "responsibility" has caused some confusion in the field. The specific meaning intended in the context of the present theory is that the person believes that he or she may be, or come to be, the cause of harm (to self or others) unless he or she takes some preventive or restorative action. The definition adopted by a group of researchers (Salkovskis et al., 1996) is as follows: "The belief that one has power which is pivotal to bring about or prevent subjectively crucial negative outcomes. These outcomes may be actual, that is, having consequences in the real world, and/or at a moral level" (p. 81). It is this appraisal of the occurrence and content of intrusions as indicating personal responsibility that results in repeated "neutralising" behavior.

An important part of the appraisal of an intrusion will concern the implications of an intrusion and the need for further action, which will be particularly heightened in sensitive individuals who perceive themselves as likely to be responsible for harm to themselves or others. At least two aspects of the intrusion are subject to appraisal: the *occurrence* and the *content*. If appraisal suggests a specific reaction (including attempts to suppress or avoid the thought), it is suggested that *controlled processing* will follow. Thus, when an intrusive cognition or its content has some direct implications for the reactions of the individual experiencing it, processing priority will increase, and further appraisal and elaboration will become more likely. This results in the strategic deployment of attention toward the control of mental activity. These attempts include trying to be sure of the accuracy of one's memory, to take account of all factors in one's decisions, to prevent the occurrence of unacceptable material, and to ensure that an outcome has been achieved when the difference between achieving it and not achieving it is imperceptible (e.g., as in deciding that one's hands are properly clean after washing to remove contamination).

In instances where *the occurrence of a particular type of thought* is appraised as an indication that the individual has become responsible for harm to him- or herself or others, then the occurrence and content of the thought becomes both a source of discomfort and an imperative signal for action that is intended to neutralize the thought and the potentially harmful consequences of its occurrence. This specific acquisition of *meaning* in terms of "responsibility" distinguishes obsessional cognitions from anxious and depressed cognitions. Appraisal of responsibility and consequent neutralizing can arise from a sensitivity to responsibility arising from a failure to control thoughts, from an increase in the level of perceived personal responsibility, and from an increased perception of the awfulness of being responsible for harm. The majority of nonclinical subjects do not regard the occurrence of intrusive thoughts as being of special significance. Once neutralizing responses to intrusive thoughts are established, they are maintained by the association with the perception of reduced responsibility and discomfort, while the recurrence of the intrusive cognitions becomes more likely as a result of the other processes just described. Thus, obsessional problems will occur in individuals who are distressed by the occurrence of intrusions and also believe the occurrence of such cognitions indicates personal responsibility for distressing harm unless corrective action is taken.

The appraisal of intrusive thoughts as having implications for responsibility for harm to self or others is therefore seen as important, because appraisal links the intrusive thought with both distress *and* the occurrence of neutralizing behavior. If the appraisal solely concerns harm or danger without an element of responsibility, then the effect is more likely to be anxiety or depression, which may become part of a mood-appraisal spiral (Teasdale, 1983) but would not result in clinical obsessions without the additional component of the responsibility-neutralizing link. Hearing someone else making blasphemous statements or talking about harming one's children *might* not be upsetting in itself. This is not to say that, if one perceives what is said as personally significant (e.g., "Perhaps this person wants to harm my children"), some emotional response (anxiety or anger) would be expected. However, without the specific appraisal of *responsibility*, an obsessional episode would not result.

An obsessional pattern would be particularly likely in vulnerable individuals when intrusions are regarded as self-initiated (e.g., resulting in appraisals such as "These thoughts might mean I want to harm the children; I must guard against losing control"). The useful comparison here is between the effects of asking an obsessional checker to lock the door or to watch someone else locking the same door. This responsibility effect is clearly demonstrated by the experiments conducted by Roper and Rachman (1976) and Roper, Rachman, and Hodgson (1973). In these important experiments, situations that usually provoked checking rituals in obsessional patients (such as locking the door) produced little or no discomfort or checking when the therapist was present, in sharp contrast to the effects of having to deal with such situations when alone (Rachman, 1993).

Responsibility appraisals are likely when particular intrusions occur in people who hold negative beliefs about thoughts such as those described by Salkovskis (1985, p. 579); for example, "not neutralising when an intrusion has occurred is similar or equivalent to seeking or wanting the harm involved in the intrusion to happen" or "thinking something is as bad as doing it." Negative interpretations will then focus on the particular meaning of the intrusion. In this way, an appraisal that is regarded as sensible is based on a thought that is itself regarded as senseless. It is, of course, quite common to be told by anxious patients that "I must be crazy because I have crazy thoughts, and I know that they are crazy thoughts. . . ."

Another important type of interpretation has been described by Shafran, Thordarson, and Rachman (1996) as thought–action fusion (TAF). This describes two types of beliefs: (1) thinking about some negative event makes it more likely to occur, and (2) having a thought about an "immoral" action is similar to carrying out such an action. Shafran et al. found a significantly higher frequency of both types of belief in obsessional individuals than in nonobsessional individuals.

The cognitive-behavioral hypothesis thus differs in crucial ways from general cognitive-deficit theories. Rather than positing a general failure of mental control, memory, or decision making, patients are hypothesized as being especially concerned about these areas; as a consequence, *they try too hard to exert control over mental processes and activity* in a variety of counterproductive and therefore anxiety-provoking ways. Efforts at overcontrol increase distress because (1) direct and deliberate attention to mental activity can modify the contents of consciousness; (2) efforts to deliberately control a range of mental activities apparently and actually meet with failure and even opposite effects; (3) attempts to prevent harm and responsibility for harm increase the salience and accessibility of the patients' concerns with harm; and (4) neutralizing directed at preventing harm also prevent disconfirmation (i.e., prevents the patient from discovering that the things he or she is afraid of will not occur). This means that exaggerated beliefs about responsibility and harm do not decline. An important implication of this approach is that people who are not suffering from obsessional problems will show phenomena characteristic of OCD if key beliefs (e.g., responsibility appraisals) and reactions (e.g., neutralizing and thought suppression) can be induced in experimental studies.

EFFECTS OF THOUGHT MONITORING, SUPPRESSION, AND NEUTRALIZING

Experimental evidence of the "paradoxical" effects of attempts to control intrusive and obsessional thoughts has been demonstrated in attempts to "suppress" unwanted thoughts, in deliberate self-monitoring, and in neutralizing. By definition, people suffering from OCD try to suppress their obsessional thoughts. The idea that active attempts to suppress particular thoughts may result in more of the thoughts has long been an assumption in clinical practice. This concept is often used to help sufferers understand why obsessional thoughts occur so frequently despite their attempts to suppress them. For example, as a behavioral experiment, obsessional patients are invited to try their hardest not to think of a giraffe; the subsequent occurrence of giraffe images is then used as the basis for educational discussion (Salkovskis & Kirk, 1989).

Wegner (1989) conducted a series of experiments on thought suppression. The results of these studies suggested that efforts to suppress did not result in an initial enhancement, but that suppression was achieved in the short term. However, during the immediately subsequent period, an enhancement (described as a "rebound") *was* observed. However, another group (Lavy & Van den Hout, 1990; Merckelbach, Muris, Van den Hout, & de Jong, 1991) did find the expected paradoxical enhancement of emotionally neutral stimuli, and did not find a rebound. Subsequently, Clark, Ball, and Pape (1991) and Clark, Winton, and Thynn (1993) again failed to find an immediate enhancement effect, using vivid, emotionally neutral stimuli (green rabbits) from a previously heard, taped story. Clark and colleagues suggested that studies that found enhancement had failed to control for the effects of the frequency with that the to-be-suppressed target was mentioned prior to the suppression task.

There are major methodological differences between such studies which present major problems of interpretation. For example, some studies used a thought counting procedure, while others used "streaming," in which subjects are asked to verbalize their stream of consciousness, which is later coded, often with the "target" thought being represented as a percentage of total thoughts. Target stimuli have varied in terms of how commonplace and relevant they are, ranging from green rabbits to kitchen utensils; most did not concern "intrusive" thoughts as usually defined, and did not focus on naturally occurring thoughts. Salkovskis and Campbell (1994) targeted personally relevant and naturally occurring negative intrusive thoughts that subjects reported they normally attempt to suppress to some extent. Thus, a characteristic of such intrusions is that subjects find them personally unacceptable and are self-motivated to remove or suppress such intrusions. In the study, 75 nonclinical subjects were allocated to one of five experimental conditions: thought suppression, mention control, and suppression under three different distraction conditions. This initial experimental period was followed by a standard "think anything" period. The design therefore allowed assessment of both suppression and rebound effects. Thought frequency was measured by means of a counter. This study showed that the subjects asked simply to suppress experienced significantly more intrusive thoughts during both first and second experimental periods when compared to the mention control group. Distraction instructions significantly decreased frequency only when a specific engaging task was provided. Effects on evaluative components of the intrusive thought (discomfort and acceptability) were observed only in the condition that involved the specific distracting task.

Clearly, laboratory studies involving brief suppression periods (typically a few minutes) have limited applicability to obsessions in which subjects describe struggling to exclude thoughts *most of the time*. In a study designed to investigate the longer-term impact of thought suppression in naturally occurring intrusive thoughts, subjects were asked to record intrusions only, to suppress, or to "think through" over a period of 4 days (Trinder & Salkovskis, 1994). Again, suppression was found to enhance intrusion. This study is key in bridging the gap between the phenomenology of OCD and thought suppression experiments. A further important development is linking the effects of suppression to the perception of heightened responsibility, as described later.

Assumptions and Appraisals

The cognitive theory proposes that people are predisposed to making particular appraisals because of assumptions that are learned over longer periods from childhood onward or that may be formed as a result of unusual or extreme events and circumstances. Some assumptions that characterize OCD patients are described in Salkovskis (1985) and include the following:

> "Having a thought about an action is like performing the action."
> "Failing to prevent (or failing to try to prevent) harm to self or others is the same as having caused the harm in the first place."
> "Responsibility is not reduced by other factors, such as something being improbable."
> "Not neutralizing when an intrusion has occurred is similar or equivalent to seeking or wanting the harm involved in the intrusion to happen."
> "One should (and can) exercise control over one's thoughts."

If someone holds these attitudes very strongly, then the overt and covert behaviors characteristic of people suffering from obsessional problems tend to follow. There are studies demonstrating that such beliefs are prominent in obsessional patients relative to people suffering from other anxiety disorders. The effects of these type of assumptions are often described in terms of "thinking errors" (Beck, 1976); thinking errors are characteristic distortions that influence whole classes of reactions. Thinking errors are not of themselves pathological; in fact, most people make judgments by employing a range of "heuristics," many of which can be fallacious (Nisbett & Ross, 1980).

The cognitive hypothesis suggests that OCD patients show a number of characteristic thinking errors that link to their obsessional difficulties; probably the most typical and important is the idea that "any influence over negative outcome = responsibility for that outcome." If the person believes that such responsibility can be manifest simply by thinking (as in TAF), then obsessional rumination seems to be an almost inevitable consequence. Responsibility assumptions and appraisals have both been found to differentiate obsessional patients from nonclinical and anxious controls (Freeston, Ladoucer, Gagnon, & Thibodeau, 1993; Salkovkis et al., 1998).

The author's group has also suggested that there may be an important set of factors concerning responsibility through inaction (things the person believes that he or she may fail to do) as opposed to action. As outlined earlier, Salkovskis (1985) suggests that the belief that "failing to prevent (or failing to try to prevent) harm to self or others is the same as having caused the harm in the first place" may be a key assumption in the generation of obsessional problems. Recently, Spranca, Minsk, and Barron (1991) demonstrated what they refer to as "omission bias" in nonclinical subjects. They showed that normal subjects judge responsibility for negative consequences to be diminished when an omission is involved as opposed to when some specific action was involved in bringing about the negative consequence. This is true in normal subjects even when the element of intention (i.e., the extent to which the person wishes the "negative" outcome to occur) is controlled for. Thus, most people appear to regard themselves as more responsible for what they actively do than what they fail to do. Clinical experience suggests that obsessional patients do not seem to show evidence of this type of omission bias with respect to their obsessional concerns. Preliminary results suggest that this effect may be idiosyncratic in that it affects obsessional patients' most prominent concerns rather than being a generalized phenomenon or bias.

The general belief that "ANY influence over outcome = responsibility for outcome" may increase concern with omissions; consideration of the phenomenology of obsessional problems suggests ways in which omissions may become more specific and troublesome to a vulnerable individual. An important factor in judgments concerning responsibility is the perception of "agency," meaning that one has chosen to bring something about. Particular importance is usually given to *premeditation* in the sense of being able to foresee possible harmful outcomes.
Thus:

> Responsible means "to some extent culpable (either morally or in law according to the context) for *one's own* acts or omissions." The ascription of responsibility in this sense on what we believe to have been the person's mental state at or before the time of the act or omission. "Premeditation" usually makes an objectionable act seem more culpable. *If the actor foresaw a real possibility of his causing harm*—for example by his way of driving—his act or omission will be called "reckless" and blamed accordingly. (Gregory & Zangwill, 1987, p. 681; emphasis added)

And:

> More often it is the actor's state of mind at the time of the act . . . that determines the degree to which he is regarded as blameworthy. If the act seems to have been

quite accidental—if for instance he knocks over a child whom he did not see in his path—he is not blamed, unless we think that he should have been aware of this as a real possibility. (Gregory & Zangwill, 1987, p. 681)

One of the problems experienced by obsessional patients is that it is often in the nature of the condition that they frequently foresee (and attempt to foresee) a wide range of possible negative outcomes; that is, the intrusive thoughts often concern things that could go wrong unless dealt with (such as transmitting contamination, hurting someone accidentally, leaving the door unlocked or the gas turned on). Sometimes it is not even permissible for an obsessional individual to try not to foresee problems/disasters, because this would mean that he or she had deliberately chosen this course, which again increases responsibility. When aware of this, some patients regard it as a *duty* to try to foresee negative outcomes. However, if in any case a negative outcome is foreseen even as an intrusive thought, responsibility is established, because to do nothing, the person would have to decide not to act to prevent the harmful outcome; that is, deciding *not* to act, despite being aware of possible disastrous consequences, becomes an active decision, making the person a causal agent in relation to those disastrous consequences. Thus, the occurrence of intrusive/obsessional thoughts transforms a situation where harm can only occur by omission into a situation where the person has "actively" chosen to allow the harm to take place. This might mean that the apparent absence of omission bias in obsessionals is mediated by the occurrence of obsessional thoughts.

Deciding not to do something results in a sense of "agency"; thus, patients will not be concerned about sharp objects they has not seen, and will not be concerned if they did not consider the possibility of harm. However, if something is seen and it occurs to him or her that they could or should take preventive action, the situation changes, because NOT acting becomes an active decision. In this way, the actual occurrence of intrusive thoughts of harm and/or responsibility for it come to play a key role in the perception of responsibility for their contents. Suppression, as described earlier, will further increase this effect by increasing the thoughts in precisely the situations that the obsessional most wishes to exclude any intrusion. Thus, having locked the door, the person tries not to think that it could be open, experiences the thought again, and is therefore constrained to act or risk being responsible through having chosen not to check. The motivation to suppress will increase, but it is very difficult to suppress a thought that is directly connected to an action just completed, so the action serves as a further cue for intrusion/suppression, and so on in the nightmarish way that obsessionals find themselves being tortured.

DECIDING WHEN TO DESIST: TRYING TOO HARD

Many of the areas problematic for obsessional patients concern activities that are, in others, usually relatively automatic, in that no particular conscious effort is devoted to them (e.g., deciding when to stop washing, recalling what has been said during a conversation, deciding whether a door is locked or the gas has been turned off). Again, obsessionals appear to try too hard in ways that interfere with the decision-making process itself. This problem may again be mediated by the occurrence of intrusions; to disregard intrusions concerning harm would be to actively disregard threat, as described earlier. Obsessionals tend to use two main strategies: (1) They repeat the action until it they are sure that it "feels right," or (2) they conduct the activity in such a way as to ensure some objective token of "completeness."

In the first instance, obsessionals use their mood or some other psychological state or mental sensation to confirm their decision to stop neutralizing activity. The basis for such judgments varies from person to person but most commonly involves feeling "comfortable" to a particular level, having "the right attitude," getting rid of feelings of unease or discomfort, or carrying out the neutralizing without experiencing the obsessional thought. In the first two instances, preexisting mood disturbance (depression or anxiety) makes finishing particularly difficult, as the obsessional patient needs to achieve the sense of rightness regardless of general mood. Furthermore, the person who excessively repeats an action often begins to develop *stronger* feelings of discomfort as time passes (and is perceived as wasted); thus, the strategy can become ever more counterproductive. The person is, however, trapped, as he or she believes it to be wrong to adopt any other strategy for the completion of the activity. Trying not to have the obsessional thought while ritualizing is a particularly difficult version of thought suppression, in that there is almost invariably a link between the obsession and the neutralizing activity. If someone washes because of a thought that he or she may be contaminated, terminating washing without thoughts of contamination presents special difficulties. Candida Richards, from the author's research team, has recently collected data identifying the use of unusual strategies to terminate checking in obsessional patients compared to controls.

SUMMARY AND CONCLUSIONS

Both phenomenology and current experimental studies are most consistent with the hypothesis that obsessional problems are the result of the specific appraisal of intrusive thoughts rather than a general neurological and cognitive deficit. Negative appraisals may give rise to deficits in some areas as a result of the strategies employed by obsessional patients. Obsessional problems can thus be regarded as arising from a pattern of specific responses to key stimuli to which the sufferer has acquired emotional sensitivity. Other problems such as reported memory and decision-making difficulties, and "failures of inhibition" are regarded as secondary to the emotional arousal and particularly to counterproductive coping strategies deployed by the sufferer. In other words, obsessional patients tend to try too hard to control their own cognitive functioning, and other cognitive functions suffer as a result of competition for processing resources.

The principal aim of cognitive-behavioral *treatment* for obsessional problems therefore follows directly from the theory. Therapy aims to help the patient conclude that obsessional thoughts, however distressing, are irrelevant to further action. Teaching the patient to control the occurrence of intrusive thoughts will be beneficial only if it alters the way in which their occurrence is interpreted, such as by convincing the patient that intrusive thoughts are at least partially under his or her own control and therefore are of no special significance. Thus, the key to control of obsessional thoughts may be to learn that the exercise of such control is unnecessary. Apart from the obvious therapy-outcome trials, further experimental investigations are required into pathways to overresponsibility, how best to reduce responsibility in both the short and long term, and specific investigations into ways in which the psychological formulation accounts for what appear to be general deficits, but which the theory suggests are the results of the sufferer trying too hard.

REFERENCES

Beck, A. T. (1976). *Cognitive therapy and the emotional disorders.* New York: International Universities Press.

Clark, D. M. (1986). A cognitive approach to panic. *Behaviour Research and Therapy, 24,* 461–470.

Clark, D. M., Ball, S., & Pape, D. (1991). An experimental investigation of thought suppression. *Behaviour Research and Therapy, 29,* 253–257.

Clark, D. M., Winton, E., & Thynn, L. (1993). A further experimental investigation of thought suppression. *Behaviour Research and Therapy, 31,* 207–210.

Enright, S. (1996). Obsessive compulsive disorder as a schizotype. In R. Rapee (Ed.), *Current controversies in the anxiety disorders.* New York: Guilford Press.

Freeston, M. H., Ladouceur, R., Gagnon, F., & Thibodeau, N. (1993). Beliefs about obsessional thoughts. *Journal of Psychopathology and Behavioral Assessment, 15,* 1–21.

Freeston, M. H., Ladouceur, R., Thibodeau, N., & Gagnon, F. (1991). Cognitive intrusions in a non-clinical population: I. Response style, subjective experience, and appraisal. *Behaviour Research and Therapy, 29,* 585–597.

Freeston, M. H., Ladouceur, R., Thibodeau, N., & Gagnon, F. (1992). Cognitive intrusions in a non-clinical population: II. Associations with depressive, anxious, and compulsive symptoms. *Behaviour Research and Therapy, 30,* 263–271.

Gregory, R. L., & Zangwill, O. L. (1987). *The Oxford companion to the mind.* Oxford, UK: Oxford University Press.

Kasvikis, Y., & Marks, I. M. (1988). Clomipramine, self-exposure, and therapist-accompanied exposure in obsessive–compulsive ritualizers: Two-year follow-up. *Journal of Anxiety Disorders, 2,* 291–298.

Lavy, E. H., & Van den Hout, M. (1990). Thought suppression induces intrusions. *Behavioural Psychotherapy, 18,* 251–258.

Maki, W. S., O'Neill, H. K., & O'Neill, G. W. (1994). Do nonclinical checkers exhibit deficits in cognitive control?: Tests of an inhibitory control hypothesis. *Behaviour Research and Therapy, 32,* 183–192.

Merckelbach, H., Muris, P., Van den Hout, M., & de Jong, P. (1991). Rebound effects of thought suppression: Instruction-dependent? *Behavioural Psychotherapy, 19*, 225–238.

Metzner, R. (1963). Some experimental analogs of obsessions. *Behaviour Research and Therapy, 1*, 231–236.

Meyer, V. (1966). Modification of expectations in cases with obsessional rituals. *Behaviour Research and Therapy, 4*, 273–280.

Mowrer, O. H. (1947). On the dual nature of learning—a re-interpretation of "conditioning" and "problem-solving." *Harvard Educational Review, 17*, 102–148.

Mowrer, O. H. (1960). *Learning theory and behavior.* New York: Wiley.

Nisbett, R. E., & Ross, R. L. (1980). *Strategies and shortcomings of social judgment.* Englewood Cliffs, NJ: Prentice-Hall.

Parkinson, L., & Rachman, S. J. (1981). The nature of intrusive thoughts. *Advances in Behavior Research and Therapy, 3*, 101–110.

Rachman, S. J. (1971). Obsessional ruminations. *Behaviour Research and Therapy, 9*, 225–238.

Rachman, S. J. (1993). Obsessions, responsibility and guilt. *Behaviour Research and Therapy, 31*, 149–154.

Rachman, S. J., & De Silva, P. (1978). Abnormal and normal obsessions. *Behaviour Research and Therapy, 16*, 233–248.

Rachman, S. J., & Hodgson, R. J. (1980). *Obsessions and compulsions.* Englewood Cliffs, NJ: Prentice-Hall.

Rachman, S. J., Hodgson, R., & Marks, I. M. (1971). The treatment of chronic obsessional neurosis. *Behaviour Research and Therapy, 9*, 237–247.

Roper, G., & Rachman, S. (1976). Obsessional–compulsive checking: Experimental replication and development. *Behaviour Research and Therapy, 14*, 25–32.

Roper, G., Rachman, S., & Hodgson, R. (1973). An experiment on obsessional checking. *Behaviour Research and Therapy, 11*, 271–277.

Salkovskis, P. M. (1985). Obsessional–compulsive problems: A cognitive-behavioural analysis. *Behaviour Research and Therapy, 23*, 571–583.

Salkovskis, P. M. (1988). Phenomenology, assessment and the cognitive model of panic. In S. J. Rachman & J. Maser (Eds.), *Panic: Psychological perspectives.* Hillsdale, NJ: Erlbaum.

Salkovskis, P. M. (1989a). Cognitive-behavioural factors and the persistence of intrusive thoughts in obsessional problems. *Behaviour Research and Therapy, 27*, 677–682.

Salkovskis, P. M. (1989b). Obsessive and intrusive thoughts: Clinical and non-clinical aspects. In P. M. G. Emmelkamp, W. T. A. M. Everaerd, & M. J. M. van Son (Eds.), *Fresh perspectives on anxiety disorders.* Amsterdam: Swets & Zeitlinger.

Salkovskis, P. M. (1991). The importance of behaviour in the maintenance of anxiety and panic: A cognitive account. *Behavioural Psychotherapy 19(1)*, 6–19.

Salkovskis, P. M., & Campbell, P. (1994). Thought suppression induces intrusion in naturally occurring negative intrusive thoughts. *Behaviour Research and Therapy, 32*, 1–8.

Salkovskis, P. M., & Harrison, J. (1984). Abnormal and normal obsessions—a replication. *Behaviour Research and Therapy, 22*, 549–552.

Salkovskis, P. M., & Kirk, J. (1989). Obsessional disorders. In K. Hawton, P. M. Salkovskis, J. Kirk, & D. M. Clark (Eds.), *Cognitive behavioural treatment for psychiatric disorders: A practical guide.* Oxford, UK: Oxford University Press.

Salkovskis, P. M., Rachman, S. J., Ladouceur, R., Freeston, M., Taylor, S., Kyrios, M., & Sica, C. (1996). Defining responsibility in obsessional problems. *Proceedings of the Smith College Women's Room—after the Toronto Cafeteria.*

Salkovskis, P. M., & Westbrook, D. (1989). Behaviour therapy and obsessional ruminations: Can failure be turned into success? *Behaviour Research and Therapy, 27(2)*, 149–60.

Salkovskis, P. M., Wroe, A., Richards, H. C., Morrison, N., Gledhill, A., Thorpe, S., Forrester, E., & Reynolds, M. (1998). *Responsibility assumptions and appraisals in obsessive–compulsive disorder.* Manuscript submitted for publication.

Seligman, M. E. P. (1971). Phobias and preparedness. *Behavior Therapy, 2,* 307–320.

Shafran, R., Thordarson, D. S., & Rachman, S. (1996). Thought–action fusion in obsessive compulsive disorder. *Journal of Anxiety Disorders, 10*(5), 379–391.

Sher, K. J., Frost, R. O., Kushner, M., Crews, T. M., & Alexander, J. E. (1989). Memory deficits in compulsive checkers: Replication and extension in a clinical sample. *Behaviour Research and Therapy, 27*(1), 65–69.

Solomon, R. L., & Wynne, L. C. (1954). Traumatic avoidance learning: The principles of anxiety conservation and partial irreversibility. *Psychological Review, 61,* 353–385.

Spranca, M., Minsk, E., & Baron, J. (1991). Omission and commission in judgement and choice. *Journal of Experimental Social Psychology, 27*(1), 76–105.

Teasdale, J. D. (1983). Negative thinking in depression: Cause, effect on reciprocal relationship? *Advances in Behavior Research and Therapy, 5,* 3–26.

Trinder, H., & Salkovskis, P. M. (1994). Personally relevant intrusions outside the laboratory: Long-term suppression increases intrusion. *Behaviour Research and Therapy, 32*(8), 833–842.

Wegner, D. M. (1989). *White bears and other unwanted thoughts; Suppression, obsession and the psychology of mental control.* New York: Viking.

Chapter 3

COGNITIVE AND BEHAVIORAL FEATURES OF OBSESSIVE–COMPULSIVE DISORDER

S. Rachman
Roz Shafran

The very concept of obsessive–compulsive disorder (OCD), and its precise definition, explicitly include cognitive and behavioral features—the obsessions are the cognitive element, and the compulsions are the behavioral element. The purpose of this chapter is to describe each of these elements and to give an account of the interplay between the two. In some cases, the problem is primarily or solely compulsions, and in others it is obsessive, but most often, both features are present (Lensi et al., 1996; Rachman & Hodgson, 1980; Rasmussen & Eisen, 1991). The disorder is not common but can be disabling and distressing for the affected person and also for friends and relatives who rarely escape the adverse consequences of this problem (Rasmussen & Eisen, 1991). Obsessions and compulsions are strongly associated with anxiety and even driven by anxiety (for these reasons, OCD is classified as an anxiety disorder in the DSM system). Obsessions and compulsions are also closely associated with depression (Black, Noyes, Goldstein, & Blum, 1992; Ricciardi & McNally, 1995).

OBSESSIONS

An obsession is an intrusive, repetitive thought, image, or impulse that is unacceptable or unwanted and gives rise to subjective resistance. It is generally regarded by the person as being repugnant, and it produces distress. It is characteristically difficult to control or remove. The person usually acknowledges the

51

senselessness of the impulse or idea. The content of an obsession is repugnant, worrying, threatening, blasphemous, obscene, nonsensical, or all of these. The major themes of obsessions are unacceptable, sexual, aggressive, or blasphemous ideas, for example, repetitive, blasphemous, obscene images of the Virgin Mary, or aggressive thoughts about attacking and harming elderly or infirm people, or having intrusive thoughts about unacceptable sexual acts.

The majority of naturally occurring obsessions are generated internally, but they can also be provoked promptly and with ease by external stimulation, such as by the sight of a sharp object that might then be incorporated into an unacceptable aggressive obsession. For example, a fond mother was tortured by thoughts that she might stab her young children and as a result was terrified of being left alone near knives or other sharp objects.

Horowitz (1975) demonstrated that after being exposed to stressful events, people tend to experience intrusive and repetitive thoughts. Consistent evidence was collected by Parkinson and Rachman (1980), who studied the experiences of a group of mothers whose children were being admitted to hospital for elective surgery. The mothers experienced extremely high levels of anxiety accompanied by a steep increase in unwanted and distressing thoughts. Reassuringly, the high level of anxiety and distressing thoughts decreased rapidly when the parents were informed that their children were safe again.

Progress in analyzing obsessions was made when it was assumed, and later demonstrated, that most people experience unwanted, intrusive thoughts that bear a qualitative similarity to obsessions, even though there are considerable differences in intensity and frequency (Rachman & De Silva, 1978; Salkovskis & Harrison, 1984). The identification of "normal" and "abnormal" obsessions was a step to addressing the following questions: What is the origin of these unacceptable thoughts, what function if any do they play, and why are they so difficult to control?

There are some similarities (and differences) between the intrusive, unwanted images of everyday life and certain aspects of clinical obsessions. Obsessions in the form of thoughts, images, or impulses certainly are a common experience. The large majority of nonclinical respondents report experiencing unwanted intrusive thoughts of the type that bear a strong similarity to obsessions. The form and the content of obsessions reported by nonclinical respondents and by obsessional patients are similar, but those experienced by the patients are more intense, more vivid, and longer-lasting. The following are some examples of obsessions described by patients (De Silva & Rachman, 1992):

- The thought of causing harm to children or elderly people.
- Blasphemous thoughts during prayers.
- The thought of "unnatural" sexual acts.
- The impulse to violently attack and kill a dog.
- The impulse to disrupt the peace at a gathering (e.g., shout obscenities or throw things).

Clinical obsessions also provoke significantly higher levels of anxiety, are hard to resist, and difficult to dismiss. It is precisely the anxiety-provoking and distressing obsessions that are the most difficult to control. The "normal obsessions" reported by the non-clinical respondents can be dismissed, blocked, or diverted with little effort or difficulty (Rachman & Hodgson, 1980).

It is possible that the observed connection between the distressing effects of the thought and its consequent adhesiveness are associated. There is a limited amount of evidence of a correlation between disturbed mood and the difficulty in dismissing an intrusive and unwanted thought (e.g., Sutherland & Rachman, 1982), and we also have evidence that the frequency of obsessions is significantly increased by increments in anxiety, even if the anxiety is not directly related to the content of the obsession. In a cognitive re-analysis of this and related questions, Salkovskis (1985) suggested that the distress and adhesiveness of obsessions arise from the person's overinterpretation or total misinterpretation of the significance of the relevant thoughts. Given that almost everyone experiences unwanted and even repugnant thoughts or images or impulses from time to time, a great deal depends on how the affected person interprets the significance of these thoughts. Salkovskis argued that insofar as they interpret these unwanted thoughts as being of great significance (e.g., if they interpret the thoughts as revealing some utterly repugnant but important aspect of their true personality), they will experience a significant increase in anxiety and other adverse emotions. These emotional disturbances in turn will interfere with the person's ability to deal with these thoughts. A full account of the cognitive approach to obsessions can be found in Rachman (1997, 1998).

Dealing with the Obsession

People who experience obsessions usually engage in behavior that is intended to provide "relief" from their distress. Three main types of behavior are commonly caused by obsessions: avoidance behavior, compulsive behavior, and neutralization. The particular avoidance has a clear, explicit relationship to the content of the obsession. For example, a patient troubled by obsessions of shouting obscenities avoided attending church; a patient distressed by thoughts of harming children avoided visiting her nephews and nieces, and so on. In addition to avoidance, the majority of people with obsessions engage in compulsive behavior designed to prevent harm and/or reduce distress. Neutralization is an attempt to "put right" the obsession, to cancel its effects, or prevent a feared outcome. Neutralization can be overt or covert (see pp. 56–57).

COMPULSIONS

The compulsive behavior that is characteristic of many people who suffer from OCD is in many ways the purest example of abnormal behavior. Compulsions are repetitive, stereotyped, intentional acts. The necessary and sufficient conditions for describing repetitive behavior as compulsive are an experienced sense of pressure to act, and the attribution of this pressure to internal sources. The occurrence of resistance is an important confirmatory feature, but it is not necessary or sufficient. The compulsions may be wholly unacceptable or, more often, partly acceptable, but are regarded by the person as being excessive, exaggerated, or, especially when judged in calmer moments, senseless. For these people, the repetitive intentional execution of purposeful but irrational actions generally provokes subjective resistance that conflicts with their strong compulsion to act. Although the particular activities are within the person's voluntary control (i.e., they can be delayed, extended, postponed, or reduced—or even carried out by other people), the urge to carry out the acts can be so strong that people execute the urges against their rational inclinations. Patients are driven to repeat their behavior, such as washing their hands, over and over again—almost always with the purpose and expectation of gaining some relief from their discomfort/anxiety. The compulsive behavior is a source of considerable distress, and people experience a sense of reduced volition, but the compulsive activity is repeatedly reinforced by its temporary anxiolytic properties.

Types of Compulsive Behavior

The classical examples of compulsive behavior are repetitive, excessive, stereotyped *cleaning* and comparably stereotyped *checking*, especially to ensure safety in the home and at work (e.g., repeatedly checking the safety of the stove, doors, windows). This division arises from clinical observation and has been confirmed by factor-analytic and other psychometric studies (Rachman & Hodgson, 1980, Chap. 10 this volume), but many people with obsessional compulsive problems have elements of both of these forms of compulsions. The less common types of compulsion are obsessional slowness in which the person carries out everyday self-care activities in a stereotyped meticulous order (e.g., 6 hours to wash and dress), hoarding, an excessive need for orderliness, and obsessional doubting (see Black et al., 1992; Rachman, 1974; Rachman & Hodgson, 1980; Rasmussen & Eisen, 1991, Veale, 1993).

COMPULSIVE CLEANING

Cleaning compulsions share some of the properties of checking compulsions but have in addition a significant element of passive avoidance, that is, taking steps to avoid coming into contact with the stimulus or situation that might provoke the urge to clean (e.g., avoiding contaminating contact with persons or places that might have an association with the AIDS virus). When these acts of passive avoidance fail, the person feels impelled to escape. The immediate purpose of carrying out cleaning compulsions is restorative, but they can also have longer-term aims. Cleaning compulsions are characterized by high levels of anxiety and share some similarities with phobias. The relation between the main forms of compulsions and phobias is illustrated in Figure 3.1.

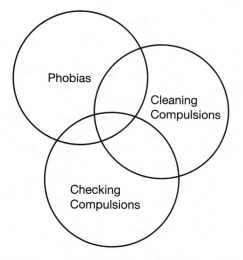

FIGURE 3.1. The overlap between phobias, cleaning compulsions, and checking compulsions.

In rare but striking instances, the cleaning compulsions are an attempt to re-move dirt or pollution that is not observable (such as invisible, bacteria-like "mind-germs"). These attempts to remove "mental pollution" (Rachman, 1994) are inevitably unsuccessful. In these cases, two, five, or even 10 showers fail to produce a feeling of cleanliness. For example, one patient tried with indifferent success to wash away the fear and guilt induced by obsessive images of killing his relatives or acquaintances.

COMPULSIVE CHECKING

Checking compulsions are intended to prevent harm from coming to someone and are almost invariably oriented toward the future. For the most part, they can be construed as a form of preventive behavior (actively avoiding the prospect of some adverse event). Checking compulsions, more often than cleaning compul-sions, are associated with doubting and indecisiveness, take a long time to com-plete, have a slow onset, evoke internal resistance, and tend to be accompanied by feelings of anger or tension.

COMPULSIVE REASSURANCE SEEKING

Sometimes, in response to their tiring obsessions, people make repeated requests for reassurance (which is a form of checking by proxy) in their search for mean-ing and, they hope, release. Seeking reassurance is equivalent to compulsive be-havior and often is an undisguised attempt to enlist someone else to help in one's checking. Although it appears to be a request for information, it generally is an attempt to reduce one's anxiety; in virtually all instances, the patient is fully aware of the answer to the question.

COMPULSIVE HOARDING

Another form of compulsive behavior, compulsive hoarding, can result in an accumulation of piles of objects that occupy a steadily increasing amount of living space, with the affected person and family members having to navigate their way through mounds of clutter. When a room becomes virtually unusable, it is closed off, and the space is turned into an overflow storage area. For example, a patient who lived in a single-bedroom apartment built up a collection of articles (mainly gifts that she might want to donate) that gradually occupied the entire bedroom, forcing her to sleep on the couch in the sitting room. Even in this remaining space, she had to thread her way through steadily rising mounds of objects. The objects were placed on the floor and on all the furniture, including the bed, with the exception of one chair, which she used for sitting when she ate or watched television.

Compulsive hoarding sometimes is part of a broader OCD and shares some characteristics of other forms of compulsive behavior, such as repeated checking. It has been pointed out that indecisiveness is strongly associated with compulsive hoarding, and both appear to be driven by a strong tendency to avoid making mistakes. Compulsive hoarders, for example, will explain their ever-growing collections as a need to ensure that they have the object or item should the need ever arise; they have an inflated fear of the consequences of falling short at some unforeseen time in the future. The indecisiveness is also connected with the great difficulty that people have in discarding items from their collection. They experience inordinate difficulty in deciding which items can be discarded and which items it is necessary to retain (Frost & Hartl, 1995, 1996). In these extreme cases, the compulsive need to collect and retain unnecessary objects is at first an embarrassment and inconvenience, but then evolves into a source of distress and an inability to function normally.

COVERT NEUTRALIZATION

In addition to avoidance and overt compulsive behavior such as washing, checking, hoarding, and so on, people with obsessions may also engage in neutralizing (e.g., "undoing" the thought), which is functionally equivalent to overt compulsions (see Freeston & Ladouceur, 1997). The purpose of neutralizing activities, which often are covert, is to put matters right—to reduce the moral discomfort caused by a repugnant thought or impulse and/or to reduce the likelihood of the nasty event occurring, or to reduce the effects of the event. It is mainly directed at undoing the effects of a person's own thought or action. At best, these neutralizing activities will provide transient relief, but in the long run, they serve to confirm the significance of the intrusive thoughts. Hence, they contribute to the persistence of the problem.

Neutralization is said to resemble overt compulsions, because the neutralizations and compulsions are both attempts to reduce anxiety, one mainly covert (neutralization) and the other mainly overt. The main purpose of checking is to prevent the event, whereas neutralization is aimed at canceling the effects of a person's thought or action, and this may or may not be an attempt to prevent the event. Neutralization is considered to be a compulsion when the same neutralization method is repeatedly used in response to an obsession and the neutralization is carried out in a stereotypical, fixed manner each time the obsession occurs. If different neutralization methods are used in response to an obsession, and if the type of neutralization method is flexible, then neutralization is not compulsive but is just one technique that the patient is using to obtain relief. It is a tactic rather than a compulsion.

In his cognitive analysis of OCD, Salkovskis (1985) attaches considerable significance to the role and effects of neutralization and connects it to the concept of inflated responsibility and the need for reassurance. Neutralization, compulsive acts, and reassurance seeking share common features and all can be construed as attempts to reduce the probability of an adverse event or its effects, and also to reduce one's responsibility for any such anticipated misfortune (Salkovskis, 1996). The clinical implications of neutralization are fully described by Salkovskis and Kirk (1997).

Most attempts at neutralization are covert and difficult to access. So for the purposes of experimentation, it is necessary to use a method for externalizing neutralization, and hence to make it accessible and open to manipulation. In a recent experimental investigation, the hypothesis that neutralization resembles overt compulsions was examined (Rachman, Shafran, Mitchell, Trant, & Teachman, 1996). In particular, it was predicted that (1) neutralization reduces the anxiety evoked by unacceptable thoughts, and (2) if neutralization is delayed, anxiety and the urge to neutralize will decay naturally. To test the hypothesis, 63 subjects prone to a cognitive bias known to be associated with obsessional complaints (thought–action fusion, TAF; to be discussed) were asked to write a sentence about harm coming to a relative or friend in order to evoke anxiety. Measures of anxiety (and other variables of interest such as guilt, responsibility, and the likelihood of harm) were taken. Subjects were then instructed either immediately to neutralize ($n = 29$) or delay for 20 minutes ($n = 34$), after which time anxiety and urge to neutralize were re-assessed. The participants who had neutralized were then instructed to delay, and those who had delayed were now instructed to neutralize, after which time the final assessments were taken. The results confirmed the predictions and supported the hypothesis that neutralization resembles overt compulsions. Of note, there were no differences between anxiety reduction after a 20-minute delay, and after immediate neutralization (see Figure 3.2).

The Role of Anxiety in the Maintenance of Compulsive Behavior

One of the most puzzling aspects of obsessive–compulsive behavior is its persistence. There is no obvious reason for people to engage in this repetitive, tiring, embarrassing, and unwanted, self-defeating compulsive behavior. Even more puzzling is the persistent recurrence of intrusive, unacceptable, and distressing

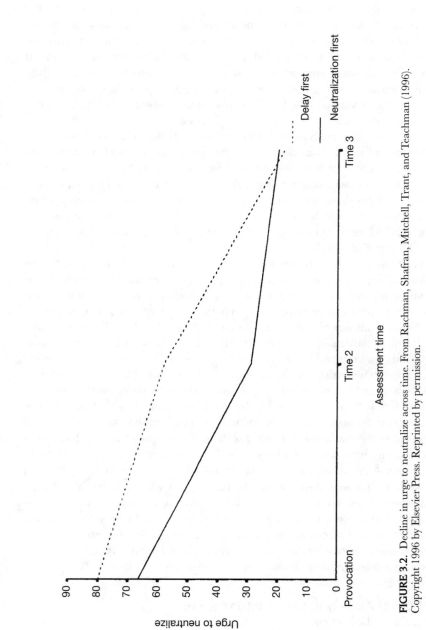

FIGURE 3.2. Decline in urge to neutralize across time. From Rachman, Shafran, Mitchell, Trant, and Teachman (1996). Copyright 1996 by Elsevier Press. Reprinted by permission.

thoughts. The persistence of these abnormal experiences and behavior is the core of the problem.

The most favored answer is that compulsive behavior persists because it reduces anxiety. This view was proposed in one form or another before and during the development of modern behavior theory and therapy, and received support from most psychologists who attempted to explain this type of abnormal behavior. For many years Mowrer's (1939, 1960) two-stage theory of fear and avoidance, stating that successful avoidance behavior paradoxically preserves fear, was incorporated into many accounts of obsessive–compulsive behavior (Eysenck & Rachman, 1965; Rachman & Hodgson, 1980), and it had a profound influence on the way in which we construe this problem. The reports given by people who have OCD can be accommodated with ease into Mowrer's view, and the theory served well for a period. The inadequacies of the theory, described elsewhere (Rachman & Hodgson, 1980), gradually became apparent, and the theory can no longer provide a comprehensive account of obsessional–compulsive behavior. Patients commonly say that they have to carry out their compulsive acts in order to achieve relief from tension or anxiety. However, this kind of information is not conclusive, and there is a difficulty at source, because a small proportion of patients deny that the completion of their compulsive behavior is followed by a sense of relief (Beech, 1971, 1974). A combination of clinical investigations, psychometric studies, and experimental analyses has introduced a measure of clarity into the nature and functions of compulsive acts.

In a number of experiments, it was found that when patients with OCD are deliberately stimulated by contact with one of their provocative stimuli (e.g., touching dirt); they almost invariably report a steep increase in anxiety and an accompanying urge to carry out the relevant compulsive act (e.g., cleaning) (see Rachman & Hodgson, 1980, for a review). If the compulsive act is carried out, the anxiety declines promptly. If in other experimental conditions they are asked to delay carrying out the compulsive activity (such as cleaning), their anxiety level tends to persist for a while, then gradually declines. In other words, the execution of the relevant compulsive act is followed by a quicker decline in anxiety (Rachman & Hodgson, 1980). An illustration of this relationship is given in Figure 3.3.

The direct prediction that compulsive activities are followed by a reduction in anxiety was the subject of a series of connected experiments in which a simple procedure was used (see Rachman & Hodgson, 1980). The patients were relaxed as far as possible and then asked to carry out some "prohibited" activity that would give rise to an immediate increase in anxiety, such as touching a dirty carpet. Once the anxiety and the associated urge were evoked, the patients were asked to carry out the appropriate compulsive act (such as washing) and report on the strength of the compulsive urges and the amount of anxiety experienced at each stage of the experiment. In the majority of these cases, the completion of the compulsive activity was indeed followed by a reduction in anxiety, and in the strength of the accompanying urge.

Among patients with cleaning compulsion, very few exceptions were en-

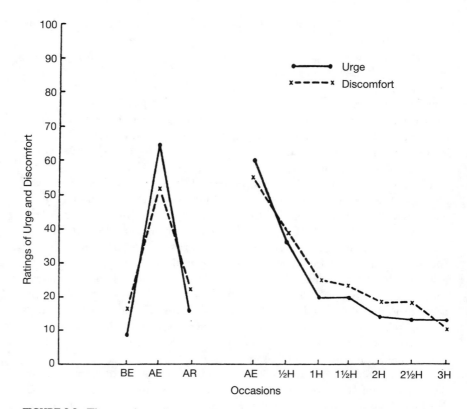

FIGURE 3.3. The experimental provocation of anxiety and compulsive cleaning urges. Mean ratings for urge and discomfort across occasions ($n = 11$). The measurement occasions plotted on the horizontal axis are as follows: BE, before exposure to provoking stimulus; AE, after exposure; AR, after ritual; AE, after second exposure; and half-hourly intervals up to 3 hours. From Rachman and Hodgson (1980). Copyright 1980 by S. Rachman. Reprinted by permission.

countered. Among patients with checking compulsions, however, a number of exceptions occurred in which the completion of the compulsive checking either left the anxiety unchanged or, in exceptional circumstances, was followed by a slight increment in anxiety. Notably, the amount of anxiety that could be provoked under these experimental conditions was larger (and easier) among patients with cleaning compulsions than among those who engaged predominantly in checking compulsions (Figure 3.4). The significance of the difference was missed at the time, only to emerge when Salkovskis (1985) drew attention to the important effects of inflated responsibility (to follow).

Compulsive Urges

There is a close and probably causal relationship between compulsive urges and compulsive acts, with the former producing the latter. Using the same experi-

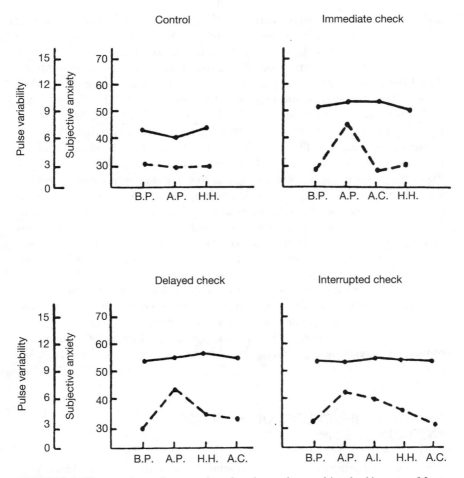

FIGURE 3.4. The experimental provocation of anxiety and compulsive checking urges. Means for subjective anxiety/discomfort (broken line) and pulse rate (continuous line) under four conditions. B.P., measurements before provocation; A.P., measurements after provocation; A.C., measurements taken after check; H.H., measures after half-hour intervals; A.I., measures after an interrupted check From Rachman and Hodgson (1980). Copyright 1980 by S. Rachman. Reprinted by permission.

mental methods, an attempt was made to collect information about the nature and the course of compulsive urges. For purposes of the experiments, compulsive urges were defined as impelling forces directed toward a goal, and it was implied that the source of the prompting was internal, even if the urge itself was partially evoked by an external event. In a psychological sense, the compulsive urges are the psychological activity that lies between an obsessional thought and the execution of a compulsive action (Rachman & Hodgson, 1980)

As in the experiments on investigating the persistence of compulsive behavior, each patient was first exposed to a provoking situation that led to a significant increase in anxiety and compulsive urges. Again, it was found that the anxiety and urges can be provoked regularly, reliably, and without difficulty. The natural course of these compulsive urges, their relation to anxiety, and the extent to which they could be modified were analyzed in two experiments.

It was found that completion of the appropriate compulsion promptly reduced the anxiety and the urges, leaving only a minimal amount of residual anxiety. After the anxiety and urges had been provoked, a 3-hour observation period was used in order to trace the time course of the so-called "spontaneous" decay of anxiety and urges. In most cases, the anxiety and urges underwent a significant decline at the end of the first hour of the observation period, and by 3 hours at the outside, almost complete dissipation occurred (see Figure 3.3). When the person was allowed to carry out the compulsive action, a rapid and steep decline in the urges was reported. It became evident that the completion of the relevant compulsion serves a function in the sense that it produces *quicker* relief. In view of the relative slowness with which compulsive urges and anxiety decay under spontaneous conditions, it is understandable why compulsive behavior develops in the first place. It produces quicker relief from intense anxiety.

Therapeutic experience revealed that when patients learn that they can expect relief from their anxiety and compulsive urges, even if they refrain from carrying out the appropriate compulsion, the compulsions begin to weaken. After repeated experiences of the natural, spontaneous decay of anxiety and compulsive urges, a lasting decrement in the anxiety and compulsive urges takes place.

RELATIONSHIP BETWEEN OBSESSIONS AND COMPULSIONS

Obsessions and compulsions are closely related, and in the study by Akhtar, Wig, Verma, Pershod, and Verma (1975), it was found that only 25% of the patients had obsessions that were not associated with overt acts. In a study of 150 obsessional patients, Wilner, Reich, Robins, Fishman, and van Doren (1976) reported that 69% of the patients complained of both obsessions and compulsions, 25% had obsessions only, and 6% had compulsions only.

Most commonly, compulsions follow the obsessions. The experience of an obsession is almost always distressing and generally prompts the affected person to take steps to reduce the unease. These steps can take the form of observable compulsions or avoidance behavior, and, frequently, attempts to neutralize the probability and/or anticipated effects of the obsession. Repeated requests for reassurance usually are a disguised form of compulsion.

Occasionally, the compulsive behavior gives rise to an obsession, for instance, repeated checking of the gas stove can be followed by obsessive doubts about one's mental stability and reliability (perhaps another example of Arntz, Ravner, & Van den Hout's [1995] post hoc reasoning, in which the occurrence of fear is taken to signify the presence of a danger).

INFORMATION PROCESSING AND OCD

The widespread adoption of cognitive analyses of anxiety disorders, including OCD, is reflected in the growing research into how information is perceived, selected, stored, and recalled by people who are anxious. In respect to OCD, two questions about information processing are of particular interest. How can we account for the extreme sensitivity to "threat" stimuli exhibited by people with OCD, and how can we explain the apparently contradictory evidence regarding their memorial ability/functioning? The curious inability of many OCD patients who engage in repetitive checking to remember whether they have or have not switched off the electrical appliances, locked the doors, and so on, gave rise to the hypothesis that people with OCD suffer from a memory deficit (Brown, Kosslyn, Breiter, Baer, & Jenike, 1994; Foa, Ilai, McCarthy, Shoyer, & Murdoch, 1993; MacDonald, Antony, MacLeod, & Richter, 1997; Rubenstein, Peynircioglu, Chambless, & Pigott, 1993; Sher, Mann, & Frost, 1984. (And, in the view of some researchers, the deficit is a result of biological dysfunction or damage [Boone, Ananth, Philpott, Kaur, & Djenderedjian, 1991; Tallis, 1995; Zielinski, Taylor, & Juzwin, 1991]).

The study of information processing in OCD is best appreciated within the broader context of studies of information processing in anxiety disorders generally (Barlow, 1988; Rachman, 1998). It is assumed that people vary in their proneness to experience anxiety, and that the vulnerable ones become hypervigilant when entering a novel or potentially intimidating situation. Their hypervigilance promotes rapid and global scanning, which then turns to an intense, narrow focus if a threat is detected. The detection of a threat triggers an inhibition of ongoing behavior (Gray, 1982), often characterized by attentive stillness and high arousal. The relevant cognitive schemas are activated and used to evaluate and assign meaning to the event (Beck & Emery, 1985); the perceived information, whether from an external or internal source, is then interpreted as signifying safety or danger. If safe, the person can then resume the ongoing behavior but if there is danger of harm, anxiety arises and may be followed by escape–avoidance–coping or, in the case of OCD, compulsive and neutralizing behavior.

The early detection of threat is of survival value, and appropriately apprehensive anxiety has obvious functional significance. It follows that there should be a selective attentional bias favoring threat, especially when one is entering circumstances that are unfamiliar or have a history of threat and danger. This selective attention is a combination of conscious, deliberate, scanning and automatic, nonconscious scanning (Mathews & MacLeod, 1994). A particularly clear account of the nature of anxious hypervigilance and attention is given by Michael Eysenck (1992), who regards this phenomenon as both a reaction to potential threat and a component of cognitive vulnerability to anxiety (see also Mathews, MacLeod, & Tata, 1986; Williams, Watts, MacLeod, & Mathews, 1988). According to Eysenck, people who are predisposed to anxiety manifest hypervigilance in these ways: They engage in a "high rate of environmental scanning which involves numerous rapid eye movements throughout the visual field, . . . a propensity to attend selectively to threat-related rather than neutral stimuli; a broadening of attention prior to the detection of such stimuli, and a narrowing of attention when a salient stimulus is being processed" (1992, p. 43). He argues that hypervigilance is a vulnerability factor for anxiety disorders and is evident in patients and in non-patient groups who are high in trait anxiety.

Hypervigilance is especially obvious under stressful conditions. In clinical practice with patients suffering from anxiety disorders, the occurrence of hypervigilance and selective attention is an obvious and daily occurrence. In extreme cases, the attentional processes are so distorted that the patients engage in rapid visual scanning in virtually all new or ambiguous situations. For example, a 38-year-old accountant who was suffering from a severe OCD that centered on his fear of disease contamination, and in particular of AIDS, engaged in rapid, broad, visual scanning whenever he left his home. The scanning was particularly intense and agitated whenever he went into situations in which he thought that the risk of encountering AIDS-contaminated material was increased. During one treatment session that took place on the grounds of a large hospital, he carried out vigorous visual scanning of the parking lot, searching for any signs of discarded hypodermics or other medical materials, which he regarded as presenting a serious threat to his health. It was extraordinarily difficult to persuade him to stop scanning the ground around him and instead to look upward at the buildings ahead of him. Whenever he observed a suspicious object, and this included an astonishingly wide range of perfectly neutral stimuli, he rapidly concentrated his full attention on the suspect object. Where he could risk it, he would then approach very gingerly to make a precise determination of what the object was and whether it might constitute a danger. If he was able to satisfy himself that it was indeed a harmless object, he would then return to his broad, general scanning. On those occasions, however, when his narrow, intense focusing of attention on the object led him to conclude that it might be some contaminated medical material, he rapidly escaped and was disinclined to go anywhere near that part of the hospital for the remainder of the treatment session.

Another patient with obsessive–compulsive problems, who had a severe fear of diseases, including AIDS, was particularly frightened by the prospect of encountering other people's blood, which she felt would constitute a serious threat to her health, even if it was the smallest trace of dried blood, and even if she approached no closer than 3 or 4 feet from the spot of dried blood. Her interpretation of the threat emanating from other people's blood, including people who were wearing the smallest piece of bandage to cover a minor nick, was indeed a gross catastrophic misinterpretation of the probability of harm coming to her and an over-estimation of the seriousness of any contact. Nevertheless, her fear of other people's blood was so intense that whenever she went into a public place, she would rapidly scan the physical environment and also the people she encountered constantly looking for evidence of blood, cuts, bandages, adhesive tape, and so forth. She had trained herself so well that she could indeed pick up traces of red spots at a considerable distance and was usually accurate. However, her perception of red spots was grossly in error in overperceiving the occurrence of red spots of blood. She tended to misperceive as blood a wide range of spots of different colors along the color continuum, so that spots of almost any dark hue were mistaken as evidence of blood (e.g., spots of mud or small pieces of waste paper, etc.).

It is assumed that people who are vulnerable to anxiety enter most situations, particularly if they are novel or known to be intimidating, with well-formed expectations, and they are selectively tuned to attend to stimuli that might be threatening. If the information is given a benign interpretation, the anxiety generated up to this point will decline. If, however, the person misinterprets the cues as signifying danger, high levels of anxiety, even of panic, can be expected.

Important misinterpretations tend to have two dimensions. They can be misinterpretations in which the probability of an aversive event occurring is exaggerated, or the misinterpretation can be an over-estimation of the seriousness of the anticipated event (or, of course, a combination of high probability and high seriousness). We already know that people who suffer from excessive levels of anxiety or depression are much inclined to over-estimate the probability and the seriousness of unfortunate events (Butler & Mathews, 1983), and the research findings of Clark (1988) and of Ehlers (1992) confirm this observation.

Anxiety has "by-products" that include inattentiveness to other people or stimuli, the impairment of desired concentration, and feelings of fatigue. Much to the bewilderment of friends and relatives, people who suffer from OCD can complain of being extremely tired even though they have spent the entire day housebound and physically inactive. In fact, the hypervigilance, selective attention, and concentrated attempts to deal with anxiety all require considerable effort, and it should not be surprising that people who experience persistent anxiety so often report feeling drained.

Clinically, it is apparent that patients with OCD do selectively attend to threat (e.g., patients who fear contracting the AIDS virus will selectively attend to signs of blood). Selective attention to this set of stimuli arises from a biased recall of threatening information regarding AIDS and because of past encounters with blood spots and traces. The selectivity of anxious attention is determined in large part by their particular memories, some of which are definitely skewed. Often, their memories were more disturbed (and disturbing) than the original events that were the subject of their recall. Comparatively mild events can become transformed into remembered catastrophes. But not all of these memories are errors of negative bias. Some of the memories are enhanced, that is, positively biased.

Attentional bias in OCD has been investigated using information-processing paradigms that examine hyperviligance for threat words. Using explicit memory measures (incidental recall and recognition) and priming (reading speed), patients with OCD demonstrated a normal performance on explicit memory tasks but failed to show feature-specific priming, leading the authors to conclude that they may have attended more focally on the priming task compared with normal controls (Wiggs, Martin, Altemus, & Murphy, 1996). Numerous studies consistently report that OCD patients with contamination fears selectively attend to relevant threat words (Foa & McNally, 1986; Foa et al., 1993; Tata, Leibowitz, Prunty, Cameron, & Pickering, 1996). The same has not been found for other OCD patients, such as checkers. It has also been demonstrated that the specific vigilance of OCD patients with "contamination" fears diminishes with successful treatment (Foa & McNally, 1986). In the most recent of these studies, using a visual dot-probe test, OCD subjects showed a content-specific vigilance for threat words compared to mood-matched high-trait-anxious controls; the reverse was true for social anxiety words. Both OCD and high-trait-anxious controls showed a general threat interference effect that was not content specific (Tata et al., 1996). These results are similar to those of Mathews et al. (1986) for anxious patients, and the authors conclude that "the attentional disturbance in OCD may be of a parallel kind to those found in anxiety disorders" (Tata et al., 1996, p. 58). Somewhat surprisingly, there is an "absence of a negative bias in explicit memory for patients with generalized anxiety disorder . . . and it is all the more surprising because there is substantial evidence for the existence of such a bias in depressed patients" (Williams et al., 1988, p. 96). And again, "anxious patients definitely do not have a negative memory bias in explicit memory, but there are indications that they may possess a negative implicit memory bias" (Eysenck, 1992, p. 96).

Bradley, Mogg, and Williams (1995) produced evidence of explicit and implicit memory biases in depressed patients but found no evidence of these biases in anxious patients. These results were consistent with their view that "depressives show memory biases in explicit memory tasks . . . such as free recall or recognition. . . . There is little evidence that they are biased in early attentional processes. By contrast anxiety is associated with early attentional mood-congruent biases but there is little consistent evidence of such biases in explicit memory tasks" (Bradley et al., 1995, p. 755). These results and conclusions are consistent with most of the available evidence, but there are reasons to expect that ultimately it will be found that these cognitive biases in attention and memory operate in both anxiety and in depression (Rachman, 1998).

Interestingly, although a number of studies have shown that there are attentional biases in anxious subjects, there is only weak and contradictory evidence of *memory* biases in these subjects. The studies showing memory biases in depressed subjects have not been replicated in people with anxiety. "It appears that different emotions may be more specific in their effects on cognitive processing than was originally thought. One possible interpretation of the data is that anxious subjects, but not depressed subjects, orient their attention towards threat. Depressed subjects (but not generally anxious subjects) may selectively remember negative material" (Williams et al., 1988, p. 168).

For elaborate reasons, Williams et al. (1988) and Mathews, Mogg, May, and Eysenck (1989) argued that clinically anxious people should display a negative bias in implicit memory but not in explicit memory. "The weight of empirical evidence suggests strongly that facilitated ability to recall emotionally negative information is a characteristic of elevated depression, but not of elevated anxiety" (Mathews & MacLeod, 1994, p. 34). Williams et al. (1988, p. 167) report that "repeated attempts to demonstrate a relation between anxiety and recall have failed."

These failures speak to the elusiveness of the phenomenon, rather than its non-existence. The surprising failures are ironic, because one of the earliest and prized examples of implicit memory, confirming the operation of non-conscious processes in memory, was provided by Claparède (1911) in a clinical situation in which anxiety may well have been operative. In the large and growing literature on the subject of memory functions in relation to anxiety, the findings are inconsistent (see also Edelmann, 1992; Eysenck, 1992; Williams et al., 1988). Cloitre, Shear, Cancienne, and Zeitlin (1994) found that patients with panic disorder showed biased explicit and implicit memory for catastrophic associations to bodily sensation words, and memory deficits have been reported in patients with posttraumatic stress disorder (Cloitre et al., 1994; McNally, Lasko, Macklin, & Pitman, 1995). On the other hand, several studies have failed to find a relationship between anxiety and memory bias (Chambless & Hope, 1996; Dalgelish, 1994; Rapee, McCallum, Melville, Ravenscroft, & Rodney, 1994).

One of the reasons that the memory-deficit hypothesis regarding OCD attracts attention is that it has face validity—compulsive checkers do report that they cannot clearly recall checking the stove (for example), even when the action has been completed moments previously. However, it is also evident to clinicians that many patients with OCD have well-developed memorial abilities and can recall precise details of situations and experiences (e.g., contact with contaminants) that were disturbing or threatening in the past. So, for example, a patient who was intensely frightened of disease-related contaminants, and consequently engaged in extensive avoidance behavior, could recall in detail the types of bloodstain or other threatening material that he had encountered in particular places as far back as 12 years ago. The same patient also had a milder fear of making errors and, as a result, engaged in a certain amount of checking behavior, especially to ensure that the stove had been switched off. As is common in compulsive checking, he frequently had difficulty remembering whether he had correctly turned off the stove, and on numerous occasions, he felt compelled to return to the kitchen to check his memory. So we have a not uncommon example in this type of disorder of a curious combination of excellent and precisely accurate memory relating to some threats and a patchy and infirm recollection of other activities. (Incidentally this kind of intra-person inconsistency in memorial ability and performance is not easily compatible with assumptions of a biological causation of significant memory and other cognitive impairments in the anxiety disorders).

This curious combination of excellent memory for some threats and poor recollection for others may be responsible for the inconsistencies regarding memory deficits reported in the literature. Studies by Sher and colleagues (Sher, Frost, & Otto, 1983; Sher et al., 1984; Sher, Frost, Kushner, Crews, & Alexander, 1989) found that nonclinical "checkers" had poorer recall for past actions than noncheckers, and that the "checkers" had significantly lower Memory Quotients, measured using the Wechsler Memory Scale (WMS; Wechsler & Stone, 1945).

However, all "checkers" scored within the normal range on the WMS, and the studies did not use clinical subjects with a diagnosis of OCD. Similar findings were reported by Rubenstein and colleagues (1993), again using subclinical "checkers" rather than clinical cases of OCD. In their study, both normal controls and subclinical checkers remembered self-generated words better than read ones, but they were more likely to confuse whether they had read or generated the words, they recalled fewer actions overall, and they more often misremembered whether they had performed, observed, or written these actions.

These findings have not been replicated using subjects with a diagnosis of OCD. McNally amd Kohlbeck (1993) did not find a deficit in the ability of OCD checkers or OCD noncheckers to distinguish between memories for performed actions and memories for imagined actions. Using different paradigms, patients with OCD discriminated seen from imagined words significantly better than normal control subjects (Brown et al., 1994; Constans, Foa, Franklin, & Mathews, 1995). The same pattern of results has been reported using a recognition measure to show that clinically compulsive checkers were unimpaired in their memory, as compared to noncheckers and nonclinical controls (MacDonald et al., 1997). Despite the accuracy of their memory, in the majority of these studies, the subjects with OCD demonstrated significantly less confidence in their memory judgments relative to controls or reported that they desired higher levels of memory vividness than they were able to produce.

Neuropsychological measures, including the Rey–Osterrieth complex figure (Rey, 1941; Osterrieth, 1944), have also been utilized to test the "memory deficit" hypothesis. On these measures, patients with OCD show some visual memory deficits relative to normal controls (Boone et al., 1991; Christensen, Kim, Dyksen, & Hoover, 1992; Cox, Fedio, & Rapoport, 1989; Martinot et al., 1990; Zielinski et al., 1991). On the basis of these neuropsychological studies, it has been concluded that "all the evidence above suggests the presence of a visual memory deficit and/or a visual–spatial memory deficit in patients with OCD" (Tallis, 1995; p. 96).

In summary, the results regarding memory deficits are inconsistent, and the conclusions are dependent upon the paradigm used to test the hypothesis. However, at present, the hypothesis that patients with OCD may suffer from a *lack of confidence* in their memory in particular settings is gaining empirical support (MacDonald et al., 1997; McNally & Kohlbeck, 1993).

THOUGHT SUPPRESSION AND OCD

In some circumstances, attempts to suppress a particular thought result in a paradoxical increase in that very thought. If confirmed and clarified, this phenomenon may have a direct bearing on the frequency and persistence of obsessions. Given the fact that obsessions and compulsions usually give rise to resistance, especially in the early stages (Rachman & Hodgson, 1980), these attempts at thought suppression may inadvertently add to the problem.

The paradoxical effect of attempts at thought suppression is part of the common knowledge of philosophers but was brought to the attention of psychologists by Wegner (Wegner, Schneider, Carter, & White, 1987). The original claims of the widespread, invariable effects of thought suppression have been tempered by the accumulating research (Lavy & Van den Hout, 1990), but the current evidence does support the idea that in particular circumstances, the paradoxical effect will occur (Clark & Ball, 1991; Gold & Wegner, 1995; Salkovskis & Campbell, 1994; Wegner & Zanakos, 1994). It has also been reported that the method of thought suppression used by patients with OCD differs from that of normal controls, with patients using more punishment, worry, reappraisal, and social control than controls (Cashman, Amir, & Foa, 1996). It now seems possible that attempts to suppress thoughts that are misinterpreted as being of catastrophic significance are most likely to cause a paradoxical increase in frequency (Rachman, 1997).

OTHER COGNITIVE FEATURES OF OCD

Exaggerated Sense of Responsibility

Important advances have been made in the cognitive analysis of various types of abnormal behavior and experience, such as panic, and Salkovskis applied this approach in his stimulating, fresh analysis of obsessional disorders (Salkovskis, 1985; Salkovskis & Kirk, 1997). He emphasizes the important role of feelings of responsibility, with responsibility defined as "the belief that one has power which is pivotal to bring about or prevent subjectively crucial negative outcomes" (Salkovskis, Rachman, Ladouceur, & Freeston, 1992).

An exaggerated sense of responsibility can take various forms: It can be too extensive, too intense, too personal, and too exclusive—or all of these. The sense of responsibility can reach extraordinary extremes in which affected persons "confesses" to the police that they have been responsible for crimes or accidents of which they in fact have little or no knowledge. A sense of excessive responsibility typically is manifested at home and at work but can spread to any situation in which people may come to harm—if the affected person feels a sense of belongingness in the place.

They also have a tendency to experience guilt, not only for their own actions but also for those of other people. A person who harbors it will be inclined to feel excessive responsibility for his or her intrusive thoughts, in addition to any actions or omissions that might form the basis for compulsive checking. Hence, the exaggerated sense of responsibility that is evident in obsessive–compulsive phenomena, notably in compulsive checking, is also at play in obsessional thinking, so that when the affected person experiences an unwanted obsessional thought, he or she feels unduly responsible for the thought and its significance.

They feel intensely responsible for their obsessional impulses to harm others and for their unacceptable sexual or other images. These obsessional experiences carry for them a penalty, for which they feel moral as well as psychological re-sponsibility. When they assign blame for these obsessional thoughts to them-selves, they experience guilt. Given that obsessions are experienced as one's own mental products (Rachman, 1973), this assignment of blame is difficult to avoid. One cannot assign the blame to an external agent, a process that may produce anger rather than guilt.

In their series of experiments on compulsive behavior, Rachman and Hodg-son (1980) incidentally encountered the effects of inflated responsibility when they discovered that cleaners and checkers sometimes responded differentially, and that the checkers reported significantly less discomfort after deliberate, ex-perimental provocation. "Patients with washing compulsions reported more anx-iety/discomfort when provoked than did patients with checking rituals. The ma-jor difference between the groups occurred immediately after provocation, but non-performance, of the ritual" (p. 177). It was often difficult to elicit discomfort in people with checking compulsions, and they concluded that

> the most probable explanation for this relative failure is . . . that the presence of an-other person, especially someone in a responsible position, apparently inhibits the arousal of discomfort, and the experimenter was always present or easily accessible throughout the experiment. What seems to happen is this: the S reasons that the ex-perimenter is unlikely to allow the gas taps (or whatever) to be left on, and even if he or she did, then the responsibility for the ensuing harm from this act of carelessness would rest with the experimenter, not the S. If the obsessional S is divested wholly or partly of responsibility for the act, he or she experiences little discomfort. (p. 177)

Consistent with this analysis, it was found that compulsive checkers expe-rienced more discomfort and difficulty when they carried out the relevant ac-tivity in their own homes, away from the structure and safety of the laboratory or clinic. An inflated sense of responsibility is a common characteristic of com-pulsive checkers (and doubters) but appears to be less intense and less common among compulsive cleaners. Within this broadened sense of responsibility, how-ever, some curious features can be observed. Even the most dedicated posses-sors of elevated responsibility acknowledge sharp borders. Characteristically, af-fected people will experience little or no responsibility in the homes or workplaces of other people. They feel responsible within their own psychologi-cal territory, and it is fascinating to watch responsibility grow in a new situation. After admission to hospital, patients initially feel relieved of responsibility, have little tension, and checking behavior is minimized; however, when patients be-come accustomed to the ward and their sense of responsibility grows, the ten-sion returns, and they begin checking on the ward, usually within a few days. A similar process of emerging responsibility can be seen when affected people go on holidays, but, sadly, as they start to feel comfortable ("at home"), the sense of territory emerges, and this is followed by the growth of responsibility—and tension. (This suggests that they will more easily tolerate brief holidays, or hol-idays in which they keep moving and avoid staying in one place long enough to feel responsible.) The emergence of the sense of responsibility under these conditions (new places, etc.) provides an ideal opportunity for studying the nature and growth of (elevated) responsibility.

Among obsessional patients, there is a curious asymmetry between their elevated sense of responsibility for *negative* events and their normal (or even lower than normal?) acceptance of responsibility for positive events. This imbalance is not confined to people with obsessional neurotic problems, but is also evident among people who are socially phobic. Unlike members of the population at large, who tend to accept and retain positive information about themselves and to discount or forget negative information, social phobics appear to reverse the signs. They appear to discount positive information about their social behavior and appearance, and accept and retain negative information. There may be similarities between the asymmetric use of information by social phobics and the asymmetric assignment of personal responsibility by people with obsessional disorders.

A range of psychometric and experimental evidence is consistent with Salkovskis's cognitive-behavioral analysis emphasizing the role of responsibility appraisals (e.g., Freeston, Ladouceur, Thibodeau, & Gagnon, 1992; Lopatka & Rachman, 1995; Shafran, 1997). For example, Lopatka and Rachman (1995) suggested that changes in perceived responsibility are followed by corresponding changes in the urge to check compulsively; the idea was tested on 30 subjects who qualified for a DSM-III-R (American Psychiatric Association, 1987) diagnosis of OCD. The manipulation succeeded in increasing–decreasing perceived responsibility, as required for the experiment. Decreased responsibility was followed by significant declines in discomfort and the urge to carry out the compulsive checking. Increased responsibility was followed by increases in discomfort and urges, but these failed to reach a statistically significant level.

Responsibility has since been manipulated using a variety of different techniques (Ladouceur et al., 1995; Shafran, 1997). For example, Shafran (1997) manipulated responsibility indirectly by varying the presence–absence of the experimenter during a behavioral task. The responsibility manipulation was successful in that perceived responsibility for threat was higher when the subject was alone than when the experimenter was present. In the high-responsibility condition, estimates of the urge to neutralize, discomfort, and probability of threat were all significantly higher than in the low-responsibility condition; however, estimates of responsibility for thoughts and control over the threat did not change significantly between the conditions. This supports the observation that the presence of the experimenter or clinician leads to a reduction of compulsive responses and provides a "brief holiday" from obsessional complaints (Rachman, 1993; Rachman & Hodgson, 1980). It was concluded that the results provided some support for the hypothesis that obsessive–compulsive phenomena are a function of perceived responsibility for threat.

Psychological Fusion of Thoughts and Actions

There is a tendency for people who are afflicted by unwanted intrusions to fuse thoughts and actions, most notably in instances of blasphemous, sexual, or aggressive thoughts, images, or impulses (Rachman, 1993). Fusion refers to the psychological phenomenon in which the patient appears to regard the obsessional thought and the forbidden action as being morally equivalent and/or feeling that the obsessional thought increases the probability of the feared event (e.g., morally, it is as wicked to even think of pushing an old man onto a railway track as it would be to actually push him; the obsessional image of having sex with a religious figure is immoral; therefore, one is morally corrupt). These ideas lead to guilt and self-denigration.

In brief, TAF appears to have two components:

1. *The belief that thinking about an unacceptable/disturbing event makes it more probable, more likely to happen in reality (the likelihood type of TAF).* For example, if a husband experiences an intrusive thought of his wife being in a car accident, he is likely to feel that his wife is at greater risk of having a car accident, *because* he has had the thought. As he has placed his wife in danger, he feels that it is his responsibility to prevent harm coming to her, perhaps by mentally "neutralizing" the thought. Another example is provided by the patient mentioned earlier, who was tormented by repetitive thoughts that his family might be involved in a serious motor accident. He felt that every time he had this thought and the accompanying horrific image, he increased the probability that his family would indeed be involved in such an accident. Naturally this raised his sense of responsibility and ensuing guilt, as well as inflating his anxiety.

2. *The interpretation of obsessional thoughts and forbidden actions as being morally equivalent.* The person feels that his or her unacceptable thoughts, images, or impulses are (almost) as bad as the event. For example, if a mother experiences the intrusive thought that she is going to harm her child, she is likely to feel (almost) as morally responsible as if she had harmed her child in reality. It is possible that the mother interprets such an intrusion as revealing her "true" nature, that is, "Only wicked people have this type of thought; I am wicked," or "Perhaps I really want to do this; I am wicked." This is the moral type of TAF.

TAF may be most intense in instances of obsessional impulses. This is not surprising, because impulses are a step closer to action than are ruminations. In obsessional impulses, the form of the action (and often the victim of the action) is clearer than in the case of ruminations.

TAF forms a coherent subscale that is strongly related to measures of obsessionality. The TAF factor correlates consistently and strongly with the checking subscale of the Maudsley Obsessional–Compulsive Inventory in particular ($r =$ .41 and $r =$ .38 in two separate studies; Rachman, Thordarson, Shafran, & Woody, 1995; Shafran, Thordarson, & Rachman, 1996). The association between TAF and checking behavior is independent of the effects of depression, and TAF has been shown to be a highly reliable construct in student, adult, and obsessional samples.

People who resist this type of psychological fusion, that is, the overwhelming majority of people, successfully distinguish between their uninvited and repugnant thoughts and their actions. They readily dismiss the thoughts and regard them as mental flotsam. Psychological fusion can serve to inflate the significance of the obsessional thinking, and learning to distinguish between the obsessional thought and actions serves to deflate the significance of the obsession. It is assumed here, largely on the basis of research on so-called "normal obsessions" (Rachman & Hodgson, 1980), that "significant" thoughts are far more difficult to control (by dismissal or blocking) than are insignificant thoughts.

In addition to behavior therapy that is directed at the abnormal behavior, it may be necessary to directly tackle the role of responsibility and TAF in the maintenance of the obsessions and compulsions. Helping to reduce the patient's inflated sense of responsibility can be difficult; broad and lasting changes generally require full cognitive analysis and persistent attention, but brief reductions can be achieved for specific therapeutic actions.

A number of patients will agree to a brief transfer of responsibility to the therapist for a specific, circumscribed purpose. For example, a patient might agree to transfer the responsibility for a particular action, say, using the gas stove, on the understanding that it leaves unaltered the patient's responsibility for related actions. Sometimes patients are unable to agree to a transfer but will agree to share some portion of the responsibility with the therapist. The effects of a full transfer or partial transfer probably differ only in degree.

This sharing or transfer of responsibility often produces substantial, brief changes in behavior. A person who has been tormented for years by the need to conduct meticulous, repeated, slow checks of each use of the gas stove may revert within minutes to completely normal use of the stove—if he or she agrees to the transfer of responsibility (for the actions and their possible consequences). Some patients are unwilling or unable to share or transfer responsibility and resist it totally. However, in those cases when it is possible to share or transfer, it can be put to effective therapeutic uses, enabling the patient and therapist to gain increasing control of the abnormal behavior, opening the way to an improved understanding of the cognitions that guide, drive, and limit the related behavior.

The identification of a fusion of thoughts and actions can also provide an avenue for the therapist to begin challenging the beliefs. Techniques that have until now dealt only with the frequency of intrusive thoughts (e.g., thought stopping), would not be helpful if the underlying belief in TAF remains unchanged. Similarly, targeting compulsive behavior, as with exposure and response prevention, will be less effective if core beliefs about TAF are not challenged.

SUMMARY AND CONCLUSIONS

In summary, obsessions are defined as intrusive, unwanted, recurrent thoughts, images, or impulses that give rise to distress and subjective resistance. They give rise to avoidance and compulsive activity in the form of overt behavior and (usually) covert neutralization. Compulsions are repetitive, intentional, stereotyped acts that are performed against the person's rational inclinations, often in response to an obsession. Checking and cleaning are the two main forms of compulsive activity, but patients also engage in neutralization (i.e., attempts to reduce the discomforting effects of an intrusive thought, image, or impulse). Information-processing biases and the effects of thought suppression in OCD have been investigated and, although the results are inconsistent, there is evidence to support the hypothesis that people with OCD lack confidence in their memory as opposed to having a memory deficit. In addition to obsessions, the other cognitive aspects of OCD include a sense of inflated responsibility and a cognitive bias called TAF.

Salkovskis's influential cognitive-behavioral analysis of OCD emphasizes the role of the inflated responsibility in compulsive checking. The psychological fusion of thoughts and actions is believed to play a part in inflating the significance of intrusive thoughts. The cognitive-behavioral analysis carries with it a range of implications and issues that remain to be addressed.

REFERENCES

Akhtar, S., Wig, N. H., Verma, V. K., Pershod, D., & Verma, S. K. (1975). A phenomenological analysis of the symptoms of obsessive–compulsive neuroses. *British Journal of Psychiatry*, 127, 342–348.

American Psychiatric Association. (1987). *Diagnostic and statistical manual of mental disorders* (3rd ed., rev.). Washington, DC: Author.

Arntz, A., Rauner, M., & Van den Hout, M. (1995). "If I feel anxious, there must be danger": Ex-consequential reasoning in inferring danger in anxiety disorders. *Behaviour Research and Therapy*, 33, 917–925.

Barlow, D. H. (1988). *Anxiety and its disorders: The nature and treatment of anxiety and panic.* New York: Guilford Press.

Beck, A. T., & Emery, G., with Greenberg, R. (1985). *Anxiety disorders and phobias: A cognitive perspective.* New York: Basic Books.

Beech, H. R. (1971). Ritualistic activity in obsessional patients. *Journal of Psychosomatic Research*, 15, 417–422.

Beech, H. R. (Ed.). (1974). *Obsessional states.* London: Methuen.

Black, D. W., Noyes, R., Goldstein, R. B., & Blum, N. (1992). A family study of obsessive–compulsive disorder. *Archives of General Psychiatry*, 49, 362–368.

Boone, K., Ananth, J., Philpott, L., Kaur, A., & Djenderedjian, A. (1991). Neuropsychological characteristics of nondepressed adults with obsessive disorder. *Neuropsychiatry, Neuropsychology, and Behavioural Neurology*, 4, 96–109.

Bradley, B. P., Mogg, K., & Williams, R. (1995). Implicit and explicit memory for emotion-congruent information in clinical depression and anxiety. *Behaviour Research and Therapy*, 33, 755–770.

Brown, H. D., Kosslyn, S. M., Breiter, H. C., Baer, L., & Jenike, M. A. (1994). Can patients with obsessive–compulsive disorder discriminate between percepts and mental images?: A signal detection analysis. *Journal of Abnormal Psychology*, 103, 445–454.

Butler, G., & Mathews, A. (1983). Cognitive processes in anxiety. *Advances in Behaviour Research and Therapy*, 5, 51–62.

Cashman, L., Amir, N., & Foa, E. B. (1996, November). *Thought suppression in OCD.* Poster presented at the 30th Annual Convention of the Association for Advancement of Behavior Therapy, New York, NY.

Chambless, D., & Hope, D. (1996). Cognitive approaches to the psychopathology and treatment of social phobia. In P. M. Salkovskis (Ed.), *Frontiers of cognitive therapy.* New York: Guilford Press.

Christensen, K., Kim, S. W., Dyksen, M. W., & Hoover, K. M. (1992). Neuropsychological performance in obsessive–compulsive disorder. *Biological Psychiatry, 31,* 4–18.

Claparède, M. (1911). Recognition et moiité. *Archives de Psychologie Génève, 11,* 79–90.

Clark, D. M. (1988). A cognitive model of panic attacks. In S. Rachman & J. Maser (Eds.), *Panic: Psychological perspectives.* Hillsdale, NJ: Erlbaum.

Clark, D., & Ball, S. (1991). An experimental investigation of thought suppression. *Behaviour Research and Therapy, 29,* 253–257.

Cloitre, M., Shear, M. K., Cancienne, J., & Zeitlin, S. B. (1994). Implicit and explicit memory for catastrophic associations to bodily sensation words in panic disorder. *Cognitive Therapy and Research, 18,* 225–240.

Constans, J. I., Foa, E. B., Franklin, M. E., & Mathews, A. (1995). Memory for actual and imagined events in OC checkers. *Behaviour Research and Therapy, 33,* 665–671.

Cox, C. S., Fedio, P., & Rapoport, J. (1989). Neuropsychological testing of obsessive–compulsive disorder in adolescents. In J. Rapoport (Ed.), *Obsessive–compulsive disorder in children and adolescents.* Washington, DC: American Psychiatric Press.

Dalgleish, T. (1994). The relationship between anxiety and memory biases for material that has been selectively processed in a prior task. *Behaviour Research and Therapy, 32,* 227–231.

Edelmann, R. J. (1992). *Anxiety: Theory, research and intervention in clinical and health psychology.* Chichester, UK: Wiley.

Ehlers, A. (1992). Interoception and panic disorder. *Advances in Behavior Research and Therapy, 115,* 3–21.

Eysenck, H. J., & Rachman, S. (1965). *Causes and cures of neurosis.* London: Routledge.

Eysenck, M. W. (1992). *Anxiety: The cognitive perspective.* Hove, UK: Erlbaum.

Foa, E. B., Ilai, D., McCarthy, P. R., Shoyer, B., & Murdoch, T. (1993). Information-processing in obsessive–compulsive disorder. *Cognitive Therapy and Research, 17,* 173–189.

Foa, E. B., & McNally, R. J. (1986). Sensitivity to feared stimuli in obsessive–compulsives: A dichotic listening analysis. *Cognitive Therapy and Research, 10,* 477–485.

Freeston, M. H., & Ladouceur, R. (1997). What do patients do with their obsessive thoughts? *Behaviour Research and Therapy, 35,* 335–348.

Freeston, M. H., Ladouceur, R., Thibodeau, N., & Gagnon, F. (1992). Cognitive intrusions in a non-clinical population: I. Response style, subjective experience and appraisal. *Behaviour Research and Therapy, 29,* 585–597.

Frost, R. O., & Hartl, T. (1995). The value of possessions in compulsive hoarding: Patterns of use and attachment. *Behaviour Research and Therapy, 33,* 897–902.

Frost, R. O., & Hartl, T. (1996). A cognitive-behavioral model of compulsive hoarding. *Behaviour Research and Therapy, 34,* 341–350.

Gold, D. B., & Wegner, D. M. (1995). Origins of ruminative thought: Trauma, incompleteness, nondisclosure, and suppression [Special issue: Rumination and intrusive thoughts]. *Journal of Applied Social Psychology, 25,* 1245–1261.

Gray, J. A. (1982). *The neuropsychology of anxiety: An enquiry into the functions of the septo-hippocampal system.* Oxford, UK: Oxford University Press.

Horowitz, M. J. (1975). Intrusive and repetitive thoughts after experimental stress. *Archives of General Psychiatry, 32,* 1457–1463.

Ladouceur, R., Rhéaume, J., Freeston, M., Aublet, F., Jean, K., Lachance, S., Langlois, F., & DePokomandy-Morin, K. (1995). Experimental manipulation of responsibility in a non-clinical population: An analogue test for models of obsessive–compulsive disorder. *Behaviour Research and Therapy, 33,* 937–946.

Lavy, E. H., & Van den Hout, M. A. (1990). Thought suppression induces intrusions. *Behavioural Psychotherapy, 18,* 251–258.

Lensi, P., Cassano, B., Correddu, G., Ravagli, S., Kunovac, J. L., & Akiskal, H. S. (1996). Obsessive–compulsive disorder: Familial–developmental history, symptomatology, comorbidity and course. *British Journal of Psychiatry, 169,* 101–107.

Lopatka, C., & Rachman, S. (1995). Perceived responsibility and compulsive checking: An experimental analysis. *Behaviour Research and Therapy, 33,* 673–684.

MacDonald, P., Antony, M. M., MacLeod, C., & Richter, M. A. (1997). Memory and confidence in memory judgments among individuals with obsessive compulsive disorder and non-clinical controls. *Behaviour Research and Therapy, 35,* 497–505.

Martinot, J. L., Allilaire, J. F., Mazoyer, B. M., Hantouche, E., Huret, J. D., Legaut-Demare, F., Deslauriers, A. G., Hardy, P., Pappata, S., Baron, J. C., & Syrota, A. (1990). Obsessive–compulsive disorder: A clinical, neuropsychological and positron emission tomography study. *Acta Psychiatrica Scandinavica, 82,* 233–242.

Mathews, A., & MacLeod, C. (1994). Cognitive approaches to emotion and emotional disorders. *Annual Review of Psychology, 45,* 25–50.

Mathews, A., MacLeod, C., & Tata, P. R. (1986). Attentional bias in emotional disorders. *Journal of Abnormal Psychology, 95,* 15–20.

Mathews, A., Mogg, K., May, J., & Eysenck, M. (1989). Implicit and explicit memory bias in anxiety. *Journal of Abnormal Psychology, 98,* 236–240.

McNally, R. J., & Kohlbeck, P. A. (1993). Reality monitoring in obsessive–compulsive disorder. *Behaviour Research and Therapy, 31,* 249–253.

McNally, R. J., Lasko, N. B., Macklin, M. L., & Pitman, R. K. (1995). Autobiographical memory disturbance in combat-related post traumatic stress disorder. *Behaviour Research and Therapy, 33,* 619–630.

Mowrer, O. H. (1939). A stimulus–response theory of anxiety. *Psychological Review, 46,* 553–65.

Mowrer, O. H. (1960). *Learning theory and behavior.* New York: Wiley.

Osterrieth, P. A. (1944). Le test de copie d'une figure complexe. *Archives de Psychologie, 30,* 206–356.

Parkinson, L., & Rachman, S. (1980). Speed of recovery from an uncontrived stress. In S. Rachman (Ed.), *Unwanted intrusive cognitions.* Oxford, UK: Pergamon Press.

Rachman, S. (1973). Some similarities and differences between obsessions and preoccupations. *Canadian Psychiatric Association Journal, 18,* 71–74.

Rachman, S. (1974). Primary obsessional slowness. *Behaviour Research and Therapy, 11,* 463–471.

Rachman, S. (1993). Obsessions, responsibility, and guilt. *Behaviour Research and Therapy, 31,* 149–154.

Rachman, S. (1994). Pollution of the mind. *Behaviour Research and Therapy, 32,* 311–314.

Rachman, S. (1997). A cognitive theory of obsessions. *Behaviour Research and Therapy, 35,* 793–802.

Rachman, S. (1998). *Anxiety.* Hove, UK: Psychology Press.

Rachman, S., & De Silva, P. (1978). Abnormal and normal obsessions. *Behaviour Research and Therapy, 16,* 233–248.

Rachman, S., & Hodgson, R. (1980). *Obsessions and compulsions.* Englewood Cliffs, NJ: Prentice-Hall.

Rachman, S., Shafran, R., Mitchell, D., Trant, J., & Teachman, B. (1996). How to remain neutral: An experimental analysis of neutralization. *Behaviour Research and Therapy, 34,* 889–898.

Rachman, S., Thordarson, D. S., Shafran, R., & Woody, S. R. (1995). Perceived responsibility: Structure and significance. *Behaviour Research and Therapy, 33,* 779–784.

Rapee, R. M., McCallum, S. L., Melville, L. F., Ravenscroft, H., & Rodney, J. M. (1994). Memory bias in social phobia. *Behaviour Research and Therapy, 32,* 89–99.

Rasmussen, S., & Eisen, J. L. (1991). Phenomenology of obsessive–compulsive disorder: Clinical subtypes, heterogeneity and coexistence. In J. Zohar, T. Insel, & S. Rasmussen (Eds.), *The psychobiology of obsessive–compulsive disorder* (Vol. 4). New York: Springer.

Rey, A. (1941). L'examen psychologique dans les cas d'encephalopathie traumatique. *Archives de Psychologie, 112,* 286–340.

Ricciardi, J. N., & McNally, R. J. (1995). Depressed mood is related to obsessions, but not to compulsions, in obsessive–compulsive disorder. *Journal of Anxiety Disorders, 9,* 249–256.

Rubenstein, C. F., Peyniricioglu, Z. F., Chambless, D. L., & Pigott, T. A. (1993). Memory in sub-clinical obsessive–compulsive checkers. *Behaviour Research and Therapy, 27,* 65–69.

Salkovskis, P. M. (1985). Obsessional–compulsive problems: A cognitive-behavioral analysis. *Behaviour Research and Therapy, 23,* 571–583.

Salkovskis, P. M. (1996). Obsessive–compulsive disorder: Understanding is not improved by redefining it as something else. In R. M. Rapee (Ed.), *Current controversies in the anxiety disorders.* New York: Guilford Press.

Salkovskis, P. M., & Campbell, P. (1994). Thought suppression induces intrusion in naturally occurring negative intrusive thoughts. *Behaviour Research and Therapy, 32,* 1–8.

Salkovsksis, P. M., & Harrison, M. (1984). Abnormal and normal obsessions: A replication. *Behaviour Research and Therapy, 22,* 549–552.

Salkovskis, P. M., & Kirk, J. (1997). Obsessive–compulsive disorder. In D. M. Clark & C. Fairburn (Eds.), *The science and practice of cognitive behavior therapy.* Oxford, UK: Oxford University Press.

Salkovksis, P. M., Rachman, S. J., Ladouceur, R., & Freeston, M. (1992, September). *The definition of "responsibility."* World Congress of Cognitive Therapy, Toronto, Canada.

Shafran, R. (1997). The manipulation of responsibility in obsessive–compulsive disorder. *British Journal of Psychology, 36,* 397–408.

Shafran, R., Thordarson, D. S., & Rachman, S. (1996). Thought–action fusion in obsessive compulsive disorder. *Journal of Anxiety Disorders, 10,* 379–391.

Sher, K., Frost, R., Kushner, M., Crews, T., & Alexander, J. (1989). Memory deficits in compulsive checkers: Replication and extension in a clinical sample. *Behaviour Research and Therapy, 27,* 65–69.

Sher, K., Frost, R., & Otto, R. (1983). Cognitive deficits in compulsive checkers: An exploratory study. *Behaviour Research and Therapy, 27,* 65–69.

Sher, K., Mann, B., & Frost, R. (1984). Cognitive dysfunction in compulsive checkers: Further explorations. *Behaviour Research and Therapy, 22,* 493–502.

Sutherland, G., & Rachman, S. (1982). Experimental investigations of mood and intrusive cognitions. *British Journal of Medical Psychology, 55,* 127–138.

Tallis, F. (1995). *Obsessive compulsive disorder: A cognitive and neuropsychological perspective*. Chichester, UK: Wiley.

Tata, P. R., Leibowitz, J. A., Prunty, M. J., Cameron, M., & Pickering, A. D. (1996). Attentional bias in obsessional compulsive disorder. *Behaviour Research and Therapy, 34*, 53–60.

Veale, D. (1993). The classification and treatment of obsessional slowness. *British Journal of Psychiatry, 162*, 198–203.

Wechsler, D., & Stone, C. (1945). *Manual for the Wechsler Memory Scale*. New York: Psychological Corporation.

Wegner, D. M., Schneider, D. J., Carter, S. III, & White, T. (1987). Paradoxical effects of thought suppression. *Journal of Personality and Social Psychology, 53*, 5–13.

Wegner, D. M., & Zanakos, S. (1994). Chronic thought suppression [Special Issue: Psychodynamics and social cognition: Perspectives on the representation and processing of emotionally significant information.] *Journal of Personality, 62*, 615–640.

Wiggs, C. I., Martin, A., Altemus, M., & Murphy, D. L. (1996). Hypervigilance in patients with obsessive–compulsive disorder. *Anxiety, 2*, 123–129.

Williams J. M. G., Watts, F. N., MacLeod, C., & Mathews, A. (1988). *Cognitive psychology and emotional disorders*. Chichester, UK: Wiley.

Wilner, A., Reich, T., Robins, I., Fishman, R., & van Doren, T. (1976). Obsessive–compulsive neurosis. *Comprehensive Psychiatry, 17*, 527–539.

Zielinski, C. M., Taylor, M. A., & Juzwin, K. R. (1991). Neuropsychological deficits in obsessive–compulsive disorder. *Neuropsychiatry, Neuropsychology and Behavioural Neurology, 4*, 110–126.

Chapter 4

PERSONALITY AND OBSESSIVE–COMPULSIVE DISORDER

Laura J. Summerfeldt
Veronika Huta
Richard P. Swinson

Interest in the role of personality factors in obsessive–compulsive disorder (OCD) has a long history in psychiatry and psychology. Despite this, a clear understanding of the nature of the relationship has remained elusive. This is largely due to a fundamental problem, clearly articulated by Tallis, Rosen, and Shafran (1996): "Investigations [have] fail[ed] to move beyond repeated and unsatisfactory attempts at confirming that such a relationship exists at all" (p. 649). This, in part, reflects a basic lack of consensus about how best to approach personality as a concept. Several bodies of research, reflecting different conceptual frameworks and levels of analysis, theoretical orientations, and personality models, have evolved in relative isolation from one another. Consequently, the volume of the current literature on personality and OCD is characterized by a remarkable lack of consistency.

This chapter reviews core dimensions of personality associated with OCD that appear as common themes running through quite disparate bodies of research, theory, and clinical observation. Our choice and discussion of these dimensions has been guided by several current issues in the general literature on OCD. These include debates regarding the nosological placement of OCD as an anxiety disorder (see Clark, Watson, & Reynolds, 1995; Enright & Beech, 1990), the evidence for heterogeneity within OCD itself (Pigott, Myers, & Williams, 1996; Rasmussen & Eisen, 1989, 1990, 1992), and the relationship of OCD to such disorders as Tourette's syndrome and trichotillomania—the hypothesized obsessive–compulsive spectrum (see Hollander, 1993a, 1993b). Consideration of personality factors may contribute to the understanding of these topics. In this context, we will also consider more traditional accounts of a distinctive "obsessional personality."

Personality has been defined in many ways (Endler & Parker, 1990, 1992). For the purposes of the present discussion, the conceptualization offered in the fourth edition (DSM-IV) of the *Diagnostic and Statistical Manual of Mental Disorders* (American Psychiatric Association, 1994) will be used: "Personality traits are enduring patterns of perceiving, relating to, and thinking about the environment and oneself that are exhibited in a wide range of social and personal contexts" (p. 630). Multiple causal influences likely contribute to these patterns. These include specific genetic and neuroanatomical factors (e.g., Cloninger, 1987; Eysenck, 1967) and psychosocial determinants (see Millon, 1981, for a review). Regardless of the distal etiological factors involved, it is their expression in motivational, cognitive, and affective consistencies that serves, proximally, to define personality.

HISTORICAL CONTEXT: ANAL AND ANANKASTIC PERSONALITIES

Approaches to the relationship between OCD and a distinctive obsessional personality derive from two main traditions. The most widely recognized account was proposed by Freud. In 1913, he suggested that obsessional neurosis was most likely to develop in an individual with an anal character or personality structure, defined by the specific triad of orderliness, parsimony, and obstinacy (see Freud, 1908). Both symptoms and traits were thought to reflect the operations of defense mechanisms against unconscious anxiety, a point made more central in subsequent psychoanalytic discussions of this personality pattern (e.g., Salzman, 1968). Unlike Freud's theoretical formulations of the anal character's development and its relationship to the disorder, his clinical descriptions have had an enduring influence. The principal features of the anal triad continue to be incorporated into DSM-IV diagnostic criteria for the obsessive–compulsive personality disorder (OCPD), as has the importance of anxiety, implicit in the pattern's inclusion in the "anxious" Cluster C of Axis II.

It is regrettable that Freud's formulations obscured a body of work published a decade earlier by Pierre Janet. In his *Les Obsessions et la Psychasthénie,* Janet (1903) provided a detailed description of the development of obsessive–compulsive symptoms, and of the foundational role played by particular personality features. Janet's work has been praised for containing the best clinical descriptions of OCD ever written (Pitman, 1987; Reed, 1985; Slater & Roth, 1977). Despite this, it has been largely neglected in North America, chiefly due to its lack of congruence with the DSM system of classification. Contrary to current opinion, Janet considered anxiety to be secondary in OCD, arising in response to the symptoms, rather than the converse. Most central to the problem, he thought, is an inner sense of imperfection, connected with the perception that actions or intentions have been incompletely achieved: "This is perhaps the most basic factor in the illness, out of which the symptomatic agitations and efforts arise" (Janet, 1903, cited in Pitman, 1987, p. 226). Janet located this feature in what he called the "psychasthenic state," the first stage in the illness, which, if prolonged, would be appropriately considered a personality precursor. Although there is some overlap in the traits hypothesized by Freud and Janet, Janet's central emphasis upon uncertainty, indecisiveness, and "incompleteness" is unique. In many ways, the psychasthenic state shares key features with European conceptualizations of the compulsive, or "anankastic," personality (e.g., World Health Organization, 1978, 1992), which emphasize uncertainty and perfectionism, and have been less influenced by Freud's anxiety-driven anal triad than North American definitions (Pitman, 1987). "Indecisiveness," in fact, was dropped altogether from DSM-IV diagnostic criteria for OCPD (American Psychiatric Association, 1994; see Pfohl & Blum, 1991), despite the cardinal position assigned "doubt" in the criteria for anankastic personality disorder in the current *International Classification of Diseases* (ICD-10; World Health Organization, 1992).

These two conceptualizations, of which the Freudian approach has been by far the more influential, are of a personality pattern unique to OCD. Subsequent research has concentrated both on this, and on nonspecific general patterns and dimensions of personality. In both cases, efforts at clarification have been hampered by several basic difficulties.

METHODOLOGICAL AND CONCEPTUAL ISSUES

Any discussion of personality and OCD should address a number of conceptual and methodological difficulties. It is generally accepted that the most common pattern in OCD is of onset in late adolescence or early adulthood, with a chronic waxing and waning course (American Psychiatric Association, 1994). In the case of such a lifelong disorder, in which symptoms are always present to some degree, the meaningfulness of speaking of personality and symptoms as orthogonal or discrete phenomena is questionable. As Black, Noyes, Pfohl, Goldstein, and Blum (1993) noted, this is even more difficult in early-onset cases, where symptoms become part of a long-standing response pattern. This feature has prompted suggestions that the degree of impairment associated with OCD confounds the assessment of personality (e.g., Ricciardi et al., 1992), as the disorder itself becomes a stable part of the experience and behavioral repertoire of the individual. These complications are particularly noteworthy in efforts to link OCD with categorical personality disorders. General diagnostic guidelines imply that these patterns, with few exceptions, have not reliably coalesced until adolescence, or early adulthood. Consequently, definitive statements about "predisposing" Axis II patterns are problematic, as their diagnosis temporally overlaps with the developmental window for onset of the symptom syndrome itself.

These clinical issues, in addition to practical constrictions, result in a significant limitation in this literature. As noted elsewhere (Baer & Jenike, 1992; Stein, Hollander, & Skodol, 1993) the majority of studies published in this area, both of categorical and dimensional personality factors, are not prospective. Personality has, for the most part, been assessed following the onset of OCD, and while symptoms are present. This practice warrants interpretive vigilance for several reasons. Primarily, it precludes conclusions about the direction of cause in the relationship, a point often overlooked in the interpretation of correlational results, where "prediction" is used in the statistical, not temporal, sense. Additionally, this method renders findings vulnerable to the distorting influence of current state, such as distress and symptoms, upon trait measurement (see Loranger et al., 1991). Tallis et al. (1996), for example, found that when the effects of anxiety (measured as a trait) and depression were statistically controlled for in their clinical sample, obsessive–compulsive symptoms remained associated with only two, rather than nine, Axis II disorders (see also Rosen & Tallis, 1995).

The results of empirical investigations of personality factors and OCD are commonly reported as statistical "associations" between the two phenomena. This is a common practice in the study of personality and psychopathology, and obscures the fact that the direction of causality is often not clear. Personality patterns may render an individual vulnerable to particular clinical disorders (Klerman, 1973), or to certain environmental stressors that, in interaction with such predispositions, result in clinical syndromes (see McKeon, Roa, & Mann, 1984). This diathesis–stress model is illustrated by a recent investigation of cues predictive of exacerbation of symptoms in subjects already diagnosed with OCD. Ristvedt, MacKenzie, and Christenson (1993) found a significant relationship between severity scores on a measure of Axis II disorders and negative affect (e.g., depression) as a cue. This was interpreted as evidence for the potentiating effect of emotional stress on personality pathology, with negative affect being considered as a precipitant of symptoms (p. 728). Alternatively, both characterological features and OCD may share a common cause or third factor. It has been suggested that obsessive–compulsive symptoms and traits may share a common genetic source (e.g., Diaferia et al., 1997; Lenane et al., 1990), perhaps associated with Tourette's syndrome (see Siever & Davis, 1991). A third and more contemporary causal focus is on the impact of clinical disorders upon personality—the "scar" hypothesis. The experience of symptoms may irrevocably change the individuals' habitual pattern of thought, behavior, and emotional regulation. Thomsen and Mikkelsen (1993) have reported the findings of a follow-up study of personality disorders, evident in early adulthood, in individuals who had been diagnosed with OCD in childhood. Consistent with many other comorbidity studies, avoidant personality disorder was found to be the most prevalent. More interesting was its foremost association with chronic rather than phasic forms of the disorder. The causal implication was made explicit by the authors: "People with OCD get isolated and develop an avoidant personality" (p. 640). A similar interpretation has been made by Baer and Jenike (1992) of their findings that the development of mixed personality disorder was associated with longer duration of OCD (Baer et al., 1990), and that in a sample of individuals with comorbid personality disorders and OCD, all but one of the individuals who responded to pharmacological and/or behavioral treatment for OCD no longer met Axis II criteria (Ricciardi et al., 1992). It has been suggested that the obsessive–compulsive personality pattern has a similarly adaptive residual function to symptoms (e.g., Swedo et al., 1989), although this view has not been widely adopted.

The phenomenological overlap of symptoms and traits has been indicated as a methodological confound in the literature on personality and anxiety disorders (Stein et al., 1993). This may be particularly true in the case of OCD. First, as episodic partial remission, rather than full amelioration, of symptoms is common (American Psychiatric Association, 1994), it may be difficult for both the sufferer, and the clinician, to distinguish between obsessive–compulsive traits and subclinical symptoms, which by definition cause neither significant impairment or distress. For this reason, Black et al. (1993) advocated as a methodological standard the differentiation of traits and both clinical and subclinical obsessive–compulsive symptoms. The task of distinguishing traits from symptoms has traditionally been guided by their disparate motivations (i.e.. symptoms function to alleviate distress) and associated subjective experience. In contrast to ego-syntonic traits, OCD symptoms were characterized as intrusive, unwanted, irrational, and distressing (American Psychiatric Association, 1987; see Foa & Kozak, 1995). However, this distinction is not useful in the case of subclinical obsessive–compulsive behavior. Perhaps more important, a growing body of researchers and clinicians, aware of variability in the ego-dystonicity of clinical symptoms, has questioned its universal applicability to the disorder itself (e.g., Rasmussen & Eisen, 1992; Tallis, 1996).

Second, the content of symptoms and traits also often overlaps, further complicating their differential assessment. Reassurance seeking is commonly considered a functional equivalent of checking in OCD (Rasmussen & Eisen, 1992), and is included in widely used symptom checklists (e.g., Yale–Brown Obsessive–Compulsive Scale [Y-BOCS]), but it is also an essential feature of the DSM-IV dependent personality disorder. Similarly, it has been suggested that "criterion contamination" in self-report measures used to assess schizotypal personality disorder may inflate estimates of its prevalence in OCD (Salkovskis, 1996). Items used to assess such diagnostic criteria as cognitive distortions and magical thinking (e.g., "No matter how hard I try to concentrate, unrelated thoughts always creep into my mind"; Claridge & Broks, 1984) may unintentionally tap OCD symptoms. Although detailed clinical enquiry may clarify phenomenological differences, reliance upon standardized interviews (see Pfohl & Blum, 1991, p. 370), and self-report measures—a mainstay of personality research—may preclude this (for general discussion, see Loranger, 1992; Tallis, 1995).

CATEGORICAL PERSONALITY DISORDERS AND OCD

Early investigations of personality pathology in OCD, guided primarily by psychodynamic theory, reported high rates of comorbidity for the obsessional (anal) personality pattern (e.g., Ingram, 1961; see Black, 1974, for a review). Since that time, improvements in the reliability and validity of assessment techniques, and the adoption of objective and standardized criteria for the diagnosis of personality disorders, have led to a more diverse literature. This section summarizes trends that have emerged in studies published in the last decade. Their results and key features are presented in Table 4.1.

TABLE 4.1. Comorbidity of Personality Disorders in Obsessive–Compulsive Disorder

Study	n	Method of OCD diagnosis	Method of PD diagnosis	% with any PD	% with >1 PD	% with avoidant PD	% with dependent PD	% with schizotypal PD	% with histrionic PD	% with compulsive PD	% with borderline PD
Baer et al. (1990)	96	DSM-III	SIDP	52	6	5	12	5	9	6	3
Baer et al. (1992)	55	Unclear	SIDP	60	27	25	24	9	7	16	9
Baer & Jenike (1992)	59	DSM-III	SIDP-R	—	—	—	—	—	—	25	—
Black, Yates, Noyes, Pfohl, & Kelley (1989)	21	SADS	PDQ	33	—	0	24	14	24	0	24
Black, Noyes, Pfohl, Goldstein, & Blum (1993)	32	DSM-III-R	SIDP	88	—	22	50	19	9	28	19
Cassano, Del Buono, & Catapano (1993)	31	DSM-III	PDE	55	39	32	16	10	6	17	16
Diaferia et al. (1997)	88	DIS-R	SIDP-R	—	—	23	28	3	28	31	8
Hermesh, Shahar, & Munitz (1987)	39	Unclear	Unclear	—	—	—	—	—	—	—	20
Jenike, Baer, Minichiello, Schwartz, & Carey (1986)	43	Unclear	DSM-III[a]	—	—	—	—	33	—	—	—
Joffe, Swinson, & Regan (1988)	23	SADS-L	MCMI	83	—	57	57	17	17	4	39
Mavissakalian, Hamann, & Jones (1990a)	43	DSM-III	PDQ	53	30	30	19	16	26	2	5

Study	N	Interview	Questionnaire							
Mavissakalian, Hamann, & Jones (1990b)	51	DSM-III	PDQ	49	27	26	20	14	24	2	4
Mavissakalian, Hamann, & Jones (1990c)	27	DSM-III	PDQ	56	33	30	26	15	26	4	4
Mavissakalian, Hamann, Haidar, & deGroot (1993)	51	DSM-III	PDQ	50	28	26	20	14	24	2	4
Minichiello, Baer, & Jenike (1987)	29	Unclear	DSM-III[a]	—	—	—	—	35	—	—	—
Rasmussen & Tsuang (1986)	44	DSM-III	DSM-III[b]	—	—	—	5	—	9	55	—
Sanderson, Wetzler, Beck, & Betz (1994)	21	SCID-P	SCID-II	—	5	5	5	—	5	5	—
Sciuto et al. (1991)	30	DSM-III-R	SIDP-R	—	10	27	13	0	23	3	3
Stanley, Turner, & Borden (1990)	25	ADIS-R	SCID-II	48	—	12	4	8	12	28	0
Steketee (1990)	26	DSM-III-R	PDQ-R	50	42	27	39	35	31	4	12
Thomsen & Mikkelsen (1993)	47	Unclear	SCID-II	68	42	23	17	4	4	17	6
Torres & Del Porto (1995)	40	DSM-III-R	SIDP-R	70	58	53	40	5	20	18	—

Note. ADIS-R, Anxiety Disorders Interview Schedule—Revised (semistructured interview, assesses Axis I DSM-III-R disorders); DIS-R, Diagnostic Interview Schedule—Revised (structured interview, assesses Axis I DSM-III-R disorders); SADS, Schedule for Affective Disorders and Schizophrenia (semistructured interview, assesses Axis I DSM-III-R disorders); SADS-L, Schedule for Affective Disorders and Schizophrenia for DSM-III-R—Lifetime Version (semistructured interview, assesses Axis I disorders); SCID-P, Structured Clinical Interview for DSM-III-R Axis I Disorders—Patient Version (semistructured interview); SCID-II, Structured Clinical Interview for DSM-III-R Axis II Disorders (semistructured interview); SIDP, Structured Interview for the DSM-III Personality Disorders (semistructured interview); SIDP-R, Structured Interview for the DSM-III Personality Disorders—Revised (semistructured interview); MCMI, Millon Clinical Multiaxial Inventory (self-rating scale); PDE, Personality Disorder Examination Assessing DSM-III Axis II Disorders (semistructured interview); PDQ, Personality Diagnostic Questionnaire Assessing DSM-III Axis II Disorders (self-rating scale); PDQ-R, Personality Diagnostic Questionnaire Assessing DSM-III Axis II Disorders—Revised (self-rating scale).

[a]Diagnoses established retrospectively.

[b]Diagnoses based on DSM-III symptom checklist.

Axis II Comorbidity

There is considerable variability in the findings reported in this literature. Methodological inconsistencies may be partly responsible (Baer & Jenike, 1992). These include sampling bias and differences across studies in the methods and standards used to diagnose both OCD and personality disorders. For example, significant changes were made in diagnostic criteria for many personality disorders between DSM-III and DSM-III-R. This was particularly true in the case of OCPD (see Pfohl & Blum, 1991), where DSM-III-R revisions resulted in the addition of four criteria, with five of nine (versus four of five) needing to be met for diagnosis. This served to increase prevalence rates (Baer et al., 1990). Most studies have relied on open-ended interviews and clinical judgment for the diagnosis of OCD, and few have used standardized structured interviews (see Table 4.1). Similar problems are evident in the methods used for the diagnosis of personality disorders. Approximately half of the summarized studies used a standardized interview designed for this purpose, whereas the rest have relied on self-report measures of varying degrees of validity and reliability.

The proportion of OCD patients with Axis II comorbidity is quite high—in studies published in the last 10 years, it has ranged from 33% to 83% and has typically been between 50% and 65%. At the same time, studies comparing the frequency of personality disorders in OCD and in other anxiety disorders, such as panic disorder and generalized anxiety disorder, have found the profiles of personality disorder diagnoses to be somewhat similar (e.g., Mavissakalian, Hamann, Haidar, & de Groot, 1993; Mavissakalian, Hamann, & Jones, 1990b; Sanderson, Wetzler, Beck, & Betz, 1994). Despite this, OCD appears unique in the heterogeneity of personality pathology associated with it. "Mixed" personality disorder, when reported as a category, tends to occur relatively frequently (e.g., Baer et al., 1990). Furthermore, generally more than half of those OCD sufferers diagnosed with any personality disorder are diagnosed with more than one, typically two to four, though two studies reported six or more comorbid Axis II disorders (Baer et al., 1992; Steketee, 1990).

Despite the variability in findings, a pattern of results is evident in the recent literature on Axis II comorbidity in OCD. A group of personality disorders is diagnosed relatively frequently: This includes avoidant, dependent, histrionic, schizotypal, and, to a slightly lesser degree, obsessive–compulsive patterns. In contrast, some personality disorders appear to be rarely diagnosed, including narcissistic, schizoid, and antisocial patterns. In the studies reviewed, these personality disorders were reported in less than 5% of cases of OCD and most commonly were not diagnosed at all. The remaining Axis II disorders, including borderline, passive–aggressive (DSM-III-R), and paranoid, have been reported, but not consistently.

The most frequently diagnosed personality disorders—avoidant, dependent, histrionic, schizotypal, and OCPD—are typically diagnosed in 5–30% of patients with OCD. There is a wide range in comorbidity figures reported for frequently occurring Axis II disorders in studies published in the last decade (reported in Table 4.1). Thus, it is difficult to determine whether some personality disorders within this group occur more frequently than others, though avoidant personality disorder, on average, seems to be diagnosed slightly more often, and OCPD slightly less often, than others in this group. Most commonly, the proportion of subjects with OCD exhibiting avoidant personality disorder has been around 30%, dependent between 10% and 20%, histrionic between 5% and 25%, and schizotypal around 15%. Prevalences of OCPD have exhibited a particularly wide range, though they have not usually been higher than 20%; the median reported rate is 6%.

When individuals with OCD have more than one personality disorder, they tend to have a combination of four of the personality disorders most commonly diagnosed in OCD: dependent, avoidant, schizotypal, and histrionic; OCPD occurs in conjunction with other personality disorders much less often (see Baer et al., 1992; Mavissakalian et al., 1990a, 1990b; Torres & Del Porto, 1995). Steketee (1990) found that in a sample of 26 OCD subjects, the most common co-occurring personality disorders were avoidant/dependent, schizotypal/histrionic (both present in 6 subjects), and all four personality disorders together, present in 4 subjects.

To summarize, a pattern has emerged from our review of recent empirical evidence for the relationship between OCD and categorical personality disorders, similar to that reported in other recent reviews (e.g., Baer & Jenike, 1992). First, considerable heterogeneity in personality pathology continues to be associated with OCD. Second, it shares with other anxiety syndromes a predominance of "anxious cluster" (i.e., avoidant and dependent patterns) personality disorders. Last, OCPD, although evident, is not the most prevalent pattern. OCPD appears to be less frequent in OCD than would be predicted from traditional psychodynamic models and early empirical reports derived from them (e.g., Ingram., 1961). Not surprisingly, there is currently some consensus that OCPD is not a necessary prerequisite to the development of OCD, with the two commonly considered distinct but related phenomena (see Pollack, 1979, 1987). Nonetheless, there is still considerable inconsistency in this literature. In a recent study, DSM-III-R OCPD criteria were found to successfully discriminate patients with OCD from those with panic or major depressive disorders (Diaferia et al., 1997). There appears to be some specificity of OCPD to OCD; There is also evidence for its uniqueness from other Axis II Cluster C disorders (Mulder & Joyce, 1997).

Comment

Results from studies of categorical Axis II disorders continue to be varied and have done little to advance our understanding of the role of personality in OCD beyond a basic recognition of high prevalence rates for multiple categories of personality pathology. Increasingly, clinicians, theorists, and researchers are questioning the heuristic value of the categorical approach adopted by the DSM system (see Frances, Widiger, & Fyer, 1990). Criticism has focused on its implicit assumption that disorders represent distinct, nonoverlapping entities qualitatively different from nonpathological behavior. This is particularly true in the case of personality. Opponents of this approach, citing ongoing problems with the reliable and valid assessment and discrimination of Axis II categories, have maintained that the personality traits that constitute them are neither dichotomous or discontinuous—they are evident in varying degrees in all individuals (see Clark, 1992; Frances, 1993; Widiger, 1992; Zimmerman, 1994). Therefore, the information necessary to describe personality functioning may be better provided by a *dimensional* perspective.

Axis II disorders are constellations of traits, which themselves represent a continuum ranging from normal adaptive behavior to pathology. Furthermore, broad, normally distributed personality dimensions may underlie multiple Axis II categories. This is a marked contrast to a categorical system, where overlap in content of Axis II criteria is often considered a psychometric weakness (see Pfohl & Blum, 1991, for a relevant account of the withdrawal of indecisiveness from DSM-IV OCPD criteria). Not surprisingly, OCD researchers have begun to show interest in a range of dimensional personality variables, as have clinicians: Their consideration in clinical assessment and treatment planning is being increasingly recommended (e.g., Andrews, 1996; Steketee, 1994).

DIMENSIONS OF PERSONALITY AND OCD

A dimensional approach to personality and OCD does not preclude the many conceptual and methodological problems already discussed. It may, however, make them more easily apparent. Traditionally, investigators have not elaborated on categorical personality findings, making it impossible to determine whether they reflected the predominant influence of certain core features, or dimensions. The limitations of this approach are made clear by the results of a recent investigation of the specificity of DSM-III personality disorder traits to common anxiety disorders, including OCD. Mavissakalian et al. (1993) found that although the OCD group did not differ from comparison groups in the prevalence of global compulsive, dependent, or histrionic personality disorders, they did score significantly higher on a number of their constituent traits (e.g., perfectionism, indecisiveness, and allowing others responsibility). Dimensional perspectives may reveal meaningful relationships that would be missed in a categorical analysis.

In the following section, we will review recent findings in the literature on dimensional personality variables and obsessive–compulsive phenomena. This is not intended as an exhaustive catalogue of every trait ever associated with OCD. Instead, we have chosen to focus on dimensions of personality that meet the following three criteria: (1) They are central features of the categorical Axis II disorders most often associated with OCD (see Mulder & Joyce, 1997); (2) they are incorporated into current models of personality structure and recognized in the mainstream literature; and (3) they have been the focus of empirical, clinical, or theoretical interest in the literature on OCD. These dimensions—harm avoidance/trait anxiety, impulsivity, perfectionism, and associated hypothetical personality concepts (i.e., *constructs*)—serve to bridge several disparate bodies of research and theory. We hope that this discussion will shed light on other themes emerging in the recent literature on OCD, including its diagnostic heterogeneity, its nosological placement, and its role in the obsessive–compulsive spectrum.

Harm Avoidance and Related Constructs

Avoidant and dependent personality disorders are frequently associated with anxiety disorders (Stein et al., 1993). Our review suggested that this is also true, albeit less consistently, in the case of OCD. Investigations of empirical bases for grouping personality disorders have consistently identified avoidant and dependent patterns as a single factor (e.g., Dowson & Berrios, 1991; Schroeder & Livesley, 1991). Mulder and Joyce (1997), who replicated this finding, characterized this factor as "asthenic," indicative of anxious, fearful, and harm-avoidant behaviors displayed as cross-situationally consistent traits.

The presence of anxiety in OCD plays a pivotal role not only in its DSM-IV nosological placement, but also in clinical models influencing treatment design. Exposure and response prevention, the building blocks of behavioral interventions used with OCD, rest on the premise that compulsive rituals, like phobic avoidance, serve to alleviate anxiety. This reflects the ongoing influence of traditional conditioning models of the acquisition and maintenance of fear and avoidance behaviors (e.g., Mowrer, 1939; see Foa, Steketee, & Milby, 1980; Marks, 1987). Cognitive-behavioral models emphasize, additionally, the continuous interaction of anxious affect with cognitive structures and processes (e.g., Foa & Kozak, 1995; Tallis, 1995; Warren & Zgourides, 1991).

NEUROTICISM

In the personality literature, broad dimensional constructs such as *neuroticism* (Costa & McCrae, 1992; Eysenck & Eysenck, 1975), *negative emotionality* and *negative affectivity* (Tellegen, 1985; Watson & Clark, 1984), and *negative temperament* (Watson & Clark, 1993) have all been posited as stable predispositions to respond to a wide range of stimuli with negative emotional states, including anxiety. High levels of neuroticism, similar to those found in other anxiety disorders, have been reported in the literature on OCD (e.g., Gray, 1981; Stanley, Swann, Bowers, Davis, & Taylor, 1991; Zinbarg & Barlow, 1996). However, such findings are of questionable value. The construct is extremely broad, leading even proponents of its inclusion in diagnostic frameworks (e.g., Costa & McCrae, 1986: Watson, Clark, & Harkness, 1994) to regard it as a general vulnerability factor in nearly all clinical disorders.

It is important to revisit the issue of problems associated with the assessment of personality in the presence of current OCD symptoms. This may be particularly salient in the case of the neuroticism–negative affectivity construct. Measures typically include such subdimensions as anxiety, depression, and somatic complaints (e.g., Costa & McCrae, 1992). The reliance of most studies on self-report data obtained with currently anxious individuals severely restricts conclusions about the status of neuroticism–negative affectivity as a vulnerability factor (see Zinbarg & Barlow, 1996). Concerns regarding the sensitivity of these instruments to cross-situationally stable personality traits versus current symptoms (e.g., Ormel, 1983) seem particularly warranted in OCD, where chronicity of symptoms and comorbidity with other mood and anxiety disorders (see Kolada, Bland, & Newman, 1994) may elevate general distress. This, and the construct's breadth, may limit its explanatory potential with this population.

TRAIT ANXIETY

Trait anxiety, a personality construct thought to reflect stable individual differences in the propensity to experience anxiety states (Endler, 1975; Spielberger, 1972), is generally subsumed under the broader dimension of neuroticism. Our review of OCD and Axis II comorbidity has revealed a preponderance of anxious/fearful cluster disorders, although this relationship is not as consistent and compelling as that observed in other anxiety disorders (Stein et al., 1993). Trait anxiety can be regarded as the common underlying feature of this cluster of personality disorders. Models of the development of anxiety syndromes incorporate this concept as a diathesis (e.g., Andrews, 1991, 1996; Gray, 1982), and there is empirical evidence that it is a shared feature of Axis I anxiety syndromes (Andrews, 1991; Zinbarg & Barlow, 1996).

In recent years, references to the inadequacy of the current classification of OCD as an anxiety disorder have become common (e.g., Clark et al., 1995; Enright, 1996a; Enright & Beech, 1990, 1993a, 1993b; Hollander, 1993b; O'Connor & Robillard, 1995; Reed, 1991; Tallis, 1996). Debates have been fueled not only by OCD's similarity to quite taxonomically disparate syndromes (e.g., tic-related disorders, trichotillomania), but also by its dissimilarity to the rest of the anxiety disorders. Although the DSM system has been lauded for its theoretical neutrality regarding etiology, the use of groupings does represent some unarticulated theories about relationships among disorders. As Stein and Hollander (1993b) have noted, the classification of OCD as an anxiety disorder suggests that its linkage with those syndromes—the presence of anxiety—is stronger than those with other disorders (see also Brown, 1996; Zinbarg & Barlow, 1996). In other words, within-group variability is considered less than that between groups. However, support for this assumption is equivocal. Discrepancies between the defining features of OCD and those of other anxiety disorders (see Insel, Zahn, & Murphy, 1985) are made more evident, according to Enright and Beech (1990), by treatment failures, inadequate conceptual models, complex comorbidity patterns, and clinical observations. These authors have been quite clear on the implications: "OCD is a distinct disorder qualitatively different from other anxiety disorder categories" (p. 625). Trait anxiety, a feature that is common among the anxiety disorders, may be a particularly informative construct.

Findings from self-report measures of trait anxiety, which commonly include somatic and cognitive–worry components (e.g., Endler, Edwards, & Vitelli, 1991; Spielberger, Gorsuch, & Lushene, 1970) are generally noncontroversial. Elevated levels of trait anxiety, indistinguishable from those observed in comparison groups with panic disorder, social phobia, and generalized anxiety disorder, have been reported repeatedly in samples of individuals with OCD (e.g., Andrews, Pollock, & Stewart, 1989; Turner, McCann, Beidel, & Mezzich, 1986). In a nonclinical sample, Gershuny and Sher (1995) found that compulsive checkers could not be distinguished from generally anxious, nonchecking controls on the basis of trait anxiety. More recently, however, McKay, Danyko, Neziroglu, and Yaryura-Tobias (1995) found that trait anxiety was correlated with obsessions but not compulsions.

The findings of a recent study are more provocative. Seeking to identify a hierarchical model of anxiety disorders sensitive to both shared and unique characteristics, Zinbarg and Barlow (1996) analyzed measures of key anxiety-related variables (e.g., tension, somatic anxiety, specific fears) in a large sample of patients representing a range of anxiety disorders. These authors found loadings of OCD symptoms on the higher-order shared factor to be among the lowest of all the variables included. Despite the indication of some shared features, these data also point to the uniqueness of OCD with regard to a single, nonspecific vulnerability factor, similar to trait anxiety. This point is underscored by recent comorbidity findings. Crino and Andrews (1996) have reported that whereas comorbid anxiety disorders are not uncommon in OCD, comorbid OCD in other anxiety disorders is significantly less frequent, and suggested that "in addition to a general or common vulnerability factor, specific vulnerability factors may be important in the development of OCD" (p. 45).

It is possible that although anxiety may be one among many mood states experienced by those with OCD, trait anxiety may not have the primary and etiological role that it may have in other disorders. In the absence of prospective longitudinal data, these findings cannot be interpreted as evidence that a trait-like predisposition to respond anxiously represents a vulnerability factor in OCD. The use of self-report measures may further complicate findings. In individuals currently suffering with symptoms, reports of how they "typically" respond may be profoundly influenced by current (state) levels of anxiety. Alternative sources of information might clarify this issue.

Although subjects with OCD have been found to score high on self-report measures of anxiety (e.g., Hoehn-Saric, McLeod, Zimmerli, & Hipsley, 1993), the presumed physiological substrate of these reports has not been conclusively demonstrated (Benkelfat et al., 1991; Hollander et al., 1991). Models of OCD that attribute a causal role to anxiety often rest on the assumed predisposing presence of heightened autonomic sensitivity, or hyperarousal (see Edelmann, 1992), as do many definitions of anxiety itself (e.g., Andrews, 1991; Barlow, 1991). In an attempt to determine whether hyperarousal is indeed essential, Hoehn-Saric, McLeod, and Hipsley (1995) administered a battery of physiological tests to subjects with OCD and controls. Resting levels on these measures were found to be the same for the two groups. The implications of this negative finding were made clear by the authors: "OCD symptoms trigger anxiety. . . . Clinically observable anxiety in patients [may be] a consequence rather than a cause of OCD" (p. 690). This point echoes others. Following a detailed review of the then current clinical and empirical literatures on OCD, Reed (1985) was adamant: "Where [anxiety] can be identified it seems to be a result rather than a cause of compulsive activity" (p. 137).

Additional evidence for the elusiveness of trait anxiety's role in OCD is provided by a quite different source. In the cognitive experimental literature, the association of anxiety with a selective attentional bias, favoring the processing of personally relevant threatening information, has proven to be robust and highly replicable (for reviews, see Dalgleish & Watts, 1990; MacLeod, 1991; Mathews & MacLeod, 1994; Mineka & Sutton, 1992). Its repeated demonstration in both a range of clinical anxiety disorders and nonclinical samples high in trait anxiety has led to its status as a "well-established" marker (Mogg, Mathews, Eysenck, & May, 1991). A few investigators have sought to identify processing biases in OCD samples similar to those observed with other anxiety disorders (e.g., Foa, Ilai, McCarthy, Shoyer, & Murdock, 1993; Lavy, van Oppen, & Van den Hout, 1994; Tata, Leibowitz, Prunty, Cameron, & Pickering, 1996). These, and similar efforts, have failed to produce robust support for trait-anxiety-related cognitive tendencies in OCD. The few studies that have been done present problematic results, both in the form of anomalous or ambiguous findings (e.g., Foa et al., 1993; McNally, Riemann, Luro, Lukach, & Kim, 1992), or in their simple inability to demonstrate these effects (e.g., McNally, Kaspi, Riemann, & Zeitlin, 1990). Moreover, the studies that do provide some evidence of attentional biases exhibit various methodological flaws (e.g., Foa et al., 1993; Tata et al., 1996) that render determination of the source of these effects difficult. Finally, in the few cases where there have been results consistent with the general literature, they have been associated with only one portion of subjects with OCD—those with contamination concerns (e.g., Foa et al., 1993; Tata et al., 1996).

Trait anxiety, as a general vulnerability factor in the development of anxiety syndromes, may be best conceptualized as a mediating variable, or an effect that interacts with the expression of other traits more unique to OCD. Rosen and Tallis (1995) investigated the relationship between obsessive–compulsive personality traits and symptoms by using a nonclinical sample and controlling for the effects of trait anxiety and depression. This procedure substantially simplified their original finding that 10 out of 13 measured personality disorders were associated with obsessive–compulsive symptoms. The only significant relationship remaining, after the two variables were controlled for statistically, was between select obsessive–compulsive symptoms (i.e., doubting, checking, and slowness) and obsessive–compulsive personality traits.

It appears that trait anxiety may be significant in its influence relative to other personality dimensions (e.g., perfectionism), particularly when distinct symptom subtypes are taken into consideration. This general idea has been articulated most clearly by Rasmussen and Eisen (1989, 1992, 1994). These authors, on the basis of a conceptual analysis of clinical interviews, have identified *abnor-*

mal risk assessment, or harm avoidance, as a core feature of OCD, cutting across manifest symptom profiles. The expression of this characteristic relies not only on its robustness, but also on its dominance relative to other core features. Its manifestation may influence, and be influenced by, the presence of other OCD-specific traits. In some forms of OCD, the trait may be very pervasive, resulting in phenomenological presentation, treatment responsiveness, and comorbidity patterns similar to those seen in other anxiety disorders. Rasmussen and Eisen (1992) have suggested that it is most manifest in OCD contamination and washing symptoms: "Of all the obsessive subtypes, their fear structure is linked most closely to the phobias. Both are precipitated by specific external stimuli, both are accompanied by a high level of anxiety, and for both, the coherence of the fear network is high" (p. 749; see also Rachman, 1976).

Impulsivity and Related Constructs

Proponents of the concept of an obsessive–compulsive spectrum of disorders (see Hollander, 1993a, 1993b) have pointed to the utility of a dimensional model, with compulsivity–impulsivity as a central continuum, along which syndromes such as OCD, trichotillomania, Tourette's, and body dysmorphic disorder can be situated (Hollander, 1993c; Oldham, Hollander, & Skodol, 1996). There is some inconsistency regarding OCD's placement on this impulsivity continuum: It has been described as the "low" pole of the spectrum by some (Hollander, 1993a; Skodol & Oldham, 1996), whereas others have emphasized its phenomenological similarity to disorders of impulse control (Lopez-Ibor, 1990). Alternatively, Hoehn-Saric and Barksdale (1983) proposed a broad distinction between impulsive and nonimpulsive subgroups of OCD.

In the personality literature, conceptualizations of impulsivity have varied widely (Cloninger, 1996). Most have incorporated risk taking, instability, a lack of reflection and restraint, and a proclivity to engage in behaviors associated with immediate gratification. Temperamental impulsivity has been identified as the common dimension underlying borderline and antisocial personality disorders (Dowson & Berrios, 1991; Zimmerman & Coryell, 1990). Although our review suggested that these are not commonly observed in OCD samples, the potential relevance of impulsivity, as a personality dimension, to current "spectrum" debates warrants some exploration.

Research findings are inconsistent. Individuals with obsessive–compulsive symptoms have been found to score lower than nonclinical controls on measures of impulsivity (e.g., Frost, Steketee, Cohn, & Greiss, 1994). Other studies, with clinical samples, have found these differences to be statistically nonsignificant (e.g., Pfohl, Black, Noyes, Kelley, & Blum, 1990; Richter, Summerfeldt, Joffe, & Swinson, 1996), which suggests that the link is tenuous. Findings with this population may be dependent upon the operational definition given to the impulsivity construct (i.e., the measure used). Researchers interested in the value of this personality dimension in the understanding of obsessive–compulsive spectrum disorders should be aware of differences in the content of items used to measure it.

Despite their similar labels, scales differ fundamentally in their emphasis upon the perceived strength of urges and thoughts, and one's own inability to resist (e.g., Barratt & Patton, 1983)—the basic subjective component, perhaps, of most general relevance to OCD and spectrum research—rather than its distal social and moral implications. Thus, different measures of impulsivity–inhibition vary from being highly predictive (Stein, Hollander, Simeon, & Cohen, 1994), to completely unrelated (Scarabelloti, Duck, & Dickerson, 1995) with respect to symptom severity.

The dimension of impulsivity, as it is generally defined by personality theorists, may only partly capture behavioral and cognitive tendencies of primary interest to obsessive–compulsive spectrum researchers. The exception to this may be in understanding the unique features of those individuals with OCD who exhibit self-regulatory deficits, such as acting out, explosive outbursts of anger, and high levels of hostility (see Stein & Hollander, 1993a). These are features of such disorders as borderline personality disorder, pathological gambling, and the paraphilias (see Hollander & Wong, 1995) whose inclusion in the obsessive–compulsive spectrum remains controversial (Rasmussen, 1994; see also Black, Goldstein, Noyes, & Blum, 1994). Hoehn-Saric and Barksdale (1983) found that highly impulsive OCD subjects, compared to nonimpulsive OCD controls, exhibited more behavioral dysregulation, conduct disturbance in childhood, and a greater range of psychopathology in adulthood. Similarities between obsessive–compulsive symptoms and the stereotyped and ritualistic behaviors seen in tic-related and grooming disorders (e.g., trichotillomania and compulsive skin picking)—the more uncontroversial members of the obsessive–compulsive spectrum (see Jenike, 1990)—may lend themselves more to exploration via other personality characteristics.

Related Constructs: Responsibility and Indecisiveness

Despite the limitations associated with the impulsivity construct, two central trends in its conceptualization correspond to well-developed areas of interest in the clinical and research literatures on OCD. One of these emphasizes its shared features with *psychopathy*, a personality dimension encompassing pathological egocentricity and an absence of guilt, found to be highly related to antisocial tendencies (Hare, Hart, & Harpur, 1991). Millon (1990) proposed the term "irresponsible" as a key descriptor of this personality disorder. This contrasts dramatically with observations made of "obsessional" characteristics. Frost et al. (1994) suggested that avoidance of risk, in this case, may reflect a heightened sense of personal responsibility. The distorted appraisal of responsibility in OCD has become a popular focus of investigation. The second trend in approaches to impulsivity is an emphasis on cognitive features. Cloninger, Przybeck, Svrâkic, and Wetzel (1994), for example, have incorporated this into the Impulsivity versus Reflection subscale of their Novelty Seeking dimension: "(Low scorers) tend to be analytical and require detailed information when making a decision or forming an opinion" (p. 22). This corresponds to a much older tradition. Kagan (1965), writing in the context of the "new look" movement in cognitive psychology, proposed the trait-like cognitive style of *reflection–impulsivity*, defined as "the degree to which a subject considers alternative hypotheses with minimal consideration of their probable validity" (Grigorenko & Sternberg, 1995, p. 208). This parallels a central theme in the literature on OCD, where much attention has been paid the related personality attributes of indecisiveness, uncertainty, and doubt.

RESPONSIBILITY AND GUILT

These characteristics of OCD have been considered common enough to be designated as associated descriptive features in the DSM-IV (American Psychiatric Association, 1994). Guilt and a pathological sense of responsibility, conceptualized as traits, are also the focus of a growing research literature. Although a key component of psychodynamic formulations, their involvement in this disorder has most recently been interpreted along cognitive frameworks, the most influential of which is the Salkovskis (1985, 1989) model of dysfunctional responsibility schemata. This suggests that distorted appraisals of the power of one's actions to produce or prevent harm, and the consequent assignment of disproportionate significance to intrusive thoughts, ultimately result in distress and anxiety-reducing rituals. In his discussion of the conceptual implications of this model, Rachman (1993) alluded to both the causal and perpetuating roles of perceived responsibility in obsessive–compulsive phenomena. Relevantly, Tallis (1994) described two cases in which responsibility and extreme guilt were considered instrumental in the development of OCD.

Efforts to demonstrate empirically the relationship between responsibility and OCD have had mixed results. In a treatment study, Freeston (1994; cited in Rhéaume, Freeston, Dugas, LeTarte, & Ladouceur, 1995) found that excessive responsibility was not apparent in his clinical sample. This contrasted with a previously observed association between this characteristic and obsessive–compulsive symptoms in nonclinical samples (Freeston, Ladouceur, Gagnon, & Thibodeau, 1992, 1993). In a multiple regression analysis of the relative value of perfectionism and responsibility in the prediction of obsessive–compulsive symptom severity in a nonclinical sample, Rhéaume et al. (1995) found responsibility to account for significantly more of the variance. Other correlational studies using self-report measures, by comparison, have reported insubstantial or nonexistent relationships between responsibility and obsessive–compulsive symptoms (e.g., Frost et al., 1994; Steketee & Frost, 1993). Similarly inconsistent findings have been reported with different operationalizations. It has been suggested that guilt, as a symptom, may be an indirect index of exaggerated appraisals of responsibility (Reynolds & Salkovkis, 1991). These authors, on these grounds, sought to replicate an earlier finding that trait guilt was a chief predictor of the frequency of, and distress associated with, negative intrusive thoughts in a normal population (Niler & Beck, 1989). The results were not replicated with this more robust sample; the only significant predictor variable was current distress (i.e., depression). Relevantly, Steketee, Quay, and White (1991) found that their clinical OCD sample did not differ on a measure of guilt from a sample of individuals with other anxiety disorders.

Despite the elegance of Salkovskis's model and its ability to explain such frequently observed phenomena as the short-term remission of obsessive–compulsive symptoms in supervised (i.e., institutional) settings (see Rachman, 1993; Rachman & Hodgson, 1980), empirical support for the model is scant. This may partially reflect qualitative differences between clinical and nonclinical OC symptoms. Unambiguous support is evident in nonclinical samples, despite Frost et al.'s (1994) observation that Salkovskis's model "may only apply to severely affected individuals" (p. 54). The lack of evidence may also indicate that in clinical samples, responsibility may have an interactive role in symptom expression or severity. The trait's influence may be determined by the presence of situational variables (e.g., familiarity of surroundings; Lopatka & Rachman, 1995; Rachman & Hodgson, 1980; see also Ladouceur, Rhéaume, & Aublet, 1997). Alternatively, it may combine with other personality variables (see Rhéaume et al., 1995) or be sensitive to the mediating effects of current (state) affect (see Reynolds & Salkovskis, 1991, for a discussion). Cognitive models maintain that it is the adverse mood created by the distorted appraisals that results in exacerbation of symptoms (see Beck, Emery, & Greenberg, 1985; Salkovskis, 1985, 1989), and so the relationship may then be an indirect one.

It is possible that varied findings may also be an artifact of researchers' treatment of OCD as a homogeneous entity. As Enright (1996b) has maintained, a substantial proportion of obsessive–compulsive symptoms simply do not fit a unitary syndrome profile. Clinically, inflated responsibility and concomitant guilt are most evident in individuals displaying pathological checking and associated obsessions regarding fear of harm befalling others (Rachman, 1976, 1993; Rasmussen & Eisen, 1989, 1992). There is empirical support for this observation. Rachman and Hodgson (1980) reported that lessened responsibility—encouraged by the presence of another person—alleviated discomfort in checkers but not washers. Ladouceur, Leger, and Rhéaume (1995, cited in Rhéaume et al., 1995) reported the therapeutic impact upon 4 patients' checking rituals of corrections of exaggerated appraisals of personal responsibility. This differential association of responsibility with symptoms may explain the construct's effects in nonclinical samples. The prevalence of checking behaviors in the general population, and their association with clinically pertinent subjective experiences of distress, has led to their current status as a nonclinical analogue of OCD (see Frost & Sher, 1989; Frost, Sher, & Geen, 1986). As such, variance in nonclinical samples in self-report measures of obsessive–compulsive symptoms may primarily reflect checking behaviors. The greater range of obsessions and compulsions in clinical samples may disguise this relationship.

In summary, although there is little evidence to support the global involvement of trait responsibility in OCD, its association with checking symptoms is compelling. It is interesting to note that such findings are quite discordant with the reported prevalence of dependent personality disorder in OCD in general. This is made clear in the second diagnostic criterion for this personality disorder: "needs others to assume responsibility for most major areas of his or her life" (American Psychiatric Association, 1994, p. 668). In order to understand this discrepancy, it is likely necessary to consider the intersection of other dependent features with other personality dimensions. As was already mentioned, reliance on others for reassurance and difficulty initiating projects—key diagnostic criteria for this pattern—may reflect personality attributes that have long been associated with obsessionality: uncertainty, indecisiveness, and doubt.

UNCERTAINTY AND INDECISIVENESS

Clinical accounts have noted the link between obsessional phenomena and indecisiveness, a trait manifested in a particular constellation of tendencies involving meticulous and prolonged decision making, attention to detail, and the weighing of all possible alternatives in making choices or reaching solutions (Fenichel, 1945; Rado, 1974). Although some of these features are evident in the current diagnostic criteria for OCPD (American Psychiatric Association, 1994), indecisiveness itself is not. Interestingly, this construct provides a bridge between the impulsivity literature and another relatively independent body of work on perfectionism.

Indecisiveness and uncertainty, and their behavioral repercussions (e.g., obsessional slowness; see Veale, 1993) may be overt indices of more fundamental cognitive tendencies, independent of symptoms and their circumscribed subject matter. Empirical evidence can be found in the difficulties experienced by subjects with OCD in the completion of timed performance tasks (see Reed, 1991). In one early example, Milner, Beech, and Walker (1971) found that although OCD subjects did not differ from controls on actual performance of a signal detection task, their requests for repetition of trials was much higher. Other studies have reported data similarly indicative of obsessional individuals' need for more information before coming to a decision. These include overall time taken to complete tasks with multiple strategic solutions (Goodwin & Sher, 1992), amount of evidence required for the solution of a probabilistic inference task (Volans, 1976; see also O'Connor & Robillard, 1995), and difficulties, in nonclinical and clinical samples, in efficient assignment to categories of lexical stimuli (Frost, Lahart, Dugas, & Sher, 1988; Persons & Foa, 1984). Nonexperimental methodologies have produced analogous findings. The centrality of intolerance of uncertainty in OCD was evident in a recent study by Richter et al. (1996) using Cloninger's (1987) Tridimensional Personality Questionnaire. It was found that the OCD group's high scores on the Harm Avoidance (HA) dimension were almost entirely due to elevations on one subscale: Fear of Uncertainty. Furthermore, this effect was unique to OCD; unlike other HA subscales, no further variance in scores was accounted for by the presence of additional comorbid anxiety disorders.

Although methodological problems may make precise interpretation difficult (see Rachman & Hodgson, 1980), such results suggest that individuals with OCD may represent the extreme pole of the reflectivity–impulsivity cognitive domain. They are also highly congruent with clinical observation. Frost and Hartl (1996), for example, indicted such decision-making tendencies in the genesis and maintenance of obsessional hoarding: "[It] results from a higher threshold for deciding what to discard" (p. 343). Importantly, these effects are manifested in a wide range of tasks and are not restricted to anxiety-evoking, symptom-relevant material (see Frost et al., 1988). This supports the conceptualization of indecisiveness as part of a general response style. Perhaps the most compelling evidence of its operation may be found in obsessional doubting. Reed (1985) suggested that this symptom, in OCD, is a subjective state consequent to decision making. This author has maintained that doubt, or uncertainty, represents a fundamental lack of conviction about the adequate completion and proper termination of a task or sequence. Historically, particularly in French psychiatry, this cognitive characteristic has been considered primary to the disorder (see Berrios, 1989), hence its appellation as the "doubting disease" (Ribot, 1904). In general, this emphasis has been lost under the influence of psychodynamic and behavioral models, in which anxiety is considered the primary driving force behind the disorder. Exceptions may be found outside of North America: Beech (1971, 1974; Walker & Beech, 1969) suggested that obsessive–compulsive symptoms may well arise from disturbance in affect but that this is itself primarily the result of profound difficulties in decision making. It is worthy of note that in a study using DSM-III-R (American Psychiatric Association, 1987) criteria for OCPD—which included indecisiveness—Tallis et al. (1996) found this personality pattern to be uniquely associated with doubting symptoms in an OCD sample.

This topic may shed light on the comorbidity of OCD with dependent personality disorder. Although this pattern is commonly characterized in terms of interpersonal sensitivity (American Psychiatric Association, 1994; Millon, 1990), a closer examination of its diagnostic criteria reveals other features more congruent with clinical accounts of OCD. The first criterion is "has difficulty making everyday decisions without an excessive amount of advice and reassurance from others" (American Psychiatric Association, 1994, p. 668). This is considered part of a larger pattern of submissiveness, motivated by a need to elicit nurturance from others. However, quite different motivations may produce overtly similar behaviors. Indecisiveness, in reflecting basic, trait-like cognitive tendencies, may result in similar compensatory activities. Relevantly, DSM-III-R diagnostic criteria for OCPD (American Psychiatric Association, 1987, p. 356) specified that indecisiveness must precede, rather than reflect, an excessive need for reassurance from others. The need for such qualifications, so at odds with the DSM's minimization of subjective variability, likely contributed to the exclusion of indecisiveness in subsequent versions.

In recent years, increasing focus on the cognitive characteristics of OCD has renewed interest in the precise nature of indecisiveness (e.g., Frost & Shows, 1993). In a work predating this trend, Reed (1985) identified this trait as crucial to the understanding of both the disorder and its personality concomitants. Basing his conclusions upon a detailed review of the then-current cognitive experimental literature, Reed contended that contrary to its classification, OCD is primarily a cognitive disorder. He suggested that obsessional doubting and indecisiveness reflect impairments in the spontaneous organization and integration of acquired information, and that clinical markers of the disorder, obsessions and compulsions, represent compensatory attempts to impose an otherwise unobtainable structure. In this view, the need to repeat tasks an arbitrary number of times, or rigidly adhere to a precise sequence in the completion of routine activities, are clinical examples of the deliberate structuring of functions that for most individuals are self-regulatory and automatic. Reed (1985) suggested that obsessive–compulsive personality traits serve a similarly compensatory function, and that this basic processing tendency is their link with the disorder.

Reed's cognitive–structural account has not been widely adopted as an investigative framework (see Jakes, 1996). Despite this, it has been increasingly cited in recent years by those interested in information processing and personality characteristics unique to OCD (e.g., Frost & Hartl, 1996; Frost & Shows, 1993; Rubenstein, Peynircioglu, Chambless, & Pigott, 1993). Cognitive anomalies of the sort discussed by Reed (1985, 1991) in such areas as concept formation, categorization, and the subjective experience of remembering, have been most commonly associated with nonwashing obsessive–compulsive symptoms (e.g., Constans, Foa, Franklin, & Mathews, 1995; Frost & Hartl, 1996; Frost et al., 1988; Maki, O'Neill, & O'Neill, 1994; McNally & Kohlbeck, 1993). It is not surprising, then, that Rasmussen and Eisen (1989, 1990, 1992; Rasmussen, 1994) have included *pathological doubt* as one of their three core features of OCD, which, although a common component of all symptom manifestations, is "seen in its purest form" (Rasmussen & Eisen, 1992, p. 750) in those with predominant checking behaviors. According to these authors, although this tendency is intensified by the threatening content of obsessions (e.g., the remote possibility that one might harm a family member), it is evident even in appraisals of the most mundane activities (e.g., deciding whether the refrigerator door is completely shut).

Attempts have been made to quantify this personality trait. Frost and Gross (1993), who were interested in its role in provoking compulsive hoarding, developed a self-report measure of indecisiveness. These authors suggested that by hoarding, the individual is able to avoid or postpone both decisions about the relative merits of discarding rather than keeping items, and tormenting doubts once the decision is made (see Frost & Hartl, 1996, for a general overview). Frost and Shows (1993) sought to extend this work by exploring the relationship in nonclinical samples between a range of obsessive–compulsive behaviors and trait indecisiveness. It was found to interfere with a variety of life domains, including social and familial functioning. Scores on the self-report measure were also predictive of decision-making latencies in an experimental task involving nonthreatening everyday choices (e.g., between menu offerings or articles of clothing). Perhaps most interestingly, these authors found that indecisiveness, in a nonclinical sample, was associated with compulsive checking but not with compulsive washing.

Theoretical accounts have often referred to the link between indecisiveness and perfectionism (e.g., Salzman, 1968; Straus, 1948), with the former—displayed in prolonged deliberation over options and the "best" choice—often seen as consequence of the latter (Guidano & Liotti, 1983). Alternatively, Reed (1985) has suggested that both arise from a more basic cognitive organizational deficit. Here, uncertainty and indecisiveness result from an impaired ability to use information, and perfectionism represents a compensatory effort to impose absolute conceptual limits. Whatever its direction, an empirical relationship has been found to exist between the two personality constructs (e.g., Frost & Shows, 1993).

Perfectionism

Generally defined as a striving to achieve excessively high standards while adopting stringent self-evaluations (Frost, Marten, Lahart, & Rosenblate, 1990), perfectionism has been regarded both as an adaptive personality trait and a debilitating vulnerability factor (see Blatt, 1995; Pacht, 1984). It was also considered by the DSM-IV Axis II Work Group to be among the "essential features" of OCPD (Pfohl & Blum, 1991) and is similarly prominent in the anankastic pattern of the ICD-10 (World Health Organization, 1992). Its association with both OCD and the obsessive–compulsive personality pattern has long been noted. Rado (1974) considered the obsessional "the ultimate perfectionist," an appraisal shared by other psychodynamically oriented writers (e.g., Jones, 1948; Mallinger, 1984; Salzman, 1968). Authors having other theoretical orientations have offered similar descriptions (e.g., Millon, 1981, 1990; McFall & Wollersheim, 1979).

The link between perfectionism and OCD was articulated most explicitly by Janet (1903). As already mentioned, he assigned a chief (and predisposing) role in the evolution of obsessive–compulsive symptoms to the *psychasthenic state*. This was thought to be characterized by subjective appraisals of the inadequacy of ones performance and perceptions, and the elusiveness of feelings of satisfaction: "Psychasthenics are continually tormented by an inner sense of imperfection" (cited in Pitman, 1987, p. 226). More recent clinical reports provide some support for the predisposing role of perfectionism in OCD. Rasmussen and Eisen (1989) found in their interviews with adult OCD patients that childhood perfectionistic traits were frequently reported. Similarly, Rasmussen and Tsuang (1986) and Honjo et al. (1989) described the majority of their patients as perfectionistic and fastidious.

Such global descriptions may require some refinement. Recent developments in the psychometric literature on perfectionism have demonstrated its multidimensionality (e.g., Frost et al., 1990; Hewitt & Flett, 1989, 1991). There is some consensus about these core features, despite differences in the content and labeling of subscales intended to assess them. Frost et al. (1990), in their detailed review, identified the following: the adoption of high personal standards, an exaggerated concern with mistakes, the perception of others' high expectations and the associated risk of criticism, a proclivity for organization, and doubts about the quality of one's performance.

Two more basic dimensions may underlie these key features. Some seem to reflect the motivating influence of social evaluation concerns and a need to meet the standards imposed by others—a dimension that Hewitt and Flett (1991) have termed *socially prescribed perfectionism*. A number of references have been made in the literature to this facet of perfectionism in the obsessive–compulsive personality pattern. McFall and Wollersheim (1979) have identified it as part of the dysfunctional obsessive–compulsive belief system, wherein anything less than perfect performance may result in "criticism or disapproval by others or oneself . . . punishment or condemnation" (p. 335). Similarly, Veale (1993) wrote of the compulsively perfectionistic individual: "In such cases there may be a close association with social anxiety or phobia—the patient may fear being rejected or isolated because of the perceived criticism of others if he was unclean or imperfect" (p. 200). As such, this dimension of perfectionism might be conceptualized as a form of social-harm avoidance (see Frost & Marten, 1990; Mallinger, 1984). This emphasis is quite congruent with psychodynamic formulations, which assign a central role in the development of both obsessive–compulsive traits and symptoms to the experience of overly critical and harsh parenting. Psychodynamic theorists have described obsessive–compulsive perfectionism as an attempt to maintain control, which serves to minimize harm and produce a sense of personal security (Mallinger, 1984; Salzman, 1968; Straus, 1948).

The few existing studies of perfectionism and obsessive–compulsive symptoms do not support this approach. In a nonclinical sample using self-report measures, Frost et al. (1994; Sample 1) found that overall levels of perfectionism were highly related to subclinical symptoms. Despite this, subclinical and noncompulsive subjects did not differ on subscales measuring more socially prescribed components of perfectionism (e.g., Parental Expectations and Parental Criticism). These findings were replicated by Rhéaume et al. (1995), also with a nonclinical sample. Such results, although suggestive, have limited generalizability due to the use of nonclinical subjects. In a recent study comparing perfectionism across several anxiety disorders, Antony, Huta, and Swinson (1996) obtained comparable results with a clinical sample. Subjects diagnosed with OCD were found to have lower scores on Hewitt and Flett's (1989) Socially Prescribed perfectionism subscales than did panic disorder and social phobia comparison groups. Not surprisingly, they were also significantly lower on the Parental Expectations subscale of Frost et al.'s (1990) measure.

These studies suggest that the role played in obsessional experience by perfectionism is not captured by its socially prescribed component. This is not surprising. In the self-reports of many individuals with OCD, one finds repeated reference to a profound sense of dissatisfaction concerning the need to have something absolutely certain, flawless, or exact. Clinical examples include having expressed a thought completely unambiguously with the best-chosen words, having left an elevator in just the right way, having one's clothing exert equal pressure on both sides of the body, and maintaining one's belongings in pristine and untouched condition. Perfectionism, here, appears to correspond to a sense of internal tension and a need for experiences to conform precisely to certain arbitrary criteria: "In some cases, individuals perform rigid or stereotyped acts according to idiosyncratically elaborated rules without being able to indicate why they are doing them" (American Psychiatric Association, 1994, p. 418). Most recently, Rasmussen and Eisen (1989, 1992, 1994), drawing heavily on the work of Janet (1903), have described this as the *incompleteness* phenomenon and proposed it as a core feature of OCD. These authors have adeptly described the subjective experience of obsessive–compulsive individuals tormented by an inner drive for certainty and perfection. Because this state of affairs is so elusive, and because the criteria for achieving it are not easily articulated, a feeling of incompleteness and dissatisfaction predominates. In those instances in which a perfect state is attained, the individual describes the experience of "the perfect feeling"—described over 80 years ago by Janet as "the occasional brief appearance of sublime ecstasy" (1903, cited in Pitman, 1987, p. 227).

Within the perfectionism literature, a strikingly similar description was provided by Hamachek (1978) in his distinction between normal and neurotic perfectionists. Of the latter, he suggested that "they are unable to feel satisfaction because in their own eyes they never seem to do things good enough to warrant that feeling" (p. 32). Other authors have placed similar emphasis on this unique subjective sense of uncertainty or incompleteness: Slade (1982) considered it central in distinguishing *satisfied* from *dissatisfied* perfectionism.

Perfectionistic tendencies, in OCD, appear to be self-prescribed or internally motivated, and seem to reflect a fundamental uncertainty about the criteria to be used in processing a wide range of experiences. This has been proposed elsewhere: "(The majority of patients) report that their parents were not the ones who set impossible standards for them to achieve. Instead they describe an inner drive that is connected to a wish to have things perfect, absolutely certain, and under total control" (Rasmussen & Eisen, 1991, p. 39). Results from empirical studies are supportive. In their nonclinical sample, Rhéaume et al. (1995) found the highest correlations between self-report measures of obsessive–compulsive symptoms and multidimensional perfectionism to exist for subscales assessing Concern over Mistakes and Doubts about Actions. As Frost et al. (1990) have indicated, both these features reflect a certain inflexibility regarding the standards that must be met for a performance to be considered acceptable. Similarly, Frost et al. (1994; Study 1) found that these two dimensions of perfectionism, along with Personal Standards (e.g., "Other people seem to accept lower standards for themselves than I do") distinguished between subclinically obsessive–compulsive and noncompulsive subjects. This trend has also been observed in clinical samples. Antony et al. (1996) found that only on the Doubting dimension did their OCD group score higher than a comparison group with panic disorder. Similarly, Frost and Steketee (1997) reported that despite their OCD subjects' elevated Total Perfectionism scores compared to nonpatient controls, when compared to a clinical control group (panic disorder with agoraphobia), they differed only in their higher scores on the Doubts about Actions facet.

These psychometric findings are lent added weight by the outcomes of other methodologies not commonly cited in the personality literature. In an experimental analysis of the dissatisfaction (i.e., *incompleteness*) quality of perfectionism, Slade, Newton, Butler, and Murphy (1991) employed a series of performance tasks designed to be sensitive to categorization and concept-formation tendencies. Drawing upon a larger cognitive style literature, these authors postulated that perfectionistic striving for absolute accuracy and flawlessness may reflect *underinclusiveness* (Zazlow, 1950), or a general tendency to set overly stringent criteria for membership in classes of phenomena. In category-formation tasks, in which the subject is expected to sort discrete stimuli into classes according to shared features, underinclusiveness is manifested in a tendency to form small categories. This is thought to reflect an inability to discount unique "irrelevant" characteristics in the interest of broader conceptual commonalities. Slade et al. (1991) found underinclusiveness in task performance to be significantly correlated with general dissatisfaction in two out of three tasks.

Underinclusiveness, identified by these authors as a central feature of the dissatisfied perfectionism construct, had actually been proposed as a key feature of obsessional phenomena more than 20 years earlier. In a body of work cited by Slade et al. (1991) as support for their conceptualization of perfectionism, Reed (1969a, 1969b, 1985, 1991) proposed that underlying both obsessive–compulsive traits (including perfectionism) and symptoms is a basic deficit in the cognitive structuring of information, and that this is manifested in a compensatory "over-structuring" processing style. Maintaining that this should be reflected in rigid and highly restricted conceptual limits, Reed (1969b) asked clinical subjects with obsessive–compulsive symptoms and traits, and matched controls to sort blocks into "classes" according to shared features, and to do so in the smallest number of groups. As predicted, obsessionals allocated fewer stimulus items to each class and required more "overly precise" classes to do so. These and similar findings (e.g., Reed, 1969a) prompted Reed's conclusion that OCD is characterized by an underinclusive (i.e., overly precise and maladaptively restrictive) cognitive style.

Other authors have reported results congruent with Reed's conceptualization. Persons and Foa (1984) reported that in a card-sorting task (which requires the subjects to identify cards that "go together" according to similar meanings), subjects with OCD took more time than controls to do the sorting task and used a significantly greater number of piles. The authors considered this support for a *complex concepts* hypothesis, specifying that OCD is associated with an overly narrow and complex approach to defining category membership. These results have been partially replicated in a nonclinical sample (Frost et al., 1988). Here, although subjects in the obsessive–compulsive group did require more time to sort components of a concept into subcategories—congruent with the complex concepts and underinclusion hypotheses—they did not require more piles to do so. Interestingly, the eventual "normality" of subjects' concept formation, while temporally impaired, may have reflected their nonclinical status. Similar cognitive tendencies have been revealed by different investigative methods. Goodwin and Sher (1992), studying "set-shifting" in nonclinical compulsive checkers, used the Wisconsin Card Sorting Test, which requires individuals to form and maintain cognitive sets by extracting information about larger-order categories from single stimuli. The "checker" group not only made significantly more total and perseverative errors than controls, but also took longer to complete trials, a relatively stable tendency also observed at a 5-month follow-up. Although such outcomes are usually interpreted as signs of perseverative difficulties, the checker group's "total error" score points to impairments in the ability to organize stimuli on the basis of shared general principles—or concept formation (Lezak, 1983). Analogous problems were evident in the nonclinical checkers studied by Maki et al. (1994). Their "inhibitory deficit" data provide evidence of these subjects' difficulties with concept organization and definition: They committed more errors in identifying members of categories and in decisions regarding the semantic relatedness of words.

In short, studies adopting a range of methodologies and operational definitions suggest an association between OCD and internally motivated "dissatisfied" perfectionism. This dimension is distinct from harm avoidance–trait anxiety (see Flett, Hewitt, Endler, & Tassone, 1995); as such, it may be the unique component of the obsessional/anankastic pattern that leads to its consistent empirical independence from "anxious cluster" personality disorders (e.g., Mulder & Joyce, 1997). Clinically, pathological perfectionism is most clearly manifested in a group of OCD sufferers who display little or no anxious apprehension, but rather a strong sense of dissatisfaction concerning the need to have things absolutely certain, flawless, or exact. This trait appears most emergent in symmetry and exactness obsessions, and compulsions involving ordering, precision, and repeating (Rasmussen & Eisen, 1989, 1992, 1994; see also Tallis, 1996). It may also, in extreme expression, underlie the "primary obsessional slowness" variant of OCD (see Rachman, 1976; Takeuchi et al., 1997; Veale, 1993).

Comment

It is clear from our review of both categorical and dimensional personality concepts that the obsessive–compulsive personality pattern—as it is conventionally described in North America—is neither globally nor consistently associated with obsessive–compulsive symptoms. There is evidence to suggest that the psychodynamic influence on this pattern's definition is in part responsible. Pitman and Jenike (1989), using the Lazare–Klerman–Armor Trait Scale's obsessive subscale, which measures classic anal personality traits, found that it did not distinguish OCD patients from healthy controls. Review of their results reveals that of the eight items that *did* discriminate the two groups, only two—doubting and indecisiveness—were elevated in OCD patients. Scores on the traditional anal traits of obstinacy, emotional constriction, and orderliness were actually higher in normal controls. Despite this, clinician ratings of the two groups on DSM-III-R OCPD traits, *which included perfectionism and indecisiveness,* were significantly different. In short, the obsessional/anankastic, but not the obsessional/anal, pattern had discriminative utility.

There are other sources of evidence for the uniqueness of these two constellations of "obsessional" traits. In factor analyses of the Lazare–Klerman–Armor

Scales (e.g., Lazare, Klerman & Armour, 1966, 1970; Torgersen, 1980), doubt and indecisiveness have not been found to load on the obsessional (i.e., anal character) dimension. Interestingly, Pfohl and Blum (1991) cited this point in their literature review as support for the recommended (and subsequently adopted) excision of indecisiveness from OCPD diagnostic criteria. One might equally regard it as evidence of the failure of psychodynamic models to capture a personality feature considered essential to obsessionality by those outside the Freudian tradition for over a century.

A recent factor analytic study by Baer (1994) is similarly illustrative. Baer sought to determine empirically the structure of OCD symptoms and their differential relationships with Axis I and Axis II disorders (i.e., tic-related disorders and OCPD). Three factors were obtained and labeled as symmetry/hoarding, contamination/checking, and pure obsessions. Only the first of these was predictive of comorbid tics and Tourette's syndrome. It was also the only factor related to a constellation of personality traits that adhered quite closely to the anankastic pattern (World Health Organization, 1992), comprising indecision, preoccupation with details, and perfectionism. Intriguingly, the traits central in Freud's (1908) model—overconscientiousness, devotion to work, authoritarianism, and stinginess—displayed unique variance and a complete lack of relationship with any OCD factor.

Baer's findings serve to coalesce several themes that we have discerned in our review of the amorphous literature on personality factors and OCD, and attempted to communicate throughout this chapter. First, substantial empirical evidence now exists for what has long been alluded to in theoretical and clinical accounts: differential relationships exist among personality dimensions and specific OCD symptom profiles. Second, by equating *the obsessive–compulsive personality pattern* with Freudian notions and neglecting other conceptual traditions, such as that of Janet, researchers have discounted its lasting value. Finally, this "anankastic" constellation of traits—with incompleteness, indecisiveness/uncertainty/doubt, and pathological (dissatisfied) perfectionism at their core—may be the common elements between OCD and obsessive–compulsive spectrum disorders. This last idea, first articulated by Rasmussen and Eisen (1989), is perhaps the most important; its heuristic value is evident in its ability to clarify findings reported elsewhere.

PERSONALITY AND THE OBSESSIVE–COMPULSIVE SPECTRUM

In a study of the phenomenology of compulsive symptoms in subjects with tic disorders, Leckman, Walker, Goodman, Pauls, and Cohen (1994) focused on such individuals' often-reported need to perform behaviors until they feel "just right." In an intriguing adaptation of the then 90-year-old psychasthenia concept (Janet, 1903), these authors asked subjects to indicate whether they associated feelings (i.e., an inner sense) of incompleteness, imperfection, and insufficiency with their symptoms. Eighty-one percent of the subjects with OCD and Tourette's syndrome reported such experiences, and qualitative responses showed remarkable similarity with Janet's description: "Most respondents emphasized a sense of imperfection and the need to perform a task until a certain feeling of satisfaction or completion was obtained" (Leckman et al., 1994, p. 677). A subsequent study found this to be true of individuals with OCD, both with and without tics (Leckman et al., 1995). Such overlap has likely contributed to the clinical difficulty of distinguishing some tics from compulsions (see Pitman, Green, Jenike, & Mesulam, 1987).

An interesting parallel is found in the subjective experience often reported by individuals suffering from pathological hair pulling, or trichotillomania. Clinical features frequently include a similar sense of inner tension and an intolerance of imperfections, seen in the irresistible need to remove anomalous or "different" hairs (see Swedo & Leonard, 1992), whose "removal is necessary in order to make the hair feel 'just right'" (Swedo, 1993, p. 96).

There is evidence for similar affective and motivational underpinnings in anorexia nervosa, a disorder proposed as a member of the obsessive–compulsive spectrum (e.g., Hollander, 1993c; Hollander & Wong, 1995). In a recent investigation of posttreatment characteristics of individuals with anorexia, Srinivasagam et al. (1995) found that even after long-term recovery, these subjects showed higher levels of perfectionistic traits than a control group. They also exhibited significantly higher levels of the obsessive–compulsive symptoms identified by Baer (1994) as statistically related to both anankastic traits and tic-related disorders—symmetry obsessions, and ordering and repeating compulsions. The authors were clear about the implications: "Such behaviors (may be) traits expressing a biological vulnerability" (p. 1634). Similarly suggestive results were reported by Bastiani, Rao, Weltzin, and Kaye (1995). In a sample of individuals diagnosed with anorexia nervosa, elevated scores (which persisted following recovery) were found on such dimensions of perfectionism as Doubts about Actions and Organization, Order, and Precision. These standards were reported to be self-imposed, rather than responses to perceived social expectations and evaluations.

In short, a coherent constellation of obsessive–compulsive traits, closer to the anankastic pattern than to that influenced by psychodynamic theory, may represent the personality commonality of a number of nosologically distinct disorders. This, rather than any superficial similarities in manifest symptoms (i.e., compulsiveness, or the presence of irresistible and uncontrollable behaviors; see Rasmussen, 1994) may be one key to the understanding of the hypothesized obsessive–compulsive spectrum. Furthermore, this personality pattern appears inextricably linked to a specific group of obsessive–compulsive symptoms, revolving around symmetry obsessions and counting, ordering, and repeating compulsions (Baer, 1994). This possibility may account for ongoing difficulties establishing a definitive empirical link among the obsessive–compulsive spectrum disorders; most current studies do not incorporate heterogeneity within OCD into their analyses (e.g., Black et al., 1994).

SUMMARY

This review has suggested that the research literature on categorical personality disorders in OCD has done little to advance our basic understanding of the relationship between personality factors and this disorder. However, a closer examination of specific dimensions of personality has proven fruitful. Empirical evidence from a wide range of methodologies and research paradigms points to the possibility that a small number of core dimensions may provide the personality context for OCD. These dimensions—harm avoidance/trait anxiety, such impulsivity-linked constructs as responsibility and indecisiveness, and self-oriented perfectionism—may also serve as keys to some of the issues under debate in the current OCD literature. Additionally, it is likely that much of the lack of consensus in the literature on personality factors in this disorder has arisen from a failure to incorporate heterogeneity within OCD into research designs. Differential relationships appear to exist between these personality dimensions (or their predominance, relative to the others) and distinct subtypes of OCD. As was made evident in our review, this basic point is also relevant to current debates regarding the syndrome's categorization as an anxiety disorder and its relationship with the hypothesized obsessive–compulsive spectrum disorders. Last, this dimensional analysis has also been of value in determining the enduring value of one traditional account of a distinctive "obsessional personality": that of Pierre Janet (1903). All of these possibilities have potential etiological, clinical, and theoretical implications, and merit further exploration.

ACKNOWLEDGMENT

The first author would like to acknowledge the support of the Social Sciences and Humanities Research Council of Canada (SSHRC), in the form of a doctoral fellowship.

REFERENCES

American Psychiatric Association. (1987). *Diagnostic and statistical manual of mental disorders* (3rd. ed., rev.). Washington, DC: Author.

American Psychiatric Association. (1994). *Diagnostic and statistical manual of mental disorders* (4th ed.). Washington, DC: Author.

Andrews, G. (1991). Anxiety, personality and anxiety disorders. *International Review of Psychiatry, 3*, 293–302.

Andrews, G. (1996). Comorbidity in neurotic disorders: The similarities are more important than the differences. In R. M. Rapee (Ed.), *Current controversies in the anxiety disorders* (pp. 3–20). New York: Guilford Press.

Andrews, G., Pollock, C., & Stewart, G. (1989). The determination of defense style by questionnaire. *Archives of General Psychiatry, 46*, 455–460.

Antony, M. M., Huta, V., & Swinson, R. P. (1996, November). *Perfectionism across the anxiety disorders.* Paper presented at the meeting of the Association for Advancement of Behavior Therapy, New York, NY.

Baer, L. (1994). Factor analysis of symptom subtypes of obsessive compulsive disorder and their relation to personality and tic disorders. *Journal of Clinical Psychiatry, 55,* 18–23.

Baer, L., & Jenike, M. A. (1992). Personality disorders in obsessive compulsive disorder. *Psychiatric Clinics of North America, 55,* 803–812.

Baer, L., Jenike, M. A., Black, D. W., Treece, C., Rosenfeld, R., & Greist, J. (1992). Effects of Axis II diagnoses on treatment outcome with clomipramine in 55 patients with obsessive–compulsive disorder. *Archives of General Psychiatry, 49,* 862–866.

Baer, L., Jenike, M. A., Ricciardi, J. N., Holland, A. D., Seymour, R. J., Minichiello, W. E., & Buttolph, M. L. (1990). Standardized assessment of personality disorders in obsessive–compulsive disorder. *Archives of General Psychiatry, 47,* 826–830.

Barlow, D. H. (1991). Disorders of emotion. *Psychological Inquiry, 2,* 58–71.

Barratt, E., & Patton, J. (1983). Impulsivity: Cognitive, behavioral, and psychophysiological correlates. In M. Zuckerman (Ed.), *Biological bases of impulsiveness and sensation seeking.* (pp. 77–116). Hillsdale, NJ: Erlbaum.

Bastiani, A. M., Rao, R., Weltzin, T., & Kaye, W. H. (1995). Perfectionism in anorexia nervosa. *International Journal of Eating Disorders, 17,* 147–152.

Beck, A. T., Emery, G., & Greenberg, R. L. (1985). *Anxiety disorders and phobias: A cognitive perspective.* New York: Basic Books.

Beech, H. R. (1971). Ritualistic activity in obsessional patients. *Journal of Psychosomatic Research, 15,* 417–422.

Beech, H. R. (1974). *Obsessional states.* London: Methuen.

Beech, H. R., & Liddell, A. (1974). Decision-making, mood states and ritualistic behaviour among obsessional patients. In H. R. Beech (Ed.), *Obsessional states* (pp. 143–160). London: Methuen.

Benkelfat, C., Mefford, I. N., Masters, C. F., Nordhal, T. E., King, A. C., Cohen, R. M., & Murphy, O. L. (1991). Plasma catecholamines and their metabolites in obsessive–compulsive disorder. *Psychiatry Research, 37,* 321–331.

Berrios, G. E. (1989). Obsessive–compulsive disorder: Its conceptual history in France during the 19th century. *Comprehensive Psychiatry, 30,* 283–295.

Black, A. (1974). The natural history of obsessional neurosis. In H. R. Beech (Ed.), *Obsessional states* (pp. 1–23). London: Methuen.

Black, D. W., Goldstein, R. B., Noyes, R., & Blum, N. (1994). Compulsive behaviors and obsessive–compulsive disorder (OCD): Lack of a relationship between OCD, eating disorders, and gambling. *Comprehensive Psychiatry, 35,* 145–148.

Black, D. W., Noyes, R., Pfohl, B., Goldstein, R. B., & Blum, N. (1993). Personality disorder in obsessive–compulsive volunteers, well comparison subjects, and their first-degree relatives. *American Journal of Psychiatry, 150,* 1226–1232.

Black, D. W., Yates, W. R., Noyes, R., Pfohl, B., & Kelley, M. (1989). DSM-III personality disorder in obsessive–compulsive study volunteers: A controlled study. *Journal of Personality Disorders, 3,* 58–62.

Blatt, S. J. (1995). The destructiveness of perfectionism: Implications for the treatment of depression. *American Psychologist, 50,* 1003–1020.

Brown, T. A. (1996). Validity of the DSM-III-R and DSM-IV classification systems for anxiety disorders. In R. M. Rapee (Ed.), *Current controversies in the anxiety disorders* (pp. 21–45). New York: Guilford Press.

Cassano, D., Del Buono, G., & Catapano, F. (1993). The relationship between obsessive compulsive personality and obsessive–compulsive disorder: Data obtained by the Personality Disorder Examination. *European Psychiatry, 8,* 219–221.

Claridge, G. S., & Broks, P. (1984). Schizotypy and hemisphere function: I. Theoretical considerations and the measurement of schizotypy. *Personality and Individual Differences, 5,* 633–648.

Clark, L. A. (1992). Resolving taxonomic issues in personality disorders: The value of large-scale analyses of symptom data. *Journal of Personality Disorders, 6,* 360–376.

Clark, L. A., & Watson, D. (1991). Tripartite model of anxiety and depression: Psychometric evidence and taxonomic implications. *Journal of Abnormal Psychology, 100,* 316–336.

Clark, L. A., Watson, D., & Mineka, S. (1994). Temperament, personality, and the mood and anxiety disorders. *Journal of Abnormal Psychology, 103,* 103–116.

Clark, L. A., Watson, D., & Reynolds, S. (1995). Diagnosis and classification of psychopathology: Challenges to the current system and future directions. *Annual Review of Psychology, 46,* 121–153.

Cloninger, C. R. (1986). A unified biosocial theory of personality and its role in the development of anxiety states. *Psychiatric Development, 3,* 167–226.

Cloninger, C. R. (1987). A systematic method for clinical description and classification of personality variance: A proposal. *Archives of General Psychiatry, 44,* 573–588.

Cloninger, C. R. (1996). Assessment of the impulsive-compulsive spectrum of behavior by the seven-factor model of temperament and character. In J. M. Oldham, E. Hollander, & A. E. Skodol (Eds.), *Impulsivity and compulsivity* (pp. 59–96). Washington, DC: American Psychiatric Press.

Cloninger, C. R., Przybeck, T. R., Svrâkic, D. M., & Wetzel, R. D. (1994). *The Temperament and Character Inventory: A guide to its development and use.* St. Louis, MO: Center for Psychobiology of Personality.

Constans, J. I., Foa, E. G., Franklin, M. E., & Mathews, A. (1995). Memory for actual and imagined events in OC checkers. *Behaviour Research and Therapy, 33,* 665–671.

Costa, P. T., & McCrae, R. R. (1986). Personality stability and its implications for clinical psychology. *Clinical Psychology Review, 6,* 407–423.

Costa, P. T., & McCrae, R. R. (1992). *Revised NEO Personality Inventory (NEO-PI-R) and NEO Five-Factor Inventory (NEO-FFI) professional manual.* Odessa, FL: Psychological Assessment Resources.

Crino, R. D., & Andrews, G. (1996). Obsessive–compulsive disorder and Axis I comorbidity. *Journal of Anxiety Disorders, 10,* 37–46.

Dalgleish, T., & Watts, F. N. (1990). Biases of attention and memory in disorders of anxiety and depression. *Clinical Psychology Review, 10,* 599–604.

Diaferia, G., Bianchi, I., Bianchi, M. L., Cavedini, P., Erzegovesi, S., & Bellodi, L. (1997). Relationship between obsessive–compulsive personality disorder and obsessive–compulsive disorder. *Comprehensive Psychiatry, 38,* 38–42.

Dowson, J. H., & Berrios, G. E. (1991). Factor structure of DSM-III-R personality disorders shown by self-report questionnaire: Implication for classifying and assessing personality disorders. *Acta Psychiatrica Scandinavica, 86,* 555–560.

Edelmann, R. J. (1992). *Anxiety: Theory, research and intervention in clinical and health psychology.* Toronto: Wiley.

Endler, N. S. (1975). A person–situation interaction model of anxiety. In C. D. Spielberger & I. G. Sarason (Eds.), *Stress and anxiety* (Vol. 1, pp. 145–164). Washington, DC: Hemisphere.

Endler, N. S., Edwards, J. M., & Vitelli, R. (1991). *Endler Multidimensional Anxiety Scales: Manual.* Los Angeles: Western Psychological Services.

Endler, N. S., & Parker, J. D. A. (1990). Personality research: Theories issues and methods. In M. Hersen, A. E. Kazdin, & A. S. Bellack (Eds.), *The clinical psychology handbook* (2nd ed., pp. 258–275). Toronto: Pergamon.

Endler, N. S., & Parker, J. D. A. (1992). Interactionism revisited: Reflections on the continuing crisis in the personality area. *European Journal of Personality, 6,* 177–198.

Enright, S. J. (1996a). Obsessive–compulsive disorder: Anxiety disorder or schizotype? In R. M. Rapee (Ed.), *Current controversies in the anxiety disorders* (pp. 161–190). New York: Guilford Press.

Enright, S. J. (1996b). Reply to Salkovskis and to Pigott et al. Forwards, backwards, and sideways: Progress in OCD research. In R. M. Rapee (Ed.), *Current controversies in the anxiety disorders* (pp. 209–213). New York: Guilford Press.

Enright, S. J., & Beech, A. R. (1990). Obsessional states: Anxiety disorders or schizotypes. An information processing and personality assessment. *Psychological Medicine, 20,* 621–627.

Enright, S. J., & Beech, A. R. (1993a). Reduced cognitive inhibition in obsessive–compulsive disorder. *British Journal of Clinical Psychology, 32,* 67–74.

Enright, S. J., & Beech, A. R. (1993b). Further evidence of reduced cognitive inhibition in obsessive–compulsive disorder. *Personality and Individual Differences, 14,* 387–395.

Eysenck, H. J. (1967). *Biological bases of personality.* Springfield, IL: Charles C Thomas.

Eysenck, H. J., & Eysenck, S. B. J. (1975). *Manual of the Eysenck Personality Questionnaire.* Kent, UK: Hodder & Stoughton.

Fenichel, O. (1945). *The psychoanalytic theory of neurosis.* New York: Norton.

Flett, G. L., Hewitt, P. L., Endler, N. S., & Tassone, C. (1995). Perfectionism and components of state and trait anxiety. *Current Psychology: Developmental, Learning, Personality, and Social, 13,* 326–350.

Foa, E. B., Ilai, D., McCarthy, P. R., Shoyer, B., & Murdock, T. (1993). Information processing in obsessive–compulsive disorder. *Cognitive Therapy and Research, 17,* 173–189.

Foa E. B., & Kozak, M. J. (1995). DSM-IV field trial: Obsessive–compulsive disorder. *American Journal of Psychiatry, 152,* 90–96.

Foa, E. B., Steketee, G., & Milby, J. B. (1980). Differential effects of exposure and response prevention in obsessive–compulsive washers. *Journal of Clinical and Consulting Psychology, 48,* 71–79.

Frances, A. (1993). Dimensional diagnosis of personality: Not whether, but when and which. *Psychological Inquiry, 4,* 110–111.

Frances, A., Widiger, T., & Fyer, M. R. (1990). The influence of classification methods an comorbidity. In J. D. Maser & C. R. Cloninger (Eds.), *Comorbidity of mood and anxiety disorders* (pp. 42–59). Washington, DC: American Psychiatric Association Press.

Freeston, M. H., Ladouceur, R., Gagnon, F., & Thibodeau, N. (1992, June). *Intrusive thoughts, worry, and obsessions: Empirical and theoretical distinctions.* Paper presented at the World Congress of Cognitive Therapy, Toronto, Canada.

Freeston, M. H., Ladouceur, R., Gagnon, F., & Thibodeau, N. (1993). Beliefs about obsessional thoughts. *Journal of Psychopathology and Behavioral Assessment, 15,* 1–21.

Freud, S. (1908). Character and anal erotism. In J. Strachey (Ed. & Trans.), *Standard edition of the complete psychological works of Sigmund Freud* (Vol. 9, pp. 169–175). London: Hogarth Press.

Freud, S. (1913). The disposition to obsessional neurosis. In J. Strachey (Ed. & Trans.), *Standard edition of the complete psychological works of Sigmund Freud* (Vol. 12, pp. 317–326). London: Hogarth Press.

Frost, R. O., & Gross, R. C. (1993). The hoarding of possessions. *Behaviour Research and Therapy, 31,* 367–381.

Frost, R. O., & Hartl, T. L. (1996). A cognitive-behavioral model of compulsive hoarding. *Behaviour Research and Therapy, 34,* 341–350.

Frost, R. O., Lahart, C. M., Dugas, K. M., & Sher, K. J. (1988). Information processing among non-clinical compulsives. *Behaviour Research and Therapy, 26,* 275–277.

Frost, R. O., & Marten, P. (1990). Pefectionism and evaluative threat. *Cognitive Therapy and Research, 14,* 449–468.

Frost, R. O., Marten, P., Lahart, C., & Rosenblate, R. (1990). The dimensions of perfectionism. *Cognitive Therapy and Research, 14,* 449–468.

Frost, R. O., & Sher, K. J. (1989). Checking behavior in a threatening situation. *Behaviour Research and Therapy, 27,* 385–389.

Frost, R. O., Sher, K. J., & Geen, T. (1986). Psychopathology and personality characteristics of nonclincial compulsive checkers. *Behaviour Research and Therapy, 24,* 133–143.

Frost, R. O., & Shows, D. L. (1993). The nature and measurement of compulsive indecisiveness. *Behaviour Research and Therapy, 31,* 683–692.

Frost, R. O., & Steketee, G. (1997). Perfectionism in obsessive–compulsive disorder patients. *Behaviour Research and Therapy, 35,* 291–296.

Frost, R. O., Steketee, G., Cohn, L., & Griess, K. (1994). Personality traits in subclinical and non-obsessive–compulsive volunteers and their parents. *Behaviour Research and Therapy, 32,* 47–56.

Gershuny, B., & Sher, K. (1995). Compulsive checking and anxiety in a nonclinical sample: Differences in cognition, behavior, personality, affect. *Journal of Psychopathology and Behavioral Assessment, 17,* 19–38.

Goodwin, A. H., & Sher, K. J. (1992). Deficits in set-shifting ability in non-clinical compulsive checkers. *Journal of Psychopathology and Behavioral Assessment, 14,* 81–91.

Gray, J. A. (1981). A critique of Eysenck's theory of personality. In H. J. Eysenck (Ed.), *A model for personality* (pp. 246–276). New York: Springer-Verlag.

Gray, J. A. (1982). *The neuropsychology of anxiety: An enquiry into the functions of the septo-hippocampal system.* Oxford, UK: Oxford University Press.

Grigorenko, E. L., & Sternberg, R. J. (1995). Thinking styles. In D.H. Saklofske & M. Zeidner (Eds.), *International handbook of personality and intelligence* (pp. 205–230). New York: Plenum.

Guidano, V., & Liotti, G. (1983). *Cognitive processes and emotional disorders.* New York: Guilford Press.

Hamachek, D. E. (1978). Psychodynamics of normal and neurotic perfectionism. *Psychology, 15,* 27–72.

Hare, R. D., Hart, S. D., & Harpur, T. J. (1991). Psychopathy and DSM-IV criteria for antisocial personality disorder. *Journal of Abnormal Psychology, 100,* 391–398.

Hermesh, H., Shahar, A., & Munitz, H. (1987). Obsessive–compulsive disorder and borderline personality disorder. *American Journal of Psychiatry, 144,* 120–121.

Hewitt, P. L., & Flett, G. L. (1989). The Multidimensional Perfectionism Scale: Development and validation. *Canadian Psychology, 30,* 339 (abstract).

Hewitt, P. L., & Flett, G. L. (1991). Perfectionism in the self and social contexts: Conceptualization, assessment, and association with psychopathology. *Journal of Personality and Social Psychology, 60,* 456–470.

Hoehn-Saric, R., & Barksdale, V. C. (1983). Impulsiveness in obsessive–compulsive patients. *British Journal of Psychiatry, 143,* 177–182.

Hoehn-Saric, R., McLeod, D. R., Hipsley, P. (1995). Is hyperarousal essential to obsessive–compulsive disorder? *Archives of General Psychiatry, 52*, 688–693.

Hoehn-Saric, R., McLeod, D. R., Zimmerli, W. D., & Hipsley, P. A. (1993). Symptoms and physiologic manifestations in obsessive–compulsive patients before and after treatment with clomipramine. *Journal of Clinical Psychiatry, 54*, 272–276.

Hollander, E. (1993a). Introduction. In E. Hollander (Ed.), *Obsessive–compulsive related disorders* (pp. 1–16). Washington, DC: American Psychiatric Association Press.

Hollander, E. (Ed.). (1993b). *Obsessive–compulsive related disorders.* Washington, DC: American Psychiatric Association Press.

Hollander, E. (1993c). Obsessive–compulsive spectrum disorders: An overview. *Psychiatric Annals, 23*, 355–358.

Hollander, E., DeCaria, C., Nitescu, A., Cooper, T., Stover, B., Gully, R., Klein, D. F., & Liebowitz, M. R. (1991). Noradrenergic function in obsessive–compulsive disorder: Behavioural and neuroendocrine responses to clonidine and comparison to healthy controls. *Psychiatry Research, 37*, 161–177.

Hollander, E., & Wong, C. M. (1995). Body dysmorphic disorder, pathological gambling, and sexual compulsions. *Journal of Clinical Psychiatry, 56*, 7–12.

Honjo, S., Hirano, C., Murase, S., Kaneko, T., Sugiyama, T., Ohtaka, K., Aoyamam, T., Takel, Y., Inoko, K., & Wakabayashi, S. (1989). Obsessive compulsive symptoms in childhood and adolescence. *Acta Psychiatrica Scandinavica, 80*, 83–91.

Ingram, I. M. (1961). The obsessional personality and obsessional illness. *American Journal of Psychiatry, 117*, 1016–1019.

Insel, T. R., Zahn, T., & Murphy, D. L. (1985). Obsessive–compulsive disorder: An anxiety disorder? In A. T. Tuma & J. Maser (Eds.), *Anxiety and the anxiety disorders* (pp. 577–589). Hillsdale, NJ: Erlbaum.

Jakes, I. (1996). *Theoretical approaches to obsessive–compulsive disorder.* Cambridge, UK: Cambridge University Press.

Janet, P. (1903). *Les obsessions et la psychasthénie* (Vols. 1 & 2, 2nd ed.). Paris: Alcan.

Jenike, M. A. (1990). Illnesses related to obsessive–compulsive diosrder. In M. A. Jenike, L. B. Baer, & W. E. Minichiello (Eds.), *Obsessive–compulsive disorders: Theory and management* (2nd ed., pp. 39–60). Chicago: Year Book Medical.

Jenike, M. A., Baer, L., Minichiello, W. E., Schwartz, C. E., & Carey, R. J. (1986). Concommitant obsessive–compulsive disorder and schizotypal personality disorder. *American Journal of Psychiatry, 143*, 530–532.

Joffe, R. T., Swinson, R. P., & Regan, J. J. (1988). Personality features of obsessive–compulsive disorder. *American Journal of Psychiatry, 145*, 1127–1129.

Jones, E. (1948). Anal-erotic character traits. In E. Jones (Ed.), *Papers on psychoanalysis* (2nd ed., pp. 413–437). London: Balliere, Tindall, & Cox.

Kagan, J. (1965). Individual differences in the resolution of response uncertainty. *Journal of Personality and Social Psychology, 2*, 154–160.

Klerman, G. L. (1973). The relationship between personality and clinical depressions: Overcoming the obstacles to verifying psychodynamic theories. *International Journal of Psychiatry, 11*, 227–233.

Kolada, J. L., Bland, R. C., & Newman, S. C. (1994). Obsessive–compulsive disorder. *Acta Psychiatrica Scandinavica, 89*, 24–35.

Ladouceur, R., Rhéaume, J., & Aublet, F. (1997). Excessive responsibility in obsessional concerns: A fine-grained experimental analysis. *Behaviour Research and Therapy, 35*, 423–427.

Lavy, E., van Oppen, P., Van den Hout, M. N. (1994). Selective processing of emotional information in obsessive compulsive disorder. *Behaviour Research and Therapy, 32,* 243–246.

Lazare, A., Klerman, G., & Armor, D. J. (1966). Oral, obsessive and hysterical personality patterns. *Archives of General Psychiatry, 14,* 624–630.

Lazare, A., Klerman, G., & Armor, D. J. (1970). Oral, obsessive and hysterical personality patterns: Replication of factor analysis in an independent sample. *Journal of Psychiatric Research, 7,* 275–279.

Leckman, J. F., Brice, D. E., Barr, L. C., de Vries, A. L. C., Martin, C., Cohen, D. J., Mc-Dougle, C. J., Goodman, W. K., & Rasmussen, S. A. (1995). Tic-related vs. non-tic-related obsessive compulsive disorder. *Anxiety, 1,* 208–215.

Leckman, J. F., Walker, D. E., Goodman, W. K., Pauls, D. L., & Cohen, D. J. (1994). "Just right" perceptions associated with compulsive behaviour in Tourette's syndrome. *American Journal of Psychiatry, 151,* 675–680.

Lenane, M. C., Swedo, S. E., Leonard, H., Pauls, D. L., Sceery, W., & Rapaport, J. L. (1990). Psychiatric disorders in first degree relatives of children and adolescents with obsessive–compulsive disorder. *Journal of the American Academy of Child and Adolescent Psychiatry, 29,* 407–412.

Lezak, M. D. (1983). *Neuropsychological assessment* (2nd ed.). New York: Oxford University Press.

Lopatka, C., & Rachman, S. (1995). Perceived responsibility and compulsive checking: An experimental analysis. *Behaviour Research and Therapy, 33,* 673–684.

Lopez-Ibor, J. J. (1990). Impulse control in obsessive–compulsive disorder: A biopsychopathological approach. *Prognostic Neuropsychopharmacologic Biological Psychiatry, 14,* 709–718.

Loranger, A. W. (1992). Are current self-report and interview measures adequate for epidemiological studies of personality disorders? *Journal of Personality Disorders, 6,* 313–325.

Loranger, A. W., Lenzenweger, M. F., Gartner, A. F., Lehmann, S. V., Herzig, J., Zammit, G. K., Gartner, J. D., Abrams, R. C., & Young, R. C. (1991). Trait–state artifacts and the diagnosis of personality disorders. *Archives of General Psychiatry, 48,* 720–728.

MacLeod, C. (1991). Clinical anxiety and the selective encoding of threatening information. *International Review of Psychiatry, 3,* 279–292.

Maki, W. S., O'Neill, H. K., & O'Neill, G. W. (1994). Do non-clinical checkers exhibit deficits in cognitive control?: Tests of an inhibitory control hypothesis. *Behaviour Research and Therapy, 32,* 183–192.

Mallinger, A. E. (1984). The obsessive's myth of control. *Journal of the American Academy of Psychoanalysis, 12,* 147–165.

Marks, I. M. (1987). *Fears, phobias, and rituals: Panic, anxiety, and their disorders.* Oxford, UK: Oxford University Press.

Mathews, A., & MacLeod, C. (1994). Cognitive approaches to emotion and emotional disorders. *Annual Review of Psychology, 45,* 25–50.

Mavissakalian, M. R., Hamann, M. S., Haidar, S. A., & deGroot, C. M. (1993). DSM-III personality disorders in generalized anxiety, panic/agoraphobia, and obsessive–compulsive disorders. *Comprehensive Psychiatry, 34,* 243–248.

Mavissakalian, M. R., Hamann, M. S., & Jones, B. (1990a). Correlates of DSM-III personality disorder in obsessive–compulsive disorder. *Comprehensive Psychiatry, 31,* 481–489.

Mavissakalian, M. R., Hamann, M. S., & Jones, B. (1990b). A comparison of DSM-III personality disorders in panic/agoraphobia and obsessive–compulsive disorder. *Comprehensive Psychiatry, 31,* 238–244.

Mavissakalian, M. R., Hamann, M. S., & Jones, B. (1990c). DSM-III personality disorders in obsessive–compulsive disorder: Changes with treatment. *Comprehensive Psychiatry, 31,* 432–437.

McFall, M. E., & Wollersheim, J. P. (1979). Obsessive–compulsive neurosis: A cognitive-behavioral formulation and approach to treatment. *Cognitive Therapy and Research, 3,* 333–348.

McKay, D., Danyko, S., Neziroglu, F., & Yaryura-Tobias, J. A. (1995). Factor structure of the Yale–Brown Obsessive–Compulsive Scale: A two dimensional measure. *Behaviour Research and Therapy, 33,* 865–869.

McKeon, J., Roa, B., & Mann, A. (1984). Life events and personality traits in obsessive compulsive neurosis. *British Journal of Psychiatry, 144,* 185–189.

McNally, R. J., Kaspi, S. P., Riemann, B. C., & Zeitlin, S. B. (1990). Selective processing of threat cues in panic disorder. *Behaviour Research and Therapy, 28,* 407–412.

McNally, R. J., & Kohlbeck, P. A. (1993). Reality monitoring in obsessive–compulsive disorder. *Behaviour Research and Therapy, 31,* 249–253.

McNally, R. J., Riemann, B. C., Luro, C. E., Lukach, B. M., & Kim, E. (1992). Cognitive processing of emotional information in panic disorder. *Behaviour Research and Therapy, 30,* 143–149.

Millon, T. (1981). *Disorders of personality: DSM-III, Axis II.* New York: Wiley Interscience.

Millon, T. (1990). *Toward a new personology: An evolutionary model.* Toronto: Wiley.

Milner, A. D., Beech, H. R., & Walker, V. J. (1971). Decision processes and obsessional behaviour. *British Journal of Social and Clinical Psychology, 10,* 88–89.

Mineka, S., & Sutton, S. K. (1992). Cognitive biases and the emotional disorders. *Psychological Science, 3,* 65–69.

Minichiello, W. E., Baer, L., & Jenike, M. A. (1987). Schizotypal personality disorder: A poor prognostic indicator for behavior therapy in the treatment of obsessive–compulsive disorder. *Journal of Anxiety Disorders, 1,* 273–276.

Mogg, K., Mathews, A., Eysenck, M., & May, J. (1991). Biased cognitive operations in anxiety: Artifact, processing priorities, or attentional search? *Behaviour Research and Therapy, 29,* 459–467.

Mowrer, O. H. (1939). Stimulus response theory of anxiety. *Psychological Review, 46,* 553–565.

Mulder, R. T., & Joyce, P. R. (1997). Temperament and the structure of personality disorder symptoms. *Psychological Medicine, 27,* 99–106.

Niler, E. R., & Beck, S. J. (1989). The relationship among guilt, dysphoria, and anxiety and obsessions in a normal population. *Behaviour Research and Therapy, 27,* 213–220.

O'Connor, K., & Robillard, S. (1995). Inference processes in obsessive–compulsive disorder: Some clinical observations. *Behaviour Research and Therapy, 33,* 887–896.

Oldham, J. M., Hollander, E., & Skodol, A. E. (Eds.). (1996). Impulsivity and compulsivity. Washington, DC: American Psychiatric Association Press.

Ormel, J. (1983). Neuroticism and well-being inventories: Measuring traits or states? *Psychological Medicine, 13,* 165–176.

Pacht, A. R. (1984). Reflections on perfection. *American Psychologist, 39,* 386–390.

Persons, J. B., & Foa, E. B. (1984). Processing of fearful and neutral information by obsessive–compulsives. *Behavior Research and Therapy, 22,* 259–265.

Pfohl, B., Black, D., Noyes, R., Kelley, M., & Blum, N. (1990). A test of the tridimensional personality theory: Association with diagnosis and platelet imipramine binding in obsessive–compulsive disorder. *Biological Psychiatry, 28,* 41–46.

Pfohl, B., Black, D. W., Noyes, R., et al. (1991). Axis I and Axis II comorbidity findings:

Implications for validity. In J. M. Oldham (Ed.), *Personality disorders: New perspectives on diagnostic validity* (pp. 147–161). Washington, DC: American Psychiatric Association Press.

Pfohl, B., & Blum, N. (1991). Obsessive–compulsive personality disorder: A review of available data and recommendations for DSM-IV. *Journal of Personality Disorders, 5,* 363–375.

Pigott, T. M., Myers, K. R., & Williams, D. A. (1996). Obsessive–compulsive disorder: A neuropsychiatric perspective. In R. M. Rapee (Ed.), *Current controversies in the anxiety disorders* (pp. 134–160). New York: Guilford Press.

Pitman, R. K. (1987). Pierre Janet on obsessive–compulsive disorder (1903). *Archives of General Psychiatry, 44,* 226–232.

Pitman, R. K., Green, R. C., Jenike, M. A., & Mesulam, M. M. (1987). Clinical comparison of Tourette's disorder and obsessive–compulsive disorder. *American Journal of Psychiatry, 144,* 1166–1171.

Pitman, R. K., & Jenike, M. A. (1989). Normal and disordered compulsivity: Evidence against a continuum. *Journal of Clinical Psychiatry, 50,* 450–452.

Pollack, J. M. (1979). Obsessive–compulsive personality: A review. *Psychological Bulletin, 86,* 225–241.

Pollack, J. M. (1987). Relationship of obsessive–compulsive personality to obsessive–compulsive disorder: A review of the literature. *Journal of Psychology, 121,* 137–148.

Rachman, S. (1976). Obsessive compulsive checking. *Behaviour Research and Therapy, 14,* 269–277.

Rachman, S. (1993). Obsessions, responsibility and guilt. *Behaviour Research and Therapy, 31,* 149–153.

Rachman, S. J., & Hodgson, R. J. (1980). *Obsessions and compulsions.* Englewood Cliffs, NJ: Prentice-Hall.

Rado, S. (1974). Obsessive behavior: A so-called obsessive–compulsive neurosis. In S. Arieti (Ed.), *American handbook of psychiatry* (Vol. III, 2nd ed., pp. 195–208). New York: Basic Books.

Rasmussen, S. A. (1994). Obsessive compulsive spectrum disorders. *Journal of Clinical Psychiatry, 55,* 89–91.

Rasmussen, S. A., & Eisen, J. L. (1989). Clinical features and phenomenology of obsessive–compulsive disorder. *Psychiatric Annals, 19,* 67–72.

Rasmussen, S. A., & Eisen, J. L. (1990). Epidemiology and clinical features of obsessive–compulsive disorder. In M. A. Jenike, L. Baer, & W. E. Minichiello (Eds.), *Obsessive compulsive disorders: Theory and management* (2nd ed., pp. 10–27). London: Year Book Medical Publishers.

Rasmussen, S. A., & Eisen, J. L. (1991). Phenomenology of obsessive–compulsive disorder: Clinical subtypes, heterogeneity, and coexistence. In J. Zohar, T. Insel, & S. A. Rasmussen (Eds.), *The psychobiology of obsessive–compulsive disorder* (pp. 13–43). New York: Springer.

Rasmussen, S. A., & Eisen, J. L. (1992). The epidemiology and clinical features of obsessive compulsive disorder. *Psychiatric Clinics of North America, 15,* 743–758.

Rasmussen, S. A., & Eisen, J. L. (1994). Clinical features and phenomenology of obsessive–compulsive disorder. *Psychiatric Annals, 19,* 67–73.

Rasmussen, S. A., & Tsuang, M. T. (1986). DSM-III obsessive compulsive disorder: Clinical characteristics and family history. *American Journal of Psychiatry, 143,* 317–322.

Rasmussen, S. A., & Tsuang, M. T. (1987). Obsessive–compulsive disorder and borderline personality disorder: Drs. Rasmussen and Tsuang reply. *American Journal of Psychiatry, 144,* 121.

Reed, G. F. (1969a). "Under-inclusion"—a characteristic of obsessional personality disorder: I. *British Journal of Psychiatry, 115,* 781–785.

Reed, G. F. (1969b). "Under-inclusion"—a characteristic of obsessional personality disorder: II. *British Journal of Psychiatry, 115,* 787–709.

Reed, G. F. (1985). *Obsessional experience and compulsive behaviour: A cognitive-structural approach.* Toronto: Academic Press.

Reed, G. F. (1991). The cognitive characteristics of obsessional disorder. In P. A. Magaro (Ed.), *Cognitive bases of mental disorders* (pp. 77–99). London: Sage.

Reynolds, M., & Salkovskis, P. M. (1991). The relationship among guilt, dysphoria, anxiety and obsessions in a normal population—an attempted replication. *Behaviour Research and Therapy, 29,* 259–265.

Rhéaume, J., Freeston, M. H., Dugas, M. J., LeTarte, H., & Ladouceur, R. (1995). Perfectionism, responsibility, and obsessive–compulsive symptoms. *Behaviour Research and Therapy, 33,* 785–794.

Ribot, T. (1904). *Les maladies de la volonté.* Paris: Alcan.

Ricciardi, J. N., Baer, L., Jenike, M. A., Fischer, S. C., Sholtz, D., & Buttolph, M. (1992). Changes in axis II diagnoses following treatment of obsessive–compulsive disorder. *American Journal of Psychiatry, 149,* 829–831.

Richter, M. A., Summerfeldt, L. J., Joffe, R. T., & Swinson, R. P. (1996). The Tridimensional Personality Questionnaire in obsessive–compulsive disorder. *Psychiatry Research, 65,* 185–188.

Ristvedt, S. L., MacKenzie, T. B., & Christenson, G. A. (1993). Cues to obsessive–compulsive symptoms: Relationships with other patient characteristics. *Behaviour Research and Therapy, 31,* 721–729.

Rosen, K. V., & Tallis, F. (1995). Investigation into the relationship between personality traits and OCD. *Behaviour Research and Therapy, 33,* 445–450.

Rubenstein, C. S., Peynircioglu, Z. F., Chambless, D. L., & Pigott, T. A. (1993). Memory in sub-clinical obsessive–compulsive checkers. *Behaviour Research and Therapy, 31,* 759–765.

Salkovskis, P. M. (1985). Obsessional–compulsive problems: A cognitive-behavioural analysis. *Behaviour Research and Therapy, 25,* 571–583.

Salkovskis, P. M. (1989). Cognitive-behavioural factors and the persistence of intrusive thoughts in obsessional problems. *Behaviour Research and Therapy, 27,* 677–682.

Salkovskis, P. M. (1996). Reply to Pigott et al. and to Enright: Understanding of obsessive–compulsive disorder is not improved by redefining it as something else. In R. M. Rapee (Ed.), *Current controversies in the anxiety disorders* (pp. 191–200). New York: Guilford Press.

Salzman, L. (1968). *The obsessive personality: Origins, dynamics and therapy.* New York: Aronson.

Sanderson, W. C., Wetzler, S., Beck, A. T., & Betz, F. (1994). Prevalence of personality disorders among patients with anxiety disorders. *Psychiatry Research, 51,* 167–174.

Scarrabelotti, M. B., Duck, J. M., & Dickerson, M. M. (1995). Individual differences in obsessive–compulsive behaviour: The role of Eysenckian dimensions and appraisals of responsibility. *Personality and Individual Differences, 18,* 413–421.

Schroeder, M. L., & Livesley, W. J. (1991). An evaluation of DSM-III-R personality disorders. *Acta Psychiatrica Scandinavica, 84,* 512–519.

Sciuto, G., Diaferia, G., Battaglia, M., Perna, G., Gabriele, A., & Bellodi, L. (1991). DSM-

III-R personality disorders in panic and obsessive–compulsive disorder: A comparison study. *Comprehensive Psychiatry, 32,* 450–457.

Siever, L. J., & Davis, K. L. (1991). A psychobiological perspective on the personality disorders. *American Journal of Psychiatry, 142,* 1017–1031.

Skodol, A. E., & Oldham, J. M. (1996). Phenomenology, differential diagnosis, and comorbidity of the impulsive-compulsive spectrum of disorders. In J. M. Oldham, E. Hollander, & A. E. Skodol (Eds.), *Impulsivity and compulsivity* (pp. 1–36). Washington, DC: American Psychiatric Association Press.

Slade, P. D. (1982). Towards a functional analysis of anorexia nervosa and bulimia nervosa. *British Journal of Clinical Psychology, 21,* 167–179.

Slade, P. D., Newton, T., Butler, N. M., & Murphy, P. (1991). An experimental analysis of perfectionism and dissatisfaction. *British Journal of Clinical Psychology, 30,* 169–176.

Slater, E., & Roth, M. (Eds.). (1977). *Clinical psychiatry.* London: Ballière–Tindall.

Spielberger, C. D. (1972). Anxiety as an emotional state. In C. D. Spielberger (Ed.), *Anxiety: Current trends in theory and research* (Vol. 1, pp. 10–30). New York: Academic Press.

Spielberger, C. D., Gorsuch, R. L., & Lushene, R. E. (1970). *Manual for the State–Trait Anxiety Inventory.* Palo Alto, CA: Consulting Psychologists Press.

Srinivasagam, N. M., Kaye, W. H., Plotnicov, K. H., Greeno, C., Weltzin, T. E., & Rao, R. (1995). Persistent perfectionism, symmetry, and exactness after long-term recovery from anorexia nervosa. *American Journal of Psychiatry, 152,* 1630–1634.

Stanley, M. A., Swann, A. C., Bowers, T. C., Davis, M. L., & Taylor, D. J. (1991). A comparison of clinical features in trichotillomania and obsessive–compulsive disorder. *Behaviour Research and Therapy, 30,* 39–44.

Stanley, M. A., Turner, S. M., & Borden, J. W. (1990). Schizotypal features in obsessive–compulsive disorder. *Comprehensive Psychiatry, 31,* 511–518.

Stein, D. J., & Hollander, E. (1993a). Impulsive aggression and obsessive–compulsive disorder. *Psychiatric Annals, 23,* 389–395.

Stein, D. J., & Hollander, E. (1993b). The spectrum of obsessive–compulsive-related disorders. In E. Hollander (Ed.), *Obsessive–compulsive-related disorders* (pp. 241–271). Washington, DC: American Psychiatric Association Press.

Stein, D. J., Hollander, E., Simeon, D., & Cohen, L. (1994). Impulsivity scores in patients with obsessive–compulsive disorder. *Journal of Nervous and Mental Disease, 182,* 240–241.

Stein, D. J., Hollander, E., & Skodol, A. E. (1993). Anxiety disorders and personality disorders: A review. *Journal of Personality Disorders, 7,* 87–104.

Steketee, G. (1990). Personality traits and disorders in obsessive–compulsives. *Journal of Anxiety Disorders, 4,* 351–364.

Steketee, G. (1994). Behavioral assessment and treatment planning with obsessive compulsive disorder: A review emphasizing clinical application. *Behavior Therapy, 25,* 613–633.

Steketee, G., & Frost, R. O. (1993, September). *Measurement of risk-taking in obsessive–compulsive disorder.* Paper presented at the meeting of the Association of Advancement of Behavior Therapy, Atlanta, GA.

Steketee, G., Quay, S., & White, K. (1991). Religion and guilt in obsessive–compulsive patients. *Journal of Anxiety Disorders, 5,* 359–367.

Straus, E. W. (1948). On obsession: A clinical and methodological study. *Nervous and Mental Disease Monograph, 73.*

Swedo, S. E. (1993). Trichotillomania. In E. Hollander (Ed.), *Obsessive–compulsive related disorders* (pp. 93–111). Washington, DC: American Psychiatric Association Press.

Swedo, S. E., & Leonard, H. L. (1992). Trichotillomania: An obsessive compulsive spectrum disorder? *Psychiatric Clinics of North America, 15,* 777–790.

Swedo, S. E., Rapoport, J. L., Leonard, H., et al. (1989). Obsessive–compulsive disorder in children and adolescents: Clinical phenomenology of 70 consecutive cases. *Archives of General Psychiatry, 138,* 231–233.

Takeuchi, T., Nakagawa, A., Harai, H., Nakatani, E., Fujikawa, S., Yoshizato, C., & Yamagami, T. (1997). Primary obsessional slowness: Long-term findings. *Behaviour Research and Therapy, 35,* 445–450.

Tallis, F. (1994). Obsessions, responsibility, and guilt: Two case reports suggesting a common and specific aetiology. *Behaviour Research and Therapy, 32,* 143–145.

Tallis, F. (1995). *Obsessive compulsive disorder: A cognitive and neuropsychological perspective.* Toronto: Wiley.

Tallis, F. (1996). Compulsive washing in the absence of phobic and illness anxiety. *Behaviour Research and Therapy, 34,* 361–362.

Tallis, F., Rosen, K., & Shafran, R. (1996). Investigation into the relationship between personality traits and OCD: A replication employing a clinical population. *Behaviour Research and Therapy, 34,* 649–653.

Tata, P. R., Leibowitz, J. A., Prunty, M. J., Cameron, M., & Pickering, A. D. (1996). Attentional bias in obsessional compulsive disorder. *Behaviour Research and Therapy, 34,* 53–60.

Tellegen, A. (1985). Structures of mood and personality and their relevance to assessing anxiety with an emphasis on self-report. In A. H. Tuma & J. D. Maser (Eds.), *Anxiety and the anxiety disorders* (pp. 681–706). Hillsdale, NJ: Erlbaum.

Thomsen, P. H., & Mikkelsen, H. U. (1993). Development of personality disorders in children and adolescents with obsessive–compulsive disorder. *Acta Psychiatrica Scandinavica, 87,* 456–462.

Torgersen, S. (1980). Hereditary–environmental differentiation of general neurotic, obsessive, and impulsive hysterical personality traits. *Acta Genetica Medica, 29,* 193–207.

Torres, A. R., & Del Porto, J. A. (1995). Comorbidity of obsessive–compulsive disorder and personality disorders. *Psychopathology, 28,* 322–329.

Turner, S. M., McCann, M., Beidel, D. C., & Mezzich, J. E. (1986). DSM-III classification of the anxiety disorders: A psychometric study. *Journal of Abnormal Psychology, 95,* 168–172.

Veale, D. (1993). Classification and treatment of obsessional slowness. *British Journal of Psychiatry, 162,* 198–203.

Volans, P. J. (1976). Styles of decision-making and probability appraisal in selected obsessional and phobic patients. *British Journal of Social and Clinical Psychology, 15,* 36–39.

Walker, V. J., & Beech, H. R. (1969). Mood state and the ritualistic behavior of obsessional patients. *British Journal of Psychiatry, 115,* 1261–1263.

Warren, R., & Zgourides, G. D. (1991). *Anxiety disorders: A rational–emotive perspective.* Elmsford, NY: Pergamon.

Watson, D., & Clark, L. A. (1984). Negative affectivity: The disposition to experience aversive emotional states. *Psychological Bulletin, 96,* 465–490.

Watson, D., & Clark, L. A. (1993). Behavioural disinhibition versus constraint: A dispositional perspective. In D. M. Wegner & J. W. Pennebaker (Eds.), *Handbook of mental control* (pp. 506–527). Englewood Cliffs, NJ: Prentice-Hall.

Watson, D., Clark, L. A., & Harkness, A. R. (1994). Structures of personality and their relevance to psychopathology. *Journal of Abnormal Psychology, 103,* 18–34.

Widiger, T. A. (1992). Categorical versus dimensional classification: Implications from and for research. *Journal of Personality Disorders, 6,* 287–300.

World Health Organization. (1978). *Mental disorders: Glossary and guide to their classification in accordance with the ninth revision of the international classification of diseases.* Geneva: Author.

World Health Organization. (1992). *The ICD-10 classification of mental and behavioral disorders: Clinical descriptions and diagnostic guidelines.* Geneva: Author.

Zazlow, R. W. (1950). A new approach to the problem of conceptual thinking in schizophrenia. *Journal of Consulting Psychology, 14,* 335–339.

Zimmerman, M. (1994). Diagnosing personality disorders: A review of issues and research methods. *Archives of General Psychiatry, 51,* 225–245.

Zimmerman, M., & Coryell, W. H. (1990). DSM-III personality disorder dimensions. *Journal of Nervous and Mental Disease, 178,* 686–692.

Zinbarg, R. E., & Barlow, D. H. (1996). Structure of anxiety and the anxiety disorders: A hierarchical model. *Journal of Abnormal Psychology, 105,* 181–193.

Chapter 5

FAMILIES OF INDIVIDUALS WITH OBSESSIVE–COMPULSIVE DISORDER

Gail Steketee
Nina A. Pruyn

The present chapter examines several familial aspects of obsessive–compulsive disorder (OCD) and is focused mainly, but not exclusively, on adults and their family members. We begin with comments about the characteristics of patients with OCD pertinent to family aspects and follow this with anecdotal reports and empirical findings regarding the effect of obsessive–compulsive symptoms on family life, including the marital relationships of people with OCD. Whether OCD is partly derived from family factors is a complex question we only superficially address in this chapter. The remainder of the chapter concerns family factors identified as predictors of treatment outcome, clinical assessment of family matters prior to and during therapy, and family involvement in treatment. This latter topic covers a range of treatments, including family support groups, spouse and family-assisted behavior therapy, and multifamily group treatment of OCD. We close with comments about the clinical advantages of including family members in the assessment and intervention process.

FAMILY CHARACTERISTICS OF OCD

It is interesting to observe that the majority of epidemiological and psychopathology studies indicate that a surprisingly high percentage of adults with OCD do not marry. Some studies have reported that 60–70% of patients were single (e.g., Coryell, 1981; Hafner, 1988; Steketee, 1993). However, other studies have found much lower figures. For example, Steketee, Grayson, and Foa (1985) noted that 37% of their sample of 75 adult patients had never married, and 25% continued to live with their parents. These figures nonetheless are higher than national norms that show that 73.2% of men and 80.6% of women marry (U.S. Bureau of Census, 1996). Even among studies with higher marriage rates, it appears that men may be especially prone to remaining single, with several studies reporting that approximately 65% of men in their samples were unmarried compared to 25–40% of women (e.g., Ingram, 1961; Khanna, Rajendra, & Channabasavanna, 1986; Lo, 1967). We suspect that this is related to the well-demonstrated earlier onset age of OCD in males, who typically experience symptoms in early adolescence compared to females, whose onset usually occurs during late teens or early 20s (cf., Eisen & Steketee, 1997).

EFFECT OF OCD ON FAMILIES

Regardless of whether patients with OCD live with partners or with parents or other relatives, it is clear that OCD can have an adverse effect on the quality of family life and family interaction. Many families become dysfunctional as a result of a family member's OCD symptoms and the family's involvement in those symptoms. Some family members become involved in the sufferer's avoidance behaviors and compulsions in an effort to relieve the fear and anxiety that the sufferer is feeling. Most reports about the effect of OCD symptoms on family situation have been anecdotal. For example, Van Noppen and colleagues illustrated the devastating impact that OCD can have on family functioning (Van Noppen, Steketee, & Pato, 1997b). The sister of a patient enrolled in the clinic described OCD symptoms in her 23-year-old sister who lived in her parent's house and "barricaded herself in the living room," refusing to allow entry to anyone, including family members, because of contamination fears. The sister noted that the upstairs and living room were filled with empty cans that created a "vile" odor, apparently the result of urinating and defecating into tin cans to avoid using the much-feared toilet. The sister feared that her efforts to keep the peace between her mother and her very controlling sister would eventually erupt into violence and sought clinical advice to prevent this. No one had entered the sister's bedroom in the past 4 years.

An adolescent patient, whose OCD symptoms consisted of ordering and other rituals, became convinced that she must keep her neat stacks of magazines on top of her parents' bed. She erupted in a tantrum whenever her parents made attempts to remove the piles. To keep the peace, they abandoned their bedroom to sleep in the living room on the couch.

In another circumstance described to us by the wife of a man with extreme hoarding rituals, the wife had raised her children in a single room of a large home, which her husband had filled completely with papers, wood, and a variety of objects from the trash that he considered potentially useful. He became violent whenever she had attempted to remove items or insist that he do so. Over time, he filled their yard with large appliances and building items that others had thrown out, and when this spilled over into neighbors' yards and onto city-owned property, the city filed suit for removal of these items. This resulted in city re-

moval of appliances and other objects that were outside his yard but had no effect on his hoarding within his own property. Situations such as these leave clinicians wondering why adult family members elect to remain in a home where they
have no control over large areas of living space, and indeed, many family members choose to leave under these circumstances. Although these cases may represent extreme circumstances, OCD rarely leaves the family system unaffected and
often seems to pull members inexorably into the patient's pathology.

To date, only two studies have closely examined the familial effects of OCD,
both focusing on family accommodation. Calvocoressi et al. (1995) surveyed family accommodation to OCD symptoms by interviewing 34 family members of
patients who were diagnosed with OCD. She reported that nearly one-third of
family members reported frequently (three or more times per week) reassuring
the patient. A third participated in behaviors related to the patient's compulsions,
and the same number reported taking over activities that were the patient's responsibility. Family and leisure-time routines and activities were modified at least
moderately in order to accommodate the patient for 35–40% of families. These
modifications in family plans appeared to be at least partly efforts to manage the
patient's distress, as evident from the moderate to severe anxiety and anger reactions shown by 40% of patients. Clearly, these accommodation efforts also led
family members to experience distress, with 35% showing moderate distress and
23% severe or extreme distress.

In a second study, Shafran, Ralph, and Tallis (1995) used a questionnaire to
record the reactions of 98 family members (67% spouses or partners; 17%
parents; 16% child, sibling or other) of volunteers who scored high on obsessive–compulsive symptoms (not necessarily diagnosed OCD). Of these relatives,
60% were involved in conducting or observing rituals or avoiding feared stimulus. These rituals included checking doors and outlets, and giving reassurance.
Interestingly, 40% sometimes felt responsible for their relative's difficulties. Only
10% of respondents reported experiencing no interference in their lives as a result of living with someone with OCD, and 20% reported severe interference.
More than half of family members wanted help, including information, counseling, and discussion, with other relatives of individuals with OCD. Responses
from family members in these two studies clearly indicated that living with OCD
can often lead relatives to try to help alleviate some of the patient's fear and anxiety, but also results in feelings of frustration, anger, and guilt.

MARITAL RELATIONSHIP AND OCD

Emmelkamp, de Haan, and Hoogduin (1990) found that nearly half of their
sample of 50 married OCD sufferers reported experiencing marital distress, with
patients and partners scoring very similarly on standardized measures of marital
adjustment and interactional problem solving. As Table 5.1 indicates, a very similar figure (47%) was reported by Riggs, Hiss, and Foa (1992) using a different
measure of marital satisfaction in 54 married individuals with OCD, and these

TABLE 5.1. **Marital Relationship in OCD**

Study	% unmarried	Marital quality
Ingram (1961)	68% (M), 40% (F)	
Bellodi, Sciuto, Diaferia, Ronchi, & Smeraldi (1992)	89% (M), 48% (F), 68% (all)	
Khanna, Rajendra, & Channabasavanna (1986)	61% (M), 25% (F)	
Kringlen (1965)	39% (M), 38% (F)	46% unhappy
Lo (1967)	61% (M), 42% (F)	
Welner, Reich, Robins, Fishman, & Van Doren (1976)	39% (young sample)	35% unhappy
Coryell (1981)	72%	
Hafner (1988)	67%	
Balslev-Olesen & Geert-Jorgensen (1989)		Generally happy
Freund & Steketee (1989)		Mean LWMAT scores in the maladjusted range
Emmelkamp, de Haan, & Hoogduin (1990)		50% distressed (MMQ)
Riggs, Hiss, & Foa (1992)		47% distressed (LWMAT)
Chambless & Steketee (1997)		Mean DAS scores in normal range; 32% scored in distressed range

Note. LWMAT, Locke–Wallace Marital Adjustment Test; MMQ, Maudsley Marital Questionnaire; DAS, Dyadic Adjustment Scale.

figures accord with the 46% rate of unhappy marriages reported by Kringlen (1965). Interestingly, this rate is similar to that reported for major depression (Beach, O'Leary, & Sandeen, 1991) but considerably higher than the 20% maritally distressed rate reported for agoraphobics (e.g., Arrindell, Emmelkamp, & Sanderman, 1986). However, other studies have reported that marital satisfaction in OCD patients is not significantly different than that of the general population (e.g., Balslev-Olesen & Geert-Jorgensen, 1989). According to Khanna et al. (1986), married patients sought treatment later than unmarried ones. Perhaps marriage provided needed emotional support that enabled some patients to delay therapy, or clients who were able to marry may have had less severe symptoms and greater functioning capacity.

Whether OCD symptoms influence marital satisfaction or vice versa has received little study. Riggs et al. (1992) demonstrated a link between marital discord, depression, and intensity of obsessive–compulsive symptoms. Prior to treatment, the level of marital distress was not associated with the severity of obsessions and compulsions or depression, although there was a modest connection to avoidance: More distress was related to more avoidance. Hand (1988) has suggested that in some cases, a spouse or family member might develop their own obsessive–compulsive symptoms in response to a patient's symptoms, but this assertion has only anecdotal support.

FAMILY FUNCTIONING AND OCD SYMPTOMS

Livingston-Van Noppen, Rasmussen, Eisen, and McCartney (1990) hypothesized that family responses to obsessive–compulsive symptoms fall on a continuum of behavioral interaction patterns. This spectrum can be visualized as having two polar opposites. On one end are families who give in to and often assist in compulsions and avoidance, as demonstrated by Calvocoressi et al. (1995) and Shafran et al.'s (1995) findings reported earlier. On the other end are families who completely oppose OCD behaviors. According to Livingston-Van Noppen and colleagues (1990), enmeshed families lie on the accommodating end of the spectrum, showing a lack of boundaries, poor limit setting, and avoidance of conflict in an effort to keep peace and reduce the patient's anxiety. Antagonistic families are rigid, demanding, and intolerant of symptoms; they show high levels of criticism, leading to patients' feeling little control and experiencing an increase in symptoms. Between these extremes, split families are often inconsistent and divided in their response to symptomology, with one family member antagonistic, whereas another is understanding and indulgent. Most families fall in the middle of the continuum and waver back and forth as anger and frustration grow. Regardless of the family response pattern, both patient and family often feel confused and anxious.

Anecdotal reports in the literature and contact with clinic patients suggest that OCD rarely leaves the family system unaffected. Marital discord, divorce and separation, alcohol abuse, and poor school performance are commonly reported results of the stress that OCD puts on the patient and family members. In addition, guilt, blame, and social stigma affect patients and relatives alike. Forty percent of family members blamed themselves for their child's or spouse's illness, according to Shafran et al. (1995), and Tynes, Salins, Skiba, and Winstead (1992) observed that relatives felt moderately guilty on average about their role in the patient's problems. Parents, in particular, may fear that early childhood traumas or their own child-rearing practices are causative. Advice from friends and relatives may further reinforce the family's sense of guilt and shame as they are told that the patient is "just going through a phase" or are given suggestions that more discipline or more attention is the solution to the patient's problem. Family members are often uncertain whether prolonged rituals and constant need for reassurance are part of the illness or willful rebellion (especially for adolescents) and demands for attention and control. OCD patients may try to hide their rituals and not divulge their thoughts out of shame. Preoccupied with the needs of the patient, and feeling blamed and burdened, family members may pull away from their usual social contacts and become increasingly isolated themselves.

Coping with a family member with OCD appears to be quite different than coping with a family member's physical illness. As Cooper (1993) noted, "Grief responses in OCD families are unique because their losses are partial and incomplete. The family member survives, but with marginal abilities and ongoing deterioration" (p. 306). Coping with such situations on a daily basis leads to frustration and anxiety for all involved. Tynes et al. (1990) stressed the importance of the attitudes of those around the OCD patient as contributory to the severity of the illness. Many people do not understand patients' inability to control their symptoms and become angry about the intrusion of obsessions and compulsions into their lives. Severely negative or rejecting reactions would exacerbate anxiety and depression, as well as obsessions and compulsions.

Consistent with the foregoing comments, some research evidence demonstrates that families with an OCD member have difficulty functioning effectively. Livingston-Van Noppen et al. (1990) assessed each family member of 50 patients with OCD using the Family Assessment Device (FAD; Miller, Epstein, Bishop, & Keitner, 1985). The FAD measures family problem solving, communication, roles, affective responsiveness, affective involvement, behavior control, and global functioning. In this sample, 61% of patients were living with a spouse or partner and 39% with parents. The results showed that 52% of the OCD families scored in the unhealthy range of functioning on at least one dimension of the FAD. The worst scores were on affective responsiveness and roles, with problem solving and behavior control also representing problematic areas of functioning. Somewhat surprisingly, the best scores were on communication. Compared with control families, families of OCD patients had a higher percentage of unhealthy scores on all dimensions of family function except communication. Patients and family members generally agreed in their assessment of the family, lending credence to the findings. This study suggests that OCD often occurs in families with a significant degree of unhealthy functioning. It is unclear, however, whether OCD symptoms adversely affect family functioning, or whether poor family interactions exacerbate anxiety symptoms.

FAMILY ROLE IN OCD SYMPTOMS; MODELS OF OCD DEVELOPMENT

There is little support for the role of specific precipitating factors causing the development of OCD, though over half of cases report a distinct traumatic event at onset of symptoms (see Black, 1974). Almost all patients can point to an increase in symptoms in response to life stresses. In many cases, an adult or child believes that he or she must behave in a certain way to protect him- or herself from causes of anxiety and obsessions. Many of these behaviors are thought to be learned from the person's environment, and family models can be applied to the understanding of causality. In some cases, parental, school, or religious expectations are considered to be the root of the obsessive–compulsive behaviors.

Research indicates that, to some extent, OCD is a genetically transmitted disorder. Relatively recent studies using current diagnostic nomenclature and assessment show that the frequency of diagnosis of OCD found in parents is approximately 20–25% (e.g., Pauls, Raymond, & Robertson, 1991; Riddle et al., 1990; Swedo et al., 1989), although some studies put this figure considerably lower (see Table 5.2). Findings from an Italian study indicated that the frequency of OCD in parents was 3.3 % (Bellodi, Sciuto, Diaferia, Ronchi, & Smeraldi, 1992), with a substantially higher risk ratio for major depression among parents, especially parents of adult children who had OCD plus major depression (15%). More commonly, obsessive–compulsive symptoms (Riddle et al., 1990) and obsessional personality traits occur in parents of children with OCD. Honjo et al. (1989) found that 42% of mothers were obsessional, and Steketee et al. (1985) reported that 50% of patients with checking rituals and 18% of those with washing rituals identified their mothers as meticulous. Perfectionism is another common trait found among parents of those with OCD, reported in 13% to 53% of patients (Balslev-Olesen & Geert-Jorgensen, 1959; Honjo et al., 1989; Lo, 1967).

Overprotection from parents, especially mothers, has also been thought a precursor to development of OCD in children, although findings suggest that this trait is not especially common, occurring in 13% of parents (Honjo et al.,

TABLE 5.2. Frequency of Parental Symptoms and Traits for OCD Patients

Study	% with OCD	% with personality traits
Lewis (1936)		37% obsessional
Balslev-Olesen & Geert-Jorgensen (1959)		45% perfectionistic
Kringlen (1965)	8% fathers, 12% mothers	
Lo (1967)		9% obsessional, 26% perfectionistic, 13% overprotective
Coryell (1981)	0	
Insel, Hoover, & Murphy (1983)	0	30% obsessional (LOI)
Hafner (1988)		High mean scores on overprotection (PBI)
Honjo et al. (1989)	0	42% obsessional (mothers), 53% perfectionistic (fathers), 13% overprotective (mothers)
Swedo et al. (1989)	25%	
Riddle et al. (1990)	19% (52% obsessive–compulsive symptoms)	
Hibbs et al. (1991)	8% mothers, 21% fathers	
Pauls, Raymond, & Robertson (1991)	22%	

Note. LOI, Leyton Obsessional Inventory; PBI, Parental Bonding Inventory.

1989; Lo, 1967). A recent report indicated that most adult OCD patients rated their parents as using affectionless control (overprotective and less caring) in their upbringing (Chambless, Gillis, Tran, & Steketee, 1996). However, parents had a different view, rating themselves as providing optimal care and protection. Of special interest was the finding that excessive protection and inadequate caring were associated with poor social adjustment and more anxious personality traits in patients.

Another area of interest in familial characteristics associated with OCD is the concept of expressed emotion (EE) derived from studies of schizophrenic and depressed patients. EE is comprised mainly of critical comments, hostile attitudes, and emotional over involvement expressed by relatives during a standard interview. EE may be particularly applicable to our understanding of and treatment approach with OCD patients and their families. Hibbs and colleagues (1991) reported that 46% of fathers and 76% of mothers of 49 children with OCD symptoms exhibited high levels of EE, rates that were two to three times higher for parents of OCD children than for parents of nonpsychiatric controls. Parents with high EE ratings had more psychiatric diagnoses, as well as more family conflict and marital discord (Hibbs, Hamburger, Kruesi, & Lenane, 1993; Hibbs et al., 1991).

Hand (1988) has suggested that onset and aggravation of obsessive–compulsive symptoms may sometimes be caused by family conflict or changing family roles. He reported two cases in which couples experiencing marital difficulties and lack of communication observed the onset of obsessive–compulsive symptoms in their son. Hand proposed that the son displayed these symptoms to remain close to his mother in order to relieve her depression resulting from her failed marriage. In so doing, the child took the role of "parent" in the family interactions, bringing both parents to be treated in therapy, where they were able to examine their relationship and its link to the child's obsessive–compulsive symptoms. This family systems model of onset of OCD, however, is not supported by Hibbs et al.'s (1993) finding that parents of OCD children did not have poorer marriages than parents of normal children.

MARITAL AND FAMILY FACTORS PREDICTING TREATMENT OUTCOME

Some clinicians consider family members' reactions to OCD behavior during and after treatment to be critical to recovery, although relatively few investigators have studied this issue. Steketee and Foa (1985) noted that some relatives are impatient, expecting treatment to lead to swift and total symptom remission, whereas others continue to "protect" the patient from situations that previously induced high anxiety, reinforcing avoidance behaviors. Years of accommodating the patient's obsessions and compulsions, creating behavior patterns that are difficult to break, may lead to relapse. Furthermore, continuing to live in negative family environments in which communication is poor and family members' attitudes are critical or even hostile is likely to increase stress and exacerbate OCD and depressive symptoms. To date, although researchers have not yet examined the effects on treatment outcome of continued accommodation to patient obsessive–compulsive symptoms, several studies do shed light on the effects of marital discord and the climate of the familial environment on treatment gains and maintenance.

Reporting on a series of cases, Hafner (1982) noted that 5 patients, all women, had relapsed after returning home to conflictual marriages. Hoover and Insel (1984) also reported that a series of 10 patients who were living with parents had relapsed slightly upon returning home after behavioral therapy, and that separation from their parents contributed to further improvement. Findings from these anecdotal reports have also been supported by empirical studies of aspects of family interaction and functioning as predictors of immediate and long-term treatment benefits.

Studies of behaviorally treated adults with OCD have yielded conflicting findings regarding family variables that are associated with outcome. Some researchers have proposed that family support is necessary for clients to benefit from behavioral therapy (Hafner, 1992; Marks, 1973). However, both Riggs et al. (1992) and Emmelkamp et al. (1990) found that the outcome of patients in distressed marriages did not differ from that of patients who reported having good marriages; both groups benefited from behavioral treatment. These research teams also noted that patients who were satisfied with their marriages before therapy remained satisfied after treatment, and improvement in OCD patients did not provoke adjustment problems in their partners (Emmelkamp et al., 1990). Interestingly, both studies also reported improved marital satisfaction after behavior therapy for OCD, although this did not persist in the Emmelkamp et al. study. According to Riggs and colleagues, demandingness and dependency were especially reduced after an intensive course of behavioral treatment, and 42% of initially dissatisfied couples experienced improvement in marital satisfaction as obsessive–compulsive symptoms declined. These two studies support earlier findings on very small samples that exposure-based treatment for OCD and phobic conditions accompanied by marital distress improved both the anxiety targets and the marital problems (Cobb, McDonald, Marks, & Stern, 1980).

Steketee (1993) directly examined self- and relative-reported family interactions in relation to outcome 9 months after behavior therapy ended. In this study, poor social and family functioning, and household interactions characterized by anger and criticism, as reported by the patient before therapy, predicted fewer gains on OCD symptoms at follow-up. Conversely, patient-perceived positive interactions in the household were associated with more improvement. A possible model for this process is given in Figure 5.1. According to this model, relatives' criticism and expressed anger would be likely to increase negative emotions such as anxiety and guilt, reducing coping capacity to fight urges to perform compulsions in response to obsessive fear. Ultimately, obsessive–compulsive symptoms would therefore increase in frequency. Relatives' beliefs that OCD patients were malingering and could "just stop" their rituals were also strongly associated with

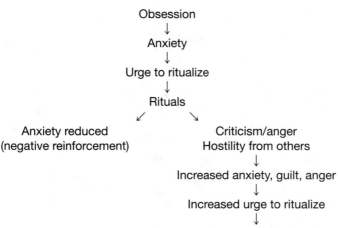

FIGURE 5.1. Chain of events leading to rituals.

poor outcome. Illustrative of such beliefs are several comments by family members of relapsing patients:

> "Why can't she just stop? She used to be so easygoing. More willpower would have helped. It makes me angry that she doesn't push herself when she gets stuck."
> "She could control her behavior if she really made up her mind."
> "I'm sure he has control over his problem. He's very stubborn. But he's a nice guy and my friends tell me I should put up with it." (Steketee, 1987, p. 162)

It is, of course, possible that at least in some cases, the relative's belief in the patient's self-control of obsessive–compulsive symptoms is an accurate assessment. Such notions, however, are contradicted by clinical observations of most patients who evidence high anxiety when confronted with obsessional situations and prevented from ritualizing.

Steketee's findings are reminiscent of reports that high expressed emotion (mainly criticism) in family members predicted poor outcome in studies of schizophrenia, depression, and anorexia (see Hooley, 1985; Hooley, Orley, & Teasdale, 1986; Szmukler, Eisler, Russell, & Dare, 1985). Studies of family functioning and EE in children with OCD have indicated that high EE was associated with parental psychopathology (Hibbs et al., 1991; Leonard et al., 1993), which in turn predicted poor long-term outcome (Leonard et al., 1993). The children in Leonard et al.'s study were treated mainly with psychopharmacology; therefore, their conclusions about parental pathology and outcome may not pertain to behavioral treatment since few received this therapy.

Emmelkamp, Kloek, and Blaauw (1992) have proposed a model for relapse in OCD in which they hypothesized that patients who lack coping skills or social support, or who experience criticism in the face of stressors after treatment, are likely to relapse. They suggested that patients' OCD problems will be further compounded if they view their symptoms as a disease over which they have little control. In a partial test of this model, Emmelkamp and colleagues found that the combination of EE ratings, avoidant coping style, and life events and daily hassles significantly predicted relapse. Consistent with other findings that social support did not influence gains from behavior therapy (Steketee, 1993), Emmelkamp and colleagues also reported that general social support did not predict outcome. Criticism and hostility were evident in three of their four clear relapses, although not in either of the two partial relapses. Unfortunately, these EE variables were assessed at follow-up but not at pretreatment, so the influence of EE factors prior to treatment is not known. Emmelkamp and colleagues (1992) recommended involving spouses or family members in treatment that emphasized empathic listening skills and communication training, and the use of group treatments for the OCD clients who had problems with social interaction. Such proposals have been pursued recently by Van Noppen and colleagues in research reported later in this chapter.

Pertinent to models of expressed emotion as predictors of therapy outcome, Chambless and Steketee (1997) have reported preliminary findings from an ongoing trial examining family variables as predictors of behavioral treatment outcome in a sample of patients with OCD and agoraphobia. Patient-rated perceived criticism predicted poorer outcome both after treatment and at 6-month follow-up. More traditional measures of EE using a standard interview showed a trend in this direction: 38% from high EE homes failed to improve at 6 months, whereas only 9% from low EE homes failed. These findings are only preliminary, but they do suggest that familial reactions and interactions with patients may have important effects on OCD symptoms and on patients' responsiveness to treatment. Of particular interest in this regard are findings pertinent to the potential benefits of including family members in the therapy itself.

ASSESSMENT OF FAMILY MATTERS

In order to determine whether the family functioning and interaction are problematic for patients and could interfere with progress during therapy, it is important to conduct an assessment of family life. Some families accommodate OCD symptoms to such an extent that their lifestyles revolve around the patient's requests. Many families become isolated, losing contact with extended family and friends outside of the home. Within the home, living situations can often become very restricted due to cleaning and washing rituals, fear of contamination, and hoarding that confines living space. To assess the nature and extent of family concerns, several strategies are appropriate in a clinical context.

The first of these is interviews with family members who are living with the patient, or who have daily contact that appears to have a significant influence on the patient's functioning. It is rare for OCD patients to resist such requests, and many are grateful for the clinician's interest in the broader lifestyle picture. Not surprisingly, family members are also relieved to be able to participate in at least the assessment process, which enables them to offer their observations, express frustration, and ask questions about the patient's symptoms and advice about their own behavior toward the patient. We recommend that a family interview cover the following topics: recall of onset of OCD symptoms and possible reasons for this, assessment of family self-blame or sense of responsibility, observations about the course of symptoms, perceived family burden, family involvement and accommodation to obsessive–compulsive symptoms, the realistic nature of family members' beliefs about the patient's capacity to overcome obsessive–compulsive symptoms, family strategies for responding to various contexts in which symptoms are displayed, degree of patient and family social isolation, and family hopes and fears about treatment. In the context of questioning family members and responding to their questions and stated concerns, the clinician will uncover areas of misinformation about OCD that can be corrected verbally or with recommended reading. If family involvement in therapy is planned, the clinician can prepare family members for their role during the intervention.

In addition to the preceding interview information, the Family Accommodation Scale (Calvocoressi et al., 1995) is an excellent way to collect specific information about particular behaviors and forms of accommodating to patients' requests and apparent needs. This 13-item scale is easy to administer and can provide a convenient method for examining this area. Van Noppen and colleagues (1997a) have used the Family Assessment Device (Miller et al., 1985) to study family functioning across a range of dimensions including problem solving, communication, roles, affective responsiveness, affective involvement, behavior control, and general functioning. Several of these areas have relevance to the obsessive–compulsive symptom context, and the availability of normative scores for nonclinical families can be useful in determining whether some areas are especially problematic for a particular family. Several other standardized self-report measures with good reliability and validity are available to assess family functioning, but since few of these have been employed with families of OCD patients, we have not included them here.

As noted earlier, a number of investigators have sought to study emotional overinvolvement and criticism (EE) of parents, spouses, and other relatives in OCD families. Unfortunately, the most common means of assessing these dimensions has been a lengthy interview (the Camberwell Family Interview) and even more lengthy coding process that requires well-trained coders. Because this is a very labor-intensive process, we cannot recommend it for clinical use. Instead, Hooley has developed a simple likert-type scale to assess perceived criticism and the degree of upset experienced in response to criticism (Hooley & Teasdale, 1989). These are assessed on a scale from 1 to 10. Generally good validity has been demonstrated by an independent group of researchers (Riso, Klein, Anderson, Ouinette, & Lizardi, 1996), making this a very simple instrument to administer. In our own treatment program, we have used this measure on a frequent basis to provide ongoing information about the patient's perceptions of the family context as treatment progresses.

Thus, a careful family interview is essential to understanding the family context in planning treatment of patients with OCD. In addition, the clinician is encouraged to obtain further information about family accommodation and might also wish to consider the use of a standardized assessment of family functioning and patient-perceived criticism. Recent findings from our studies indicate that perceived criticism from spouses and parents may have different effects. It is possible that criticism from parents may not always be negative, but may sometimes serve to motivate patients who strive to improve further.

FAMILY INVOLVEMENT IN TREATMENT

Support Groups

Support groups for OCD patients and their families provide one avenue for examining the effect of involving family members in treatment of patients with OCD. Marks, Hodgson, and Rachman (1975) considered involvement of the family in treatment to be "crucial in some cases" (p. 361). Some patients participated in a mixed patient and relative group that met every few weeks while the patient participated in individual behavioral therapy. Other researchers have also reported on the benefits of combined patient–family or family-only support groups (Black & Blum, 1992; Cooper, 1993; Tynes, Salins, Skiba, & Winstead, 1992). Such groups usually include a psychoeducational component, as well as mutual aid to group members. Education about OCD and its effects is considered an essential component designed to increase hope and alleviate fear in patients and their family members. Support from other families that share similar experiences is experienced as reassuring by members of the group. Furthermore, family group discussions typically offer shared strategies for managing difficult problems such as reassurance seeking and requests to participate in obsessive–compulsive behaviors (Marks et al., 1975). Such groups are reported to enhance families members' abilities to cope with situations that often provoke considerable anxiety and distress for all involved. Support groups constituted conjointly with the patients and their significant others have included topics such as symptoms, theories behind OCD, treatment possibilities, medications, complications, and relapse prevention (Tynes et al., 1992). Participants have reported good satisfaction with such psychoeducational/support groups, but unfortunately no outcome data are available regarding their effects on patient symptoms.

Family-Assisted Treatment

Numerous studies have shown that behavior therapy using exposure and response prevention with or without medication has a lasting effect on the reduction of obsessive–compulsive behaviors (see Chapters 11 and 12 of this volume; for reviews see Christensen, Hadzi-Pavlovic, Andrews, & Mattick, 1987; Steketee & Lam, 1993). Not surprisingly, in view of the evidence, behavior therapy has become a treatment of choice for OCD. Efforts to further improve this treatment for the 25–30% who have not benefited, as well as efforts to address evident family problems, have led researchers to examine the effects of exposure therapy that included family assistance. Several of these studies are listed in Table 5.3.

A handful of studies have employed a parent, spouse, or other family member to act as coach or supervisor during exposure homework, with explicit guidelines from the therapist. Hafner (1992) sought to prevent exacerbation of OCD symptoms that he had observed when wives returned to conflictual marriages by including spouses in the behavioral treatment. He reported that 5 such patients showed clear improvement when treatment included their spouses. Similar benefits have also been described in case studies of parental involvement in behavioral treatment of children (e.g., Dalton, 1983; Fine, 1973; March, Mulle, & Herbel, 1994) and of adolescents and adults (Hafner, Gilchrist, Bowling, & Kalucy, 1981; Hoover & Insel, 1984). For example, Hafner et al. (1981) reported a case of a 16-year-old boy who did not improve after several attempts at treatment. When the previously uncooperative parents finally consented to be involved, the family was able to express uncommunicated feelings and, after many sessions, the boy's symptoms subsided. Of course, this and other case studies do not clarify the specific roles in outcome of family communication content and style, behavioral

TABLE 5.3. Marital and Parental Involvement in Treatment

Study	Sample	Findings
Cobb, McDonald, Marks, & Stern (1980)	12 OCD and phobic adults	Improved with spouse-aided BT
Emmelkamp & DeLange (1983)	12 adults	Spouse-aided BT > BT alone at posttest; spouse-aided BT = BT alone at 6-month follow-up
Emmelkamp, de Haan, & Hoogduin (1990)	50 adults	Spouse-aided BT = BT alone at 1-month follow-up; no effect of marriage quality
Dalton (1983)	1 (age 9)	Improved following parent training in BT
Fine (1973)	2 (age 9, 11)	Improved following BT and joint family meetings
Hafner, Gilchrist, Bowling, & Kalucy (1981)	2 (age 16, 24)	BT failed; improved following family therapy
Hoover & Insel (1984)	10 adults	Improved patients relapsed partly on return home; separation from parents led to improvement
Mehta (1990)	30 adults	Family-assisted BT > BT alone; firm, nonanxious family members most helpful
Van Noppen et al. (1997a)	19 adults	Multifamily groups were effective, benefits evident in OCD and family functioning

Note. BT, behavior therapy.

treatment, learning of alternative responses to the patient's OCD symptoms, and other possible curative factors.

An uncontrolled trial of family treatment included efforts to reduce relatives' involvement in OCD symptoms. This inpatient treatment program in Great Britain emphasized self-treatment and teaching relatives to assist in the therapy program for inpatients with a variety of diagnoses, including OCD (Thornicroft, Colson, & Marks, 1991). Individual behavior therapy consisted of exposure, response prevention, self-control, and social skills training. This treatment was combined with a family component that focused on training relatives to monitor patient behavior and encourage self-exposure in a noncritical manner. Assisting relatives were supervised by the therapist on the ward. The 45 mostly OCD patients participating in this treatment program experienced a 45% decrease in symptoms at discharge. For the 22 patients available at 6-month follow-up, a 60% reduction was apparent, with concomitant improvement in functioning. Such gains can be considered good success for this severe inpatient population, who scored in the extreme range on disability from OCD symptoms.

It is clear that case reports and uncontrolled trials argue for the benefits of family involvement in behavior therapy. However, including family members has produced somewhat mixed results in larger controlled trials. Emmelkamp and colleagues conducted two studies of the benefits of spousal assistance during exposure and response prevention therapy, comparing this treatment with individual behavior therapy. In the first study of 12 patients, spousal participation in therapy and assistance with homework assignments benefited patients more than did individual treatment, but this apparent advantage did not persist at follow-up (Emmelkamp & DeLange, 1983). In a later trial on a larger sample, spouse-aided exposure made no difference either after treatment or at follow-up, despite improvement in marital satisfaction in the spouse-aided group (Emmelkamp et al., 1990). It may be important to note that in these two trials, spouses were not specifically trained in communication with patients regarding their symptoms, although in a later report, Emmelkamp and colleagues emphasized empathic communication as an important factor in outcome (Emmelkamp et al., 1992) .

Sharply contrasting findings resulted from a study conducted in India of 15 OCD patients who were assisted in exposure therapy by family members, including 6 spouses, 7 parents, and 2 adult children. This group was compared to 15 patients who received comparable but unassisted behavior therapy. Mehta (1990) found that patients who were aided by a family member during treatment benefited significantly more than patients who received no family participation and were more likely to maintain their gains than individually treated patients, who showed somewhat more relapse. The emotional support and supervision of a nonanxious, firm family member proved especially effective in treatment. The discrepancy between Emmelkamp and colleagues' findings with spousal participation and Mehta's results with family members is puzzling. The greater intensity of treatment in the Indian trial (24 sessions twice weekly vs. 8 sessions in 5 weeks in the Dutch study) may have enabled investigators to identify significant differences that were only trends in Emmelkamp et al.'s data. Another explanation may be found in the response styles of relatives from different cultures. For example, in Indian culture, levels of EE (criticism) in families of schizophrenics have been reported to be lower than EE levels in Western countries such as England (Leff et al., 1987), and thus Mehta's family members may have been less critical or expectant than Emmelkamp's spouses. Futhermore, patients' reactions to spousal involvement may be different than their reactions to other family members' participation.

Multifamily Group Treatment

Van Noppen and colleagues have begun to investigate the benefits of family group treatments that combine elements of family support groups and family-assisted behavior therapy described earlier. Treatment began with one or more individual sessions with a therapist, who would later colead the multifamily group. In these first sessions, the clinician collected information about OCD and other psychological symptoms, history of OCD and of previous mental health treatment, as well as general history about family and social relationships. Therapists then used the collected information about OCD symptoms to generate a hierarchy for use during group sessions. The multifamily behavioral therapy (MFBT) sessions included patient and family education about OCD symptoms and behavioral treatment in an effort to reduce isolation and stigma associated with the disorder. To this end, participants read a pamphlet entitled *Learning to live with OCD* (Van Noppen, Pato, & Rasmussen, 1993). Patients and family members were also asked to read selected chapters from Steketee and White's (1990) self-help book to facilitate learning about their symptoms and treatment strategies. Group exchange of information was intended to provide opportunities for cross-family modeling of coping strategies.

In most MFBT sessions, the coleaders demonstrated *in vivo* exposure (and imaginal exposure if appropriate for selected patients) and gave specific instructions for response prevention during and outside of sessions. Discussion of family reactions to and involvement in OCD symptoms set the stage for behavioral contracting among family members regarding exposure and response prevention. Patients and family members jointly participated in planning *in vivo* exposure during the session and selecting homework exposures. *In vivo* demonstrations of exposure and response prevention for individual patients and families were employed throughout the session whenever possible. Through behavioral contracting tasks during sessions, families improved communication regarding expression of wishes and limiting of family involvement in compulsive behaviors during and between sessions. Patients were assigned exposure homework and asked to report on this at each session. At the end of each session, each patient chose a behavioral homework task and rehearsed it mentally or behaviorally in the group.

Group cohesiveness was fostered by including all group members in discussion whenever possible and encouraging group suggestions for other members' dilemmas when appropriate. In-session review of homework assignments encouraged patients and family members to follow these behavioral contracts for exposure and limiting of rituals. Thus, the family group served to enhance motivation and reinforce progress throughout. At the last session, group members discussed progress and further plans, and arranged to meet for 6-month discussion sessions to review intervening experiences. At the 6-month sessions, families reviewed progress, identified areas for further contracting and exposure, and discussed strategies for improving and/or maintaining gains with other families. A detailed description of this treatment with examples is available in Van Noppen et al. (1997b).

Van Noppen, Steketee, McCorkle, and Pato (1997a) examined the effects of the preceding format for 19 patients treated with multifamily group treatment and compared it to the effects on 17 OCD patients treated with a comparable group therapy without family involvement. Patients in the MFBT group experienced significant reductions in obsessive–compulsive symptom severity and in scores on a measure of family functioning. Patients who received group therapy also benefited on obsessive–compulsive symptoms but not on family variables. More of the MFBT patients were clinically significantly improved (reliably changed and scoring in the nonclinical range on OCD symptoms) at posttest (47%) and at 1-year follow-up (58%) compared to the group treatment patients (31% at posttest and 43% at follow-up). Overall, then, the multifamily intervention was quite effective, although some patients did not show strong gains. These researchers also attempted to determine whether family variables played a role in treatment outcome. Interestingly, poorer family functioning with respect to roles and communication predicted less benefit on obsessive–compulsive symptoms, and several additional components of family functioning also predicted posttreatment disability scores; that is, poorer family functioning was associated with more disability. However, this relationship did not hold up at 1-year follow-up, in part because the sample size was small.

Results from multifamily behavioral treatment were comparable to those achieved by individual behavior therapy. From this research, then, it appears that multifamily group therapy is another option for treatment in which the participation of family members might enhance outcome for patients whose families can benefit substantially from training in communication, role functioning, and reduced involvement in obsessive–compulsive symptoms.

IMPLICATIONS FOR PRACTICE

The literature on family responses to OCD and on family involvement in treatment for this disorder has several implications for clinical practice. It is clear that assessment of family involvement in symptoms and emotional reactions to the patient (criticism, anger) is needed to determine how to advise family members in order to best assist the patient during treatment. Overinvolvement in symptoms will necessitate a therapeutic discussion about withdrawing from these situations. Excessive criticism may improve with education and family discussion about symptoms, but may also necessitate encouraging the patient to seek support elsewhere during behavioral treatment and minimizing contact with the critical relative.

Inclusion of family members in therapy may be advantageous, as several studies suggest, but we suspect that very hostile family members may impede treatment and should be included only later, after some significant reduction in obsessive–compulsive symptoms has been achieved. If family members are included, they will need training in how and when to assist, as agreed with the patient. Certainly, many family members are grateful to be able to learn more about how to manage very frustrating family situations. Recent research on the benefits of family group behavioral treatment make this an attractive and cost-effective alternative for clinical settings in which sufficient numbers of patients with OCD are available for therapy. These groups need not be restricted to relatives but can also include close friends as patient assistants. Overall, we strongly recommend inclusion of families in some aspects of the therapy, if only the assessment.

REFERENCES

Arrindell, W. W., Emmelkamp, P. M. G., & Sanderman, R. (1986). Marital quality and general life adjustment in relation to treatment outcome in agoraphobia. *Advances in Behaviour Therapy, 19,* 335–338.

Balslev-Olesen, T., & Geert-Jorgensen, E. (1989). The prognosis of obsessive–compulsive disorder. *Acta Psychiatrica Scandinavica, 34,* 232–241.

Beach, S. R. H., O'Leary, K. D., & Sandeen, E. E. (1990). *Depression in marriage: A model for etiology and treatment.* New York: Guilford Press.

Bellodi, L., Sciuto, G., Diaferia, G., Ronchi, P., & Smeraldi, E. (1992). Psychiatric disorders in the families of patients with obsessive–compulsive disorder. *Psychiatry Research, 42,* 111–120.

Black, A. (1974). The natural history of obsessional neurosis. In H. R. Beech (Ed.), *Obsessional states* (pp. 19–54). London: Methuen.

Black, D. W., & Blum, N. S. (1992). Obsessive–compulsive disorder support groups: The Iowa model. *Comprehensive Psychiatry, 33,* 65–71.

Calvocoressi, L., Lewis, B., Harris, M., Trufan, S. J., Goodman, W. K., McDougle, C. J., & Price, L. H. (1995). Family accommodation in obsessive–compulsive disorder. *American Journal of Psychiatry, 152,* 441–443.

Chambless, D. L., Gillis, M. M., Tran, G. Q., & Steketee, G. S. (1996). Parental bonding reports of clients with obsessive–compulsive disorder and agoraphobia. *Clinical Psychology and Psychotherapy, 3,* 77–85.

Chambless, L. L., & Steketee, G. (1997, November). *Expressed emotion and the outcome of treatment for agoraphobia and OCD.* Paper presented at the meeting of the Association for Advancement of Behavior Therapy, Miami, FL.

Christensen, H., Hadzi-Pavlovic, D., Andrews, G., & Mattick, R. (1987). Behavior therapy and tricyclic medication in the treatment of obsessive–compulsive disorder: A quantitative review. *Journal of Consulting and Clinical Psychology, 55,* 701–711.

Cobb, J., McDonald, R., Marks, I., & Stern, R. (1980). Marital versus exposure therapy: Psychological treatment of co-existing marital and phobic–obsessive problems. *Behavioural Analysis and Modification, 4,* 3–16.

Cooper, M. (1993, May). A group for families of obsessive–compulsive persons. *Families in Society: The Journal of Contemporary Human Services*, 301–307.

Coryell, W. (1981). Obsessive–compulsive disorder and primary unipolar depression: Comparisons of background, family history, course, and mortality. *Journal of Nervous and Mental Disease, 169*, 220–224.

Dalton, P. (1983). Family treatment of an obsessive–compulsive child: A case report. *Family Process, 22*, 99–108.

Eisen, J., & Steketee, G. (1997). Course of illness of OCD. In M. Pato & G. Steketee (Section Eds.), Obsessive–compulsive disorder across the life cycle. In L. J. Dickstein, M. B. Riba, & J. M. Oldhan (Eds.), *Annual review of psychiatry* (Vol. 16). Washington, DC: American Psychiatric Press.

Emmelkamp, P. M. G., de Haan, E., & Hoogduin, C. A. L. (1990). Marital adjustment and obsessive–compulsive disorder. *British Journal of Psychiatry, 156*, 55–60.

Emmelkamp, P. M. G., & DeLange, I. (1983). Spouse involvement in the treatment of obsessive–compulsive patients. *Behaviour Research and Therapy, 21*, 341–346.

Emmelkamp, P. M. G., Kloek, J., & Blaauw, E. (1992). Obsessive–compulsive disorders in principles and practice of relapse prevention. In P. H. Wilson (Ed.), *Principles and practice of relapse prevention* (pp. 213–234). New York: Guilford Press.

Fine, S. (1973). Family therapy: A behavioral approach to childhood obsessive compulsive neurosis. *Archives of General Psychiatry, 28*, 695–697.

Hafner, R. J. (1982). Marital interaction in persisting obsessive–compulsive disorders. *Australian and New Zealand Journal of Psychiatry, 16*, 171–178.

Hafner, R. J. (1988). Anxiety disorders. In I. R. H. Falloon (Ed.), *Handbook of behavioral family therapy* (pp. 203–230). New York: Guilford Press.

Hafner, R.J. (1992). Anxiety disorders and family therapy. *Australian and New Zealand Journal of Family Therapy, 13*, 99–104.

Hafner, R. J., Gilchrist, P., Bowling, J., & Kalucy, R. (1981). The treatment of obsessional neurosis in a family setting. *Australian and New Zealand Journal of Psychiatry, 15*, 145–151.

Hand, I. (1988). Obsessive–compulsive patients and their families. In I. R. H. Falloon (Ed.), *Handbook of behavioral therapy* (pp. 231–256). New York: Guilford Press.

Hibbs, E. D., Hamburger, S. D., Kruesi, M. J. P., & Lenane, M. (1993). Factors affecting expressed emotion in parents of ill and normal children. *American Journal of Orthopsychiatry, 63*, 103–112.

Hibbs, E. D., Hamburger, S. D., Lenane, M., Rapoport, J. L., Kruesi, M. J. P., Keysor, C. S., & Goldstein, M. J. (1991). Determinants of expressed emotion in families of disturbed and normal children. *Journal of Psychology and Psychiatry, 32*, 757–770.

Honjo, S., Hirano, C., Murase, S., Kaneko, T., Sugiyama, T., Ohtaka, K., Aoyama, T., Takel, Y., Inoko, K., & Wakabayashi, S. (1989). Obsessive–compulsive symptoms in childhood and adolescence. *Acta Psychiatrica Scandinavica, 80*, 83–91.

Hooley, J. M. (1985). Expressed emotion: A review of the critical literature. *Clinical Psychology Review, 5*, 119–139.

Hooley, J. M., Orley, J., & Teasdale, J. D. (1986). Levels of expressed emotion and relapse in depressed patients. *British Journal of Psychiatry, 148*, 642–647.

Hooley, J.M., & Teasdale, J.D. (1989). Predictors of relapse in unipolar depressives: Expressed emotion, marital relapse, and perceived criticism. *Journal of Abnormal Psychology, 98*, 223–235.

Hoover, C. F., & Insel, T. (1984). Families of origin in obsessive–compulsive disorder. *Journal of Nervous and Mental Disease, 172*, 223–228.

Ingram, I. M. (1961). Obsessional illness in mental hospital patients. *Journal of Mental Science, 107,* 382–402.

Khanna, S., Rajendra, P. N., & Channabasavanna, S. M. (1986). Sociodemographic variables in obsessive compulsive disorder in India. *International Journal of Social Psychiatry, 32,* 47–54.

Kringlen, E. (1965). Obsessional neurotics: A long-term follow-up. *British Journal of Psychiatry, 111,* 709–722.

Leff, J., Wig, N., Ghosh, A., Bedi, H., Menon, D., Kuipers, L., Korten, A., Ernberg, G., Day, R., Sartorius, N., & Jablensky, A. (1987). Influence of relatives' expressed emotion on the course of schizophrenia in Chandigarh. *British Journal of Psychiatry, 151,* 166–173.

Leonard, H. L., Swedo, S. E., Lenane, M. C., Rettew, D. C., Hamburger, S. D., Bartko, J. J., & Rapoport, J. L. (1993). A 2- to 7-year follow-up study of 54 obsessive–compulsive children and adolescents. *Archives of General Psychiatry, 50,* 429–439.

Livingston-Van Noppen, B., Rasmussen, S. A., Eisen, J., & McCartney, L. (1990). Family function and treatment in obsessive–compulsive disorder. In M. A. Jenike, L. Baer, & W. E. Minichiello (Eds.), *Obsessive–compulsive disorder: Theory and treatment* (pp. 325–340). Chicago: Year Book Medical Publishers.

Lo, W. H. (1967). A follow-up study of obsessional neurotics in Hong Kong Chinese. *British Journal of Psychiatry, 113,* 823–832.

March, J. S., Mulle, K., & Herbel, B. (1994). Behavioral psychotherapy for children and adolescents with obsessive–compulsive disorder: An open trial of a new protocol-driven treatment package. *Journal of the American Academy of Child and Adolescent Psychiatry, 33,* 333–341.

Marks, I. M. (1973). The reduction of fear: Towards a unifying theory. *Journal of the Canadian Psychiatric Association, 18,* 9–12.

Marks, I. M., Hodgson, R., & Rachman, S. (1975). Treatment of chronic obsessive–compulsive neurosis by in-vivo exposure: A two-year follow-up and issues in treatment. *British Journal of Psychiatry, 127,* 349–364.

Mehta, M. (1990). A comparative study of family-based and patient-based behavioural management in obsessive–compulsive disorder. *British Journal of Psychiatry, 157,* 133–135.

Miller, I., Epstein, N. B., Bishop, D. S., & Keitner, G. I. (1985). McMaster Family Assessment Device: Reliability and validity. *Journal of Marital and Family Therapy, 11,* 345–356.

Pauls, D. L., Raymond, C. L., & Robertson, M. (1991). The genetics of obsessive–compulsive disorder: A review. In J. Zohar, T. Insel, & S. Rasmussen (Eds.), *The psychobiology of obsessive–compulsive disorder* (pp. 89–100). New York: Springer.

Riddle, M. A., Scahill, L., King, R., Hardin, M. T., Towbin, K. E., Ort, S. I., Leckman, J. F., & Cohen, D. J. (1990). Obsessive compulsive disorder in children and adolescents: Phenomenology and family history. *Journal of the American Academy of Child and Adolescent Psychiatry, 29,* 766–772.

Riggs, D. S., Hiss, H., & Foa, E. B. (1992). Marital distress and the treatment of obsessive compulsive disorder. *Behavior Therapy, 23,* 585–597.

Riso, L. P., Klein, D. N., Anderson, R. L., Ouinette, P. C., & Lizardi, H. (1996). Convergent and discriminant validity of perceived criticism from spouses and family members. *Behavior Therapy, 27,* 129–138.

Shafran, R., Ralph, J., & Tallis, F. (1995). Obsessive–compulsive symptoms and the family. *Bulletin of the Menninger Clinic, 59,* 472–479.

Steketee, G. (1987). Predicting relapse following behavioral treatment for obsessive compulsive disorder: The impact of social support (Doctoral dissertation, Bryn Mawr College, 1987). *Dissertation Abstracts International, 48/05,* 1320.

Steketee, G. (1993). Social support and treatment outcome of obsessive compulsive disorder at 9-month follow-up. *Behavioural Psychotherapy, 21,* 81–95.

Steketee, G., & Foa, E. B. (1985). Obsessive–compulsive disorder. In D. H. Barlow (Ed.), *Clinical handbook of psychological disorders: A step-by-step treatment manual* (pp. 69–144). New York: Guilford Press.

Steketee, G., Grayson, J. B., & Foa, E. B. (1985). Obsessive–compulsive disorder: Differences between washers and checkers. *Behaviour Research and Therapy, 23,* 197–201.

Steketee, G., & Lam, J. (1993). Obsessive compulsive disorder. In T. R. Giles (Ed.), *Handbook of effective psychotherapy: A comparative outcome approach* (pp. 253–278). New York: Plenum.

Steketee, G., & White, K. (1990). When once is not enough. Oakland, CA: New Harbinger.

Swedo, S. E., Rapoport, J. L., Leonard, H., et al. (1989). Obsessive compulsive disorder in children and adolescents. *Archives of General Psychiatry, 46,* 335–345.

Szmukler, G. I., Eisler, I., Russell, G. F., & Dare, C. (1985). Anorexia nervosa, parental "expressed emotion" and dropping out of treatment. *British Journal of Psychiatry, 147,* 265–271.

Thornicroft, G., Colson, L., & Marks, I. M. (1991). An inpatient behavioural psychotherapy unit description and audit. *British Journal of Psychiatry, 158,* 362–367.

Tynes, L. L., Salins, C., Skiba, W., & Winstead, D. K. (1992). A psycho educational and support group for obsessive–compulsive disorder patients and their significant others. *Comprehensive Psychiatry, 33,* 197–201.

Tynes, L. L., Salins, C., & Winstead, D. K. (1990, October). Obsessive compulsive patients: Familial frustration and criticism. *Journal of Louisiana State Medical Society,* pp. 24–29.

U.S. Bureau of Census. (1996). *Statistical abstract of the United States: 1996* (116th ed.). Washington, DC: U.S. Government Printing Office.

Van Noppen, B., Pato, M., & Rasmussen, S. (1993). *Learning to live with OCD.* Milford, CT: Obsessive–Compulsive Foundation.

Van Noppen, B., Steketee, G., McCorkle, B. H., & Pato, M. (1997a). Group and multifamily behavioral treatment for obsessive compulsive disorder: A pilot study. *Journal of Anxiety Disorders, 11,* 431–446.

Van Noppen, B., Steketee, G., & Pato, M. (1997b). Group and multifamily behavioral treatments for OCD. In E. Hollander & Stein (Eds.), *Obsessive–compulsive disorders: Diagnosis, etiology and treatment* (pp. 331–336). New York: Marcel Dekker.

Chapter 6

BIOLOGICAL MODELS OF OBSESSIVE–COMPULSIVE DISORDER
The Serotonin Hypothesis

Raz Gross
Yehuda Sasson
Miriam Chopra
Joseph Zohar

Many psychiatric disorders are believed to be associated with serotonin (5-hydroxytryptamine, or 5-HT) subsystems. Alterations in the sensitivity of 5-HT receptors have been hypothesized to be involved in both the pathogenesis and the pharmacological treatment of these disorders. Because 5-HT has been implicated in many functions, including food intake, temperature regulation, sleep, circadian rhythms, sexual activity, memory, motor activity, pain, and neuroendocrine systems, it is not surprising that the 5-HT system plays such a significant role in disorders involving anxiety (Humphrey, Hartig, & Hoyer, 1993; Lesch, 1991; Murphy et al., 1996).

Abnormalities in the serotonin system, and particularly a hypersensitivity in the postsynaptic 5-HT receptors, have been the leading hypothesis for the underlying pathophysiology of obsessive–compulsive disorder (OCD) since the 1980s (Zohar & Insel, 1987). The serotonergic hypothesis has been supported by several different lines of research. First, evidence has emerged demonstrating that the efficacy of antiobsessional medications is a function of serotonin reuptake inhibition (Zohar & Kindler, 1992). In addition, studies of biological markers and probes have provided further evidence for the serotonin hypothesis. For example, treatment response has been shown to be related to reductions in 5-HT activity in platelet studies (Flament, Rapoport, Murphy, Lake, & Berg, 1987) and with decreased 5-hydroxyindolacetic acid (5-HIAA) levels within the cerebrospinal fluid of patients with OCD (Thoren, Asberg, Gronholm, Jornestedt, &

Traskman, 1980). Lending further support to the serotonin hypotheses is evidence from observations of the behavioral and physiological responses observed following challenges with serotonin agonists such as meta-chlorophenylpiperazine (mCPP), a compound with high affinity for 5-HT_{1A}, 5-HT_{1D}, and 5-HT_{2C} receptors (Zohar et al., 1987a). This chapter includes a review of the evidence pointing to the involvement of the serotonergic system in the pathophysiology of OCD. The types of studies relevant to this review include studies addressing the specificity of drug response, peripheral markers of the serotonergic system function, and pharmacological challenge studies with serotonergic agonists or antagonists (Pigott et al., 1993).

DRUG RESPONSE PROFILE

It is possible to differentiate OCD from other anxiety disorders on the basis of the preferential response of patients with OCD to medications possessing a serotonergic profile. Indeed, the serotonergic hypothesis of OCD was initially derived from these clinical observations. Clomipramine (CMI) and other serotonin reuptake inhibitors (SRIs) have been demonstrated to be superior not only to placebo in OCD, but also to other antidepressants, including the noradrenergic tricyclic antidepressant desipramine (Leonard et al., 1989, 1991) and other related medications such as nortriptyline and imipramine (Anath, Pecknold, Van den Steen, & Engelsman, 1981; Montgomery et al., 1993; Volavka, Neziroglu, & Yaryura-Tobias, 1985). Moreover, other nontricyclic selective serotonin reuptake inhibitors (SSRIs) such as fluvoxamine, fluoxetine, paroxetine, and sertraline, have also been reported to be effective antiobsessional drugs (Greist et al., 1995; Insel, Mueller, Alterman, Linnoila, & Murphy, 1985; Wheadon, Bushnell, & Steiner, 1993).

In order to examine involvement of the serotonergic system in the therapeutic effect of CMI, Flament et al. (1987) compared levels of platelet serotonin content in 29 adolescent patients with OCD and 31 age- and sex-matched normal controls. In this study, the levels of platelet serotonin were compared before and after CMI treatment. Before treatment with CMI, no significant differences were noted. However, posttreatment results indicated a significant relationship ($r = .77$) between clinical improvement and decreased platelet serotonin levels. In addition, the plasma levels of CMI, but not of its primary metabolite, desmethyl-CMI, have been found to correlate significantly with reductions in OCD symptoms in some studies (Insel, 1992; Stern, Marks, Wright, & Luscombe, 1980).

Considered together, these findings are consistent with the hypothesis that the antiobsessional effects of serotonergic medications are mediated by the serotonergic system. However, the issue of whether OCD patients have a psychobiological abnormality involving serotonergic functioning is an entirely different question, which is best addressed by studying peripheral markers of the serotonergic system in drug-free OCD patients or by examining behavioral and endocrine changes following serotonergic challenges.

PERIPHERAL MARKERS OF FUNCTION

Cerebrospinal Fluid Studies

A number of biochemical studies have supported the view that serotonergic pathways mediate the antiobsessional properties of the SRI medications. One approach that has been used to evaluate serotonergic activity is to investigate serotonergic abnormalities in the cerebrospinal fluid (CSF). Because levels of CSF serotonin are too low to be measured directly, studies have focused instead on measuring CSF concentrations of 5-HIAA, the primary metabolite of serotonin. Thoren and coworkers (1980) found nonsignificant increases in the levels of 5-HIAA in the lumbar CSF of 24 patients with OCD compared to 37 normal controls. Confirming this finding, Insel et al. (1985) demonstrated that the levels of 5-HIAA in the CSF were significantly elevated in 8 patients with OCD compared to 23 matched normal controls. In contrast, Lydiard, Ballenger, Ellinwood, Fossey, and Laraia (1990) failed to demonstrate significant differences between 23 patients with OCD and 17 normal controls on levels of 5-HIAA in the CSF.

Blood Studies

Studies of peripheral markers of central serotonergic function are based on the assumption that these peripheral markers reflect central serotonergic activity. In a study comparing 18 non-medicated patients with OCD to 18 sex- and age-matched normal controls, Weizman et al. (1986) found that patients had reduced levels of [3H]imipramine binding-site density, which is related to serotonin transport systems. These findings were replicated by Marazziti, Hollander, Lensi, Ravagli, and Cassano (1992), who also reported lower [3H]imipramine binding sites in 17 drug-free OCD patients compared to normal controls and patients with other anxiety disorders. Twenty-four of these patients were subsequently entered into a double-blind treatment study, receiving either CMI or fluvoxamine. Reassessment after 8 weeks of treatment showed that [3H]imipramine density had significantly increased over baseline in both treatment groups toward normal values. This suggests that the 5-HT transporter has a role in OCD and may be linked to recovery and positive response to serotonergic drugs. In another study (Bastani, Arora, & Meltzer, 1991), 20 OCD patients were compared to 53 normal controls. This study found significantly reduced affinity for serotonin uptake in OCD patients. However, in two large studies, these findings were not replicated (Kim, Dysken, Pandey, & Davis, 1991, Vitiello et al., 1991). In summary, the studies that examined peripheral markers of serotonergic function in OCD may suggest a serotonergic abnormality, although results are inconclusive.

Pharmacological Challenge Studies

In order to clarify the nature of the putative abnormality in serotonin functioning, as well as the mechanisms by which SSRI produce their therapeutic effects,

OCD patients have been acutely administered serotonin agonists and antagonists by means of a pharmacological challenge paradigm. By focusing on dynamic changes produced by the introduction of serotonergic probes, challenge studies differ from the investigation of biological markers, which examine systems in equilibrium (Barr, Goodman, Price, McDougle, & Charney, 1992; Goodman, Price, et al., 1991).

L-Tryptophan Challenge Studies

L-Tryptophan is a serotonin precursor, whose exact mechanism of action has yet to be ascertained. It has been used to examine the function of the serotonergic system in several psychiatric disorders (Sandyk, 1992). Addition of exogenous tryptophan increases endogenous serotonin synthesis (Barr, Goodman, & Price, 1993; Barr et al., 1992). However, this does not necessarily indicate that there is an increase in the activity of the serotonin system. Charney et al. (1988) has demonstrated a small but significant rise in prolactin in response to intravenous administration of tryptophan in 21 OCD patients compared to 21 normal controls. However, in a study comparing 16 patients with OCD to 16 healthy controls, Fineberg, Cowen, Kirk, and Montgomery (1994) did not find group differences in L-tryptophan induced prolactin release. However, individuals with OCD did show a greater increase in plasma growth hormone following intraveneous L-tryptophan relative to controls.

L-Tryptophan Depletion

The effects of short-term tryptophan depletion were examined in 15 patients with OCD who had responded to treatment with various SRIs, such as CMI, fluvoxamine, and fluoxetine. These patients were subjected to tryptophan depletion under double-blind, placebo-controlled conditions. Reduction of tryptophan had no significant effects on either obsessions or compulsions, but mean depression ratings were significantly increased during tryptophan depletion. This rather surprising finding suggests a different serotonergic mechanism for depression versus OCD, since tryptophan depletion is associated with transient exacerbation in depressed patients who have responded to treatment with SRIs, but not in OCD patients under the same conditions (Barr et al., 1994).

Fenfluramine

The nonspecific serotonin agonist fenfluramine has been used in challenge studies with inconclusive results. Several studies (e.g., Hollander et al., 1992; McBride et al., 1992) have failed to find differences between patients with OCD and healthy controls in response of prolactin to a fenfluramine challenge. In contrast, Hewlett, Vinogradov, Martin, Berman, and Czernansky (1992) found a prolactin response, restricted to female OCD patients. Lucey, Butcher, Clare, and Dinan (1993) reported on a significantly attenuated prolactin response to fenfluramine in 8 OCD patients compared to 8 normal controls. However, despite the effect of fenfluramine on prolactin levels in some studies, administration of fenfluramine has not been found to influence OCD symptoms.

mCPP

The only serotonergic agonist associated with a brief exacerbation of obsessive–compulsive symptoms is mCPP. mCPP is a metabolite of trazodone, an atypical antidepressant. It is a synthetic, non-indole, aryl-substituted piperazine derivative that rapidly penetrates the blood–brain barrier (Zohar, Insel, Zohar-Kadouch, & Murphy, 1988). mCPP possesses only weak affinity for dopamine, acetylcholine, and alpha-1-adrenergic and beta-adrenergic receptors (Hamik & Peroutka, 1989). Its agonistic activity is greatest for the 5-HT_{2C} and 5-HT_3 receptor subtypes, and to a lesser extent, for the 5-HT_{1A} and 5-HT_{1D} subtypes (Barr et al., 1992).

In preclinical biochemical studies, mCPP was shown to decrease central serotonin synthesis and turnover. This effect has been attributed to a negative feedback mechanism following postsynaptic receptor stimulation. It has also been noted in animal studies that mCPP produced typical changes in serotonin-mediated behavior, such as decreased food consumption and decreased locomotion. The first report on the use of mCPP in OCD patients came from Zohar and coworkers (1987a) in an investigation of the "serotonin hypothesis" of OCD. The behavioral and neuroendocrine effects of mCPP were studied in patients with OCD and healthy controls. Twelve patients and 20 controls were given a single dose of 0.5 mg/kg of mCPP, administered orally under double-blind, placebo-controlled, random-assignment conditions. Following mCPP, but not following placebo, about half of the patients with OCD experienced an acute, transient exacerbation of their obsessive–compulsive symptoms. Moreover, compared with healthy controls, patients exhibited greater changes in other behavioral variables (e.g., increases in anxiety and depression) following mCPP administration. In contrast, there were no differences on endocrinological or thermal measures. These findings were consistent with a special role for the neurotransmitter serotonin in OCD psychopathology.

Another study that examined the effect of oral mCPP was carried out by Hollander et al. (1992). This study also found a transient worsening of OCD symptoms in a group of 20 patients with OCD, relative to 10 normal volunteers. Unlike patients in the Zohar et al. (1987a) study, those in the Hollander et al. study showed no significant difference in anxiety or depression, using visual analogue scales. With respect to neuroendocrine measures, Hollander and colleagues found no cortisol difference between patients and controls, but prolactin response in the patient group was blunted compared with controls. Charney et al. (1988) used intravenous mCPP and found no exacerbation in obsessive–compulsive symptoms. However, they noted a significantly higher rise in anxiety and depression among OCD patients. They also reported a blunted prolactin response but no cortisol difference between female OCD patients and female controls.

A third study employing oral mCPP was conducted by Pigott et al. (1992) and involved a comparison of the effects of oral versus intravenous mCPP. After oral mCPP, there were no significant differences between OCD patients ($n = 17$) and healthy volunteers ($n = 10$), nor were there significant differences from baseline in either group. However, following intravenous mCPP, there were significant increases in anxiety and obsessive–compulsive symptoms in the OCD group. Despite the findings noted in this study, a more recent study by Goodman et al. (1995) found no evidence for increased obsessive–compulsive symptoms following either oral or intraveneous administration of mCPP. Explanations for this discrepancy include the possible effects of variations in the amount of time elapsing before mCPP reaches the receptor, as well as limitations with respect to the reliability of the psychometric instruments used to assess changes in frequency and severity of obsessive–compulsive symptoms, namely, the challenge version of the Yale–Brown Obsessive–Compulsive Scale (YBOCS). This scale, which is the assessment instrument most widely used during provocation studies (Goodman, Price, Woods, & Charney, 1991; Goodman et al., 1989a, 1989b), may be unable to detect singular changes in obsessions or compulsions. Furthermore, a study of nonclinical volunteers by Murphy, Mueller, Hill, Tolliver, and Jacobsen (1989) found that different routes of mCPP administration elicited distinct responses, with intravenous administration inducing more anxiety and physical symptoms than oral administration.

In order to evaluate whether the behavioral effects of mCPP in OCD patients might be attributable to activity in serotonergic receptors, Pigott et al. (1991, 1993) pretreated participants with a single dose (4 mg) of metergoline, 1 hour prior to mCPP administration. Metergoline is a nonselective serotonin receptor antagonist, known to have an effect on 5-HT$_{1A}$, 5-HT$_{1D}$, and 5-HT$_{2C}$ receptors. Indeed, the addition of metergoline eliminated the behavioral and endocrine response of OCD patients to mCPP. This effect was noted regardless of whether mCPP was administered orally or intravenously.

Some of the studies reviewed here suggest that mCPP administration is associated with a transient exacerbation of obsessive–compulsive symptoms. However, they fail to reach a consensus regarding prolactin, cortisol, and other neuroendocrine parameters. Any conclusions made from these investigations must take into account our incomplete knowledge of the mechanism of action of mCPP and the complex interaction between different brain circuits and other moaminergic systems in the brain. However, the exacerbation of obsessive–compulsive symptoms following administration of mCPP is in line with the serotonergic hypothesis of OCD and suggests that OCD patients are behaviorally hypersensitive to activation of their serotonergic system.

mCPP has also been used to examine whether the behavioral, thermal, and endocrine responses of OCD patients to mCPP might be modified by therapeutic agents used for OCD treatment. In a study by Zohar, Insel, Zohar-Kadouch, Hill, and Murphy (1988), OCD patients treated for an average of 4 months with CMI showed attenuated behavioral responses to mCPP readministration. Temperature response was also attenuated, but prolactin and cortisol responses did not significantly differ from those of untreated patients. Similar results were found by Hollander et al. (1991), using orally administered mCPP in patients taking fluoxetine chronically. These findings suggest that the therapeutic effects of SRIs are associated with the development of an adaptive down-regulation of the serotonergic subsystems affected by mCPP.

Ipsapirone

An azipirone similar to buspirone, ipsapirone is a selective 5-HT$_{1A}$ ligand. In a study by Lesch, Hoh, Schulte, Osterheider, and Mueller (1991), ipsapirone was administered to 12 drug-free OCD patients and 20 control volunteers. All received a single dose of 0.3 mg/kg of ipsapirone or placebo orally, under double-blind, random-assignment conditions. The results of this study showed that ipsapirone had neither a notable effect on behavioral measures nor did it produce thermoregulatory or neuroendocrine responses that were significantly different between the two groups. This study suggests that 5-HT$_{1A}$ does not play a crucial role in mediating obsessive–compulsive symptoms in OCD patients. When the effects of ipsapirone were reexamined in patients treated for their obsessive–compulsive symptoms with fluoxetine, the hypothermia and release of adrenocorticotropic hormone (ACTH) and of cortisol were significantly attenuated compared to pretreatment levels (Lesch, 1991). These findings support the development of an adaptive down-regulation following treatment with SRIs.

MK-212

Evidence for the diminished responsivity of the serotonergic system in mediating the endocrine response has been provided by using the serotonin agonist MK-212 as a pharmacological probe. MK-212 has an affinity for 5-HT$_{1A}$ and 5-HT$_{2C}$ receptors (Zohar & Kindler, 1992). Differences between OCD patients and normal controls in response to challenge with MK-212 have been investigated by Bastani, Nash, and Meltzer (1990). Patients demonstrated a blunted cortisol but no prolactin response to this agent compared with normal controls. MK-212 was not found to produce any significant changes in obsessive–compulsive symptoms or other behaviors.

WHICH SEROTONERGIC RECEPTOR IS IMPLICATED IN OCD?

Because only mCPP has been associated with an exacerbation of obsessive–compulsive symptoms, the differences in receptor affinity between mCPP on the one hand, and MK-212 and ipsapirone on the other hand could provide us with important clues about the receptor subtype associated with the provocation of obsessive–compulsive symptoms. mCPP shows affinity for 5-HT$_{1A}$, 5-HT$_{1D}$ and 5-HT$_{2C}$, whereas MK-212 has affinities mainly for 5-HT$_{1A}$ and 5-HT$_{2C}$. The principal difference between mCPP and MK-212 is the 5-HT$_{1D}$ receptor affinity.

This suggests that the 5-HT$_{1D}$ receptor subtype might warrant further investigation as a possible candidate for the mediation of obsessive–compulsive behavior in OCD patients.

Following this rationale, sumatriptan, a 5-HT$_{1D}$ receptor agonist, was compared to mCPP and placebo in a group of 10 OCD patients and 5 normal controls. Behavioral and neuroendocrine measures were examined. Following a sumatriptan challenge, OCD patients reported a transient, statistically significant rise in obsessive–compulsive symptoms. No rise was noted in prolactin or cortisol levels (Cohen et al., 1995). This pilot report supports a possible role for 5-HT$_{1D}$ in mediating obsessive–compulsive symptoms.

ARE OCD PATIENTS SENSITIVE TO OTHER ANXIOGENIC CHALLENGES?

Various anxiogenic challenges have been studied in panic disorder (PD), among them lactate, yohimbine, caffeine, carbon dioxide, and cholesystokinin (CCK). These challenges cause panic-like attacks in approximately 60% of all patients with PD. The response to these challenges is completely different among OCD patients. Although occasionally a patient may respond with a rise in anxiety, or, rarely, with a panic attack, as a group, anxiogenic challenges do not lead to any behavioral alteration among OCD patients (Gorman et al., 1985; Gorman, Fyer, Liebowitz, & Klein, 1987; Rasmussen, Goodman, Woods, Heninger, & Charney, 1987; Weizman, Zohar, & Insel, 1991; Zohar, Mueller, Insel, Zohar-Kadouch, & Murphy, 1987b). These studies call into question the linkage between OCD and other anxiety disorders. Yet they strengthen the specificity of the mCPP challenge in OCD, as so far, only mCPP (and probably sumatriptan) have been associated with an exacerbation of obsessive–compulsive symptoms (Weizman et al., 1991).

In an adrenergic challenge study, Rasmussen et al. (1987) administered yohimbine (an alpha-2-adrenergic antagonist) to 12 drug-free OCD patients and 12 healthy subjects. No significant group differences were found in the anxiogenic effects of yohimbine, although in one of the two patients with a history of panic attacks, yohimbine induced an attack. Hollander et al. (1988) compared the anxiogenic effects of clonidine (an alpha-2-adrenergic autoreceptor agonistic) to placebo in 6 OCD patients. In contrast to the findings with the yohimbine challenge, clonidine was reported to be associated with an amelioration of obsessive–compulsive symptoms. To the best of our knowledge, this finding has not been replicated.

Besides yohimbine, challenge studies have also included the CCK analogue, pentagastrin, whose effect in inducing panic attacks has been demonstrated by Abelson and Nesse (1990). den Boer & Westenberg (1997) examined the effect of pentagastrin in 7 female OCD patients and 7 healthy controls. Five of the 7 OCD patients responded with a panic-like attack, compared to 1 in the control group. However, no changes in obsessive–compulsive symptoms were found during the pentagastrin challenge (den Boer et al., 1993).

CONCLUSION

The most robust evidence for the involvement of the serotonergic system in OCD comes from the specific efficacy of serotonergic medication in the treatment of obsessive–compulsive symptoms. Overall, the results of pharmacological challenge studies are consistent with this hypothesis and suggest that dysregulation of the serotonergic system might be involved in this disorder, although the exact mechanism remains elusive. Future research directions in OCD include the development and administration of other selective probes that will enable more specific examination of different subreceptor systems. However, the relationship and interactions between the serotonergic system and other neurotransmitter systems await further clarification as well. The boundaries of research have therefore extended beyond serotonin to other systems such as dopamine, neuropeptides, and the autoimmune system.

REFERENCES

Abelson, J. L., & Nesse, R. M. (1990). Cholecystokinin-4 and panic. *Archives of General Psychiatry, 47*, 395.

Ananth, J., Pecknold, J. C., Van den Steen, N., & Engelsman, F. (1981). Double-blind comparative study of clomipramine and amitriptyline in obsessive neurosis. *Progress in Neuropsychopharmacology, 5*, 257–262.

Barr, L. C., Goodman, W. K., McDougle, C. J., Delgado, P. L., Heninger, G. R., Charney, D. S., & Price, L. H. (1994). Tryptophan depletion in patients with obsessive compulsive disorder who respond to serotonin reuptake inhibitors. *Archives of General Psychiatry, 51*, 309–317.

Barr, L. C., Goodman, W. K., & Price, L. H. (1993). The serotonin hypothesis of obsessive compulsive disorder. *International Clinical Psychopharmacology, 8*, 79s–82s.

Barr, L. C., Goodman, W. K., Price, L. H., McDougle, C. J., & Charney, D. S. (1992). The serotonin hypothesis of obsessive compulsive disorder: Implications of pharmacologic challenge studies. *Journal of Clinical Psychiatry, 4*, 17s–28s.

Bastani, B., Arora, R.C., & Meltzer, H. Y. (1991). Serotonin uptake and imipramine binding in the blood platelets of obsessive–compulsive disorder patients. *Biological Psychiatry, 30*, 131–139.

Bastani, B., Nash, J. F., & Meltzer, H. Y. (1990). Prolactin and cortisol responses to MK-212, a serotonin agonist, in obsessive–compulsive disorder. *Archives of General Psychiatry, 47*, 833–839.

Charney, D. S., Goodman, W. K., Price, L. H., Woods, S. W., Rasmussen, S. A., & Heninger, G. R. (1988). Serotonin function in obsessive–compulsive disorder. *Archives of General Psychiatry, 45*, 177–185.

Cohen, R., Zohar, J., Kindler, S., Sasson, Y., Gross, R., & Iseroff, R. (1995). *Specific seroton-*

ergic receptors in obsessive–compulsive disorder. Paper presented at the second meeting of the Israeli Society for Biological Psychiatry, Kfar Giladi, Israel.

den Boer, J. A., & Westenberg, H. G. M. (1997). Challenge studies in obsessive–compulsive disorder. In J. A. den Boer & H. G. M. Westenberg (Eds.), *Focus on obsessive compulsive spectrum disorder* (pp. 123–134). Amsterdam: Syn-Thesis.

Fineberg, N. A., Cowen, P. J., Kirk, J. W., & Montgomery, S. A. (1994). Neuroendocrine responses to intravenous L-tryptophan in obsessive compulsive disorder. *Journal of Affective Disorders, 32,* 97–104.

Flament, M. F., Rapoport, J. L., Murphy, D. L., Berg, C. J., & Lake, C. R. (1987). Biochemical changes during clomipramine treatment of childhood obsessive–compulsive disorder. *Archives of General Psychiatry, 44,* 219–225.

Goodman, W. K., McDougle, C., Price, L. H., Barr, L. C., Hills, O. F., Caplik, J. F., Charney, D. S., & Heninger, G. K. (1995). M-Chlorophenylpiperazine in patients with obsessive compulsive disorder: Absence of symptom exacerbation. *Biological Psychiatry, 38,* 138–149.

Goodman, W. K., Price, L. H., Rasmussen, S. A., Mazure, C., Delgado, P., Heninger, G. R., & Charney, D. S. (1989a). The Yale–Brown Obsessive–Compulsive Scale: II. Validity. *Archives of General Psychiatry, 46,* 1012–1016.

Goodman, W. K., Price, L. H., Rasmussen, S. A., Mazure, C., Fleishmann, R. L., Hill, C. L., Heninger, G. R., & Charney, D. S. (1989b). The Yale–Brown Obsessive–Compulsive Scale: I. Development, use, and reliability. *Archives of General Psychiatry, 46,* 1006–1011.

Goodman, W. K., Price, L. H., Woods, S. W., & Charney, D. S. (1991). Pharmacologic challenges in obsessive compulsive disorder. In J. Zohar, T. R. Insel, & S. Rasmussen (Eds.), *The of obsessive–compulsive disorder* (pp. 162–186). New York: Springer-Verlag.

Gorman, J. M., Fyer, A. J., Liebowitz, M. R., & Klein, D. F. (1987). Pharmacologic provocation of panic attacks. In H. Y. Meltzer (Ed.), *Psychopharmacology, the third generation of progress* (pp. 985–993). New York: Raven Press.

Gorman, J. M., Liebowitz, M. R., Fyer, A. J., Dillon, D., Davies, S. O., Stein, J., & Klein, D. F. (1985). Lactate infusions in obsessive–compulsive disorder. *American Journal of Psychiatry, 142,* 864–866.

Greist, J., Chouinard, G., & DuBoff, E. (1995). Double blind parallel comparison of three doses of sertraline and placebo in the treatment of outpatients with obsessive compulsive disorder. *Archives of General Psychiatry, 52,* 289–295.

Hamik, A., & Peroutka, S. (1989). 1-m-chlorophenyl piperazine (*m*CPP) interactions with neurotransmitter receptors in human brain. *Biological Psychiatry, 25,* 569–575.

Hewlett, W. A., Vinogradov, S., Martin, K., Berman, S., & Czernansky, J. G. (1992) Fenfluramine stimulation of prolactin in obsessive compulsive disorder. *Psychiatry Research, 42,* 81–92.

Hollander, E., DeCaria, C. M., Gully, R., Nitescu, A., Suckow, R. F., Gorman, J. M., Klein, D. F., & Liebowitz, M. E. (1991). Effects of chronic fluoxetine treatment on behavioral and neuroendocrine responses to meta-chlorophenyl-piperazine in obsessive–compulsive disorder. *Psychiatry Research, 36,* 1–17.

Hollander, E., DeCaria, C. M., Nitescu, A., Gully, R., Suckow, R., Cooper, T., Gorman, J., Klein, D., & Liebowitz, M. (1992). Serotonergic function in obsessive–compulsive disorder: Behavioral and neuroendocrine responses to oral m-chlorophenylpiperazine and fenfluramine in patients and health volunteers. *Archives of General Psychiatry, 49,* 21–28.

Hollander, E., Fay, M., Cohen, B., Campeas, R., Gorman, J. M., & Liebowitz, M. R.

(1988). Serotonergic and noradrenergic sensitivity in obsessive–compulsive disorder: Behavioral findings. *American Journal of Psychiatry, 145,* 1015–1017.

Humphrey, P. P., Hartig, P., & Hoyer, D. (1993). A proposed new nomenclature for 5-HT receptors. *Trends in Pharmacological Sciences, 14,* 233–236.

Insel, T. R. (1992). Towards a neuroanatomy of obsessive compulsive disorder. *Archives of General Psychiatry, 49,* 739–744.

Insel, T. R., Mueller, E. A., Alterman, I., Linnoila, M., & Murphy, D. L. (1985). Obsessive–compulsive disorder and serotonin: Is there a connection? *Biological Psychiatry, 20,* 1174–1188.

Kim, S. W., Dysken, M. W., Pandey, G. N., & Davis, J. M. (1991). Platelet ^{3}H-imipramine binding sites in obsessive–compulsive disorder. *Archives of General Psychiatry, 48,* 548–555.

Leonard, H., Swedo, S., Koby, E., Rapoport, J. L., Lenane, M., Cheslow, D., & Hamburger, S. (1989). Treatment of obsessive compulsive disorder with clomipramine and desmethylimipramine in children and adolescents: A double-blind crossover comparison. *Archives of General Psychiatry, 46,* 1088–1092.

Leonard, H., Swedo, S., Lenane, M., Rettew, D., Cheslow, D., Hamburger, S., & Rapoport, J. (1991). A double-blind desipramine substitution during long-term clomipramine treatment in children and adolescents with obsessive–compulsive disorder. *Archives of General Psychiatry, 48,* 922–927.

Lesch, K. P., Hoh, A., Disselkamp-Tietze, J., Weismann, M., Osterheider, M., & Schulte, H. (1991). 5-Hydroxytryptamine$_{1A}$ (5-HT$_{1A}$) receptor responsivity in obsessive–compulsive disorder: Comparison of patients and controls. *Archives of General Psychiatry, 48,* 540–547.

Lesch, K. P., Hoh, A., Schulte, H. M., Osterheider, M., & Mueller, T. (1991). Long-term fluoxetine treatment decreases 5-HT$_{1A}$ receptor responsivity in obsessive–compulsive disorder. *Psychopharmacology, 105,* 415–420.

Lucey, J. V., Butcher, G., Clare, A. W., & Dinan, T. G. (1993). The anterior pituitary responds normally to protirelin in obsessive–compulsive disorder: Evidence to support a neuroendocrine serotonergic deficit. *Acta Psychiatrica Scandinavica, 87,* 384–388.

Lydiard, R. B., Ballenger, J. C., Ellinwood, E., Fossey, M. A., & Laraia, M. T. (1990, May). *CSF monamine metabolites in obsessive–compulsive disorder.* Paper presented at the 143rd annual meeting of the American Psychiatric Assciation, New York.

Maguire, K. P., Norman, T. R., Apostopoulos, M., Judd, F. K., & Burrows, G. D. (1995). Platelet [^{3}H]paroxetine binding in obsessive–compulsive disorder. *Human Psychopharmacology, 10,* 141–146.

Marazziti, D., Hollander, E., Lensi, P., Ravagli, S., & Cassano, G. B. (1992). Peripheral markers of serotonin and dopamine function in obsessive–compulsive disorder. *Psychiatry Research, 42,* 41–51.

McBride, P. A., DeMeo, M. D., Sweeney, J. A., Halper, J., Mann, J. J., & Shear, M. K. (1992). Neuroendocrine amd behavioral responses to challenge with indirect serotonin agonist *dl*-fenfluramine in adults with obsessive–compulsive disorder. *Biological Psychiary, 31,* 19–34.

Montgomery, S. A., McIntyre, A., Osterheider, M., Sarteschi, P., Zitterl, W., Zohar, J., Birkett, M., & Wood, A. J. (1993). A double-blind, placebo controlled study of fluoxetine in patients with DSM-III-R obsessive compulsive disorder. The Lilly European Obsessive–Compulsive Disorder Study Group. *European Neuropsychopharmacology, 3,* 143–152.

Murphy, D. L., Greenberg, B., Altemus, M., Benjamin, J., Grady, T., & Pigott, T. (1996).

The neuropharmacology and neurobiology of obsessive compulsive disorder: An update on the serotonin hypothesis. In H. G. M. Westenberg, J. A. den Boer, & D. L. Murphy (Eds.), *Advances in the neurobiology of anxiety disorders* (pp. 279–297). New York: Wiley.

Murphy, D. L., Mueller, E. A., Hill, J. L., Tolliver, T. J., & Jacobsen, F. M. (1989). Comparative anxiogenic, neuroendocrine, and other physiologic effects of m-chlorophenyl-piperazine given intravenously or orally to healthy volunteers. *Psychopharmacology, 98,* 275–282.

Pigott, T. A., Grady, T. A., Bernstein, S. E., L'Heureux, F., Hill, J. L., Rubenstein, C. S., & Murphy, D. L. (1992). A comparison of oral and IV m-CPP in patients with obsessive compulsive disorder. *Biological Psychiatry, 31,* 173A.

Pigott, T. A., Hill, J. L., Grady, T. A., L'Heureux, F., Bernstein, S. E., Rubenstein, C. S., & Murphy, D. L. (1993). A comparison of the behavioral effects of oral versus intravenous *m*CPP administration in OCD patients and the effect of metergoline prior to i.v. *m*CPP. *Biological Psychiatry, 33,* 3–14.

Pigott, T. A., Zohar, J., Hill, J. L., Bernstein, S. E., Grover, G. N., Zohar-Kadouch, R. C., & Murphy, D. L. (1991). Metergoline blocks the behavioral and neuroendocrine effects of orally administered m-chlorophenylpiperazine in patients with obsessive–compulsive disorder. *Biological Psychiatry, 29,* 418–426.

Rasmussen, S. A., Goodman, W. K., Woods, S. W., Heninger, G. R., & Charney, D. S. (1987). Effects of yohimbine in obsessive compulsive disorder. *Psychopharmacology, 93,* 308–313.

Sandyk, R. (1992). Tryptophan in neuropsychiatric disorders. *International Journal of Neuroscience, 67,* 127–144.

Stern, R. S., Marks, I. M., Wright, J., & Luscombe, D. K. (1980). Clomipramine: Plasma levels, side-effects and outcome in obsessive compulsive neurosis. *Postgraduate Medical Journal, 56,* 134–139.

Thoren, P., Asberg, M., Gronholm, B., Jornestedt, L., & Traskman, L. (1980). Clomipramine treatment of obsessive–compulsive disorder: A controlled clinical trial. *Archives of General Psychiatry, 37,* 1281–1285.

Vitiello, B., Shimon, H., Behar, D., Stoff, D., Bridger, W. H., & Friedman, E. (1991). Platelet imipramine binding and serotonin uptake in obsessive–compulsive patients. *Acta Psychiatrica Scandinavica, 84,* 29–32.

Volavka, J., Neziroglu, F., & Yaryura-Tobias, J. A. (1985). Clomipramine and imipramine in obsessive compulsive disorder. *Psychiatry Research, 14,* 85–93.

Weizman, A., Carmi, M., Hermesh, H., Shahar, A., Apter, A., Tyano, S., & Rehavi, N. (1986). High affinity imipramine binding and serotonin uptake in platelets of eight adolescent and ten adult obsessive–compulsive patients. *American Journal of Psychiatry, 143,* 335–339.

Weizman, A., Zohar, J., & Insel, T. R. (1991). Biological markers in obsessive–compulsive disorder. In J. Zohar, T. R. Insel, & S. Rasmussen (Eds.), *The psychobiology of obsessive–compulsive disorder* (pp. 46–161). New York: Springer-Verlag.

Wheadon, D. E., Bushnell, W. D., & Steiner, M. (1993, December). *A fixed dose comparison of 20, 40 or 60 mg paroxetine to placebo in the treatment of OCD.* Paper presented at the annual Meeting of the American College of Neuropsychopharmacology, San Juan, Puerto Rico.

Zohar, J., & Insel, T. R. (1987). Obsessive–compulsive disorder: Psychobiological approaches to diagnosis, treatment and pathophysiology. *Biological Psychiatry, 22,* 667–687.

Zohar, J., Insel, T. R., Zohar-Kadouch, R. C., Mueller, E. A., & Murphy, D. L. (1988). Serotonergic role in obsessive–compulsive disorder. In V. Chan-Palay & S. L. Palay (Eds.), *Progress in catecholamine research: Part C. Clinical aspects* (pp. 386–391). New York: Liss.

Zohar, J., Insel, T. R., Zohar-Kadouch, R. C., Hill, J. L., & Murphy, D. L. (1988). Serotonergic responsivity in obsessive–compulsive disorder: Effects of chronic clomipramine treatment. *Archives of General Psychiatry, 45,* 167–172.

Zohar, J., & Kindler, S. (1992). Serotonergic probes in obsessive compulsive disorder. *International Clinical Psychopharmacology, 7,* 39s–40s.

Zohar, J., Mueller, E. A., Insel, T. R., Zohar-Kadouch, R. C., & Murphy, D. L. (1987a). Serotonergic role in obsessive–compulsive disorder. In R. H. Belmaker, M. Sandler, & A. Dahlström (Eds.), *Progress in catecholamine research: Part C. Clinical aspects* (pp. 385–391). New York: Liss.

Zohar, J., Mueller, E. A., Insel, T. R., Zohar-Kadouch, R. C., & Murphy, D. L. (1987b). Serotonergic responsivity in obsessive–compulsive disorder: Comparison of patients and healthy controls. *Archives of General Psychiatry, 44,* 946–951.

Chapter 7

NEUROIMAGING AND NEUROANATOMICAL ISSUES IN OBSESSIVE–COMPULSIVE DISORDER
Toward an Integrative Model— Perceived Impulsivity

Jean Cottraux
Daniel Gérard

Until the early 1970s obsessive–compulsive disorder (OCD) was viewed as a disorder of psychological origin. Learning theories and behavior therapies based mainly on the model of habituation tried to bridge the gap between biology and psychology (Marks, 1987). Since then, the advent of increasingly sophisticated technologies has greatly facilitated the more in-depth exploration of possible genetic and neurological substrates underlying this disorder. Now, both genetic and environmental influences are considered to be factors underlying OCD and related OCD spectrum disorders. Pauls, Asobrock, Goodman, Rasmussen, and Leckman (1995) demonstrated that OCD was five times as frequent in families of OCD probands compared to control families. Moreover, they suggested a genetic heterogeneity with three forms of OCD: familial cases with tics or Gilles de la Tourette syndrome, familial cases with only obsessions and compulsions, and nonfamilial cases.

Although speculative, a relationship between Syndenham's chorea and OCD symptoms in children has been suggested by Swedo et al. (1989a). In line with this finding, some studies have suggested that antineural antibodies against caudate and putamen might be implicated in tics and OCD symptoms (Kiessling, Marcotte, & Culpepper, 1994). In addition, stereotactic leukotomy, which interrupts orbital cortex pathways from the hypothalamus, thalamus, and the limbic system, has shown some results in intractable OCD, though at the cost of impulse control impairment and activation of aggressive tendencies in some patients (Chiocca & Martuza, 1990). Thus, whatever the respective roles of genetics and environment, there is evidence for neural network impairment in at least some OCD subtypes compared with controls. Since Baxter, Thompson, et al.'s (1987) seminal study of OCD with positron emission tomography (PET) technology, neuroimaging techniques have been used extensively in OCD research. Data from over the last 10 years suggest that OCD is associated with dysfunction within particular neural pathways.

A good general model of OCD should account for abnormalities in information processing related to specific neural networks and the biology of the habituation process. It should examine the psychological effects of intrusive thoughts, their relation to cognitive schemas, and their development from early learning experiences. Such a model should also account for the therapeutic effects of exposure therapy, cognitive therapy, and serotonergic antidepressants (see related chapters in this book). To summarize, then, structural and functional neuroanatomy may help us to understand the neural networks and neurochemistry mediating the obsessive–compulsive process. Psychology may help us to understand the relationships among obsessional stimuli, the content in obsessive cognitive schemas, and their respective neural networks. Evolutionary psychology may also be considered in order to raise hypotheses about the survival value of obsessions and compulsions. In this chapter, we review the evidence drawn from controlled studies in structural and functional neuroimaging and attempt to integrate this evidence into a new model of OCD that we term "perceived impulsivity."

STRUCTURAL NEUROIMAGING STUDIES

Early case studies reported lesions in the basal ganglia of patients with compulsive behavior associated with brain disease. Laplane et al. (1989) reported eight cases with anoxic or toxic encephalopathy that had atrophy of the basal ganglia based on magnetic resonance imaging (MRI) and frontal hypometabolism based on PET. Trillet, Croisile, Tourniaire, and Schott (1990) reported three similar cases based on MRI showing atrophy in the caudate nucleus, and a fourth case by Pénisson-Besnier, Le Gall, and Dubas (1992) confirmed these findings. Weilburg et al. (1989) found left caudate and putamen abnormalities with MRI in a young OCD patient. To date, 11 controlled studies have been conducted with medicated and unmedicated samples with the use of computed tomography (CT) or MRI. Table 7.1 summarizes the outcomes.

Five of the 12 studies using either CT or MRI found no differences between OCD and controls. The remaining seven studies that reported differ-

TABLE 7.1. Structural Studies: OCD Patients versus Control Subjects

Study	Technique	Results
Insel, Donnelly, Lalakea, Alterman, & Murphy (1983)	CT	OCD = controls
Behar, Rapoport, & Berg (1984)	CT	VBR larger in OCD
Luxenberg et al. (1988)	CT	Caudate OCD < controls
Garber, Ananth, Chiu, Griswold, & Oldendorf (1989)	MRI	OCD: abnormalities in frontal white matter
Kellner et al. (1991)	MRI	OCD = controls
Scarone et al. (1992)	MRI	Head of caudate: OCD > controls
Stein et al. (1993)	CT	OCD = controls
Calabrese, Colombo, Bonfanti, Scotti, & Scarone (1993)	MRI	OCD: Left caudate > right caudate; no asymmetry in controls
Robinson et al. (1995)	MRI	Caudate: OCD < controls
Aylard et al. (1996)	MRI	OCD = controls
Jenike et al. (1996)	MRI	White matter: OCD < controls; total cortex and opercular volume: OCD > controls
Stein, Coetzer, Lee, Davids, & Bouwer (1997)	MRI	OCD = trichotillomania = controls

Note. VBR, ventricle–brain ratio.

ences are summarized here. In two CT studies (Luxenberg et al., 1988; Robinson et al., 1995), the head of the caudate nucleus was smaller in OCD patients than in controls. The head of the right caudate was enlarged in one MRI study (Scarone et al., 1992), and in another study, the left caudate volume was enlarged (Calabrese, Colombo, Bonfanti, Scotti, & Scarone, 1993). Abnormalities in frontal white matter were found using MRI by Garber, Ananth, Chiu, Griswold, and Oldendorf (1989), who suggested that the frontal lobe and anterior cingulate gyrus play a role in the expression of OCD symptoms. A morphometric MRI study (Jenike et al., 1996) found relatively diffuse white matter decrease in OCD subjects, compared to controls. The total cortex volume as well as the volume of the operculum was significantly greater in OCD subjects and OCD severity was correlated with the volume of the opercular region. This study suggests that the structural brain abnormality underlying obsessive–compulsive symptoms may be more widely distributed than previously thought.

In summary, 36%, or five of the 12 controlled studies using CT or MRI found no differences between OCD subjects and controls. The seven positive studies reported discrepant findings that suggest involvement of the caudate nucleus and/or frontal lobes, or, alternatively, a pervasive brain abnormality in some OCD patients.

FUNCTIONAL NEUROIMAGING STUDIES: PET, SPECT, AND FUNCTIONAL MRI

Technical Aspects of Functional Neuroimaging

Neuroanatomy and pathophysiology have been examined using PET, single photon emission compited tomography (SPECT), and functional MRI in controlled studies. These techniques have provided new data on areas of the brain whose dysfunction may mediate OCD symptomatology.

PET and SPECT are emission and tomographic techniques. The source of radiation is within the patient, and the computerized reconstruction techniques are similar to those employed by CT technology. PET is a high-resolution imaging technique in which trace amounts of biochemicals of interest are labeled with unstable nuclei that emit positrons. When the positrons collide with electrons in the body, they produce a pair of photons that are picked up by detectors. In contrast, SPECT is based on the counting of each "single photon" emitted by the radioisotope or radiopharmaceutical administered. PET takes advantage of the short physical half-lives of the commonly used positron-emitting radionuclides (^{11}C, ^{13}N, ^{15}O, ^{18}F). Scans performed with ^{18}fluorodeoxyglucose (^{18}FDG) show the sum of all cerebral glucose consumption occurring during the uptake phase of approximately 30 minutes; thus, the cumulative ^{18}FDG method cannot capture transitory events. Brief "snapshots" of brain activity are possible, however, by measuring regional cerebral blood flow (rCBF) after administration of ^{15}O-labeled water. Because the 2-minute half-life of ^{15}O allows for repeated measures in a single session, comparisons between baseline and several treatment conditions are possible. Imaging technology is expanding rapidly and the resolution of scanners has improved in recent years. A typical reconstructed resolution value for PET is now in the range of 4–6 mm, whereas the spatial resolution for SPECT has advanced from about 20 mm a decade ago to between 6 and 9 mm today. With these advances, the biggest problem currently concerns not resolution, but image analysis.

The very first studies using image analysis were aimed at quantifying absolute metabolic rates in localized cerebral regions or "regions of interest" (ROIs). Yet large intra- and intersubject variability made statistical comparisons difficult. Moreover, determining input function and calculating absolute metabolism or cerebral blood flow was limited to a few methods, with substantial discrepancies among them. To avoid this difficulty, investigators began to standardize their data by calculating the ratio between a defined ROI and a larger section of the brain. Unfortunately, different normalization methods have been used (e.g., ipsilateral hemisphere; global activity of gray matter, visual cortex, cerebellum, etc.), and the delineation of ROIs varies considerably, depending on whether they are drawn manually, with the aid of a brain atlas, or by superimposing the functional images on the subject's own brain CT or MRI scan.

Today other approaches are used when analyzing data obtained from repeated PET scans. Stereotactic normalization reduces differences in brain position, size, and shape by mapping data onto a standard stereotactic space, as defined in Talairach and Tournoux's (1988) *Co-Planar Stereotactic Atlas of the Human Brain*. A new technique called statistical parametric mapping (SPM) refers to the creation of images whose pixel values are distributed according to a statistical test. The SPM technique provides what can be described as images of change significance (Friston, Frith, Liddle, & Frackowiack, 1991). SPM has now become the international standard for communicating PET results. Unfortunately, most of the studies conducted with OCD patients involve data collected from earlier methodologies, not SPM, making direct comparisons between them difficult. Figure 7.1 represents some recent and unpublished outcomes that our group obtained with SPM.

In contrast to PET and SPECT, functional MRI does not rely on ionizing radiation. Therefore, subjects can be studied repeatedly without discomfort. Moreover, new functional MRI techniques do not require a contrast agent. The

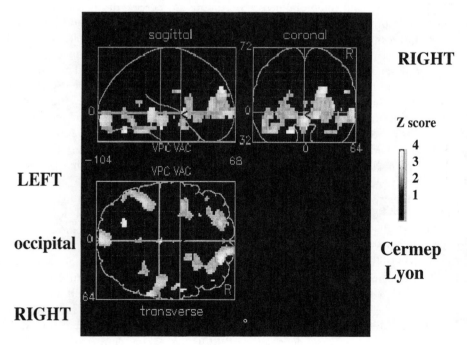

FIGURE 7.1. Statistical parametric mapping: Controls (*n* = 9) were subtracted from OCD (*n* = 8). rCBF was greater for OCD patients than controls in the following regions of interest: superior and middle frontal lobe bilaterally; temporal lobe: superior (left) and middle (right) and fusiform gyrus (left), caudate (right), putamen (left), visual occipital cortex (bilaterally). From Gérard, Grégoire, Cottraux, & Cinotti (unpublished data).

blood oxygen level–dependent (BOLD) method allows assessment of rCBF as indicated by the change in hemoglobin from an oxy to a deoxy state. Thus, an increase in rCBF reflects neuronal activation (Breiter et al., 1996).

CONTROLLED STUDIES OF FUNCTIONAL NEUROIMAGING IN OCD

A Medline search on the Internet found 27 studies that used either a within-groups, baseline-controlled design or a between-groups design. Three approaches to neuroimaging studies have been used in the last 10 years: the study of the brain during its "resting state" (see Table 7.2); the study of the brain under stimulation (see Table 7.3); and study of the brain before and after successful treatment using pharmacological or psychological interventions (see Table 7.4).

Resting State Studies

PET STUDIES

Initially, studies were conducted comparing neurometabolic abnormalities in OCD subjects with normal control subjects during resting states. Seven studies in total have been published. The first and most influential study was conducted by Baxter, Phelps, et al. (1987), who studied 14 OCD patients with PET, using [18]FDG. These patients were compared with 14 normal controls and 14 patients with unipolar depression. Results showed that unipolar depression patients and OCD subjects did not differ in levels of anxiety, tension, or depression. In OCD, metabolic rates were significantly increased in the left orbital gyrus and bilaterally in the caudate nuclei when compared with both controls and individuals with unipolar depression. In addition, there was a tendency toward an increased metabolic rate in the right orbital gyrus on all comparisons. The metabolic rates in the left orbital gyrus/ipsilateral hemisphere were significantly elevated compared to those in the controls and in the depressed subjects, and remained high even after successful drug treatment. Initially, the metabolic ratio for the caudate/hemisphere was in the normal range; when OCD symptoms improved after drug treatment, the ratio increased uniformly and significantly bilaterally. This ratio did not increase in those who did not respond to treatment. In this study, OCD subjects showed cerebral glucose metabolic patterns that differed from controls in both the symptomatic and recovered states.

In another study, Baxter et al. (1988) compared cerebral glucose metabolism using PET in 10 nondepressed OCD patients with 10 normal controls. The groups were matched for sex and age. Patients showed significantly elevated metabolic rates in the entire cerebral hemisphere, heads of the caudate nuclei, the orbital gyri, and the orbital gyrus/ipsilateral hemisphere ratio bilaterally. Nordhal et al. (1989) partially confirmed earlier findings from Baxter et al. This study looked at the possible influence of mental activity on PET results. Subjects with OCD and nonclinical controls were asked to close their eyes while continuous auditory performance tasks were administered. [18]FDG PET data on 8 nondepressed patients with OCD were compared with data on 30 normal volunteers. Significantly higher normalized region-specific metabolism, both in the right and left orbital frontal cortex, was observed in OCD patients. No normalized glucose metabolic differences appeared in basal ganglia structures for those with OCD when compared to controls.

Swedo et al. (1989b) studied cerebral metabolic rates for glucose in 18 adults with childhood-onset OCD and matched controls using [18]FDG PET. Both groups were scanned in a resting state with reduced auditory and visual stimulation (eyes closed). The OCD group showed increased glucose metabolism in the left orbital frontal, right sensorimotor and bilateral prefrontal, and anterior cingulate region, compared to controls. The ratio of regional activity to mean cortical gray matter metabolism was increased for the right prefrontal and left anterior cingulate regions in the OCD subjects. There was a significant relationship between metabolic activity, obsessive–compulsive state and trait anxiety, and response to clomipramine.

Sawle, Hymas, Lees, and Frackowiak (1991) compared 6 OCD subjects with extreme slowness with 6 healthy volunteers. PET scans were taken with the tracers [15]O and [^{18}F]Dopa. OCD was associated with hypermetabolism in the orbito-frontal region and the premotor and midfrontal cortex. Dopa uptake was normal in the caudate, putamen, and medial frontal cortex.

Martinot et al. (1990) failed to confirm previous findings. Using [18]FDG, 16 OCD patients showed decreased metabolism in the whole and prefrontal cortex. Retrospectively, however, the observed hypometabolism might be explained by the generally observed finding of decreased metabolism in medicated patients (e.g., Baxter et al., 1992; Martinot et al., 1990). Ten of the 16 individuals in the Martinot et al. study had been medicated at the time of the PET examination.

A [^{11}C]glucose study (Mindus, Nyman, Mogard, Meyerson, & Ericson, 1989) reported lower metabolism in the left orbital gyrus of 5 impaired OCD patients before capsulotomy; after capsulotomy, metabolism in the orbital gyri and caudate nuclei decreased. Whether these OCD patients were receiving pharmocotherapy was not specified. Patients included in the study were probably too exhausted to carry out rituals, which may explain the observed lower metabolism, if we accept the hypothesis that a frontal increase in rCBF reflects the patient's struggle against his or her obsessions and urges to ritualize (Insel, 1992). Another explanation could be the use of [^{11}C]glucose, which metabolizes more rapidly than [18]FDG (Brody & Saxena, 1996).

In summary, despite a few discrepant findings, the outcomes of the controlled [18]FDG PET studies point to dysfunctional circuitry involving orbito-frontal regions and possibly the basal ganglia, particularly the head of the caudate nuclei. It should be noted that Baxter's findings were replicated in other studies with respect to the orbito-frontal region findings only.

SPECT STUDIES

Six SPECT studies on OCD have been reported in the literature so far. Machlin et al. (1991) compared 10 OCD subjects with 8 nonclinical volunteers and demonstrated a higher ratio of medial–frontal to entire cortex blood flow, which was unrelated to obsessive–compulsive symptom severity but was correlated with other measures of anxiety. Rubin, Villanueva-Meyer, Ananth, Trajmar, and Mena (1992) found no significant difference in resting states between OCD subjects and controls when ^{133}Xe SPECT was used. In contrast, when [^{99m}Tc]HMPAO was used, a relative increase of rCBF in the orbital gyri and superior parietal cortex, and decreased rCBF in the head of the caudate nuclei, was reported.

Harris, Hoehn-Saric, Lewis, Pearlson, and Streeter (1994) compared 10 OCD patients to 7 nonclinical controls and found higher relative perfusion in the medial–frontal and right frontal cortex as well as in the cerebellum. Perfusion was reduced in the right visual association cortex. No between-group difference was found for the caudate nuclei. Edmonstone et al. (1994) reported discrepant findings. Twelve OCD patients were investigated during resting states using SPECT with [^{99m}Tc]exametazime. The uptake of [^{99m}Tc]exametazime was expressed relative to the calcarine/occipital cortex. OCD patients were matched for drug treatment with 12 patients receiving pharmacotherapy for a major depressive episode. A control group was used. Significant bilateral decreases in tracer uptake were limited to the basal ganglia in the OCD group. Although the findings were consistent with altered function in the basal ganglia, the direction of change contradicts Baxter, Phelps, et al.'s (1987) and Baxter et al.'s (1992) results.

Adams, Warneke, McEwan, and Fraser (1993) evaluated 11 symptomatic OCD patients using SPECT. Compared with a control group, 8 of the 11 patients demonstrated asymmetric perfusion of the basal ganglia; the left side showed hypoperfusion in 6 patients and the right side showed hypoperfusion in 2 patients.

A more recent study using the same technique also failed to confirm previous findings. Lucey et al. (1995) compared 30 subjects with OCD to 30 healthy controls. rCBF was measured as the uptake of [^{99m}Tc]HMPAO in 15 ROIs. During a resting state, significant reductions were found in rCBF in the right and left superior frontal cortex, right inferior frontal cortex, left temporal cortex, left parietal cortex, right caudate nucleus, and right thalamus in the OCD group. Reduced blood flow to the right inferior frontal cortex correlated significantly with OCD severity. Interestingly, the study used multivariate analysis to correlate two specific dimensions of the rated symptomatology with the functional neuroanatomy data. An obsession–compulsion dimension, including obsessions, compulsions, and low mood, was significantly negatively correlated with left inferior frontal, medial–frontal, and right parietal rCBF. A dimension combining anxiety and avoidance was significantly positively correlated with left and right superior frontal, right inferior frontal, medial frontal cortical, and right and left caudate and thalamic rCBF.

In summary, four SPECT experiments demonstrated higher perfusion in

TABLE 7.2. Functional Neuroimaging Studies: Rest Studies

Study	Technique	Comparison groups	Changes observed in local metabolism or rCBF in OCD subjects
PET studies			
Baxter et al. (1987)	^{18}FDG PET	Normals Depressives	Increased metabolism in left orbital gyrus and bilaterally in caudate nuclei
Baxter et al. (1988)	^{18}FDG PET	Depressives	Increased metabolism in entire cerebral hemisphere, heads of caudate nuclei, orbital gyri, and bilaterally in orbital gyrus/ipsilateral hemisphere
Mindus, Nyman, Mogard, Meyerson, & Ericson (1989)	^{11}C-G-PET	Normals	Decreased metabolism in left orbital gyrus
Nordhal et al. (1989)	^{18}FDG PET	Normals	Increased normalized region specific metabolism in right and left orbito-frontal cortex
Swedo et al. (1989)	^{18}FDG PET	Normals	Increased glucose metabolism in left orbito-frontal, right sensorimotor, and bilateral prefrontal and anterior cingulate region
Martinot et al. (1990)	^{18}FDG PET	Normals	Decreased metabolism in the whole and prefrontal cortex
Sawle, Hymas, Lees, & Frackowiak (1991)	^{15}O PET	Normals	Increased metabolism in orbito-frontal region, premotor, and midfrontal cortex
	[^{18}F]Dopa		Dopa uptake normal into caudate, putamen, and medial–frontal cortex
SPECT studies			
Machlin et al. (1991)	[^{99m}Tc]HMPAO	Normals	Higher ratio of medial–frontal to whole cortex blood flow correlated with anxiety
Rubin, Villanueva-Meyer, Ananth, Trajmar, & Mena (1992)	^{133}Xe SPECT [^{99m}Tc]HMPAO	Normals	No significant difference in resting states Increased rCBF in orbital gyri and superior parietal cortex; decreased rCBF in heads of caudate nuclei
Adams, Warneke, McEwan, & Fraser (1993)	[^{99m}Tc]HMPAO	Normals	Asymmetric perfusion of the basal ganglia
Edmonstone et al. (1994)	[^{99m}Tc]HMPAO	Normals, depressives	Decreased tracer uptake bilaterally in basal ganglia
Harris, Hoehn-Saric, Lewis, Pearlson, & Streeter (1994)	[^{99m}Tc]HMPAO	Normals	Increased perfusion in medial–frontal and right frontal cortex and cerebellum; decreased perfusion in right visual association cortex
Lucey et al. (1995)	[^{99m}Tc]HMPAO	Normals	Decreased rCBF in right and left superior frontal cortex, right inferior frontal cortex, left temporal cortex, left parietal cortex, right caudate nucleus and right thalamus

Note. rCBF, regional cerebral blood flow.

the frontal structures of OCD patients, and two studies reported decreased rCBF in the basal ganglia.

Stimulation Studies: SPECT, PET, and Functional MRI

The second stage in neuroimaging studies came about in order to establish the relationship between the possible neural circuitry involved in OCD and stimuli having specific content and obsessive properties. To this end, the notion of "resting state" has undergone reanalysis. Since neuroimaging using [18]FDG lasts about 45 minutes, it has been proposed that environmental influences (e.g., lighting in the room, noise level) and emotions brought about by PET technology may interact with a patient's metabolic responses. Moreover, inner monologues, obsessive themes, and cognitive schemas may influence the way the environment is perceived, potentially activating some specific brain regions. In the Baxter, Phelps, et al. (1987), Baxter et al. (1988), and Sawle et al. (1991) studies, patients' eyes were open during the scan. In contrast, Swedo et al. (1989) recommended that patients have their eyes closed. The partial replication of Baxter's findings by Nordhal et al. (1989), who attempted to control for cognitive activity, was a step forward. The notion of resting state was later refined by Andreasen et al. (1995) in a [15O]H$_2$O PET study on memory. The short, 2-minute half-life of [15]O allowed repeated measurements. The study showed that free mental activity or "random episodic silent thinking" (REST) produced a pervasive activation of the associative cortex, whereas focused episodic memory (recall of past experience) activated a network including the medial–frontal regions, cingulate gyrus, thalamus, and cerebellum. A control task exploring semantic memory was related to activation of Broca's area. Thus, matching environmental and/or inner stimuli to patients' symptomatology was found to be of critical importance for PET research.

To date, seven activation studies have been published. The effects of imagined and actual stimulation effects were studied with SPECT (Zohar et al., 1989) in 10 OCD patients with contamination fears and washing rituals. Three conditions were compared: a "relaxed" state, imagined exposure, and exposure *in vivo* to "contaminants." During *in vivo* exposure, a decrease in rCBF in the parieto–occipital regions was reported, whereas imagined exposure showed increased rCBF in the temporal region. It was suggested that habituation was linked to brain-stem activity accompanied by a decrease of higher order functions. Repeated *in vivo* exposure could be associated with increased cerebral blood flow reflecting the reestablishment of higher order functions with a greater degree of cognitive processing as a result of "reality testing."

A serotonergic probe was used by Hollander et al. (1991) to study rCBF in OCD. The partial serotonin agonist meta-chlorophenylpiperazine (*m*CPP) has been reported to increase obsessive–compulsive symptoms in some patients with OCD. OCD symptoms provoked by *m*CPP were related to SPECT hyperfrontality in 10 OCD subjects. Another study from the same group found less specific outcomes (Hollander, Prohovnik, & Stein, 1995). In this study, 14 patients with

OCD were investigated with the SPECT Xenon-133 method after administration of oral mCPP (0.5 mg/kg). Seven individuals who responded to mCPP with symptomatic exacerbation had a significant increase in global cortical perfusion (18.1%). This contrasted with the seven nonresponders to mCPP, who showed no change. These results suggest that mCPP exacerbation of OCD symptoms is associated with increased cortical blood flow. The finding of a global increase in rCBF (rather than an increase in specific brain structures) may be due to the low resolution of SPECT. Some PET or functional MRI studies investigating mCPP activation in specific brain structures such as the orbito-frontal cortex and head of the caudate regions are warranted.

In a PET study with ^{15}O, Rauch et al. (1994) used the SPM method. Using a within-group design, the investigators compared neutral and individually tailored OCD-related stimuli in a group of eight patients (two checkers and six cleaners–washers). Omnibus subtraction images demonstrated a statistically significant increase in relative rCBF in the right caudate nucleus, left anterior cingulate cortex, and bilateral orbito-frontal cortex during the OCD symptomatic state versus the resting state; an observed increase in the left thalamus was of borderline statistical significance. Again, the data implicated the orbito-frontal cortex, caudate nucleus, and anterior cingulate cortex in the pathophysiology of OCD.

Another ^{15}O PET study (McGuire, Bench, Marks, Frackowiak, & Dolan, 1994) was performed using SPM technology. This study used a within-group, repeated measures design of 4 patients with washing rituals, who received 12 scans in total. The study demonstrated a positive correlation between symptoms and blood flow in the right inferior frontal gyrus, caudate nucleus, putamen, globus pallidus, and thalamus, and the left hippocampus and posterior cingulate gyrus. There was also a negative correlation in the right superior frontal cortex and temporo-parietal junction.

Cottraux et al. (1996) studied the effect of exposure to intrusive obsessive thoughts on the rCBF of OCD checkers and nonclinical control subjects. Three independent surveys have shown that more than 80% of nonclinical subjects have obsessive thoughts with contents similar to those found in OCD (Freeston, Ladouceur, Thibodeau, & Gagnon, 1991; Rachman & De Silva, 1978; Salkovskis & Harrison, 1984). We refer to these as "normal" obsessions to distinguish them from the obsessive thoughts ("abnormal" obsessions) that occur in people suffering from OCD. "Abnormal" and "normal" intrusive thoughts have been found to differ not in content but in the duration, frequency, habituation, and ease with which they are rejected. Although most individuals experience the same kinds of intrusive thoughts as people with OCD, they habituate quickly and are not compelled to ritualize. This study (Cottraux et al., 1996) compared stimulation of OCD patients with their "abnormal" obsessions and stimulation of control subjects with their "normal obsessions." The dependent variables were the subjective response to stimulation and rCBF in ROIs, whose involvement in OCD had been suggested in previous studies. In order to have a homogeneous group of patients with specific cognitive disturbances, only checkers were included in the study. Our hypothesis was that exposure to abnormal obsessions would modify rCBF in the

ROIs of OCD patients, unlike those of normal controls, whose rCBF would not be modified when provoked with normal obsessions. Thus, a group × condition (neutral vs. obsessive stimulation) interaction was expected in specific structures. Ten nondepressed individuals meeting DSM-III-R criteria for OCD (American Psychiatric Association, 1987) with predominant checking rituals were compared to 10 sex- and age-matched controls. Hemispheric rCBF was measured with PET ($[^{15}O]H_2O$) across four conditions: rest, auditory stimulation with idiosyncratic normal or abnormal obsessions, auditory stimulation with neutral verbal stimuli, and rest again. The order of neutral and obsessive stimulation was randomized. At rest, there was a group effect in the superior temporal gyri: rCBF was higher in OCD subjects than in controls. A higher subjective response to obsessive rather than to neutral stimulation was found in both groups; subjective responses were higher in OCD subjects when obsessive stimulation was presented first. A four-way analysis of variance (ANOVA) for group × stimulation order × hemisphere × condition type (neutral or obsessive stimulation) was performed on stimulation minus rest-normalized rCBF values. Controls had significantly higher rCBF in the thalamus and putamen. A trend toward higher rCBF in OCD was found in the superior temporal regions. When neutral stimulation was presented first, rCBF was higher in the caudate region of controls. Obsessive stimulation produced higher rCBF than neutral stimulation in orbito-frontal regions in both groups. Under obsessive stimulation, superior temporal and orbito-frontal activities were correlated in OCD patients but not in controls.

The data might be interpreted as reflecting a three-stage process with specific features in OCD. First, in resting states, individuals with OCD checking rituals may have basal abnormalities, as reflected by higher rCBF in the superior temporal regions. Second, processing of both obsessive and neutral stimulation increases rCBF in superior temporal regions in OCD patients. This illness-specific effect is coupled with a nonspecific "common frontal worry" effect in OCD subjects and controls or increased activity in the orbito-frontal areas when processing obsessive-like stimulation. Moreover, in OCD, there was a significant correlation of subtracted rCBF values between the superior temporal region, middle orbito-frontal, and inferior orbito-frontal regions when subjects were obsessing. In controls, these correlations were not significant. Third, inhibition of the basal ganglia in OCD may result from temporal and orbito-frontal activation.

Finally, Breiter et al. (1996) used a new technique, functional MRI, to study 10 OCD patients and 5 controls. Despite the small sample size, they confirmed the outcomes of early PET studies and showed activation in the medial orbito-frontal, anterior temporal, anterior cingulate, and insular cortex, as well as caudate, lenticulate, and amygdala in 70% of the patients. There was no activation in any brain regions of the control subjects. To provoke obsessions, either imagined flooding using patients' primary obsessional foci or *in vivo* exposure was administered. Of the 10 individuals studied, 5 patients had contamination obsessions, and 5 had doubting accompanied by checking or sexual obsessions without compulsions.

In summary, activation studies suggest some degree of orbito-frontal-area dysfunction in OCD, as well as involvement of the basal ganglia. Moreover, the

TABLE 7.3. Functional Neuroimaging Studies: Stimulation Studies

Study	Technique	Design	Method of stimulation	Changes observed in local metabolism or rCBF in OCD subjects
Zohar et al. (1989)	SPECT	Within-group	*In vivo* exposure	Decreased rCBF in parieto-occipital regions related to *in vivo* exposure
			Imagined exposure	Increased rCBF in temporal region related to imagined exposure
Hollander et al. (1991)	SPECT	Within-group	*m*CPP	Increased rCBF in frontal lobes
McGuire et al. (1994)	^{15}O PET	Within-group	*In vivo* exposure	Positive correlation between symptoms and blood flow in right inferior frontal gyrus, caudate nucleus, putamen, globus pallidus, thalamus, left hippocampus and posterior cingulate gyrus; negative correlation between symptoms and rCBF in right superior frontal cortex and temporo-parietal junction
Rauch et al. (1994)	^{15}O PET	Within-group	*In vivo* exposure	Increased rCBF in right caudate nucleus, left anterior cingulate cortex, and bilateral orbitofrontal cortex
Hollander et al. (1995)	SPECT	Within-group	*m*CPP	Increase in global cortical perfusion for those who responded to *m*CPP
Cottraux et al. (1996)	^{15}O PET	Between-group, normal controls, factorial design	Content of obsessions presented auditorily	Increased rCBF in superior gyri temporal correlated with increase in orbito-frontal regions in OCD; increased rCBF in orbito-frontal regions in both controls and OCD; decreased rCBF in basal ganglia
Breiter et al. (1996)	Functional MRI	Between-group, normal controls	Imaginal exposure or *in vivo* exposure	Activation in medial orbito-frontal, anterior temporal, anterior cingulate, insular cortex, caudate nucleus, lenticulate, and amygdala

*Note. m*CPP, meta-chlorophenylpiperazine.

two studies with normal control groups (Cottraux et al., 1996; Breiter et al., 1996) suggest that temporal regions might also be implicated in the information processing of obsessive stimuli. The contradictory finding of a relative decrease in rCBF in basal ganglia in OCD reported by Cottraux et al. (1996) might be related to the fact that only checkers were included in this study: Individuals with this symptom profile may have been able to covertly ritualize in response to provocation with obsessional stimuli. Under PET examination, it is impossible for cleaner–washers to ritualize adequately.

Effect of Successful Treatment on Neuroimaging Findings

The third type of imaging investigations has looked at the effects of psychological and pharmacological treatments on neuroimaging outcomes. Seven studies dealing with resting states have been reported in the literature. Thus far, no studies utilizing stimulation methods pre- and posttreatment have been published.

The effects of trazodone hydrochloride treatment were studied by Baxter, Thompson, et al. (1987) in a group of 10 OCD patients, some of whom were being treated with a monoamine oxidase inhibitor (MAOI). Changes in symptoms correlated with changes in local cerebral metabolic rates for glucose, as measured by [18]FDG PET. All those who responded to drug treatment showed a relative increase in glucose metabolism in the heads of the caudate nuclei when compared with the metabolic rate in the ipsilateral hemisphere as a whole.

Subsequent findings from the same group of investigators (Baxter et al., 1992) failed to confirm these findings in a group of OCD patients who participated in a study using [18]FDG PET before and after being treated with either fluoxetine hydrochloride or behavior therapy. The posttreatment ratio of glucose metabolic rate in the right caudate/ipsilateral hemisphere showed a significant decrease compared with pretreatment values in those who responded to both drug and behavior therapy. Percentage change in OCD symptom ratings correlated significantly with change in the right caudate/ipsilateral hemisphere ratio in the drug therapy condition, and there was a trend toward significance for this same correlation with behavior therapy. By lumping together all those who responded to either treatment, right orbital cortex/hemisphere was significantly correlated with ipsilateral caudate/hemisphere and thalamus/hemisphere before treatment but not after. Differences before and after treatment were significant.

Schwartz, Stoessel, Baxter, Martin, and Phelps (1996) studied 9 OCD patients using [18]FDG PET before and after 10 weeks of structured treatment including exposure, response prevention, and cognitive therapy. Results were analyzed both alone and in combination with the results of 9 similar subjects from the Baxter et al. (1992) study. Those who responded to behavior therapy had significant bilateral decreases in caudate glucose metabolic rates, which were greater than those seen in subjects who did not respond to treatment. Before treatment, there were significant correlations in brain activity among the orbital gyri, the head of the caudate nucleus, and the orbital gyri and thalamus on the right. These correlations decreased significantly in those who responded to treatment. This study nicely replicated the Baxter et al. (1992) findings.

Swedo et al. (1992) repeated [18]FDG PET scans in 13 OCD adults from their 1989 study. Ten of these same subjects had received at least 1 year of pharmacotherapy with clomipramine or fluoxetine. On the whole, the patients reported significant improvement on all OCD and anxiety-related measures. PET demonstrated a significant decrease in normalized orbito-frontal regional cerebral glucose metabolism bilaterally. Among the treated patients, the decrease in right orbito-frontal metabolism was directly correlated with two measures of OCD improvement.

Benkelfat et al. (1990) expanded on the Nordhal et al. (1989) study. Eight patients with OCD who had previously been scanned while untreated were scanned again during treatment with clomipramine. Comparisons of local cerebral glucose metabolic rates with [18]FDG PET before and after treatment showed a relative decrease in the orbito-frontal cortex and the left caudate regions, and

TABLE 7.4. Functional Neuroimaging Studies: Effects of Successful Treatment

Study	Technique	Treatment	Design	Posttreatment effects
Baxter et al. (1987)	[18]FDG PET	Trazodone	Within-group	Increased glucose metabolism in heads of the caudate nuclei
Benkelfat et al. (1990)	[18]FDG PET	Clomipramine	Within-group	Decreased glucose metabolism in orbito-frontal cortex and left caudate
				Increased glucose metabolism in basal ganglia and right anterior putamen
Hoehn-Saric et al. (1991)	SPECT	Fluoxetine	Within-group	Decreased hyperfrontality
Baxter et al. (1992)	[18]FDG PET	Fluoxetine or behavior therapy	Within-group	Decreased glucose metabolism in right caudate/ipsilateral hemisphere in those that responded to treatment
Swedo et al. (1992)	[18]FDG PET	Clomipramine or fluoxetine	Within-group	Decrease in normalized orbito-frontal regional cerebral glucose metabolism bilaterally
Perani et al. (1995)	[18]FDG PET	SSRI	Between-group	Decreased glucose metabolism in thalamus, cingulate cortex, and putamen–pallidum
Schwartz, Stoessel, Baxter, Martin, & Phelps (1996)	[18]FDG PET	Behavior therapy	Within-group	Decreased glucose metabolism in caudate nucleus bilaterally

Note. SSRI, selective serotonin reuptake inhibitor.

an increase in other areas including the basal ganglia and the right anterior puta-men. When comparing responders to nonresponders, significant decreases in metabolism were reported in the left caudate of responders only. This is dis-crepant with the right caudate changes observed in Baxter, Thompson, et al. (1987) and Baxter et al. (1992).

Hoehn-Saric, Pearlson, Harris, Machlin, and Camargo (1991b) found a de-crease in hyperfrontality measured using SPECT in 6 previously drug-free OCD patients treated with fluoxetine. This was accompanied by a decrease in the rated symptomatology. Finally, Perani et al. (1995) found higher glucose metabolism in the thalamus, cingulate cortex, and putamen/pallidum with PET [18]FDG in 11 OCD subjects compared with 15 controls. This hypermetabolism was reduced by various SSRI treatments and was correlated with symptomatic improvement.

In summary, using PET, hypermetabolism in the frontal lobes and basal ganglia has been identified as a state marker that is reversible with successful pharmacological or behavioral treatment. Serotonergic antidepressants de-creased metabolism both in the orbito-frontal regions and the basal ganglia in three independent PET [18]FDG studies (Baxter et al., 1992; Benkelfat et al., 1990; Perani et al., 1995). Decreased hyperfrontality due to SSRI treatment was con-firmed by one SPECT study (Hoehn-Saric, Pearlson, Harris, Machlin, et al., 1991b). One discrepant study (Baxter, Thompson, et al., 1987) reported an in-crease of caudate metabolic activity with Trazodone.

SYNTHESIS OF NEUROANATOMICAL FINDINGS

The most consistent findings across all studies have been hyperfrontality during resting or provoked states and changes in frontal lobe activity (typically decreased hyperfrontality) following treatment. Nineteen of the 27, or 70%, of the studies showed these results. In addition, two case studies using PET reported untoward side effects of fluoxetine (Hoehn-Saric, Pearlson, Harris, Cox, et al., 1991a) and fluvoxamine (George & Trimble, 1992), respectively, which triggered clinical frontal syndrome with hypofrontality. Of note, there were three stimulation stud-ies using PET (Cottraux et al., 1996; McGuire et al., 1994; Rauch et al., 1994) and one using functional MRI (Breiter et al., 1996) that revealed the common finding of orbito-frontal hyperactivity resulting from provocation of either "ab-normal" or "normal" obsessions.

In contrast, basal ganglia involvement was only found in 15 of the 26 stud-ies (57%). Moreover, the hemisphere involved (i.e., left, right, bilateral), the direc-tion of change following treatment, and the specific between-group differences (hyper- or hypofunctioning) varied across studies.

The observation that behavior therapy is as effective as SSRIs, both clinical-ly and at a neuroanatomical level, suggests that the local brain hyperactivity state found in neuroimaging studies might mirror the struggle between compulsions and the attempt to control them. Regardless, neuropharmacological studies on orbito-frontal cortex and basal ganglia are warranted, as serotonin regulation is involved in the modulation of these regions. Insel (1992) demonstrated that the brain regions showing the greatest binding with the SSRI Citalopram are the ventro-medial caudate and nucleus accumbens. Some studies have shown that SSRIs also act selectively on orbito-frontal cortex in animals (Mansari, Bouchard, & Blier, 1995).

EXISTING NEUROANATOMICAL MODELS OF OCD

Baxter, Schwartz, Guze, Bergman, and Szuba (1990) proposed a tentative model of OCD. They suggested that the caudate nucleus serves as a mediator between the orbito-frontal cortex, the thalamus, and obsessive–compulsive behaviors. Obsessive impulses and thoughts are processed by the striatum, the left orbital-fronto cortex, and the cingulate gyri. The striatum normally may suppress thoughts, sensations, and actions without conscious intervention of cortical structures. In OCD, a defect in frontal inhibition would result in a tendency for perseveration of disturbing thoughts when initiated by worries in the frontal cortex. Rituals are then initiated through conscious orbital mechanisms to cope with the worry. In this model, the function of the caudate might be viewed as similar to "repression" and that of the orbital gyri as a "conscious orchestrator" of coping mechanisms. Strong repression by way of the caudate nucleus, and/or strong magical belief (orbito-frontal hyperactivity) would result in the reduction of anxiety. Although the theory has some Freudian connotations, Baxter et al. (1990) insist that they do not pay allegiance to a psychoanalytic causal model.

More recently Brody and Saxena (1996) proposed a more sophisticated pathophysiological model. They hypothesized that two pathways may be involved in OCD: a direct pathway projecting from the cortex to the striatum, then on to the globus pallidus and thalamus before returning to the cortex. A second indirect pathway projects from the cortex to striatum, then from the striatum via the external segment of the globus pallidus to the subthalamic nucleus before returning to the globus pallidus, the thalamus, and the cortex. The direct pathway would provide a positive feedback loop and the indirect pathway a negative one. The role of the indirect pathway would be to break up the repetitive behaviors driven by the direct pathway. OCD may result from an imbalance between these two pathways, due to chemical mechanisms. Alterations in the balance of neuromediators, particularly serotonin, dopamine, and acetylcholine, may modify these projections.

TOWARD A NEW MODEL: "PERCEIVED IMPULSIVITY" AND "COMPENSATORY COMPULSIVITY"

Presentation of the Model

This model (Cottraux, 1995) attempts to synthesize the recent advances in information processing studies, cognitive-behavioral therapy, pharmacology, and the neuroimaging studies reviewed earlier. This model also integrates some aspects of Baxter et al.'s model (1990). It should be noted that this model is highly speculative and may apply best to a subset of OCD patients, those who check excessively.

To sum up the model, OCD derives both from biological vulnerability and environmental influences. There may be innate biological vulnerability for increased impulsivity that is compensated for with compulsive behavior. The interaction between the social environment and impulsivity shapes the patient's responsibility–culpability cognitive schemas. The patient believes that he or she is potentially dangerous to others. This negative self-appraisal is termed "perceived impulsivity." Similarly, patients perceive themselves as potentially antisocial and develop a cognitive-behavioral system (rituals) that is intended to prevent the danger they see themselves inflicting on others. Doubt and other cognitive factors such as visual memory deficits and/or faulty monitoring of actions result in rituals. In this model, the orbito-frontal hyperactivity reported through the use of PET scans may be a state marker that reflects the obsessive struggle to control impulsivity. Figure 7.2 depicts the different levels of the model.

The Biological Level of "Perceived Impulsivity"

Serotonin and dopamine imbalances play a role in this dysfunction. Elevations observed in rCBF and metabolism in the orbito-frontal, caudate, and temporal regions using PET, SPECT, or functional MRI reflect the abnormal information processing resulting from the biological trait.

Further support for this hypothesized impulsivity trait comes from a study conducted by the author investigating the effect of SSRIs and behavior therapy in OCD. Cottraux et al. (1990) randomly assigned 60 nondepressed OCD patients to three treatment groups: fluvoxamine with antiexposure instructions (F), fluvoxamine combined with exposure (Fe), and placebo with exposure (Pe) for a 24-week period. Fluvoxamine and exposure were synergistic in the short term, and exposure reduced subsequent antidepressant use in the year following inital medication discontinuation (Cottraux, Mollard, Bouvard, & Marks, 1993). Data from the Minnesota Multiphasic Personality Inventory (MMPI) at posttest (Cottraux & Mollard, 1992) revealed an interesting finding in favor of the combined condition. When the three groups were compared at posttest time, the only significant difference was a greater reduction in scores on the psychopathic deviation (Pd) item in the Fe condition, compared to the Pe condition and the F condition which fell in between the two (see Figure 7.3).

The Pd scale on the MMPI reflects a disregard for social norms, incapacity to learn through experience, and impulsivity. Previous studies have reported that scores on hostility scales are similar for those with OCD and those with antisocial personalities (Hoehn-Saric & Barksdale, 1983; Marks, 1965). As there is no comorbidity between antisocial personality and OCD (Baer & Jenike, 1990), this suggests that OCD patients may have a distorted perception of themselves as

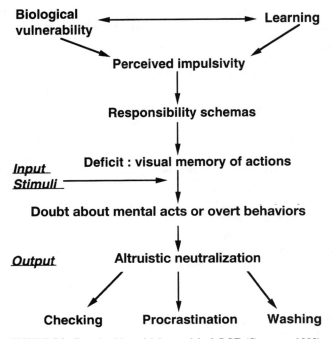

FIGURE 7.2. Perceived impulsivity model of OCD (Cottraux, 1995).

dangerous or antisocial. This negative self-appraisal may be related to perceived impulsivity (which triggers compulsive behaviors). The patient believes that he or she is unable to resist images, thoughts, or urges with content involving common antisocial impulses—as there is no difference in content between normal and abnormal obsessions (Rachman & De Silva, 1978). This belief triggers a struggle against cognitive intrusions designed to control possible behaviors that may harm others. Compulsions that have an altruistic function may be the product of doubt related to uncertainty about self-control.

The correlation between change in the MMPI Pd scale results, and responses to treatment (behavioral or pharmacological) suggest a role for both the environment and specific neuromediator imbalance. The frontal lobe, which is activated during the obsessive struggle (as demonstrated by PET scan studies), may be where modulation of perceived impulsivity occurs. As suggested by Ridley (1994), the production of maladaptive and repetitive behaviors is frequent in higher animals and humans. The environment can affect the way in which the nervous system develops, and brain plasticity may result in synapse stabilization. The frontal lobes exert a modulating effect on the initiation of motor activity by the basal ganglia, on the facilitation of voluntary behaviors, and on the neural mechanisms that control perception, memory, and thinking. Failures in these three functions could result in excessive and repetitive motor activity, stimulus-

MMPI: pre-test

No between-group difference

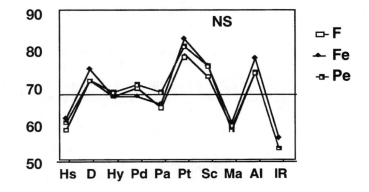

MMPI: post-test

Fluvoxamine + Exposure > Placebo + Exposure

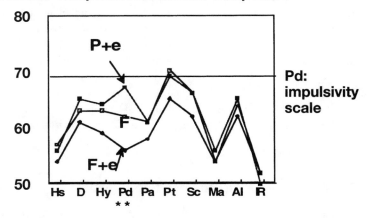

FIGURE 7.3. Effects of fluvoxamine and exposure on impulsivity. *Groups:* F, fluvoxamine + antiexposure instructions; Fe, fluvoxamine + exposure; Pe, placebo + exposure. *MMPI subscales:* Hs, hypochondriasis, D, depression, Hy, hysteria, Pd, psychopathic deviation, Pa, paranoia, Pt, psychasthenia, Sc, schizophrenia, Ma, mania, AI, anxiety index, IR, internalization ratio; a score above 70 on any MMPI scale is considered to be clinically significant.

bound behaviors, and decreases in volitional and creative behaviors, all of which are found in OCD.

The Neuropsychological Level of Perceived Impulsivity: Doubt and Memory

Impairment in attention and short-term visual memory has been shown in studies of individuals from mixed OCD subtypes (Christensen, Won Kim, Dysken, & Hoover, 1992; Dirson, Bouvard, Cottraux, & Martin, 1995; Rosen, Hollander, Stannick, & Liebowitz, 1988; Savage et al., 1996; Zielinski, Taylor, & Juzwin, 1991) as well as studies specifically investigating patients who check excessively. (Sher, Frost, Kushner, Crews, & Alexander, 1989; Sher, Frost, & Otto, 1983; Sher, Mann, & Frost, 1984). In addition, Bouvard and Cottraux (1997) found that 13 nondepressed OCD checkers had difficulties recalling details of meaningful verbal sequences and impaired immediate visual reproduction compared to 13 matched controls. However, several studies have failed to show actual deficits in memory, suggesting instead that checkers lack confidence in their ability to remember (e.g., Constans, Foa, Franklin, & Mathews, 1995; MacDonald, Antony, MacLeod, & Richter, 1997; MacNally & Kohlbeck, 1993). In summary, several studies appear to support a deficit in visual short- and long-term memory in OCD. The relationship of this deficit to doubts about memory ability versus actual impairment in monitoring actions remains to be resolved. Regardless, memory impairment might be a link between a biological perceived-impulsivity trait and doubt about the actual consequences of impulsivity. Of note are the two stimulation studies (one with MRI and one with PET) (Breiter et al., 1996; Cottraux et al., 1996) that pointed out temporal lobe abnormalities (increased rCBF) in OCD subjects as compared with controls. This area is used in the processing of auditory information and memory.

From Perceived Impulsivity to Cognitive Schemas

The interaction between the social and familial environment and perceived impulsivity may shape responsibility schemas. A range from normal altruistic beliefs to almost delusional beliefs regarding the impact of one's behavior on others can be found in OCD, each point on the continuum reflected by pseudorational statements stemming from the familial and/or social environment. Examples may include the following:

1. Normal altruistic beliefs: "People should not cause harm to others."
2. Checking: "Checking prevents harm."
3. Procrastination: "Doing nothing means avoidance of danger."
4. Washing: "Prevent contamination of others."
5. Thought–action fusion: "Control the thoughts that may kill others."

6. Magical thinking: "Some special thought may kill—intention is as bad as a deed."
7. Schizotypal belief: "Magical forces are running the world."

Perceived impulsivity correponds to a specific cognitive set. That the patient believes he or she is dangerous might be related to thought–action fusion (Shafran, Thonardson, & Rachman, 1996).

Effective Treatments and Perceived Impulsivity

Three effective treatments may modify perceived impulsivity based on their underlying assumptions. First, biological treatments such as medication may modify the biological trait (and emotional state) leading to perceived impulsivity. Second, exposure and response prevention may lead to increased self-control and reality-testing capabilities. Finally, cognitive therapy may decrease the illusion or delusion of magical control over people or events. The combination of these three treatment methods may yield the best outcomes.

CONCLUSION

This chapter reviewed the tremendous advances over the past decade in understanding the neural basis of OCD. Many issues remain to be resolved, but we have good reasons to believe that they will be clarified in the near future. First, there is a lack of convergent validity across studies. This may be due to variability in the techniques used across neuroimaging studies. Second, studies tend not to differentiate among the various OCD subtypes, despite evidence that OCD is a heterogeneous condition. The delineation of subgroups based on clinical subtypes, genetics, and psychological/psychobiological dimensions will be critical in understanding the results of neuropharmacological, behavioral, cognitive, and functional imaging studies in the future. Larger, collaborative studies with standard methodologies may help to improve our understanding regarding the etiology of OCD and thereby improve available treatments.

REFERENCES

Adams, B. L., Warneke, L. B., McEwan, A. J., & Fraser, B. A. (1993). Single photon emission computerized tomography in obsessive compulsive disorder: A preliminary study. *Journal of Psychiatry and Neurosciences, 18,* 109–112.

American Psychiatric Association. (1987). *Diagnostic and statistical manual of mental disorders* (3rd ed., rev.). Washington, DC: Author.

Andreasen, N. C., O'Leary, D., Cidzadlo, T., Arndt, S., Rezai, K., Watkins, L., Boles, L. L., Ponto, L. L., & Hichwa, R. D. (1995). Remembering the past: Two facets of episodic memory explored with positron emission tomography. *American Journal of Psychiatry, 152,* 1576–1585.

Aylard, E. H., Gordon, J. H., Hoehn-Saric, R., Barta, P. E., Machlin, S. R., & Pearlson, G. D. (1996). Normal caudate nucleus in obsessive–compulsive disorder assessed by quantitative neuroimaging. *Archives of General Psychiatry, 53,* 577–584.

Baer, L., & Jenike, M. A. (1990). Personality disorders in obsessive–compulsive disorder. In M. A. Jenike, L. Baer, & W. E. Minichiello (Eds.), *Obsessive–compulsive disorder: Theory and management* (pp. 76–88). Chicago: Year Book Medical Publishers.

Baxter, L., Phelps, M., Mazziota, J., Guze, B., Schwartz, J., & Selin, C. (1987a). Local cerebral glucose metabolic rates in obsessive–compulsive disorder. *Archives of General Psychiatry, 44,* 211–218.

Baxter, L., Schwartz, J., Bergman, K., Szuba, M., Guze, B., Mazziota, J., Alazraki, A., Selin, C., Huan-Kwang, F., Munford, P., & Phelps, M. (1992). Caudate glucose metabolic rate changes with both drug and behavior therapy for obsessive–compulsive disorder. *Archives of General Psychiatry, 49,* 681–689.

Baxter, L., Schwartz, J., Guze, B., Bergman, K., & Szuba, M. P. (1990). Neuroimaging in obsessive–compulsive disorder: Seeking the mediating anatomy. In M. A. Jenike, L. Baer, & W. E. Minichiello (Eds.), *Obsessive–compulsive disorder: Theory and management* (pp. 167–188). Chicago: Year Book Medical Publishers.

Baxter, L., Schwartz, J., Mazziotta, J., Phelps, M., Pahl, J., Guze, B., & Fairbanks, L. (1988). Cerebral glucose metabolic rates in non-depressed obsessive–compulsives. *American Journal of Psychiatry, 145,* 1560–1563.

Baxter, L. R., Thompson, J. M., Schwartz, J. M., Guze, B. H., Phelps, M. E., Mazziotta, J. C., Selin, C. E., & Moss, L. (1987b). Trazodone treatment response in obsessive–compulsive disorder-correlated with shifts in glucose metabolism in the caudate nuclei. *Psychopathology, 20*(Suppl. 1), 114–122.

Behar, D., Rapoport, J. L., & Berg, C. J. (1984). Computerized tomography and neuropsychological test measures in adolescents with obsessive compulsive disorder. *American Journal of Psychiatry, 141,* 363–368.

Benkelfat, C., Nordhal, T., Semple, W., King, C., Murphy, D., & Cohen, R. (1990). Local cerebral glucose metabolic rates in obsessive–compulsive disorder. *Archives of General Psychiatry, 47,* 840–848.

Bouvard, M., & Cottraux, J. (1997). Etude comparative chez le sujet normal et le sujet obsessif–compulsif des pensées intrusives et de la mémoire. [A comparative study of intrusive thoughts and memory in normal subjects and obsessive–compulsive patients]. *L'Encéphale, 23,* 175–179.

Breiter, H. C., Tuach, S. L., Kwong, K. K, Baker, J. R, Weisskoff, R. M., Kennedy, D. M., Kendrick, A. D., Davis, T. L., Jiang, A., Cohen, M. S., Stern, C. S., Belliveau, J. W., Baer, L., O'Sullivan, R. L., Savage, C. R., Jenike, M. A., & Rosen, B. R. (1996). Functional magnetic resonance imaging of symptom provocation in obsessive–compulsive disorder. *Archives of General Psychiatry, 53,* 595–606.

Brody, A. L., & Saxena, S. (1996). Brain imaging in obsessive–compulsive disorder: Evidence for the involvement of frontal-subcortical circuitery in the mediation of symptomatology. *CNS-Spectrums, 1,* 27–41.

Calabrese, G., Colombo, C., Bonfanti, A., Scotti, G., & Scarone, S. (1993). Caudate nucleus abnormalities in obsessive–compulsive disorder: Measurement of MRI signal intensity. *Psychiatry Research: Neuroimaging, 50,* 89–123.

Chiocca, A. E., & Martuza, R. L. (1990). Neurosurgical therapy of obsessive–compulsive disorder. In M. A. Jenike, L. Baer, & W. E. Minichiello (Eds.), *Obsessive–compulsive disorder: Theory and management* (pp. 283–294). Chicago: Year Book Medical Publishers.

Christensen, K. J., Won Kim, S., Dysken, W., & Hoover, K. M. (1992). Neuropsychological performance in obsessive compulsive disorder. *Biological Psychiatry, 31,* 4–18.

Constans, J. I., Foa, E. B., Franklin, M. E., & Mathews, A. (1995). Memory for actual and imagined events in OC checkers. *Behaviour Research and Therapy, 33,* 665–671.

Cottraux, J. (1995). Les modèles comportementaux et cognitifs des troubles anxieux. *Confrontations Psychiatriques, 36,* 231–251.

Cottraux, J., Gérard, D., Cinotti, L., Froment, J. C., Deiber, M. P., Le Bars, D., Galy, G., Millet, P., Labb,, C., Lavenne, F., Bouvard, M., & Mauguière, F. (1996). A controlled PET scan study of neutral and obsessive auditory stimulations in obsessive–compulsive disorder. *Psychiatry Research, 60,* 101–112.

Cottraux, J., & Mollard, E. (1992). La place de la thérapie comportementale et des antidépresseurs dans le traitement des obsessions–compulsions. *Journal de Thérapie Comportementale et Cognitive, 2,* 14–17.

Cottraux, J., Mollard, E., Bouvard, M., & Marks, I. (1993). One year follow up after exposure and/or fluvoxamine in depressed obsessive–compulsive disorder. *Psychiatry Research, 49,* 63–75.

Cottraux, J., Mollard, E., Bouvard, M., Marks, I., Sluys, M., Nury, A. M., Douge, R., & Cialdella, P. (1990). A controlled study of fluvoxamine and exposure in obsessive–compulsive disorder. *International Clinical Psychopharmacology, 5,* 17–20.

Dirson, S., Bouvard, M., Cottraux, J., & Martin, R. (1995). Visual memory impairment in patients with obsessive–compulsive disorder: A controlled study. *Psychotherapy and Psychosomatics, 63,* 22–31.

Edmonstone, Y., Austin, M. P., Prentice, N., Dougall, N., Freeman, C. P., Ebmeier, K. P., & Goodwin, G. M. (1994). Uptake of [99mTc]exametazime shown by single photon emission computerized tomography in obsessive–compulsive disorder compared with major depression and normal controls. *Acta Psychiatrica Scandinavica, 90,* 298–303.

Freeston, M. H., Ladouceur, R., Thibodeau, H., & Gagnon, F. (1991). Cognitive intrusions in non-clinical populations: I-Response style subjective experience and appraisal. *Behaviour Research and Therapy, 29,* 585–597.

Friston, K., Frith, C., Liddle, P., & Frackowiack, R. (1991). Comparing functional (PET) images: The assessment of significant change. *Journal of Cerebral Blood Flow and Metabolism, 11,* 690–699.

Garber, H. J., Ananth, J. V., Chiu, L. C., Griswold, V. J., & Oldendorf, W. H. (1989). Nuclear magnetic resonance study of obsessive–compulsive disorder. *American Journal of Psychiatry, 146,* 1001–1005.

George, M., & Trimble, M. (1992). A fluvoxamine induced frontal lobe syndrome in a patient with comorbid Gilles de laTourette's syndrome and obsessive–compulsive disorder. *Journal of Clinical Psychiatry, 53,* 379–380.

Harris, G. J., Hoehn-Saric, R., Lewis, R., Pearlson, R. L., & Streeter, C. (1994). Mapping SPECT cerebral perfusion abnormalities in obsessive–compulsive disorder. *Human Brain Mapping, 2,* 237–248.

Hoehn-Saric, R., & Barksdale, V. (1983). Impulsiveness in obsessive–compulsive disorder. *British Journal of Psychiatry, 143,* 177–182.

Hoehn-Saric, R., Pearlson, G., Harris, G., Cox, C., Machlin, S., & Camargo, E. (1991a). A fluoxetine-induced frontal lobe syndrome in an obsessive–compulsive patient. *Journal of Clinical Psychiatry, 52,* 131–133.

Hoehn-Saric, R., Pearlson, G., Harris, G., Machlin, S., & Camargo, E. (1991b). Effects of fluoxetine on regional cerebral blood flow in obsessive–compulsive patients. *American Journal of Psychiatry, 148,* 1243–1245.

Hollander, E., De Caria, C., Saoud, J., Trungold, S., Stein, D., Liebowitz, M., & Prohovnik, I. (1991). m-CPP activated regional cerebral blood flow in obsessive–compulsive disorder. *Biological Psychiatry, 29*, 170A.

Hollander, E., Prohovnik, I., & Stein, D. J. (1995). Increased cerebral blood flow during
m-CPP exacerbation of obsessive–compulsive disorder. *Journal of Neuropsychiatry and
Clinical Neurosciences, 7*, 485–490.

Insel, T. (1992). Toward a neuroanatomy of obsessive–compulsive disorder. *Archives of General Psychiatry, 49*, 739–744.

Insel, T., Donnelly, E., Lalakea, M., Alterman, S., & Murphy, D. (1983). Neurological
studies of patients with obsessive–compulsive disorder. *Biological Psychiatry, 18*,
742–751.

Jenike, M. A., Breiter, H. C., Baer, L., Kennedy, D. N., Savage, C. A., Olivares, M. J.,
O'Sullivan, R. L., Shera, D. M., Rauch, S. L., Keuthen, N., Rosen, B. L., Caviness,
V. S., & Filipek, P. (1996). Cerebral structural abnormalities in obsessive–compulsive
disorder. *Archives of General Psychiatry, 53*, 625–632.

Kellner, C. H., Joller, R. R., Holgate, R. C., Austin, L., Lidyard, R. B., Laraia, M., & Ballenger, J. C. (1991). Brain MRI in obsessive compulsive disorder. *Psychiatry Research,
36*, 45–49.

Kiessling, L. S., Marcotte, A. C., & Culpepper, L. (1994). Antineural antibodies: Tics and
obsessive–compulsive symptoms. *Journal of Developmental and Behavioral Pediatrics, 15*,
421–425.

Laplane, D., Levasseur, M., Pillon, B., Dubois, B., Baulac, M., Mazoyer, B., Tran Dinh, S.,
Sette, G., Danze, F., & Baron, J. C. (1989). Obsessive–compulsive and other behavioural changes with bilateral basal ganglia lesions. *Brain, 112*, 699–725.

Lucey, J. V., Costa, D. C., Blanes, T., Busatto, G. F., Pilowsky, L. S., Takei, N., Marks, I. M.,
Ell, P. J., & Kerwin, R. W. (1995). Regional cerebral blood flow in obsessive–compulsive disordered patients at rest: Differential correlates with obsessive–compulsive and
anxious–avoidant dimensions. *British Journal of Psychiatry, 167*, 629–634.

Luxenberg, J., Swedo, S., Flament, M., Friedland, R., Rapoport, J., & Rapoport, S.
(1988). Neuroanatomical abnormalities in obsessive–compulsive disorder detected
with quantitative X-Ray computed tomography. *American Journal of Psychiatry, 145*,
1089–1093.

MacDonald, P., Antony, M. M., MacLeod, C., & Richter, M. A. (1997). Memory and confidence in memory judgments among individuals with obsessive compulsive disorder
and non-clinical controls. *Behaviour Research and Therapy, 35*, 497–505.

Machlin, S., Harris, G., Pearlson, G., Hoehn-Saric, R., Jeffery, P., & Camargo, E. (1991).
Elevated medial-frontal cerebral blood flow in obsessive–compulsive patients: A
SPECT study. *American Journal of Psychiatry, 148*, 1240–1242.

MacNally, R. J., & Kohlbeck, P. A. (1993). Reality monitoring in obsessive compulsive disorder. *Behaviour Research and Therapy, 31*, 249–253.

Mansari, M. E., Bouchard, C., & Blier, P. (1995). Alteration of serotonin release in the
guinea pig orbito-frontal cortex by selective serotonin reuptake inhibitors. *Neuropsychopharmacology, 13*, 117–127.

Marks, I. M. (1965). *Patterns of meaning in psychiatric patients*. London: Oxford University
Press.

Marks, I. M. (1987). *Fears, phobias and rituals: Panic, anxiety, and their disorders*. Oxford, UK:
Oxford University Press.

Martinot, J. L., Allilaire, J. F., Mazoyer, B., Hantouche, E., Huret, J. D., Legaut-Demare,
F., Deslauriers, A., Hardy, P., Pappata, S., Baron, J. C., & Syrota, A. (1990). Obses-

sive–compulsive disorder: A clinical, neuropsychological and positron emission to-mography study. *Acta Psychiatrica Scandinavica, 82,* 233–242.

McGuire, P. K., Bench, C. D., Marks, I. M., Frackowiak, R. S. J., & Dolan, R. J. (1994). Graded activation of symptoms in obsessive compulsive disorder. *British Journal of Psychiatry, 164,* 459–468.

Mindus, P., Nyman, H., Mogard, J., Meyerson, B., & Ericson, K. (1989). Orbital and cau-date glucose metabolism studied by positron emission tomography (PET) in patients undergoing capsulotomy for obsessive compulsive disorder. In M. Jenike & M. Ash-berg (Eds.), *Understanding obsessive compulsive disorder (OCD)* (pp. 52–57). Toronto: Hogrefe & Huber.

Nordahl, T., Benkelfat, C., Semple, W., Gross, M., King, A., & Cohen, M. (1989). Cere-bral glucose metabolic rates in obsessive compulsive disorder. *Neuropsychopharmacology, 2,* 1–7.

Pauls, D. L., Asobrock, J. P., Goodman, W., Rasmussen, S., & Leckman, J. F. (1995). A fam-ily study of obsessive–compulsive disorder. *American Journal of Psychiatry, 152,* 76–84.

Pénisson-Besnier, I., Le Gall, D., & Dubas, F. (1992). Comportement compulsif d'allure obsessionnelle (arithmomanie): Atrophie des noyaux caudés. *Revue Neurologique, 148,* 262–267.

Perani, D., Colombo, C., Bressi, A., Bonfanti, A., Grassi, F., Scarone, S., Bellodi, L., Smeraldi, E., & Fazio, F. (1995). ^{18}FDG PET in obsesssive–compulsive disorder: A clinical-metabolic correlation study after treatment. *British Journal of Psychiatry, 166,* 244–250.

Rachman, S., & de Silva, P. (1978). Abnormal and normal obsessions. *Behaviour Research and Therapy, 16,* 233–248.

Rauch, S., Jenike, M., Alpert, N., Baer, L., Breiter, H., Savage, C., & Fischman, A. (1994). Regional cerebral blood flow measured during symptom provocation in obsessive–compulsive disorder using oxygen-15 labeled carbon-dioxide and positron emission tomography. *Archives of General Psychiatry, 51,* 62–70.

Ridley, R. M. (1994). The psychology of perserverative and stereotyped behaviour. *Progress in Neurobiology, 44,* 221–231.

Robinson, D., Wu, H., Munne, R. A., Ashtari, M., Alvir, J. M. A., Lerner, G., Koreen, A., Cole, K., & Bogerts, B. (1995). Reduced caudate nucleus volume in obsessive–com-pulsive disorder. *Archives of General Psychiatry, 52,* 393–398.

Rosen, W., Hollander, E., Stannick, V., & Liebowitz, M. R. (1988). Task performance variables in obsessive–compulsive disorder. *Journal of Clinical and Experimental Neuropsy-chology, 10,* 73.

Rubin, R. T., Villanueva-Meyer, J., Ananth, J., Trajmar, P. G., & Mena, I. (1992). Region-al Xenon-133 cerebral blood flow and technetium [^{99m}]HMPAO uptake in unmed-icated patients with obsessive compulsive disorder and matched normal control sub-jects. *Archives of General Psychiatry, 49,* 695–702.

Salkovskis, P., & Harrison, J. (1984). Abnormal and normal obsessions: A replication. *Be-haviour Research and Therapy, 22,* 549–552.

Savage, C. R., Keuthen, N. J., Jenike, M. A., Brown, H. D., Baer, L., Kendrick, A., Miguel, E. C., Rauch, S. L., & Albert, M. S. (1996). Recall and recognition memory in obsessive compulsive disorder. *Journal of Neuropsychiatry and Clinical Neurosciences, 8,* 99–103.

Sawle, G., Hymas, N., Lees, A., & Frackowiak, R. (1991). Obsessional slowness: Function-al studies with positron emission tomography. *Brain, 114,* 2191–2202.

Scarone, S., Colombo, C., Livian, S., Abbruzese, M., Ronchi, P., Locaelli, M., Scoti, G., &

Smeraldi, E. (1992). Increased right caudate nucleus size in obessive–compulsive disorder: Detection with magnetic resonance imaging. *Psychiatry Research, 45,* 115–121.

Schwartz, J. M., Stoessel, P. W., Baxter, L. R., Martin, K. M., & Phelps, M. E. (1996). Systematic changes in cerebral glucose metabolic rate after successful behavior modification treatment of obsessive–compulsive disorder. *Archives of General Psychiatry, 53,* 109–113.

Shafran, R., Thonardson, D. S., & Rachman, S. (1996). Thought–action fusion in obsessive–compulsive disorder. *Journal of Anxiety Disorders, 10,* 379–391.

Sher, K. J., Frost, R. O., Kushner, M., Crews, T. M., Alexander, J. E. (1989). Memory deficits in compulsive checkers: Replication and extension in a clinical sample. *Behaviour Research and Therapy, 27,* 65–69.

Sher, K. J., Frost, R. O., & Otto, R. (1983). Cognitive deficits in compulsive checkers: An exploratory study. *Behaviour Research and Therapy, 21,* 357–363.

Sher, K. J., Mann, B., & Frost, R. (1984). Cognitive dysfunction in compulsive checkers: Further explorations. *Behaviour Research and Therapy, 22,* 493–502.

Stein, D. J., Coetzer, R., Lee, M., Davids, B., & Bouwer, C. (1997). Magnetic resonance brain imaging in women with obsessive–compulsive disorder and trichotillomania. *Psychiatry Research Neuroimaging, 74,* 177–182.

Stein, D., Hollander, E., Chan, S., De Caria, C. M., Hilal, S., Liebowitz, M. R., & Klein, D. (1993). Computed neurology and enurological soft signs in obsessive–compulsive disorder. *Psychiatry Research: Neuroimaging, 50,* 143–150.

Swedo, S. E., Pietrini, P., Leonard, H. L., Schapiro, M. B., Rettew, D. C., Goldberger, E. L., Rapoport, S. I., Rapoport, J. L., & Grady, C. L. (1992). Cerebral glucose metabolism in childhood-onset obsessive–compulsive disorder: Revisualization during pharmacotherapy. *Archives of General Psychiatry, 49,* 690–694.

Swedo, S. E., Rapoport, J. L., Cheslow, D. L., Leonard, H. L., Ayoub, E. M., Hosier, D. M., & Wald, E. R. (1989a). High prevalence of obsessive–compulsive symptoms in patients with Sydenham's chorea. *American Journal of Psychiatry, 146,* 246–249.

Swedo, S. E., Schapiro, M., Grady, C., Cheslow, D., Leonard, H., Kumar, A., Friedland, R., Rapoport, S., & Rapoport, J. (1989b). Cerebral glucose metabolism in childhood-onset obsessive–compulsive disorder. *Archives of General Psychiatry, 46,* 518–523.

Talairach, J., & Tournoux, P. (1988). *Co-planar stereotactic atlas of the human brain.* New York: Thieme.

Trillet, M., Croisile, B., Tourniaire, D., & Schott, B. (1990). Perturbation de l'activité motrice volontaire et lésions des noyaux caudés. *Revue Neurologique, 5,* 338–344.

Weilburg, J., Mesulam, M., Weintraub, S., Buonanno, F., Jenike, M., & Stakes, J. (1989) Focal striatal abnormalities in a patient with obsessive–compulsive disorder. *Archives of Neurology, 46,* 233–235.

Zielenski, C. M., Taylor, M. A., & Juzwin, K. R. (1991). Neuropsychological deficits in obsessive compulsive disorder. *Neuropsychiatry, Neuropsychology and Behavioural Neurology, 4,* 110–126.

Zohar, J., Insel, T., Foa, E., Steketee, G., Berman, K., Weinberger, D., Kozak, M., & Cohen, R. (1989). Physiological and psychological changes during in vivo exposure and imaginal flooding of obsessive compulsive disorder patients. *Archives of General Psychiatry, 46,* 505–510.

Chapter 8

GENETICS OF OBSESSIVE–COMPULSIVE DISORDER

Elizabeth A. Billett
Margaret A. Richter
James L. Kennedy

Over the years, many clinicians have made the observation that obsessive–compulsive disorder (OCD) tends to be familial. Today, there is growing acceptance in the literature that, indeed, many psychiatric diseases are likely to have a strong genetic component (Ashall, 1994; Crowe, 1993; Pato, Pato, & Kennedy, 1993). This acceptance came about not just from clinicians' personal experiences, but from well-designed family, twin, and adoption studies that provided convincing evidence for the role of heritable factors in psychiatric illness. Building on this base, researchers are now using molecular genetic technology to determine the precise genes involved. Molecular genetic techniques have been used extensively over the past 10 years to further our understanding of bipolar affective disorder, schizophrenia, familial Alzheimer's disease, and Tourette's syndrome. The successful identification of several genes involved in Alzheimer's disease has proven that molecular strategies are powerful tools in our quest to comprehend neuropsychiatric illness.

Despite extensive interest in genetic research in psychiatry, to date, little effort has been focused on the genetics of OCD. There is, however, strong evidence for a genetic diathesis in the disorder. Several family and twin studies have been performed over the better part of this century, and on the whole, they support a role for genetic factors in OCD. In addition, segregation studies have shown that the pattern of inheritance in OCD is consistent with a single, major gene. Based on these foundations, molecular genetic efforts have begun at the DNA level, directed at finding the genes responsible for OCD. Thus far, these efforts have been preliminary; only a few candidate genes have been evaluated as yet, but the work has just begun.

This chapter discusses the family and twin studies that have been performed in OCD, and explains how the results of these studies provide evidence that OCD is familial. The molecular genetic strategies available for the study of OCD are outlined. Many current techniques depend on the selection of appropriate candidate genes. These are specific genes that are investigated based on the existence of a biological rationale supporting their involvement in the illness. Thus, biological theories that attempt to explain the etiology of OCD are important in OCD genetics. These biological theories are therefore discussed briefly in this chapter (see other chapters in this volume for more detailed discussions), and the candidate genes currently of interest in OCD are described. The chapter concludes by discussing the innovative possibilities for OCD genetic research in the future.

FAMILY AND TWIN STUDIES

Until the advent of current molecular genetic techniques, twin, adoption, and family studies were the three primary methods available to researchers attempting to investigate the relative roles of heredity versus environment in disease. Adoption and separation studies are generally rare, due to the relative scarcity of cases of adopted children or twins, reared apart, affected by the disease in question. To our knowledge, no studies involving OCD have been published. We thus review family and twin studies here.

In the world literature, from 1936 to present, there are 14 published twin studies reporting on OCD. A summary of this literature is provided in Table 8.1. These studies, taken as a whole, provide some indication of the relative rates for concordant and discordant monozygotic (MZ) and dizygotic (DZ) twin pairs. The ratio of concordant MZ:DZ twins is of particular interest as a finding of greater concordance among MZ than DZ twins suggests a genetic basis to the disease in question. The studies that we have reviewed include a total of 80 MZ twin pairs, of whom 54 were reported as concordant and 26 as discordant. Similarly, 29 DZ twin pairs are reported, of whom 9 were concordant. When this literature is analyzed as a whole (80 MZ pairs and 29 DZ pairs), the concordant MZ:DZ ratio is 2.19:1, which is very close to the 2:1 ratio considered consistent with a single susceptibility gene (Risch, 1990). In complex traits determined by many different genes (polygenic traits), the MZ:DZ ratio may provide an estimate of the number of genes involved. The higher the MZ:DZ ratio, the more likely it is that a larger number of genes is involved in the illness. This reflects the decreasing probability of finding all the etiological genes within one person as the degree of relatedness between that person and another decreases. In contrast with the 2:1 ratio found in OCD, the ratio found in schizophrenia is 3.5:1, and in bipolar disorder it is 3:1 (reviewed by Petronis & Kennedy, 1995). This suggests that, unlike in OCD, a single gene effect cannot account for these disorders.

TABLE 8.1. Twin Studies of OCD

Study	No. of twin pairs	Zygosity determination supported	Monozygous C/D[a]	Dizygous C/D[a]	Diagnostic information
Lewis (1936)	3	No	2/1		"Obsessional illness" poorly described
Rudin (1953)	10	No	6/4		"Obsessional neurosis" poorly described
Tienari (1963)	11	No	10/1		"Phobic or obsessional neurosis"
Parker (1964)	2	Yes	0/2		"Obsessional neurosis" well described
Woodruff & Pitts (1964)	1	Yes	1/0		"Obessional behavior" well described but likely organic
Ihda (1961)	20	No	10/10		"Obessional neurosis" poorly described
Inouye (1965)	14	No	9/2	1/3	"Obsessive–compulsive reaction"; 1 case likely Tourette's syndrome
Marks et al. (1969)	1	Yes	1/0		"Obsessive–compulsive neurosis" meets DSM-III-R
Tarsh (1978)	1	Yes		1/0	Good clinical description, meets DSM-III-R
Hoaken & Schurr (1980)	1	Yes	0/1		Well described but not DSM-III-R
McGuffin & Mawson (1980)	2	Yes	2/0		Well described, meets DSM-III-R
Carey & Gottesman (1981)	30	No	13/2	7/8	"Obsessional neurosis" partly described
Torgersen (1982)	12	Yes	0/3	0/9	DSM-III-R criteria
Kim et al. (1990)	1	Yes	1/0		OCD well described

[a]Concordant/discordant.

It is important, however, to keep in mind some of the limitations of this literature. First, the published literature is probably influenced by a reporting bias favoring concordant pairs. Second, most studies provide insufficient clinical data to verify if subjects would meet current standardized diagnostic criteria. Third, there is insufficient information given to definitively establish monozygosity in many cases. Last, an additional factor in evaluating these results is the greater environmental similarities for, and the impact of imitation and identification on, MZ twins. However, even if one allows for the reporting bias and these other issues by increasing the concordance ratio twofold, it would still be considered consistent with a strong genetic etiology involving a relatively small number of genes (Petronis & Kennedy, 1995; Risch, 1990).

Family studies have historically provided one of the best means of analysis of genetic factors since they enable testing of many different genetic hypotheses. Through the use of family studies, it has been repeatedly shown that rates of OCD and obsessive–compulsive behavior are increased among first-degree relatives of OCD probands. This literature is summarized in Table 8.2 (see also review by Rasmussen, 1993).

However, there are several methodological problems that must be kept in mind in reviewing this literature. Early studies (the first, by Lewis, dates back to 1936) lacked clear, consistent diagnostic criteria and did not provide sufficient information to determine if affected individuals would conform to DSM-IV criteria (Brown, 1942; Kringlen, 1965; Lewis, 1936; Lo, 1967; Rosenberg, 1967; Rudin, 1953). Another major issue is the method chosen to elicit family data: Most early studies relied on the family-history method, assessing relatives and determining diagnoses in an unstandardized fashion, based solely on information from the proband. A few studies addressed this by interviewing relatives already identified as possibly affected (Hoover & Insel, 1984; Insel, Hoover, & Murphy, 1983; McKeon & Murray, 1987). One study relied solely on a chart review to diagnose the percent of probands with at least one affected first-degree relative (Toro, Montserrat, Osejo, & Salamero, 1992). In contrast, most recent studies have used the family-study method, in which all available first-degree relatives are directly interviewed (Bellodi, Sciuto, Diaferia, Ronchi, & Smeraldi, 1992; Black, Noyes, Goldstein, & Blum, 1992; Lenane et al., 1990; Nicolini, Weissbecker, Mejia, & De Carmona, 1993; Pauls, Alsobrook, Goodman, Rasmussen, & Leckman, 1995; Riddle et al., 1990). Of these, two were based on children and adolescents as probands. Findings may differ from adult studies, as it is possible that there is greater genetic loading for childhood-onset OCD as has been reported for affective disorders (Clifford, Murray, & Fulker, 1984).

Both the family-history and family-study methods have inherent strengths and weaknesses. The family-history method is relatively quick, inexpensive, and provides information on all relatives. The family-study method is considered more sensitive and accurate; however, it has been demonstrated to underestimate significantly the prevalence of certain conditions with pejorative connotations through denial of symptoms by the subject (Mendlewicz, Fleiss, Cataldo, & Rainer, 1975). There are three negative studies (Insel et al., 1983; McKeon & Murray, 1987; Rosenberg, 1967). The earliest, by Rosenberg (1967), relied primarily on chart review and gives no clear description of the diagnostic criteria used. In the Insel et al. (1983) study, diagnosis relied on family-history data obtained clinically for parents only, in an unstandardized fashion. McKeon and Murray (1987) used a mailed general health questionnaire to screen relatives; those identified at risk then received an interview. It is likely that many relatives who were most ill and so of greatest interest were among the 12% that did not respond, negatively skewing the results obtained.

There are seven recent family studies that have used DSM-III or DSM-

TABLE 8.2. Family Studies of OCD

Study	Probands	No. of 1st-degree relatives	Diagnostic criteria	Controls	Study design[a]	Rate of OC in 1st-degree relatives (%)
Lewis (1936)	50	306	No	No	H	37 (parents) 20 (sibs) OC features
Brown (1942)	20	96	No	Yes	H	7 OC illness 25 OC features
Rudin (1953)	130	260	No	No	H	5 OC illness 5 OC features
Kringlen (1965)	91	182	No	No	H	5 (parents) 3 (sibs) OC features
Lo (1967)	86	495	No	No	H	9 (parents) 5 (sibs) OC features
Rosenberg (1967)	144	547	No	No	H	0.4 OC illness 3 "anxiety neurosis"
Hoover & Insel (1984)	10	43	DSM-III	No	Partial S	12 any psychiatric treatment
Insel, Hoover, & Murphy (1983)	27	54	DSM-III	No	Partial S	0 (parents)
Rasmussen & Tsuang (1986)	44	88	DSM-III	No	H	5 (parents) OC illness 12 (parents) OC features
McKeon & Murray (1987)	50	149	RDC	No	Partial S	0.7 hospitalized OC illness
Lenane et al. (1990)	46	146	DSM-III	No	S	12 OCD 23 OC features
Riddle et al. (1990)	21	36	DSM-III-R	No	S	11 OCD 31 OC features
Bellodi, Sciuto, Diaferia, Ronchi, & Smeraldi (1992)	92	370	DSM-III-R	No	H	3.4 OCD
Black, Noyes, Goldstein, & Blum (1992); Black, Noyes, Pfohl, Goldstein, & Blum (1993)	32	120	DSM-III-R	Yes	S	3 OCD 21 OC features 10.8 compulsive personality disorder
Toro, Montserrat, Osejo, & Salamero (1992)	72	?	DSM-III-R	Yes	Chart review	15.3 of probands had relative with OCD
Pauls, Alsobrook, Goodman, Rasmussen, & Leckman (1995)	100	466	DSM-III-R	Yes	S	10.3 OCD 7.9 subthreshold
Richter et al. (unpublished data)	26	94	DSM-III-R RDC	Yes	H[b]	18 OCD 9 OC behavior

[a]H, family history study design; S, family study design.
[b]With structured interview for diagnosis of relatives.

III-R criteria, and collectively, these studies found the rate of OCD to be 3–12% among the first-degree relatives of OCD probands (Bellodi et al., 1992; Black et al., 1992; Hoover & Insel, 1984; Lenane et al., 1990; Pauls et al., 1995; Rasmussen & Tsuang, 1986; Riddle et al., 1990). This is significantly higher that the 2–3% lifetime prevalence rate for OCD in the general population (Bland, Orn, & Newman, 1988; Feehan, McGee, Nada Raja, & Williams, 1994; Robins et al., 1984). The reported rates of obsessive–compulsive behavior (or subclinical OCD) in first-degree relatives was reported as 8–31%, according to these same seven family studies. In those studies examining both OCD and obsessive–compulsive behavior, the total percentage of relatives affected ranges from 17% to 35% (Black et al., 1992; Lenane et al., 1990; Pauls et al., 1995; Rasmussen & Tsuang, 1986; Riddle et al., 1990). The results of these family studies are thus overwhelmingly in favor of a heritable factor in OCD. Moreover, symptom patterns have generally been observed to differ between probands and affected relatives, making an environmental or "learned behavior" explanation less likely.

In an ongoing study conducted by one of the authors (M.A.R.), many of these issues are addressed through a refinement of the family-history method. This investigation utilizes standardized psychiatric interviews for assessment and diagnosis of probands, as well as for the obtaining of diagnostic information on first-degree relatives (Richter et al., unpublished data). It is hoped that most of the advantages of the family-study method will be gleaned while still using the family-history method. Data on a matched sample of control probands free of psychiatric disorder have been collected and are currently being analyzed. In Richter's study, results to date indicate that 18% of first-degree relatives meet criteria for OCD, whereas a further 9% demonstrate obsessive–compulsive behavior. Thus, 27% of all relatives have clinical or subclinical OCD, in the middle of the range reported by other investigators. In total, 40% of probands have a positive family history of OCD, which is consistent with other published studies.

To summarize, the investigation of families and twins has been key in establishing the importance of genetic factors in the development of OCD. However, family studies have also formed the basis for the next step in furthering understanding of the role of genetic factors. Family data can be used from studies such as those reported earlier to generate different testable mathematical models of the mode of inheritance of the illness in question. This approach is known as segregation analysis. Two studies to date have investigated the genetic mode of inheritance of OCD. The first, by Nicolini, Hanna, Baxter, Weissbacker, and Spence (1990), performed segregation analysis on 24 families, recruited through the University of California–Los Angeles psychiatric service. OCD was diagnosed using a standardized interview in 12 first-degree and 12 second-degree relatives. Results suggested an autosomal dominant, single major-locus model of transmission with 80% penetrance. A more recent study by Cavallini et al. (1995) utilized a larger sample of 107 OCD families and demonstrated best fit with either an unrestricted or a single major locus-model, with 66% penetrance. When the phenotype was widened to include Tourette's syndrome and other tic disorders, the same best fit was obtained. Thus, these results are consistent with the findings of the twin and family literature in supporting the role of at least one gene of major effect in the etiology of OCD, although the existence of a small number of additional modifying genes cannot be ruled out and may prove most likely in time.

The Genetic Relationship with Other Anxiety Disorders and OCD Spectrum Disorders

One of the major problems confronting researchers in psychiatric genetics is the establishment of clear boundaries regarding the phenotype of the disorders under investigation. The diagnosis of many medical conditions is facilitated by the presence of objectively measurable abnormalities on serological or other forms of testing, such as the glucose tolerance test in diabetes. Alternatively, many disorders have specific symptomatology that defines them (e.g., the presence of seizures in epilepsy). Unfortunately, most psychiatric disorders (and OCD specifically) currently lack unambiguous, objectively measurable markers. The absence of clear markers, and subsequent reliance on clinical presentation for diagnosis, can result in a number of possible errors when determining whom to include in genetic studies. Phenocopies may mistakenly be included; these may be defined as individuals who demonstrate symptoms consistent with the disorder of interest due to causes other than the underlying genetic roots. A related problem is the identification of individuals who have inherited the same biological diathesis as unaffected, when the disorder is either expressed differently or not at all. Additionally, the frequent overlap between disorders in the same individual (comorbidity) can further confuse the picture. It is therefore crucial that genetic research take these factors into account.

Other anxiety disorders, such as specific and social phobia and panic disorder, are found with increased frequency among OCD patients (Rasmussen & Eisen, 1994). It seems as though individuals with OCD may thus be predisposed to develop other anxiety disorders as well. This may reflect an underlying genetic diathesis that is shared between OCD and these other disorders. OCD patients also have an increased chance (when compared to the general population) of suffering from major depression. Sixty-seven percent of OCD patients will suffer from at least one episode of major depression over the course of their lives (Rasmussen & Eisen, 1994). These observations emphasize the overlap between anxiety disorders and depressive illness; there may be a common genetic susceptibility to both conditions. However, unlike the relationship with the disorders discussed later, this inherited diathesis appears to be quite nonspecific, as family studies examining the prevalence rate of OCD in first-degree relatives of probands with panic disorder and major depression have not generally observed an increase (see Goldstein et al., 1994). In other words, there may be genetic factors that generally predispose individuals toward anxiety and/or mood disorders; however, interaction with another, more specific "OCD" gene may be required for OCD to develop. For further discussion of comorbidity and the nature of the relationship between OCD, other anxiety disorders, and depression, please refer to Chapters 1 and 9.

There are a number of other disorders that have been postulated to be part of an obsessive–compulsive spectrum of disorders. This hypothetical relationship is based on similarities with OCD on features such as phenomenology, epidemiology, clinical course, family history, biology, treatment response, and the like. This relationship is discussed in detail in Chapters 17 and 18. There is evidence in the literature to support a putative genetic link between OCD and some of these "spectrum" conditions specifically. Gilles de la Tourette's syndrome (TS) is a hereditary neuropsychiatric condition, characterized by chronic intermittent motor and vocal tics. It has been repeatedly shown to have a strong genetic basis (Nee et al., 1980; Pauls et al., 1986, 1990). The most widely accepted model proposes a single autosomal dominant gene with sex-influenced expression (Curtis, Robertson, & Gurling, 1992; Devor, 1990; Pauls et al., 1990). OCD and obsessive–compulsive behavior are found in 45–90% of TS patients' families (Nee et al., 1980; Pitman et al., 1987). Furthermore, similar rates of OCD in relatives are observed regardless of whether the proband has OCD in addition to TS (Pauls & Leckman, 1986). Last, the rate of tic disorders (TS and chronic tics) has also been observed to be significantly higher in relatives of OCD probands (4.6%) than in relatives of comparison subjects (1%)(Pauls et al., 1995). Therefore at least some forms of OCD and TS appear genetically related. Trichotillomania, an impulse control disorder characterized by compulsive hair pulling, also tends to occur relatively frequently as a comorbid condition with OCD. Like TS, it has been shown to be associated with a greater prevalence of OCD in first-degree relatives of probands with the condition (6.4%) as compared to relatives of controls (0%)(Lenane et al., 1992). These observations suggest that conditions such as tic disorders and trichotillomania are variant phenotypes arising from the same genetic diathesis. This leads to the conclusion that genetic studies of OCD should attempt to take at least these spectrum conditions into consideration when determining the phenotypic status of individuals.

MOLECULAR GENETIC STRATEGIES IN OCD

As has been described, family and twin studies provided the first evidence that genetic factors are important in OCD. With this established, work in OCD using DNA technology was begun in earnest. The study of OCD at the DNA level should eventually result in the determination of precisely which genes are involved in the disorder. There is reason to believe that this knowledge will pave the way to a clearer understanding of the etiology of OCD, and to more specific therapeutic options. Molecular genetic strategies currently available consist of two different research designs: linkage analysis in families, and association studies across unrelated individuals.

Linkage analysis, which, if successful, leads to positional cloning of the gene, requires the collection of families that have multiple affected members.

These studies use information from the familial relationship of pedigree members to identify a region of a given chromosome that is coinherited with the illness. There is therefore no requirement for any a priori hypothesis regarding involvement of a specific DNA region. Traditionally, psychiatric studies utilizing this strategy have relied on large multigenerational families, with many affected individuals. However, there are several disadvantages with the large-pedigree method. First, any linked gene found may represent forms of the illness other than that typically found in clinical practice, where families with only one or a few affected individuals are the norm. This problem was found to have influenced results of an epilepsy study (Greenberg, 1992). Second, linkage results with large families are very sensitive to typing errors or change in diagnosis, as was demonstrated by the change in lod score (an indicator of linkage) by orders of magnitude for affective disorder in the Amish (Egeland et al., 1987; Kelsoe et al., 1989). Last, the effort and expense required simply to collect these relatively rare families is wasted if linkage is not found.

Recent work suggests that an equally effective strategy is to focus on the common form of the illness seen in the more easily found small families containing just a few affected individuals (Greenberg, 1992). Modern methods now allow linkage analysis to be performed on sets of pairs of related individuals with the condition of interest. The Affected Relative Pair method (ARP) uses these pairs of affected relatives (such as siblings or cousins) to calculate a maximum likelihood-ratio test statistic from which linkage can be derived. Either linkage method also offers the advantage of reducing genetic heterogeneity in the test population, as all subjects must have affected relatives for inclusion.

With linkage methods, all the individuals in the study are typed for a genetic marker (defined later) at the DNA level. The typings are then analyzed to look for cosegregation of the disease with a particular variant of the marker. This is typically done with a computer program that calculates the likelihood that a marker is being inherited with the disease. If linkage is found, it can be inferred that a causative gene is either upstream or downstream from the marker. Linkage analysis has met with great success in recent years, finding the genes responsible for dozens of illnesses including Huntington's disease, Alzheimer's, and cystic fibrosis.

In contrast to linkage methods, association studies utilize a case–control approach to investigate "candidate genes." These are genes that, based on biological or other evidence, are hypothesized to be involved in the etiology of the disorder. Currently, candidates generating the most interest have mainly been genes in the serotoninergic and dopaminergic systems. The association study involves typing a group of affected people and a group of matched controls for a marker that is located close to or within the candidate gene. The typings are then analyzed to look for differences between the affected group and the controls. Association studies are well suited to the investigation of complex traits (Risch & Merikangas, 1996). This is because, unlike traditional linkage analysis, one does not need to specify a mode of gene transmission (e.g., autosomal dominant) to perform the analysis. To see an example of how productive association studies can be, we need look no further than the genetic research that has been done in Type I diabetes. Association studies have played an important role in determining the genes involved in this polygenic disease (see Davies et al., 1994; Julier et al., 1994).

Association methods have advanced in recent years with the development of sophisticated modifications. The Haplotype Relative Risk method (HRR) employs the proband and the two parents, the "HRR triplet," as the focus of analysis. DNA marker data from those parental chromosomes not inherited by the proband are used to generate a hypothetical person's genotype, which becomes the control sample. With this refinement, the HRR strategy overcomes sampling biases usually inherent in a traditional control sample. This method has led to impressive success in studies of susceptibility genes for diabetes and cleft lip and palate (Khoury, 1994; Khoury & Flanders, 1996).

The "genetic marker" is a tool common to both linkage analysis and association studies. A genetic marker is a variable site in the DNA, known as a polymorphism. At this site, the DNA sequence varies in the population, so that there is more than one allelic form. Several types of markers have been used in molecular genetic research. *Microsatellites* are two- or three-base nucleotide units (e.g., CA) that are repeated over and over again. The number of repeats varies across individuals. The *variable number tandem repeat* (VNTR) is a longer, repeating DNA sequence comprising numerous nucleotide units, and as with microsatellites, the number of repeats varies from person to person. A *restriction fragment length polymorphism* (Botstein, White, Skolnick, & Davis, 1980) is a point mutation of a single nucleotide that is within a recognition sequence for a specific DNA cutting enzyme (a restriction endonuclease).

Contemporary typing methods employ the polymerase chain reaction (PCR) to detect DNA polymorphisms. This method of "amplifying" a small amount of DNA was developed in the late 1980s and revolutionized molecular genetics. A sample of the subject's DNA is placed in a test tube, along with a DNA synthesis enzyme (Taq polymerase) and a set of DNA "primers," which are short nucleotide fragments used for the synthesis of copies of the original DNA site. The test tube is then put through a "cycle" consisting of three temperature changes. The cycle is repeated 20 to 30 times, resulting in the production of millions of copies of the original DNA sequence. This large number of copies can be seen with the naked eye under ultraviolet light, and comparisons of the same DNA site can be made easily across many individuals. Another relatively new technique, called single-strand conformation polymorphism (SSCP) can be used on any PCR product to detect most sequence variations. Thousands of PCR-based markers distributed over all the human chromosomes are currently available to researchers studying the molecular genetics of OCD.

BIOLOGICAL THEORIES OF OCD

As outlined earlier, etiological theories are an important consideration for modern genetic researchers in OCD. A large number of biological factors may be involved in the pathology, including neurochemical, neuroanatomic, and genetic factors. Theories regarding the neurochemical basis of this condition provide the field of genetics with appropriate candidate genes, enabling association studies to be performed. Candidate genes can also be used in linkage analysis, in place of an exhaustive and expensive genome scan. The most accepted neurochemical theories of OCD proposed to date involve the serotonin and dopamine neurotransmitter systems. There is also a new hypothesis just beginning to emerge, regarding an autoimmune etiology, which may also guide geneticists to target additional gene candidates. Although a detailed review is beyond the scope of this chapter, we briefly cover these three hypotheses.

The serotonin hypothesis of OCD was borne out of the successful treatment of OCD with clomipramine, a potent serotonin reuptake inhibitor (Collaborative Study Group, 1991). Further support was gleaned by the well-demonstrated efficacy of the selective serotonin reuptake inhibitors, such as fluoxetine, fluvoxamine, and sertraline (Chouinard, 1992; Goodman et al., 1989a; Jenike et al., 1989; Liebowitz et al., 1989). These observations have led OCD research toward analysis of the serotonin system and its function in OCD patients. A number of parameters in the serotonin (5-hydroxytryptamine, or 5-HT) system have been measured in people with OCD. These include cerebrospinal fluid (CSF) 5-hydroxyindoleacetic acid (the major metabolite of serotonin) (Kruesi et al., 1990; Lydiard et al., 1990; Thoren et al., 1980; Zohar, Mueller, Insel, Zohar-Kadouch, & Murphy, 1987), whole blood levels of 5-HT (Hanna, Yuwiler, & Cantwell, 1991; Hanna et al., 1995; Yaryura-Tobias & Bhagavan, 1977), platelet 5-HT concentrations (Flament, Rapoport, Murphy, Berg & Lake, 1987), and platelet imipramine binding (thought to be reflective of 5-HT uptake)(Bastani, Arora, & Meltzer, 1991; Insel, Mueller, Alterman, Linnoila, & Murphy, 1985; Marazziti, Hollander, Lensi, Ravagli, & Cassano, 1992; Ravizza et al., 1991; Weizman et al., 1986). Taken as a whole, the results of these studies are not fully consistent, but they suggest that 5-HT dysfunction is important in OCD.

Pharmacological challenges have also been conducted in OCD patients. These have used agents such as L-tryptophan, fenfluramine (a serotonin-releasing agent), and meta-chlorophenylpiperazine (mCPP) (see Charney et al., 1988; Goodman et al., 1995; Hollander et al., 1993; Pigott et al., 1993; Zohar et al., 1987). No firm conclusions can be made about the specific nature of the serotonergic dysfunction in OCD based on these challenge studies. Some investigators have suggested that OCD patients may suffer from a behavioral hypersensitivity to serotonin coupled with a neuroendocrine hyposensitivity, as suggested by the findings with mCPP (Barr, Goodman, Price, McDougle, & Charney, 1992; Goodman, Price, Woods, & Charney, 1991).

The idea that the dopamine neurotransmitter system may be involved in OCD has not received as much attention as has the serotonin system. Nevertheless, it is an idea that is worth considering, because it is based on converging evidence from diverse sources. To begin with, Tourette's syndome is thought to be dopaminergically mediated, because of the successful use of haloperidol and other dopamine antagonists in its treatment (Shapiro, Shapiro, & Eisenkraft,

1983). Tourette's syndrome and OCD have been associated, because they tend to occur in the same individual (and in an affected individual's family) more often than expected based on chance alone (Pauls et al., 1995). Further support for a "dopaminergic hypothesis" comes from pharmacological challenges of OCD patients. With d-amphetamine, OCD symptoms were observed to improve (Insel, Hamilton, Guttmacher, & Murphy, 1983), although methylphenidate had no effect (Swinson & Joffe, 1988). Evidence for the involvement of dopamine in OCD also comes from a connection between OCD and the basal ganglia (Baxter, Schwartz, & Guze, 1991). Serotonin and dopamine systems are known to interact in this area of the brain. Finally, there is indirect evidence for the involvement of the dopamine system in OCD derived from clinical pharmacological experience. Several case reports have been published describing the emergence of de novo obsessive–compulsive symptoms in patients on clozapine (see Ghaemi et al., 1995). Clomipramine and fluoxetine, two drugs that effectively treat OCD, may have antidopaminergic activity (Austin et al., 1991; Lipinski, Mallya, Zimmerman, & Pope, 1989). There is also documented research on the benefit of potentiating serotonin reuptake inhibitor (SRI) responders with neuroleptics (McDougle et al., 1994). Taken together, all of the outlined evidence provides enough impetus for further study of the dopamine system in the etiology of OCD.

Going beyond the realm of neurotransmitters, there is a new hypothesis emerging in OCD research. The intriguing autoimmune hypothesis of OCD was proposed by Allen, Leonard, and Swedo (1995) after a thoughtful review of literature reports. The potential role of autoantibodies in childhood neuropsychiatric disorders is further discussed in a paper by Swedo and Kiessling (1994). An association was drawn between infection with group A beta-hemolytic *Streptococcus* (as well as other agents, including viruses), and the onset or exacerbation of OCD in some children. The mechanism may be similar to that of Sydenham's chorea, with infection triggering an autoimmune response that affects the basal ganglia or another area of the brain. The importance of this hypothesis cannot yet be determined, however, because it is not known how many child-onset cases of OCD can be accounted for by this sort of an autoimmune process. It may be that inherited genetic factors interact with the autoimmune mechanisms, making a person more or less susceptible to the cross-reaction created by the infection. Genetic variants in the human leukocyte antigen (HLA) system may be interesting candidates to examine in this group of OCD subjects.

CANDIDATE GENES IN OCD

Because of the biological theories of OCD that are prevailing, the candidate genes currently being investigated come from the serotonin and dopamine systems. The genes for the dopamine receptors were the first to be cloned and tested. Since that time, the gene sequences for other components of the systems have become available. A few of these genes in the dopamine and serotonin systems have been employed in genetic association studies of OCD. These have had negative or inconclusive results, as described later. The candidate genes drawn from the autoimmune hypothesis of OCD are outlined, although studies of these genes have not yet emerged in the literature.

Over the past 5 years, there has been a rapid increase in our understanding of the receptors, transporters, and enzymes involved in serotonergic function in the periphery and in the central nervous system. Seven classes of receptors have been identified so far (5-HT$_1$–5-HT$_7$), with several subclasses. All of the receptor classes are coupled to G-proteins except for 5-HT$_3$, which is directly linked to a ligand-gated cation membrane channel (Mattes et al., 1993; Ruat et al., 1993; Shen et al., 1993; Zifa & Fillion, 1992). Polymorphisms have been identified in a number of serotonin receptors, the serotonin transporter, and the rate-limiting enzyme tryptophan hydroxylase (see Table 8.3). Association studies investigating a relationship between OCD and the receptor polymorphisms have begun, but there have not been any definitive results as of yet.

The gene for the serotonin transporter has also been cloned and sequenced (Lesch, Wolozin, Estler, Murphy, & Riederer, 1993; Ramamoorthy et al., 1993), and localized to chromosome 17q (Gelernter, Pakstis, & Kidd, 1995a). The serotonin transporter (5-HTT) is responsible for the reuptake of serotonin back into the presynaptic terminal. Tricyclic antidepressants and selective SRIs bind to the 5-HTT but their exact mechanism of action is unknown. Altemus, Murphy, Greenberg, and Lesch (1996) sequenced the coding region of the 5-HTT gene in 22 OCD patients and 4 controls. No sequence differences were observed. In the promoter region of the 5-HTT gene, there is a 44 base-pair insertion/deletion polymorphism (Heils et al., 1996). Lesch et al. (1996) investigated this promoter polymorphism in a group of 505 normal subjects that had been rated for personality and psychological traits. There was a small but significant association between one allele of the serotonin transporter promoter polymorphism and the anxiety ratings of the subjects. This same polymorphism was investigated by Billett et al. (1997) in an association study consisting of 74 OCD patients and 74 matched controls. No significant difference was observed between the two groups. Billett et al. (1997) also tested the polymorphism for its ability to predict the response of OCD patients to SRIs. No such ability was detected, but the sample size was small, and the possibility of an effect could not be ruled out. In the second intron of the 5-HTT gene, there is another polymorphism, a VNTR (Lesch et al., 1994). A possible role for this marker in OCD has not yet been the subject of research. Another potentially interesting genetic polymorphism in the serotonin system is the SSCP/PCR polymorphism in the tryptophan hydroxylase gene (Nielsen, Dean, & Goldman, 1992). Tryptophan hydroxylase is the rate-limiting enzyme in the metabolic process generating 5-HT, and thus may be involved in susceptibility to OCD.

The dopamine system includes five subtypes of receptors (D1–D5), all G-protein coupled. The dopamine receptors can be grouped into two classes, based on their similarity to either D1 or D2. The "D1-like" receptors are D1 and D5; they are positively coupled to adenylate cyclase and have no introns. The D2,

TABLE 8.3. List of Candidate Genes from the Serotonin System

Locus symbol	Name of gene	Chromosome	Reference	Polymorphism
TPH	Tryptophan hydroxylase	11p	Nielsen, Dean, & Goldman (1992)	SSCP
5-HTT	Serotonin transporter	17q	Lesch et al. (1994)	VNTR
			Heils et al. (1996)	5′ ins/del PCR
HTR1A	Serotonin 1A receptor	5q	Khan, Isenberg, Aschauer, & Devor (1990)	SacI RFLP
			Melmer et al. (1991)	TaqI RFLP
			Bolos, Goldman, & Dean (1993)	CA & alu repeat
HTR1Dβ	Serotonin 1Dβ receptor	6q	Sidenberg et al. (1993)	HincII RFLP
			Nothen, Erdmann, Shimron-Abarbanell, & Propping (1994)	SSCP
HTR1Dα	Serotonin 1Dα receptor	1p	Kasapi et al. (1994)	SSCP
			Ozaki et al. (1995)	PCR-RFLP
HTR1E	Serotonin 1E receptor	6q	Shimron-Abarbanell et al. (1995)	SSCP, PCR-RFLP
HTR1F	Serotonin 1F receptor		Shimron-Abarbanell et al. (1996)	SSCP, PCR-RFLPs
HTR2A	Serotonin 2A receptor	13q	Warren, Peacock, Rodriguez, & Fink (1993)	PCR-RFLP
			Erdmann et al. (1996)	His/Tyr PCR-RFLP
			Nothen et al. (1996)	5′ PCR-RFLP
HTR2C	Serotonin 2C receptor	Xq	Lappalainen et al. (1995)	SSCP, Cys/Ser PCR-RFLP
HTR6	Serotonin 6 receptor	1p	Kohen et al. (1996)	PCR-RFLP
HTR7	Serotonin 7 receptor	10q	Gelernter et al. (1995)	HincII RFLP

D3, and D4 receptors are known as "D2-like," because they are all negatively coupled to adenylate cyclase, and they all have introns. All of the dopamine receptor genes have been cloned and have readily tested polymorphisms available (see Table 8.4). There has been a preliminary association study published examining the role of the D3 dopamine receptor MscI polymorphism in 97 OCD patients and 97 controls (Catalano et al., 1994). The results were negative. Novelli, Nobile, Diaferia, Sciuto, and Catalano (1994) sequenced the D2 gene in 45 OCD patients and 26 controls, but found no nucleotide substitutions. Billett et al. (in press) investigated the D2, D3, and D4 dopamine receptor genes in OCD, and association studies showed no significant role for D2 or D3. An interesting

TABLE 8.4. List of Candidate Genes from the Dopamine System

Locus symbol	Name of gene	Chromosome	Source	Polymorphism
DRD1	Dopamine receptor D1	5q	Cichon, Nothen, Erdmann, & Propping (1994)	SSCP
DRD2	Dopamine receptor D2	11q	Castiglione et al. (1995)	TaqIA, TaqIB, STR
DRD3	Dopamine receptor D3	3q	Lannfelt et al. (1992)	MscI
DRD4	Dopamine receptor D4	11p15.5	Van Tol et al. (1992); Petronis, Van Tol, & Kennedy (1994)	VNTR, SmaI
DRD5	Dopamine receptor D5	4p	Sherrington et al. (1993)	$(CA)_N$
DAT	Dopamine transporter	5p	Vandenbergh, Persico, & Uhl (1992); Byerley, Hoff, Holik, Caron, & Giros (1993)	VNTR1, VNTR2, Taq1
TH	Tyrosine hydroxylase	11p15.5	Edwards, Hammond, Jin, Caskey, & Chakraborty (1992)	STR

trend was observed, however, in the D4 data. The seven-repeat (long) allele of the VNTR was less frequent among the OCD patients than it was among the controls. The long allele has been associated with the personality trait of Novelty Seeking in two independent reports (Benjamin et al., 1996; Ebstein et al., 1996). This may lead to an interesting hypothesis, because the personality characteristics of individuals with OCD tend to be the opposite of novelty seekers. For the most part, people with OCD are more rigid and reflective in their behavior.

In addition to the dopamine receptors, genes for other components of the dopamine system have been cloned. The sequence for the dopamine transporter gene has been elucidated and a VNTR polymorphism identified within the gene (see Table 8.4). Billett et al. (in press) found no association between this polymorphism and OCD.

There are other candidate genes on the horizon for OCD, based on biological theories of OCD and psychiatric illness in general. Given the burgeoning evidence for involvement of autoimmune mechanisms in OCD, genes of the HLA system may be promising candidates. Associations have been demonstrated between HLA-system genes and several autoimmune diseases, such as rheumatoid arthritis, systemic lupus erythematosus, and ankylosing spondylitis (for a review, see Boitard & McDevitt, 1992). These findings may indicate a genetic susceptibility to such conditions in predisposed individuals. In the field of psychiatric genetics, there has been recent interest in genes with repeating trinucleotide sequences. These polymorphisms, which have been termed "unstable DNA," have the ability to expand with each generation. The resulting increased number of trinucleotide repeats has been demonstrated to be the genetic mechanism responsible for several neuropsychiatric diseases, including Huntington's disease, fragile-X mental retardation, and myotonic dystrophy (Petronis & Kennedy, 1995; Warren, 1996). Families affected by these diseases have been observed to display genetic anticipation, meaning the disease has a lower age of onset and greater severity with each succeeding generation. This non-Mendelian mode of transmission can now be explained by the instability in these DNA sequences. It is not known if OCD families display anticipation, as this has never been directly studied. Moreover, retrospectively establishing age of onset is a significant difficulty in this condition. Nevertheless, brain cDNAs with unstable sequences, including those cloned by Li, McInnis, Margolis, Antonarakis, and Ross (1993), and Riggins, Lokey, and Warren (1992), may be important candidates in OCD.

FUTURE DIRECTIONS

Although the molecular genetic association studies of OCD reviewed here have been valuable beginnings, the sample sizes for these studies will need to be increased substantially in order to obtain more definitive results. In addition, other research strategies need to be employed. The HRR method, in which untransmitted alleles of the proband's parents are used as controls, is one strategy that may prove fruitful. Collection of affected sibling pairs and larger families with multiple OCD cases will allow for a scan of all the chromosomes using a set of several hundred genetic markers. This latter approach has the advantage of not requiring an a priori hypothesis, and the technology for typing large sets of DNA markers is becoming more efficient at a rapid pace.

The powerful technology in the DNA laboratory is not currently the rate-limiting step in molecular genetic studies of OCD. Rather, the complexity of the diagnosis in the absence of unambiguous physical markers for this condition, and the definition of the phenotype, are the most problematic areas. Great advances have been made in reliability of assessments of OCD through standardization of diagnostic criteria such as DSM-IV, refinements of structured interviews such as the Structured Clinical Interview for DSM-IV (First, Spitzer, Gibbon, & Williams, 1996), and severity rating scales such as the Yale–Brown Obsessive–Compulsive Scale (Goodman et al., 1989b, 1989c). However, the phenotype of OCD remains relatively broad for the purposes of genetic studies, and efforts to subclassify patients using biological variables need to be developed. One useful approach, for example, may be to subdivide patients according to their response to selective SRI medication. These two groups of patients could then be compared using genetic polymorphisms from the serotonin system, as outlined by Billett et al. (1997). Numerous other dimensions of phenotypic subdivision also warrant exploration. These include presence or absence of tics, response to mCPP or fenfluramine challenge, autoimmune status, or comparison of symptom subgroups such as fear of contamination versus need for symmetry.

Time may prove that dissecting out a contribution of genetic factors to the development of illness will be yet another beginning. The traditional approach in psychiatric genetics has relied on the assumption that environmental effects act much like "noise" on the genetic signal, and should be relatively simple to extract out if large and clean enough samples are utilized. However, there is increasing recognition that the relative roles played by heredity and environment may interact in far more complex ways than are currently considered in most genetic research. For example, elegant work has been conducted on the heritability of aggressive and antisocial behavior. This literature, according to Kendler (1995), may be interpreted as follows: Predisposing genes may have limited impact in early years, whereas in adulthood, their effect "become(s) amplified; not only can they have a direct impact on the probability of committing any (antisocial) acts, but they can indirectly increase the probability of self-selection into a social environment that further encourages (antisocial) traits" (p. 896). This interaction may therefore cause a correlation between genetic and environmental effects. Although, traditionally, it has been assumed that the family environment remains relatively similar for siblings, parenting may in fact differ in response to the individual child (Plomin & Neiderhiser, 1992).

Another related consideration is that genetic factors may act not by causing illness, but by increasing vulnerability to other environmental factors. This has been discussed in work investigating the impact of maternal smoking and the risk of developing cleft lip or palate in genetically predisposed offspring (Khoury, 1994). In a related vein, it has similarly been shown that the risk of developing major depression following exposure to stress is differently affected depending on inherited vulnerability; those who are already more susceptible genetically experience a greater increase in risk (Kendler et al., 1995).

It may be that current reliance on diagnosis as our indicator of susceptbility genes is too crude. Measures of temperament, or other subtler variations in personality, may be the required indices for future research. However, as our sophistication with both the clinical phenotype and the molecular neurobiology of psychiatric illness develops, it will converge with the dramatic advances in methods for study of the human genetic code. It is here that the mysteries of OCD etiology will begin to reveal themselves.

REFERENCES

Allen, A. J., Leonard, H. L., & Swedo, S. E. (1995). Case study: A new infection-triggered, autoimmune subtype of pediatric OCD and Tourette's syndrome. *Journal of the American Academy of Child and Adolescent Psychiatry, 34,* 307–311.

Altemus, M., Murphy, D. L., Greenberg, B., & Lesch, K. P. (1996). Intact coding region of the serotonin transporter gene in obsessive–compulsive disorder. *American Journal of Medical Genetics (Neuropsychiatric Genetics), 67,* 409–411.

Ashall, F. (1994). Genes for normal and diseased mental states. *Trends in Genetics, 10,* 37–39.

Austin, L. S., Lydiard, B., Ballenger, J. C., Cohen, B. M., Laraia, M. T., Zelaberg, J. J., Fossey, M. D., & Ellinwood, E. J. (1991). Dopamine blocking activity of

198   PSYCHOPATHOLOGY AND THEORETICAL PERSPECTIVES

clomipramine in patients with obsessive–compulsive disorder. *Biological Psychiatry, 30*, 225–232.

Barr, L. C., Goodman, W. K., Price, L. H., McDougle, C. J., & Charney, D. S. (1992). The serotonin hypothesis of obsessive compulsive disorder: Implications of pharmacologic challenge studies. *Journal of Clinical Psychiatry, 53*(Suppl. 4), 17–28.

Bastani, B., Arora, R. C., & Meltzer, H. Y. (1991). Serotonin uptake and imipramine binding in the blood platelets of obsessive–compulsive disorder patients. *Biological Psychiatry, 30*, 131–139.

Baxter, L. R., Schwartz, J. M., & Guze, B. H. (1991). Brain imaging: Toward a neuroanatomy of OCD. In J. Zohar, T. Insel, & S. Rasmussen (Eds.), *The psychobiology of obsessive–compulsive disorder.* New York: Springer.

Bellodi, L., Sciuto, G., Diaferia, G., Ronchi, P., & Smeraldi, E. (1992). Psychiatric disorders in the families of patients with obsessive–compulsive disorder. *Psychiatry Research, 42*, 111–120.

Benjamin, J., Li, L., Patterson, C., Greenberg, B. D., Murphy, D. L., & Hamer, D. H. (1996). Population and familial association between the D4 dopamine receptor gene and measures of Novelty Seeking. *Nature Genetics, 12*, 81–84.

Billett, E. A., Richter, M. A., King, N., Heils, A., Lesch, K. P., & Kennedy, J. L. (1997). Obsessive compulsive disorder: Response to serotonin reuptake inhibitors and the serotonin transporter gene. *Molecular Psychiatry, 2*(5), 403–406.

Billett, E. A., Richter, M. A., Swinson, R. P., King, N., Badri, F., Sasaki, T., Buchanan, J. A., & Kennedy, J. L. (in press). Investigation of dopamine system genes in obsessive compulsive disorder. *Psychiatric Genetics.*

Black, D. W., Noyes, R., Goldstein, R. B., & Blum, M. (1992). A family study of obsessive–compulsive disorder. *Archives of General Psychiatry, 49*, 362–370.

Black, D. W., Noyes, R., Pfohl, B., Goldstein, R. B., & Blum, N. (1993). Personality disorder in obsessive–compulsive volunteers, well comparison subjects, and their first-degree relatives. *American Journal of Psychiatry, 150*, 1226–1232.

Bland, R. C., Orn, H., & Newman, S. C. (1988). Lifetime prevalence of psychiatric disorders in Edmonton. *Acta Psychiatrica Scandinavica, 338*, 24–32.

Boitard, C., & McDevitt, H. O. (1992). The biological basis of autoimmune disease. In R. A. King, J. I. Rotter, & A. G. Motulsky (Eds.), *The genetic basis of common diseases* (pp. 115–129). New York: Oxford University Press.

Bolos, A. M., Goldman, D., & Dean, M. (1993). Dinucleotide repeat and alu repeat polymorphisms at the 5-HT1A (HTR1A) receptor gene. *Psychiatric Genetics, 3*, 235–240.

Botstein, D., White, R. L., Skolnick, M., & Davis, R. (1980). Construction of a genetic linkage map in man using restriction fragment length polymorphisms. *American Journal of Human Genetics, 32*, 314–331.

Brown, F. W. (1942). Heredity in the psychoneuroses. *Proceedings of the Royal Society of Medicine, 35*, 785–790.

Byerley, W., Hoff, M., Holik, J., Caron, M. G., & Giros, B. (1993). VNTR polymorphism for the human dopamine transporter gene (DAT1). *Human Molecular Genetics, 2*, 335.

Carey, G., & Gottesman, I. I. (1981). Twin and family studies of anxiety, phobic and obsessive disorders. In D. F. Klein & J. Radkin (Eds.), *Anxiety: New research and changing concepts* (pp. 117–135). New York: Raven Press.

Castiglione, C. M., Deinard, A. S., Speed, W. C., Sirugo, G., Rosenbaum, H. C., Zhang, Y., Grandy, D. K., Grigorenko, E. L., Bonne-Tamir, B., Pakstis, A. J., Kidd, J. R., & Kidd, K. K. (1995). Evolution of haplotypes at the DRD2 locus. *American Journal of Human Genetics, 57*, 1445–1456.

Catalano, M., Sciuto, G., Di Bella, D., Novelli, E., Nobile, M., & Bellodi, L. (1994). Lack of association between obsessive compulsive disorder and the dopamine D3 receptor gene: Some preliminiary considerations. *American Journal of Medical Genetics (Neuropsychiatric Genetics), 54,* 253–255.

Cavallini, M. C., Macciardi, F., Pasquale, L., Bellodi, L., & Smeraldi, E. (1995). Complex segregation analysis of obsessive compulsive and spectrum related disorders. *Psychiatric Genetics 5(supp 1),* s31.

Charney, D., Goodman, W., Price, L., Woods, S., Rasmussen, S., & Heninger, G. (1988). Serotonin function in obsessive–compulsive disorder. *Archives of General Psychiatry, 45,* 177–185.

Chouinard, G. (1992). Sertraline in the treatment of obsessive compulsive disorder: Two double-blind, placebo-controlled studies. *International Clinical Psychopharmacology, 7*(Suppl. 2), 37–41.

Cichon, S., Nothen, M. M., Erdmann, J., & Propping, P. (1994). Detection of four polymorphic sites in the human dopamine D1 receptor gene (DRD1). *Human Molecular Genetics, 3,* 209.

Clifford, C. A., Murray, R. M., & Fulker, D. W. (1984). Genetic and environmental influences on obsessional traits and symptoms. *Psychological Medicine, 14,* 791–800.

Collaborative Study Group. (1991). Clomipramine in the treatment of patients with obsessive–compulsive disorder. *Archives of General Psychiatry, 48,* 730–738.

Crowe, R. R. (1993). Candidate genes in psychiatry: An epidemiological perspective. *American Journal of Medical Genetics (Neuropsychiatric Genetics), 48,* 74–77.

Curtis, D., Robertson, M. M., & Gurling, H. M. D. (1992). Autosomal dominant gene transmission in a large kindred with Gilles de la Tourette syndrome. *British Journal of Psychiatry, 160,* 845–849.

Davies, J., Kawaguchi, Y., Bennet, S., Copeman, J., Cordell, H., Pritchars, L., Reed, P., Gough, S., Jenkins, S., Palmer, S., Balfour, K., Rowe, B., Farrall, M., Barnett, A., Bain, S., & Todd, J. (1994). A genome-wide search for human type 1 diabetes susceptibility genes. *Nature, 371,* 130–136.

Devor, E. J. (1990). Untying the Gordian knot: The genetics of Tourette syndrome. *Journal of Nervous and Mental Disease, 178*(11), 1073–1077.

Ebstein, R. P., Novick, O., Umansky, R., Priel, B., Osher, Y., Blaine, D., Bennett, E. R., Nemanov, L., Katz, M., & Belmaker, R. H. (1996). Dopamine D4 receptor (D4DR) exon III polymorphism associated with the human personality trait of Novelty Seeking. *Nature Genetics, 12,* 78–80.

Edwards, A., Hammond, H. A., Jin, L., Caskey, C. T., & Chakraborty, R. (1992). Genetic variation at five trimeric and tetrameric tandem repeat loci in four human population groups. *Genomics, 12,* 241–253.

Egeland, J. A., Gerhard, D. S., Pauls, D. L., Sussex, J. N., Kidd, K. K., Allen, C. R., Hostetter, A. M., & Housman, D. E. (1987). Bipolar affective disorders linked to DNA markers on chromosome 11. *Nature, 325,* 783–787.

Erdmann, J., Shimron-Abarbanell, D., Rietschel, M., Albus, M., Maier, W., Korner, J., Bondy Brigitta, B., Chen, K., Shih, J. C., Knapp, M., Propping, P., & Nothen, M. M. (1996). Systematic screening for mutations in the human serotonin-2A (5HT2A) receptor gene: Identification of two naturally occurring receptor variants and association analysis in schizophrenia. *Human Genetics, 97,* 614–619.

Feehan, M., McGee, R., Nada Raja, S., & Williams, S. M. (1994). DSM-III-R disorders in New Zealand 18-year-olds. *Australian and New Zealand Journal of Psychiatry, 28,* 87–99.

First, M. B., Spitzer, R. L., Gibbon, M., & Williams, J. B. W. (1996). *Structured Clinical Inter-*

view for DSM-IV Axis I Disorders—Patient Edition (SCID-I/P, version 2.0). New York: Biometrics Research, New York State Psychiatric Institute.

Flament, J., Rapoport, J., Murphy, D., Berg, C., & Lake, R. (1987). Biochemical changes during clomipramine treatment of childhood obsessive–compulsive disorder. *Archives of General Psychiatry, 44,* 219–225.

Gelernter, J., Pakstis A. J., & Kidd, K. K. (1995a). Linkage mapping of the serotonin transporter protein gene SLC 6A4 on chromosome 17. *Human Genetics, 95,* 677–680.

Ghaemi, S. N., Zarate, C. A. Jr., Popli, A. P., Pillay, S. S., & Cole, J. O. (1995). Is there a relationship between clozapine and obsessive–compulsive disorder?: A retrospetive chart review. *Comprehensive Psychiatry, 36,* 267–270.

Goldstein, R. B., Weissman, M. M., Adams, P. B., Horwath, E., Lish, J. D., Charney, D., Woods, S. W., Sobin, C., & Wickramaratne, P. J. (1994). Psychiatric disorders in relatives of probands with panic disorder and/or major depression. *Archives of General Psychiatry, 51,* 383–394.

Goodman, W. K., McDougle, C. J., Price, L. H., Barr, L. C., Hillis, O. F., Caplik, J. F., Charney, D. S., & Heninger, G. R. (1995). *m*-Chlorophenylpiperazine in patients with obsessive-compulsive disorder: Absence of symptom exacerbation. *Biological Psychiatry 38,* 138–149.

Goodman, W. K., Price, L. H., Rasmussen, S. A., Delgado, P. L., Heninger, G. R., & Charney, D. S. (1989a). Efficacy of fluvoxamine in obsessive–compulsive disorder: A double-blind comparison with placebo. *Archives of General Psychiatry, 46,* 36–44.

Goodman, W. K., Price, L. H., Rasmussen, S. A., Mazure, D., Delgado, P., Heninger, G. R., & Charney, D. S. (1989b). The Yale–Brown Obsessive–Compulsive Scale: Part II. Validity. *Archives of General Psychiatry, 46,* 1012–1016.

Goodman, W. K., Price, L. H., Rasmussen, S. A., Mazure, D., Fleischmann, R. L., Hill, C. L., Heninger, G. R., & Charney, D. S. (1989c). The Yale–Brown Obsessive–Compulsive Scale: Part I. Development, use and reliability. *Archives of General Psychiatry, 46,* 1006–1011.

Goodman, W. K., Price, L. H., Woods, S. W., & Charney, D. S. (1991). Pharmacologic challenges in obsessive–compulsive disorder. In J. Zohar, T. Insel, & S. Rasmussen (Eds.), *The psychobiology of obsessive–compulsive disorder* (pp. 162–186). New York: Springer.

Greenberg, D. A. (1992). There is more than one way to collect data for linkage analysis. *Archives of General Psychiatry, 49,* 745–750.

Hanna, G. L., Yuwiler, A., & Cantwell, D. P. (1991). Whole blood serotonin in juvenile obsessive–compulsive disorder. *Biological Psychiatry, 29,* 738–744.

Hanna, G. L., Yulwiler, A., & Coates, J. K. (1995). Whole blood serotonin and disruptive behaviors in juvenile obsessive–compulsive disorder. *Journal of the American Academy of Child and Adolescent Psychiatry 34,* 28–35.

Heils, A., Teufel, A., Petri, S., Stober, G., Riederer, P., Bengel, D., & Lesch, K. P. (1996). Allelic variation of human serotonin transporter gene expression. *Journal of Neurochemistry, 66,* 2621–2624.

Hoaken, P. C. S., & Schurr, R. (1980). Genetic factors in obsessive–compulsive neurosis? *Canadian Journal of Psychiatry, 25,* 167–172.

Hollander, E., Cohen, L. J., DeCaria, C., Saoud, J. B., Stein, D. J., Cooper, T. B., Islam, N. N., Liebowitz, B. R., & Klein, D. F. (1993). Timing of neuroendocrine responses and effect of m-CPP and fenfluramine plasma levels in OCD. *Biological Psychiatry, 34,* 407–413.

Hoover, C., & Insel, T. (1984). Families of origin in obsessive compulsive disorder. *Journal of Nervous and Mental Disorders, 172,* 207–215.

Ihda, S. (1961). A study of neurosis by twin method. *Psychiatric Neurology of Japan, 62*, 861–892.

Inouye, E. (1965). Similar and dissimilar manifestations of obsessive–compulsive neurosis in monozygotic twins. *American Journal of Psychiatry, 121*, 1171–1175.

Insel, T. R., Hamilton, J. A., Guttmacher, L. B., & Murphy, D. L. (1983). D-Amphetamine in obsessive–compulsive disorder. *Psychopharmacology, 80*, 231–235.

Insel, T. R., Hoover, C., & Murphy, D. L. (1983). Parents of patients with obsessive–compulsive disorder. *Psychological Medicine, 13*, 807–811.

Insel, T., Mueller, E., Alterman, I., Linnoila, M., & Murphy, D. (1985). Obsessive–compulsive disorder and serotonin: Is there a connection? *Biological Psychiatry, 20*, 1174–1188.

Jenike, M. A., Buttolph, L., Baer, L., et al. (1989). Open trial of fluoxetine in obsessive–compulsive disorder. *Journal of Clinical Psychopharmacology, 5*, 207–212.

Julier, C., Lucassen, A., Villedieu, P., Delepine, M., Levy-Marchal, C., Danze, P., Bianchi, F., Boitard, C., Froguel, P., Bell, J., & Lathrop G. (1994). Multiple DNA variant association analysis: Application to the insulin gene region in type 1 diabetes. *American Journal of Human Genetics, 55*, 1247–1254.

Kasapi, M., Holik, J., Shah, M., Hoff, M., Coon, H., & Byerley, W. (1994). SSCP at the HTR1Da locus. *Human Molecular Genetics, 3*(8), 1444.

Kelsoe, J. R., Ginns, E. I., Egland, J., Gerhard, D. S., Goldstein, A. M., Bale, S. J., Pauls, D. L., et al. (1989). Re-evaluation of the linkage relationship between chromosome 11p loci and the gene for bipolar affective disorder in the Old Order Amish. *Nature, 342*, 238–243.

Kendler, K. S. (1995). Genetic epidemiology in psychiatry: Taking both genes and environment seriously. *Archives of General Psychiatry, 52*, 895–899.

Kendler, K. S., Kessler, R. C., Walters, E. E., MacLean, C. J., Sham, P. C., Neale, M. C., Heath, A. C., & Eaves, L. J. (1995). Stressful life events, genetic liability and onset of an episode of major depression in women. *American Journal of Psychiatry, 152*, 833–842.

Khan, M. A. R., Isenberg, K. E., Aschauer, H., & Devor, E. J. (1990). A SacI RFLP is detected with the 5-HT1a serotonin receptor probe G21. *Nucleic Acids Research, 18*, 691.

Khoury, M. J. (1994). Case–parental control method in the search for disease-susceptibility genes. *American Journal of Human Genetics, 55*, 414–415.

Khoury, M. J., & Flanders, W. D. (1996). Nontraditional epidemiologic approaches in the analysis of gene-environment interaction: Case–control studies with no controls. *American Journal of Epidemiology, 144*, 207–213.

Kim, S. W., Dysken, M. W., & Kline, M. D. (1990). Monozygotic twins with obsessive–compulsive disorder. *British Journal of Psychiatry, 156*, 435–438.

Kohen, R., Metcalf, M. A., Khan, N., Druck, T., Huebner, K., Lachowicz, J. E., Meltzer, H. Y., Sibley, D. R., Roth, B. L., & Hamblin, M. W. (1996). Cloning, characterization, and chromosomal localization of a human 5-HT6 serotonin receptor. *Journal of Neurochemistry, 66*(1), 47–56.

Kringlen, E. (1965). Obsessional neurotics: A long-term follow-up. *British Journal of Psychiatry, 111*, 709–722.

Kruesi, M. J., Rapoport, J. L., Hamburger, S., et al. (1990). Cerebrospinal fluid monoamine metabolites, aggression, and impulsivity in disruptive behavior disorders of children and adolescents. *Archives of General Psychiatry, 47*, 419–426.

Lannfelt, L., Sokoloff, P., Martres, M.-P., Pilon, C., Giros, B., Jonsson, E., Sedvall, G., & Schwartz, J.-C. (1992). Amino acid substitution in the dopamine D3 receptor as a useful polymorphism for investigating psychiatric disorders. *Psychiatric Genetics, 2,* 249–256.

Lappalainen, J., Zhan, L., Dean, M., Oz, M., Ozaki, N., Yu, D. H., Virkkunen, M., Weight, F., Linnoila, M., & Goldman, D. (1995). Identification, expression, and pharmacology of Cys23-Ser23 substitution in the human 5-HT2C receptor gene (HTR2C). *Genomics, 27*(2), 274–279.

Lenane, M. C., Swedo, S. E., Leonard, H., et al. (1990). Psychiatric disorders in first degree relatives of children and adolescents with obsessive compulsive disorder. *Journal of the American Academy of Child and Adolescent Psychiatry, 29,* 407–412.

Lenane, M. C., Swedo, S. E., Rapoport, J. L., Leonard, H., Sceery, W., & Guroff, J. J. (1992). Rates of obsessive compulsive disorder in first degree relatives of patients with trichotillomania: A research note. *Journal of Child Psychology and Psychiatry, 33*(5), 925–933.

Lesch, K. P., Balling, U., Gross, J., Strauss, K., Wolozin, B. L., & Murphy, D. L. (1994). Organisation of the human serotonin transporter gene. *Journal of Neural Transmission, 95,* 157–162.

Lesch, K. P., Dietmar, B., Heils, A., Sabol, S. Z., Greenberg, B. D., Petri, S., Benjamin, J., Müller, C. R., Hamer, D. H., Murphy, D. L. (1996). Association of anxiety-related traits with a polymorphism in the serotonin transporter gene regulatory region. *Science, 274,* 1527–1531.

Lesch, K. P., Wolozin, B. L., Estler, H. C., Murphy, D. L., & Riederer, P. (1993). Isolation of a cDNA encoding the human brain serotonin transporter. *Journal of Neural Transmission, 91,* 67–72.

Lewis, A. (1936). Problems of obsessional illness. *Proceedings of the Royal Society of Medicine, 29,* 325–36.

Li, S., McInnis, M. G., Margolis, R., Antonarakis, S., & Ross, C. (1993). Novel triplicate repeat containing gene in human brain: Cloning, expression and length polymorphisms. *Genomics, 16,* 572–579.

Liebowitz, M. R., Hollander, E., Schneier, F., et al. (1989). Fluoxetine treatment of obsessive–compulsive disorder: An open clinical trial. *Journal of Clinical Psychopharmacology, 9,* 423–427.

Lipinski, J. F., Mallya, G., Zimmerman, P., & Pope, H. G. (1989). Fluoxetine-induced akathisia: Clinical and theoretical implications. *Journal of Clinical Psychiatry, 50,* 339–342.

Lo, W. J. (1967). A follow-up study of obsessional neurotics in Hong Kong Chinese. *British Journal of Psychiatry, 113,* 823–832.

Lydiard, F. B., Ballenger, J. C., Ellinwood, E., et al. (1990). *CSF monoamine metabolites in obsessive–compulsive disorder.* Paper presented at the 143rd Annual Meeting of the American Psychiatric Association, New York.

Marks, I. M., Crowe, M., Drewe, E., et al. (1969). Obsessive–compulsive neurosis in identical twins. *British Journal of Psychiatry, 115,* 991–998.

Marazziti, D., Hollander, E., Lensi, P., Ravagli, S., & Cassano, G. B. (1992). Peripheral markers of serotonin and dopamine function in obsessive–compulsive disorder. *Psychiatry Research, 42,* 41–51.

Mattes, H., Boschert, U., Amlaiky, N., Grailhe, R., Plassa, J.-L., Muscatelli, R., Mattei, M. G., & Hen, R. (1993). Mouse 5-hydroxytryptamine$_{5A}$ and 5-hydroxytryptamine$_{5B}$ receptors define a new family of serotonin receptors: Cloning, functional expression, and chromosomal localization. *Molecular Pharmacology, 43,* 313–319.

McDougle, C., Goodman, W., Leckman, J., Lee, N., Heninger, G., & Price, L. (1994).

Haloperidol addition in fluvoxamine-refractory obsessive–compulsive disorder. *Archives of General Psychiatry, 51,* 302–308.

McGuffin, P., & Mawson, D. (1980). Obsessive–compulsive neurosis: Two identical twin pairs. *British Journal of Psychiatry, 137,* 285–287.

McKeon, P., & Murray, R. (1987). Familial aspects of obsessive–compulsive neurosis. *British Journal of Psychiatry, 151,* 528–534.

Melmer, G., Sherrington, R., Mankoo, B., Kalsi, G., Curtis, D., & Gurling, H. M. D. (1991). A cosmid clone for the 5-HT1A receptor (HTR1A) reveals a TaqI RFLP that shows tight linkage to DNA loci D5S6, D5S39, and D5S76. *Genomics, 11,* 767–769.

Mendlewicz, J., Fleiss, J. L., Cataldo, M., & Rainer, J. D. (1975). Accuracy of the family history method in affective illness. *Archives of General Psychiatry, 32,* 309–314.

Nee, L., Caine, E. D., Polinsky, R. J., et al. (1980). Gilles de la Tourette's syndrome: Clinical and family study of 50 cases. *Annals of Neurology, 7,* 41–49.

Nicolini, H., Hanna, G., Baxter, L., Weissbacker, K., & Spence, M. A. (1990). Segregation analysis of obsessive–compulsive and associated disorders. *American Journal of Human Genetics, 47*(3), A141.

Nicolini, H., Weissbecker, K., Mejia, J., & De Carmona, M. (1993). Family study of obsessive compulsive disorder in a Mexican population. *Archives of Medical Research, 24*(2), 193–198.

Nielsen, D. A., Dean, M., & Goldman, D. (1992). Genetic mapping of the human tryptophan hydroxylase gene on chromosome 11, using an intronic conformational polymorphism. *American Journal of Human Genetics, 51,* 1366–1371.

Nothen, M. M., Erdmann, J., Shimron-Abarbanell, D., & Propping, P. (1994). Identification of genetic variation in the human serotonin 1D beta receptor gene. *Biochemical and Biophysical Research and Communication, 205,* 1194–1200.

Nothen, M. M., Erdmann, J., Shimron-Abarbanell, D., Rietschel, M., Albus, M., Maier, W., Chen, K., Shih, J. C., & Propping, P. (1996). Investigation of the serotonin 2A receptor gene in schizophrenia. *American Journal of Human Genetics, 59*(Suppl.), A230.

Novelli, E., Nobile, M., Diaferia, G., Sciuto, G., & Catalano, M. (1994). A molecular investigation suggests no relationship between obsessive compulsive disorder and the dopamine D2 receptor. *Neuropsychobiology, 29,* 61–63.

Ozaki, N., Lappalainien, J., Dean, M., Virkkunen, M., Linnoila, M., & Goldman, D. (1995). Mapping of the serotonin 5-HT1Da autoreceptor gene (HTR1D) on chromosome 1 using a silent polymorphism in the coding region. *Neuropsychiatric Genetics, 60,* 162–164.

Parker, N. (1964). Close identification in twins discordant for obsessional neurosis. *British Journal of Psychiatry, 110,* 496–504.

Pato, C. N., Pato, M. T., & Kennedy, J. L. (1993). Summary of the Third World Congress on Psychiatric Genetics. *American Journal of Medical Genetics (Neuropsychiatric Genetics), 48,* 234–237.

Pauls, D. L. (1992). The genetics of obsessive compulsive disorder and Gilles de la Tourette's syndrome. *Psychiatric Clinics of North America, 15*(4), 759–766.

Pauls, D. L., Alsobrook, J. P., Goodman, W., Rasmussen, S., & Leckman, J. F. (1995), A family study of obsessive compulsive disorder. *American Journal of Psychiatry, 152,* 76–84.

Pauls, D. L., & Leckman, J. F. (1986). The inheritance of Gilles de la Tourette's syndrome and associated behaviors. *New England Journal of Medicine, 315,* 993–997.

Pauls, D. L., Pakstis, A. J., Kurlan, R., Kidd, K. K., Leckman, J. F., Cohen, D. J., Kidd, J. R., Como, P., & Sparkes, R. (1990). Segregation and linkage analyses of Tourette's syndrome and related disorders. *Journal of the American Academy of Child and Adolescent Psychiatry, 29*(2), 195–203.

Pauls, D. L., Towbin, K. E., Leckman, J. F., et al. (1986). Gilles de la Tourette's syndrome and obsessive–compulsive disorder. *Archives of General Psychiatry, 43,* 1180–1182.

Petronis, A., & Kennedy, J. L. (1995). Unstable genes—unstable mind? *American Journal of Psychiatry, 152,* 164–172.

Petronis, A., Van Tol, H. H. M., & Kennedy, J. L. (1994). A SmaI PCR-RFLP in the 5' noncoding region of the human D4 dopamine receptor gene (DRD4). *Human Heredity, 44,* 58–60.

Pigott, T. A., Hill, J. L., Grady, T. A., K'Heureux, F., Bernstein, S., Rubenstein, C. S., & Murphy, D. L. (1993). A comparison of the behavioral effects of oral versus intravenous *m*CPP administration in OCD patients and effect of metergoline prior to IV *m*CPP. *Biological Psychiatry 33,* 3–14.

Pitman, R. K., Green, R. C., Jenike, J. A., et al. (1987). Clinical comparison of Tourette's disorder and obsessive–compulsive disorder. *American Journal of Psychiatry, 144,* 1166–1171.

Plomin, R., & Neiderhiser, J. M. (1992). Genetics and experience. *Current Directions in Psychological Science, 1*(5), 160–163.

Ramamoorthy, S., Bauman, A. L., Moore, K. R., Han, H., Yang-Feng, T., Chang, A. S., Ganapathy, V., & Blakely, R. D. (1993). Antidepressant- and cocaine-sensitive human serotonin transporter: Molecular cloning, expression, and chromosomal localization. *Proceedings of the National Academy of Science, 90,* 2542–2546.

Rasmussen, S. A. (1993). Genetic studies of obsessive–compulsive disorder. *Annals of Clinical Psychiatry, 5,* 241–248.

Rasmussen, S. A., & Eisen, J. L. (1991). Phenomenology of OCD: Clinical subtypes, heterogeneity and coexistence. In J. Zohar, T. Insel, & S. Rasmussen (Eds.), *The psychobiology of obsessive–compulsive disorder.* New York: Springer.

Rasmussen, S. A., & Eisen, J. L. (1994). The epidemiology and differential diagnosis of obsessive compulsive disorder. *Journal of Clinical Psychiatry, 55*(10), 5–10.

Rasmussen, S. A., & Tsuang, M. T. (1986). Clinical characteristics and family history in DSM-III obsessive–compulsive disorder. *American Journal of Psychiatry, 143,* 317–322.

Ravizza, L., Rocca, P., Maina, G., et al. (1991). An analysis of ^{3}H-imipramine binding in OCD. *Biological Psychiatry, 29*(11S), 440S–441S.

Riddle, M. A., Scahill, L., King, R., et al. (1990). Obsessive compulsive disorder in children and adolescents: Phenomenology and family history. *Journal of the American Academy of Child and Adolescent Psychiatry, 29,* 766–772.

Riggins, G. J., Lokey, L., & Warren, S. (1992). CGG repeat polymorphism at the c-Ha-ras oncogene locus. *Human Molecular Genetics, 1,* 775.

Risch, N. (1990). Linkage strategies for genetically complex traits: I. Multilocus traits. *American Journal of Human Genetics, 46*(2), 222–228.

Risch, N., & Merikangas, K. (1996). The future of genetic studies of complex human diseases. *Science, 273,* 1516–1517.

Robins, L. N., Helzer, J. I., Weissman, M. M., et al. (1984). Lifetime prevalence of specific psychiatric disorders in three sites. *Archives of General Psychiatry, 41,* 949–959.

Rosenberg, C. M. (1967). Familial aspects of obsessional neurosis. *British Journal of Psychiatry, 113,* 405–413.

Ruat, M., Traiffort, E., Leurs, R., Tardivel-Lacombe, J., Diaz, J., Arrang, J. M., & Schwartz, J. C. (1993). Molecular cloning, characterization, and localization of a high-affinity serotonin receptor (5-HT$_7$) activating cAMP formation. *Proceedings of the National Academy of Science, 90,* 8547–8551.

Rudin, E. (1953). Ein Beitrag zur Frage der Zwangskrankheit insbesondere ihrer hereditaren Beziehungen. *Archive für Psychiatrie und Zeitschrift für Neurologie, 191,* 14–54.

Shapiro, A. K., Shapiro, E., & Eisenkraft, G. J. (1983). Treatment of Gilles de la Tourette syndrome with pimozide. *American Journal of Psychiatry, 140,* 1183–1186.

Shen, Y., Monsma, F. J., Metcalf, M. A., Jose, P. A., Hamblin, M. W., & Sibley, D. R. (1993). Molecular cloning and expression of a 5-hydroxytryptamine$_7$ serotonin receptor subtype. *Journal of Biological Chemistry, 268,* 18200–18204.

Sidenberg, D. G., Basset, A. S., Demchyshyn, L., Niznik, H. B., Macciardi, F., Kamble, A. B., Honer, W. G., & Kennedy, J. L. (1993). New polymorphism for the human serotonin 1D receptor variant not linked to schizophrenia in five Canadian pedigrees. *Human Heredity, 43,* 315–318.

Sherrington, R., Mankoo, B., Attwood, J., Kalsi, G., Curtis, D., Buetow, K., Povey, S., & Gurling, H. (1993). Cloning of the human dopamine D5 receptor gene and identification of a highly polymorphic microsatellite for the DRD5 locus that shows tight linkage to the chromosome 4p reference marker RAF 1P1. *Genomics, 18,* 423–425.

Shimron-Abarbanell, D., Harms, H., Erdmann, J., Albus, M., Maier, W., Rietschel, M., Korner, J., Weigelt, B., Franzek, E., Sander, T., Knapp, M., Propping, P., & Nothen, M. M. (1996). Systematic screening for mutations in the human serotonin 1F receptor gene in patients with bipolar affective disorder and schizophrenia. *American Journal of Medical Genetics (Neuropsychiatric Genetics), 67,* 225–228.

Shimron-Abarbanell, D., Nothen, M. M., Erdmann, J., & Propping, P. (1995). Lack of genetically determined structural variants of the human serotonin-1E (5-HT1E) receptor protein points to its evolutionary conservation. *Molecular Brain Research, 29,* 387–390.

Swedo, S. E., & Kiessling, L. S. (1994). Speculations on antineuronal antibody-mediated neuropsychiatric disorders of childhood. *Pediatrics, 93*(2), 323–326.

Swinson, R. P., & Joffe, R. T. (1988). Biological challenges in obsessive compulsive disorder. *Progress in Neuropsychopharmacology and Biological Psychiatry, 12,* 269–275.

Tarsh, M. (1978). Severe obsessional illness in dizygotic twins treated by leukotomy. *Comprehensive Psychiatry, 19*(2), 165–169.

Thoren, P., Asberg, M., Bertillson, L., Mellstrom, B., Pharm, M., Sjoqvist, R., & Traskman, L. (1980). Clomipramine treatment of obsessive–compulsive disorder: II. Biochemical aspects. *Archives of General Psychiatry, 37,* 1289–1294.

Tienari, P. (1963). Psychiatric illnesses in identical twins. *Acta Psychiatrica Scandinavica, 39*(Suppl. 171), 3–195.

Torgersen, S. (1983). Genetic factors in anxiety disorder. *Archives of General Psychiatry, 40,* 1085–1089.

Toro, J., Montserrat, C., Osejo, E., & Salamero, M. (1992). Obsessive–compulsive disorder in childhood and adolescence: A clinical study. *Journal of Child Psychology and Psychiatry, 33*(6), 1025–1037.

Vandenbergh, D. J., Persico, A. M., & Uhl, G. R. (1992). A human dopamine transporter cDNA predicts reduced glycosylation, displays a novel repetitive element and provides racially dimorphic TAQI RFLPs. *Molecular Brain Research, 15,* 161–166.

Van Tol, H. H. M., Wu, C. M., Guan, H.-C., Ohara, K., Bunzow, J. R., Civelli, O., & Kennedy, J. L., Seeman, P., Niznik, H., & Jovanovic, V. (1992). Multiple dopamine D4 receptor variants in the human population. *Nature, 358,* 149–152.

Warren, J. T. Jr., Peacock, M. L., Rodriguez, L. C., & Fink, J. K. (1993). An MspI polymorphism in the human serotonin receptor gene (HTR2): Detection by DGGE and RFLP analysis. *Human Molecular Genetics, 2*(3), 338.

Warren, S. T. (1996). The expanding world of trinucleotide repeats. *Science, 271,* 1374–1375.

Weizman, A., Carmi, M., Hermesh, H., Shahar, A., Apter, A., Tyano, S., & Rehavi, M. (1986). High-affinity imipramine binding and serotonin uptake in platelets of eight adolescent and ten adult obsessive–compulsive patients. *American Journal of Psychiatry 143,* 335–339.

Woodruff, R., & Pitts, F. N. Jr. (1964). Monozygotic twins with obsessional illness. *American Journal of Psychiatry, 120,* 1075–1080.

Yaryura-Tobias, J., & Bhagavan, H. (1977). L-tryptophan in obsessive–compulsive disorders. *American Journal of Psychiatry, 134,* 1298–1299.

Zifa, E., & Fillion, G. (1992). 5-Hydroxytryptamine receptors. *Pharmacology Review, 44,* 401–458.

Zohar, J., Mueller, E., Insel, T., Zohar-Kadouch, R., & Murphy, D. (1987). Serotonergic responsivity in obsessive–compulsive disorder. *Archives of General Psychiatry, 44,* 946–951.

Chapter 9

THE RELATIONSHIP BETWEEN OBSESSIVE–COMPULSIVE DISORDER AND OTHER ANXIETY-BASED DISORDERS

Timothy A. Brown

Although obsessive–compulsive disorder (OCD) has existed in our classification systems of mental disorders for decades, perhaps no disorder has undergone greater scrutiny with regard to its relationship or distinctiveness to other diagnoses. At the request of the editors, this chapter focuses on the extant literature bearing on the overlap and distinctiveness of OCD and its constituent features to other anxiety-based disorders such as generalized anxiety disorder (GAD) and selected somatoform disorders (e.g., hypochondriasis, body dysmorphic disorder). Nevertheless, although the majority of research addressing the diagnostic and symptomatic boundary of OCD has involved anxiety-based disorders, it is interesting to note that, unlike other anxiety disorders, OCD has been considered as potentially overlapping with or related to almost all other major classes of psychopathology, including the mood disorders (e.g., Hudson & Pope, 1990; Insel, Zahn, & Murphy, 1985), the personality disorders (e.g., Baer, Jenike, & Ricciardi, 1990; Joffe, Swinson, & Regan, 1988; Pfohl, 1996), the eating disorders (e.g., Pigott et al., 1991; Rubenstein, Altemus, Pigott, Hess, & Murphy, 1995; Thiel, Broocks, Ohlmeier, Jacoby, & Schüßler, 1995), the impulse control disorders (i.e., trichotillomania; e.g., Stein, Simeon, Cohen, & Hollander, 1995), the tic disorders (e.g., Leckman & Chittenden, 1990; Pauls, Towbin, Leckman, Zahner, & Cohen, 1986), and the schizophrenic disorders (e.g., Enright, 1996; Insel & Akiskal, 1986; for reviews, see McElroy, Phillips, & Keck, 1994; Rasmussen & Eisen, 1992; Tynes, White, & Steketee, 1990).

Before turning to the review of evidence bearing on the relationship of

OCD to other anxiety-based disorders, a relatively new issue pertaining to the boundary between OCD and the schizophrenic disorders merits brief mention. It is interesting to note that, in addition to the recognition of "mental" compulsions (i.e., mental acts, such as counting or repeating prayers, aimed at preventing or reducing distress, or preventing a feared outcome associated with an obsession), the major revision to the diagnostic criteria for OCD in DSM-IV was the deemphasis on the requirement that persons with OCD recognize their obsessions and compulsions as excessive or unreasonable (Foa & Kozak, 1995). Indeed, in DSM-IV, the diagnosis of OCD can now be assigned with the specifier "poor insight type" to reflect cases in which, for most of the time during the disturbance, the person does not recognize that the obsessions and compulsions are excessive or unreasonable (American Psychiatric Association, 1994). Although these revisions have no foreseeable implications for obfuscating or clarifying the boundary between OCD and other anxiety-based disorders,[1] these changes may bear on the distinction between OCD and the delusional and schizophrenic disorders. Indeed, whereas researchers had begun to converge on the conclusion that the empirical evidence does not support a relationship between OCD and the schizophrenic disorders (Tynes et al., 1990; cf. Enright, 1996), this revision to the DSM-IV criteria for OCD is likely to renew clinical and empirical interest in the potential boundary problems between overvalued obsessions and delusional beliefs (e.g., what are the quantitative or qualitative differences between delusions vs. obsessions that are strongly maintained by the person with OCD as being sensible and reasonable?; cf. Foa & Kozak, 1995; Kozak & Foa, 1994).

SUPPORT FOR OCD AT THE DIAGNOSTIC AND STRUCTURAL LEVELS

Despite the wide number of diagnoses considered potentially to have salient relationships or boundary problems with OCD, relative to the other anxiety disorders, the diagnostic reliability of OCD has been quite favorable. For instance, in a recent study examining the reliability of DSM-III-R (American Psychiatric Association, 1987) anxiety disorders as assessed by the Anxiety Disorders Interview Schedule—Revised (ADIS-R; Di Nardo & Barlow, 1988), the principal diagnosis of OCD was associated with excellent diagnostic reliability (kappa = .80; based on two independent administrations of the ADIS-R), second only to simple phobia (kappa = .82; Di Nardo, Moras, Barlow, Rapee, & Brown, 1993). Preliminary evidence based on a limited number of patients with anxiety or mood disorders ($n = 75$) who were evaluated with the Anxiety Disorders Interview Schedule for DSM-IV—Lifetime Version (ADIS-IV-L; Di Nardo, Brown, & Barlow, 1994) suggests that the DSM-IV diagnosis of OCD is associated with excellent diag-

---

[1]However, Foa and Kozak (1995) assert that acknowledgment in DSM-IV of the existence of mental compulsions may foster the clarification of the boundary between OCD and GAD and the mood disorders, because the presence of mental rituals is specific to OCD.

nostic reliability as well (kappa = .90; Di Nardo, Brown, Lawton, & Barlow, 1995).

Previously (e.g., Brown, 1996), we have speculated that the high rates of interrater agreement for the diagnosis of OCD may be fostered by the fact that the disorder is usually associated with an overt behavioral marker (i.e., behavioral compulsions). Findings from a recent study support this assertion (Chorpita, Brown, & Barlow, in press). In this study, Chorpita et al. conducted an in-depth analysis of the sources of diagnostic disagreement using the sample reported on previously by Di Nardo et al. (1993). Results indicated that of the 14 cases in which both interviewers independently assigned a diagnosis of OCD, all involved patients who evidenced behavioral compulsions. Conversely, two-thirds of the diagnostic disagreements (six of nine) involved clinical presentations of obsessions only. Indeed, the association between the presence–absence of compulsions and diagnostic (dis)agreement was statistically significant ($p < .05$, based on Fisher's exact test).

In addition, data from family and genetic studies are pertinent to the validity of OCD at the diagnostic level. Findings from such investigations have provided mixed support for the empirical basis of OCD. Whereas several twin studies have produced findings attesting to the genetic aggregation in OCD (i.e., concordance rates are highest in monozygotic twins; for a review, see Rasmussen & Tsuang, 1986), others have indicated that genetic factors exert a nonspecific influence for the development of anxiety disorders in general (Andrews, Stewart, Allen, & Henderson, 1990; Torgerson, 1983; cf. Kendler, Neale, Kessler, Heath, & Eaves, 1992). Although initial family studies found no significant elevations in risk for OCD in first-order relatives of patients with the disorder (e.g., McKeon & Murray, 1987), recent investigations employing more sophisticated methodologies (e.g., direct interview of relatives) have found the rates of OCD to be higher in relatives of probands compared to relatives of control subjects (e.g., Black, Noyes, Goldstein, & Blum, 1992; Pauls, Alsobrook, Goodman, Rasmussen, & Leckman, 1995). For example, Pauls et al. (1995) administered structured interviews to 466 first-degree relatives of 100 probands with OCD, and to 113 first-degree relatives of 33 persons with no mental disorder. The rates of OCD and subthreshold OCD were significantly greater among the relatives of probands with OCD (10.3% and 7.9%, respectively) than among relatives of comparison subjects (1.9% and 2.0%, respectively). Interestingly, the rate of tic disorders was also significantly greater among relatives of probands (4.6%) than among relatives of comparison subjects (1.0%), supporting prior evidence and conceptual speculation of an interrelationship between OCD and the tic disorders (cf. Pauls et al., 1986). Thus, although more research is needed to reconcile inconsistent findings from earlier studies, evidence from more recent investigations has been largely supportive of the familial nature of OCD.

Of studies that bear on the validation of the classification of anxiety and mood disorders, the majority have been conducted at the diagnostic level (e.g., family and twin studies), or have examined dimensional features within a diagnostic category (e.g., across-diagnosis comparisons to determine if a given disorder is distinguished from other disorders on a given dimension). As has been discussed at length elsewhere (e.g., Brown, 1996; Brown & Chorpita, 1996; Livesley, Schroeder, Jackson, & Jang, 1994), the categorical approach to analysis has many limitations. For instance, studies conducted at the diagnostic level are restricted by their adherence to the disorders defined by the classification system; that is, by using diagnoses as the units of analysis, researchers are implicitly accepting or are bound to the nosology they are evaluating. Moreover, as most researchers would agree that psychopathological phenomena operate on a continuum, analyses at the diagnostic level rely largely on data that do not reflect the dimensional nature of these features. Categorization of dimensional variables usually forfeits meaningful information by artificially (and often erroneously) collapsing variability above and below an arbitrary threshold (e.g., presence–absence of a DSM-IV disorder). Conversely, if assessment was performed at the dimensional level, the interrelationships among symptoms and syndromes could be examined, as could the extent to which the latent structure of these features corresponds to the structure forwarded by major classification systems such as DSM-IV.

Analyses of this nature are beginning to appear in the literature. For example, Zinbarg and Barlow (1996) administered questionnaires of key features of anxiety and related dimensions—including panic, sensitivity to social evaluation, anxiety sensitivity, depression, worry, obsessions, compulsions, and specific fears—to 432 patients and 32 normal controls. Results of exploratory and confirmatory factor analyses of these measures produced a factor structure that was largely consistent with the DSM-III-R nosology. Specifically, the six factors obtained from these solutions were clearly identified as relating to Social Anxiety, Generalized Dysphoria, Agoraphobia, Fear of Fear, Obsessions and Compulsions, and Simple Fears. All six factors loaded significantly (loadings ranged from .33 to .82) onto a higher-order general factor (i.e., a higher-order factor without indicators), which was labeled by the authors as Negative Affect. Support for DSM-III-R was also provided by discriminant function analyses indicating that selected diagnostic groups (defined by principal DSM-III-R diagnoses established by ADIS-R interviews) evidenced characteristic profiles in factor scores generated from a higher-order factor analysis. Of particular relevance to the present chapter was the finding of one statistically significant discriminant function that differentiated patients with OCD from the seven other groups examined (i.e., panic disorder, panic disorder with agoraphobia, GAD, simple phobia, major depression, social phobia, no mental disorder). Germane to issues discussed later in this chapter, the results of this analysis also indicated that, while scoring significantly below patients with OCD, patients with a principal diagnosis of GAD scored above persons with panic disorder, panic disorder with agoraphobia, simple phobia, social phobia, and no mental disorder. The finding that these patients showed an intermediate elevation on the obsessions and compulsions function may be viewed in support of the notion that GAD and OCD are more closely related to each other than they are to other anxiety disorders.

Although the findings of Zinbarg and Barlow (1996) provide encouraging evidence for the discriminant validity of the DSM-III-R anxiety disorder constructs, as noted by the authors, the results were limited by a number of factors, including the sole reliance on self-report measures in the analyses of latent structure (e.g., method variance could account in part for the structure observed). For example, in the various factor analyses, the Obsessions and Compulsions factor was defined exclusively by three subscales from the Maudsley Obsessional–Compulsive Inventory (MOCI; Hodgson & Rachman, 1977), thus raising the possibility that method variance contributed strongly to its emergence as a distinct factor. The most optimal approach for evaluating the shared and distinctive features of anxiety and mood disorders would entail structural analyses of dimensional data generated from multiple assessment modalities (e.g., clinician ratings, self-report).

Along these lines, we have recently examined the structural relationships of dimensions of key features of selected DSM-IV disorders and dimensions of the tripartite model of anxiety and depression (Clark & Watson, 1991) in a sample of 350 patients with DSM-IV anxiety and mood disorders (Brown, Chorpita, & Barlow, in press). The five DSM-IV constructs evaluated in this study (i.e., mood disorders, GAD, panic disorder/agoraphobia, OCD, social phobia) were defined by both questionnaires and dimensional clinician ratings from the ADIS-IV-L. Results of confirmatory factor analysis supported the discriminant validity of DSM-IV for the five constructs examined. Specifically, relative to models that collapsed across all or various disorders (e.g., a one-factor model and a four-factor model, where GAD and mood disorders were combined as a single factor), the five-factor model (i.e., mood disorders, GAD, panic disorder/agoraphobia, OCD, social phobia) provided the best fit for the data.

While upholding the discriminant validity of these domains, inspection of the zero-order correlations among these latent factors highlighted areas of potential overlap. For instance, the OCD latent factor had its strongest correlation with the GAD latent factor ($r = .52$), supporting previous contentions that the closest "neighbor" to OCD among the various anxiety and mood disorders is GAD. Other factor correlations were also in accord with prior evidence and conceptual assertions (i.e., correlations between the OCD latent factor and other factors were .43, .29, and .30 for mood disorders, panic disorder/agoraphobia, and social phobia, respectively, consistent with evidence that OCD may have stronger associations with depression than with some anxiety disorders; cf. Brown & Barlow, 1992).

In addition, Brown et al. (in press) comparatively evaluated several structural models of the interrelationships among the five DSM-IV disorder latent factors and three latent factors corresponding to the tripartite model of anxiety and depression (i.e., negative affect, positive affect, autonomic arousal). Consistent with theoretical predictions (cf. Clark, Watson, & Mineka, 1994), superior data fit was associated with a model that specified Negative Affect and Positive Affect as higher-order factors to the DSM-IV disorder factors (with significant paths from Negative Affect to each of the five DSM-IV factors, and significant paths from Positive Affect to the Mood Disorder and Social Phobia factors only), and that specified Autonomic Arousal as a lower-order factor (with significant paths from

Panic Disorder/Agoraphobia and Generalized Anxiety Disorder to Autonomic Arousal).[2] Thus, these results are consistent with predictions based on the tripartite model, where negative affect is considered as a dispositional (vulnerability) trait that is common to both anxiety and mood disorders, and positive affect is viewed as a dispositional factor to the development of depression, and perhaps social phobia (although these interpretations require verification from longitudinal research). However, of interest to the present chapter were findings indicating that although strong and statistically significant paths were obtained from Negative Affect to both GAD (.74) and OCD (.43), modification indices generated by LISREL suggested that model fit would improve significantly if correlated residuals were specified between the OCD and GAD latent factors. Indeed, model fit was enhanced by this revision (correlated error between OCD and GAD was .18, $p < .001$).

Collectively, the results of Zinbarg and Barlow (1996) and Brown et al. (in press) indicate that whereas the constituent features of OCD and GAD do evidence considerable differentiation, relative to the other anxiety and mood disorders, these features possess the highest degree of overlap. Also, the finding from Brown et al. (in press) that indicated correlated residuals of the OCD and GAD latent factors suggests that the relationship between these disorders may be due in part to the influence of a shared high-order factor that is specific to these two disorders.

DIAGNOSTIC AND DIMENSIONAL DISTINCTIVENESS OF OCD AND GAD

The potential boundary problems between OCD and GAD were the topic of considerable discussion and debate during the process of evaluating and revising the diagnostic criteria for anxiety disorders in DSM-IV (cf. Brown, Barlow, & Liebowitz, 1994). These discussions centered mainly around the resemblance and possible poor discriminant validity in the constructs of chronic worry and obsessions (i.e., both are excessive and uncontrollable cognitive processes associated with high levels of negative affect). Literature reviews of this area commissioned by the DSM-IV Anxiety Disorders Workgroup indicated a paucity of empirical data bearing on the distinctiveness and interrelationship of worry and obsessions (and the diagnoses of OCD and GAD). As summarized by Turner, Beidel, and Stanley (1992), at the time, no compelling data existed to attest to whether worry and obsessions reflect "uniquely different cognitive phenomena or whether they simply refer to the same mental process, perhaps reflecting different degrees of intensity" (p. 231). Potentially adding to the obfuscation of the

[2]Interestingly, the path from Generalized Anxiety Disorder to Autonomic Arousal was negative (completely standardized coefficient = −.22), consistent with laboratory-based findings indicating that the key symptoms of DSM-IV generalized anxiety disorder (i.e., chronic worry) are associated with autonomic suppression.

boundary between OCD and GAD are findings that worry is present to some degree in all emotional disorders (cf. Brown et al., 1994) and may in fact have etiological significance to the progression of subclinical intrusive thoughts to clinical obsessions (cf. Salkovskis, 1989). Fortunately, the issues raised during the process of developing DSM-IV have since spawned research in this important area.

For example, shortly after this issue was raised by the DSM-IV Anxiety Disorders Workgroup, an investigation was initiated at our center to examine the diagnostic and symptom distinguishability of OCD and GAD (Brown, Moras, Zinbarg, & Barlow, 1993). Participants were 31 patients with a principal DSM-III-R diagnosis of OCD and 46 patients with a principal DSM-III-R diagnosis of GAD, who were assessed with ADIS-R and a variety of questionnaires. Slightly over half (53%; $n = 41$ of 77) of the sample was administered the ADIS-R on two occasions (on separate days, by two independent evaluators) for purposes of examining diagnostic reliability. Results from the diagnostic reliability subsample indicated that of the 12 diagnostic disagreements that occurred (8 of 24 for GAD; 4 of 17 for OCD), in no instance did one interviewer assign a diagnosis of OCD and the other, GAD. Thus, diagnostic disagreements in this sample did not involve differential diagnosis or diagnostic boundary problems between OCD and GAD. In fact, the four diagnostic disagreements associated with the principal diagnosis of OCD involved the diagnoses of panic disorder ($n = 2$), social phobia, and anxiety disorder not otherwise specified (NOS), disorders that are usually not considered as posing boundary problems with OCD. Further evidence that OCD and GAD were distinct at the diagnostic level was provided by findings pertaining to rates and patterns of comorbidity associated with these diagnoses. Consistent with the findings of larger-scale comorbidity studies (e.g., Brawman-Mintzer et al., 1993; Brown & Barlow, 1992; Sanderson, Di Nardo, Rapee, & Barlow, 1990), results indicated that GAD and OCD co-occurred infrequently. Specifically, only one patient with a principal diagnosis of GAD received an additional diagnosis of OCD, and only two patients with a principal diagnosis of OCD received an additional diagnosis of GAD. Although the low rate of co-occurrence of OCD and GAD (as well as the absence of diagnostic disagreements involving these two disorders) could be interpreted in support of the position that the features of these disorders do not overlap or covary extensively, it is still possible that diagnosticians did indeed observe overlapping features but opted to subsume the features of one disorder under the disorder that was assigned as the principal diagnosis. Nevertheless, Brown et al. (1993) concluded that this possibility was unlikely, particularly in light of between-group comparisons indicating that OCD and GAD could be differentiated on disorder-specific measures (e.g., patients with OCD obtained significantly higher scores than patients with GAD on the MOCI; patients with GAD obtained significantly higher scores than patients with OCD on the Penn State Worry Questionnaire, a measure of the trait of chronic worry; cf. Brown, Antony, & Barlow, 1992).

Nevertheless, comparisons at the diagnostic level do not address directly the degree of overlap and distinguishability between the constructs of obsessions and chronic worry. As suggested earlier in this chapter, the optimal approach to examining this issue would best conducted at the dimensional level. Dimensionalization of these constructs should follow from formal definitions provided in DSM-IV: "obsessions"—recurrent and persistent thoughts, impulses, or images that are experienced, at some time during the disturbance, as intrusive and inappropriate and that cause marked anxiety and distress; "chronic worry"—excessive apprehensive expectation, occurring more days than not for at least 6 months, about a number of events or activities (e.g., work or school performance) that person finds difficult to control (American Psychiatric Association, 1994). The DSM-IV definition of worry has been elaborated upon by several investigators. Perhaps the most widely recognized is the definition provided by Borkovec (1994) who defines worry as a predominantly verbal–linguistic attempt to avoid future aversive events, that is, experienced by the worrier as negative-affect laden and uncontrollable. A predominance of thought activity may be particularly salient to the phenomenology and distinctiveness of worry given initial evidence that worry is associated with a suppression of physiological activity (autonomic arousal), because worrisome thinking may foster cognitive avoidance of threat- and affect-laden imagery (Borkovec & Hu, 1990; Borkovec & Inz, 1990; Borkovec, Lyonfields, Wiser, & Diehl, 1993; Hoehn-Saric, McLeod, & Zimmerli, 1989; Lyonfields, Borkovec, & Thayer, 1995). If borne out by future research, these findings may elucidate important differences between worry and obsessions; for instance, worry may exclusively take the form of cognitive activity, whereas obsessions may manifest in a variety of forms (e.g., thoughts, impulses, images). Similarly, given initial findings suggesting that chronic worry is associated with low vagal tone and autonomic inflexibility, it would be of interest to examine the physiological concomitants and sequelae of obsessions to determine the extent of overlap or distinction with worry.

In their review of the literature for DSM-IV, Turner et al. (1992) highlighted several similarities and differences between obsessions and worry that merit future research attention. Similarities underscored by Turner et al. (1992) included the following: (1) both obsessions and worry are present in varying degrees in clinical and nonclinical populations; (2) both possess a similar form and content (although note the considerations discussed in the preceding paragraph); (3) heightened frequency and perceptions of uncontrollability foster clinical and subclinical delineations of both phenomena; (4) both are mediated by negative affect, which in turn is mediated by attentional biases and negative attributions (cf. Salkovskis, 1989). Nevertheless, Turner et al. (1992) also noted several dimensions that might demarcate the boundaries between obsessions and worry: (1) Worry is more likely to be self-initiated or precipitated by common circumstances of daily living (whereas obsessions may be more apt to experienced as intrusive or uncued); (2) the content of worry is more apt to be linked to common circumstances of daily living (e.g., concern about finances, family, worry, etc.; whereas the content of obsessions may be more apt to be bizarre or outside the range of the person's typical life circumstances);[3] and (3) though both chronic worry and obsessions may be experienced as uncontrollable, obsessions may be associated with a greater degree of resistance and perceptions of unacceptability (although this distinction may not apply to some cases, as reflected by the revision introduced in DSM-IV that provides diagnostic coverage for persons with "poor insight type" of OCD).

Research that existed around the time of Turner et al.'s (1992) review provided indirect, descriptive support for several of their proposed distinctions including precipitants (e.g., Craske, Rapee, Jackel, & Barlow, 1989; Rachman & De Silva, 1978), content (e.g., Borkovec, Shadick, & Hopkins, 1991; Rachman & Hodgson, 1980), form (e.g., Borkovec & Inz, 1990; Rachman & Hodgson, 1980), and acceptability (e.g., Rachman & Hodgson, 1980; Roemer & Borkovec, 1993). Although clinical research conducted since Turner et al.'s (1992) review has not addressed these points directly (i.e., no research with clinical patients has directly compared persons with obsessions to persons with chronic worry on the dimensions outlined by Turner et al.), a number of studies have since appeared that have examined the extent of overlap in self-report measures of these constructs.

For instance, in the aforementioned study by Brown et al. (1993), the interrelationships of the subscales of the MOCI and the Penn State Worry Questionnaire (PSWQ; Meyer, Miller, Metzger, & Borkovec, 1990) were examined in a combined sample of 501 patients with DSM-III-R anxiety and mood disorders and 32 persons with no mental disorder. Correlations between the PSWQ and the MOCI Doubting and Checking subscales (rs = .45 and .43, respectively) were significant larger than correlations between the PSWQ and the MOCI Washing and Repetition subscales (rs = .22 and −.02, respectively). Thus, as expected, greater overlap was observed in measures of obsessions and worry than in measures of compulsions and worry. However, reliable differentiation was indicated by a significantly larger correlation between the MOCI Doubting and Checking subscales (r = .58) than between both these obsession subscales and the PSWQ.

A similar pattern of correlations was obtained in a study by Freeston et al. (1994) in which the PSWQ and the Padua Inventory (PI; Sanavio, 1988; a 60-item measure of obsessive and compulsive symptoms that is scored as a total score and four subscales) were administered to 145 outpatients awaiting medical services in a hospital waiting room. Consistent with the results of Brown et al. (1993), who observed greater overlap in worry and obsessions than in worry and compulsions, results indicated that the PSWQ had a significantly strong correlation (r = .66) with the PI Mental Control subscale (a measure of obsessions, intrusive thoughts, doubts, etc.) than with the PI subscales of Contamination (r = .26), Checking (r = .36), and Impulses (r = .34).

---

[3]This parameter is underscored in DSM-IV in the differential diagnosis of OCD and GAD. Specifically, DSM-IV states that "generalized anxiety disorder is characterized by excessive worry, but such worries are distinguished from obsessions by the fact that the person experiences them as excessive concerns about real-life circumstances" (American Psychiatric Association, 1994, p. 421).

Results from nonclinical samples have also produced evidence that worry and obsessions represent distinct constructs. For example, Gross and Eifert (1990) conducted a factor analysis of a variety of measures of anxiety that had been administered to 162 college students. Findings indicated that worry and intrusive thought items loaded onto separate factors, which was interpreted as upholding the position that worry and intrusive thoughts could be differentiated. Similarly, Tallis and De Silva (1992) administered the Worry Domains Questionnaire (WDQ; Tallis, Eysenck, & Mathews, 1992) and the MOCI to 235 nonclinical subjects. The WDQ Total score was correlated significantly (but weakly, perhaps due to range restriction in the nonclinical sample) with the MOCI Checking and Doubting subscales (rs = .17 and .18, respectively), but not with the MOCI Washing or Repetition subscales (rs = .09 and .07, respectively). Although the authors concluded that these findings suggest that worry and checking are functionally similar (e.g., both are oriented toward future threat), these data provide further evidence of the differential pattern of relationships between worry and obsessions, and worry and compulsions, and support the notion that obsessions and worry display considerable differentiation (nonoverlap) at the nonclinical level.

Although no study to date has conducted a fine-grained analysis of parameters that may differentiate clinical obsessions and pathological worry (cf. Turner et al., 1992), this issue has been addressed in a study of normal worry and normal intrusive thoughts in a sample of 30 college students (Wells & Morrison, 1994). Based on dimensional ratings of obsessions and worries recorded during a 2-week self-monitoring period, the following differences were noted: Relative to obsessions, worries were rated by participants as consisting of significantly greater verbal content, greater duration, more realistic, more voluntary, and associated with a greater urge to act. No differences were obtained in dimensional self-ratings of intrusiveness, controllability, distress, resistance, and attention grabbing. Obviously, the extent that these similarities and differences apply to clinical obsessions and worry awaits replication and extension in patient samples.

As noted earlier, most of the extant research bearing on the boundary between OCD and GAD has focused on the relationship between obsessions and chronic worry. However, it is interesting to note that the behavioral features of these disorders may represent another point of overlap. Research indicates that the majority of persons with OCD engage in behavioral compulsions that are completed in attempt to neutralize or reduce distress associated with an obsession (Foa & Kozak, 1995). Although not part of any formal diagnostic definition of GAD, research has indicated that a large percentage of persons with this disorder engage in behaviors that are executed to cope with or prevent a feared outcome associated with their worry (e.g., Craske et al., 1989). For example, a person who worries excessively about receiving a negative job evaluation might repetitively reexamine paperwork to ensure that he or she has completed it correctly. In fact, because these behaviors are common and are believed to be functionally related to the maintenance of GAD, they represent formal targets of many current psychosocial treatments of this disorder (cf. Brown, O'Leary, &

Barlow, 1993). Although such safety behaviors are not necessarily unique to GAD (e.g., some patients with panic disorder repetitively check their pulse to allay concerns of cardiac dysfunction), these symptoms represent another potential point of overlap with OCD and thus are worthy of future empirical attention (e.g., can OCD compulsions be distinguished from GAD worry behaviors by such dimensions as their time-consuming, repetitive, or bizarre/superstitious nature?).

DISTINCTIVENESS OF OCD AND THE SOMATOFORM DISORDERS AND ILLNESS PHOBIA

In addition to GAD, disorders involving persistent anxiety about somatic concerns may pose boundary and differential diagnostic problems with certain forms of OCD. Specifically, the features of the anxiety disorder, specific phobia (other type, illness phobia), and the somatoform disorder, hypochondriasis, may possess considerable overlap with cases of OCD that involve contamination or somatic obsessions. This potential boundary issue is particularly salient in light of evidence that contamination and somatic fears are among the most common forms of obsessions in OCD (for instance, in the DSM-IV field trial for OCD, contamination obsessions were the most prevalent type of primary obsessions [endorsed by 37.8% of a sample of 425 patients with OCD]; somatic obsessions were the fourth most common [7.2%]; Foa & Kozak, 1995). In fact, in an earlier study of 100 patients with OCD, it was found that 34% evidenced somatic obsessions that compelled them to undergo repetitive examinations for reassurance of having no serious illness (Rasmussen & Tsuang, 1986). Although none of the patients in this sample was assigned hypochondriasis as a comorbid diagnosis, as Tynes et al. (1990) note, this could simply be an artifact of the hierarchical rules of the diagnostic system in place at the time (i.e., DSM-III; American Psychiatric Association, 1980), which discouraged the simultaneous assignment of these diagnoses. An avenue for future research would be to examine symptom and syndrome comorbidity of OCD and hypochondriasis as defined by DSM-IV, which does not contain the diagnostic hierarchy rules of earlier systems (i.e., both OCD and hypochondriasis can be assigned as formal diagnoses if the criteria for both are met). Data from a small sample of patients with hypochondriasis ($n = 42$) diagnosed by DSM-III-R criteria indicate that, although higher than a nonhypochondriacal control group (2.6%), the rate of comorbid OCD was low (9.5%; Barsky, Wyshak, & Klerman, 1992).

Nevertheless, the fear of having or contracting a physical disease may be a feature common to specific phobias of illness, hypochondriasis, and many presentations of OCD. Although to date no large-scale studies have addressed this issue, the similarities or overlap across disorders has been discussed in case reports (e.g., Fallon, Javitch, Hollander, & Liebowitz, 1991), review articles (Tynes et al., 1990), etiological models of these syndromes (e.g., Salkovskis & Warwick, 1986), and literature reviews commissioned by the DSM-IV Anxiety Disorders

Workgroup to guide revisions of the diagnostic criteria for OCD and specific phobia (e.g., Craske et al., 1996; Foa et al., 1996). Whereas earlier conceptions of these disorders suggested that OCD could be distinguished from hypochondriasis by the ego–dystonic nature of obsessions (i.e., unlike the beliefs of a person with hypochondriasis, obsessions are perceived by the patient with OCD as nonsensical and intrusive; cf. Salkovskis & Warwick, 1986), this distinction is blurred by recent data and revisions to DSM-IV criteria indicating that a large portion of persons with OCD do not regard their obsessions as unreasonable or excessive (Foa & Kozak, 1995). Unlike specific phobia of illness, which entails a *fear* of *contracting* an illness (cf. Craske et al., 1996), both OCD and hypochondriasis may be associated with a *conviction* that one *has* a serious illness (Insel & Akiskal, 1986). Thus, DSM-IV provides the following as a guideline for the distinction between OCD and hypochondriasis: "If recurrent distressing thoughts are exclusively related to fears of having, or the idea that one has, a serious disease based on misinterpretations of bodily symptoms, then hypochondriasis should be diagnosed instead of OCD" (American Psychiatric Association, 1994, p. 421). Thus, this guideline underscores the specificity of concerns as a key parameter for differential diagnosis; that is, OCD might be warranted over hypochondriasis when the obsessions and compulsive behaviors are not restricted to concerns about illness. In differentiating OCD from specific phobias of illness, DSM-IV underscores the presence–absence of rituals (compulsions), in addition to the specificity of health-related concerns. Specifically, DSM-IV states that "if the major concern is about contracting an illness (rather than having an illness), and no rituals are involved, then a specific phobia of illness may be the more appropriate diagnosis" (American Psychiatric Association, 1994, p. 421). The presence of rituals may also foster the differentiation of OCD from hypochondriasis if the clinical presentation involves checking rituals other than just numerous visits to the doctor (cf. Foa et al., 1996).

However, it should be noted that the aforementioned diagnostic provisions were formulated for DSM-IV in the absence of an appreciable research literature. Future research should address how well these parameters demarcate the boundaries between OCD, hypochondriasis, and illness phobia. For instance, the presence–absence of compulsive behaviors may not contribute to these distinctions substantially given evidence that most anxiety-based disorders are associated with recurrent safety behaviors (e.g., hypochondriasis is often characterized by repetitive reassurance-seeking behaviors such as doctor's visits and self-exams). Along the lines of the research discussed in the first section of this chapter (e.g., Brown et al., in press; Zinbarg & Barlow, 1996), in addition to investigations carried out at the diagnostic level (e.g., genetic and family studies), the discriminant and construct validity of these disorders should be examined at the dimensional level to determine whether the latent structure of these symptoms corresponds to the DSM-IV nosology and to evaluate if these disorders differ more in degree than in kind (e.g., do some cases of OCD characterized by somatic or contamination obsessions differ from cases of illness phobia only by the extent of overt compulsions triggered by these fears?).

In addition to hypochondriasis, it has been suggested that the DSM-IV somatoform disorder referred to as body dysmorphic disorder (BDD) could be regarded as an obsessive–compulsive spectrum disorder (e.g., Foa et al., 1996; Phillips, McElroy, Hudson, & Pope, 1995; Simeon, Hollander, Stein, Cohen, & Aronowitz, 1995). The key feature of BDD is an obsessive preoccupation with an imagined body defect; although not a formal diagnostic criterion in DSM-IV, BDD is frequently associated with compulsive-checking behavior (e.g., checking the "defect" in mirrors or other reflecting surfaces can consume many hours per day; Phillips, McElroy, Keck, Pope, & Hudson, 1993). Thus, given the presence of symptoms of an obsessive–compulsive nature in BDD, its potential overlap or relationship to OCD has been considered.

Researchers have interpreted findings relating to the patterns and rates of comorbidity in OCD and BDD as evidence of a possible association between these disorders. In patients with a principal diagnosis of OCD, the lifetime prevalence of BDD has been estimated to range from 8% to 37% (Brawman-Mintzer et al., 1995; Phillips et al., 1995; Simeon et al., 1995). Estimates of lifetime OCD in patients with BDD have been as high as 29% (Phillips et al., 1995). In addition, Phillips et al. reported that in their sample of 130 patients with BDD, major depression was the most prevalent lifetime diagnosis (83%). Given evidence of high rates of co-occurrence between mood disorders and OCD, the authors viewed this result as further indication that BDD may be an obsessive–compulsive spectrum disorder.

Initial findings indicate that OCD may occur frequently in first-order relatives of probands with BDD (Hollander, Cohen, & Simeon, 1993; McElroy et al., 1993). For instance, Hollander et al. (1993) found OCD to be the most common disorder in relatives of patients with BDD (prevalence = 17%), although this result appeared to be influenced in part by the high rate of comorbid OCD in the probands (78%). Other indicators of a possible relationship between OCD and BDD include evidence that the disorders have similar ages of onset, sex ratios, courses of disturbance, and levels of distress/impairment (e.g., Brawman-Mintzer et al., 1995; Phillips et al., 1995; Simeon et al., 1995). Another line of evidence that has been taken as support of the link between BDD and OCD is BDD's preferential response in open trials to selective serotonin reuptake inhibitors (SSRIs; Brady, Austin, & Lydiard, 1990; Hollander, Liebowitz, Winchel, Klumker, & Klein, 1989; Phillips, McElroy, Keck, Hudson, & Pope, 1994), although this line of reasoning is controversial (cf. Liebowitz et al., 1988). In addition to the difficulties inherent to drawing conclusions about the (dis)similarities of disorders based on their response to treatment, any favorable response to the SSRIs does not appear to be specific to OCD and BDD (i.e., initial evidence suggests that a variety of disorders may respond favorably to SSRIs).

Researchers contributing to the preparation of DSM-IV concluded that, although descriptive evidence suggests that OCD and BDD share similarities with regard to phenomenology, demographic and associated features, etiology, and treatment response, the lack of systematic research on BDD prohibited an assessment of the validity of BDD as a subgroup of OCD (Foa et al., 1996). These investigators noted the diagnostic difficulties currently associated with BDD, asserting that there appeared to be even less evidence linking BDD to the somatoform disorders (where BDD resides in DSM-IV) than to OCD (e.g., unlike the other somatoform disorders, the symptoms of BDD more frequently progress to delusional intensity). Thus, it was concluded that although revisions to the placement or definition of BDD or OCD in DSM-IV were not merited in the absence of a sufficient research literature, the close relationship between these disorders should be mentioned in the text. Indeed, these similarities are acknowledged in DSM-IV, and it is stated that the specificity of the obsessive–compulsive symptoms should be weighed heavily in the differential diagnosis of BDD and OCD (i.e., OCD is assigned when the obsessions and compulsions are not restricted to concerns about appearance). Based on their extensive clinical experience, Phillips et al. (1995) highlight other potential distinguishing features of BDD that are worthy of future investigation. Although maintaining that BDD should be conceptualized as an obsessive–compulsive spectrum disorder, these researchers note that compared to OCD, BDD is associated with a higher prevalence of delusional or overvalued ideation (including delusions of references); moreover, BDD preoccupations appear to be more often associated with profound feelings of shame, rejection sensitivity, and low self-esteem, and BDD behaviors (e.g., mirror checking) are more likely than OCD rituals to increase rather than decrease anxiety.

SUMMARY

The available evidence suggests that the anxiety-based disorders discussed in this chapter (GAD, specific phobia, hypochondriasis, BDD) have varying degrees of similarity to OCD. However, given the descriptive nature of these data (e.g., comorbidity, familial aggregation, demographic and associated features), conclusions about how these findings bear on the boundaries among these disorders are limited. For instance, evidence of symptom overlap or diagnostic co-occurrence could be interpreted from a variety of perspectives. These perspectives are sufficiently wide-ranging to either support or invalidate the DSM-IV classification of these disorders. In support of the DSM-IV, it could be concluded that the covariation or overlap in OCD and the other anxiety-based disorders is due to the fact that they share the same diathesis (e.g., biological or trait vulnerabilities), or perhaps because the features of one disorder act as risk factors for other disorders (Blashfield, 1990; Brown, 1996; Frances, Widiger, & Fyer, 1990). Conversely, high covariation or overlap could be viewed in support of the position that the anxiety-based disorders in DSM-IV represent an artificial separation of a broader syndromes (e.g., BDD has been erroneously classified as a distinct disorder when, in fact, it represents a discrete manifestation of OCD).

In attempt to account for the relationships and comorbidity among the emotional disorders, we (Barlow, 1988; Brown, 1996; Brown et al., in press), have speculated that although these disorders share common diatheses, they perhaps differ on important dimensions (e.g., key features) to an extent that differentiation is warranted (e.g., these distinctions have important clinical implications, such as treatment selection). However, empirical efforts to evaluate the nature or validity of the various emotional disorders have usually been conducted at the descriptive level, and have focused on a single disorder at a time. As has been discussed previously (e.g., Brown et al., in press; Clark et al., 1994), these strategies fail to consider the possibility that although the DSM-IV nosology is meaningful and reasonably valid, there may exist shared higher-order traits or dimensions (e.g., negative affect, neuroticism) that have greater significance to the understanding of the course, co-occurrence, prognosis, and so forth, of the emotional disorders. We hope that future research efforts on the validation of the anxiety-based disorders will possess one or more of the following methodological refinements: (1) include dimensional as well as diagnostic (categorical) data as the units for analysis; (2) examine a wide range of disorders simultaneously as opposed to a single disorder in isolation; (3) evaluate the features of disorders in the context of conceptually relevant, higher-order or shared biological or trait dimensions; (4) utilize longitudinal assessments (e.g., what disorder-specific or common dimensions predict longitudinal course or the emergence of comorbid symptoms or syndromes?). In addition to improving our nosology of these psychopathological phenomena, the results of such empirical endeavors should substantially foster the prevention and treatment of these disorders.

REFERENCES

American Psychiatric Association. (1980). *Diagnostic and statistical manual of mental disorders* (3rd ed.). Washington, DC: Author.

American Psychiatric Association. (1987). *Diagnostic and statistical manual of mental disorders* (3rd ed., rev.). Washington, DC: Author.

American Psychiatric Association. (1994). *Diagnostic and statistical manual of mental disorders* (4th ed.). Washington, DC: Author.

Andrews, G., Stewart, G., Allen, R., & Henderson, A. S. (1990). The genetics of six neurotic disorders: A twin study. *Journal of Affective Disorders, 19*, 23–29.

Baer, L., Jenike, M. A., & Ricciardi, J. (1990). Standardized assessment of personality disorders in obsessive–compulsive disorder. *Archives of General Psychiatry, 47*, 826–830.

Barlow, D. H. (1988). *Anxiety and its disorders: The nature and treatment of anxiety and panic.* New York: Guilford Press.

Barsky, A. J., Wyshak, G., & Klerman, G. L. (1992). Psychiatric comorbidity in DSM-III-R hypochondriasis. *Archives of General Psychiatry, 49*, 101–108.

Black, D. W., Noyes, R., Goldstein, R. B., & Blum, N. (1992). A family study of obsessive–compulsive disorder. *Archives of General Psychiatry, 49*, 362–368.

Blashfield, R. K. (1990). Comorbidity and classification. In J. D. Maser & C. R. Cloninger (Eds.), *Comorbidity of mood and anxiety disorders* (pp. 61–82). Washington, DC: American Psychiatric Association Press.

Borkovec, T. D. (1994). The nature, functions, and origins of worry. In G. Davey & F. Tallis (Eds.), *Worrying: Perspectives on theory, assessment, and treatment* (pp. 5–33). New York: Wiley.

Borkovec, T. D., & Hu, S. (1990). The effect of worry on cardiovascular response to phobic imagery. *Behaviour Research and Therapy, 28,* 69–73.

Borkovec, T. D., & Inz, J. (1990). The nature of worry in generalized anxiety disorder: A predominance of thought activity. *Behaviour Research and Therapy, 28,* 153–158.

Borkovec, T. D., Lyonfields, J. D., Wiser, S. L., & Diehl, L. (1993). The role of worrisome thinking in the suppression of cardiovascular response to phobic imagery. *Behaviour Research and Therapy, 31,* 321–324.

Borkovec, T. D., Shadick, R., & Hopkins, M. (1991). The nature of normal and pathological worry. In R. M. Rapee & D. H. Barlow (Eds.), *Chronic anxiety: Generalized anxiety disorder and mixed anxiety–depression* (pp. 29–51). New York: Guilford Press.

Brady, K. T., Austin, L., & Lydiard, R. B. (1990). Body dysmorphic disorder: The relationship to obsessive–compulsive disorder. *Journal of Nervous and Mental Disease, 178,* 538–540.

Brawman-Mintzer, O., Lydiard, R. B., Emmanuel, N., Payeur, R., Johnson, M., Roberts, J., Jarrell, M. P., & Ballenger, J. C. (1993). Psychiatric comorbidity in patients with generalized anxiety disorder. *American Journal of Psychiatry, 150,* 1216–1218.

Brawman-Mintzer, O., Lydiard, R. B., Phillips, K. A., Morton, A., Czepowicz, V., Emmanuel, N., Villareal, G., Johnson, M., & Ballenger, J. C. (1995). Body dysmorphic disorder in patients with anxiety disorders and major depression: A comorbidity study. *American Journal of Psychiatry, 152,* 1665–1667.

Brown, T. A. (1996). Validity of the DSM-III-R and DSM-IV classification systems for anxiety disorders. In R. M. Rapee (Ed.), *Current controversies in the anxiety disorders* (pp. 21–45). New York: Guilford Press.

Brown, T. A., Antony, M. M., & Barlow, D. H. (1992). Psychometric properties of the Penn State Worry Questionnaire in a clinical anxiety disorders sample. *Behaviour Research and Therapy, 30,* 33–37.

Brown, T. A., & Barlow, D. H. (1992). Comorbidity among anxiety disorders: Implications for treatment and DSM-IV. *Journal of Consulting and Clinical Psychology, 60,* 835–844.

Brown, T. A., Barlow, D. H., & Liebowitz, M. R. (1994). The empirical basis of generalized anxiety disorder. *American Journal of Psychiatry, 151,* 1272–1280.

Brown, T. A., & Chorpita, B. F. (1996). On the validity and comorbidity of the DSM-III-R and DSM-IV anxiety disorders. In R.M. Rapee (Ed.), *Current controversies in the anxiety disorders* (pp. 48–52). New York: Guilford Press.

Brown, T. A., Chorpita, B. F., & Barlow, D. H. (in press). Structural relationships among dimensions of the DSM-IV anxiety and mood disorders and dimensions of negative affect, positive affect, and autonomic arousal. *Journal of Abnormal Psychology.*

Brown, T. A., Moras, K., Zinbarg, R. E., & Barlow, D. H. (1993). Diagnostic and symptom distinguishability of generalized anxiety disorder and obsessive–compulsive disorder. *Behavior Therapy, 24,* 227–240.

Brown, T. A., O'Leary, T. A., & Barlow, D. H. (1993). Cognitive-behavioral treatment of generalized anxiety disorder. In D. H. Barlow (Ed.), *Clinical handbook of psychological disorders: A step-by-step treatment manual* (2nd ed., pp. 137–188). New York: Guilford Press.

Chorpita, B. F., Brown, T. A., & Barlow, D. H. (in press). Patient and evaluator parameters affecting diagnostic reliability of the DSM-III-R anxiety disorders. *Behavior Modification.*

Clark, L. A., & Watson, D. (1991). Tripartite model of anxiety and depression: Psychometric evidence and taxonomic implications. *Journal of Abnormal Psychology, 100,* 316–336.

Clark, L. A., Watson, D., & Mineka, S. (1994). Temperament, personality, and the mood and anxiety disorders. *Journal of Abnormal Psychology, 103*, 103–116.

Craske, M. G., Barlow, D. H., Clark, D. M., Curtis, G. C., Hill, E. M., Himle, J. A., Lee, Y. J., Lewis, J. A., McNally, R. J., Öst, L. G., Salkovskis, P. M., & Warwick, H. M. C. (1996). Specific (simple) phobia. In T. A. Widiger, A. J. Frances, H. A. Pincus, R. Ross, M. B. First, & W. W. Davis (Eds.), *DSM-IV sourcebook* (Vol. 2, pp. 473–506). Washington, DC: American Psychiatric Association Press.

Craske, M. G., Rapee, R. M., Jackel, L., & Barlow, D. H. (1989). Qualitative dimensions of worry in DSM-III-R generalized anxiety disorder subjects and nonanxious controls. *Behaviour Research and Therapy, 27*, 189–198.

Di Nardo, P. A., & Barlow, D. H. (1988). *Anxiety Disorders Interview Schedule for DSM-III-R (ADIS-R)*. Albany, NY: Graywind.

Di Nardo, P. A., Brown, T. A., & Barlow, D. H. (1994). *Anxiety Disorders Interview Schedule for DSM-IV— Lifetime Version (ADIS-IV-L)*. San Antonio, TX: Psychological Corporation.

Di Nardo, P. A., Brown, T. A., Lawton, J. K., & Barlow, D. H. (1995, November). *The Anxiety Disorders Interview Schedule for DSM-IV—Lifetime Version: Description and initial evidence for diagnostic reliability.* Paper presented at the meeting of the Association for Advancement of Behavior Therapy, Washington, DC.

Di Nardo, P. A., Moras, K., Barlow, D. H., Rapee, R. M., & Brown, T. A. (1993). Reliability of DSM-III-R anxiety disorder categories using the Anxiety Disorders Interview Schedule—Revised (ADIS-R). *Archives of General Psychiatry, 50*, 251–256.

Enright, S. J. (1996). Obsessive–compulsive disorder: Anxiety disorder or schizotype? In R. M. Rapee (Ed.), *Current controversies in the anxiety disorders* (pp. 161–190). New York: Guilford Press.

Fallon, B. A., Javitch, J. A., Hollander, E., & Liebowitz, M. R. (1991). Hypochondriasis and obsessive compulsive disorder: Overlap in diagnosis and treatment. *Journal of Clinical Psychiatry, 52*, 457–460.

Foa, E. B., Jenike, M., Kozak, M. J., Joffe, R., Baer, L., Pauls, D., Beidel, D. C., Rasmussen, S. A., Goodman, W., Swinson, R. P., Hollander, E., & Turner, S. M. (1996). Obsessive–compulsive disorder. In T. A. Widiger, A. J. Frances, H. A. Pincus, R. Ross, M. B. First, & W. W. Davis (Eds.), *DSM-IV sourcebook* (Vol. 2, pp. 549–575). Washington, DC: American Psychiatric Association Press.

Foa, E. B., & Kozak, M. J. (1995). DSM-IV field trial: Obsessive–compulsive disorder. *American Journal of Psychiatry, 152*, 90–96.

Frances, A., Widiger, T., & Fyer, M. R. (1990). The influence of classification methods on comorbidity. In J. D. Maser & C. R. Cloninger (Eds.), *Comorbidity of mood and anxiety disorders* (pp. 41–59). Washington, DC: American Psychiatric Association Press.

Freeston, M. H., Ladouceur, R., Rh,aume, J., Letarte, H., Gagnon, F., & Thibodeau, N. (1994). Self-report of obsessions and worry. *Behaviour Research and Therapy, 32*, 29–36.

Gross, P. R., & Eifert, G. H. (1990). Components of generalized anxiety: The role of intrusive thoughts vs. worry. *Behaviour Research and Therapy, 28*, 421–428.

Hodgson, R. J., & Rachman, S. J. (1977). Obsessional–compulsive complaints. *Behaviour Research and Therapy, 15*, 389–395.

Hoehn-Saric, R., McLeod, D. R., & Zimmerli, W. D. (1989). Somatic manifestations in women with generalized anxiety disorder: Psychophysiological responses to psychological stress. *Archives of General Psychiatry, 46*, 1113–1119.

Hollander, E., Cohen, L. J., & Simeon, D. (1993). Body dysmorphic disorder. *Psychiatric Annals, 23*, 359–364.

Hollander, E., Liebowitz, M. R., Winchel, R., Klumker, A., & Klein, D. F. (1989). Treatment of body dysmorphic disorder with serotonin reuptake blockers. *American Journal of Psychiatry, 146,* 768–770.

Hudson, J. I., & Pope, H. G. (1990). Affective spectrum disorder: Does antidepressant response identify a family of disorders with a common pathophysiology? *American Journal of Psychiatry, 147,* 552–564.

Insel, T. R., & Akiskal, H. S. (1986). Obsessive–compulsive disorder with psychotic features: A phenomenologic analysis. *American Journal of Psychiatry, 143,* 1527–1533.

Insel, T. R., Zahn, T., & Murphy, D. L. (1985). Obsessive–compulsive disorder: An anxiety disorder? In A. H. Tuma & J. D. Maser (Eds.), *Anxiety and the anxiety disorders* (pp. 577–589). Hillsdale, NJ: Erlbaum.

Joffe, R. T., Swinson, R. P., & Regan, J. J. (1988). Personality features in obsessive–compulsive disorder. *American Journal of Psychiatry, 145,* 1127–1129.

Kendler, K. S., Neale, M. C., Kessler, R. C., Heath, A. C., & Eaves, L. J. (1992). Major depression and generalized anxiety disorder: Same genes, (partly) different environments? *Archives of General Psychiatry, 49,* 716–722.

Kozak, M. J., & Foa, E. B. (1994). Obsessions, overvalued ideas, and delusions in obsessive–compulsive disorder. *Behaviour Research and Therapy, 32,* 342–353.

Leckman, J. F., & Chittenden, E. H. (1990). Gilles de la Tourette's syndrome and some forms of obsessive–compulsive disorder may share a common genetic diathesis. *L'Encéphale, 16,* 321–323.

Liebowitz, M. R., Quitkin, F. M., Stewart, J. W., McGrath, P. J., Harrison, W. M., Markowitz, J. S., Rabkin, J. G., Tricamo, E., Goetz, D. M., & Klein, D. F. (1988). Antidepressant specificity in atypical depression. *Archives of General Psychiatry, 45,* 129–137.

Livesley, W. J., Schroeder, M. L., Jackson, D. N., & Jang, K. L. (1994). Categorical distinctions in the study of personality disorder: Implications for classification. *Journal of Abnormal Psychology, 103,* 6–17.

Lyonfields, J. D., Borkovec, T. D., & Thayer, J. F. (1995). Vagal tone in generalized anxiety disorder and the effects of aversive imagery and worrisome thinking. *Behavior Therapy, 26,* 457–466.

McElroy, S. L., Phillips, K. A., & Keck, P. E. (1994). Obsessive compulsive spectrum disorder. *Journal of Clinical Psychiatry, 55*(Suppl. 10), 33–51.

McElroy, S. L., Phillips, K. A., Keck, P. E., et al. (1993). Body dysmorphic disorder: Does it have a psychotic subtype? *Journal of Clinical Psychiatry, 54,* 389–395.

McKeon, P., & Murray, R. (1987). Familial aspects of obsessive–compulsive neurosis. *British Journal of Psychiatry, 151,* 528–534.

Meyer, T. J., Miller, M. L., Metzger, R. L., & Borkovec, T. D. (1990). Development and validation of the Penn State Worry Questionnaire. *Behaviour Research and Therapy, 28,* 487–495.

Pauls, D. L., Alsobrook, J. P., Goodman, W., Rasmussen, S., & Leckman, J. F. (1995). A family study of obsessive–compulsive disorder. *American Journal of Psychiatry, 152,* 76–84.

Pauls, D. L., Towbin, K. E., Leckman, J. F., Zahner, G. E., & Cohen, D. J. (1986). Gilles de la Tourette's syndrome and obsessive–compulsive disorder. *Archives of General Psychiatry, 43,* 1180–1182.

Pfohl, B. (1996). Obsessive–compulsive personality disorder. In T. A. Widiger, A. J. Frances, H. A. Pincus, R. Ross, M. B. First, & W. W. Davis (Eds.), *DSM-IV sourcebook* (Vol. 2, pp. 777–788). Washington, DC: American Psychiatric Association Press.

Phillips, K. A., McElroy, S. L., Hudson, J. I., & Pope, H. G. (1995). Body dysmorphic disorder: An obsessive–compulsive spectrum disorder, a form of affective spectrum disorder, or both? *Journal of Clinical Psychiatry, 56*(Suppl. 4), 41–51.

Phillips, K. A., McElroy, S. L., Keck, P. E., Hudson, J. I., & Pope, H. G. (1994). A comparison of delusional and nondelusional body dysmorphic disorder in 100 cases. *Psychopharmacological Bulletin, 30*, 179–186.

Phillips, K. A., McElroy, S. L., Keck, P. E., Pope, H. G., & Hudson, J. I. (1993). Body dysmorphic disorder: 30 cases of imagined ugliness. *American Journal of Psychiatry, 150*, 302–308.

Pigott, T. A., Altemus, M., Rubenstein, C. S., Hill, J. L., Bihari, K., L'Heureux, F., Bernstein, S., & Murphy, D. L. (1991). Symptoms of eating disorders in patients with obsessive–compulsive disorder. *American Journal of Psychiatry, 148*, 1552–1557.

Rachman, S., & De Silva, P. (1978). Abnormal and normal obsessions. *Behaviour Research and Therapy, 16*, 233–248.

Rachman, S. J., & Hodgson, R. J. (1980). *Obsessions and compulsions.* Englewood Cliffs, NJ: Prentice-Hall.

Rasmussen, S. A., & Eisen, J. L. (1992). The epidemiology and differential diagnosis of obsessive compulsive disorder. *Journal of Clinical Psychiatry, 53*(Suppl. 4), 4–10.

Rasmussen, S. A., & Tsuang, M. T. (1986). Clinical characteristics and family history in DSM-III obsessive–compulsive disorder. *American Journal of Psychiatry, 143*, 317–382.

Roemer, L., & Borkovec, T. D. (1993). Worry: Unwanted cognitive activity that controls unwanted somatic experience. In D. M. Wegner & J. W. Pennebaker (Eds.), *Handbook of mental control* (pp. 220–238). Englewood Cliffs, NJ: Prentice-Hall.

Rubenstein, C. S., Altemus, M., Pigott, T. A., Hess, A., & Murphy, D. L. (1995). Symptom overlap between OCD and bulimia nervosa. *Journal of Anxiety Disorders, 9*, 1–9.

Salkovskis, P. M. (1989). Cognitive-behavioural factors and the persistence of intrusive thoughts in obsessional problems. *Behaviour Research and Therapy, 27*, 677–682.

Salkovskis, P. M., & Warwick, H. M. C. (1986). Morbid preoccupations, health anxiety, and reassurance: A cognitive-behavioural approach to hypochondriasis. *Behaviour Research and Therapy, 24*, 597–602.

Sanavio, E. (1988). Obsessions and compulsions: The Padua Inventory. *Behaviour Research and Therapy, 26*, 169–177.

Sanderson, W. C., Di Nardo, P. A., Rapee, R. M., & Barlow, D. H. (1990). Syndrome comorbidity in patients diagnosed with a DSM-III-R anxiety disorder. *Journal of Abnormal Psychology, 99*, 308–312.

Simeon, D., Hollander, E., Stein, D. J., Cohen, L., & Aronowitz, B. (1995). Body dysmorphic disorder in the DSM-IV field trial for obsessive–compulsive disorder. *American Journal of Psychiatry, 152*, 1207–1209.

Stein, D. J., Simeon, D., Cohen, L. J., & Hollander, E. (1995). Trichotillomania and obsessive–compulsive disorder. *Journal of Clinical Psychiatry, 56*(Suppl. 4), 28–34.

Tallis, F., & De Silva, P. (1992). Worry and obsessional symptoms: A correlational analysis. *Behaviour Research and Therapy, 30*, 103–105.

Tallis, F., Eysenck, M. W., & Mathews, A. (1992). A questionnaire for the measurement of nonpathological worry. *Personality and Individual Differences, 13*, 161–168.

Thiel, A., Broocks, A., Ohlmeier, M., Jacoby, G. E., & Schüßler, G. (1995). Obsessive–compulsive disorder among patients with anorexia nervosa and bulimia nervosa. *American Journal of Psychiatry, 152*, 72–75.

Torgersen, S. (1983). Genetic factors in anxiety disorders. *Archives of General Psychiatry, 40*, 1085–1089.

Turner, S. M., Beidel, D. C., & Stanley, M. A. (1992). Are obsessional thoughts and worry different cognitive phenomena? *Clinical Psychology Review, 12*, 257–270.

Tynes, L. L., White, K., & Steketee, G. S. (1990). Toward a new nosology of obsessive compulsive disorder. *Comprehensive Psychiatry, 31*, 465–480.

Wells, A., & Morrison, A. P. (1994). Qualitative dimensions of normal worry and normal obsessions: A comparative study. *Behaviour Research and Therapy, 32*, 867–870.

Zinbarg, R. E., & Barlow, D. H. (1996). Structure of anxiety and anxiety disorders: A hierarchical model. *Journal of Abnormal Psychology, 105*, 181–193.

Part II

ASSESSMENT AND TREATMENT

Chapter 10

ASSESSMENT OF OBSESSIVE–COMPULSIVE DISORDER

Steven Taylor

In order to evaluate theories and treatments of obsessive–compulsive disorder (OCD), it is necessary to have reliable diagnostic instruments and comprehensive, psychometrically sound measures of obsessive–compulsive (OC)-related signs and symptoms (e.g., measures of obsessions, compulsions, and OC-related fear and avoidance). The purpose of this chapter is to review the major classes of these measures: structured diagnostic interviews, behavioral approach tests, self-report measures, and observer-rated scales. This chapter provides an update of a previous review of OC measures (Taylor, 1995) by including new data on existing measures, and by reviewing promising measures that were not discussed previously. In recent years, there have been several new developments in the assessment of OCD, including innovations in behavioral assessment, and revisions or adaptations of existing measures. The latter include revisions to the Padua Inventory and Maudsley Obsessional–Compulsive Inventory (MOCI), and the development and validation of a self-report version of the Yale–Brown Obsessive–Compulsive Scale (YBOCS).

Due to space limitations, this chapter does not attempt to review all of the available measures of OCD. Some of the older measures have fallen from favor in recent years. Some of these measures have poor discriminant validity (e.g., the OC scales from the Symptom Checklist 90—Revised [SCL-90-R] and predecessors, and the OC scale from the Comprehensive Psychopathological Rating Scale). Although they assess OC symptoms, these measures are primarily assessments of nonspecific distress. Other measures confound important variables, such as symptom severity and degree of resistance to symptoms (e.g., the Leyton Obsessional Inventory). Accordingly, these measures are not reviewed here; see Taylor (1995) for a review.

In reviewing data on convergent and discriminant validity, I use Cohen's

(1988) classification scheme: Large correlations are defined as those ≥ .50, medium correlations are .30 to .49, and small correlations are .10 to .29. Good convergent validity is defined by medium-to-large correlations, and good discriminant validity is said to occur when an OC measure is correlated more highly with other OC measures than with measures of other constructs, such as general anxiety or depression (cf. Campbell & Fiske, 1959). Acceptable internal consistency is defined as alpha ≥ .70, and good internal consistency as alpha ≥ .80 (Nunnally, 1978). Similarly, acceptable test–retest reliability is defined as $r ≥ .70$, and good test–retest reliability as $r ≥ .80$. Criterion-related (known groups) validity is supported by demonstrating that a given measure discriminates people with OCD from people with other psychiatric disorders, and from normal controls. The rationale for these criteria is discussed in more detail elsewhere (Taylor, 1995).

STRUCTURED DIAGNOSTIC INTERVIEWS

Among the most widely used methods for diagnosing OCD are the Structured Clinical Interview for DSM-IV (SCID-IV; First, Spitzer, Gibbon, & Williams, 1996) and the Anxiety Disorders Interview Schedule for DSM-IV (ADIS-IV; Di Nardo, Brown, & Barlow, 1994). Each of these is a revision of a previous version (Di Nardo & Barlow, 1988; Spitzer, Williams, & Gibbon, 1987) developed for DSM-III-R, and each is available in several formats (e.g., lifetime and standard editions). Although psychometric studies have yet to be conducted using the newest versions of these interviews, the diagnostic criteria for OCD have changed very little from DSM-III-R to DSM-IV, and therefore the reliability findings for the DSM-III-R versions of these instruments probably can be generalized to the DSM-IV versions.

The SCID-IV provides a broad assessment of the major DSM-IV disorders. It is economical in that it elicits just enough information to establish or rule out a diagnosis. The ADIS-IV assesses fewer disorders than the SCID, but provides a more detailed assessment of anxiety disorders. The ADIS-IV also assesses disorders that are commonly comorbid with anxiety disorders or used for purposes of screening out potential participants from research trials (e.g., mood disorders, substance-use disorders, and somatoform disorders). If one desires a detailed assessment of anxiety disorders, then the ADIS-IV should be used in place of the SCID-IV. The ADIS-IV elicits more information than is needed to rule in or out a diagnosis of, say, OCD, although the extra information can be useful for research and treatment planning (e.g., ratings of the strength of belief in intrusive thoughts; percentage of time consumed by compulsions).

Like all observer-rated scales discussed in this chapter, the SCID-IV and ADIS-IV should be administered by trained clinicians. As noted by Spitzer, Williams, Gibbon, and First (1992), "Optimally, a SCID interviewer should be someone who has enough clinical experience and knowledge of psychopathology and psychiatric diagnosis to conduct a diagnostic interview without an interview guide" (p. 627). Moreover, "unlike a lay interviewer administering a completely structured interview . . . an experienced clinician can tailor an interview by phrasing questions to fit the subject's understanding, asking additional questions that clarify differential diagnoses, challenging inconsistencies in the subject's account, and judging whether the subject's description of an experience conforms to the intent of a diagnostic criterion" (p. 624).

In many research centers that use the SCID-IV or ADIS-IV, the interviewers are licensed psychologists, psychiatrists, or social workers. Given the current trend toward reduced funding for health care and clinical research, it has become increasingly necessary to use lesser-trained individuals to conduct these interviews. In our clinic, we routinely use interviewers who have either completed a BA or MA in psychology. We have found that such interviewers can reliably administer the SCID-IV and ADIS-IV interviews under supervision by a doctoral-level psychologist. In our clinic, diagnostic supervision is based on a review of the completed interview protocol, along with a discussion of the case with the interviewer. The interviews also are audiotaped to establish interrater reliability. We have found that diagnoses of OCD and other anxiety disorders obtained under these conditions generally have good interrater reliability when compared to diagnoses made by an independent doctoral-level psychologist (Taylor, Woody, Koch, McLean, & Anderson, 1996; Taylor et al., 1997; Whittal, McLean, Taylor, Söchting, & Anderson, 1997). However, close supervision by an experienced clinician is needed to accurately establish a diagnosis of OCD, especially when the patient (1) has difficulty describing the symptoms, (2) presents with atypical OC symptoms (e.g., compulsive wrist cutting in the absence of borderline personality disorder), or (3) presents with OC symptoms that are difficult to distinguish from symptoms of other disorders (e.g., obsessional doubts and ruminations can sometimes be difficult to distinguish from excessive worry: see the section on clinical considerations for further details).

With regard to the interrater reliability of the SCID, Williams et al. (1992) conducted a multisite study of 390 psychiatric patients and found that the SCID (for DSM-III-R) had adequate interrater reliability for the current diagnosis of OCD (kappa = .59) and lifetime diagnosis of this disorder (kappa = .67).[1] Williams et al. also assessed 202 nonpatients recruited from the community. The kappa for the lifetime diagnosis of OCD (.33) was substantially lower than that obtained from the patient sample, possibly due to the low base rate of the disorder in community samples compared to their clinical samples (lifetime prevalence: 4% vs. 11%, respectively). There was an insufficient number of community subjects to compute the kappa for current diagnosis of OCD.

With regard to the ADIS (for DSM-III-R), Di Nardo, Moras, Barlow, Rapee, and Brown (1993) assessed the interrater reliability for 267 outpatients presenting for treatment of anxiety disorders. For OCD, reliability was very good (kappa = .80) for assigning OCD as the principal diagnosis (in terms of severity

---

[1]Kappas ranging from .50 to .70 generally indicate fair agreement, whereas those below .50 indicate poor agreement (Fleiss, 1981).

and impairment in functioning). Reliability also was good when assigning OCD as either a principal or additional diagnosis (kappa = .75). Thus, the interrater reliability for the diagnosis of OCD was higher for the ADIS (Di Nardo et al., 1993) than it was for the SCID (Williams et al., 1992): (kappa = .75 and .59, respectively, for the diagnosis of current OCD (as either a primary or additional disorder) in patient samples. The differences in kappas does not seem to be due to differences in the base rates of current OCD in the two studies (9% vs. 7%, for Di Nardo et al. and Williams et al., respectively). However, the methods used in the studies differed in several ways (e.g., Di Nardo et al. assessed their patients from a single clinic in the United States, whereas Williams et al. sampled their patients from multiple clinics in the United States and Germany). These factors may have accounted for the differences across studies. Thus, both the SCID and ADIS can be used reliably to diagnose OCD, and the question arises as to whether the diagnosis is more reliable for the ADIS. Further research is needed to investigate this possibility. The interrater reliabilities of the DSM-IV versions of these interviews also remain to be determined.

BEHAVIORAL AVOIDANCE TESTS

Behavioral Avoidance Tests (BATs) were originally developed to assess fear and avoidance in people with circumscribed fears and phobias (e.g., Lang & Lazovik, 1963). In these tasks, the person is asked to approach as close as possible to a feared stimulus. The distance of closest approach is used as a measure of avoidance, and self-reported levels of distress at particular distances are used to measure fear. The SUD (subjective units of distress) scale is commonly used to measure fear. Here, the person provides a rating of his or her fear or distress on a 0–100 scale, where 0 = no fear/distress and 100 = extreme fear/distress.

Several types of BATs have been developed to assess OC-related fear and avoidance. The simplest is the *single-task* BAT (e.g., Foa, Steketee, Grayson, Turner, & Latimer, 1984), in which the patient is asked to approach as close as possible to the feared stimulus and then report his or her SUD level at the point of closest approach. To illustrate, a compulsive washer might be asked to approach a "contaminated" object such as a trash can. Avoidance is assessed by distance from the feared stimulus, or some other proximity measure, such as whether the patient is able to touch the object without wearing gloves, or whether he or she is willing to be exposed to the feared stimulus without engaging in compulsive rituals.

A problem with the single-task BAT is that it assesses fear and avoidance of only one stimulus, and so fails to assess the breadth of a patient's fear and avoidance. Rachman and colleagues (1979) devised a *multitask* BAT, in which OC patients each complete a number of different fear-related tasks. For example, Rachman et al. asked each patient to carry out five tasks that usually gave rise to compulsive rituals. For each task, an independent assessor scored the patient's performance (rated as 1 = task completed, and 0 = task avoided). Scores then were summed across tasks to yield a 0–5 avoidance score. The assessor also rated the patient's discomfort during each task, using a 0–8 scale (0 = no discomfort, 8 = extreme discomfort). Discomfort scores were summed to yield a 0–40 discomfort scale.

To further increase the sensitivity of the BAT, Steketee and colleagues (Steketee, Chambless, Tran, Worden, & Gillis, 1996; Woody, Steketee, & Chambless, 1995a) recently developed a *multistep–multitask* BAT. For each patient, the assessor identifies three tasks that are difficult or impossible for the patients to complete without significant anxiety or rituals (e.g., switching off electrical appliances without checking). Each task is then broken down into three to seven steps intended to provoke steadily increasing levels of discomfort. For example, the patient might be asked to drive on progressively busier streets without checking. To reduce the demand characteristics of the task, Steketee et al. (1996) instruct patients that the BATs are tests of their ability to approach feared situations as far as they can proceed comfortably without ritualizing. The patients are told that the BAT is not a test of courage, and that they are free to refuse any or all of the task.

Several different measures can be obtained from the multistep–multitask BAT. Steketee et al. (1996) reported using several measures, including SUD, measures of avoidance (3-point scale, ranging from 0 = no avoidance, to 2 = complete avoidance of the entire task), and frequency of rituals (3-point scale, ranging from 0 = no rituals, to 2 = extensive rituals). To aid in the construction of BATs, Steketee and colleagues developed a instruction guide for constructing and implementing BATs.

There have been few studies of the psychometric properties of BATs for OCD. Most of the available data are for the multistep–multitask BAT (Steketee et al., 1996; Woody et al., 1995a). The results are summarized in Table 10.1. In support of the convergent validity of the multistep–multitask BAT, Woody et al. (1995a) obtained medium-sized correlations between pretreatment BAT measures (fear and avoidance) and the YBOCS (rs = .38 to .43). Steketee et al. (1996), using a sample that partly overlapping with that of Woody et al. (1995a) also found moderate-sized correlations between pretreatment BAT measures (SUD, avoidance, and rituals) and the YBOCS (rs = .36 to .43). BAT measures of avoidance and rituals had medium-sized correlations (rs = .30 to .32) with the MOCI, and SUD ratings from the BAT were correlated .21 with the MOCI. Thus, the available data generally support the convergent validity of the multistep–multitask BAT.

Steketee et al. (1996) also obtained evidence of good discriminant validity, with BAT measures of SUD, avoidance, and rituals having small or trivial correlations with the SCL-90-R depression scale (rs = .01 to .20), and with a measure of OC personality disorder (rs = −.10 to −.03).

Each type of BAT (i.e., single-task, multitask, and multistep–multitask) has been shown to be sensitive to detecting the effects of well-established treatments for OCD, such as behavior therapy (exposure and response prevention) and clomipramine (Cottraux et al., 1990; Foa et al., 1984; Rachman et al., 1979; Steketee et al., 1996; Woody et al., 1995a). Mean pre–post effect sizes for SUD

TABLE 10.1. Measures of OC Symptoms and Signs: Psychometric Properties

	Reliability			Validity			Sensitivity to treatment effects
	Internal consistency	Interrater	Test–retest (≥ 7 days)	Criterion related	Convergent	Discriminant	
Multistep–multitask behavioral approach test	na	na	?	?	+	+	+
Maudsley Obsessional–Compulsive Inventory							
Total scale	na	na	+	+	+	+	+
Washing subscale	+	na	?	+	+	+	?
Checking subscale	+	na	?	+	+	+	?
Doubting subscale	+	na	?	+	?	?	?
Slowness subscale	—	na	?	—	?	?	?
Maudsley Obsessional–Compulsive Inventory—Revised	?	na	?	?	?	?	?
Compulsive Activity Checklist							
Self-report	+	na	+	+	+	?	+
Observer-rated	+	+	+	+	+	—	+
Padua Inventory—Revised, subscales							
Obsessional thoughts about harm to self or others	+	na	+	+	?	+	?
Obsessional impulses to harm self or others	+	na	+	+	?	+	?
Contamination obsessions and washing compulsions	+	na	+	+	?	+	?
Checking compulsions	+	na	+	+	?	+	?
Dressing and grooming compulsions	+	na	+	+	?	+	?
Likert scales							
Self-report	na	na	?	?	+	+	+
Observer-rated	na	+	?	?	+	+	+
NIMH Global Obsessive–Compulsive Scale	na	?	+	?	+	?	+
10-item Yale–Brown Obsessive–Compulsive Scale							
Self-report	+	na	+	+	?	?	?
Observer-rated	+	+	+	+	+	—	+

Note. +, good or adequate; ?, insufficient information;—, inadequate; na, not applicable.

ratings and avoidance tend to be > 1.00 *SD* units (Taylor, 1995). The sensitivity of measures from the BATs are similar to, or slightly larger than those from self-report measures of OCD (e.g., MOCI), and slightly smaller than those of observer-rated scales (e.g., YBOCS). See Taylor (1995) for a meta-analysis of the comparative sensitivities of OC scales for detecting the effects of established treatments for OCD (i.e., behavior therapy [exposure and response prevention] and clomipramine).

BATs have the advantage of providing *in vivo* measures of fear, avoidance, and rituals. They can be used either in the clinic or set for patients as homework assignments (where the patient records his or her levels of fear, avoidance, etc.). BATs are well suited for assessing fear and avoidance of "contaminated" stimuli associated with washing compulsions. It is more difficult to design BATs for patients with other types of compulsions, such as checking or ordering rituals. However, Steketee et al.'s (1996) instruction guide facilitates the construction of multistep–multitask BATs by providing detailed guidelines and examples.

In summary, available data for the most recent version of the behavioral approach test—the multistep–multitask BAT—supports its convergent validity, discriminant validity, and sensitivity to treatment-related effects. Test–retest reliability and criterion-related (known groups) validity have yet to be examined. However, it is likely that the BAT will have good criterion-related validity for many types of exposure tasks. This is because, by definition, only people with OCD will display significant fear, avoidance, and rituals in response to classic OC-related stimuli, such as "contaminants," doorlocks, and so forth. However, is also is likely that there will be conditions in which the BAT does not discriminate between diagnostic groups. For example, a BAT consisting of driving on increasingly busier streets may be fear evoking for people with OCD, and also for people with other disorders, such as panic disorder with agoraphobia and specific phobia of driving.

MOCI

The MOCI (Hodgson & Rachman, 1977) consists of four factorially derived subscales: (1) washing (i.e., OC-related washing compulsions and contamination fears; 11 items), (2) checking compulsions (9 items), (3) obsessional slowness/repetition (7 items), and (4) excessive doubting/conscientiousness (7 items). The subscales are essentially symptom checklists; that is, their scores reflect the amount of time consumed by OC symptoms. Factor-analytic studies have generally replicated all subscales except the slowness subscale (Chan, 1990; Emmelkamp, Kraaijkamp, & Van den Hout, in press; Rachman & Hodgson, 1980; Sanavio & Vidotto, 1985; Sternberger & Burns, 1990b).

Studies of clinical samples have generally obtained acceptable internal consistencies for the checking, cleaning, and doubting/conscientiousness subscales, with coefficients alpha ranging from .60 to .87 (Hodgson & Rachman, 1977; Emmelkamp et al., in press; Rachman & Hodgson, 1980; Richter, Cox, & Direnfeld,

1994). Studies of student samples have reported lower internal consistencies, ranging from .40 to .62 (Chan, 1990; Sanavio & Vidotto, 1985; Sternberger & Burns, 1980b). Lower alphas may have been due to range restriction. Studies of clinical and nonclinical samples have generally found very low internal consistencies for the slowness subscale, with alphas ranging from 0 to .44 (Chan, 1990; Emmelkamp et al., in press; Rachman & Hodgson, 1980; Sanavio & Vidotto, 1985). Very low alphas for the slowness subscales may be due to item heterogeneity.

Hodgson and Rachman (1977) examined the 4-week test–retest reliability of the MOCI in a sample of university students. Kendell's tau was used to examine the concordance between item responses across the retest interval. For the sum of MOCI items, test–retest reliability was found to be good (tau = .8). Emmelkamp et al. (in press) used the same procedure to examine the 4-week test–retest reliability in a mixed sample of OCs and depressed patients. Reliability also was good (tau = .84), and MOCI total scores correlated .92 across the test–retest interval. Sternberger and Burns (1990b), using a sample of university students, found the 6- to 7-month test–retest reliability was acceptable for the MOCI total score ($r =$ .69). In summary, the MOCI total scale has acceptable test–retest reliability over a period of at least 6 to 7 months. Test–retest reliabilities of the subscales have yet to be reported.

With regard to criterion-related validity, Hodgson, Rankin, and Stockwell (1979, unpublished, cited in Rachman & Hodgson, 1980) found the MOCI total scale discriminated between phobics and OCs. Emmelkamp et al. (in press) found the MOCI total scale reliably discriminated OCs from a normal controls, anorectics, and patients with non-OC anxiety disorders. Compared to normal controls and the combined psychiatric samples (anorexia, depression, and non-OC anxiety disorders), OCs had higher scores on all MOCI subscales, except the slowness subscale, where OCs and normals did not differ. Hodgson and Rachman (1977) and Emmelkamp et al. (in press) found that high scores on the washing subscale was associated with greater therapist-rated severity of washing compulsions. Similarly, high scores on the checking subscale were associated with greater therapist-rated severity of checking compulsions. In summary, there is support for the criterion-related validity of the MOCI total scale and for its washing, checking, and doubting/conscientiousness subscales. The only study of the slowness subscale (Emmelkamp et al., in press) failed to support its criterion-related validity.

The MOCI tends to have large correlations (rs = .23 to .77; mean = .57) with other OC measures (e.g., Compulsive Activity Checklist, Padua Inventory, YBOCS, subscales of the Leyton Obsessional Inventory; Freund, Steketee, & Foa, 1987; Goodman et al., 1989b; Hodgson & Rachman, 1977; Emmelkamp et al., in press; Richter et al., 1994; Sanavio, 1988; Steketee & Doppelt, 1986; Steketee & Freund, 1993; Sternberger & Burns, 1990a, 1990b; van Oppen, 1992; van Oppen, Hoekstra, & Emmelkamp, 1995b; Woody et al., 1995a, 1995b). These results support the convergent validity of the MOCI.

Chan (1990) found the MOCI correlated .54 with the Beck Depression Inventory, and Richter et al. (1994) found the MOCI correlated .41 with the Hamilton Depression Scale. Sternberger and Burns (1990b) found the MOCI had small-to-medium correlations with all SCL-90-R scales (rs = .26 to .36) except the SCL-90-R OC scale (r = .51). In general, the results show that correlations with non-OC measures tend to be lower than correlations with OC measures, which supports the discriminant validity of the MOCI total scale.

With regard to convergent and discriminant validity of the subscales, the MOCI washing subscale has been found to have large correlations with the Padua Inventory contamination subscale (rs = .53 to .87) and small-to-medium correlations with the Padua checking subscale (rs = .05 to .33) (Sternberger & Burns, 1990a; van Oppen, 1992; van Oppen et al., 1995b). A similar pattern of results was obtained for the MOCI checking subscale, that is, large correlations with the Padua checking subscale (rs = .62 to .84) and small-to-medium correlations with the Padua contamination subscale (rs = .24 to .35; Sternberger & Burns, 1990a; van Oppen, 1992; van Oppen et al., 1995b). The MOCI washing subscale has small-to-medium correlations with the MOCI checking subscale (rs = .25 to .46; Chan, 1990; Hodgson & Rachman, 1977; Sternberger & Burns, 1990b). These results indicate good convergent and discriminant validities of the MOCI washing and checking subscales.

The MOCI checking and washing subscales have medium-to-large correlations with the Beck Depression Inventory (BDI) and Hamilton Depression Scale (rs = .30 to .51; Chan, 1990; Richter et al., 1994). These tend to be lower than the convergent validity correlations, and so support the discriminant validity of the checking and washing subscales. There is insufficient information to evaluate the convergent and discriminant validity of the other subscales.

With regard to sensitivity to treatment effects, the pre–post effect sizes of the MOCI (mean = 1.09 SD units) tend to be as large as those of other self-report measures (e.g., the self-report Compulsive Activity Checklist), and smaller than those of observer-rated scales (e.g., the YBOCS; Taylor, 1995). The sensitivities of the subscales have yet to be examined.

In summary, the MOCI total scale has generally acceptable psychometric properties, as do its washing and checking subscales (see Table 10.1). The other subscales require further investigation. The MOCI subscales were developed on the basis of factor analysis, and subsequent studies support the factorial distinction between all but the slowness subscale. The latter has poor internal consistency, which is not surprising given its item content. Two of its items are related to ruminations, two items refer to compulsive counting and the need for routine, and only three items make direct reference to obsessional slowness.

Although the MOCI total scale has adequate psychometric properties, it also has important limitations. The MOCI assesses washing and checking compulsions, which are the most common types of compulsions (American Psychiatric Association, 1994; Rachman & Hodgson, 1980) but does not assess other important compulsions such as hoarding and covert rituals. It provides a limited assessment of obsessional ruminations (two items). The MOCI also does not assess important parameters of OCD, such as interference and resistance to compulsions. Interference can only be inferred by the number of symptoms endorsed by the respondent.

MOCI—Revised

Recently, Rachman and colleagues have begun to develop a revised MOCI (MOCI-R; Rachman, Thordarson, & Radomsky, 1995). The first version of the MOCI-R contained 84 items. Compared to the original MOCI, it was designed to assess a broader range of obsessions and compulsions, and to assess avoidance behaviors and personality characteristics (e.g., beliefs) thought to be important in OCD. In order to increase the scale's sensitivity to detecting treatment effects, the true–false response format of the original MOCI was replaced with a 5-point scale (ranging from $0 =$ not at all, to $4 =$ totally).

The MOCI-R (version 1) consisted of 17 subscales, with 3 to 12 items per subscale. The subscales were grouped into four categories. Categories (and subscales) were as follows: (1) contamination (cleaning, contamination, avoidance of contamination), (2) danger (checking, thoughts of danger, avoidance of danger), (3) other obsessions and compulsions (obscene thoughts, counting, ordering, hoarding, slowness), and (4) personality characteristics and beliefs (concern with safety, responsibility, perfectionism, indecisiveness, moral thought–action fusion, likelihood thought–action fusion).

Version 1 of the MOCI-R was administered to samples of university students and community adults (Rachman et al., 1995). Coefficients alpha ranged from .62 to .94 (mean $= .80$), indicating that internal consistency was generally adequate. The MOCI-R subscales tended to have moderate-to-large correlations with the total score of the original MOCI ($rs = .30$ to .63, mean $= .49$), and these correlations tended to be slightly higher than the correlations between the MOCI-R subscales and the BDI; $rs = .23$ to .56, mean $= .36$). Thus, overall there was encouraging evidence to support the convergent and discriminant validity of the MOCI-R. However, some of the subscales were problematic. For example, the MOCI-R cleaning subscale was correlated equally with the MOCI cleaning and checking subscales ($rs = .42$ and .43, respectively), and these correlations were little different from the correlation between the MOCI-R cleaning subscale and the BDI ($r = .35$). Moreover, and rather surprisingly, the MOCI-R was found to be unifactorial (Rachman et al., 1995), which suggests that some or many of the subscales were redundant with one another.

Since their 1995 study, Rachman and colleagues have developed version 2 of the MOCI-R by rewriting or deleting items from version 1, and by adding other items. Version 2 originally consisted of 111 items. Factor analyses led to a revision of the nature and number of subscales (Thordarson & Shafran, personal communication, June 1996). Factor analysis suggested 7- and 9-factor solutions. The best items (in terms of simple structure) were selected to form a 62-item scale, containing eight subscales: (1) contamination; (2) checking; (3) obsessions; (4) hoarding; (5) indecisiveness, perfectionism, and concern over mistakes; (6) strict routine, counting, slowness; (7) moral thought–action fusion; and

(8) likelihood thought–action fusion (Thordarson & Shafran, personal communication, June 1996).

Clearly, the MOCI-R is still under development. Further studies using clinical and nonclinical samples are required to determine the psychometric properties of the latest version of this scale. The MOCI-R offers the promise of being one of the most comprehensive measures of OCD. However, it remains to be seen whether the MOCI-R can outperform its popular predecessor, the MOCI.

COMPULSIVE ACTIVITY CHECKLIST

The Compulsive Activity Checklist (CAC) was developed originally as a 62-item interviewer-administered schedule to assess the extent to which OC symptoms interfere with everyday activities (Philpott, 1975). Each item lists an activity (e.g., using electrical appliances), which is rated on a 4-point scale, ranging from 0 (performance of activity within normal limits) to 3 (complete impairment). Impairment is rated according to four criteria: frequency, duration, avoidance, and oddity of behavior. To illustrate, a score of 3 would be given if (1) the activity takes three times longer than usual, (2) it is three times as frequent as usual, (3) it definitely appears very odd, or (4) avoidance markedly interferes with activity. Criteria for "normal" and "odd" behavior are left to the judgment of the interviewer. Interviewers are instructed to elicit concrete information to allow them to make a rating.

The CAC has been revised several times, mainly by deleting items and changing to a self-report format. Marks, Hallam, Connolly, and Philpott (1977) developed clinician-rated and self-report versions, each containing 39 items. Freund et al. (1987) developed a 38-item observer-rated version, and Cottraux, Bouvard, Defayolle, and Messy (1988) developed an 18-item self-report version. Most recently, Steketee and Freund (1993) developed a 28-item self-report version. Each revision was intended to increase item homogeneity and discriminability of OCs from other populations, although as we will see, the versions have very similar psychometric properties. Instructions and the rating scale remained essentially unchanged. To summarize, each version is a measure of global impairment due to obsessions or compulsions, taking into account duration, frequency, and avoidance.

Good internal consistency has been reported for the 37-item self-report CAC (alpha = .94; Cottraux et al., 1988) and for the 38-item observer-rated version (alpha = .91; Freund et al., 1987). Similar results were obtained for the 38-item self-report version (alphas = .86 to .95: Sternberger & Burns, 1990b; Freund et al., 1987) and for the 28-item self-report version (alpha = .87; Steketee & Freund, 1987). Internal consistency of the other, less popular versions have not been reported.

With regard to interrater reliability, Marks, Stern, Mawson, Cobb, and Mc-Donald (1980) had two independent assessors administer the 39-item CAC to a sample of OCs. Total scores correlated .95 between observers, and the observer-rated and self-report versions correlated .83. Freund et al. (1987) obtained moderate interrater agreement (r = .64) for the 38-item CAC. The mean CAC score, averaged across raters, correlated .94 with the 38-item self-report CAC. These results suggest the observer-rated CAC has adequate interrater reliability.

Freund et al. (1987) averaged CAC ratings from two interviewers to examine the test–retest reliability of the 38-item CAC. Test–retest reliability was r = .68 for a retest interval ranging from 5–60 days (mean = 37 days). Cottraux et al. (1988) administered the 37-item self-report CAC to a sample of normal controls and found the 1-month test–retest reliability was r = .62. Sternberger and Burns (1990b), using a sample of university students, obtained a 6- to 7-month test–retest reliability of r = .74. Thus, it appears that the self-report and observer-rated versions have good test–retest reliability over a period of weeks, if not months.

Using the 37-item self-report CAC, Cottraux et al. (1988) found that OCs had higher scores than panic-disordered patients, social phobics, and normal controls. Steketee and Freund (1993) compared OCs to patients with other anxiety disorders and to university students. OCs had significantly higher scores on 29 of 38 items of the self-report CAC. These findings support the criterion-related validity of the CAC.

The self-report and observer-rated CACs tend to have medium correlations (rs = .19 to .84, mean = .40) with other OC measures (i.e., MOCI, Padua Inventory, SCL-90-R OC scale, and Likert scale ratings of symptom severity: Cottraux et al., 1988; Freund et al., 1987; Marks et al., 1980; Steketee & Freund, 1993; Sternberger & Burns, 1990b). These results support the convergent validity of the CAC.

Concerning discriminant validity, Freund et al. (1987) found that the 38-item observer-rated CAC had a medium-sized correlation with the SCL-90-R OC scale (r = .38) and slightly smaller correlations with the other SCL-90-R scales (rs = .14 to .31). Foa, Steketee, Kozak, and Dugger (1987) found that the observer-rated CAC had medium correlations (rs = .33 to .47) with measures of depression (i.e., the BDI, and patient and observer-rated Likert measures of depression severity).

To summarize, the observer-rated CAC has correlations with non-OC measures that tend to be similar in magnitude to correlations with OC measures. This indicates weak discriminant validity. The same conclusion probably holds for the self-report CAC, because the self-report and observer-rated CACs are highly correlated.

The self-report CAC tends to be as sensitive to treatment-related effects as other self-report scales such as the MOCI, and the observer-rated CAC tends to be more sensitive than the self-report CAC (mean effect sizes = 1.64 and 0.88 SD units, respectively; Taylor, 1995). The observer-rated CAC tends to as sensitive as other observer-rated measures of OCD (Taylor, 1995). The psychometric properties of the CACs are summarized in Table 10.1.

In summary, the 28–38 item self-report and observer-rated versions of the CAC have very similar psychometric properties. Psychometric properties are generally adequate, with the exception of discriminant validity. A further problem with each version of the CAC is that it confounds slowness, avoidance, and "oddity" of behavior. Moreover, the CAC does not directly assess OC symptoms; it merely assesses interference in everyday activities that may be due to obsessions, compulsions, or both. The CAC provides no indication as to the nature of the interference, because its ratings confound slowness, avoidance, and "oddity" of behavior. This means that high scores on the CAC are ambiguous; they could arise from obsessional slowness, compulsive repeating, avoidance, and/or obsessional doubting and indecision.

The lack of a structured interview is a further limitation for the observer-rated CAC, because the psychometric properties may depend on the skill and training experiences of the interviewer(s) rather than the properties inherent to the CAC.

PADUA INVENTORY

In 1988, Sanavio observed that existing self-report measures of OCD fail to adequately assess obsessions. Accordingly, he developed the Padua Inventory, which contains four subscales: (1) checking, (2) contamination fears, (3) mental dyscontrol (impaired control of mental activities), and (4) fear of behavioral dyscontrol (urges and worries about losing control of one's behavior). The Padua Inventory is highly correlated with other OC measures, such as the MOCI ($rs = .74$ to .75: Kyrios, Bhar, & Wade, 1996; van Oppen, 1992). However, it is also highly correlated with measures of general distress, such as measures of neuroticism ($r = .60$), trait anxiety ($r = .58$), depression ($rs = .55$ to .61), and trait worry ($r = .57$; Freeston et al., 1994; Kyrios et al., 1996; Sternberger & Burns, 1990a; van Oppen, 1992).

The high correlations with general distress may be because some items of the Padua Inventory appear to be measures of general worry rather than obsessions (Freeston et al., 1994). Worry and obsessions share many features, although they can be distinguished conceptually (Turner, Beidel, & Stanley, 1992).

Burns, Keortge, Formea, and Sternberger (1996) recently revised the Padua Inventory, primarily with the purpose of deleting items that assess worry. The inventory was reduced from 60 to 39 items, which formed five content-related subscales: (1) obsessional thoughts about harm to oneself or others (7 items), (2) obsessional impulses to harm oneself or others (9 items), (3) contamination obsessions and washing compulsions (10 items), (4) checking compulsions (10 items), and (5) dressing and grooming compulsions (3 items).

Burns et al. (1996) administered the revised inventory to a very large sample of university students ($N = 5,010$), and a measure of trait worry—the Penn State Worry Questionnaire (PSWQ)—was completed by a subset of this sample ($N = 2,970$). The revised Padua subscales were shown to be factorially distinct and had good internal consistency (alphas = .77 to .88). The subscales correlated .22 to .57 with one another. Test–retest reliability over a 6- to 7-month rest interval was good, with retest correlations ranging from .61 to .84. These correlations were significantly higher than cross-correlations over the retest interval (i.e., the correlation between subscale A, completed at time 1, and subscale B, completed at time 2). The cross-correlations ranged from .17 to .51 (mean = .34).

The subscales tended to have small-to-medium correlations with the PSWQ (rs = .08 to .37; Burns et al., 1996). Improved discriminant validity of the revised Padua Inventory, compared to the original inventory, was suggested by the finding that total score of the revised inventory had only 12% of shared variance with the PSWQ, whereas the original inventory shared 34% of its variance with the PSWQ (Freeston et al., 1994). Burns et al. (1996) also found that 15 people with OCD had significantly higher scores than normal controls on all five subscales, thus providing preliminary support for the criterion-related validity of the revised inventory.

The revised Padua Inventory has yet to be evaluated in terms of convergent validity and sensitivity to treatment effects. However, the original inventory performed well in terms of convergent validity (discussed previously). The original Padua Inventory also was sensitive to treatment effects, although its effect size (0.92 SD units) was smaller than that of the YBOCS (1.82 SD units; van Oppen, Emmelkamp, van Balkom, & van Dyck, 1995a).

In summary, the revised Padua Inventory is a promising measure of OCD. It is among the most comprehensive self-report measures of OCD and has performed well in psychometric evaluations using nonclinical and OC samples. It probably has good convergent validity, and is probably sensitive to treatment effects, although further evaluation is required.

LIKERT SCALES

A variety of single-item, 9-point Likert scales have been developed to assess various aspects of OCD. These include global measures of severity of obsessions and compulsions, and specific scales, such as measures of OC-related fear, avoidance, time spent ritualizing, and severity of urges to ritualize (e.g., Emmelkamp, 1982; Foa, Kozak, Steketee, & McCarthy, 1992; Foa et al., 1983). The scales may be rated by the patient or by an interviewer.

Foa et al. (1983) obtained high interrater correlations for Likert measures of severity of obsessions and Likert measures severity of compulsions (rs = .92 to .97). Cottraux et al. (1990) reported large correlations (rs = .74 to .89) between a self-report and observer-rated versions of two types of Likert measures (OC-related anxiety/discomfort and duration of compulsions). Large correlations also have been obtained among the patient's, therapist's, and independent observer's ratings of various OC features, including main fear, avoidance, and compulsion severity (rs = .64 to .83; Foa et al., 1987). Thus, there is evidence of good interrater reliability and high correlations between self-report and observer-rated Likert scales.

Steketee, Freund, and Foa (1988) reported that the test–retest reliability of Likert scales (assessing main fear, avoidance, general functioning, anxiety, or depression) ranged from .40 to .87 for self-report ratings, and .20 to .50 for observer ratings over a mean 60-day interval. These data suggest considerable variation in test–retest reliabilities. Unfortunately, reliabilities were not reported for individual scales (only the aforementioned ranges were given), and so it is not possible to identify which scales had the lowest reliability. Accordingly, the test–retest reliability of Likert scales requires further evaluation.

There have been no published studies of the criterion-related validity of these scales. It may be assumed that they have good criterion-related validity, because patients without OCD would have low (or zero) scores on items measuring global severity of obsessions, compulsions, and so forth. However, this assumption may not be warranted, because unwanted, intrusive thoughts often occur in people without OCD (e.g., Rachman & De Silva, 1978; Salkovskis & Harrison, 1984), and compulsion-like behaviors (e.g., excessive checking) can occur in patients with disorders other than OCD (e.g., generalized anxiety disorder; Brown, Moras, Zinbarg, & Barlow, 1993; Schut, Castonguay, Plummer, & Borkovec, 1995) and in community samples (Muris, Merckelbach, & Clavan, 1997).

Likert measures of OC symptoms generally have moderate correlations (rs = .17 to .62, mean = .32) with other OC measures, including the CAC, YBOCS, SCL-90-R OC scale (and predecessors), and original Padua Inventory (Cottraux et al., 1988; Foa et al., 1983; Freund et al., 1987; Steketee & Doppelt, 1986; van Oppen et al., 1995a; Woody et al., 1995a, 1995b). This suggests that the Likert scales generally have acceptable convergent validity.

With regard to discriminant validity, Foa et al. (1983) reported that Likert measures of OC symptoms had small-to-medium correlations with Hopkins Symptom Checklist measures of depression, somatization, anxiety, and interpersonal sensitivity (rs = .09 to .36). Foa et al. (1987) found Likert ratings of the patient's main fear and severity of compulsions had small-to-medium correlations with self-report and observer ratings of depression (rs < .30). These correlations tend to be smaller than the convergent validity correlations, and thereby suggest that the Likert measures have adequate discriminant validity.

Likert scales have been shown to be sensitive to treatment effects, with mean effect sizes ranging from 1.56 to 3.47 (Taylor, 1995). There is little difference in the sensitivity of self-report and observer-rated versions. They tend to be more sensitive that self-report inventories such as the MOCI and self-report CAC, and their sensitivities are as good or better than those of the YBOCS (Taylor, 1995).

Likert scales generally have good psychometric properties (Table 10.1) and are popular in treatment studies because of their ease of administration and scoring. However, a limitation of these scales is that investigators using them have provided little information on the instructions accompanying the self-report versions, and no information on the questions used by interviewers using the observer-rated versions. This makes it difficult to determine whether different investigators are administering the measures in the same way. It also makes it difficult for other researchers or clinicians to know whether they are administering the scales in a reliable and valid manner.

NIMH GLOBAL OBSESSIVE–COMPULSIVE SCALE

The NIMH Global Obsessive–Compulsive Scale (GOCS; Insel et al., 1983) is a single-item, Likert-like measure of the overall severity of OC symptoms. It is a clinician-rated scale based on other NIMH global rating scales, such as the global measures of mania and depression (Murphy, Pickar, & Alterman, 1982). It differs from the Likert scales in the previous section in two ways: the number of rating points (15 vs. 9), and the clustering of descriptors on the scale. The observer completes the GOCS by selecting 1 of 15 severity levels, ranging from 1 (minimal symptoms or within normal range) to 15 (very severe). Severity levels are clustered into five main groups (i.e., ratings of 1–3, 4–6, 7–9, 10–12, and 13–15), with detailed descriptors for each cluster. For example, ratings from 10–12 represent severe OC behavior, defined as "symptoms that are crippling to the patient, interfering so that daily activity is an `active struggle.' Patient may spend full time resisting symptoms. Requires much help from others to function" (cited in Insel et al., 1983).

Interrater reliability of the GOCS has yet to be determined. Two studies have examined test–retest reliability. Kim, Dysken, and Kuskowski (1992) reported a 2-week intraclass correlation of .98, and Kim, Dysken, Kuskowski, and Hoover (1993) obtained a 2-week intraclass correlation of .87. There have been no studies of criterion-related validity or discriminant validity. With regard to convergent validity, one study found the GOCS had a medium correlation ($r = .33$) with the SCL-90-R OC scale, and several studies obtained large correlations with the YBOCS ($rs = .63$ to .77, mean = 69; Black, Kelly, Myers, & Noyes, 1990; Goodman et al., 1989b; Kim et al., 1992, 1993). The convergent validity of the GOCS appears adequate, although in need of further evaluation using measures apart from the YBOCS. Correlations between the GOCS and YBOCS may have been spuriously inflated, because, in each case, the scales were administered by the same interviewer. This means that ratings made on the YBOCS may have influenced those on the GOCS, and vice versa.

The GOCS has been used in several treatment outcome studies. It is sensitive to treatment effects (mean effect size = 1.74 SD units), and tends to be more sensitive than many self-report measures such as the MOCI, and equally as sensitive as most observer-rated measures such as the YBOCS (Taylor, 1995).

The GOCS has the advantage of being a simple, one-item scale, which no doubt accounts for its popularity in treatment outcome studies. However, much remains unknown about its reliability and validity (see Table 10.1). GOCS ratings are based on unstructured clinical interviews, and so its psychometric properties may vary widely from one study to the next, depending on the adequacy of the interviews. The GOCS provides only a global assessment of OC symptoms and fails to capture information about the severity of different types of OC symptoms.

YBOCS

The YBOCS is a semistructured interview designed to assess symptom severity and response to treatment for patients diagnosed with OCD (Goodman et al., 1989a, 1989b, 1989c). It consists of three sections. The first section contains definitions and examples of obsessions and compulsions, which the interviewer reads to the patient. The second section contains a symptom checklist, consisting of more than 50 common obsessions and compulsions. The interviewer asks the patient whether the symptoms have been present currently or in the past. The interviewer then asks the patient to list the most prominent obsessions, compulsions, and OC-related avoidance behaviors.

The third section of the YBOCS consists of 10 core items and 11 investigational items. The latter are included on a provisional basis and require further evaluation. The core items assess five parameters of obsessions (items 1–5) and compulsions (items 6–10): (1) duration/frequency, (2) interference in social and occupational functioning, (3) associated distress, (4) degree of resistance, and (5) perceived control over obsessions or compulsions. Thus, the YBOCS assesses parameters of symptom severity independent of symptom content.

Each core item of the YBOCS proper is rated by the interviewer on a 5-point scale, ranging from 0 (none) to 4 (extreme). The rater must determine whether the patient is presenting with real obsessions or compulsions and not symptoms of another disorder such as paraphilia. All items are accompanied by probe questions, and written definitions accompany each point on the 0–4 scales. Items are rated in terms of the average severity of each parameter over the past week. To illustrate, item 1 assesses the average time spent on all obsessions over the past week. The accompanying rating scale ranges from 0 (no obsessions) to 4 (extreme, greater than 8 hours/day or near constant intrusions). Scores on the 10 core items are summed to yield scores for the obsessions subscale, the compulsions subscale, and the total (10-item) YBOCS scale.

The YBOCS investigational items assess the following: amount of time free of obsessions or compulsions, insight into the irrationality of obsessions and compulsions, avoidance, degree of indecisiveness, overvalued sense of personal responsibility, obsessive slowness/inertia, pathological doubting, global severity, overall response to treatment, and reliability of information obtained from the patient. They are rated by the interviewer on 0–4 or 0–6 scales, similar to those used for the core items.

YBOCS resistance items are rated such that greater resistance is associated with lower scores, because greater resistance is associated with less impairment in social and occupational functioning. This scoring rule is supported by the finding that resistance scores are correlated with less severe OC symptoms, as assessed by other YBOCS items (Goodman et al., 1989a; Woody et al., 1995a).

In practice, most published treatment outcome studies used only the sum of the 10 core items. Scores on the obsession and compulsion subscales are infrequently used, and the Symptom Checklist has yet to be used as an outcome measure. The following review is confined to the psychometric properties of the 10-item YBOCS, because there is little or no available information on the properties of the Symptom Checklist or the investigational items.

Results of several studies suggest that the YBOCS has excellent interrelater reliability. Price, Goodman, Charney, Rasmussen, and Heninger (1987) obtained an intraclass correlation of .99 when the YBOCS was administered by two independent raters to 10 OCs. Goodman et al. (1989a) had six trained raters evaluate videotaped interviews of 6 OCs. The intraclass correlation was .80. In a second study reported in the same article, four trained raters evaluated videotaped interviews of 40 OCs, yielding an intraclass correlation of .98. Jenike et al. (1990) used four raters to assess 40 OCs and obtained an intraclass correlation of .96 for the YBOCS. Woody et al. (1995a) had an interviewer obtain YBOCS ratings from live interviews of 30 OCs, and then a second rater listened to audiotapes of the interviews. The intraclass correlation was .93.

It is possible that interrater reliability may have been spuriously inflated in some of these studies. The reliability estimates were obtained by having one evaluator rerate taped interviews of another evaluator. This shows that one can score another's interview reliably, but not that one can administer the instrument reliably.

The YBOCS has acceptable-to-good internal consistency, with coefficients alpha ranging from .69 to .91 (Goodman et al., 1989a; Richter et al., 1994; Woody et al., 1995a). With regard to test–retest reliability, Kim et al. (1990, 1992, 1993) administered the YBOCS to three samples of OCs three times over a 2-week period. Intraclass correlations ranged from .81 to .97. Woody et al. (1995a) administered the YBOCS to 24 OCs on two occasions over test–retest intervals ranging from 10 to 103 days (mean = 49 days). The intraclass correlation was .61, and was reduced, probably because of the large retest interval. The findings suggest the YBOCS has good test–retest reliability over at least a 2-week interval.

The YBOCS was intended for use with patients diagnosed with OCD, and so there has been only one study of its criterion-related validity. Rosenfeld, Dar, Anderson, Kobak, and Greist (1992) found that patients with OCD had higher YBOCS scores than patients with other anxiety disorders and normal controls.

The YBOCS tends to have large correlations (rs = .17 to .77, mean = .51) with other OC measures (i.e., anxiety and avoidance ratings from behavioral avoidance tests, SCL-90-R OC scale, subscales of the Leyton Obsessional Inventory, MOCI, Likert scales of symptom severity, GOCS; Black et al., 1990; Goodman et al., 1989b; Kim et al., 1990, 1992; Richter et al., 1994; Woody et al., 1995a, 1995b). These results indicate that the YBOCS has good convergent validity.

Studies of discriminant validity are less encouraging. The YBOCS has large correlations with the Hamilton Depression Scale (rs = .53 to .91, mean = .64) and large correlations with the Hamilton Anxiety Scale (rs = .47 to .85, mean = .62; Goodman et al., 1989b; Hewlett, Vinogradov, & Agras, 1992; Price et al., 1987; Richter et al., 1994). These studies show that correlations between the YBOCS and measures of depression and general anxiety tend to be as large as the convergent validity correlations. This suggests the 10-item YBOCS has poor discriminant validity.

Several studies have found the 10-item YBOCS to be sensitive to treatment effects (mean effect size = 1.75 SD units; Taylor, 1995). It is as sensitive as other observer-rated scales, and tends to be more sensitive that self-report measures (Taylor, 1995).

In summary, the 10-item YBOCS generally has good psychometric properties (Table 10.1) and provides the most comprehensive available assessment of OCD. However, its discriminant validity is poor. The reasons for this are unclear and require further investigation. The psychometric properties of the Symptom Checklist and investigational items also remain to be investigated.

The Symptom Checklist requires the assessor to inquire about a wide range of obsessive and compulsive phenomena. This is important for a comprehensive assessment, because patients may feel embarrassed or otherwise reluctant to discuss their obsessions and compulsions, and so they may not mention these symptoms unless the interviewer directly asks about them. A limitation of the Symptom Checklist is that it provides a limited assessment of cognitive compulsions (e.g., repeating special words or phrases to "undo" disturbing thoughts). The Checklist was recently expanded by Foa and Kozak to assess these phenomena (personal communication, April 1994).

The YBOCS provides separate scores to measure the severity of obsessions and compulsions. However, most outcome studies simply combine these into a total score. Kim, Dysken, and Katz (1989) observed that if a patient has only obsessions or compulsions, then the YBOCS total score may be misleadingly low, even if symptoms are severe. The use of subscales would provide more information about the effects of treatment (e.g., some treatments may have a greater effect on compulsions than obsessions), and would help circumvent the problem raised by Kim et al.

Self-Report and Computerized Versions

Recent studies have shown that computerized and self-report versions of the YBOCS perform favorably compared to the interviewer-administered version. Rosenfeld et al. (1992) developed a self-administered, computerized version of the YBOCS, which was well received by respondents and yielded comparable results to those obtained from the interview version. For the computerized and interview-administered versions of the 10-item YBOCS, the total scores of most (76%) respondents fell within 3 points of one another (out of a possible 40 points). Using a cutoff score of 16 (which is commonly used in treatment outcome studies), there was 97% agreement on the diagnosis (presence or absence) of OCD. The obsessions and compulsions subscales for the 10-item computer version correlated .86 to .88 with the corresponding subscales in the interview version.

Baer, Brown-Beasley, Sorce, and Henriques (1993) administered three versions of the YBOCS to a sample of 18 OCs: a telephone talking-computer version, an in-person telephone interview, and a self-report version. The versions were given in counterbalanced order. Scores on self-report and computer versions correlated very highly with the interview version (rs = .97 and .99), and mean scores did not differ across the three versions.

Warren, Zgourides, and Monto (1993) administered the self-report, 10-item YBOCS to a sample of university students and obtained good internal consistency for the subscales and 10-item total score (alphas = .88 to .91). Most recently, Steketee, Frost, and Bogart (1996) conducted an intensive evaluation of the self-report YBOCS (i.e., the 10-item YBOCS proper and the Symptom Checklist) in four samples (two student samples, an OCD sample, and a non-OC anxiety-disordered sample). Self-report and interview versions were administered in various combinations to the different samples. There was good agreement between self-report and interview versions of the Symptom Checklist, although respondents tended to report more symptoms on the self-report version. The 10-item YBOCS displayed generally good internal consistency (alphas = .78 to .89), although the subscales displayed somewhat more variable internal consistencies across nonclinical and OC samples (alphas = .55 to 85, mean = .74). The subscales and 10-item total scale had good test–retest reliability over a 1-week interval, with rs ranging from .82 to .88 for nonclinical and OC samples. The corresponding correlations for the interview version were .55 to .79, which suggest that the self-report version had slightly better test–retest reliability.

Across the various samples, scores on the self-report, 10-item YBOCS tended to closely agree with those of the interview version, thus indicating parallel forms validity. The self-report version discriminated between OC and non-OC patients, thereby supporting its criterion-related validity.

In summary, the results of Steketee et al. (1996) and others suggest that self-report and computerized versions of the YBOCS produce similar results to the interview version. Thus, the self-report and computerized versions represent less costly and more time-efficient alternatives to the interview version. It remains to be seen whether the self-report and computerized versions have acceptable convergent validity, and whether they are sensitive to treatment effects. It also remains to be determined whether they suffer the poor discriminant validity that is characteristic of the interview version.

CLINICAL CONSIDERATIONS IN THE ASSESSMENT OF OCD

Despite the usefulness of many of the measures described in this chapter, each has their limitations. The purpose of this section is to review some of the clinical problems that arise when using structured interviews, observer-rated scales, and self-report measures in the assessment of OCD. Two particular issues are important: (1) procedural difficulties in administering the measures, and (2) problems in distinguishing obsessions and compulsions from related phenomena, that is, problems of ensuring that a given measures is, in fact, assessing obsessions and compulsions in a given respondent.

Procedural Problems

There are a variety of reasons why people with OCD have difficulty describing their obsessions and compulsions. Sometimes patients are embarrassed about their symptoms. Thus, the clinician needs to be sensitive to these concerns and appropriately empathic about the difficulties inherent in describing these symptoms to others. Clearly, the interview will be facilitated if the interviewer does not appear shocked or disturbed by the patient's symptoms. Structured interviews such as the YBOCS can further help put the patient at ease. The YBOCS contains an extensive Symptom Checklist. The interviewer can introduce the items on this checklist as symptoms that are commonly reported by people with OCD. As the patient is taken through the checklist, he or she often comes to realize that other people have similar symptoms, and that the interviewer has encountered these symptoms before.

Patients sometimes may have difficulty describing the contents of their obsessions because of belief in "thought–action fusion," that is, the belief that discussing (i.e., thinking about) a particular thought increases the likelihood that the thought will be translated into action. This is illustrated, for example, by the belief that thinking about harming someone will increase the likelihood that one will actually commit an act of harm. When thought–action fusion interferes with the assessment, this problem usually can be overcome by gently but persistently encouraging the patient to describe his or her obsessions. Once the patient describes these thoughts, he or she may engage in neutralizing compulsions (e.g., replacing a harm-related obsession with a "good" thought).

A similar problem occurs when patients with contamination fears are concerned about handling questionnaires and writing materials, and therefore have difficulty completing the assessment. Again, we have found that persistent encouragement is often helpful. If necessary, one can remind the patient that he or she can always engage in cleaning rituals after completing the questionnaires.

A further problem is that patients sometimes attempt to minimize their symptoms. For example, people with hoarding compulsions may present for treatment at the urging of significant others, who find that hoarding has made living conditions intolerable. Some people with hoarding rituals do not regard these compulsions as problematic and may be reluctant to participate in assessment and treatment. When symptom minimization is suspected, it can be useful to conduct a home visit along with an interview with significant others.

A related assessment problem concerns the person's awareness ("insight") into the severity of his or her compulsions. For example, a patient may not realize that he or she engages in frequent reassurance seeking. Again, an interview with significant other can be illuminating.

Indecisiveness, intolerance of ambiguity, and need for reassurance are characteristic features of OCD. Occasionally, these features interfere with the assessment of OC-related signs and symptoms by greatly increasing the amount of time required to complete the assessment. For example, while conducting structured interviews such as the YBOCS, some patients can be circumstantial in their descriptions of their signs and symptoms, in an attempt to provide the interview with "all" the details. Similarly, patients completing self-report measures may repeatedly ask for clarification of the meaning of questions, and may repeatedly check their answers. These problems, when they arise, can often be addressed by patience and prompting; gently but persistently encouraging the patient to make short, concise responses; and reminding the patient of the time constraints. For self-report measures, we encourage the patient to write down the first response that comes to mind, and discourage repeated checking of answers. These simple strategies are generally effective in helping patients to complete interviews and questionnaires within a reasonable time period.

Distinguishing Obsessions and Compulsions from Related Phenomena

A clinical interview is often useful to ensure that OCD instruments (especially self-report measures) are, in fact, assessing obsessions and compulsions. This is needed to ensure that the respondent is indeed rating his or her OC symptoms, instead of making ratings for topographically similar symptoms, such as worries, paraphilias, or tics. The purpose of this section of the chapter is not to provide a complete list of differential diagnoses; that can be found in the DSM-IV (American Psychiatric Association, 1994). Instead, we focus on some of the more common diagnostic difficulties.

Tics and compulsive urges can be difficult to distinguish. The two appear to differ primarily in that compulsions are more likely to be purposive behaviors, often in response to an obsession, and intended to prevent or undo some form of harm. In some cases, it also can be difficult to distinguish obsessions from worries. Obsessional doubts and ruminations often have a worry-like quality to them (e.g., repetitive obsessional thoughts such as "What if I didn't lock the door?"). Obsessions and worries share some similarities; both are uncontrollable and appraised by the person as excessive. To complicate matters, people with excessive worry (i.e., those with generalized anxiety disorder) often engage in subclinical rituals, particularly checking compulsions (Brown et al., 1993; Schut et al., 1995).

Although obsessions can sometimes be very difficult to distinguish from worries, in most cases, experienced clinicians can reliably distinguish between the two (Brown et al., 1993), and respondents can distinguish worries from obsessions once they are given definitions of these phenomena (Wells & Morrison, 1994). In a recent review of the literature on obsessions and worries, Turner et al. (1992) identified several ways in which worries differ from obsessions. The following criteria can aid in the accurate identification of obsessions: (1) Compared to obsessions, worry is more frequently perceived (by the person) as being triggered by an internal or external event; (2) the content of worry is typically related to normal experiences of everyday living (e.g., family, finances, work), whereas the content of obsessions frequently includes themes of dirt/contamination, religion, sex, and aggression (but themes of health and illness can characterize worries and obsessions); (3) worry generally occurs in the form of a thought (i.e., a verbal/linguistic representation), whereas obsessions appear in a variety of forms (thoughts, images, impulses); (4) although worry and obsessions are both experienced as uncontrollable, worry does not appear to be resisted as strongly, nor is worry as intrusive as obsessional thinking; and (5) the content of worries, compared to obsessions, is less likely to be regarded by the person as "unacceptable" (i.e., less likely to be ego–dystonic).

CONCLUSIONS

The SCID and ADIS are the most commonly used methods for diagnosing OCD (as defined by DSM-III-R). When used by suitably trained clinicians, these interviews yield adequate interrater reliability. The data for the ADIS is particularly encouraging. The interrater reliability for the DSM-IV versions of these interviews remains to be investigated. However, the DSM-III-R and DSM-IV diagnostic criteria for OCD are very similar, and so it seems likely that the DSM-IV versions of the SCID and ADIS will have adequate reliability.

The other measures of OC-related symptoms and signs described in this chapter can be used to aid in the diagnosis of OCD. However, this is not their primary purpose. Measures such as the MOCI and YBOCS are used to characterize the nature and severity of OC symptoms, regardless of whether these symptoms exceed the threshold for defining OCD. The selection of these measures for research or clinical purposes is based on multiple criteria. Among the most important are (1) content (range of phenomena assessed), (2) reliability and validity, and whether there is sufficient available information to evaluate these properties, and (3) sensitivity to changes in symptom severity.

Some OC measures are popular measures in OCD treatment outcome studies (e.g., the GOCS), yet little is known about their psychometric properties (Table 10.1). Some measures provide only global measures of OC symptoms (e.g., CAC). Some measures confound important variables (e.g., obsessional slowness, avoidance, and oddity of behavior are confounded in the CAC).

BATs have the advantage of providing *in vivo* measures of OC-related fear, avoidance, and rituals. A major disadvantage of BATs is that they are sometimes difficult to devise and time consuming to implement. Self-report inventories are popular because of their ease of administration. They vary markedly in their breadth of measurement; some provide measures of different OC phenomena (e.g., the MOCI subscales and the revised Padua Inventory), whereas others only provide measures of global severity of OC symptoms (e.g., the CAC). In terms of breadth of assessment and psychometric properties (Table 10.1), the original MOCI and the revised Padua Inventory appear to be among the best available self-report inventories. The revised Padua Inventory has an advantage over the MOCI in that it provides a broader assessment of OC symptoms, particularly the assessment of obsessions. It remains to be seen how the MOCI-R compares to these inventories.

The YBOCS is broader still in its assessment, providing not only a detailed assessment of obsessions and compulsions (in the Symptom Checklist), but also a comprehensive evaluation of the parameters of OCD (e.g., frequency, resistance, avoidance). Each item is accompanied by detailed probe questions that structure the interview and ensure that appropriate information is collected. When breadth of measurement, reliability, and validity are considered together, the YBOCS appears to be among the best available measures for assessing OCD for clinical and research purposes. However, the poor discriminant validity of the 10-item YBOCS is an important concern. It remains to be seen whether its discriminant validity can be improved by revising the YBOCS. It is unlikely, however, that this is a weakness specific to the YBOCS, because the GOCS is highly correlated with the YBOCS, and so it may have similar problems with discriminant validity. A further drawback is that the interview-administered YBOCS can be time consuming, with interviews taking an average of 40 minutes per patient (Rosenfeld et al., 1992). However, this problem can be circumvented by using self-report or computerized versions of this scale.

Observer-rated inventories such as the YBOCS are generally more sensitive to treatment effects than self-report scales. It may be that the superior sensitivity of observer-rated scales is due to rater bias; that is, raters may tend to assign high scores if they know that the patient is presenting for treatment, and low scores if they know that the patient may have just completed treatment. However, if observer-rated scales are not biased in this regard, then it appears better to use observer-rated than self-report scales to evaluate the efficacy of treatments for OCD. Further studies of the question of rater bias may help resolve this issue and thereby improve our ability to detect treatment-related changes in OCD.

The measures covered in this chapter are useful in providing a detailed assessment of OC-related symptoms and signs. However, these measures are likely to produce an insufficient description of OC-related psychopathology. Given the growing emphasis on the role of maladaptive beliefs in OCD (e.g., Salkovskis, 1985, 1989), it seems that a comprehensive assessment of OCD will require an evaluation of OC-related beliefs and appraisals. A review of these measures is beyond the scope of the present chapter. The interested reader is referred to a recent article on the topic (Obsessive Compulsive Cognitions Work Group, 1997).

REFERENCES

American Psychiatric Association. (1994). *Diagnostic and statistical manual of mental disorders* (4th ed.). Washington, DC: Author.

Baer, L., Brown-Beasley, M. W., Sorce, J., & Henriques, A. (1993). Computer-assisted telephone administration of a structured interview for obsessive–compulsive disorder. *American Journal of Psychiatry, 150,* 1737–1738.

Black, D. W., Kelly, M., Myers, C., & Noyes, R. (1990). Tritiated imipramine binding in obsessive–compulsive volunteers and psychiatrically normal controls. *Biological Psychiatry, 27,* 319–327.

Brown, T. A., Moras, K., Zinbarg, R. E., & Barlow, D. H. (1993). Diagnostic and symptom distinguishability of generalized anxiety disorder and obsessive–compulsive disorder. *Behavior Therapy, 24,* 227–240.

Burns, G. L., Keortge, S. G., Formea, G. M., & Sternberger, L. G. (1996). Revision of the Padua Inventory for obsessive compulsive disorder symptoms: Distinctions between worry, obsessions, and compulsions. *Behaviour Research and Therapy, 34,* 163–173.

Campbell, D. T., & Fiske, D. W. (1959). Convergent and discriminant validation by the multitrait multimethod matrix. *Psychological Bulletin, 56,* 81–105.

Chan, D. W. (1990). The Maudsley Obsessional–Compulsive Inventory: A psychometric investigation on Chinese normal subjects. *Behaviour Research and Therapy, 28,* 413–420.

Cohen, J. (1988). *Statistical power analyses for the behavioral sciences* (2nd ed.). Hillsdale, NJ: Erlbaum.

Cottraux, J., Bouvard, M., Defayolle, M., & Messy, P. (1988). Validity and factorial structure of the compulsive activity checklist. *Behavior Therapy, 19,* 45–53.

Cottraux, J., Mollard, E., Bouvard, M., Marks, I., Sluys, M., Nury, A. M., Douge, R., & Cialdella, P. (1990). A controlled study of fluvoxamine and exposure in obsessive–compulsive disorder. *International Clinical Psychopharmacology, 5,* 17–30.

Di Nardo, P., & Barlow, D. H. (1988). Anxiety Disorders Interview Schedule—Revised. New York: Graywind.

Di Nardo, P., Brown, T. A., & Barlow, D. H. (1994). *Anxiety Disorders Interview Schedule for DSM-IV.* San Antonio, TX: Psychological Corporation.

Di Nardo, P., Moras, K., Barlow, D. H., Rapee, R. M., & Brown, T. A. (1993). Reliability of DSM-III-R anxiety disorder categories: Using the Anxiety Disorders Interview Schedule—Revised (ADIS-R). *Archives of General Psychiatry, 50,* 251–256.

Emmelkamp, P. M. G. (1982). *Phobic and obsessive–compulsive disorders: Theory, research, and practice.* New York: Plenum.

Emmelkamp, P. M. G., Kraaijkamp, H. J. M., & Van den Hout, M. A. (in press). The Maudsley Obsessional–Compulsive Inventory: Reliability and validity. *Behavior Modification.*

First, M. B., Spitzer, R. L., Gibbon, M., & Williams, J. B. W. (1996). *Structured Clinical Interview for DSM-IV Axis I Disorders—Patient Edition (SCID-I/P, Version 2.0).* New York: Biometrics Research Department, New York State Psychiatric Institute.

Fleiss, J. L. (1981). *Statistical methods for rates and proportions* (2nd ed.). New York: Wiley.

Foa, E. B., Grayson, J. B., Steketee, G. S., Doppelt, H. G., Turner, R. M., & Latimer, P. R. (1983). Success and failure in the behavioral treatment of obsessive–compulsives. *Journal of Consulting and Clinical Psychology, 51,* 287–297.

Foa, E. B., Kozak, M. J., Steketee, G. S., & McCarthy, P. R. (1992). Treatment of depressive and obsessive–compulsive symptoms in OCD by imipramine and behavior therapy. *British Journal of Clinical Psychology, 31,* 279–292.

Foa, E. B., Steketee, G., Grayson, J. B., Turner, R. M., & Latimer, P. R. (1984). Deliberate exposure and blocking of obsessive–compulsive rituals: Immediate and long-term effects. *Behavior Therapy, 15,* 450–472.

Foa, E. B., Steketee, G., Kozak, M. J., & Dugger, D. (1987). Effects of imipramine on depression and obsessive–compulsive symptoms. *Psychiatry Research, 21,* 123–136.

Freeston, M. H., Ladouceur, R., Rh,aume, J., Letarte, H., Gagnon, F., & Thibodeau, N. (1994). Self-report of obsessions and worry. *Behaviour Research and Therapy, 32,* 29–36.

Freund, B., Steketee, G. S., & Foa, E. B. (1987). Compulsive activity checklist (CAC): Psychometric analysis with obsessive–compulsive disorder. *Behavioral Assessment, 9,* 67–79.

Goodman, W. K., Price, L. H., Rasmussen, S. A., Mazure, C., Fleishmann, R. L., Hill, C. L., Heninger, G. R., & Charney, D. S. (1989a). The Yale–Brown Obsessive–Compulsive Scale: I. Development, use, and reliability. *Archives of General Psychiatry, 46,* 1006–1011.

Goodman, W. K., Price, L. H., Rasmussen, S. A., Mazure, C., Delgado, P., Heninger, G. R., & Charney, D. S. (1989b). The Yale–Brown Obsessive–Compulsive Scale: II. Validity. *Archives of General Psychiatry, 46,* 1012–1016.

Goodman, W. K., Rasmussen, S. A., Price, L. H., Mazure, C., Heninger, G. R., & Charney, D. S. (1989c). *Manual for the Yale–Brown Obsessive–Compulsive Scale (revised).* New Haven, CT: Connecticut Mental Health Center.

Hewlett, W. A., Vinogradov, S., & Agras, W. S. (1992). Clomipramine, clonazepam, and clonidine treatment of obsessive–compulsive disorder. *Journal of Clinical Psychopharmacology, 12,* 420–430.

Hodgson, R. J., & Rachman, S. (1977). Obsessional–compulsive complaints. *Behaviour Research and Therapy, 15,* 389–395.

Insel, T. R., Murphy, D. L., Cohen, R. M., Alterman, I., Kilton, C., & Linnoila, M. (1983). Obsessive–compulsive disorder: A double-blind trial of clomipramine and clorgyline. *Archives of General Psychiatry, 40,* 605–612.

Jenike, M. A., Hyman, S., Baer, L., Holland, A., Minichiello, W. E., Buttolph, L., Summergrad, P., Seymour, R., & Ricciardi, J. (1990). A controlled trial of fluvoxamine in obsessive–compulsive disorder: Implications for a serotonergic theory. *American Journal of Psychiatry, 147,* 1209–1215.

Kim, S. W., Dysken, M. W., & Katz, R. (1989). Rating scales for obsessive compulsive disorder. *Psychiatric Annals, 19,* 74–79.

Kim, S. W., Dysken, M. W., & Kuskowski, M. (1990). The Yale–Brown Obsessive–Compulsive Scale: A reliability and validity study. *Psychiatry Research, 34,* 99–106.

Kim, S. W., Dysken, M. W., & Kuskowski, M. (1992). The Symptom Checklist-90 obsessive–compulsive subscale: A reliability and validity study. Psychiatry Research, 41, 37–44.

Kim, S. W., Dysken, M. W., Kuskowski, M., & Hoover, K. M. (1993). The Yale–Brown Obsessive–Compulsive Scale and the NIMH Global Obsessive–Compulsive Scale (GOCS): A reliability and validity study. *International Journal of Methods in Psychiatric Research, 3,* 37–44.

Kyrios, M., Bhar, S., & Wade, D. (1996). The assessment of obsessive–compulsive phenomena: Psychometric and normative data on the Padua Inventory from an Australian non-clinical student sample. *Behaviour Research and Therapy, 34,* 85–95.

Lang, P. J., & Lazovik, A. D. (1963). Experimental desensitization of a phobia. *Journal of Abnormal and Social Psychology, 66,* 519–525.

Marks, I. M., Hallam, R. S., Connolly, J., & Philpott, R. (1977). *Nursing in behavioral psychotherapy.* London: Royal College of Nursing.

Marks, I. M., Stern, R. S., Mawson, D., Cobb, J., & McDonald, R. (1980). Clomipramine and exposure for obsessive–compulsive rituals: I. *British Journal of Psychiatry, 136,* 1–25.

Muris, P., Merckelbach, H., & Clavan, M. (1997). Abnormal and normal compulsions. *Behaviour Research and Therapy, 35,* 249–252.

Murphy, D. L., Pickar, D., & Alterman, I. S. (1982). Methods for the quantitative assessment of depressive and manic behavior. In E. I. Burdock, A. Sudilosky, & S. Gershon (Eds.), *The behavior of psychiatric patients* (pp. 355–392). New York: Marcel Dekker.

Nunnally, J. C. (1978). *Psychometric theory* (2nd ed.). New York: McGraw-Hill.

Obsessive–Compulsive Cognitions Work Group: Amir, N., Bouvard, M., Carmin, C., Clark, D. A., Cottraux, J., Eisen, J., Emmelkamp, P., Foa, E., Freeston, M., Frost, R., Hoekstra, R., Kozak, M., Kyrios, M., Ladouceur, R., March, J., McKay, D., Neziroglu, F., Pinard, A., Pollard, C. A., Purdon, C., Rachman, S., Rhéaume, J., Richards, C., Salkovskis, P., Sanavio, E., Shafran, R., Sica, C., Simos, G., Sookman, D., Steketee, G., Tallis, F., Taylor, S., Thordarson, D., Turner, S., van Oppen, P., Warren, R., & Yaryura-Tobias, J. (1997). Cognitive assessment of obsessive–compulsive disorder. *Behaviour Research and Therapy, 35,* 667–681.

Philpott, R. (1975). Recent advances in the behavioral assessment of obsessional illness: Difficulties common to these and other measures. *Scottish Medical Journal, 20*(Suppl. 1), 33–40.

Price, L. H., Goodman, W. K., Charney, D. S., Rasmussen, S. A., & Heninger, G. R. (1987). Treatment of severe obsessive–compulsive disorder with fluvoxamine. *American Journal of Psychiatry, 144,* 1059–1061.

Rachman, S., Cobb, J., Grey, B., McDonald, D., Mawson, D., Sartory, G., & Stern, R. (1979). The behavioral treatment of obsessive–compulsive disorders, with and without clomipramine. *Behaviour Research and Therapy, 17,* 467–478.

Rachman, S., & De Silva, P. (1978). Abnormal and normal obsessions. *Behaviour Research and Therapy, 16,* 233–248.

Rachman, S., & Hodgson, R. J. (1980). *Obsessions and compulsions.* Englewood Cliffs, NJ: Prentice-Hall.

Rachman, S., Thordarson, D. S., & Radomsky, A. S. (1995, July). *A revision of the Maudsley Obsessional–Compulsive Inventory.* Poster presented at the World Congress of Behavioural and Cognitive Therapies, Copenhagen, Denmark.

Richter, M. A., Cox, B. J., & Direnfeld, D. M. (1994). A comparison of three assessment instruments for obsessive–compulsive symptoms. *Journal of Behavior Therapy and Experimental Psychiatry, 25,* 143–147.

Rosenfeld, R., Dar, R., Anderson, D., Kobak, K. A., & Greist, J. H. (1992). A computer-administered version of the Yale–Brown Obsessive–Compulsive Scale. *Psychological Assessment, 4,* 329–332.

Salkovskis, P. M. (1985). Obsessional–compulsive problems: A cognitive-behavioural analysis. *Behaviour Research and Therapy, 25,* 571–583.

Salkovskis, P. M. (1989). Cognitive-behavioural factors and the persistence of intrusive thoughts in obsessional problems. *Behaviour Research and Therapy, 27,* 677–682.

Salkovskis, P. M., & Harrison, J. (1984). Abnormal and normal obsessions: A replication. *Behaviour Research and Therapy, 22,* 549–552.

Sanavio, E. (1988). Obsessions and compulsions: The Padua Inventory. *Behaviour Research and Therapy, 26,* 169–177.

Sanavio, E., & Vidotto, G. (1985). The components of the Maudsley Obsessional–Compulsive Questionnaire. *Behaviour Research and Therapy, 23,* 659–662.

Schut, A. J., Castonguay, L. G., Plummer, K., & Borkovec, T. D. (1995, November). *Compulsive checking behaviors in generalized anxiety disorder.* Paper presented at the 29th meeting of the Association for Advancement of Behavior Therapy, Washington, DC.

Spitzer, R. L., Williams, J. B. W., & Gibbon, M. (1987). *SCID: Structured Clinical Interview for DSM-III-R*. New York: New York State Psychiatric Institute.

Spitzer, R. L., Williams, J. B. W., Gibbon, M., & First, M. B. (1992). The Structured Clinical Interview for DSM-III-R (SCID): I. History, rationale, and description. *Archives of General Psychiatry, 49,* 624–629.

Steketee, G. S., Chambless, D. L., Tran, G. Q., Worden, H., & Gillis, M. M. (1996). Behavioral avoidance test for obsessive compulsive disorder. *Behaviour Research and Therapy, 34,* 73–83.

Steketee, G. S., & Doppelt, H. (1986). Measurement of obsessive–compulsive symptomatology: Utility of the Hopkins Symptom Checklist. *Psychiatry Research, 19,* 135–145.

Steketee, G. S., & Freund, B. (1993). Compulsive Activity Checklist (CAC): Further psychometric analyses and revision. *Behavioural Psychotherapy, 21,* 13–25.

Steketee, G., Freund, B., & Foa, E. B. (1988). Likert scaling. In M. Hersen & A. S. Bellack (Eds.), *Dictionary of behavioral assessment techniques* (pp. 289–291). New York: Pergamon.

Steketee, G., Frost, R., & Bogart, K. (1996). The Yale–Brown Obsessive–Compulsive Scale: Interview versus self-report. *Behaviour Research and Therapy, 34,* 675–684.

Sternberger, L. G., & Burns, G. L. (1990a). Obsessions and compulsions: Psychometric properties of the Padua Inventory with an American college population. *Behaviour Research and Therapy, 28,* 341–345.

Sternberger, L. G., & Burns, G. L. (1990b). Compulsive Activity Checklist and the Maudsley Obsessional–Compulsive Inventory: Psychometric properties of two measures of obsessive–compulsive disorder. *Behavior Therapy, 21,* 117–127.

Taylor, S. (1995). Assessment of obsessions and compulsions: Reliability, validity, and sensitivity to treatment effects. *Clinical Psychology Review, 15,* 261–296.

Taylor, S., Woody, S., Koch, W. J., McLean, P., & Anderson, K. (1996). Suffocation false-alarms and efficacy of cognitive-behavioural therapy for panic disorder. *Behavior Therapy, 27,* 115–126.

Taylor, S., Woody, S., Koch, W. J., McLean, P., Paterson, R., & Anderson, K. (1997). Cognitive restructuring in the treatment of social phobia: Efficacy and mode of action. *Behavior Modification, 21,* 487–511.

Turner, S. M., Beidel, D. C., & Stanley, M. A. (1992). Are obsessional thoughts and worry different cognitive phenomena? *Clinical Psychology Review, 12,* 257–270.

van Oppen, P. (1992). Obsessions and compulsions: Dimensional structure, reliability, convergent and divergent validity of the Padua Inventory. *Behaviour Research and Therapy, 30,* 631–637.

van Oppen, P., Emmelkamp, P. M. G., van Balkom, A., & van Dyck, R. (1995a). The sensitivity to change of measures for obsessive–compulsive disorder. *Journal of Anxiety Disorders, 9,* 241–248.

van Oppen, P., Hoekstra, R. J., & Emmelkamp, P. M. G. (1995b). The structure of obsessive–compulsives symptoms. *Behaviour Research and Therapy, 33,* 15–23.

Warren, R., Zgourides, G., & Monto, M. (1993). Self-report versions of the Yale–Brown Obsessive–Compulsive Scale: An assessment of a sample of normals. *Psychological Reports, 73,* 574.

Wells, A., & Morrison, A. P. (1994). Qualitative dimensions of normal worry and normal obsessions: A comparative study. *Behaviour Research and Therapy, 32,* 867–870.

Whittal, M., McLean, P., Taylor, S., Söchting, I., & Anderson, K. (1997, September). *Comparative efficacy of cognitive and behavioural therapies for obsessive–compulsive disorder.* Paper presented in the symposium, Treatment of Obsessive–Compulsive Disorder: Current Status and Future Directions (S. Taylor, Chair) at the XXVII Congress of the European Association for Behavioural and Cognitive Therapies, Venice, Italy.

Williams, J. B. W., Gibbon, M., First, M. B., Spitzer, R. L., Davis, M., Borus, J., Howes, M. J., Kane, J., Pope, H. G., Rounsaville, B., Wittchen, H.-U. (1992). The Structured Clinical Interview for DSM-III-R (SCID): II. Multisite test–retest reliability. *Archives of General Psychiatry, 49*, 630–636.

Woody, S. R., Steketee, G., & Chambless, D. L. (1995a). Reliability and validity of the Yale–Brown Obsessive–Compulsive Scale. *Behaviour Research and Therapy, 33*, 597–605.

Woody, S. R., Steketee, G., & Chambless, D. L. (1995b). The usefulness of the obsessive compulsive scale of the Symptom Checklist-90—Revised. *Behaviour Research and Therapy, 33*, 607–611.

Chapter 11

PSYCHOSOCIAL TREATMENTS FOR OBSESSIVE–COMPULSIVE DISORDER
Literature Review

Edna B. Foa
Martin E. Franklin
Michael J. Kozak

The last 30 years have brought much progress in the development of effective psychosocial treatments for obsessive–compulsive disorder (OCD). In this chapter, we first briefly review the early behavioral interventions that did not prove satisfactory. Next, we discuss the immediate and long-term efficacy of cognitive-behavioral therapy (CBT) involving exposure and ritual prevention (EX/RP), a program that emerged as quite effective in ameliorating OCD symptoms. We also describe what are thought to be the active ingredients in CBT. We then compare the relative efficacy of other treatments, including cognitive therapy, to EX/RP. Finally, we summarize the findings on prediction of treatment outcome and point to topics for further study.

EARLY PSYCHOSOCIAL TREATMENTS

Until the mid-1960s, OCD was considered a refractory psychiatric condition. Neither psychodynamic psychotherapy nor a variety of pharmacological treatments had proven successful with OCD symptoms. Several behavioral techniques derived from learning theory were also used to treat OCD. In general, these interventions involved either a form of exposure (e.g., systematic desensitization) or reinforcement procedures (e.g., aversion). Results varied widely across reports, and methodological flaws made the findings difficult to interpret. The use of systematic desensitization for OCD was examined in case studies and small-case series. For the most part, the reported efficacy of this procedure was very modest (Foa, Steketee, & Ozarow, 1985). For example, Cooper, Gelder, and Marks (1965) found that only 3 of 10 patients treated with systematic desensitization improved. It did seem that *in vivo* desensitization was more effective than imaginal (Beech & Vaughn, 1978).

Paradoxical intention, that is, *in vivo* confrontation with stimuli that evoke the obsessions coupled with instructions to elaborate the obsessional material, was also employed with OCD. Gertz (1966) reported 66% responders in a small-case series; Solyom, Garza-Perez, Ledwidge, and Solyom (1972) reported that 5 of 10 treated patients were markedly improved at posttreatment.

Other exposure procedures have been examined in single-case reports. Noonan (1971) reported that after 7 sessions of implosive therapy, the patients was symptom free; McCarthy (1972) found that prolonged imaginal exposure to feared consequences produced symptom remission in another patient. Broadhurst (1976) found that imaginal exposure to menstrual blood resulted in mild improvement for one patient at posttreatment, with further improvement at long-term follow-up.

With nonritualizers, exposure did not prove particularly effective in a study conducted by Emmelkamp and Kwee (1977), with only 1 of 3 patients showing improvement after 5 one-hour sessions. Similarly, satiation, which involves having patients verbalize their obsessive ruminations in 1-hour sessions, resulted in improvement for only 2 of 7 treated patients (Stern, 1978).

A series of studies examining exposure in combination with aversion relief found some evidence for the efficacy of this program. Treatment consisted of exposure to taped narratives of obsessive thoughts. These narratives were periodically interrupted by 20-second silences followed by a mild electric shock. Shock was terminated by the patient, at which point the taped narratives resumed. Results indicated improvement for patients with a variety of obsessive concerns (Solymon & Kingstone, 1973; Solymon, Zamanzadeh, Ledwidge, & Kenny, 1971).

Several studies reported about the efficacy of procedures aimed at compulsions. Rabavilas, Boulougouris, and Stefanis (1977) instructed 4 patients with checking rituals to continue checking beyond their urge to do so. Patients did not comply with the instructions, yet showed a substantial decrease in ritualizing at follow-up anyway. Perhaps the mechanism underlying this intervention is similar to that involved in paradoxical intention, which was also effective in several case studies.

Reinforcement procedures have also been utilized to treat OCD. An aversion relief paradigm was examined in which OCD washers received electric shocks when they began ritualizing; these shocks were terminated upon contact with the contaminant. Patients in two studies evidenced some improvement in compulsive behavior with this technique (Marks, Crowe, Drewe, Young, & Dewhurst, 1969; Rubin & Merbaum, 1971). Aversion procedures without relief upon contact with feared stimuli were also examined, with improvement noted in 3 of 5 treated patients in one study (Kenny, Mowbray, & Lalani, 1978) and in 1 compulsive washer (LeBoeuf, 1974). A patient with ordering rituals treated with another variant of aversion therapy, covert sensitization, was also treated successfully (Wisocki, 1970).

Other types of blocking procedures have aimed to reduce obsessions, with some positive case outcomes reported for delivery of shock following obsessional thoughts (e.g., Kenny, Solyom, & Solyom, 1973; McGuire & Vallance, 1964). Thought stopping, which involves shouting "Stop!" in response to obsessive intrusions, was also found effective in case examples (Gullick & Blanchard, 1973; Leger, 1978; Stern, 1970). However, when treatment by relaxation training alone was compared to relaxation plus thought stopping conducted during tape-recorded presentations of obsessional scenes, only 4 of 11 patients improved in the combined treatment (Stern, Lipsedge, & Marks, 1975). Similarly, a study using therapist presentation of scenes was also ineffective, with 2 of 7 patients showing only slight improvement (Stern, 1978); Emmelkamp and Kwee (1977) found that 1 of 2 patients treated with thought stopping as a first treatment improved.

In summary, the literature on the early behavioral treatments for OCD is mixed. Of course, as is customary with innovations in treatment development, most of these reports were either case studies or uncontrolled case series, and long-term outcome was not reported. With the gift of hindsight, the primary impression to be gleaned from these reports is that the procedures used were not very powerful, except perhaps to the extent that they employed actual exposure, as in the paradoxical intention studies. Also, the treatments that used reinforcement procedures to inhibit ritualizing showed some promise. Despite their limitations, these early studies served to generate new hypotheses about treatment efficacy and mechanisms of change, advancing the development of the treatment procedures that have since proven highly effective, such as exposure and ritual prevention.

EXPOSURE AND RITUAL PREVENTION

The prognostic picture for OCD has improved dramatically since Victor Meyer (1966) reported on 2 patients treated successfully with a treatment that included prolonged exposure to obsessional cues and strict prevention of rituals. This procedure, known at the time as exposure and response prevention, was subsequently found to be extremely successful in 10 of 15 cases and partly effective in the remainder; at a 5-year follow-up, only 2 of 15 patients had relapsed (Meyer & Levy, 1973; Meyer, Levy, & Schnurer, 1974).

Descendants of Meyer's (1966) procedure, current EX/RP programs typically include both exposure and ritual blocking. Exposure exercises are often done in real-life settings (*in vivo*), such as by asking the patient who fears contamination from germs to sit on the floor. Feared consequences are often addressed via imaginal exposure. Both forms of exposure are designed specifically to prompt obsessional distress; repeated, prolonged exposure without ritualizing or avoiding is thought to provide information that disconfirms mistaken associations and evaluations held by the patients and promotes habituation to previously fearful thoughts and situations (Foa & Kozak, 1986). Exposure is usually gradual, with situations provoking moderate distress confronted before more upsetting ones. Exposure exercises conducted between treatment sessions are also assigned. Patients are also asked to refrain from rituals between sessions.

Since Meyer's (1966) initial reports of the efficacy of EX/RP, numerous uncontrolled and controlled studies of EX/RP have shown that the majority of EX/RP treatment completers are responders at posttreatment and remain so at follow-up. Foa and Kozak's (1996) review of 12 outcome studies ($N = 330$) that reported number of treatment responders revealed that among treatment completers, an average of 83% were responders immediately after treatment. In 16 studies reporting long-term outcome ($N = 376$; mean follow-up interval of 29 months), 76% were responders.

EX/RP has been found quite effective in reducing OCD and has produced great durability of gains following treatment discontinuation. These findings appear to be particularly robust: They are consistent across different sites and procedural variations. As there are many variants of EX/RP treatment, we review the literature of the relative efficacy of the ingredients that comprise EX/RP.

EX/RP TREATMENT VARIABLES

Exposure versus Ritual Prevention versus EX/RP

Most studies on the efficacy of exposure therapy for OCD included also ritual prevention (e.g., Foa & Goldstein, 1978; Rachman et al., 1979; Rachman, Hodgson, & Marks, 1971), thus confounding the effects of each procedure. To separate these effects, Foa, Steketee, Grayson, Turner, and Latimer (1984) randomly assigned patients with washing rituals to either treatment by exposure only (EX), ritual prevention only (RP), or their combination (EX/RP). Each treatment was conducted intensively (15 daily 2-hour sessions conducted over 3 weeks) and followed by a home visit. Although symptom reductions were observed in each condition at both posttreatment and follow-up, the combined treatment was superior to the single-component treatments on almost every symptom measure at posttreatment and follow-up. Notably, patients who received exposure alone reported lower anxiety when confronting feared contaminants than patients who had received only ritual prevention, whereas the ritual prevention–alone group reported greater decreases in urge to ritualize than did the exposure-alone group. Thus, it appeared that exposure and ritual prevention affect symptoms differently. The implication of these results is that EX/RP should be implemented concurrently; treatments that do not include both components yield inferior outcome.

Duration of Exposure

Duration of exposure is thought to be important for outcome: Prolonged continuous exposure is better than short interrupted exposure (Rabavilas, Boulougouris, & Stefanis, 1976). How much time is adequate? There is no hard-and-fast rule. Clinical observations suggest that exposure should continue until the patient notices a decrease in obsessional distress. Indeed, reduction in anxiety (habituation) within the exposure session to the most distressing item, as well as reduction in the peak anxiety across sessions, were associated with improvement following EX/RP treatment (Kozak, Foa, & Steketee, 1988). Studies indicated that continuous exposure of approximately 90-minutes duration is needed for reduction of anxiety (Foa & Chambless, 1978) and for decrease in urges to ritualize (Rachman, De Silva, & Roper, 1976); this is a useful rule of thumb, but exposure should sometimes be continued beyond 90 minutes if the patient has not felt some relief within that time, or terminated if substantial reduction in obsessional distress occurs earlier.

Gradual versus Abrupt Exposures

Patients who confront the most distressing situations from the start of therapy have achieved the same gains as patients who confront less distressing situations before confronting the most distressing one (Hodgson, Rachman, & Marks, 1972). However, most patients appear to be more satisfied with a gradual approach. Because patients' willingness to comply with treatment procedures is such a critical aspect of successful EX/RP, situations of moderate difficulty are usually confronted first, followed by several intermediate steps before the most distressing exposures are accomplished.

Frequency of Exposure Sessions

Optimal frequency of exposure sessions is unknown. Intensive exposure therapy programs that have achieved excellent results (cf. Foa, Kozak, Steketee, & McCarthy, 1992) typically involve daily sessions, but quite favorable outcomes have also been achieved with more widely spaced sessions (e.g., de Araujo, Ito, Marks, & Deale, 1995). Weekly sessions may suffice for patients whose OCD symptoms are mild, and who readily understand the importance of daily exposure homework. Clinical impression suggests that patients who have severe symptoms or exhibit difficulty complying with exposure homework or ritual prevention benefit from a more intensive regimen.

Therapist-Assisted versus Self-Exposure

The role of the therapist in EX/RP is unclear. Although one study found that modeling of exposure by the therapists did not enhance overall treatment efficacy (Rachman, Marks, & Hodgson, 1973), patients in this study did prefer modeling. Moreover, clinical experience suggests that patients appear more willing to confront feared situations in the presence of the therapist, and some patients find modeling helpful. Evaluations of the presence of a therapist during exposure have yielded inconsistent results. In one study, patients with OCD who received therapist-aided exposure were more improved immediately posttreatment than those receiving clomipramine and self-exposure, but this difference disappeared by 1-year follow-up (Marks et al., 1988). However, the design of the study introduced confounds, and therefore the results are difficult to interpret. In a second study with OCD, no differences between therapist-assisted treatment and self-exposure were detected either at posttreatment or at follow-up (Emmelkamp & van Kraanen, 1977). However, the number of patients in each condition was too small to render these results conclusive.

In contrast to the negative results just described, therapist presence enhanced the efficacy of a single, 3-hour exposure session for persons with specific phobia compared to self-exposure of equal length (Ost, 1989). Because specific phobias are on the whole less debilitating and easier to treat than OCD, one would expect that therapist presence could also enhance exposure with OCD. The effects of therapist presence on treatment of OCD awaits a well-controlled study with a sufficiently large sample to afford the necessary power to detect group differences.

Use of Imaginal Exposure

The addition of imaginal exposure to a program that includes *in vivo* EX/RP appeared to enhance maintenance of treatment gains for OC patients (Foa, Steketee, Turner, & Fischer, 1980; Steketee, Foa, & Grayson, 1982). In contrast, one study did not find such differences (de Araujo et al., 1995). However, the treatment program in the Foa and colleagues studies differed from that of de Araujo et al. on several parameters (e.g., 90-minute vs. 30-minute imaginal exposures, respectively), and thus the source of the disparate findings cannot be identified.

Clinically, we find imaginal exposure to be useful primarily for patients whose obsessional fears focus on disastrous consequences and/or those whose fears are not readily translated into *in vivo* exposure exercises. Also, the addition of imagery to *in vivo* exposure may circumvent the cognitive avoidance strategies used by patients who evade thinking about the consequences of exposure while confronting feared situations *in vivo*. In summary, although imaginal exposure does not appear essential for successful outcome, it may enhance long-term maintenance and is often a useful adjunct to *in vivo* exercises for patients with fears focusing on disastrous consequences. For patients who do not report any feared disasters consequent to refraining from rituals (other than being extremely distressed), imaginal exposure may not be helpful.

Implementation of Ritual Prevention

In Meyer's (1966) treatment program, hospital staff actually stopped the patients from performing rituals (e.g., turning off water supply in patient's room). Accordingly, this treatment procedure was labeled "response prevention" (here termed "ritual prevention"). However, physical intervention by others to prevent patients from ritualizing is no longer typical or recommended. In addition to concerns that actual physical prevention is too coercive to be acceptable, it is believed that reliance upon this technique may limit generalizability to nontherapy situations in which staff are not present to prevent rituals. Instead of physical prevention, instructions and encouragement to refrain from ritualizing and avoidance are much more common procedures in implementing ritual prevention (e.g., Rachman et al., 1971). As noted earlier, although exposure reduces obsessional distress, in itself, it is not so effective in reducing compulsions. To maximize improvement, the patient needs to voluntarily refrain from ritualizing while engaging in programmatic exposure exercises. Therapists should assist with this difficult task by providing support, encouragement, and suggestions about how to refrain from ritualizing in particular situations.

FAMILY INVOLVEMENT VERSUS STANDARD EX/RP TREATMENT

Influenced by findings that efficacy of exposure therapy for panic disorder with agoraphobia is enhanced by partner assistance, Emmelkamp, de Haan, and Hoogduin (1990) examined whether such assistance would also enhance the efficacy of EX/RP for OCD. Patients who were married or living with a romantic partner were randomly assigned to receive EX/RP either with or without partner involvement in treatment. Each treatment lasted 5 weeks and consisted of eight 45- 60-minute sessions with the therapist; exposures were not practiced in session. Results indicated that OCD severity was significantly reduced immediately after treatment for both groups. No group differences were detected, and initial marital distress did not predict outcome. Notably, although mean symptom reduction reached statistical significance, the reduction in anxiety/distress reported for the sample as a whole was modest (33%). This may have resulted from the shorter treatment and absence of in-session *in vivo* exposure.

Mehta (1990) also examined the adjunctive role of family involvement in EX/RP treatment in a study conducted in India. In order to adapt the treatment to serve the large numbers of young, unmarried people seeking OCD treatment and the "joint family system" prevalent in India, a family-based rather than spouse-based treatment approach was utilized. Patients previously nonresponsive to pharmacotherapy were randomly assigned to receive treatment by systematic desensitization and EX/RP, either with or without family assistance. Sessions in both conditions were held twice per week for 12 weeks; response prevention was gradual. In the family condition, a designated family member (parent, spouse, or adult child) assisted with homework assignments, supervised relaxation therapy, participated in response prevention, and was instructed to be supportive. On self-reported OCD symptoms, a greater improvement was found for the family-based intervention at posttreatment and 6-month follow-up. Although the study had methodological problems that complicate interpretation of findings (e.g., use of self-report OCD measures only, unclear description of treatment procedures), it offers convergent evidence that family involvement may enhance OCD treatment.

EX/RP VERSUS COGNITIVE THERAPIES

Dissatisfaction with formulations of treatment as mediated by autonomic processes such as extinction (Stampfl & Levis, 1967) or habituation (Watts, 1973), and the increased interest in cognitive therapy (e.g., Beck, 1976; Ellis, 1962) prompted researchers to examine the efficacy of cognitive procedures for OCD. Emmelkamp, van der Helm, van Zanten, and Plochg (1980) compared self-instructional training (Meichenbaum, 1975) plus EX/RP to EX/RP alone. Treatment was conducted twice weekly and sessions were of 2-hour duration. Both groups improved on all outcome measures; on assessor-rated avoidance associated with main compulsion, a superiority of EX/RP alone emerged. Thus, self-instructional training may have slightly hindered, rather than enhanced, efficacy.

The failure to find an additive effect for self-instructional training led Emmelkamp, Visser, and Hoekstra (1988) to examine the efficacy of rational–emotive therapy (RET), a cognitive therapy program that focuses on irrational beliefs. Patients were randomly assigned to EX/RP or RET. Treatment consisted of 10 sessions (60 minutes each) conducted over 8 weeks. In the EX/RP condition, exposure exercises were not practiced during treatment sessions. Instead, patients were assigned exposure exercises from their treatment hierarchy to perform at home twice per week for at least 90 minutes. RET involved determining the irrational thoughts that mediated negative feelings, confronting these thoughts via cognitive techniques, and modifying them with the aim of reducing anxiety and thereby decreasing the need to ritualize. In the RET condition, irrational beliefs were challenged Socratically by the therapist during sessions; patients were instructed to continue challenging their irrational thinking for homework. Patients receiving RET were not instructed to expose themselves to feared situations, nor were they explicitly instructed to refrain from such exposure. Results indicated that both groups were improved at posttreatment, and no group differences emerged. On ratings of anxiety/discomfort associated with the main OCD problem, the RET group showed an average posttreatment improvement of 40%, and the EX/RP, 51%. Long-term comparisons were confounded by the large number of individuals who received additional treatment during the follow-up period.

Emmelkamp and Beens (1991) sought to replicate the findings of Emmelkamp et al. (1988) and also to examine whether a combined package of cognitive therapy plus EX/RP would enhance the effects of EX/RP. They compared a program that included six sessions of RET alone followed by six sessions of RET plus self-controlled EX/RP to a program that included 12 sessions of self-controlled EX/RP. In both programs the first six sessions were followed by 4 weeks of no treatment, after which the additional six sessions were delivered. As in Emmelkamp et al.'s (1988) study, treatment sessions were conducted approximately once per week and lasted for 60 minutes each. EX/RP sessions did not include therapist-assisted exposure, and patients were assigned twice-weekly exposure-homework exercises. The first six sessions of the RET program were equivalent to that employed in the Emmelkamp et al. (1988) study and did not include exposure homework. When self-controlled EX/RP was introduced following the first 6 RET-only sessions, the latter was focused on irrational thoughts that occurred in response to exposure homework exercises. Immediately following the completion of six sessions of cognitive therapy without exposure and EX/RP (week 9), mean reduction of anxiety associated with main obsessive–compulsive problems was 25% for RET and 23% for EX/RP. Following six more sessions (RET + EX/RP in one condition and EX/RP only in the other), both groups continued to improve on most measures compared to pretreatment; no significant group differences emerged. Notably, approximately 30% of the sample dropped out during treatment, which is higher than reported in several other studies and may limit generalizability of the findings.

In a further examination of the efficacy of cognitive therapy for OCD, van Oppen et al. (1995) compared the efficacy of self-controlled EX/RP and a cognitive intervention developed to correct specific cognitive distortions hypothesized by Salkovskis (1985) to underlie OCD. Patients were randomly assigned to receive 16 sessions of cognitive therapy or EX/RP. In order to examine the effects of "purer" versions of cognitive therapy and EX/RP, behavioral experiments (exposures) were not introduced into the cognitive treatment until after session 6 and, conversely, in the first six EX/RP sessions, care was taken by the therapist to specifically avoid any discussion of disastrous consequences. Sessions in both treatment conditions lasted for 45 minutes.

Results were similar to the studies of cognitive therapy just reviewed. After six sessions of cognitive therapy without behavioral experiments, and EX/RP without discussion of disastrous consequences, OCD symptom reductions of 20% were observed for cognitive therapy and 23%, for EX/RP. At posttreatment, both groups continued to improve on almost all measures, with trends favoring cognitive therapy over EX/RP. However, inspection of the reduction in Yale–Brown Obsessive–Compulsive Scale scores (YBOCS; Goodman et al., 1989) for the EX/RP condition suggests that outcome for EX/RP at posttreatment (32% for EX/RP) was inferior to that typically achieved in other studies of EX/RP (e.g., de Araujo et al., 1995; Hiss, Foa, & Kozak, 1994). It also appeared that there was very little effect for adding discussion of disastrous outcomes in EX/RP at midtreatment (10% reduction from midtest to posttreatment).

Hiss et al. (1994) investigated whether adding a formal relapse prevention program following intensive EX/RP enhanced maintenance of therapeutic gains. In this study, all components typically included to address relapse prevention (e.g., discussion of lapse vs. relapse, posttreatment exposure instructions, themes of guilt and personal responsibility) were removed from the 15 daily sessions of the intensive phase. All patients received the modified EX/RP, followed by either a relapse prevention treatment or a psychosocial control treatment (associative therapy). All patients were responders to EX/RP at posttreatment (defined as 50% or greater reduction in OCD symptoms). At 6-month follow-up, gains were better maintained in the relapse prevention group than in the associative therapy condition. Using the criterion of 50% OCD symptom reduction as measured by the YBOCS, the percentage of responders at follow-up were 75% and 33%, respectively.

As can be seen from the previous review, the results of studies examining the relative and combined efficacy of EX/RP and cognitive interventions have been mixed: One study found that the addition of self-instructional training to EX/RP hindered outcome compared to EX/RP only (Emmelkamp et al., 1980), and one found no difference between RET and EX/RP (Emmelkamp et al., 1988). A third study comparing cognitive therapy that excluded any exposure, with EX/RP that excluded discussions of feared consequences, found no significant differences between these procedures (van Oppen et al., 1995). Notably, the EX/RP treatments used in these studies were compromised versions (e.g., shorter sessions, fewer sessions, absence of therapist-assisted exposure) of the procedures that have been found to yield the largest improvements. These diluted programs resulted in attenuated outcome compared to programs that used intensive regimens (e.g., 80% reduction on assessors ratings of rituals; Foa et al., 1992; 60% and 66% reduction on the YBOCS; Hiss et al., 1994). The import of the results of studies comparing attenuated versions of EX/RP to variants of cognitive therapy is unclear.

The issue of whether cognitive therapy improves the efficacy of EX/RP is of theoretical interest but may be practically moot, because most EX/RP specialists customarily discuss dysfunctional thinking and mistaken beliefs during exposure sessions, as part of the rationale for exposure therapy. Notably, Foa and Kozak (1986) argued that a crucial mechanism underlying the efficacy of exposure is the disconfirmation of erroneous associations and beliefs. For example, a patient and therapist sitting on the bathroom floor in a public restroom, conducting an exposure to contaminated surfaces, often discuss risk assessment, probability overestimation, and so on, as the therapist helps the patient achieve the cognitive modification necessary for improvement. In our clinic, therapists routinely discuss patients' mistaken beliefs, but these discussions anticipate and accompany exposure rather than compete with it.

EX/RP VERSUS PHARMACOTHERAPY

Studies examining the relative and combined efficacy of EX/RP and pharmacotherapy are openly summarized here, because they are detailed in Chapter 15 of this volume. The mounting evidence that EX/RP and serotonin reuptake inhibitors are individually neither completely nor universally helpful has prompted investigation of their combined efficacy. However, there is little evidence from these investigations for the superiority of such combined treatment over the individual treatments. Several studies have combined antidepressants with EX/RP (Amin, Ban, Pecknold, & Klingner, 1977; Cottraux et al., 1990; Foa et al., 1992;

Hembree, Cohen, Riggs, Kozak, & Foa, 1992; Marks et al., 1988; Marks, Stern, Mawson, Cobb, & McDonald, 1980; Neziroglu, 1979), but for the most part, methodological issues with these studies preclude strong conclusions about (1) the relative efficacy of the individual treatments; (2) the combined efficacy versus each treatment individually; or (3) whether the addition of EX/RP to pharmacotherapy reduces the problem of relapse after drug discontinuation.

A multicenter study in progress at Allegheny University of the Health Sciences and Columbia University examining the relative and combined efficacy of clomipramine (CMI) and intensive EX/RP (Kozak, Liebowitz, & Foa, in press) has sought to address some of these lingering questions. In this study, an EX/RP program that includes an intensive phase (15 two-hour sessions conducted over 3 weeks) and follow-up phase (six brief sessions delivered over 8 weeks) is compared to CMI, EX/RP + CMI, and pill placebo. Preliminary findings with treatment completer data as well as intent-to-treat data suggest that the active treatments appear superior to placebo, EX/RP appears superior to CMI, and the combination of the two treatments does not appear superior to EX/RP alone. However, the design used in the Allegheny–Columbia study may not have been optimal for promoting an additive effect of CMI, because the intensive portion of the EX/RP program was largely completed before the medication effects could be realized.

In summary, there is ample evidence about the efficacy of both pharmaceutical and EX/RP treatments, but information about their relative and combined efficacy is scarce, because most of the studies that addressed these issues have been methodologically limited. With this caveat in mind, no study has found clear, long-term superiority for combined pharmacotherapy plus EX/RP over EX/RP alone. The absence of conclusive supportive findings notwithstanding, many experts continue to advocate combined procedures as the treatment of choice for OCD (e.g., Greist, 1992).

In our view, the results of the outcome studies on the whole lead to a conclusion that EX/RP is the best available treatment for patients who are willing or able to complete it. Whether EX/RP is superior for patients overall, and whether a pharmacotherapy plus EX/RP combination would be generally superior, is yet unclear. Monotherapy by certain serotonergic medications is also of established efficacy. If the patient refuses EX/RP, or if it is unavailable, serotonergic medications are attractive.

INDIVIDUAL VERSUS GROUP EX/RP

Intensive individual EX/RP, although of demonstrated efficacy, can pose practical problems such as high cost for treatment and difficulty scheduling daily therapy sessions. Additionally, because experts in EX/RP treatment are scarce, individual patients may need to wait for long periods of time, or travel substantial distances, in order to receive treatment.

Uncontrolled explorations of group therapy for OCD (e.g., Enright, 1991) prompted a controlled trial by Fals-Stewart, Marks, and Schafer (1993). OCD patients were randomly assigned to EX/RP conducted individually, group EX/RP treatment, or a psychosocial control condition (relaxation). Each of the active treatments was 2 weeks long, with sessions held twice weekly, and included daily exposure-homework assignments. Reductions in obsessive–compulsive symptoms were obtained only with the two active treatments. Moreover, no differences between individual and group EX/RP were detected immediately posttreatment or at 6-month follow-up, although profile analysis of OCD symptom ratings collected throughout treatment indicated a faster reduction in symptoms for patients receiving individual treatment.

These results offer evidence for the efficacy of group treatment. Patients were excluded from this study if they were diagnosed with *any* personality disorder or with comorbid major depression based on Beck Depression Inventory (BDI; Beck, Ward, Mendelson, Mock, & Erbaugh, 1961) score greater than 22. These exclusion criteria, together with the relatively low pretreatment severity and the fact that all 93 patients had received no previous treatment of any kind for OCD, renders the sample somewhat atypical, and inferences about a broader population merit caution.

PREDICTORS OF TREATMENT OUTCOME

Pretreatment Depression

Several early reports in the literature suggest that patients with severe depression responded poorly to behavioral interventions (e.g., Foa, 1979; Marks, 1973). However, a controlled prospective study revealed that both depressed and nondepressed groups responded favorably to EX/RP, and that the reduction of depression by imipramine prior to EX/RP did not enhance EX/RP outcome (Foa et al., 1992). Generally, the literature is inconclusive about whether pretreatment depression predicts outcome of either EX/RP or medication. In 6 of 10 available studies, depression was not predictive of outcome; in the remaining four studies, it predicted poor outcome (Buchanan, Meng, & Marks, 1996; for a review, see Steketee & Shapiro, 1995).

Pretreatment OCD Severity

Examinations of overall pretreatment OCD severity as a predictor of EX/RP outcome have yielded negative findings (Foa, Grayson, Steketee, Doppelt, Turner, & Latimer, 1983; Hoogduin & Duivenvoorden, 1988; Marks et al., 1980; O'Sullivan, Noshirvani, Marks, Monteiro, & Lelliott, 1991; Steketee, 1993a), whereas severity of *specific* OCD symptoms (e.g., behavioral avoidance, rituals, obsessions) have predicted poor outcome of treatment by medications plus EX/RP (Basoglu, Lax, Kasvikis, & Marks, 1988; Cottraux, Mollard, Bouvard, & Marks, 1993). With respect to the relationship between EX/RP outcome and type of ritual (washing vs. checking), findings have been inconsistent. No relationship with EX/RP outcome was found in two studies (Foa et al., 1983; Rachman et al., 1973). However, one study found that checking predicted good outcome (Drummond, 1993), and three studies found that washing predicted good outcome (Basoglu et al., 1988; Boulougouris, 1977; Buchanan et al., 1996). In summary, it appears that overall OCD severity may not be predictive, but certain specific OCD symptoms may be related to outcome.

Personality Disorders

Comorbid personality disorders of any kind were predictive of poor behavior therapy outcome in two studies (AuBuchon & Malatesta, 1994; Fals-Stewart & Lucente, 1993), whereas specific personality disorder diagnoses have also been found related to poor response to serotonin reuptake inhibitors (SRIs; Baer et al., 1992, Jenike, Baer, & Carey, 1986; Minichiello, Baer, & Jenike, 1987; Ravizza, Barzega, Bellino, Bogetto, & Maina, 1995). Only one study failed to find a relationship between presence of personality disorders and medication treatment outcome (Mavissakalian, Hamann, & Jones, 1990). Thus, the presence of personality disorders, especially schizotypal and borderline, predicts poor outcome for *both* SRIs and EX/RP.

Expectancy of Outcome

Patients' expectations of treatment benefits were found to influence EX/RP outcome in one study (Cottraux et al., 1993) but not in another (Lax, Basoglu, & Marks, 1992). It may also be the case that patients with the lowest expectations of EX/RP treatment benefit refuse to enter EX/RP; thus, the predictive value of expectancy may be underestimated in studies that do not consider treatment refusal as an outcome variable.

Motivation and Compliance with Treatment

Several studies found that motivation (and compliance) influenced EX/RP outcome (Hoogduin & Duivenvoorden, 1988; Keijsers, Hoogduin, & Schaap, 1994; O'Sullivan et al., 1991). However, one study (Lax et al., 1992) failed to find such a relationship. Clinically, we have found that motivation and compliance with treatment procedures are important mediators of EX/RP success.

CONCLUSIONS AND FUTURE DIRECTIONS

In summary, results of the outcome studies conducted so far have indicated that EX/RP is a highly effective treatment for adult OCD, but several limitations should be noted. A relatively high number of patients refuse to participate in intensive EX/RP treatment programs for various reasons, one of which is that EX/RP sounds too threatening for some patients. Despite the availability of detailed treatment manuals (Kozak & Foa, 1997; Steketee, 1993b), access to clinicians who are proficient with EX/RP remains limited. Moreover, the specialty centers that have produced most of the outcome research may be nonrepresentative not only in their level of expertise, but also in the kinds of patients they attract and accept for treatment.

Whether centers not specialized in EX/RP can obtain similar success has yet to be determined. Preliminary results from the Allegheny–Columbia multicenter study (Kozak et al., in press) suggest that a pharmacological center can obtain efficacy comparable to that obtained in centers that specialize in EX/RP treatment. In addition to the scarcity of experts, the increasing demands placed on clinicians for fewer and shorter sessions by market factors (e.g., managed care policies) may prevent even experts from conducting treatment in a manner that will maximize outcome.

Although a great deal is already known about the efficacy of EX/RP for OCD, some issues await further investigation. One current criticism of EX/RP is that its overall effectiveness is limited by the fact that many patients reject it because they are too afraid. Future research should explore methods to decrease refusals. Perhaps the optimal treatment for patients who are too frightened to try EX/RP should involve medication at the start, followed by EX/RP implemented after medication has lessened the OCD symptoms, and thereby increase the acceptability of EX/RP.

As we discussed in this chapter, several factors have been found associated with poor outcome. Further investigation on factors that mediated treatment response is needed to help clinicians determine what type of treatment is likely to help a given patient. A related issue is the influence of treatment choice on outcome. Because most carefully controlled outcome studies use random assignment to treatment conditions, the effect of patients' treatment choice on outcome is obscured. We also have no knowledge of whether a patient who does not respond to his or her first choice (e.g., EX/RP) is likely to respond to a subsequent application of a different treatment modality (e.g., medication). These questions are best addressed using a naturalistic design that includes patient choice of treatment. Because patients treated outside expert clinical research settings typically end up choosing their treatment, studies that incorporate choice will inform us about the generalizability of findings from well-controlled treatment outcome studies to the applied clinical settings where many OCD sufferers receive care.

ACKNOWLEDGMENT

This chapter was supported in part by Grant No. MH45404 awarded to the first author.

REFERENCES

Amin, M. D., Ban, T. A., Pecknold, J. C., & Klingner, A. (1977). Clomipramine (Anafranil) and behavior therapy in obsessive–compulsive and phobic disorders. *Journal of International Medical Research, 5,* 33–37.

AuBuchon, P. G., & Malatesta, V. J. (1994). Obsessive compulsive patients with comorbid personality disorder: Associated problems and response to a comprehensive behavior therapy. *Journal of Clinical Psychiatry, 55*, 448–453.

Baer, L., Jenike, M. A., Black, D. W., Treece, C., Rosenfeld, R., & Greist, J. (1992). Effect of Axis II diagnoses on treatment outcome with clomipramine in 55 patients with obsessive–compulsive disorder. *Archives of General Psychiatry, 49*(11), 862–866.

Basoglu, M., Lax, T., Kasvikis, Y., & Marks, I. M. (1988). Predictors of improvement in obsessive–compulsive disorder. *Journal of Anxiety Disorders, 2*(4), 299–317.

Beck, A. T. (1976). *Cognitive therapy and the emotional disorders.* New York: International Universities Press.

Beck, A. T., Ward, C. H., Mendelson, M., Mock, J. E., & Erbaugh, J. K. (1961). An inventory for measuring depression. *Archives of General Psychiatry, 4*, 561–571.

Beech, H. R., & Vaughn, M. (1978). *Behavioral treatment of obsessional states.* New York: Wiley.

Boulougouris, J. (1977). Variables affecting the behaviour modification of obsessive–compulsive patients treated by flooding. In J. C. Boulougouris & A. D. Rabavilas (Eds.), *The treatment of phobic and obsessive–compulsive disorders* (pp. 73–84). Oxford, UK: Pergamon Press.

Broadhurst, A. (1976). It's never too late to learn: An application of conditioned inhibition to obsessional ruminations in an elderly patient. In H. J. Eysenck (Ed.), *Case studies in behaviour therapy* (pp. 173–183). London: Routledge & Kegan Paul.

Buchanan, A. W., Meng, K. S., & Marks, I. M. (1996). What predicts improvement and compliance during the behavioral treatment of obsessive compulsive disorder? *Anxiety, 2*, 22–27.

Cooper, J. E., Gelder, M. G., & Marks, I. M. (1965). Results of behaviour therapy in 77 psychiatric patients. *British Medical Journal, 1*, 1222–1225.

Cottraux, J., Mollard, E., Bouvard, M., & Marks, I. (1993). Exposure therapy, fluvoxamine, or combination treatment in obsessive–compulsive disorder: One-year follow-up. *Psychiatry Research, 49*(1), 63–75.

Cottraux, J., Mollard, E., Bouvard, M., Marks, I., Sluys, M., Nury, A. M., Douge, R., & Ciadella, P. (1990). A controlled study of fluvoxamine and exposure in obsessive–compulsive disorder. *International Clinical Psychopharmacology, 5*, 17–30.

de Araujo, L. A., Ito, L. M., Marks, I. M., & Deale, A. (1995). Does imagined exposure to the consequences of not ritualising enhance live exposure for OCD? A controlled study: I. Main outcome. *British Journal of Psychiatry, 167*(1), 65–70.

Drummond, L. M. (1993). The treatment of severe, chronic, resistant obsessive compulsive disorder: An evaluation of an in-patient program using behavioral psychotherapy in combination with other treatments. *British Journal of Psychiatry, 163*, 223–229.

Ellis, A. (1962). *Reason and emotion in psychotherapy.* New York: Lyle Stuart.

Emmelkamp, P. M. G., & Beens, H. (1991). Cognitive therapy with obsessive–compulsive disorder: A comparative evaluation. *Behaviour Research and Therapy, 29*, 293–300.

Emmelkamp, P. M. G., de Haan, E., & Hoogduin, C. A. L. (1990). Marital adjustment and obsessive–compulsive disorder. *British Journal of Psychiatry, 156*, 55–60.

Emmelkamp, P. M. G., & Kwee, K. G. (1977). Obsessional ruminations: A comparison between thought-stopping and prolonged exposure in imagination. *Behaviour Research and Therapy, 15*, 441–444.

Emmelkamp, P. M. G., van der Helm, M., van Zanten, B. L., & Plochg, I. (1980). Treatment of obsessive–compulsive patients: The contribution of self-instructional training to the effectiveness of exposure. *Behaviour Research and Therapy, 18*, 61–66.

Emmelkamp, P. M. G., & van Kraanen, J. (1977). Therapist-controlled exposure *in vivo*: A comparison with obsessive–compulsive patients. *Behaviour Research and Therapy, 15,* 491–495.

Emmelkamp, P. M. G., Visser, S., & Hoekstra, R. J. (1988). Cognitive therapy vs. exposure *in vivo* in the treatment of obsessive–compulsives. *Cognitive Therapy and Research, 12,* 103–114.

Enright, S. J. (1991). Group treatment for obsessive–compulsive disorder: An evaluation. *Behavioural Psychotherapy, 19*(2), 183–192.

Fals-Stewart, W., & Lucente, S. (1993). An MCMI cluster typology of obsessive–compulsives: A measure of personality characteristics and its relationship to treatment participation, compliance and outcome in behavior therapy. *Journal of Psychiatric Research, 27*(2), 139–154.

Fals-Stewart, W., Marks, A. P., & Schafer, J. (1993). A comparison of behavioral group therapy and individual behavior therapy in treating obsessive–compulsive disorder. *Journal of Nervous and Mental Disease, 181*(3), 189–193.

Foa, E. B. (1979). Failure in treating obsessive–compulsives. *Behaviour Research and Therapy, 17,* 169–176.

Foa, E. B., & Chambless, D. L. (1978). Habituation of subjective anxiety during flooding in imagery. *Behaviour Research and Therapy, 16,* 391–399.

Foa, E., & Goldstein, A. (1978). Continuous exposure and complete response prevention in the treatment of obsessive–compulsive neurosis. *Behavior Therapy, 9,* 821–829.

Foa, E. B., Grayson, J. B., Steketee, G. S., Doppelt, H. G., Turner, R. M., & Latimer, P. R. (1983). Success and failure in the behavioral treatment of obsessive–compulsives. *Journal of Consulting and Clinical Psychology, 51,* 287–297.

Foa, E. B., & Kozak, M. J. (1986). Emotional processing of fear: Exposure to corrective information. *Psychological Bulletin, 99,* 20–35.

Foa, E. B., & Kozak, M. J. (1996). Psychological treatment for obsessive–compulsive disorder. In M. R. Mavissakalian & R. F. Prien (Eds.), *Long-term treatments of anxiety disorders* (pp. 285–309). Washington, DC: American Psychiatric Association Press.

Foa, E. B., Kozak, M. J., Steketee, G. S., & McCarthy, P. R. (1992). Treatment of depressive and obsessive–compulsive symptoms in OCD by imipramine and behavior therapy. *British Journal of Clinical Psychology, 31*(3), 279–292.

Foa, E. B., Steketee, G., Grayson, J. B., Turner, R. M., & Latimer, P. (1984). Deliberate exposure and blocking of obsessive–compulsive rituals: Immediate and long-term effects. *Behavior Therapy, 15*(5), 450–472.

Foa, E. B., Steketee, G. S., & Ozarow, B. J. (1985). Behavior therapy with obsessive–compulsives: From theory to treatment. In M. Mavissakalian (Ed.), *Obsessive–compulsive disorders: Psychological and pharmacological treatments* (pp. 49–129). New York: Plenum.

Foa, E. B., Steketee, G., Turner, R. M., & Fischer, S. C. (1980). Effects of imaginal exposure to feared disasters in obsessive–compulsive checkers. *Behaviour Research and Therapy, 18,* 449–455.

Gertz, H. O. (1966). Experience with the logotherapeutic technique of paradoxical intention in the treatment of phobic and obsessive–compulsive patients. *American Journal of Psychiatry, 123,* 548–553.

Goodman, W. K., Price, L. H., Rasmussen, S. A., Mazure, C., Fleischmann, R. L., Hill, C. L., Heninger, G. R., & Charney, D. S. (1989). The Yale–Brown Obsessive–Compulsive Scale: I. Development, use, and reliability. *Archives of General Psychiatry, 46*(11), 1006–1011.

Greist, J. H. (1992). An integrated approach to treatment of obsessive compulsive disorder. *Journal of Clinical Psychiatry, 53*(Suppl. 4), 38–41.

Gullick, E. L., & Blanchard, E. B. (1973). The use of psychotherapy and behavior therapy in the treatment of an obsessional disorder: An experimental case study. *Journal of Nervous and Mental Disease, 156,* 427–431.

Hembree, E. A., Cohen, A., Riggs, D., Kozak, M. J., & Foa, E. B. (1992). *The long-term efficacy of behavior therapy and serotonergic medications in the treatment of obsessive–compulsive ritualizers.* Unpublished manuscript.

Hiss, H., Foa, E. B., & Kozak, M. J. (1994). Relapse prevention program for treatment of obsessive–compulsive disorder. *Journal of Consulting and Clinical Psychology, 62*(4), 801–808.

Hodgson, R. J., Rachman, S., & Marks, I. M. (1972). The treatment of chronic obsessive–compulsive neurosis: Follow-up and further findings. *Behaviour Research and Therapy, 10,* 181–189.

Hoogduin, C. A. L., & Duivenvoorden, H. J. (1988). A decision model in the treatment of obsessive–compulsive neurosis. *British Journal of Psychiatry, 152,* 516–521.

Jenike, M. A., Baer, L., & Carey, R. J. (1986). Coexistent obsessive–compulsive disorder and schizotypal personality disorder: A poor prognostic indicator. *Archives of General Psychiatry, 43*(3), 296.

Keijsers, G. P. J., Hoogduin, C. A. L., & Schaap, C. P. D. R. (1994). Predictors of treatment outcome in the behavioural treatment of obsessive–compulsive disorder. *British Journal of Psychiatry, 165*(6), 781–786.

Kenny, F. T., Mowbray, R. M., & Lalani, S. (1978). Faradic disruption of obsessive ideation in the treatment of obsessive neurosis: A controlled study. *Behavior Therapy, 9,* 209–221.

Kenny, F. T., Solyom, L., & Solyom, C. (1973). Faradic disruption of obsessive indiation in the treatment of obsessive neurosis. *Behavior Therapy, 4,* 448–451.

Kozak, M. J., & Foa, E. B. (1997). *Mastery of obsessive–compulsive disorder: A cognitive behavioral approach.* San Antonio, TX: Psychological Corporation.

Kozak, M. J., Foa, E. B., & Steketee, G. (1988). Process and outcome of exposure treatment with obsessive–compulsives: Psychophysiological indicators of emotional processing. *Behavior Therapy, 19,* 157–169.

Kozak, M. J., Liebowitz, M. R., & Foa, E. B. (in press). Cognitive behavior therapy and pharmacotherapy for OCD: The NIMH-sponsored collaborative study. In W. K. Goodman, M. Rudorfer, & J. Maser (Eds.), *Treatment challenges in obsessive compulsive disorder.* Mahwah, NJ: Erlbaum.

Lax, T., Basoglu, M., & Marks, I. M. (1992). Expectancy and compliance as predictors of outcome in obsessive–compulsive disorder. *Behavioural Psychotherapy, 20,* 257–266.

LeBoeuf, A. (1974). An automated aversion device in the treatment of a compulsive handwashing ritual. *Journal of Behavior Therapy and Experimental Psychiatry, 5,* 267–270.

Leger, L. A. (1978). Spurious and actual improvement in the treatment of preoccupying thoughts by thought-stopping. *British Journal of Social and Clinical Psychology, 17,* 373–377.

Marks, I. M. (1973). New approaches to the treatment of obsessive–compulsive disorder. *Journal of Nervous and Mental Disease, 156,* 420–426.

Marks, I. M., Crowe, E., Drewe, E., Young, J., & Dewhurst, W. G. (1969). Obsessive–compulsive neurosis in identical twins. *British Journal of Psychiatry, 15,* 991–998.

Marks, I. M., Lelliott, P. T., Basoglu, M., Noshirvani, H., Monteiro, W., Cohen, D., & Kasvikis, Y. (1988). Clomipramine, self-exposure and therapist-aided exposure for obsessive–compulsive rituals. *British Journal of Psychiatry, 152,* 522–534.

Marks, I. M., Stern, R. S., Mawson, D., Cobb, J., & McDonald, R. (1980). Clomipramine and exposure for obsessive–compulsive rituals—I. *British Journal of Psychiatry, 136*, 1–25.

Mavissakalian, M., Hamann, M. S., & Jones, B. (1990). DSM-III personality disorders in obsessive–compulsive disorder: Changes with treatment. *Comprehensive Psychiatry, 31*, 432–437.

McCarthy, B. W. (1972). Short term implosive therapy: Case study. *Psychological Reports, 30*, 589–590.

McGuire, R. J., & Vallance, M. (1964). Aversion therapy by electric shock: A simple technique. *British Medical Journal, 1*, 151–153.

Mehta, M. (1990). A comparative study of family-based and patients-based behavioural management in obsessive–compulsive disorder. *British Journal of Psychiatry, 157*, 133–135.

Meichenbaum, D. (1975). Self-instructional methods. In F. H. Kanfer & A. P. Goldstein (Eds.), *Helping people change* (pp. 357–392). New York: Pergamon Press.

Meyer, V. (1966). Modification of expectations in cases with obsessional rituals. *Behaviour Research and Therapy, 4*, 273–280.

Meyer, V., & Levy, R. (1973). Modification of behavior in obsessive–compulsive disorders. In H. E. Adams & P. Unikel (Eds.), *Issues and trends in behavior therapy* (pp. 77–136). Springfield, IL: Charles C Thomas.

Meyer, V., Levy, R., & Schnurer, A. (1974). The behavioural treatment of obsessive–compulsive disorders. In H. R. Beech (Ed.), *Obsessional states* (pp. 233–258). London: Methuen.

Minichiello, W. E., Baer, L., & Jenike, M. A. (1987). Schizotypal personality disorder: A poor prognostic indicator for behavior therapy in the treatment of obsessive–compulsive disorder. *Journal of Anxiety Disorders, 1*(3), 273–276.

Neziroglu, F. (1979). A combined behavioral–pharmacotherapy approach to obsessive–compulsive disorder. In J. Oriols, C. Ballus, M. Gonzalez, & J. Prijol (Eds.), *Biological psychiatry today* (pp. 591–596). Amsterdam: Elsevier/North Holland Press.

Noonan, J. R. (1971). An obsessive–compulsive reaction treated by induced anxiety. *American Journal of Psychotherapy, 25*, 293–295.

Ost, L.-G. (1989). One-session treatment for specific phobias. *Behaviour Research and Therapy, 27*, 1–7.

O'Sullivan, G., Noshirvani, H., Marks, I., Monteiro, W., & Lelliott, P. (1991). Six-year follow-up after exposure and clomipramine therapy for obsessive compulsive disorder. *Journal of Clinical Psychiatry, 52*(4), 150–155.

Rabavilas, A. D., Boulougouris, J. C., & Stefanis, C. (1976). Duration of flooding sessions in the treatment of obsessive–compulsive patients. *Behaviour Research and Therapy, 14*, 349–355.

Rabavilas, A. D., Boulougouris, J. C., & Stefanis, C. (1977). Compulsive checking diminished when over-checking instructions were disobeyed. *Journal of Behavior Therapy and Experimental Psychiatry, 8*, 111–112.

Rachman, S., Cobb, J., Grey, S., McDonald, B., Mawson, D., Sartory, G., & Stern, R. (1979). The behavioural treatment of obsessional–compulsive disorders, with and without clomipramine. *Behaviour Research and Therapy, 17*, 467–478.

Rachman, S., De Silva, P., & Roper, G. (1976). The spontaneous decay of compulsive urges. *Behaviour Research and Therapy, 14*, 445–453.

Rachman, S., Hodgson, R., & Marks, I. M. (1971). The treatment of chronic obsessive–compulsive neurosis. *Behaviour Research & Therapy, 9*, 237–247.

Rachman, S., Marks, I. M., & Hodgson, R. (1973). The treatment of obsessive–compulsive neurotics by modelling. *Behaviour Research and Therapy, 8,* 383–392.

Ravizza, L., Barzega, G., Bellino, S., Bogetto, F., & Maina, G. (1995). Predictors of drug treatment response in obsessive–compulsive disorder. *Journal of Clinical Psychiatry, 56*(8), 368–373.

Rubin, R. D., & Merbaum, M. (1971). Self-imposed punishment versus desensitization. In R. D. Rubin, H. Gensterheim, A. A. Lazarus, & C. M. Franks (Eds.), *Advances in behavior therapy* (pp. 85–91). New York: Academic Press.

Salkovskis, P. M. (1985). Obsessional compulsive problems: A cognitive behavioral analysis. *Behaviour Research and Therapy, 23,* 571–583.

Solymon, L., Garza-Perez, B. L., Ledwidge, L., & Solymon, C. (1972). Paradoxical intention in the treatment of obsessive thoughts: A pilot study. *Comprehensive Psychiatry, 13*(3), 291–297.

Solymon, L., & Kingstone, E. (1973). An obsessive neurosis following morning glory seed ingestion treated by aversion relief. *Journal of Behavior Therapy and Experimental Psychiatry, 4,* 293–295.

Solymon, L., Zamanzadeh, D., Ledwidge, B., & Kenny, F. (1971). Aversion relief treatment of obsessive neurosis. In R. D. Rubin (Ed.), *Advances in behavior therapy* (pp. 93–109). New York: Academic Press.

Stampfl, T. G., & Levis, D. J. (1967). Essentials of implosive therapy: A learning-theory-based psychodynamic behavioral therapy. *Journal of Abnormal Psychology, 72*(6), 496–503.

Steketee, G. (1993a). Social support and treatment outcome of obsessive compulsive disorder at 9-month follow-up. *Behavioural Psychotherapy, 21*(2), 81–95.

Steketee, G. S. (1993b). *Treatment of obsessive–compulsive disorder.* New York: Guilford Press.

Steketee, G. S., Foa, E. B., & Grayson, J. B. (1982). Recent advances in the treatment of obsessive–compulsives. *Archives of General Psychiatry, 39,* 1365–1371.

Steketee, G., & Shapiro, L. J. (1995). Predicting behavioral treatment outcome for agoraphobia and obsessive compulsive disorder. *Clinical Psychology Review, 15*(4), 317–346.

Stern, R. S. (1970). Treatment of a case of obsessional neurosis using thought-stopping technique. *British Journal of Psychiatry, 117,* 441–442.

Stern, R. S. (1978). Obsessive thoughts: The problem of therapy. *British Journal of Psychiatry, 132,* 200–205.

Stern, R. S., Lipsedge, M. S., & Marks, I. M. (1975). Obsessive ruminations: A controlled trial of thought-stopping technique. *Behaviour Research and Therapy, 11,* 650–662.

van Oppen, P., de Haan, E., Van Balkom, A. J. L. M., Spinhoven, P., Hoogduin, K., & van Dyck, R. (1995). Cognitive therapy and exposure *in vivo* in the treatment of obsessive compulsive disorder. *Behaviour Research and Therapy, 33*(4), 379–390.

Watts, F. N. (1973). Desensitization as an habituation phenomenon: II. Studies of interstimulus interval length. *Psychological Reports, 33,* 715–718.

Wisocki, P. A. (1970). Treatment of obsessive–compulsive behavior by covert sensitization and covert reinforcement: A case report. *Journal of Behavior Therapy and Experimental Psychiatry, 1,* 233–239.

Chapter 12

PSYCHOSOCIAL TREATMENTS FOR OBSESSIVE–COMPULSIVE DISORDER
Clinical Applications

Melinda A. Stanley
Patricia M. Averill

As is apparent from the review of the treatment literature in Chapter 11, exposure and response prevention (ERP) is the psychosocial treatment of choice for obsessive–compulsive disorder (OCD). Although other interventions (e.g., cognitive approaches, thought stopping) have received some attention in the literature, ERP has received by far the strongest empirical support for treating this chronic and severe condition. As such, this chapter reviews in some detail the procedures for planning and implementing this approach. Strategies for the maintenance of treatment gains following exposure and response prevention also are discussed, as are issues related to patient management, potential problems in treatment implementation, and special considerations for the treatment of patients without overt rituals.

ASSESSMENT AND TREATMENT PLANNING

The assessment of OCD can be time consuming and complex for several reasons (see Chapter 10 of this volume). First, although there tend to be central categories into which many obsessions and compulsions fall (e.g., fears of contamination or hurting someone, ritualistic cleaning or checking), more unusual fears or behaviors often are reported. In particular, sexual, aggressive, and/or religious themes (e.g., images of having sex with Christ or fears of defecating on religious symbols such as a Bible or a cross) are often present. In addition, cognitive rituals (e.g., repetitive praying, counting, or visualization of certain geometric shapes) are sometimes difficult to assess. Second, patients often experience shame or guilt associated with OCD symptoms. They also may be afraid that discussing their fears may "cause" them to happen or exacerbate them (Turner & Beidel, 1988), or they may fear negative evaluation by the clinician if they report socially unacceptable obsessions (such as fear of hurting children). For all of these reasons, patients may be reluctant to report their fears or behaviors. Finally, patients may no longer recall underlying fears associated with ritualistic behaviors, or they may have engaged in some behaviors for so long that they no longer recognize them as symptomatic of OCD.

Because of the heterogeneous nature of OCD symptoms and patient variables that may impede reporting of symptoms, the accurate diagnosis of OCD and characterization of the clinical picture may require several modes of assessment (e.g., clinical interviews, self-report, self-monitoring, behavioral observation), tapping cognitive, behavioral, and physiological symptoms. Chapter 10 provides a full review of standardized measures in this regard, and these are not described here. Instead, the focus in this chapter is on general assessment strategies useful for the planning and implementation of ERP. Generally, the three assessment phases include (1) the initial assessment phase, during which the goal is to evaluate the full diagnostic picture; (2) an assessment of the patient's motivation for behavioral treatment; and (3) a more in-depth assessment to gather specific details of fears and rituals in preparation for treatment planning. These phases of the assessment process are described here.

Initial Diagnostic Assessment

During the initial phase of assessment, the first goal is to confirm the diagnosis of OCD. This can be accomplished using a structured or unstructured clinical interview (see Chapter 10) and beginning with questions regarding presenting problems. As noted already, patients may be secretive about their thoughts and behaviors and therefore may need significant encouragement to discuss them openly. This can be done by asking questions that provide examples of unusual symptoms (e.g., "Do you often stare at the stove for long periods of time to be sure that it is turned off?"), and by taking a comfortable, nonjudgmental approach to patients' reports of bizarre patterns of behavior (Stanley, 1992). During this stage, it is important to assess for the presence of obsessive thoughts and fears, overt ritualistic behaviors and mental rituals, as well as levels of distress and interference. It may be beneficial to determine whether patients perceive their fears and/or rituals as excessive, although recent literature suggests that overvalued ideation may not effect treatment outcome (Foa & Kozak, 1995; Kozak & Foa, 1994; Stanley & Turner, 1995; see also Chapter 11).

As well as assessing for the presence of OCD, it is important to assess for coexistent Axis I disorders (e.g., additional anxiety disorders, affective disorders, or psychosis). In general, patients who are psychotic should not be treated with behavioral interventions for OCD (Steketee, 1993). On the other hand, patients with a coexistent anxiety disorder may be treated concomitantly for both disorders using behavioral interventions, if appropriate. Steketee (1993) also has suggested that anxiolytics may be of some benefit in these cases, provided the dosage does not interfere with the client's ability to experience arousal during ERP. We do not recommend the use of anxiolytics, however, since it has been hypothesized that arousal is necessary for fear reduction (Foa & Kozak, 1986). Finally, patients with an affective disorder may need antidepressant medication in conjunction with, or before, behavioral treatment, particularly if they report suicidal ideation (Baer, 1991; Stanley, 1992). It is well known that many of these medications, in particular the serotonin reuptake inhibitors (SRIs), also may be useful in reducing the severity of obsessive–compulsive symptoms (see Chapter 13 of this volume for a review).

Coexistent personality disorders may have treatment implications and therefore should be assessed at this stage. For example, Baer et al. (1992) conducted a prospective study suggesting that coexistent schizotypal, borderline, or avoidant personality disorders may be associated with increased symptoms at baseline and poorer outcome. Earlier research also suggested a relation between schizotypal, borderline, and passive–aggressive personality traits and poor outcome (e.g., Hermesh, Shahar, & Munitz, 1987; Jenike, Baer, Minichiello, Schwartz, & Carey, 1986; Steketee, 1990). Although more prospective data are needed in this regard, it is clear that the assessment of coexistent Axis II disorders is important in this initial diagnostic phase.

Another component of the initial assessment is to determine whether clients are using alcohol or drugs (recreational or prescriptive) to reduce anxiety, since these may interfere with treatment efficacy. Excessive alcohol use should be discontinued prior to treatment, and we also recommend discontinuation of anxiolytic medications, given their potential to interfere with the experience of arousal during ERP. If this is difficult for patients, consideration should be given to hospitalization for detoxification prior to treatment implementation (Stanley, 1992).

All patients should receive a medical evaluation before starting treatment to rule out any physical factors that may contraindicate a behavioral approach (Turner & Beidel, 1988; Stanley, 1992). For example, clients with cardiovascular problems may not be suitable candidates for behavioral treatment, because the increased arousal associated with ERP may trigger cardiac symptoms. In such a case, it may be necessary to modify treatment by using a gradual approach to treatment implementation (Stanley, 1992).

Treatment Motivation

After the initial diagnostic evaluation indicates that the patient is an appropriate candidate for ERP, the therapist should educate the patient about the disorder, preferably including examples from the patient's own reported symptoms. Patients often have little knowledge about the nature and prevalence of OCD and therefore benefit from this type of general overview. In addition, a rationale for treatment and a general description of ERP, including a brief review of the treatment outcome literature, should be provided (Stanley, 1992). Patients should be informed that some symptoms may persist after the completion of treatment so as to set realistic expectations for treatment outcome. The therapist should ensure that adequate time and encouragement are provided for patients to ask questions. Patients' responses to this educational material, including their reported expectations of treatment outcome, may provide information regarding their motivation and willingness to participate (Steketee, 1993). Patients also should be advised of the significant time commitment involved in successful treatment, including the requirement that they engage in various activities between sessions as well as during sessions (Stanley, 1992). For example, during the assessment phase, patients will need to monitor symptoms and complete questionnaires. Compliance with these procedures may, in fact, indicate the patient's motivation for treatment (Steketee, 1993). Later, patients will need to commit significant blocks of time to exposure sessions and homework tasks, and they will need to continue working to maintain gains after the treatment phase is complete (see Maintenance of Treatment Gains, below). Although it is recommended that treatment be described in somewhat general terms, sufficient detail should be provided so that patients have a clear understanding of the level of commitment involved. As such, it is likely that a clearer assessment of a patient's level of motivation will be gathered (Steketee, 1993).

The availability of social support also may have treatment implications, and family members may serve as motivators or saboteurs. In a review of the literature, Steketee (1993) indicated mixed findings regarding the role of social support in treatment outcome. For example, some studies have found that spouse- or family-assisted therapy has led to improvements (Hafner, 1982, 1988; Mehta, 1990), whereas others have found no advantages of including spouses or family members in treatment (e.g., Emmelkamp, de Haan, & Googduin, 1990; Emmelkamp & De Lange, 1983; Hoover & Insel, 1984). Despite these conflicting reports in the literature, our clinical judgment is that family characteristics need to be considered during the assessment phase. Some data have indicated that relapse may be associated with criticism from close relatives (Steketee, 1987), suggesting that relatives who may be involved in treatment be brought to the assessment center so that the interactions between the patient and the relative can be assessed. These interactions also can be observed during the home visit (see Treatment Implementation, below). Additionally, it is important to assess whether family members are assisting in patients' ritualistic behavior. For example, family members may take showers and change their clothes immediately upon entering the home so as to prevent contamination. In these cases, family members will need to be instructed to stop such behaviors when treatment is initiated.

In-Depth Assessment

During the final assessment phase, the focus is on gathering more detailed information about ritualistic behaviors and avoidance, as well as specific obsessive thoughts and fears, in preparation for treatment planning. Specific information is needed in each of these areas so that treatment can target key symptoms accurately.

Specific behavioral rituals can be assessed by observational methods in conjunction with the clinical interview, self-monitoring, and self-report questionnaires. Observation of rituals can occur during a home visit (see Treatment Implementation, below) or, if the behavior is transportable, during an office visit (Stanley, 1992). For example, if the patient takes excessive time to write checks, he or she can be asked to bring bills to the office to pay them. Naturally, observational methods cannot be used for private behaviors (such as bathing) or cognitive rituals. In these cases, detailed questioning about sequences of behaviors is necessary. In addition to direct behavioral observation, self-monitoring sheets can be helpful in providing details about the time involved in a ritual, the number of repetitions in a day, and the specific sequences of behavior (see Figure 12.1). To enhance accuracy, it is preferable for patients to complete the forms immediately after each ritual, while details are vivid. They can be instructed to start completing self-monitoring sheets after the initial interview, so that more detailed information can be gathered quickly in preparation for treatment planning.

Some of the necessary information at this phase can be gathered using a

BEHAVIOR MONITORING FORM

NAME: _____   DATES: FROM: _____ TO:_____

DATE	BEGINNING TIME	BEGINNING SUDS* RATING (0-100)	BEHAVIOR	ENDING TIME	ENDING SUDS* RATING (0-100)

*Subjective Units of Discomfort Scale

0	50	100
NO ANXIETY	MODERATE ANXIETY	WORST ANXIETY EVER

FIGURE 12.1 Sample self-monitoring form.

more in-depth clinical interview, although patients often cannot recall the specific details surrounding their obsessive–compulsive symptoms. In these cases, details of ritualistic behavior can be provided by family members, who often are aware of rituals that may be overlooked by the patient (Steketee, 1993). Another helpful method for gathering accurate information involves asking patients to describe their behaviors during a typical day (Steketee, 1993), placing particular emphasis on times when rituals are most disturbing. For example, if the patient has difficulty arriving at work on time due to morning cleansing rituals, it may be helpful to ask the patient to describe specifically the behaviors that occur between waking and leaving the home.

In addition to gathering information about overt behavioral rituals, it is essential to assess the presence of cognitive rituals. These are, of course, more difficult to assess because evaluation depends entirely upon self-report. Furthermore, patients may not be aware that they are engaging in repetitive cognitive activity that serves to reduce anxiety. As such, it is important to ask directly whether such rituals are present, particularly if patients report certain fears but do not report associated behavioral rituals. For example, one patient assessed in our clinic reported repetitious, irrational thoughts of failure, but no associated behavioral rituals. Further questioning, however, indicated that he tended to review his schedule for the subsequent day repeatedly in his mind to alleviate associated anxiety. We also have assessed patients whose anxiety about obsessional thoughts was reduced by visualizing certain geometric patterns, silently repeating certain prayers or phrases, or imagining repetitively a significant other's reassurance.

Apart from obtaining detailed information about overt and cognitive rituals, the therapist needs to assess for any avoidance that serves to reduce obsessive fears. For example, patients fearing contamination may avoid using public rest rooms or sitting on chairs in public areas. Some avoidance behaviors are fairly common and quite obvious, whereas others may require extensive questioning or careful observation. For example, we evaluated one patient who wanted to make coffee for the therapist during a long home visit. When he went to the pantry, he found that he was out of instant coffee. The examiner noted aloud that he had a can of ground coffee, but the patient became very anxious and reluctant to open the can. Further questioning indicated that opening the can would result in a serrated lid being available, which the patient feared he might use as a "weapon" to slit somebody's throat. Indeed, the patient then acknowledged that he had not opened any cans in 2 years, although he had not mentioned this type of avoidance during the assessment phase. Another method of gathering avoidance information may be to assess premorbid functioning (Steketee, 1993). Structured interviews and self-report questionnaires also may be useful in tapping avoidance behaviors.

In addition to assessing ritualistic and avoidance behaviors, another central task in this phase involves gathering detailed information about obsessional thoughts and fears. Some of these fears may be externally driven, such as fear of exposure to asbestos in old buildings, or fear of becoming contaminated when shaking hands. Other fears are internally driven, such as images of using profane language in public or hurting a loved one. In both cases, it is important to evaluate the external and internal cues that provoke obsessional fears. Generally, however, fears seem to revolve around central themes, and we believe that it is important to identify the "core fear" and target that fear in treatment. For example, the individual described earlier, who avoided opening cans, had a primary belief that he was a bad person. More specifically, he feared that he had left the home while he was asleep and, without awareness, engaged in raping and/or murdering innocent women. Numerous cues provoked this fear, including reading about murders in the newspaper or seeing them on television, and seeing knives or other sharp objects in his kitchen. For this individual, it was important to obtain a comprehensive evaluation of the fear cues, although it was clear that all cues led to the same core fear, which was then targeted for treatment.

Despite careful gathering of detailed information, it is not unusual to find that important information has been omitted, possibly due to shame or because patients do not consider the information to be important. Sometimes, such details do not become apparent until the early stages of treatment and may necessitate changes in the ERP plan.

In assessing fears, it is important to gather information regarding the degree of subjective discomfort experienced. Typically, the therapist teaches the patient how to rate his or her discomfort using the Subjective Units of Discomfort Scale (SUDS). Usually, this scale is described as ranging from 0 to 100, with a zero rating indicating no discomfort at all and 100 indicating total discomfort. It is helpful to ask patients to rate themselves at the time the scale is described and at various times while assessing fears. SUDS ratings also are used during treatment implementation in assessing anxiety and habituation (see Treatment Implementation, below).

After assessment is complete, decisions need to be made regarding the use of *in vivo* versus imaginal exposure. As mentioned earlier, it is important to tap the primary fear during treatment. If this can be done using *in vivo* techniques, this generally is the preferred method of treatment. For example, one patient we treated was fearful that certain clothing had become "contaminated" by asbestos as a result of walking past old buildings. These clothes were kept in a separate pile, apart from his "safe" clothing. He also did not wash the contaminated clothing for fear of contaminating the washing machine. In this case, *in vivo* treatment, involving mixing the clothes together, washing them, storing them, and wearing them, was effective because it tapped the primary fear of asbestos contamination. However, some fears do not lend themselves to *in vivo* treatments; for example, fears of future or past harm (Steketee, 1993) may be better tapped using imaginal scenes. The patient mentioned previously, who feared raping and murdering many women while he was asleep, responded well to imaginal scenes describing the details of feared past events. Imaginal techniques also can be useful when the fear involves contaminants to which the patient should not be exposed, such as feces or blood products.

TREATMENT IMPLEMENTATION

ERP consists of two components: exposure to fear-producing obsessions and prevention of ritualistic responses typically performed to reduce anxiety. Although it is clear from the empirical literature that the combination of these approaches produces optimal improvement (Steketee, Foa, & Grayson, 1982; see also Chapter 11, this volume), procedures for implementing the two components are reviewed separately here.

Response Prevention

In order for exposure to produce habituation of the fear response, rituals designed to reduce anxiety must be prevented. A response prevention (RP) plan is therefore developed to provide instructions for the patient about how to carry out daily-life activities without the performance of rituals. Some ERP programs that have produced impressive improvement rates (e.g., Foa, Steketee, Grayson, Turner, & Latimer, 1984; Foa, Kozak, Steketee, & McCarthy, 1992) recommend very strict RP, for example, requiring that patients with washing rituals take a 10-minute shower only once or twice a week and discontinue all handwashing except under unusual circumstances such as spilled grease or ink (Steketee, 1993). However, we believe it is important that patients never be asked to engage in any behavior that is unsanitary or unsafe or, in fact, any behavior that the therapist would not be willing to do (Stanley, 1992; Turner & Beidel, 1988). In this vein, we are more likely to ask patients with washing compulsions to take a 10-minute shower once a day and to restrict handwashing to a limited amount of time before eating and after using the rest room. We believe it is important to block rituals and avoidance behaviors such that "normal" daily activities can be completed without repetition. A sample RP plan for a patient with contamination fears and related rituals is presented in Table 12.1.

In our clinic, implementation of the RP plan typically begins with a home visit, wherein the therapist reviews the plan in detail and assists the patient in completing all assigned tasks. During the home visit, the need for revisions in the plan also can be evaluated based on observations of undisclosed rituals. If family members are to be included in the RP plan (i.e., if they will be asked to discontinue engaging in rituals with the patient or completing tasks for the patient to minimize his or her fear), it is beneficial for them to be present during the home visit to review instructions for their participation. The family's support of the patient during a difficult treatment course also can be encouraged at this time, although participating family members should be reminded that they need to refrain from providing repetitive reassurance to the patient that changes in behavior will not lead to disastrous consequences. Patients frequently seek this type of reassurance, but the therapist and family members should remember that this verbal "checking" can serve the same function as other rituals and therefore should not be reinforced. When patients pose such questions, they can be asked to try and answer the question themselves. They also can be reminded that the

TABLE 12.1. Response Prevention Plan for a Patient with Contamination Fears and Related Rituals

1. Clothes may be washed only once, one time per week, and they must be worn at least once to be washed.

2. After doing laundry, clothes should be placed directly on top of the bed (instead of on an undersheet) for folding. They then should be put away and not washed again until worn at least once.

3. No more than 15 minutes per day should be spent on straightening up your home. More extensive cleaning should be done only once a week, for no more than 2½ hours.

4. Hands should be washed only after using the bathroom or before eating. Washing hands should take no more than 30 seconds. Only soap and water (not rubbing alcohol) should be used for this activity.

5. Showers should be taken no more than once per day, for no more than 15 minutes.

6. Teeth should be brushed only after meals, at bedtime, and after getting up in the morning. This activity should take no more than 1 minute each time.

function of such questioning is ritualistic, and therefore the questions cannot be answered more than once (Steketee, 1993).

During the home visit, the therapist should assume a confident and directive approach, providing specific instructions about how the RP plan should be carried out and challenging the patient to perform new behaviors. If necessary, the therapist can model the appropriate way to engage in daily activities without rituals (e.g., how to wash hands quickly, how to leave the home without rechecking appliances, locks, etc.), although patients should never be physically pushed to perform any action. Here, it is important to emphasize the choice the patient is making to perform the new behavior and to increase the patient's perception of his or her responsibility for change. Often, it is tempting for patients to attribute responsibility for discontinuing rituals (and, consequently, any disastrous outcomes) to the therapist, thereby relieving themselves of anxiety. Thus, the therapist should maximize the patient's role in deciding to discontinue compulsions (Steketee, 1993). Simultaneous with direct instructions, the therapist should express understanding of the distress the patient is undergoing, providing encouragement and reinforcement for attempts to change ritualistic behavior patterns.

The home visit usually is complete when all RP assignments have been practiced and the patient's anxiety level is low enough that rituals will not be repeated upon the therapist's departure. At this time, the patient is instructed to follow the RP plan as closely as possible until the first exposure session, which usually occurs the following day, and then throughout the entire treatment interval. Family members may be able to provide support with this assignment, and the patient may be encouraged to engage in distracting, pleasurable activities outside the home to assist in the prevention of ritualistic behavior between exposure sessions. Although distraction during exposure sessions is counterproductive (Grayson, Foa, & Steketee, 1986), our clinical impression is that distraction as a means of assisting RP during the remainder of the patient's daily functioning can be useful.

Self-monitoring procedures can be used to check on a patient's progress with this part of the treatment. It also is prudent at the beginning of each exposure session to query the patient about any difficulties in implementation of RP. At these points, the therapist can provide additional suggestions and reinforcement, modifying the plan as necessary to fit any new reports of ritualistic behavior. As treatment progresses, it is important to transfer responsibility for decision making about RP behaviors to the patient. When patients ask about how they should do certain things, it can be useful to respond by asking them to think about the purpose of the behavior, decide if it is a compulsion, and propose for themselves an alternative behavior, if necessary. As time passes, the therapist should refrain from providing specific instructions about RP, requesting that the patient make those decisions alone.

Some therapists attempt to conduct RP in a more gradual fashion, that is, by slowly reducing the number of repetitions or time spent ritualizing or by asking patients to refrain from rituals in a hierarchical fashion. We agree with Steketee (1993), however, that these methods are less than optimal. First, more gradual methods of RP are not based on empirically supported procedures, and a recent meta-analysis suggested that treatments with total RP lead to greater improvement than those with partial RP (Abramowitz, 1996). In addition, allowing patients to perform rituals during exposure treatment runs counter to the habituation–extinction model upon which the treatment originally was based. Thus, for both empirical and theoretical reasons, we recommend the more comprehensive and intense method of RP described here. If patients initially are unable to adhere to complete RP, a more gradual approach may be attempted.

Exposure

After the home visit and initiation of RP, a series of exposure sessions are conducted. In our clinic, these sessions generally occur on a daily basis for the first 2 weeks of treatment. We utilize this type of intensive program, given its demonstrated efficacy in the literature (Foa et al., 1984, 1992), although, occasionally, we treat a patient who is highly motivated, or whose symptoms are not very severe, on a less frequent basis (i.e., two to three times per week). In these instances, as suggested by Steketee and Turner (1991), we rely heavily on the patient's ability to complete additional exposure sessions at home, the assistance of a spouse or family member, and/or the use of brief telephone contacts between sessions. However, given the solid empirical support for a more intense program of exposure, we most often conduct exposure (or flooding) sessions on a daily basis for at least 2 weeks.

The specific nature of exposure is determined, based on the therapist's assessment of the patient's core fear(s). The therapist also needs to make a determination before exposure is initiated whether imaginal or *in vivo* procedures (or a combination of both) are most likely to access the primary fear. The therapist certainly should remain flexible, however, with regard to modifying the original approach if the predetermined mode of exposure fails to produce the expected levels of arousal. Exposure sessions can be conducted in a graduated fashion, with pretreatment preparation of a hierarchy of situations that require exposure (Steketee, 1993), or in a more intense manner, wherein exposure tasks are selected to create higher levels of anxiety (Turner & Beidel, 1988). We generally begin treatment with exposure tasks that create moderately high levels of anxiety that challenge patients but are not unmanageable.

Exposure sessions generally are continued until some evidence of within-session habituation is observed (i.e., subjective, observable, and/or physiological indices of anxiety are reduced before the session is ended). Although there is some evidence that 90-minute sessions can be efficacious (Steketee, 1993; Steketee & Turner, 1991; see also Chapter 11 of this volume), a general rule of thumb is to discontinue exposure when there is a 50% reduction in anxiety from peak levels (Steketee, 1993). Smaller anxiety reductions generally are sufficient for patients with high baseline levels of anxiety or those whose anxiety habituates slowly. Of most importance, however, is that sessions not be ended when anxiety levels are at their peak or rising; the habituation model upon which the intervention originally was based relies on extended contact with feared situations that allows for significant decreases in anxiety over time. If, however, an exposure session needs to be ended prematurely, the patient should be asked to return to the situation as soon as possible. Although within-session habituation is necessary for ERP to be effective, it is not sufficient; between-session habituation also must occur. This phenomenon is evident when peak levels of anxiety decrease over sessions, and when the duration of time to within-session habituation shortens over time. The therapist needs to remain aware of any apparent failure to attain either type of habituation, modifying treatment procedures as necessary (see Patient Management, Potential Problems, and Solutions, below).

IN-SESSION PROCEDURES FOR *IN VIVO* EXPOSURE

To begin the first *in vivo* exposure session, it generally is useful to review with the patient any problems with the RP plan initiated during the home visit. At the beginning of subsequent sessions, it also is important to review any homework exposure tasks assigned during the prior session, problem-solving any difficulties and modifying the assignment for future practice. Reinforcement and support at this time for all attempts to comply with treatment procedures also are important.

Immediately before beginning exposure, the therapist should review the plan for the session. During early sessions, the patient should be reminded about the goals of treatment and the theoretical model upon which the intervention is based. We also generally remind patients that the therapist's role during the exposure session is to create an environment that produces anxiety related to the patient's primary fear. Similarly, the patient's role is to participate in the session as actively as possible, refraining from any distractions or anxiety-reducing behaviors. Following this brief preparation, the exposure session should begin. It is important to note that we assume that the specific activity of the *in vivo* session is not important as long as it elicits the primary or core fear. If a graduated approach is used, all exposure tasks in the hierarchy should be representative of the same fear so that there will be generalization of fear reduction from one level to another.

In preparing to conduct *in vivo* exposure, the therapist needs to remain flexible about how best to elicit the fear. Sometimes sessions are held in the therapy office; for example, patients with hoarding compulsions might be asked to bring bags of paper or trash from home to practice throwing items away quickly; patients with contamination fears might be asked to touch objects in the therapist's office, waiting room, or other public areas; and patients with checking compulsions might bring paperwork from the office to be completed under supervision without checking. At other times, *in vivo* exposure requires leaving the therapist's office to enter situations that elicit the fear most effectively. For example, patients may be taken to hospital waiting rooms or offices, where they fear contamination; they also can be asked to drive certain routes (with the therapist in the car) or practice locking their cars in the parking lot while refraining from checking behaviors. It should be clear that creativity on the part of the therapist in developing effective exposure tasks is essential.

At the beginning of an *in vivo* session, the therapist may first model the behavior that is prescribed, for example, touching a contaminated object and then "spreading" contamination over clothes, hair, or skin; sitting in chairs that might previously have been occupied by an ill patient; locking a door without checking; or leaving a room without looking down to see if something has been dropped. The patient then should be asked to perform the same behavior. The therapist's role throughout the remainder of the session is to keep the patient's attention focused on the feared situation. This can be done by repetitively pointing out what the patient has done, and what the potential disastrous consequences might be, as well as by asking the patient repeatedly to describe his or her thoughts, feelings, physiological sensations, and expected consequences. The therapist can provide reinforcement occasionally for the patient's active participation in the session (e.g., "You did that well"), although it is important that no anxiety-reduction strategies be provided and the patient's attention remain focused on the potential disastrous outcomes (e.g., "Now pay close attention to what you have just done; notice that the contamination has been spread to all parts of your body"). Based on data documenting that distraction during exposure is countertherapeutic (Grayson et al., 1986), we do not recommend that therapists provide any reassurance, relaxation strategies, or cognitive-restructuring techniques during a session. The therapist also needs to observe the patient closely for any minor rituals or avoidance strategies that may reduce anxiety. For example, patients with contamination fears may touch a "contaminated" object, but then hold their hands away from their bodies to avoid "spreading" the contamination. In these instances, therapist modeling can encourage more thorough contact with feared situations.

During the exposure session, the therapist should assess regularly the patient's level of anxiety. In our clinic, patients provide a SUDS rating every 10–15 minutes. If the patient is engaged in a behavior that is sedentary, we also take regular measures of physiological functioning, assessing heart rate, blood pressure, or respiration rate. The session is continued until some evidence of fear reduction (habituation) is evident. At that time, the exposure session is ended. The therapist and patient then may take some time to review the session, making note of any changes that need to be made before the next exposure session. Homework assignments for additional exposure practice also can be made, and the therapist should remind the patient about the importance of continued RP.

IN-SESSION PROCEDURES FOR IMAGINAL EXPOSURE

Imaginal exposure sessions generally begin in the same way as described earlier; patients' progress on RP and other homework assignments is reviewed and reinforced, and suggestions are made for any necessary revisions in these assignments. During early sessions, the goals and theoretical rationale of treatment should be reviewed, and therapist and patient roles should be clarified. The therapist might explain that he or she will be assuming a role during imaginal scenes, emphasizing to the patient topics and ideas that produce anxiety relevant to the primary fear. In this role, the therapist may make statements that he or she would never make outside of an exposure session (e.g., "You are a bad person for what you have done"), and we find it useful to make this expectation explicit for patients. (As an aside, the role required for conducting imaginal exposure sometimes makes novice therapists uncomfortable, although we have found in our supervision of student therapists that these feelings generally dissipate after one or two sessions, when therapists themselves "habituate" to the situation and observe habituation and improvement in the patient). Patients' roles in imaginal exposure are to imagine the scene as vividly as possible and to assume a role as if they were actually "in the scene," as opposed to observing themselves as if they were actors in a movie. They also should be reminded to try not to utilize distraction techniques, but to keep their attention focused on the imaginal scene.

Before beginning imaginal exposure, it is important to determine that the patient has the ability to create relatively vivid scenes in imagination. If the patient is incapable of this process, imagery training sometimes can be useful. In other cases, a transition to *in vivo* exposure may be necessary. Even if patients have the capacity for imagery, beginning the scene with vivid descriptions of the environment (e.g., the location of furniture, the temperature of the air, the clothes the patient is wearing, etc.) can be useful for enhancing realism. Throughout the scene, the patient should be encouraged to focus attention on associated thoughts, feelings, and physiological sensations. The patient can be asked repeatedly to describe what is going on "now" in the scene, as well as what thoughts, feelings, and bodily sensations are occurring. The therapist then can maintain focus on the scene by repeating these (e.g., "Notice your palms sweating as you approach the room," "Pay close attention to the thoughts that your spouse has been harmed by your own actions"). As the patient's anxiety increases and the primary fear is experienced, the therapist should maintain the patient's focus on the thoughts, images, and feelings at this stage until habituation is apparent. The therapist should assess regularly the patient's anxiety and discontinue the session only when anxiety levels are significantly reduced relative to peak levels. Again, a 50% reduction in this domain is optimal, although smaller reductions may be acceptable for some patients. An example of a flooding scene used with the patient described earlier who feared raping and murdering women while he was asleep is described in Table 12.2.

After each imaginal exposure session, it is useful to spend some time dis-

---

TABLE 12.2. Sample Imaginal Exposure Scene

It is Friday evening and a friend is driving you home from a local bar. The radio is on, and pleasant music is playing. As you both listen, the music ends and the news begins. Suddenly, your friend turns up the radio because she has caught some words that interest her. The story is about a young woman who was brutally raped and murdered a week ago. The newscaster is saying that no new leads have been found in this case, and the family has posted a reward for any information leading to the capture of the murderer. As the story ends and the newscaster moves to a different story, your friend turns down the radio and declares that the death penalty is too lenient for such a fiend.

After hearing the news, you have difficulty concentrating on the conversation. You keep wondering whether you may have raped the murdered woman. You want to find out when the murder occurred so that you can check your date book to see whether you were out that night. You feel yourself getting very anxious. You feel hot, your muscles are very tense, and your heart is pounding. You feel paralyzed as you imagine the murder scene, with you raping and killing the woman. (*Prompt patient for any additional thoughts, feelings, or physiological sensations.*) Suddenly, you realize that your friend is looking at you strangely. She asks if you are okay. You give some excuse and try to pay attention to the conversation, but your mind keeps wandering back to the murder. As soon as you arrive home, you turn on the TV to watch the news. When the story about the murdered woman is reported, you wait anxiously to hear when the rape and murder occurred. (*Prompt for thoughts, feelings, body sensations.*) After the date is reported, you check your date book and notice that you were out drinking that night. When you try to recall your journey home, the details are fuzzy. Maybe you saw the woman on your way home and stopped to give her a ride. Maybe you drove to a quiet wooded area and brutally raped and murdered her. You try to tell yourself that you couldn't do something like that. You would never want to hurt anybody. But you really feel sick as you realize that you could have raped and murdered the woman. (*Prompt for thoughts, feelings, and body sensations.*)

As you try to sleep that night, you keep thinking about the murdered woman. You know the wooded area where her body was found is on the way home from the bar where you were drinking that night. You know you have even been there before, so it very well may have been you who committed this horrible crime. Then, a dreadful thought comes to you. If you raped and murdered this woman without knowing it, maybe you have raped and murdered many other women. What if you repeatedly go out during the night when you are asleep and commit these heinous acts? (*Prompt for thoughts, feelings, and physiological sensations.*)

How can you live with yourself after all these crimes you may have committed? How can any good thing you do begin to settle the account for such heinous acts? This new knowledge about yourself is going to ruin your life. You might as well drop out of school. You are a failure anyway. How can you ever have an intimate relationship again, knowing what you may have done to other women? (*Prompt for thoughts, feelings.*)

---

cussing the process. The patient should be asked to identify aspects of the scene that were most realistic and/or anxiety-producing, as well as types of comments on the part of the therapist that were most helpful in eliciting the primary fear. Any necessary modifications in the scene then can be made for subsequent sessions. At this point, it also is important to reemphasize the importance of RP and discuss any homework assignments. Often, following imaginal exposure, homework involves listening to audiotapes of the exposure scene. In other cases, *in vivo* exposure assignments that relate to the exposure scene might be prescribed.

Following an intensive phase of either *in vivo* or imaginal exposure that produces between-session habituation, the frequency of sessions is reduced, and the patient is given more responsibility for self-exposure. Generally, intensive exposure is followed by an additional 2 weeks during which sessions occur approximately twice a week. During this time, exposure should continue to occur on a daily basis, but patients assume increased responsibility for developing and conducting exposure sessions. Therapist support and reinforcement during this phase are important, as are strategies to increase patients' incorporation of ERP procedures into their daily lives.

Cognitive Therapy

Cognitive models of OCD are reviewed in Chapters 2 and 3 of this volume, and relevant treatment outcome literature is discussed in Chapter 11. Of relevance here, however, is the observation that beliefs about the perceived dangerousness of various situations generally change as a result of ERP (Steketee, 1993), although no study has addressed directly the impact of this intervention on all types of cognitions proposed to be characteristic of OCD (e.g., perfectionism, enhanced personal responsibility, doubt, and overestimation of risk). More important, very few controlled investigations have examined the utility of cognitive therapy as an adjunct or alternative to ERP (see review by James & Blackburn, 1995), and the studies currently available suffer from a number of methodological weaknesses. First, the cognitive procedures used vary across reports, with some studies examining the impact of self-instructional training (Emmelkamp, van der Helm, van Zanten, & Plochg, 1980), others examining the utility of rational–emotive therapy (Emmelkamp, Visser, & Hoekstra, 1989), and still others examining the effects of procedures developed from the models of Beck and Salkovskis (van Oppen, de Haan, van Balkom, Spinhoven, Hoogduin, & van Dyck, 1995). In addition, many studies utilizing cognitive approaches assign "behavioral experiments" that include elements of exposure. None of the controlled trials reported to date has demonstrated clearly that cognitive therapy alone produces effects equivalent to ERP, or that adjunctive cognitive procedures enhance the behavioral approach. Given this lack of empirical support for the efficacy of any particular set of cognitive therapy techniques, we do not incorporate cognitive interventions into the intensive phase of ERP, nor do we recommend this approach until further empirical documentation and specification of procedures are available. We do, however, recommend that this mode of intervention be incorporated into a maintenance phase of treatment, as described below.

MAINTENANCE OF TREATMENT GAINS

As noted earlier, after 2 weeks of intensive ERP, we recommend an additional 2-week period during which patients are seen for exposure sessions approximately twice a week. Steketee (1993) has advised that this phase may need to last as long as 8–10 weeks, and we concur that, at times, patients need multiple weekly sessions for a period longer than the 2 weeks we most often recommend. During this time, the patient continues daily exposure but assumes increased responsibility for making and carrying out assignments. Subsequently, frequency of treatment sessions should be reduced to once per week, with even further transfer of responsibility for continued exposure to the patient. Based on our clinical experience, the duration of treatment after this point depends on a number of factors, including the patient's continuing symptom severity, his or her ability to accept responsibility for incorporating exposure practice into daily life, the extent of family and/or social support available, and the severity of remaining interpersonal difficulties and coexistent pathology.

Empirical research only recently has begun to address systematically the efficacy of behavioral maintenance programs for OCD. In an uncontrolled report of 6 patients who received 4 weeks of intensive ERP, a 6-month maintenance program was developed to include regular, self-directed exposure and RP exercises accompanied by biweekly telephone contact with therapists (McKay, Todaro, Neziroglu, & Yaryura-Tobias, 1996). Results of this study suggested that the maintenance program was effective in maintaining treatment gains. In a more well-controlled trial, 18 patients with OCD were treated with 3 weeks of intensive ERP, then assigned randomly to receive either a formal relapse prevention program or associative therapy (Hiss, Foa, & Kozak, 1994). Relapse prevention consisted of four 90-minute sessions conducted over 1 week, with focus on identifying potential stressors that might increase obsessive–compulsive symptoms, normalizing expected fluctuations of symptom severity, providing suggestions for improving maladaptive interpersonal interactions, and instructing patients in cognitive restructuring. Following these four sessions, nine additional telephone contacts between therapist and patient were held over the subsequent 12 weeks. Results demonstrated improved maintenance of gains in this condition relative to associative therapy, a control condition that involved training in both muscle relaxation and free association about obsessive–compulsive symptoms. Both of these reports (Hiss et al., 1994; McKay et al., 1996) confirm our clinical impression that continued self-exposure, combined with less frequent therapist contact, are essential to maintenance of treatment gains following intensive ERP. Additional research is needed, however, to clarify the most effective methods for implementing this general plan. Various self-help books currently available (e.g., Foa & Wilson, 1991) may be of use in this regard.

Another relapse prevention strategy that may be of some use involves adjunctive support groups (e.g., Black & Blum, 1992; Tynes, Salins, Skiba, & Winstead, 1992). We concur with Steketee (1993), however, that this type of approach is most likely useful in maintaining gains after ERP if group membership is restricted to patients who have undergone an intensive course of this type of treatment. In this case, patients can provide suggestions and support for each other with some knowledge of the theoretical and practical approaches that have been demonstrated useful in the literature. However, the empirical literature about the role of support groups is limited.

Other maintenance tasks may include helping patients learn to fill the time that previously was spent with obsessional thoughts and compulsive behaviors, providing stress management skills, addressing impaired interpersonal relationships, and treating remaining coexistent conditions. Prior to treatment, many patients with OCD have spent multiple hours per day engaged in obsessive thoughts and compulsive rituals. As a result, occupational and interpersonal functioning often have become significantly impaired. In these cases, once obsessive–compulsive symptoms are under some control, patients may need to explore potential employment opportunities through volunteer positions and/or career counseling, and reestablish functional interpersonal relationships. Marital or family counseling, or some form of interpersonal skills training, may be required in the latter case. Providing patients with skills in stress management also can be useful, as it is inevitable that they will encounter stressful situations throughout their lives that impact their ability to maintain control over obsessive–compulsive symptoms. Continued self-directed exposure is one useful strategy in this regard, as are periodic "booster sessions" with the therapist. In addition, learning to control stress in other ways (i.e., through cognitive restructuring, enhancing problem-solving skills, and/or social skills training) can be useful. Finally, treatment during a maintenance phase may need to be directed toward any remaining coexistent conditions such as other anxiety disorders or depressive syndromes, and a variety of empirically supported procedures are available in this regard (Chambless et al., 1995).

PATIENT MANAGEMENT, POTENTIAL PROBLEMS, AND SOLUTIONS

Strategies for handling the secrecy often exhibited by patients with OCD were reviewed earlier, along with the need for extensive education about the nature of the disorder. Of importance to reiterate here, however, is the notion that ERP should not be initiated until the patient appears ready to accept the intervention fully (Stanley, 1992; Turner & Beidel, 1988). In this vein, it is necessary to clarify explicitly the rationale for treatment, as well as the expectations for participation, level of distress, time, and expense of the intervention. Although many patients express ambivalence about the intervention, it is ineffective to pressure patients into accepting a course of ERP. The treatment requires a significant amount of effort on the patient's part, and we often take a fairly "hard line" in this regard. As suggested earlier, providing homework assignments as part of the assessment phase can be a useful way of determining if a patient is ready to engage in treatment. Written contracts also can be useful if patients are having difficulty with the completion of assignments. At times, a patient's level of anxiety or depression at the start of treatment may interfere with his or her ability to engage in treatment. In these instances, a course of antidepressant medication may alleviate overall distress such that the patient is better able to tolerate the anxiety produced by ERP. Although insufficient empirical literature is available to support this perspective, we often recommend medication in these cases and sometimes will refuse to conduct behavioral treatment until the patient appears ready to engage in the intervention.

During ERP, the therapist needs to maintain a confident and understanding attitude, while concurrently providing direct instructions and maintaining high expectations about the patient's participation in the intervention. Novice therapists, who have difficulty tolerating the patient's anxiety themselves, may be unable to conduct exposure sessions in the manner required. As noted earlier, it also is important for the therapist to maintain the patient's attention on fear cues during exposure sessions and to transfer responsibility for decision making about exposure to the patient as soon as possible.

During the intense phase of ERP, certain problems can occur. As reviewed by Steketee (1993), these include the patient's failure to habituate during or between sessions, observation of subtle avoidance behaviors that may preclude the patient's full engagement in exposure, and the emergence of new fears during the course of the intervention. When patients fail to habituate, the potential impact of depressive symptoms and/or overvalued ideation should be considered. In addition, the therapist and patient should evaluate whether the primary fear has been identified accurately and the extent to which the fear cues presented in the exposure session are adequate to produce the necessary level of anxiety. In some cases, habituation may not occur, because anxiety levels are too high (Foa, Grayson, Steketee, & Doppelt, 1983). In these instances, revising the exposure session to evoke a less intense anxiety response may be helpful. Furthermore, if habituation fails to occur, it is important to evaluate whether the patient's attention has been focused as completely as possible on the fear cues presented. Cognitive rituals and/or subtle avoidance behaviors also may be interfering with the extinction process (see Assessment and Treatment Planning, above). In these cases, these behaviors should be pointed out to the patient, with suggestions for specific behavioral change that will decrease avoidance and increase exposure. Strategies for maintaining the patient's attention and reducing distraction or avoidance behaviors during imaginal exposure have been discussed previously. Finally, it is not uncommon for new fears to emerge in the process of exposure treatment. In these cases, exposure tasks need to be revised to incorporate the new information, particularly if it indicates modified conceptualization of the primary fear.

TREATING OBSESSIONS WITHOUT
OVERT COMPULSIONS

Some patients present for evaluation and treatment with obsessions but without apparent rituals. It has been proposed that such patients may be engaging in mental rituals that often are not identified during the assessment phase (Robertson, Wendiggensen, & Kaplan, 1983; Salkovskis & Westbrook, 1989). This position emphasizes the need for routine evaluation of cognitive activity designed to reduce obsessional fears. Even if no mental rituals are apparent, patients may be distracting themselves during exposure, a phenomenon that may interfere with fear reduction (habituation).

One method of treating these patients has involved prolonged exposure to obsessions (Emmelkamp & Kwee, 1977; Stern, 1978), an approach that matches the theoretical basis of the treatment procedures described earlier. This approach can involve any of the exposure procedures described, or patients can be asked to listen to tape recordings or write repeatedly about obsessional thoughts. This method, however, has led to only 50% improvement in symptoms, a figure somewhat lower than that typically reported following intensive ERP. One explanation for these reduced treatment effects is that undisclosed mental rituals are occurring during treatment, thereby reducing discomfort and strengthening rituals (e.g., Salkovskis & Westbrook, 1989). If this is the case, it is necessary to block rituals or distractions while exposing the patient to feared thoughts. One effective method of keeping patients focused on feared thoughts is to have them redirect their thoughts back to the obsessional ideas as soon as they become aware that they are no longer focused. Such techniques have been found to be effective in the treatment of obsessions without apparent compulsions (e.g., Headland & MacDonald, 1987; Hoogduin, De Haan, Schaap, & Arts, 1987; Salkovskis & Westbrook, 1989).

REFERENCES

Abramowitz, J. S. (1996). Variants of exposure and response prevention in the treatment of obsessive–compulsive disorder: A meta-analysis. *Behavior Therapy, 27,* 583–600.

Baer, L. (1991). *Getting control: Overcoming your obsessions and compulsions.* Boston: Little, Brown.

Baer, L., Jenike, M. A., Black, D. W., Treece, C., Rosenfeld, R., & Greist, J. (1992). Effect of Axis II diagnoses on treatment outcome with clomipramine in 55 patients with obsessive–compulsive disorder. *Archives of General Psychiatry, 49,* 862–866.

Black, D. W., & Blum, N. S. (1992). Obsessive–compulsive disorder support groups: The Iowa model. *Comprehensive Psychiatry, 33,* 65–71.

Chambless, D. L., et al. (1995). Training in and dissemination of empirically-validated psychological treatments: Report and recommendations. *The Clinical Psychologist, 48,* 3–23.

Emmelkamp, P. M. G., de Haan, E., & Googduin, C. A. L. (1990). Marital adjustment and obsessive–compulsive disorder. *British Journal of Psychiatry, 156,* 55–60.

Emmelkamp, P. M. G., & De Lange, I. (1983). Spouse involvement in the treatment of obsessive–compulsive patients. *Behaviour Research and Therapy, 21,* 341–346.

Emmelkamp, P. M. G., & Kwee, K. G. (1977). Obsessional ruminations: A comparison between thought-stopping and prolonged exposure in imagination. *Behaviour Research and Therapy, 15,* 441–444.

Emmelkamp, P. M. G., van der Helm, M., van Zanten, B. L., & Plochg, I. (1980). Contributions of self-instructional training to the effectiveness of exposure *in vivo*: A comparison with obsessive compulsive patients. *Behaviour Research and Therapy, 18,* 61–66.

Emmelkamp, P. M. G., Visser, S., & Hoekstra, R. J. (1988). Cognitive therapy vs. exposure *in vivo* in the treatment of obsessive–compulsives. *Cognitive Therapy and Research, 12,* 103–114.

Foa, E. B., Grayson, J. B., Steketee, G. S., & Doppelt, H. G. (1983). Treatment of obsessive–compulsives: When do we fail? In E. B. Foa & P. M. G. Emmelkamp (Eds.), *Failures in behavior therapy* (pp. 10–34). New York: Wiley.

Foa, E. B., & Kozak, W. J. (1986). Emotional processing of fear: Exposure to corrective information. *Psychological Bulletin, 99,* 20–35.

Foa, E. B., & Kozak, M. J. (1995). DSM-IV field trial: Obsessive–compulsive disorder. *American Journal of Psychiatry, 152*(1), 90–96.

Foa, E. B., Kozak, M. J., Steketee, G. S., & McCarthy, P. R. (1992). Imipramine and behavior therapy in the treatment of depressive and obsessive–compulsive symptoms: Immediate and long-term effects. *British Journal of Clinical Psychology, 31,* 279–292.

Foa, E. B., Steketee, G. S., Grayson, J. B., Turner, R. M., & Latimer, P. R. (1984). Deliberate exposure and blocking of obsessive–compulsive rituals: Immediate and long term effects. *Behavior Therapy, 15,* 450–472.

Foa, E. B., & Wilson, R. (1991). *Stop obsessing!: How to overcome your obsessions and compulsions.* New York: Bantam.

Goodman, W. K., Price, L. H., Rasmussen, S. A., Mazure, C., Fleischmann, R. L., Hill, C. L., Heninger, G. R., & Charney, D. S. (1989). Part 1. Yale–Brown Obsessive–Compulsive Scale: Development, use, and reliability. *Archives of General Psychiatry, 46,* 1006–1011.

Grayson, J. B., Foa, E. B., & Steketee, G. (1986). Exposure *in vivo* of obsessive–compulsives under distracting and attention-focusing conditions: Replication and extension. *Behaviour Research and Therapy, 24,* 475–479.

Hafner, R. J. (1982). Marital interaction in persisting obsessive–compulsive disorders. *Australian and New Zealand Journal of Psychiatry, 16,* 171–178.

Hafner, R. J. (1988). Obsessive–compulsive disorder: A questionnaire survey of a self-help group. *International Journal of Social Psychiatry, 34,* 310–315.

Headland, K., & MacDonald, B. (1987). Rapid audio-tape treatment of obsessional ruminations: A case report. *Behavioural Psychotherapy, 15,* 188–192.

Hermesh, H., Shahar, A., & Munitz, H. (1987). Obsessive–compulsive disorder and borderline personality disorder [letter to the editor]. *American Journal of Psychiatry, 144,* 120–121.

Hiss, H., Foa, E. B., & Kozak, M. J. (1994). Relapse prevention program for treatment of obsessive–compulsive disorder. *Journal of Consulting and Clinical Psychology, 62,* 801–808.

Hoogduin, K., de Haan, E., Schaap, C., & Arts, W. (1987). Exposure and response prevention in patients with obsessions. *Acta Psychiatrica Belgica, 87,* 640–653.

Hoover, C., & Insel, T. R. (1984). Families of origin in obsessive–compulsive disorder. *Journal of Nervous and Mental Disease, 172,* 207–215.

James, I. A., & Blackburn, I. M. (1995). Cognitive therapy with obsessive–compulsive disorder. *British Journal of Psychiatry, 166,* 444–450.

Jenike, M. A., Baer, L., Minichiello, W. E., Schwartz, C. E., & Carey, R. J. (1986). Concomitant obsessive–compulsive disorder and schizotypal personality disorder. *American Journal of Psychiatry, 143,* 530–532.

Kozak, M. J., & Foa, E. B. (1994). Obsessions, overvalued ideas, and delusions in obsessive–compulsive disorder. *Behaviour Research and Therapy, 32*(3), 343–353.

McKay, D., Todaro, J. F., Neziroglu, F., & Yaryura-Tobias, J. A. (1996). Evaluation of a naturalistic maintenance program in the treatment of obsessive–compulsive disorder: A preliminary investigation. *Journal of Anxiety Disorders, 10,* 211–217.

Mehta, M. (1990). A comparative study of family-based and patient-based behavioral management in obsessive–compulsive disorder. *British Journal of Psychiatry, 157,* 133–135.

Robertson, J., Wendiggensen, P., & Kaplan, I. (1983). Towards a comprehensive treatment for obsessional thoughts. *Behaviour Research and Therapy, 21,* 347–356.

Salkovskis, P. M., & Westbrook, D. (1989). Behaviour therapy and obsessional ruminations: Can failure be turned into success? *Behaviour Research and Therapy, 27,* 149–160.

Stanley, M. A. (1992). Obsessive–compulsive disorder. In S. M. Turner, K. S. Calhoun, & H. E. Adams (Eds.), *Handbook of clinical behavior therapy* (pp. 67–85). New York: Wiley.

Stanley, M. A., & Turner, S. M. (1995). Current status of pharmacological and behavioral treatment of obsessive–compulsive disorder. *Behavior Therapy, 26,* 163–186.

Steketee, G. (1987, June). *Social support systems as predictors of long term outcome following individual treatment.* Paper presented at the meeting of the Society for Psychotherapy Research, Ulm, West Germany.

Steketee, G. (1990). Personality traits and disorders in obsessive–compulsives. *Journal of Anxiety Disorders, 4,* 351–364.

Steketee, G., & Turner, S. M. (1991). When time is short, is there effective treatment for OCD? Response. *Behavior Therapist, 14,* 79.

Steketee, G. S. (1993). *Treatment of obsessive compulsive disorder.* New York: Guilford Press.

Steketee G. S., & Foa, E. B. (1985). Obsessive–compulsive disorder. In D. H. Barlow (Ed.), *Clinical handbook of psychological disorders: A step-by-step treatment manual* (pp. 69–144). New York: Guilford Press.

Steketee, G. S., Foa, E. B., & Grayson, J. B. (1982). Recent advances in the treatment of obsessive–compulsives. *Archives of General Psychiatry, 39,* 1365–1371.

Stern, R. S. (1978). Obsessive thoughts: The problem of therapy. *British Journal of Psychiatry, 132,* 200–205.

Turner, S. M., & Beidel, D. C. (1988). *Treating obsessive–compulsive disorder.* New York: Pergamon Press.

Tynes, L. L., Salins, C., Skiba, W., & Winstead, D. K. (1992). A psychoeducational and support group for obsessive–compulsive disorder patients and their significant others. *Comprehensive Psychiatry, 33,* 197–201.

van Oppen, P., de Haan, E., van Balkom, A. J. L. M., Spinhoven, P., Hoogduin, K., & van Dyck, R. (1995). Cognitive therapy and exposure *in vivo* in the treatment of obsessive compulsive disorder. *Behaviour Research and Therapy, 4,* 379–390.

Chapter 13

BIOLOGICAL TREATMENTS FOR OBSESSIVE–COMPULSIVE DISORDER

Literature Review

Teresa A. Pigott
Sheila Seay

Obsessive–compulsive disorder (OCD) is an anxiety disorder that encompasses a broad range of cognitive and behavioral symptoms. Indeed, OCD is probably a much more heterogeneous disorder than originally appreciated. Although there is considerable evidence that OCD has an early age of onset, little has been established concerning its typical clinical course. Early studies emphasized the chronic, persistent nature of OCD, but large-scale epidemiological surveys suggest more diversity. For example, Demal, Lenz, Mayrhofer, Zapotoczky, and Zitterl (1993) identified five different patterns of clinical course and subsequent long-term outcome from a retrospective analysis of 62 patients with OCD. The most common were (1) continuous, persistently severe symptomatology (27.4%); (2) continuous, but less severe symptomatology (24.4%); (3) episodic symptoms, with partial symptom improvement between exacerbations (24.2%); (4) episodic symptoms, with full symptom remission between episodes (11.3%); or (5) continuous symptomatology, with worsening severity of symptoms (9.7%).

Comorbid Axis I disorders are very common in OCD patients. The lifetime prevalence rate for an additional Axis I diagnosis in patients with primary OCD exceeds 50% in most studies. The most frequently encountered concomitant disorders appear to be mood and/or anxiety disorders. At the time of their initial psychiatric evaluation, at least 30% of OCD patients will meet current criteria for a major depressive disorder (MDD). The lifetime prevalence rate for MDD is estimated at 60–80% in OCD patients. Results from several studies suggest that 40% of patients with OCD will also fulfill criteria for an additional anxiety disorder diagnosis besides OCD (Pigott, L'Heureux, Dubbert, Bernstein, & Murphy, 1994; Rasmussen & Eisen, 1990, 1992).

BIOLOGICAL FACTORS IN OCD

Conceptual Issues

As eloquently summarized by Insel and colleagues (Insel, Moss, & Olivier, 1994), the etiology of OCD can be conceptualized from two very different but fundamental perspectives. Do aberrant, distressing thoughts concerning guilt and doubt emerge first, followed by the development of compulsive behaviors to reduce the concomitant anxiety? Or does the sudden emergence of ritualistic behaviors secondarily trigger a focus on certain cognitions as a means to explain or rationalize the senseless behaviors? The answer to this fundamental question remains undetermined. However, several lines of evidence implicate two specific brain regions, the prefrontal cortex and the basal ganglia, as the critical loci in the functional neuroanatomy of OCD.

One reason that these sites are often implicated in the development of OCD arises from their purported function. Several higher-level cognitive functions such as temporal sequencing and the interpretation of cause-and-effect relationships are mediated by the prefrontal cortex. In addition, affective states such as anticipation are linked to the prefrontal cortex. As a result, alterations in prefrontal cortex functioning could give rise to such manifestations as altered risk assessment, pathological doubt, and overconscientious behaviors. The basal ganglia, in contrast, contain neural circuits that primarily modulate motor movement. Some of the motor pathways located within the basal ganglia are speculated to modulate primitive, repetitive actions such as grooming and/or maintenance behaviors. Alterations in the pathways modulating and/or suppressing such behaviors could, hypothetically, result in the inappropriate expression of repetitive actions such as excessive checking, cleaning, arranging, or collecting behaviors. Although such speculation may seem far-fetched, data derived from neuroimaging studies also appear to confirm the importance of the prefrontal cortex and basal ganglia in the pathogenesis of OCD symptoms.

Neuroimaging Studies

Early neuroimaging studies using computed tomography (CT) or magnetic resonance imaging (MRI) techniques reported structural differences in OCD patients versus control subjects. However, these differences may have in part been due to the inclusion of childhood-onset—in comparison to adult-onset—patients with OCD, since later CT and routine MRI studies have failed to detect structural differences between OCD patients and controls. OCD patients have also been examined by volumetric MRI. A volumetric study of the caudate nuclei failed to detect significant differences between OCD patients and controls (Aylward et al., 1996), whereas a more generalized study revealed significant reductions in total white matter and increased total cortex and opercular volumes in the OCD patients (Jenike et al., 1996). Although these results suggest that subtle structural abnormalities may exist in some patients with OCD, neuroimaging studies such as positron emission tomography (PET) and single photon emission computed to-mography (SPECT) have provided more consistent evidence of regional brain abnormalities in OCD patients.

In contrast to CT scans and MRIs, neuroimaging techniques such as PET and SPECT provide a dynamic assessment of brain function by measuring and comparing the rate of regional cerebral blood flow (rCBF) and/or rate of cere-bral metabolism in different brain regions. More than 10 studies using either PET or SPECT scans have identified significant differences in brain function in OCD patients versus control subjects. The majority of these studies have corrob-orated the presence of elevated rCBF or hypermetabolism in the prefrontal cor-tex of OCD patients versus control subjects (Hoehn-Saric & Benkelfat, 1994). There have also been reports of altered basal ganglia function in OCD in com-parison to control subjects in several PET and SPECT studies (Benkelfat et al., 1990; Rubin, Villanueva-Meyer, Ananth, Trajmar, & Mena, 1992). No consistent evidence of other specific brain-area abnormalities were detected in the OCD patients during these studies. It is important to note, however, that the previous neuroimaging studies were conducted in a resting state; that is, subjects were scanned while supine and inactive. No effort to elicit OCD symptoms, anxiety, and so forth was attempted in either the OCD or control subjects.

More recent SPECT studies have also incorporated an "activation" compo-nent during the scan in an attempt to differentiate "trait" versus "state" respons-es. The activation component typically involves exposing the OCD subject to a feared stimulus (e.g., a "dirty" glove in an OCD patient with contamination ob-sessions) in an attempt to elicit an acute exacerbation in OCD symptoms during the scan. Brain activity can then be compared in the resting versus the activated state within an individual OCD subject. Using this experimental paradigm, sig-nificant increases in activity have been demonstrated in the prefrontal cortex and/or basal ganglia of the OCD patients in the activated versus resting condi-tion. Functional MRI studies completed during the activation component have also revealed remarkably similar findings. Increased activity of the prefrontal cortex, basal ganglia, and amygdala has been detected in the OCD subjects. In fact, 70% of the OCD subjects exhibited activation during the MRI scans, whereas none of the control subjects had such a response (Breiter et al., 1996).

The effect of various treatment interventions on regional brain function has also been investigated by conducting scans (PET, SPECT) pre- and posttreat-ment in OCD patients. Significant reductions in activity occurred in the pre-frontal cortex region after neurosurgical (anterior capsulotomy) or pharmacolog-ical (clomipramine, fluoxetine) interventions (Rubin, Ananth, Villanueva-Meyer, Trajmar, & Mena, 1995). A comparison of fluoxetine versus behavioral therapy revealed significant reductions in basal ganglia (caudate nucleus) activity in com-parison to the pretreatment state (Baxter, 1992). These results suggest that some of the brain-area alterations noted in OCD may shift toward a more "normal-ized" pattern of brain activity after various treatment interventions. Unfortu-nately, no significant relationship between changes in brain activity and treat-ment response were detected in the previous studies. Therefore, it cannot be excluded that the changes in brain activity that occurred reflected nonspecific medication effect(s), and so on, rather than specific antiobsessional effects.

More recent functional neuroimaging studies have revealed significant relationships between improvement in OCD symptoms and regional brain metabolism changes. Bilateral decreases in cingulate cortex metabolism occurred in OCD subjects who responded to treatment with serotonin transport inhibitors (STIs), whereas nonresponders had no significant change in cingulate cortex activity (Perani et al., 1995). Behavioral therapy responders, in contrast to nonresponders, exhibited significant bilateral decreases in caudate glucose metabolism in another study conducted in patients with OCD (Schwarz, Stoessel, Baxter, Martin, & Phelps, 1996).

Data from neuroimaging studies provide substantial support for the presence of dysfunction in specific brain regions, particularly the prefrontal cortex and basal ganglia, in patients with OCD. However, the clinical application of neuroimaging techniques to an individual patient with OCD remains elusive. Although, as will be discussed later in this chapter, promising pilot data suggest that functional neuroimaging studies may eventually prove invaluable in the selection and/or prediction of treatment response in patients with OCD. The next section summarizes information concerning the neurobiological "substrate" speculated to underlie and precipitate the functional abnormalities detected in patients with OCD.

The Neuropharmacology of OCD

Neurotransmitters are important modulators of brain function. Therefore, alterations in neurotransmitter concentrations and/or function is often implicated in the pathophysiology of psychiatric disorders. The neurotransmitter serotonin (5-hydroxytryptamine, or 5-HT) has been specifically implicated in the pathophysiology of OCD for years (Barr, Goodman, Price, McDougle, & Charney, 1992). The 5-HT hypothesis of OCD originated from the clinical observation that most antidepressant and anxiolytic agents did not significantly reduce OCD symptoms. In fact, the tricyclic antidepressant (TCA) clomipramine was the first medication to demonstrate consistent efficacy in the treatment of patients with OCD (Clomipramine Collaborative Study Group, 1991). In contrast, clinical trials of various TCAs including desipramine, amitriptyline, imipramine, as well as the monoamine oxidase inhibiting (MAOI) antidepressant phenelzine, were all associated with nonsignificant effects on OCD symptoms (Ananth, Pecknold, Van Den Steen, & Engelsman, 1981; Leonard et al., 1991; Vallejo, Olivares, Marcos, Bulbena, & Menchon, 1992; Volavka, Neziroglu, & Yaryura-Tobias, 1985).

In comparison to other TCAs, clomipramine has relatively greater potency and selectivity for blockade of the serotonin transport site (Benfield, Harris, & Luscombe, 1980; Richelson, 1994). As a result, clomipramine's unique efficacy in OCD was subsequently attributed to its effects on 5-HT. As will be discussed, extensive research efforts since that time have generated further support for the importance of serotonergic mechanisms in OCD. This section summarizes information concerning the neuropharmacology of OCD as assessed by (1) measurement of central and peripheral neurotransmitter (monoamine) concentrations, and (2) comparison of behavioral and neuroendocrine response in OCD patients versus control subjects after the acute administration of pharmacological agents designed to differentially effect neurotransmitter systems.

Central and Peripheral Markers

Measurement of central and/or peripheral concentrations of norepinephrine (NE) and/or dopamine (DA) and their respective metabolites has failed to detect evidence of differences between OCD patients and control subjects. In contrast, several studies have reported altered cerebrospinal fluid (CSF) concentrations of the 5-HT metabolite, 5-HIAA, in patients with OCD in comparison to control subjects (Flament, Rapaport, Murphy, Lake, & Berg, 1987; Insel, Mueller, Alterman, Linnoila, & Murphy, 1985; Thoren, Asberg, & Bertelsson, 1980a). This has not been a universal finding, however, as several investigators have failed to detect differences in 5-HIAA concentrations in the CSF between OCD and control subjects (Altemus, Swedo, & Leonard, 1994; Lydiard, Balllenger, Ellinwood, Fossey, & Laraia, 1990; Swedo et al., 1992).

Another means of assessing central serotonin function is provided by platelets. Although considered important to the function of platelets, serotonin cannot be produced or synthesized within the platelet. Instead, serotonin concentration within the platelet is entirely dependent on the serotonin transport mechanism. For example, administration of a medication that has serotonin transport inhibition properties such as a TCA (imipramine, clomipramine, etc.) results in a significant drop in serotonin concentration within the platelet. Prior to the recent identification and cloning of the specific serotonin transport site, tritiated imipramine binding was commonly used as a ligand to assess characteristics (e.g., binding density) of the serotonin transport site. Several tritiated imipramine binding studies of platelets have been conducted in patients with OCD. Unfortunately, the results are far from conclusive. The most recent platelet studies have reported decreased tritiated imipramine binding sites in the OCD versus control subjects (Marazziti et al., 1993; Ravizza, Maina, Rocca, & Bogetto, 1993; Weizman et al., 1986), but earlier studies reported similar (Flament et al., 1987; Insel et al., 1985) or increased (Vitiello et al., 1991) tritiated imipramine binding sites in OCD subjects in comparison to control subjects.

Pharmacological challenges have been utilized extensively to assess noradrenergic, dopaminergic, and serotoninergic function in psychiatric disorders. Patients with depression and/or panic disorder frequently demonstrate evidence of significant alterations in noradrenergic and/or serotonergic function in comparison to control subjects. OCD subjects, however, exhibit a much different response profile during pharmacological challenges.

OCD patients appear to respond similarly to control subjects when administered pharmacological agents that primarily elicit responses mediated by the noradrenergic (yohimbine, clonidine, lactate, caffeine, or carbon dioxide) system.

Similarly, evidence of altered dopaminergic responsivity was not demonstrated in OCD versus control subjects administered bromocriptine. With the exception of the 5-HT$_{1A}$ partial agonist buspirone (Norman, Apostolopoulos, Burrows, & Judd, 1994), substantial evidence of altered serotonin responsivity has been demonstrated in OCD versus control subjects (Gross-Isseroff, Kindler, Kottler, & Sassoon, 1994).

Administration of 5-HT precursors such as trytophan, or 5-HT releasers such as fenfluramine, respectively, result in blunted neuroendocrine responses in patients with OCD in comparison to healthy controls. Although 5-HT$_{1A}$ receptor alterations do not appear to be present in most patients with OCD (Lesch et al., 1991), there is considerable evidence implicating other 5-HT receptors, especially the 5-HT$_2$ subclass, as important in OCD. In particular, data elicited by the acute administration of the 5-HT$_{2C}$ partial agonist, meta-chlorophenylpiperazine (mCPP), has been of considerable interest.

Several placebo-controlled studies reported that acute administration of mCPP to unmedicated patients with OCD elicited brief but dramatic exacerbations in OCD symptoms (Hollander, DeCaria, Nitescu, Gorman, Klein, & Liebowitz, 1991b; Hollander, DeCaria, Nitescu, Gully, Suckow, Cooper, et al., 1992; Hollander et al., 1988; Hollander et al., 1991a; Pigott et al., 1991b; Zohar, Mueller, Insel, Zohar-Kadouch, & Murphy, 1987; Zohar, Mueller, Insel, Zohar-Kadouch, & Murphy, 1988). Relatively blunted mCPP-induced prolactin and/or cortisol responses were also noted in the OCD patients in comparison to the control subjects in the same studies. After chronic clomipramine or fluoxetine treatment, the exacerbation in OCD symptoms did not reoccur when the OCD patients were rechallenged with mCPP (Hollander et al., 1991b; Zohar et al., 1988). These results were met with considerable enthusiasm, in part because they appeared to represent solid confirmation of the presence of altered serotonin function in patients with OCD. Strong support was also rendered for the contention that the therapeutic effects of clomipramine or fluoxetine were mediated by their actions on serotonin.

Unfortunately, results from additional mCPP studies have been much less convincing (Charney et al., 1988; Goodman et al., 1995; Pigott et al., 1993b). In these mCPP studies, no significant changes in OCD symptoms occurred; nor was there evidence of altered behavioral sensitivity in the OCD versus the control subjects. Numerous factors such as different routes of administration (oral vs. intravenous), use of dissimilar behavioral rating scales, disparate populations of OCD patients, and so on, have been hypothesized to contribute to the discrepancy in these results. Nevertheless, significant differences in neuroendocrine responses between OCD patients and controls have been consistently reported in all of the mCPP studies to date. These results suggest that OCD patients exhibit evidence of altered serotonergic, but intact noradrenergic and dopaminergic, function.

Conversely, patients with depression or panic disorder exhibit consistent evidence of altered noradrenergic and serotonergic function (Charney, Woods, Goodman, & Heninger, 1987a, 1987b; Kahn, Asnis, Wetzler, & von-Praag,

1988). The presence of both noradrenergic and serotonergic dysregulation in depressed or panic disorder patients may help explain why a variety of therapeutic agents, regardless of neurotransmitter selectivity, possess therapeutic efficacy in these disorders. In contrast, patients with OCD demonstrate selective alterations in serotonergic function. These medications (clomipramine, fluoxetine, sertraline, paroxetine, and fluvoxamine) can be collectively labeled as STIs. The next section provides an overview of the STIs in the treatment of patients with OCD.

FIRST-LINE PHARMACOTHERAPY

The STIs represent the cornerstone of pharmacological treatment in patients with OCD. They include the tricyclic antidepressant clomipramine and the selective serotonin reuptake inhibiting (SSRI) antidepressants fluoxetine, sertraline, paroxetine, and fluvoxamine.

Clomipramine has been the most extensively studied medication for the treatment of OCD. Although clomipramine has potent effects on serotonin reuptake blockade, its major metabolite desmethyl-clomipramine (d-CMI) is a potent inhibitor of norepinephrine reuptake (Benfield et al., 1980). Clomipramine also has a relatively high affinity for adrenergic (alpha-1), dopamine (D2), and histamine (H1) central receptors (Hall & Ogren, 1981). Both clomipramine and d-CMI also have potent anticholinergic effects (Benfield et al., 1980). These anticholinergic effects are linked to many of the adverse effects observed during clomipramine administration and also contribute to its toxicity in overdosage. In addition, daily doses of clomipramine over 250 mg/day are associated with a relatively increased rate of seizures in comparison to most other antidepressant medication.

Most studies have suggested that 150–250 mg/day of clomipramine is a standard effective dose for patients with OCD. Some (Insel et al., 1983; Mavissakalian, Jones, Olsen, & Perel, 1990; Stern, Marks, & Wright, 1980), but not all (Flament et al., 1987; Kasvikis & Marks, 1988; Thoren, Asberg, Crohnholm, Jornestedt, & Trachman, 1980b) studies have suggested that clomipramine plasma levels may be significantly related to antiobsessive response in OCD patients. There is also some evidence that clomipramine response may be enhanced by an elevated clomipramine-to-d-CMI plasma concentration ratio (Mavissakalian et al., 1990).

The SSRI antidepressants selectively block the presynaptic reuptake of 5-HT, but have minimal affinity for histaminic, muscarinic, adrenergic, and serotonergic receptors (Richelson, 1994). As might be expected from their similar pharmacological effects, there is considerable overlap in the side effects associated with the SSRI antidepressants. Headache, disturbed sleep, and gastrointestinal (nausea, anorexia, diarrhea) effects appear to be the most common side effects endorsed during SSRI administration. The SSRI antidepressants are remarkably well tolerated and are characterized by low toxicity and relative safety in overdose. Considerable variance in pharmacokinetic characteristics exists within the SSRIs (DeVane, 1992). Fluoxetine has the most extensive half-life (fluoxetine, 48–72 hours; norfluoxetine, 7–10 days). Sertraline and paroxetine have a half-life similar to clomipramine and the TCAs (approximately 23–25 hours), and fluvoxamine has the shortest (15 hours) half-life.

Table 13.1 summarizes results from the U.S. multicenter, placebo-controlled trials conducted in patients with primary OCD. The Yale–Brown Obsessive–Compulsive Scale (YBOCS) is the most widely used and accepted instrument for measuring change in OCD symptoms (Goodman & Price, 1990). A mean reduction from baseline of 25–35% on the YBOCS is generally considered a clinically meaningful change in OCD symptom severity. The YBOCS was used as either the primary or one of the main efficacy variables in each of the multicenter OCD studies.

Each trial was conducted separately and compared an individual STI versus placebo in a randomized, parallel cell design. These multicenter trials were conducted at different times (clomipramine followed by fluoxetine, sertraline, fluvoxamine, and paroxetine, respectively) and at varying sites over an approximately 8-year span. Despite these differences, remarkably consistent data emerged concerning the pharmacological response of patients with OCD. Two of the most important findings were as follows: (1) At least 6–10 weeks of STI administration was necessary before significant reductions in OCD symptoms were noted; and (2) most of the OCD patients who responded to STI therapy experienced only partial improvement (mean reduction in OCD symptoms from baseline, 25–40%).

TABLE 13.1. Multicenter, Placebo-Controlled Trials

Medication studied	Dosage	Length of treatment (weeks)	OCD symptom reduction[a]	No. of patients participating
Clomipramine (Clomipramine Collaborative Study Group, 1991)	Flexible dose design, Mean dose = 249 mg/day	10	40%	400
Fluoxetine (Tollefson, Birkett, Koran, & Genduso, 1994)	Fixed dose design; 20, 40, 60[b] mg/day	13	22–27%	355
Sertraline (Greist, 1995)	Fixed dose design; 50[b], 100, 200[b] mg/day	12	24–28%	324
Fluvoxamine (Rasmussen, et al., in press)	Flexible dose design; Mean dose = 249 mg/day	10	20%	300
Paroxetine (Wheadon, et al., 1995)	Fixed dose design; 20, 40[b], 60[b], mg/day	12	25–29%	263

[a]A mean reduction greater than 25–35% from baseline as measured by the Yale–Brown Obsessive–Compulsive Scale (YBOCS) is generally considered a "response" in patients with OCD (Goodman & Price, 1990).

[b]Best dose response.

The multicenter trials also provided evidence that the pharmacological treatment of OCD has additional distinct features from the pharmacotherapy of patients with depression and/or panic disorder. Considerable placebo response rates are often associated with the pharmacological treatment of patients with depression (30–40%) or panic disorder (40–50%). In contrast, relatively few OCD patients (8–20%) had a significant response to placebo administration during the multicenter trials. Even within an individual patient, OCD symptoms appear to have a differential and autonomous response pattern in comparison to depressive symptoms. Reductions in OCD symptoms rarely coincide with changes in depressive symptoms in patients with OCD. Moreover, depressed and nondepressed OCD patients have similar levels of response to pharmacotherapy.

There is also some suggestion from the multicenter trial data that the average effective dose of STI medication for OCD may be different than the average effective dose for antidepressant and antipanic effects. Because flexible dose designs were used in the clomipramine and fluvoxamine trials, the minimal effective dose cannot be determined.

A fixed-dose design was used during the fluoxetine, paroxetine, and sertraline trials. Statistically similar reductions in OCD symptoms were noted at each of the doses (20, 40, or 60 mg/day) during the fluoxetine trial. The high doses (40 and 60 mg/day) of paroxetine were associated with significant anti-OCD effects, whereas 20 mg/day of paroxetine was similar to placebo administration. However, the multicenter trials of fluoxetine and paroxetine revealed a statistical trend for the highest doses of each medication to be associated with greater OCD symptom reduction. The results of the sertraline multicenter trial are difficult to assess, because sertraline at doses of 50 and 150 mg/day were effective, but 100 mg/day of sertraline was not significantly different than placebo administration. As illustrated in Figure 13.1, the doses associated with the greatest improvement in OCD symptoms during the multicenter trials of clomipramine (226 mg/day), fluoxetine (60 mg/day), fluvoxamine (249 mg/day), sertraline (200 mg/day), and paroxetine (60 mg/day), respectively, are relatively high in comparison to those usually associated with efficacy in patients with depression or panic disorder.

Meta-Analysis: Comparative Efficacy of STIs

The multicenter OCD trials did not, however, address the issue of the relative efficacy or tolerability of STIs in the treatment of OCD. Several groups have combed data sets from the individual OCD trials and then statistically compared response rates (using meta-analysis) between the STIs in the treatment of OCD. Greist and colleagues' (1995b) meta-analysis of the data from the multicenter OCD trials revealed significantly greater improvement in OCD symptoms during clomipramine in comparison to fluoxetine, fluvoxamine, or sertraline treatment. Two other meta-analyses also supported the superiority of

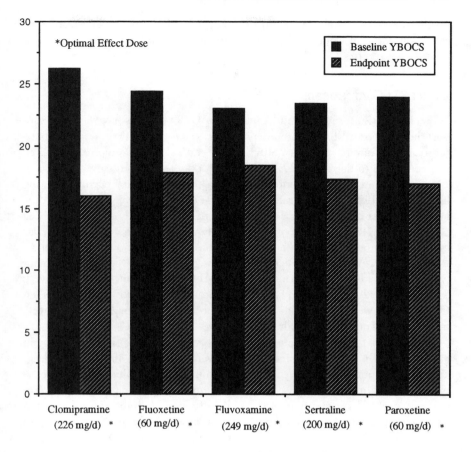

STI Medication

FIGURE 13.1. The total Yale–Brown Obsessive–Compulsive Scale (YBOCS) (mean score *y*-axis) at baseline and at the end of the study is depicted for each of the multicenter, placebo-controlled trials that were conducted separately with each STI. The mean daily dose of medication for flexible dose trials (clomipramine and fluvoxamine) or the optimal dose for fixed-dose studies (fluoxetine, sertraline, and paroxetine) is also included.

clomipramine over the SSRIs in placebo-controlled trials conducted in patients with OCD (Piccinelli, Pini, Bellantuono, & Wilkinson, 1995; Stein, Spadaccini, & Hollander, 1995). Although these results are intriguing, each of the investigators also acknowledged that methodological issues may have favored clomipramine in these statistical comparisons. For example, the SSRI trials, which were conducted after the clomipramine study, often included patients who had already failed previous trial(s) of clomipramine and/or SSRI treatment. The clomipramine trial included OCD patients more likely to be medication treatment–naive than the subsequent SSRI trials. Therefore, the clomipramine trial would be most likely to be associated with relatively robust treatment responses.

Direct STI Comparisons

Direct comparisons of STI antidepressants in OCD patients have failed to support the superiority of clomipramine over the SSRIs. In the first direct comparison of clomipramine versus an SSRI (Pigott et al., 1990), clomipramine (CMI) was compared to fluoxetine (FLX) in a small, double-blind crossover study ($n = 11$). Similar and significant improvement in OCD symptoms occurred during both CMI and FLX administration. More side effects, however, were noted during CMI than FLX treatment. In the second part of the study, a group of OCD patients ($n = 21$) who had responded favorably to CMI (mean duration of treatment, 14 months) were crossed over to FLX in a double-blind fashion. After 10 weeks of FLX, most of the patients (85%) were at a similar level of improvement to what they had achieved during chronic CMI treatment. Smeraldi, Erzegovesi, & Bianchi (1992) reported similar, and significant reductions in symptoms when OCD patients were treated with either CMI or fluvoxamine in another, relatively small ($n = 10$) comparative study.

Subsequent large-scale, multicenter trials have reported similar findings in patients with OCD. Fluvoxamine and CMI were associated with similar and significant reductions in OCD symptoms in double-blind, multicenter trials conducted in the United States ($n = 79$) and the United Kingdom ($n = 66$). More reports of postural hypotension, dry mouth, dizziness, tremor, and anorgasmia were noted in the CMI-treated group, whereas insomnia was endorsed more frequently by the fluvoxamine-treated group (Freeman, Trimble, Deakin, Stokes, & Ashford, 1994; Koran et al., 1996).

A double-blind comparison of sertraline versus CMI was conducted in 86 patients with OCD. Both medications were associated with significant antiobsessional effects. The sertraline-treated group had a statistically greater reduction in OCD symptoms in comparison to the fluvoxamine-treated group. Unfortunately, the mean dose of CMI during the study (90 mg/day) was well below the usual CMI dose recommended for OCD, whereas the mean dose of sertraline (125 mg/day) was within the range associated with antiobsessional effects (Bisserbee, 1995).

In the largest comparative trial reported, paroxetine was compared to CMI and placebo in 399 patients with OCD (Zohar & Judge, 1996). Response was defined a priori as a 25% or greater reduction from baseline as measured by the YBOCS. Both paroxetine and CMI were associated with significantly more patients meeting response criteria in comparison to placebo administration. There was evidence that paroxetine was associated with greater tolerability during the study, because significantly more adverse effects were noted during CMI in comparison to paroxetine or placebo administration.

The studies summarized in this section suggest that the STIs appear to have similar efficacy in the treatment of OCD, but that significant differences in tolerability and side-effect profiles may exist between CMI and the SSRIs.

Cross-Response

Clinical experience suggests that nonresponse to one STI does not preclude response to another STI in patients with OCD. Unfortunately, few studies have examined sequential response rates between the individual STI medications in patients with OCD; that is, if a patient with OCD fails to respond to CMI, what is the likelihood of a subsequent response to FLX and/or other SSRIs? Are OCD patients who respond to one SSRI likely to respond to other SSRIs? Information concerning "cross-response" within the STIs has considerable clinical relevance. Cross-response studies could provide valuable information concerning the optimal order of STI medication as well as the likelihood of response to subsequent STI medications in patients failing to respond to an initial STI trial. Without such available data, the most effective STI for an individual patient with OCD requires substantial trial and error.

Unfortunately, few studies have examined STI cross-response in patients with OCD. A retrospective analysis of cross-response between CMI and FLX was conducted in 81 patients with a primary diagnosis of OCD (Pigott, L'Heureux, & Murphy, 1993a). The response criterion was defined as a 25% or greater improvement in OCD symptoms (as measured by the YBOCS). Using this criterion, there was evidence of significant cross-response between CMI and FLX in the OCD patients. Responders to CMI had a 65% chance of responding to FLX, whereas 80% of FLX responders also responded to CMI treatment. However, OCD patients who failed to respond to CMI were unlikely (20% response) to improve with FLX (Pigott et al., 1993a). Previous nonresponse to FLX or CMI predicted poor response to subsequent fluvoxamine treatment in another group of OCD patients (Mattes, 1994). Although preliminary, studies of STI cross-response appear promising and suggest that further studies are indicated.

Augmentation Strategies

Combined treatment with an STI and a mood stabilizer may be indicated for a patient with OCD and bipolar disorder. Augmenting agents such as lithium carbonate or nonselective antidepressants may also be specifically beneficial in patients with OCD and mood disorders who experience breakthrough depressive symptoms during STI therapy (Hollander, DeCaria, Schneider, Liebowitz, & Klein, 1990; Pigott et al., 1991a). Adjuvant medication is also commonly prescribed in OCD patients to "augment" antiobsessive response in patients receiving ongoing medication treatment. The majority of reports concerning augmentation medication have employed an open rather than controlled study design. As will be discussed, most of the medications originally thought to be successful in enhancing response in OCD patients have not proven effective when tested under more rigorous conditions.

Lithium has been extensively investigated as a potential augmentation strategy in OCD patients. Despite promising case reports, controlled trials have failed to support the utility of lithium as an augmentation strategy in OCD patients. OCD patients receiving ongoing CMI or fluvoxamine treatment, respectively, did not experience further OCD symptom improvement when lithium was added in two separate double-blind, placebo-controlled studies (McDougle, Price, Goodman, Charney, & Heninger, 1991; Pigott et al., 1991a). There were substantial improvements noted in depressive symptoms after the addition of lithium in 6 of the 16 OCD patients during the CMI/lithium study (Pigott et al., 1991a). Thyroid hormone was also ineffective as an augmentation strategy in the CMI-treated patients with OCD (Pigott et al., 1991a).

Open-label studies suggested that buspirone is an effective augmentation agent when added to FLX (Jenike, Baer, & Buttolph, 1991; Markovitz, Stagno, & Calabrese, 1990) or sertraline (Menkes, 1995). Subsequent controlled trials, however, have not been successful. In fact, there was no difference between adding buspirone and adding placebo in patients receiving ongoing CMI (Pigott, L'Heureux, Hill, Bihari, Bernstein, & Murphy, 1992c), FLX (Grady et al., 1993), or fluvoxamine (McDougle et al., 1993) treatment, respectively, in separate controlled trials conducted in OCD patients.

Various medications that enhance 5-HT function have also been reported to be effective as augmentation agents in OCD. Case reports have suggested that the 5-HT releaser, fenfluramine (Hollander et al., 1990; Hollander & Liebowitz, 1988; Judd, Chua, Lynch, & Norman, 1991), and the 5-HT precursor, tryptophan (Rasmussen, 1984; Yaryura-Tobias & Bhagavan, 1977), are effective as augmentation agents in patients with OCD, although confirmation from controlled studies is lacking. In contrast, the 5-HT_2 antagonist ritanserin and the 5-HT_3 receptor antagonist ondansetron were both ineffective as augmentation agents when added to fluvoxamine in two separate trials conducted in OCD patients (Erzegovski, Rhonchi, & Smeraldi, 1992; Smeraldi, Erzegovesi, & Bianchi, 1992).

Blier and Bergeron (1996) sequentially administered 5-HT enhancing agents to 13 OCD patients who had failed to respond to STI therapy. Addition of the 5-HT_{1A} beta-adrenergic antagonist pindolol to an STI resulted in a rapid improvement in depressive symptoms, but no change in OCD symptoms. Addition of buspirone or the immediate precursor of 5-HT, 5-hyroxytryptophan, to the STI–pindolol regimen did not result in improvement of OCD symptoms. However, 4 weeks after the addition of the 5-HT precursor tryptophan to the STI–pindolol regimen, a significant improvement in OCD symptoms was noted in 7 of the patients who did not respond sufficiently to the previous strategies.

Case reports have suggested that clonazepam may be a useful augmentation strategy in patients with OCD (Leonard et al., 1994). A double-blind, placebo-controlled study of adjuvant clonazepam in fluoxetine- or CMI-treated OCD patients revealed some promising results. Significant reductions in anxiety symptoms, and perhaps OCD symptoms (one of the three OCD rating scales revealed improvement), occurred during the study (Pigott et al., 1992b). Although encouraging, further studies are required before clonazepam can be considered a reliable augmentation strategy for patients with OCD.

The most promising results for augmentation strategies have occurred when a neuroleptic has been added to ongoing STI therapy in OCD patients with comorbid tic disorder. Adjuvant haloperidol was added to fluvoxamine-treated OCD patients in a controlled study conducted by McDougle and colleagues (1994). Patients with OCD and tics, but not OCD alone, had significant improvement in OCD symptoms when haloperidol, but not placebo, was added to fluvoxamine during the study. The atypical neuroleptic risperidone (mean dose = 2.75 mg/day) was administered in an open-label fashion to 21 STI-refractory patients with OCD. Although 5 patients discontinued due to side effects, 14 of the 16 remaining patients exhibited significant improvement in OCD symptoms on the combined STI–risperidone regimen (Saxena, Wang, Bystritsky, & Baxter, 1996).

These results suggest that few augmentation agents purported to have efficacy in OCD are actually associated with further symptom reduction in most patients with OCD. There is evidence that neuroleptic augmentation represents a valuable strategy in OCD patients with a concomitant tic disorder. Preliminary but promising results also suggest that adjuvant clonazepam and an STI–pindolol–tryptophan combination regimen are worthy of further investigations.

PREDICTORS OF TREATMENT RESPONSE

The identification of reliable predictors of treatment response represents one of the most critical areas of investigation in OCD treatment. Several studies suggest that the type of OCD symptoms may impact on treatment response. The YBOCS Symptom Checklist is often used to assess the presence of various obsessions and compulsions in patients with OCD. Several investigators have administered the YBOCS Symptom Checklist to large samples of patients in an attempt to identify discrete subgroups of OCD patients (Baer & Jenike, 1992; Leckman, Grice, Boardman, & Zhang, 1996). The largest data set analyzed thus far (n = 306) identified four separate OCD symptom factors: obsessions and checking, symmetry and order, cleaning and washing, and hoarding. These four subtypes accounted for more than 60% of the symptoms endorsed by the OCD patient population studied (Leckman et al., 1996).

Symptom Content

Ball, Baer, and Otto (1996) recently reviewed 65 studies concerning the efficacy of behavioral interventions in patients with OCD. Most (75%) of the patients included in the behavioral therapy literature had primary cleaning and/or checking rituals. Relatively few (12%) of the patients exhibited counting, hoarding, or symmetry compulsions or multiple rituals.

These results suggest that response rates (70–80%) attributed to behavioral therapy are based upon a fairly small and homogeneous sample of OCD patients. Whether these robust response rates can be accurately extrapolated to OCD patients with other symptom constellations has not been systematically evaluated. Regardless, the presence of prominent cleaning and checking rituals suggests a good response to behavioral interventions in OCD. Poor predictors of response to behavioral therapy include the presence of (1) obsessions only, (2) severe depressive symptoms, (3) increased OCD symptom severity, and/or (4) overvalued ideation or psychotic features (Ball et al., 1996).

A young age of onset, longer illness duration, and the presence of compulsions have also been identified as poor predictors of response to CMI and/or FLX treatment in patients with OCD (Ackerman, Greenland, Bystritsky, Morgenstern, & Katz, 1994; DeVeaugh-Geiss, Katz, Landau, Goodman, & Rasmussen, 1990; Ravizza, Barzega, Bellino, Bogetto, & Maina, 1995). The presence of primary cleaning rituals and/or higher initial scores on the YBOCS was predictive of a poorer response during long-term (mean, 18.6 months) CMI treatment in a longitudinal study conducted in 45 patients with OCD (Alarcon, 1993).

Comorbid Disorders

OCD patients with prominent symmetry or hoarding symptoms appear to have an elevated rate of comorbid tic disorder (Baer, 1994; Leckman et al., 1993; Rasmussen & Eisen, 1993); the presence of comorbid tic disorder appears to be associated with a poor response to STI medication, unless neuroleptic augmentation is utilized (McDougle et al., 1994; Saxena et al., 1996). The presence of concomitant social phobia, particularly the generalized subtype, also appears to be associated with a poor response to STI therapy (Carrasco, Hollander, Schneier, & Liebowitz, 1992). In fact, patients with OCD and generalized social phobia may be more likely to respond to MAOIs, in comparison to STI therapy (Carrasco et al., 1992).

The impact of concomitant personality disorder(s) on treatment response in patients with OCD has been examined in several studies. The presence of schizotypal, borderline, or avoidant personality disorder, as well as an increased total number of personality disorders within a patient, suggested a subsequent poor response to CMI treatment in 55 patients with OCD (Baer & Jenike, 1992). Subsequent studies have also confirmed that concomitant schizotypal personality disorder is predictive of poor response to CMI or FLX treatment in OCD patients (Mundo, Erzegovesi, & Bellodi, 1995; Ravizza et al., 1995).

The absence of a concomitant personality disorder(s) in patients with OCD is predictive of a good response to behavioral therapy. OCD patients with histrionic or borderline personality disorder(s) who receive behavioral therapy are less likely to maintain treatment gains on a long-term basis (Fals-Stewart & Lucente, 1993). The presence of neurological soft signs and/or neuropsychological test abnormalities in patients with OCD does not predict diminished response to STI therapy in patients with OCD. In fact, soft signs present at baseline in a group of

OCD patients ($n = 21$) were noted to resolve after treatment with an STI medication (Thienemann & Koran, 1995). Although these results concerning predictors of treatment response are promising, further studies are clearly needed. The next section reviews the long-term pharmacological treatment of OCD.

LONG-TERM PHARMACOTHERAPY

Continuation and Maintenance Phase

Once the most effective medication is determined in a patient with OCD, a treatment duration of at least 9–12 months is generally recommended. The pharmacological treatment of patients with OCD can be divided into three phases: (1) acute treatment (the initial 4–6 months of STI therapy), (2) the continuation phase (the first 6–12 months of STI therapy), and (3) maintenance treatment (after the first 12 months of STI therapy). Data from the multicenter extension studies support the efficacy and safety of STI medications in patients with OCD during the acute and continuation phases of treatment. Fortunately, improvement in OCD symptoms appears to be sustained as long as the STI is continued (Greist, Jefferson, Koback, Katzelnick, & Serlin, 1995b; Jenike, 1992; Rasmussen, Eisen, & Pato, 1993; Steiner, Bushnell, Gergel, & Wheadon, 1995; Tollefson, Birkett, Koran, & Genduso, 1994; Wheadon & Gergel, 1995).

The optimal dose of STI medication during these respective phases has not been established. As previously discussed, there is ample suggestion that doses associated with optimal OCD symptom reduction during the acute treatment phase are relatively higher than those routinely used for STIs in the treatment of depression (see Figure 13.1). At least one report has suggested that OCD patients may also require relatively high doses of STI medication during the continuation-phase treatment (Wood, Tollefson, & Birkett, 1993). However, a second study (Mundo et al., 1995) investigated this issue under double-blind conditions. Thirty patients who had been stabilized on either CMI or fluvoxamine therapy (mean days of treatment: clomipramine, 180 days; fluvoxamine, 210 days) were randomly assigned to one of three groups: (1) control group (no dose reduction), (2) moderate reduction group (33–40% dose reduction), or (3) marked dose reduction (60–66% dose reduction). Interestingly, there were no significant differences in the cumultative proportion of patients in each group who met relapse criteria during the 102-day observation period during the study. This study provides strong evidence that lower dosages of STI medication may be effective in many patients with OCD during the continuation and, perhaps, maintenance phases of treatment.

Even fewer studies have addressed the issue of STI dosage during the maintenance phase of treatment for patients with OCD. There is some evidence that the dose of antiobsessional medication during maintenance treatment may be substantially less than the dose necessary for improvement in OCD symptoms during acute treatment (Pato, Hill, & Murphy, 1990). If significant dose reduction could be accomplished during the continuation and maintenance phases, significant progress by virtue of enhanced tolerability and/or compliance might result.

Medication Discontinuation and Relapse

The majority of patients with OCD who are treated with antiobsessive medication will rapidly relapse after the medication is discontinued. Two placebo-controlled studies have specifically assessed the rate of relapse in CMI-treated patients with OCD (Leonard et al., 1991; Pato, Zohar-Kadouch, Zohar, & Murphy, 1988). In both studies, most of the OCD patients relapsed within 4–8 weeks of CMI discontinuation. Multicenter extension trials also suggest that rapid relapse in OCD symptoms occurs when SSRI medications are discontinued and/or replaced with placebo even after long-term treatment (Steiner et al., 1995; Tollefson et al., 1994; Wheadon & Gergel, 1995).

Impact of Treatment on Prognosis

Data from several long-term studies conducted in adolescents with OCD suggest that vigorous treatment with medication and/or behavioral therapy is associated with substantial (50–60%) recovery rates and reduced symptom severity (Bolton, Luckie, & Steinberg, 1995; Tollefson et al., 1994). A 2-year follow-up of adult OCD patients treated with STI medication ($n = 85$) revealed that 87% had responded to treatment (Orloff et al., 1994).

TREATMENT-REFRACTORY OCD

Patients with OCD should not be considered "treatment resistant" unless they have failed to respond to separate trials ($\geq$ 10 weeks in duration and at the maximum tolerated dose) of CMI and at least three, if not four, of the SSRI antidepressants (FLX, fluvoxamine, sertraline, and/or paroxetine). Although earlier studies have demonstrated that failure to one STI predicted poor response to another (Mattes, 1994; Pigott et al., 1993a), further controlled trials are needed to investigate this important treatment issue.

Factors in Treatment Failure

A number of factors such as inaccurate diagnoses, presence of complicating, concurrent psychiatric disorders, and inadequate duration and/or dosage should be considered in any patient with OCD who appears resistant to standard pharmacotherapy. Treatment compliance and/or outcome expectations should also be considered in any patient who fails to respond to conventional treatment interventions. Appropriate explanation, easily understood instructions, availability of psychoeducational materials, and a sincere commitment to establishing a collaborative therapeutic relationship with patients can help to enhance a patients' compliance to recommended treatment regimens. Unreasonable expectations for treatment outcome can also contribute to poor treatment results. Some patients with OCD, and some clinicians, do not know, or cannot accept, that partial symptom reduction is the usual "response" in OCD. As a result, they can be erroneously designated "treatment failures," when they are in fact experiencing a level of symptom reduction that is "average."

Alternative Monotherapy

A number of medications have been suggested as alternatives for patients with OCD who fail to respond to STI medication(s). Monoamine oxidase inhibiting antidepressants (MAOIs) should be considered in OCD patients who fail to respond to standard pharmacotherapeutic interventions. Early case studies of the MAOI phenelzine reported improvement in OCD symptoms (Jain, Swinson, & Thomas, 1970; Jenike, Surnam, & Cassem, 1983); however, the MAOI clorgyline (Insel et al., 1983) was ineffective in reducing OCD symptoms. A more recent and controlled study revealed similar and significant reductions in OCD symptoms after phenelzine (75 mg/day) or CMI (225 mg/day) administration in 30 patients with OCD (Vallejo et al., 1992). In addition, open studies have suggested that MAOIs may be particularly beneficial in patients with OCD that have primary somatic and/or bowel obsessions. In addition, OCD patients with comorbid anxiety disorders such as social phobia or panic disorder may preferentially respond to MAOI rather than STI therapy (Carrasco et al., 1992; Jenike & Raush, 1994; Jenike et al., 1983).

There is some evidence that buspirone may be a promising alternative for treatment-refractory OCD patients. A double-blind, crossover comparison of buspirone (mean dose, 58 mg/day) versus CMI (mean dose, 225 mg/day) reported similar and significant reductions in OCD symptoms with both medications (Pato, Pigott, Hill, Grover, Bernstein, & Murphy, 1991). Because the duration of medication treatment during the crossover study was only 6 weeks and a subsequent open trial was negative (Jenike & Baer, 1988), further studies are necessary before buspirone's potential antiobsessive effects can be more fully assessed.

The benzodiazepine clonazepam has also been suggested to have some antiobsessive effects as a monotherapy. A controlled, crossover design study (Hewlett, Vinogradov, & Agras, 1992) compared clonazepam, diphenhydramine, CMI, and clonidine in patients with OCD. Clonazepam, diphenhydramine, and CMI, but not clonidine, were associated with significant reductions in OCD symptoms from baseline. Although these results suggests that clonazepam may have some efficacy in OCD, the control medication (diphenhydramine) was also associated with significant reductions in OCD symptoms during the study. Therefore, further studies are necessary before clonazepam's efficacy in OCD can be established.

Several agents have been reported to be effective in OCD in initial trials, but further trials and/or replication is currently unavailable. Venlafaxine, a potent combined 5-HT and noradrenergic-reuptake inhibitor, was effective in reducing symptoms in a placebo-controlled trial conducted in 30 patients with OCD (Yaryura-Tobias & Neziroglu, 1996). The second messenger precursor inositol was more effective than placebo in reducing OCD symptoms in a crossover study of 13 patients with OCD (Fux, Levine, Aviv, & Belmaker, 1996). A controlled study of CMI versus another phenylpiperazine, mCPP, revealed that both medications were associated with significant improvement in OCD symptoms. However, CMI was significantly more effective in reducing OCD symptoms than mCPP during the study (Pigott, L'Heureux, Bernstein, Grover, Dubbert, Hill, & Murphy, 1992b).

The phenylpiperazine antidepressant, trazodone, was ineffective in significantly reducing OCD symptoms in a controlled trial conducted in 18 patients with OCD. In fact, trazodone was no more effective than placebo during the study (Pigott et al., 1992d). A preliminary, open trial of another phenylpiperazine antidepressant, nefazodone, also failed to demonstrate significant antiobsessive effects in patients with OCD. These results suggest that monotherapy with an MAOI, buspirone, clonazepam, or perhaps venlafaxine, may represent reasonable choices for OCD patients failing to respond to STI medications.

Combined Pharmacotherapy

Combined CMI–SSRI or SSRI–SSRI regimens have been the focus of considerable interest recently. Despite apparent widespread clinical use, there have been few case reports of combined CMI and SSRI treatment for OCD. The CMI–fluoxetine combination has been reported to be effective in patients who had previously failed to respond to either drug administered as monotherapy (Browne, Horn, & Jones, 1993; Simeon, Thatte, & Wiggins, 1990). This combined strategy may also offer enhanced tolerability. For example, SSRI-induced psychomotor agitation and/or insomnia can sometimes be attenuated by the careful addition of a small dose of CMI.

The safety and tolerability of combined CMI–fluvoxamine (FLV) therapy was recently assessed in an open-label study. OCD patients receiving ongoing CMI treatment, but experiencing breakthrough depressive symptoms ($n = 22$), were augmented with FLV. The combination was well tolerated and associated with clinical improvement in most of the patients, although serum-CMI levels were markedly elevated (between 500 and 1,200 ng/ml) in 50% of the patients. The authors concluded that the combined CMI–FLV treatment was well tolerated in most patients, but recommend monitoring of plasma concentrations of CMI because elevated levels frequently occurred during coadministration of FLV (Szegedi, Wetzel, Leal, Hartter, & Hiemke, 1996).

Case reports have suggested various medication combinations for OCD patients who are treatment refractory. The addition of risperidone (Jacobsen, 1995; McDougle et al., 1995), valproate (Deltito, 1994), aminoglutethimide (Chouinard, Belanger, Beauclair, Sultan, & Murphy, 1996), bromocriptine (Ceccherini-Nelli & Guazzelli, 1994), and clonidine (Hollander et al., 1991b; Lipsedge & Prothero, 1987), respectively, to ongoing STI therapy have all been reported to "convert" treatment-refractory OCD patients to "responders" in various case reports. In the next section, "heroic strategies" will be discussed for patients with OCD who fail to respond to the previously mentioned treatment interventions.

Other Treatment Strategies

Intravenous (IV) CMI has been touted as an effective strategy for patients with OCD who have failed other treatment interventions. Koran, Faravelli, and Pallanti (1994) successfully treated five OCD patients with daily IV CMI infusions. Substantial improvements in OCD symptoms were noted after 2 weeks of IV CMI suggesting that the therapeutic effects of IV CMI occur twice as rapidly as those associated with oral CMI therapy. Despite scattered reports of the efficacy of electroconvulsive therapy (ECT) in treatment-refractory patients (Husain, Lewis, & Thornton, 1993; Maletzky, McFarland, & Burt, 1994), few OCD patients appear to respond favorably to ECT.

Neurosurgery

Several surgical procedures, including cingulotomy and anterior capsulotomy, have proven to be of significant benefit in patients with treatment-refractory OCD.

Several groups have reported long-term follow-up studies in OCD patients who received psychosurgery for intractable OCD. Baer and colleagues (1995) conducted an unblinded preoperative and follow-up assessment in 18 patients with OCD who underwent cingulotomy. At a mean follow-up of 26.8 months, 5 patients (28%) met conservative criteria for treatment responders, and 3 others (17%) were partial responders. The group improved significantly in mean functional status, and few serious adverse events were found. Improvement in OCD symptoms was strongly correlated with improvement in depressive and anxiety symptoms. A longitudinal study (mean follow-up = 10 years) of 26 patients with intractable OCD who received psychosurgery has also been reported (Hay et al., 1993). At follow-up, 38% of the patients were judged as moderately improved. In the remainder of the patients, 46% were felt to have no clinically relevant response, and 15% were judged to be worse. In patients who had significant responses, both obsessive and compulsive symptoms improved, and the change in OCD symptoms was independent of changes in anxiety and depression scores. No significant predictors of improvement were identified. Important adverse effects in the stereotactic surgery group ($n = 20$) were epilepsy (1 patient) and personality change (2 patients).

Neuropsychological performance has been evaluated in patients treated with psychosurgery. In the 10-year follow-up study previously reported (Hay et al., 1993), the psychosurgery-treated OCD patients performed relatively poorly on the Wisconsin Card Sorting Test but did not show any deterioration in Wechsler Intelligence and Memory scores. Comprehensive neuropsychological testing was completed in 17 OCD patients treated with psychosurgery and compared to control subjects in another study (Cummings, Hay, Lee, & Sachdev, 1995). The psychosurgery and control groups did not differ in intellectual or memory functioning, consistent with earlier findings that psychosurgery does not reduce global ability estimates. Similar to the previous study, the psychosurgery group performed more poorly than the control group on an adaptation of the Wisconsin Card Sorting Test during the Cummings et al. study.

Personality characteristics have also been assessed in patients ($n = 24$) before and after psychosurgery for incapacitating anxiety disorders (including OCD). Interestingly, there was no evidence of negative personality changes after surgery. In fact, significant normalization on the majority of the personality scales was detected, and significant symptomatic relief occurred in 80% of the cases. The changes on scales reflecting anxiety proneness were conspicuous in patients suffering from "pure" anxiety disorders, as compared with those suffering from OCD. In OCD patients, correlations were obtained between changes in brain metabolism studied with PET and changes in personality scores (Mindus & Nyman, 1991).

These results suggest that 25–30% of the patients who previously were unresponsive to medication and behavioral treatments are significantly improved after psychosurgery. Although psychosurgery should always be considered as a last resort, these studies suggest that complications are relatively rare, and that neuropsychological and personality functioning is not adversely effected by psychosurgery.

FUTURE RESEARCH

Critical areas for further research include (1) controlled, comparative trials of the individual STI medication with special attention to tolerability and "cross response" issues, (2) controlled studies of promising treatment alternatives for patients with OCD who fail STI therapy, and (3) further investigations to identify subtypes of OCD as well as additional, reliable predictors of treatment response.

REFERENCES

Ackerman, D., Greenland, S., Bystritsky, A., Morgenstern, H., & Katz, R. (1994). Predictors of treatment response in OCD: Multivariate analyses from a multicenter trial of clomipramine. *Journal of Clinical Psychopharmacology, 14*(4), 247–254.

Alarcon, R., Libb, J., & Spitler, D. (1993). A predictive study of OCD response to clomipramine. *Journal of Clinical Psychopharmacology, 13*, 210–213.

Altemus, M., Swedo, S., & Leonard, H. (1994). Changes in cerebrospinal fluid neurochemistry during treatment of obsessive–compulsive disorder with clomipramine. *Archives of General Psychiatry, 51*(10), 794–803.

Ananth, J., Pecknold, J., Van Den Steen, N., & Engelsman, F. (1981). Double-blind study of clomipramine and amitriptyline in obsessive neurosis. *Progress in Neuro-Psychopharmacology, 5*, 257–262.

Aylward, E. H., Harris, G. J., Hoehn-Saric, R., Barta, P. E., Machlin, S. R., & Pearlson,

G. D. (1996). Normal caudate nucleus in obsessive–compulsive disorder assessed by quantitative neuroimaging. *Archives of General Psychiatry, 53*(7), 577–584.

Baer, L. (1994). Factor analysis of symptom subtypes of obsessive–compulsive disorder and their relation to personality and tic disorders. *Journal of Clinical Psychiatry, 55*, 18–23.

Baer, L., & Jenike, M. (1992). Personality disorders in OCD. *Psychiatric Clinics of North America, 15*(4), 803–812.

Baer, L., Rauch, S. L., Ballantine, H. T. Jr., Martuza, R., Cosgrove, R., Cassem, E., Giriunas, I., Manzo, P. A., Dimino, C., & Jenike, M. A. (1995). Cingulotomy for intractable obsessive–compulsive disorder. Prospective long-term follow-up of 18 patients. *Archives of General Psychiatry, 52*(5), 384–392.

Ball, S. G., Baer, L., & Otto, M. W. (1996). Symptom subtypes of obsessive–compulsive disorder in behavioral treatment studies: A quantitative review. *Behaviour Research and Therapy, 34*(1), 47–51.

Barr, L., Goodman, W., Price, L., McDougle, C., & Charney, D. (1992). The serotonin hypothesis of obsessive–compulsive disorder: Implications of pharmacologic challenge studies. *Journal of Clinical Psychiatry, 53*(4), 17–28.

Baxter, L. (1992). Neuroimaging studies of obsessive–compulsive disorder. *Psychiatric Clinics of North America, 15*(4), 871–884.

Benfield, D., Harris, C., & Luscombe, D. (1980). Some psychopharmacological aspects of desmethylclomipramine. *Postgraduate Medicine, 56*(1), 13–18.

Benkelfat, C., Nordahl, T., Semple, W., King, C., Murphy, D., & Cohen, R. (1990). Local cerebral glucose metabolic activity in obsessive–compulsive disorder: Patients treated with clomipramine. *Archives of General Psychiatry, 47*, 840–848.

Bisserbee, C. (1995). *Sertraline versus clomipramine in OCD.* Paper presented at the American Psychiatric Association Annual Meeting, Miami, FL.

Blier, P., & Bergeron, R. (1996). Sequential administration of augmentation strategies in treatment-resistant obsessive–compulsive disorder: Preliminary findings. *International Journal of Clinical Psychopharmacology, 11*(1), 37–44.

Bolton, D., Luckie, M., & Steinberg, D. (1995). Long-term course of obsessive–compulsive disorder treated in adolescence. *Journal of American Academy of Child and Adolescent Psychiatry, 34*(11), 1441–1450.

Breiter, H. C., Rauch, S. L., Kwong, K. K., Baker, J. R., Weisskoff, R. M., Kennedy, D. N., Kendrick, A. D., Davis, T. L., Jiang, A., Cohen, M. S., Stern, C. E., Belliveau, J. W., Baer, L., O'Sullivan, R. L., Savage, C. R., Jenike, M. A., & Rosen, B. R. (1996). Functional magnetic resonance imaging of symptom provocation in obsessive–compulsive disorder. *Archives of General Psychiatry, 53*(7), 595–606.

Browne, M., Horn, E., & Jones, T. (1993). The benefits of clomipramine–fluoxetine combination in OCD. *Canadian Journal of Psychiatry, 38*, 242–243.

Carrasco, J., Hollander, E., Schneier, F., & Liebowitz, M. (1992). Treatment outcome of OCD with comorbid social phobia. *Journal of Clinical Psychiatry, 53*, 387–391.

Ceccherini-Nelli, A., & Guazzelli, M. (1994). Treatment of refractory OCD with the dopamine agonist bromocriptine. *Journal of Clinical Psychiatry, 55*(9), 415–416.

Charney, D., Woods, S., Goodman, W., & Heninger, G (1987a). Neurobiological mechanisms of panic anxiety: Biochemical and behavioral corelates of yohimbine-induced panic attacks. *American Journal of Psychiatry, 144*, 1030–1036.

Charney, D., Woods, S., Goodman, W., & Heninger, G (1987b). Serotonin function in anxiety. *Psychopharmacology, 92*, 14–24.

Chouinard, G., Belanger, M. C., Beauclair, L., Sultan, S., & Murphy, B. E. (1996). Potentiation of fluoxetine by aminoglutethimide, an adrenal steroid suppressant, in obsessive–compulsive disorder resistant to SSRIs: A case report. *Progress in Neuropsychophar-macology and Biological Psychiatry, 20*(6), 1067–1079.

Clomipramine Collaborative Study Group. (1991). Clomipramine in the treatment of patients with OCD. *Archives of General Psychiatry, 48,* 730–738.

Cumming, S., Hay, P., Lee, T., & Sachdev, P. (1995). Neuropsychological outcome from psychosurgery for obsessive–compulsive disorder. *Australian and New Zealand Journal of Psychiatry, 29*(2), 293–298.

Deltito, J. A. (1994). Valproate pretreatment for the difficult-to-treat patient with OCD [letter]. *Journal of Clinical Psychiatry, 55*(11), 500.

Demal, U., Lenz, G., Mayrhofer, A., Zapotoczky, H. G., & Zitterl, W. (1993). Obsessive–compulsive disorder and depression: A retrospective study on course and interaction. *Psychopathology, 26*(3–4), 145–150.

DeVane, C. (1992). Pharmacokinetics of the selective serotonin reuptake inhibitors. *Journal of Clinical Psychiatry, 53*(2), 13–20.

DeVeaugh-Geiss, J., Katz, R., Landau, P., Goodman, W., & Rasmussen, S. (1990). Clinical predictors of treatment response in OCD: Exploratory analyses from multicenter trials of clomipramine. *Psychopharmacology Bulletin, 26,* 54–59.

Erzegovski, S., Rhonchi, P., & Smeraldi, E. (1992). 5-HT$_2$ receptor and fluvoxamine effect in OCD. *Human Psychopharmacology, 7,* 287–289.

Fals-Stewart, W., & Lucente, S. (1993). An MCMI cluster typology of obsessive–compulsives: A measure of personality characteristics and its relationship to treatment participation, compliance and outcome in behavior therapy. *Journal of Psychiatric Research, 27*(2), 139–154.

Flament, M., Rapaport, J., Murphy, D., Lake, C., & Berg, C. (1987). Biochemical changes during clomipramine treatment of childhood obsessive–compulsive disorder. *Archives of General Psychiatry, 44,* 219–225.

Freeman, C., Trimble, M., Deakin, J., Stokes, T., & Ashford, J. (1994). Fluvoxamine versus clomipramine in the treatment of OCD: A multicenter, randomized, double-blind, parallel group comparison. *Journal of Clinical Psychiatry, 55,* 301–305.

Fux, M., Levine, J., Aviv, A., & Belmaker, R. H. (1996). Inositol treatment of obsessive–compulsive disorder. *American Journal of Psychiatry, 153*(9), 1219–1221.

Goodman, W., McDougle, C., Price, L., Barr, L., Hills, O. F., Capli, J. F., Charney, D. S., & Heninger, G. R. (1995). m-Chlorophenylpiperazine in patients with obsessive–compulsive disorder: Absence of symptom exacerbation. *Biological Psychiatry, 38*(3), 138–149.

Goodman, W., & Price, L. (1990). Rating scales for OCD. In M. Jenike, L. Baer, & W. Minichiello (Eds.), *Obsessive–compulsive disorders: Theory and management.* St. Louis: Mosby Year Book.

Grady, T. A., Pigott, T. A., L'Heureux, F., Hill, J. L., Bernstein, S. E., & Murphy, D. L. (1993). A double-blind study of adjuvant buspirone hydrochloride in fluoxetine-treated patients with OCD. *American Journal of Psychiatry, 150*(5), 819–821.

Greist, J., Chouinard, G., DuBoff, E., Halaris, A., Kim, S., Koran, L., Liebowitz, M., Lydiard, R., Rasmussen, S., White, K., et al. (1995). Double-blind parallel comparison of three dosages of sertraline and placebo in outpatients with obsessive–compulsive disorder. *Archives of General Psychiatry, 52*(4), 289–295.

Greist, J. H., Jefferson, J. W., Kobak, K. A., Chouinard, G., DuBoff, E., Halaris, A., Kim, S. W., Koran, L., Liebowtiz, M. R., & Lydiard, R. B. (1995a). A 1-year double-blind placebo-controlled fixed-dose study of sertraline in the treatment of obsessive–compulsive disorder. *International Journal of Clinical Psychopharmacology, 10*(2), 57–65.

Greist, J., Jefferson, J., Koback, K., Katzelnick, D., & Serlin, R. (1995b). Efficacy and tolerability of serotonin transport inhibitors in obsessive–compulsive disorder: A meta-analysis. *Archives of General Psychiatry, 52,* 53–60.

Gross-Isseroff, R., Kindler, S., Kottler, M., & Sassoon, Y. (1994). Pharmacological challenges. In E. Hollander, J. Zohar, D. Marazziti, & B. Olivier (Eds.), *Current insights in obsessive–compulsive disorder* (pp. 137–148). Chichester, UK: Wiley.

Hall, H., & Ogren, S. (1981). Effects of antidepressant drugs on different receptors in the rat brain. *European Journal of Pharmacology, 10*(70), 393–407.

Hay, P., Sachdev, P., Cumming, S., Smith, J. S., Lee, T., Kitchener, P., & Matheson, J. (1993). Treatment of obsessive–compulsive disorder by psychosurgery. *Acta Psychiatrica Scandinavica, 87*(3), 197–207.

Hewlett, W., Vinogradov, S., & Agras, W. (1992). Clomipramine, clonazepam, and clonidine treatment of OCD. *Journal of Clinical Psychopharmacology, 12,* 420–430.

Hoehn-Saric, R., & Benkelfat, C. (1994). Structural and functional brain imaging in OCD. In E. Hollander, J. Zohar, D. Marazziti, & B. Olivier (Eds.), *Current insights in obsessive–compulsive disorder* (pp. 183–211). Chicester, UK: Wiley

Hollander, E. A., DeCaria, C., Gully, R., Nitescu, A., Suckow, R. F., Gorman, J. M., Klein, D. F., & Liebowitz, M. E. (1991a). Effects of chronic fluoxetine treatment on behavioral and neuroendocrine responses to m-CPP in OCD. *Psychiatry Research, 36,* 1–17.

Hollander, E., DeCaria, C., Nitescu, A., Gorman, J., Klein, D., & Liebowitz, M. (1991b). Noradrenergic function in obsessive–compulsive disorder: Behavioral and neuroendocrine responses to clonidine and comparison to healthy controls. *Psychiatry Research, 137,* 161–177.

Hollander, E., DeCaria, C., Nitescu, A., Gully, R., Suckow, R., Cooper, T., Gorman, J., Klein, D., & Liebowitz, M. (1992). Serotonergic function in obsessive–compulsive disorder: Behavioral and neuroendocrine responses to oral m-CPP and fenfluramine in patients and healthy volunteers. *Archives of General Psychiatry, 49,* 21–28.

Hollander, E., DeCaria, C., Schneider, H. A., Liebowitz, M. R., & Klein, D. F. (1990). Fenfluramine augmentation of serotonin reuptake blockade antiobsessional treatment. *Journal of Clinical Psychiatry, 51,* 119–123.

Hollander, E., Fay, B., Cohen, R., Campeas, R., Gorman, J. M., & Liebowitz, M. R. (1988). Serotonergic and noradrenergic sensitivity in obsessive–compulsive disorder: Behavioral findings. *American Journal of Psychiatry, 145,* 1015–1018.

Hollander, E., & Liebowitz, M. (1988). Augmentation of antiobsessional treatment with fenfluramine. *American Journal of Psychiatry, 145,* 1314–1315.

Husain, M. M., Lewis, S. F., & Thornton, W. L. (1993). Maintenance ECT for refractory obsessive–compulsive disorder [letter]. *American Journal of Psychiatry, 150*(12), 1899–900.

Insel, T., Mueller, E., Alterman, I., Linnoila, M., & Murphy, D. (1985). Obsessive–compulsive disorder and serotonin: Is there a connection? *Biological Psychiatry, 20,* 1174–1188.

Insel, T., Moss, J., & Olivier, B. (1994). Animal models of OCD. In E. Hollander, J. Zohar, D. Marazziti, & B. Olivier (Eds.), Current insights in obsessive–compulsive disorder (pp. 117–135). Chicester, UK: Wiley.

Insel, T., Murphy, D., Cohen, R., Alterman, I., Kilts, C., & Linnolia, M., (1983). OCD: A double-blind trial of clomipramine and clorgyline. *Archives of General Psychiatry, 40,* 605–612.

Jacobsen, F. (1995). Risperidone for refractory OCD (case report). *Journal of Clinical Psychiatry, 56*(9), 423–429.

Jain, V., Swinson, R., & Thomas, J. (1970). Phenelzine in obsessional neurosis. *British Journal of Psychiatry, 117,* 237–238.

Jenike, M. (1992). Pharmacologic treatment of obsessive–compulsive disorder. *Psychiatric Clinics of North America, 15,* 895–919.

Jenike, M., & Baer, L. (1988). Buspirone in OCD: An open trial. *American Journal of Psychiatry, 145,* 1285–1286.

Jenike, M., Baer, L., & Buttolph, L. (1991). Buspirone augmentation of fluoxetine in patients with OCD. *Journal of Clinical Psychiatry, 1,* 13–14.

Jenike, M. A., Breiter, H. C., Baer, L., Kennedy, D. N., Savage, C. R., Olivares, M. J., O'Sullivan, R. L., Shera, D. M., Rauch, S. L., Keuthen, N., Rosen, B. R., Caviness, V. S., & Filipek, P. A. (1996). Cerebral structural abnormalities in obsessive–compulsive disorder. A quantitative morphometric magnetic resonance imaging study. *Archives of General Psychiatry, 53*(7), 625–632.

Jenike, M., & Raush, S. (1994). Managing the patient with treatment-resistant obsessive–compulsive disorder: Current strategies. *Journal of Clinical Psychiatry, 55,* 11–17.

Jenike, M., Surnam, O., & Cassem, N. (1983). Monoamine oxidase inhibitors in OCD. *Journal of Clinical Psychiatry, 44,* 131–132.

Judd, F., Chua, P., Lynch, C., & Norman, T. (1991). Fenfluramine augmentation of clomipramine treatment of OCD. *Australian and New Zealand Journal of Psychiatry, 25,* 412–414.

Kahn, R., Asnis, J., Wetzler, S., & von-Praag, H. M. (1988). Neuroendocrine evidence for serotonin receptor hypersensitivity in panic disorder. *Psychopharmacology, 96,* 360–364.

Kasvikis, Y., & Marks, I. (1988). Clomipramine in obsessive–compulsive ritualizers treated with exposure therapy: Relations between dose, plasma levels, outcome, and side effects. *Psychopharmacology, 95,* 113–118.

Koran, L., Faravelli, C., & Pallanti, S. (1994). Intravenous clomipramine for obsessive–compulsive disorder. *Journal of Clinical Psychopharmacology, 14*(3), 216–218.

Koran, L. M., McElroy, S. L., Davidson, J. R., Rasmussen, S. A., Hollander, E., & Jenike, M. A. (1996). Fluvoxamine versus clomipramine for obsessive–compulsive disorder: A double-blind comparison. *Journal of Clinical Psychopharmacology, 16*(2), 121–129.

Leckman, J., Grice, D., Boardman, J., & Zhang, H. (1996). A factor analysis study of OCD. *ACNP Abstracts,* 35th Annual Meeting, 216.

Leckman, J., Walker, D., Goodman, W., Rasmussen, S., Pauls, D., & Cohen, D. (1993). Just right perceptions associated with compulsive behavior in Tourette's syndrome and OCD. *First International OCD Conference Abstracts,* 82–84.

Leonard, H., Swedo, S., Lenane, M., Rettew, D., Cheslow, D., Hamburger, S., & Rapaport, J. (1991). A double-blind desipramine substitution during long-term clomipramine treatment in children and adolescents with obsessive–compulsive disorder. *Archives of General Psychiatry, 48,* 922–927.

Leonard, H., Topol, D., Bukstein, O., Hindmarsh, D., Allen, A., & Swedo, S. (1994). Clonazepam as an augmenting agent in the treatment of childhood-onset obssesive–compulsive disorder. *Journal of the American Academy of Child and Adolescent Psychiatry, 33*(6), 792–794.

Lesch, K., Hoh, A., Disselkamp-Tietze, J., Weissman, M., Osterheider, M., & Schulte, H. (1991). 5-Hyroxytryptamine$_{1A}$ receptor responsivity in obsessive–compulsive disorder: Comparison of patients and controls. *Archives of General Psychiatry, 48,* 540–547.

Lipsedge, M., & Prothero, W. (1987). Clonidine and clomipramine in OCD. *American Journal of Psychiatry, 144,* 965–966.

Lydiard, R., Ballenger, J., Ellinwood, E., Fossey, M. A., & Laraia, M. T. (1990). CSF monoamine metabolites in OCD. *143rd Annual American Psychiatric Association Meeting Abstracts.*

Maletzky, B., McFarland, B., & Burt, A. (1994). Refractory obsessive–compulsive disorder and ECT. *Convulsive Therapy, 10*(1), 34–42.

Marazziti, D., Lensi, P., Ravagli, S., Milanfranchi, S., Rotondo, A., Palego, L., Lucacchini, A., & Cassano, G. (1993). Peripheral CNS markers in OCD. *Proceedings of the First International OCD Conference*, 51.

Markovitz, P., Stagno, S., & Calabrese, J. (1990). Buspirone treatment of fluoxetine in OCD. *American Journal of Psychiatry, 147*, 798–800.

Mattes, J. (1994). Fluvoxamine in obsessive–compulsive nonresponders to clomipramine or fluoxetine. *American Journal of Psychiatry, 151*(10), 1524.

Mavissakalian, M., Jones, B., Olsen, S., & Perel, J. M. (1990). Clomipramine in obsessive–compulsive disorder: Clinical response and plasma level. *Journal of Clinical Psychopharmacology, 5*, 207–212.

McDougle, C. J., Fleischmann, R. L., Epperson, C. N., Wasylink, S., Leckman, J. F., & Price, L. H. (1995). Risperidone addition in fluvoxamine-refractory obsessive–compulsive disorder: Three cases. *Journal of Clinical Psychiatry, 56*(11), 526–528.

McDougle, C., Goodman, W., Leckman, J., Holzer, J., Barr, L., McCance-Katz, E., Heninger, G. (1993). Limited therapeutic effect of the addition of buspirone in fluvoxamine-refractory OCD. *American Journal of Psychiatry, 150*, 647–649.

McDougle, C., Goodman, W., Leckman, J., Lee, N., Heninger, G., Price, L. (1994). Haloperidol addition in fluvoxamine-refractory obsessive–compulsive disorder: A double-blind, placebo-controlled study in patients with and without tics. *Archives of General Psychiatry, 51*(4), 302–308.

McDougle, C., Price, L., Goodman, W., Charney, D., & Heninger, G. (1991). A controlled trial of lithium augmentation in fluvoxamine-refractory obsessive–compulsive disorder: Lack of efficacy. *Journal of Clinical Psychopharmacology, 11*, 175–184.

Menkes, D. B. (1995). Buspirone augmentation of sertraline [letter]. *British Journal of Psychiatry, 166*(6), 823–824.

Mindus, P., & Nyman, H. (1991). Normalization of personality characteristics in patients with incapacitating anxiety disorders after capsulotomy. *Acta Psychiatrica Scandinavica, 83*(4), 283–291.

Mundo, E., Erzegovesi, S., & Bellodi, L. (1995). Follow-up of obsessive–compulsive patients treated with proserotonergic agents [letter]. *Journal of Clinical Psychopharmacology, 15*(4), 288–289.

Norman, T., Apostolopoulos, M., Burrows, G., & Judd, F. (1994). Neuroendocrine responsis to single doses of buspirone in obsessive–compulsive disorder. *International Clinical Psychopharmacology, 9*(2), 89–94.

Orloff, L. M., Battle, M. A., Baer, L., Ivanjack, L., Pettit, A. R., Buttolph, M. L., & Jenike, M. A. (1994). Long-term follow-up of 85 patients with obsessive–compulsive disorder. *American Journal of Psychiatry, 151*(3), 441–442.

Pato, M. T., Hill, J. L., & Murphy, D. L. (1990). A clomipramine dosage reduction study in the course of long-term treatment of obsessive–compulsive disorder patients. *Psychopharmacology Bulletin, 26*(2), 211–214.

Pato, M. T., Pigott, T. A., Hill, J. L., Grover, G. N., Bernstein, S. E., & Murphy, D. L. (1991). Controlled comparison of buspirone and clomipramine in obsessive–compulsive disorder. *American Journal of Psychiatry, 148*, 127–129.

Pato, M. T., Zohar-Kadouch, R., Zohar, J., & Murphy, D. (1988). Return of symptoms after discontinuation of clomipramine in patients with obsessive–compulsive disorder. *American Journal of Psychiatry, 145*, 1521–1525.

Perani, D., Colombo, C., Bressi, S., Bonfanti, A., Grassi, F., Scarone, S., Bellodi, L., Smeraldi, E., & Fazio, F. (1995). [^{18}F]FDG PET study in obsessive–compulsive disorder. A clinical/metabolic correlation study after treatment. *British Journal of Psychiatry, 166*(2), 244–250.

Piccinelli, M., Pini, S., Bellantuono, C., & Wilkinson, G. (1995). Efficacy of drug treatment in obsessive–compulsive disorder: A meta-analytic review. *British Journal of Psychiatry, 166*(4), 424–443.

Pigott, T. A., L'Heureux, F., Bernstein, S. E., Grover, G. N., Dubbert, B., Hill, J. L., & Murphy, D. L. (1992a). A controlled comparison of clomipramine and m-chlorophenylpiperazine in patients with OCD. *NCDEU Annual Meeting Abstracts.*

Pigott, T., L'Heureux, F., Bernstein, S., Rubenstein, C., Dubbert, B., & Murphy, D. (1992b). A controlled trial of adjuvant clonazepam in clomipramine and fluoxetine treated patients with OCD. *Proceedings of the 145th Annual American Psychiatric Association Meeting, 144,* 82.

Pigott, T. A., L'Heureux, F., Hill, J. L., Bihari, K., Bernstein, S. E., & Murphy, D. L. (1992c). A double-blind study of adjuvant buspirone hydrochloride in clomipramine-treated OCD patients. *Journal of Clinical Psychopharmacology, 12,* 11–18.

Pigott, T. A., L'Heureux, F., Rubenstein, C. S., Bernstein, S. E., Hill, J. L., & Murphy, D. L. (1992d). A double-blind, placebo controlled study of trazodone in patients with obsessive–compulsive disorder. *Journal of Clinical Psychopharmacology, 12*(3), 156–162.

Pigott, T. A., L'Heureux, F., & Murphy, D. (1993a). Pharmacological approaches to treatment-resistant OCD patients. *First International OCD Conference Abstracts, Isle of Capri* (Italy), 123–125.

Pigott, T. A., Hill, J. L., Grady, T. A., L'Heureux, F., Bernstein, S. E., Rubenstein, C. S., & Murphy, D. L. (1993b). A comparison of the behavioral effects of oral vs intravenous m-CPP administration in OCD patients and a study of the effects of metergoline prior to iv m-CPP. *Biological Psychiatry, 33*(1), 3–14.

Pigott, T. A., L'Heureux, F., Dubbert, B., Bernstein, S., & Murphy, D. (1994). Obsessive–compulsive disorder: Comorbid conditions. *Journal of Clinical Psychiatry, 55*(10), 15–27.

Pigott, T. A., Pato, M. T., Bernstein, S. E., Grover, G. N., Hill, J. L., Tolliver, T. J., & Murphy, D. L. (1990). Controlled comparisons of clomipramine and fluoxetine in the treatment of obsessive–compulsive disorder. *Archives of General Psychiatry, 47,* 1543–1550.

Pigott, T. A., Pato, M. T., L'Heureux, F., Hill, J. L., Grover, G. N., Bernstein, S. E., & Murphy, D. L. (1991a). A controlled comparison of adjuvant lithium carbonate or thyroid hormone in clomipramine-treated OCD patients. *Journal of Clinical Psychopharmacology, 11*(4), 242–248.

Pigott, T. A., Zohar, J., Hill, J. L., Bernstein, S. E., Grover, G. N., Zohar-Kadouch, R. C., & Murphy, D. L. (1991b). Metergoline blocks the behavioral and neuroendocrine effects of orally administered m-CPP in patients with OCD. *Biological Psychiatry, 29,* 418–426.

Rasmussen, S. (1984). Lithium and tryptophan augmentation in clomipramine-resistant OCD. *American Journal of Psychiatry, 141,* 1283–1285.

Rasmussen, S., & Eisen, J. (1988). Clinical and epidemiologic findings of significance to neuropharmacologic trials in obsessive–compulsive disorder. *Psychopharmacology Bulletin, 24,* 466–470.

Rasmussen, S., & Eisen, J. (1990). Epidemiology and clinical features of OCD. In M. Jenike, L. Baer, & W. Minichiello (Eds.), *Obsessive–compulsive disorders: Theory and management* (pp. 10–27). St. Louis: Mosby Year Book.

Rasmussen, S., & Eisen, J. (1992). The epidemiology and clinical features of obsessive–compulsive disorder. *Psychiatric Clinics of North America, 15*(4), 743–758.

Rasmussen, S., & Eisen, J. (1993). Assessment of core features, conviction and psychosocial function in OCD. *Proceedings of the First International OCD Conference, Isle of Capri* (Italy), 32–33.

Rasmussen, S., Eisen, J., & Pato, M. (1993). Current issues in the pharmacologic management of obsessive–compulsive disorder. *Journal of Clinical Psychiatry, 54,* 4–9.

Rasmussen, S., Goodman, W., Greist, J., Jenike, M., & Kozak, M. (in press). Fluvoxamine in the treatment of OCD: A multi-center double-blind, placebo-controlled study in outpatients. *American Journal of Psychiatry.*

Ravizza, L., Barzega, G., Bellino, S., Bogetto, F., & Maina, G. (1995). Predictors of drug treatment response in obsessive–compulsive disorder. *Journal of Clinical Psychiatry, 56*(8), 368–373.

Ravizza, L., Maina, G., Rocca, P., & Bogetto, F. (1993). Biological and therapeutic aspects of OCD. *Proceedings of the First International OCD Conference, Isle of Capri* (Italy), 57–58.

Richelson, E. (1994). Pharmacology of antidepressants: Characteristics of the ideal drug. *Mayo Clinical Proceedings, 69,* 1069–1081.

Rubin, R., Ananth, J., J, V.-M., Trajmar, P., & Mena, I. (1995). Regional [133]xenon cerebral blood flow and cerebral [99mTc]HMPAO uptake in patients with obsessive compulsive disorder before and during treatment. *Biological Psychiatry, 38*(7), 429–437.

Rubin, R., Villanueva-Meyer, J., Ananth, J., Trajmar, P., & Mena, I. (1992). Regional xenon 133 cerebral blood flow and cerebral technetium [99mTc]HMPAO uptake in unmedicated patients with obsessive–compulsive disorder and matched normal control subjects. *Archives of General Psychiatry, 49,* 695–702.

Saxena, S., Wang, D., Bystritsky, A., & Baxter, L. R. Jr. (1996). Risperidone augmentation of SRI treatment for refractory obsessive–compulsive disorder. *Journal of Clinical Psychiatry, 57*(7), 303–306.

Schwartz, J. M., Stoessel, P. W., Baxter, L. R. Jr., Martin, K. M., & Phelps, M. E. (1996). Systematic changes in cerebral glucose metabolic rate after successful behavior modification treatment of obsessive–compulsive disorder. *Archives of General Psychiatry, 53*(2), 109–113.

Simeon, J., Thatte, S., & Wiggins, D. (1990). Treatment of adolescent OCD with a clomipramine–fluoxetine combination. *Psychopharmacology Bulletin, 26,* 285–290.

Smeraldi, E., Erzegovesi, S., & Bianchi, I. (1992). Fluvoxamine versus clomipramine treatment in OCD: A preliminary study. *New Trends in Experimental and Clinical Psychiatry, 8,* 63–65.

Stein, D., Spadaccini, E., & Hollander, E. (1995). Meta-analysis of pharmacotherapy trials for obsessive–compulsive disorder. *International Clinical Psychopharmacology, 10*(1), 11–18.

Steiner, M., Bushnell, W., Gergel, I., & Wheadon, D. (1995). Long-term treatment and prevention of relapse of OCD with paroxetine. *American Psychiatric Association Annual Meeting Abstracts.*

Stern, R., Marks, I., & Wright, J., (1980). Clomipramine: Plasma levels, side effects, and outcome in obsessive–compulsive neurosis. *Postgraduate Medical Journal, 56*(Suppl. 1), 134–139.

Swedo, S., Leonard, H., Kruesi, M., Rettew, D., Listwak, S., Berrettini, W., Stipetic, M., Hamburger, S., Gold, P., Potter, W., & Rappaport, J., (1992). Cerebrospinal fluid neurochemistry in children and adolescents with OCD. *Archives of General Psychiatry, 49,* 29–36.

Szegedi, A., Wetzel, H., Leal, M., Hartter, S., & Hiemke, C. (1996). Combination treatment with clomipramine and fluvoxamine: Drug monitoring, safety, and tolerability data. *Journal of Clinical Psychiatry, 57*(6), 257–264.

Thienemann, M., & Koran, L. M. (1995). Do soft signs predict treatment outcome in obsessive–compulsive disorder? *Journal of Neuropsychiatry and Clinical Neurosciences, 7*(2), 218–222.

Thoren, P., Asberg, M., & Bertelsson, L (1980a). Clomipramine treatment of OCD: II. Biochemical aspects. *Archives of General Psychiatry, 37,* 1289–1294.

Thoren, P., Asberg, M., Crohnholm, B., Jornestedt, L., & Trachman, L. (1980b). Clomipramine treatment of obsessive–compulsive disorder: I. A controlled clinical trial. *Archives of General Psychiatry, 37,* 1281–1285.

Tollefson, G., Birkett, M., Koran, L., & Genduso, L. (1994). Continuation treatment of OCD: Double-blind and open-label experience with fluoxetine. *Journal of Clinical Psychiatry, 55,* 69–78.

Vallejo, J., Olivares, J., Marcos, T., Bulbena, A., & Menchon, J. (1992). Clomipramine versus phenelzine in obsessive–compulsive disorder: A controlled clinical trial. *British Journal of Psychiatry, 161,* 665–670.

Vitiello, B., Shimon, H., Behar, D., Stoff, D., Bridger, W. H., & Friedman, E. (1991). Platelet imipramine binding and serotonin uptake in obsessive–compulsive patients. *Acta Psychiatrica Scandinavica, 84*(1), 29–32.

Volavka, J., Neziroglu, F., & Yaryura-Tobias, J. (1985). Clomipramine and imipramine in obsessive compulsive disorder. *Psychiatry Research, 14,* 85–93.

Weizman, A., Carmi, M., Hermesh, H., Shahar, A., Apter, A., Tyrano, S., & Rehavi, M. (1986). High affinity imipramine binding and serotonin uptake in platelets of eight adolescent and ten adult obsessive–compulsive disorder patients. *American Journal of Psychiatry, 143,* 335–339.

Wheadon, D., & Gergel, I. (1995). Long-term treatment with paroxetine of outpatients with OCD: An extension of the fixed dose study. Manuscript submitted for publication to *Journal of Clinical Psychiatry.*

Wood, A., Tollefson, G. D., & Birkett, M. (1993). Pharmacotherapy of obsessive compulsive disorder—experience with fluoxetine. *International Journal of Clinical Psychopharmacology, 8*(4), 301–306.

Yaryura-Tobias, J. A., & Neziroglu, F. A. (1996). Venlafaxine in obsessive–compulsive disorder [letter; comment]. *Archives of General Psychiatry, 53*(7), 653–654.

Yaryura-Tobias, J., & Bhagavan, H. (1977). L-Tryptophan in OCD. *American Journal of Psychiatry, 134,* 1298–1299.

Zohar, J., & Judge, R. (1996). Paroxetine versus clomipramine in the treatment of obsessive–compulsive disorder. OCD Paroxetine Study Investigators. *British Journal of Psychiatry, 169*(4), 468–474.

Zohar, J., Mueller, E. A., Insel, T. R., Zohar-Kadouch, R. C., & Murphy, D. L. (1987). Serotonergic responsivity in obsessive–compulsive disorder: Comparison of patients and healthy controls. *Archives of General Psychiatry, 44,* 946–951.

Zohar, J., Mueller, E. A., Insel, T. R., Zohar-Kadouch, R. C., & Murphy, D. L. (1988). Serotonergic responsivity in OCD: Effects of chronic clomipramine treatment. *American Journal of Psychiatry, 45,* 167–172.

Chapter 14

BIOLOGICAL TREATMENTS FOR OBSESSIVE–COMPULSIVE DISORDER
Clinical Applications

Michele T. Pato
Carlos N. Pato
Susan A. Gunn

Patients are usually stricken with obsessive–compulsive disorder (OCD) at a relatively young age, ranging from childhood through young adulthood, with a mean age of onset of 19.8 ± 9.6 years (Rasmussen & Eisen, 1991). Fewer than 15% of patients date the onset of their symptoms after age 35. Clinically, they present with many different types of obsessions and compulsions. When evaluating a patient for treatment, it is critical to elucidate the specific obsessions and compulsions with which a patient presents. The Symptom Checklist of the Yale–Brown Obsessive–Compulsive Scale (YBOCS) is one of the most clinically useful methods for assessing OCD (Goodman et al., 1989). Given the secretive nature and sense of embarrassment that many patients feel about their symptoms, the process of divulging these symptoms to the clinician is a critical step in building rapport with the patient. It is this rapport that often becomes the foundation for patient compliance with treatment. Designing individualized treatment by identifying the patient's specific symptoms is important in creating a plan that has a high likelihood of success. In the case of behavioral therapy in particular, the challenges and hierarchies developed must be specifically related to the symptoms present.

Obsessions are usually described as unwanted, recurrent, intrusive ideas. They are often disturbing thoughts or impulses that the patient cannot dismiss. Compulsions are behaviors that most of the time are repetitive and can be actual observable behaviors, but may also be mental rituals, such as a compulsion to go through a particular mental exercise. The compulsive behaviors are often found to reduce the anxiety engendered by obsessions. Many people may normally perform certain behaviors in a ritualistic way: repeating, checking or washing things over and over out of habit or concern. What makes OCD a clinically significant psychiatric disorder is that the experience of obsessions, and performance of rituals, reaches such an intensity or frequency that it causes significant psychological distress or interferes in a significant way with psychosocial functioning. The guideline of at least 1 hour of symptoms per day (American Psychiatric Association, 1994; Goodman et al., 1989) is a good starting point as a measure for "significant interference." However, patients may avoid situations that bring on rituals. In these cases, the actual symptoms may not take an hour, yet the impact of having to avoid objects or situations would surely be defined as interfering. We often give the example of a single mother of three who lives on welfare and throws out over $100 per week of groceries because of contamination fears. This is a major disturbance of socioeconomic functioning, yet one may be hard-pressed to demonstrate that it takes 1 hour per day to do this.

Many clinicians have been taught that the ability of patients to maintain insight into the irrational and senseless nature of their symptoms is the key to distinguishing the OCD patient from those suffering from psychotic disorders with similar presentation. However, as more and more patients have been carefully followed longitudinally, it has become apparent that patients can exhibit a full range of insight about their symptoms from complete awareness (excellent insight) to delusional insight (poor insight) (Eisen & Rasmussen, 1993; Foa & Kozak, 1995; Insel & Akiskal, 1986; Kozak & Foa, 1994; Lelliot, Noshirvani, Basoglu, Marks, & Monteiro, 1988). Therefore DSM-IV, unlike previous versions, includes a new specifier for OCD: OCD with poor insight (American Psychiatric Association, 1994). Insight or the presence of psychotic symptoms may have some bearing on treatment choice and outcome (Foa, 1979). Patients with poor insight that reaches psychotic proportions can have comorbid schizoid or schizotypal personality disorder or schizophrenia, and tend to be more treatment resistant. The addition of an antipsychotic medication may be appropriate in these psychotic or delusional patients (Eisen & Rasmussen, 1993; McDougle et al., 1990).

The design of an individually tailored treatment plan begins with a careful assessment of the clinical presentation. A typical pattern for obsessions and compulsions starts with obsessions causing a mounting sense of anxiety or concern that can only be reduced by either performing a compulsion or avoiding the situation that brings on the obsessional thinking. For example, obsessional fear of dirt, germs, or contaminants often leads to excessive washing of hands or sanitizing of objects, or refusal to touch anything that might be contaminated. The DSM-IV field trials found the most common obsessions to be of contamination and fear of harming oneself or others. The most common compulsions were checking and cleaning/washing (Foa & Kozak, 1995). Obsessions without compulsions is a rare presentation. Patients who appear to have only obsessions may actually have subtle compulsions such as repeated asking for reassurance that they did something correctly, or that something did or did not happen. The occurrence of compulsions without obsessions also appears to be quite rare, but it has been noted in young children ages 6–8 (Swedo, Rapoport, Leonard, Lenane, & Cheslow, 1989a).

The patient's clinical history often can be characterized by a progressive worsening of symptoms. For instance, patients may describe a fear that harm will come to themselves or others by contact with a feared contaminant. In the case of one 33-year-old mother of a 5-year-old, this led to keeping her son inside if she saw a Chemlawn truck on the street because of fear that he might somehow become contaminated. As her symptoms progressed, she would not buy groceries except in an organic supermarket because of fear of chemical contaminants. She even stopped cooking completely for her family, forcing them to go for meals to relatives because of her fear that she could not prepare food without contaminating it.

Patients with pathological doubt are often concerned that, as a result of their carelessness, harm will come to themselves or someone else. This can be described as a "sense of overresponsibility." Patients with symptoms such as these often tend to "catastrophize"; they are focused on the worst possible outcome, no matter how unlikely. Often, OCD patients presenting in this manner find it difficult to take medications or engage in behavioral treatment. Not only is it hard for them to take risks or feel out of control, but they are also convinced that they will experience every side effect, no matter how rare. Pathological doubt may lead to compulsive avoidance to the point of being house bound. This presentation may superficially resemble severe agoraphobia. Careful history will usually reveal that obsessions, rather than a fear of experiencing panic attacks or feared physical symptoms, lead to the avoidance.

Pathological doubt can also appear with aggressive obsessions or a fear of doing violent harm to others. This can range from an adoring aunt refusing to baby-sit her nieces and nephews, fearing that she might take a knife and stab them while they are sleeping, to a man in his 40s who could not take the subway to work because he feared he would push someone off the platform into the path of an oncoming train. No amount of reassurance that they were not violent people by nature could convince these patients they would not do harm.

The clinical approach to each patient must also consider somatic obsessions, such as worries that one will contract or has contracted an illness or disease. Common somatic obsessions include a fear of cancer, venereal disease, or AIDS (Jenike & Pato, 1986). Checking compulsions consisting of checking and rechecking the body part of concern, as well as reassurance seeking, are commonly associated with this fear. The presentation of patients with the somatic obsessions of hypochondriasis have several distinguishing features. Patients with OCD usually have a history of other, classic OCD obsessions. They are more likely to engage in classic OCD compulsions, such as checking and reassurance seeking and, unlike patients with hypochondriasis, are less likely to experience actual somatic symptoms of illness; instead, they simply worry that they might have the symptoms.

INITIATING TREATMENT

The key features of OCD, as already discussed, include obsessional doubt, the need to feel in control, and risk aversion, and these features have significant impact on the successful application of both pharmacological and behavioral treatments. Obsessional doubt and risk aversion are often initial barriers to treatment. The clinician may find that the patient does not believe that the treatment will do any good, and is not willing to deal with the risk of side effects or the anxiety that behavioral treatment will evoke. The clinician must take extra time to explain the benefits of treatment so that the potential benefits appear to be worth the perceived risks.

OCD sufferers' cognitive misperceptions may leave them convinced that they will experience each and every side effect to the most severe degree. This cognitive distortion may cause patients to experience everything in extremes. The clinician must take extra time to "inform without alarm," discussing side effects thoroughly and not simply dismissing the patient's irrational concerns and providing a corrective cognitive experience. Giving accurate data on side effects also includes correcting cognitive distortions. It is important to identify for the patient that the OCD and fear of risk is contributing to his/her concern about medications and that although there are many side effects, especially with clomipramine, not every side effect will be experienced, and it is unlikely that the intensity of the side effects will be unbearable.

The fear of losing control can also manifest itself throughout treatment. Helping patients set up their own treatment goals can help them feel in control of the pace and rate at which they move forward. Given the 6- to 10-week time lag that is usually required before a treatment response from pharmacological agents in OCD, the issue of control is less prominent with medication use because the lag is "built in." But an understanding and expectation of the lag in response helps patients through the waiting period. Otherwise, doubt can begin to affect the treatment as the patient becomes frustrated with no response in the face of significant side effects. This is why preparation of the patient in the early stages of treatment for what to anticipate over the course of treatment is very helpful in maintaining treatment compliance. When insight is poor, as in more delusional OCD, or when severe anxiety is a comorbid symptom, the patient may be unable or unwilling to engage in behavioral treatment. In these cases, it may be better to start with medication and get some initial reduction in symptoms or improvement in insight before engaging in behavioral treatment.

PHARMACOLOGICAL TREATMENTS: GENERAL CONSIDERATIONS

Assessment

The most widely used measure in treatment outcome studies is the YBOCS (Goodman et al., 1989). Unlike instruments that preceded it, this rating scale measures severity rather than simply types of symptoms. The 10 questions of the YBOCS are divided into two parallel subscales, one for obsessions and one for compulsions, each with a potential score of 20 and an overall total score of 40.

Patients scoring at least 16–18 are considered ill enough to require treatment, and those who score over 30 are considered severely ill (Pato, Eisen, & Pato, 1994). In terms of treatment outcome, a 25–35% reduction represents significant improvement in symptoms (Goodman, McDougle, Barr, Aronson, & Price, 1993).

It can also be helpful to use the YBOCS in everyday clinical practice as a measure of symptom improvement and, as such, a justification for remaining on a given medication or switching to an alternative. The key to obtaining a valid measure of severity of symptoms with the YBOCS is to obtain a careful history of the patient's specific symptoms, both obsessions and compulsions. The Patient Version of the Yale–Brown Symptom Checklist can actually be given to the patient to complete. It contains a list of symptoms with easy-to-understand explanations of each symptom. Once the checklist is obtained, a severity measure—the YBOCS—can be administered to establish a baseline symptom severity. The YBOCS can be repeated at strategic points (e.g., after 10 weeks of adequate treatment) to quantify symptom improvement or to make a decision about increasing dose or adding an augmenting agent. After another 8–10 weeks at an increased dose or following augmentation, the YBOCS should again be repeated in order to establish whether the change actually made a difference. Continuing an augmenting agent, if it had no effect on OCD symptoms, is probably not worthwhile unless it improved some ancillary symptoms such as panic attacks, general anxiety, or psychosis.

From a practical point of view, in patients who endorse many symptoms, it is not always easy to check on the progress of each symptom at every appointment. Thus, once the checklist is completed, it may be helpful for the clinician to identify a few key symptoms that will be tracked or monitored at each visit, as the benchmarks of the patient's illness. These symptoms are discussed with the patient at every visit as a concrete measure of improvement, irrespective of whether the full checklist is administered. For example, one patient in her early 60s had multiple checking rituals, including checking the well on her property many times per day from her kitchen window to make sure the cover was on, and adding up the numbers on license plates as she drove. These two symptoms were among the myriad checking and contamination obsessions and compulsions that this woman performed on a daily basis. In addition to any other specific symptoms or medication side effects, we discussed at each visit the "well checking" and the "license plate adding," both in terms of *frequency* and *intensity* of the urge to perform them, as the two benchmarks of her illness. Not only did this provide the clinician with a quick check on the patient's symptoms, but it also gave the patient a quick way to assess her improvement. The latter is often important for patients with OCD, who can often get lost in the details of their symptoms.

Medication Administration

The serotonin reuptake inhibitors (SRIs), or serotonin transport inhibitors (STIs), have been found to be the first line of pharmacological treatment of OCD.

These agents include fluvoxamine, sertraline, fluoxetine, paroxetine, and clomipramine. All are currently available in the United States and Canada, and all have OCD among their indications. Clomipramine (Anafranil) was the first agent to receive Food and Drug Administration (FDA) approval for the treatment of OCD, and thus was the first to have large, multicenter placebo control data available (Clomipramine Collaborative Study Group, 1991). Other agents have followed with similar placebo-controlled multicenter studies: fluoxetine (Prozac) (Tollefson, Birkett, Koran, & Genduso, 1994a; Tollefson, Rampey, et al., 1994b; Wood, Tollefson, & Birkett, 1993), sertraline (Zoloft) (Greist, Chouinard, Duboff, et al., 1995a; Greist, Jefferson, Kobak, Katzelnick, & Serlin, 1995b), paroxetine (Paxil) (Wheadon, Bushnell, & Steiner, 1993; Zohar, Judge, & OCD Paroxetine Study Investigators, 1996), and fluvoxamine (Luvox) (Greist et al., 1995b; Greist, Jenike, Robinson, & Rasmussen, 1995c; Koran et al., 1996; see Chapter 13 of this volume for details).

Ideally, the clinician should choose a pharmacological agent to treat OCD based on comparative efficacy of the different serotonin reuptake inhibiting agents available. However, only few studies of relative efficacy exist, and differences in side-effect profiles may actually be more relevant in the choice of a particular patient's treatment. The overall effect size seen with clomipramine has been consistently higher than with the selective serotonin reuptake inhibitors (SSRIs)—fluoxetine, sertraline, and fluvoxamine—though all have shown good efficacy compared to placebo in treating OCD (Freeman, Trimble, Deakin, Stokes & Ashford, 1994; Jefferson & Greist, 1996; Koran et al., 1996; Pigott, 1996; Zohar et al., 1996).

Clomipramine clearly has more problematic side effects than any of the SSRIs, and the great majority of patients (80–90%) on clomipramine experience some side effects (Freeman et al., 1994; Greist et al., 1995b; Jenike, Baer, & Greist, 1990a; Koran et al., 1996; Pigott et al., 1990; Tollefson et al., 1994a, 1994b; Wheadon et al., 1993; Wood et al., 1993). However, such findings must be viewed in the context of each individual patient, since it is not always easy to measure the severity or significance of side effects. For instance, is "mild impotence" less of a problem than a very dry mouth? It would have to depend on the patient's interpretation of these symptoms. Comparative dropout rates, rather than number or intensity of side effects, may be a good indirect measure of the tolerability of the medication. The results in this regard have been mixed but interesting. In comparative studies between fluvoxamine and clomipramine (Freeman et al., 1994; Koran et al., 1996), dropout rates were virtually identical with both medications, around 15%. However, in the meta-analysis conducted by Greist et al. (1995b), they note that analysis of the pooled multicenter studies revealed the lowest rates of dropout in the clomipramine group at 12%, followed by fluoxetine at 23%, fluvoxamine at 24%, and sertraline at 27%. Again, however, one must consider that at the time that the clomipramine multicenter trials were conducted, there was no FDA-approved medication for the treatment of OCD in the United States, so patients had little choice but to stay on clomipramine. In addition, it has been our clinical experience that, in general, OCD patients often tolerate very significant and bothersome side effects. For instance, it is not uncommon to detect in patients' speech the presence of dry mouth as they try to articulate, but when we ask patients if this dry mouth presents a problem to them, they often answer no—they just drink more water.

Choice of Medication

Does success or failure of one pharmacological agent predict response to another agent from the same class? Cross-responsivity is the probability of patients responding to a second antiobsessional agent if they have already responded to another antiobsessional agent. It can also be viewed as whether patients will respond to a second or third agent if they have failed to respond to previous agents. The little data that is available are hopeful. In a multicenter trial of fluvoxamine (Griest et al., 1995b), 19% of patients who had failed previous trials with clomipramine or fluoxetine responded to fluvoxamine. In an analysis of a small trial comparing fluoxetine and clomipramine, Pigott (1996) noted that only 65% of patients who responded to clomipramine also responded to fluoxetine, whereas 80% of patients who responded to fluoxetine also responded to clomipramine. However, patients who had not responded to clomipramine had only a 20% chance of responding to fluoxetine. Thus, clinically, if an initial agent is unsuccessful, it is reasonable to pursue a trial with other agents. Moreover, if patients have had a positive response to clomipramine, they have a good chance of being responsive to other agents (see case examples, below).

Dosing of Medication

Most of the initial studies of efficacy of the antiobsessional medications were done as maximum-dose studies. Such a design required researchers to go to the maximum tolerated dose, which, in the case of clomipramine, was 250 mg (doses higher than this significantly increase the risk of seizure (DeVeaugh-Geiss, Landau, & Katz, 1989), fluvoxamine 300 mg, fluoxetine 80 mg, sertraline 200 mg, and paroxetine 60 mg. This strategy was used because, in a study of treatment efficacy, it is important to give maximum doses so that negative findings cannot be viewed as being due to inadequate dosing. However, more recently, there have been some studies that have explored the "proper" dose of medication with which to treat a patient. Most of these studies have been done in the form of fixed-dose trials. However, not every medication has been systematically studied in this way. To date, fixed-dose studies are only available for fluoxetine (Tollefson et al. 1994a, 1994b; Wood et al., 1993), sertraline (Greist et al., 1995b) and paroxetine (Wheadon et al., 1993). It is the fluoxetine fixed-dose studies that provide the most valuable information on dosing (Tollefson et al., 1994a, 1994b;

Wood et al., 1993). The studies initially involved doses of 20 mg, 40 mg, and 60 mg, and in the extension phase, patients could go up to 80 mg. In the initial 13-week trial, 20 mg, 40 mg, and 60 mg were all effective, with some tendency for 60 mg to be more effective. However, in the 6-month extension phase, subjects were allowed to stay at the same dose or increase their dose. In both groups of those patients who increased the dose or stayed on the same dose for longer, many experienced further improvement (Levine, Hoffman, Knepple, & Kenin, 1989; Tollefson et al., 1994a). Many of those who chose to increase their dose of medication improved further on the higher dose. Thus, it seems reasonable to recommend upward titration as well as longer duration of treatment to improve treatment efficacy.

Different and somewhat more problematic results were noted in the paroxetine and sertraline studies. In the paroxetine study, doses of 20 mg, 40 mg, and 60 mg were all compared to placebo, and only 40 mg and 60 mg were found significantly superior to placebo (Wheadon et al., 1993). In the sertraline study, 50 mg, 100 mg, and 200 mg were used, and only 50 mg and 200 mg were found superior to placebo on the YBOCS (Greist et al., 1995b; see sertraline, below, for more discussion).

Thus, while there is no perfect dose of medication for treatment with any of these agents, the clinician would be wise to give a trial at maximum dosing for 4–7 weeks if lower dosing for 5–9 weeks has not been effective (March, Frances, Carpenter, & Kahn, 1997). As always, there is some justification for keeping the dose at a minimum, since this is likely to minimize side effects (Jefferson & Greist, 1996) as well as cost. At least one study by Pato, Hill, and Murphy (1990) also showed that once patients had responded to clomipramine for an extended period of time (12–18 months), their dose of clomipramine could be dropped about 100 mg, and they could maintain similar therapeutic efficacy with fewer side effects.

Practical Considerations of Metabolism

Much has been written about the effects of these antiobsessional medications, especially the SSRIs, on inhibiting liver enzymes of the cytochrome P-450 system, which are involved in the metabolism of many other medications, including the antiobsessional medications themselves. For an excellent and detailed review of the intricacies of this metabolism, the interested reader is referred to Devane (1994). As a general rule, fluoxetine's long half-life (see section on fluoxetine) and strong inhibition of the 2D6 enzyme can present particular problems with elevated blood levels of a variety of coadministered drugs, including various tricyclics (such as clomipramine), carbamazepine, phenytoin, and trazodone. Fluvoxamine, on the other hand, is unique among the SSRIs in that it is the only one of the four agents that causes strong inhibition of the 1A2 enzyme. This enzyme is important in the metabolism of clozapine. Some creative clinicians have used this inhibition as a way of cutting cost by decreasing the oral dose of clozapine needed to get an effective serum level. However, one should be cautious about clozapine serum levels becoming toxic when clozapine and fluvoxamine are coadministered.

Duration and Discontinuation

Clinical recommendations for duration of treatment differ significantly from the 2–4 weeks recommended in depression. Although some effects may be seen as early as 4 weeks (Greist et al., 1995a; Greist et al., 1995b), an adequate duration is generally considered to be longer (Rasmussen, Eisen, & Pato, 1993). Most OCD patients do not begin to respond until 4–6 weeks, and a full 10-week trial at adequate dosage is needed before a trial can be deemed as adequate (Goodman et al., 1989; Greist et al., 1995a; Greist et al., 1995b; Greist et al., 1995c; Jefferson & Greist, 1996; Jenike, et al., 1990b; March et al., 1997; Rasmussen et al., 1993; Koran et al., 1996).

Recent results of the consensus report (March et al., 1997) recommend at least 4–7 weeks at maximal dosage, with at least 4–8 weeks prior to that at less than maximal dosage before a trial with any one agent is considered adequate. Thus, an adequate trial with any one medication, first at a lower dose and then at the highest maximal dose, could run 15 weeks or more. This long lag before therapeutic response must enter into any consideration of patient compliance with treatment. The typical patient with OCD has suffered with symptoms for many years. Because of this, patients are often willing to endure this long treatment trial if it is part of the treatment plan and the patient's expectations are appropriate from the start of the trial.

Although there are only rare reports of loss of efficacy, the issue of how long to maintain treatment before a trial off medication has not been well explored. Unfortunately, the only data that exist in this area come from three rather small blinded discontinuation studies. All were done with clomipramine, one in adults (Pato, Zohar-Kadouch, Zohar, & Murphy, 1988) and two in children (Leonard et al., 1989, 1991). In each case, the majority of the patients (upwards of 90%) had their symptoms return within 4–7 weeks of discontinuing medication. In the adult study, placebo was substituted, whereas in the child studies, desipramine was substituted, yet results were similar. Recently, large, blinded, multicenter trials of discontinuation of fluoxetine and sertraline have been completed, but results are not yet available. Perhaps in part based on these discontinuation findings, the consensus report (March et al., 1997) suggested that clinicians in general recommend 1 year or more of treatment with medication alone before a trial off medication, and that, in addition, the withdrawal should be slow. Slow was defined as a 25% reduction in dosage every 2 months. Even when cognitive-behavioral treatment is combined with medication, the consensus clinicians still preferred 1 year of treatment prior to discontinuation. Finally, it was recommended that in patients with mild to moderate symptoms, only three to four relapses be tolerated before prescribing maintenance medication, and that in severally ill patients, only two to four relapses be tolerated before prescribing maintenance medication.

Resistance to Treatment and Augmentation Strategies

There are some data on the characteristics of patients who are more resistant to treatment or poor treatment responders, but more work is needed in this area. For instance, patients with schizotypal personality disorder, borderline personality disorder, avoidant personality disorder, and obsessive–compulsive personality disorder have shown poor response to pharmacotherapy in some studies (Jenike, 1993; Jenike, Baer, Minichiello, Schwartz, & Carey, 1986; Riccardi et al., 1992). More recently Black, Monahan, Clancy, Baker, and Gabel (1997) have reported that hoarding behavior was a predictor of poor treatment response, as indicated by regression analysis.

However, before giving a patient the label of treatment resistant, it is important to establish that an adequate dosage and duration of each medication has been tried. And, in light of the data on cross-responsivity, all five available antiobsessional medications, particularly clomipramine, should be given adequate trials. If adequate doses of primary medications have been given, the clinician should consider augmenting agents as well, especially in cases of partial response to monotherapy (Goodman et al., 1993; Jenike, 1993; Jenike et al., 1986).

The use of an augmenting agent should be considered, but it has been suggested that such agents only be considered if there has been a partial response elicited from the primary antiobsessional agent. Otherwise, if on the first primary antiobsessional drug patients show no improvement, they should just be tried on another antiobsessional agent (Jefferson & Greist, 1996). When augmenting agents are used, a trial of at least 2 weeks and, in some cases, like with buspirone, up to 8 weeks may be warranted (Goodman et al., 1993; Jenike, 1992, 1993) before abandoning the augmenting agent. In general, most augmenting agents have not stood up to systematic trials, although a number of anecdotal reports have shown efficacy in some patients (see Clinical Vignettes with Specific Agents).

One strategy for choosing an augmenting agent is to look at comorbid symptoms in the patient. For example, if psychosis or poor insight is present, one might add an antipsychotic such as pimozide (McDougle et al., 1990), olanzepine, or risperidone (Jacobsen, 1995). With prominent anxiety features or panic attacks, one might consider clonazepam or buspirone (Jenike, Baer, & Buttolph, 1991; Markovitz, Stagnos, & Calabresa, 1990; McDougle et al., 1993; Pigott et al., 1992a) and with mood lability, lithium (McDougle, Price, Goodman, Charney, & Heninger, 1991). Dosing is usually in a range typically given to treat the comorbid condition (e.g., buspirone to 60–90 mg/day, clonazepam 0.5–3.0 mg/day, and risperidone 0.5–6 mg/day) (March et al., 1997). Of course, the addition of a second medication adds with it a second constellation of side effects. So for instance, one might prefer risperidone with its decreased risk of extrapyramidal side effects over more traditional antipsychotic medications such as pimozide and haldol.

In the most treatment-resistant cases in which severe disability from OCD makes life almost unbearable, one may be considered for psychosurgery. In such cases, surgery is only considered after failed trials with all or most of the five antiobsessionals, plus augmentations, plus one or more adequate trials of behavioral therapy. Some details of this treatment are outlined in Chapter 13 of this volume.

CLINICAL VIGNETTES WITH SPECIFIC AGENTS

Fluvoxamine (Luvox)

Although fluvoxamine was not among the first agents to receive FDA approval in the United States for use in OCD, it, along with clomipramine, was among the first agents with reported efficacy in the treatment of OCD (Fernandez & Lopez-Ibor, 1967; Yayura-Tobias, Neziroglu, & Bergman, 1976 [clomipramine]; Price et al., 1987 [fluvoxamine]). It did finally receive approval for use in adults in December 1994, with amended approval in children down to age 8 in March 1997, making it, along with clomipramine (approved down to age 10), one of the only two agents approved for use in children. (In 1997 sertraline also received approval down to age 6.) Given in doses between 100 and 300 mg/day, fluvoxamine has been compared head-to-head with clomipramine and found to have comparable efficacy with fewer side effects (Koran et al., 1996). Fluvoxamine is a first-line agent in the treatment of OCD. The recent consensus report (March et al., 1997) noted that fluvoxamine and fluoxetine showed a statistically significant preference for use over sertraline and paroxetine among the 69 experts surveyed. Fluvoxamine is not prone to as much agitation as fluoxetine, but it does cause nausea and sexual dysfunction, as do the other SSRIs (March et al., 1997). However, as highlighted below, although efficacious, side effects can sometimes get in the way of long-term compliance with any of these agents.

CASE EXAMPLE: UNCOMPLICATED TREATMENT WITH EXPOSURE AND RESPONSE PREVENTION (ERP) AUGMENTATION

Mr. A was a 26-year-old single male, who presented with the chief complaint "My OCD is getting out of hand." He reported that he was obsessing about his girlfriend and constantly seeking reassurance from her after one of their dates. He would mentally replay an evening to comfort himself that she cared about him and things were okay. He further reported that he had mental images of having sex with her that was excessive and intrusive. He also telephoned her again and again to seek reassurance and would try to hold her hand or seek other physical touching even when she clearly told him she did not want to. Mr. A had more "classic" OCD symptoms as well. He had many superstitious fears and symmetry obsessions. He had repeating, ordering, and superstitious rituals (as elicited by the YBOCS Symptom Checklist). He would do things in 4's and 16's, and felt the need to touch, tap, or rub items that he admired. Fear of losing his artistic ability and/or fear that something bad would happen drove these compulsions.

On his initial visit, Mr. A reported many depressive symptoms as well. He complained of anhedonia, anergia, decreased concentration, withdrawal, amotivation, and decreased appetite, with a 10-pound weight loss and some sleep disturbance. He had vague suicidal ideation, yet most of Mr. A's depressive symptoms appeared to be precipitated by his distress secondary to his OCD. His initial YBOCS score was 26. Mr. A recalled touching and tapping behaviors as young as age 7. He did not seek treatment, however, until age 23, when symptoms worsened while he was in college. He was diagnosed with OCD at that age.

Treatment consisted of initiating fluvoxamine with eventual titration to 250 mg/day. He initially experienced some drowsiness, dizziness, and "jitteriness." After 2 weeks, these side effects had subsided. Within 8 weeks, Mr. A's YBOCS decreased to 20 from 26. After this initial medication trial, behavioral treatment (exposure and response prevention, or ERP) was added to his treatment regimen, and by the end of 5 months of treatment (20 weeks), his YBOCS score was down to 13.

CASE EXAMPLE: NONCOMPLIANCE SECONDARY TO PSYCHOLOGICAL AND PHYSICAL SIDE EFFECTS

Mr. B was a 16-year-old male who presented with his parents during the summer semester school break for treatment of recently diagnosed OCD. He was referred by a Tourette's clinic after his tic-like behaviors, on further evaluation, were determined to be repeating rituals. Mr. B's chief complaint was "If something bad happens, I have to go over it in my mind over and over." He reported aggressive obsessions in which he feared he would hurt others' feelings by saying the wrong thing or giving bad advice. He performed mental reassurance rituals of replaying conversations in his head or actively seeking reassurance from others. He also had symmetry obsessions and would look at objects with odd shapes or features that stuck out until they "felt right" or he had looked for the "right" number of times. It was these rituals that caught the attention of his parents and eventually led to the evaluation. Mr. B acknowledged symptoms of OCD since the age of 10 and acknowledged that in the past, contamination and superstitious obsessions with cleaning and avoidance had been prominent. Current symptoms began at age 15, with a notable drop in his grades, as he was an A student until the year prior to seeking treatment. Mr. B's YBOCS score was 28 on admission, indicating severe symptoms.

Treatment consisted of administering fluvoxamine, which was titrated to 200 mg within 1 month's time. Several sessions of psychoeducation for both of his parents and himself were given to make all parties more accepting of the illness and able to cope with the symptoms in the home environment. Six weeks after reaching the 200 mg dose, Mr. B's YBOCS score had already dropped to 20. However, upon his return to school in the fall, his YBOCS went back up to 29 and his symptoms exacerbated. In response, fluvoxamine was increased to 250 mg, with mild improvement, as his score dropped to 24. As he was monitored throughout the semester, Mr. B's anger with his illness became more evident as he fought with his parents and younger sibling, and began to resist coming to appointments. Although he initially reported some mild gastrointestinal distress and sedation, Mr. B usually denied side effects when questioned. Then, after 4–5 months in school, Mr. B's mother called staff and reported she was finding partially digested pills in the garbage. Upon questioning, Mr. B admitted "cheeking" his pills. He indicated that sexual dysfunction had led him to stop his medication. Despite our teaching about this side effect and encouragement to report all side effects, Mr. B had chosen to cheek his pills instead. When staff expressed concern and frank puzzlement at his behavior given their perceived "open attitude," Mr. B expressed distress at not being a "normal" teen and saw his pills and treatment as making him stand out from his peers. He reported that he would rather manage symptoms on his own than receive treatment that he felt labeled him as different, no matter how much he struggled.

Fluoxetine (Prozac)

Fluoxetine is unique among the SSRIs for the treatment of OCD because of its extremely long half-life. It is reported by the manufacturer to have a half-life of the parent compound of 4–6 days and the active metabolite norfluoxetine of 4–16 days. At least one report (Pato, Murphy & Devane, 1991) of OCD patients using 80 mg for approximately 1 year computed half-lives of 8 days for fluoxetine and 19 days for norfluoxetine. This long half-life can actually be a boon in cases of poor patient compliance, because adequate serum levels will be maintained even when doses are missed. On the other hand, this long half-life presents problems upon discontinuation. The side effects of fluoxetine persist for a long time after discontinuation; for instance, a drug-related rash could persist for days. In addition, it can be problematic starting another antiobsessional agent if fluoxetine has not worked, because a patient may end up battling two sets of side effects: those lingering from fluoxetine, and those from the new agent. Also, because of fluoxetine's strong inhibition of the cytochrome P-450 enzymes, particularly 2D6, which is involved in the metabolism of clomipramine, the serum levels of clomipramine must be carefully watched when it is given simultaneously with or following the use of fluoxetine to prevent toxicity (see section on clomipramine) (Devane, 1994). This long half-life is the reason for the warning of a 5-week waiting period before using a monoamine oxidase inhibitor (MAOI), when the MAOI follows the use of fluoxetine.

The side-effects profile of fluoxetine, however, may make it a good choice in some patients. For instance, although some patients may find it the most agitating of the SSRIs, at times even leading to akathisia, patients with severe neurovegetative depressions and hypersomnia accompanying their OCD symptoms may find this motor restlessness to be somewhat motivating, particularly if the medication is prescribed first thing in the morning. Fluoxetine is also somewhat more prone to causing headache, like sertraline. However, patients are less prone to diarrhea, and there is less risk of withdrawal syndromes because of its long half-life. Like the other SSRIs, fluoxetine can lead to sexual dysfunction; and because of its long half-life, it is not effective to treat this dysfunction with brief 1- to 2-day drug holidays when there is a desire to perform sexually, as is sometimes recommended with the other antiobsessionals.

CASE EXAMPLE: UNCOMPLICATED RESPONSE WITHOUT ERP

Mr. C was a 17-year-old male with severe contamination obsessions and fears regarding AIDS. He was seen with his mother for his first psychiatric contact when she noted he was washing his hands more than 40 times per day. He also reported perfectionism and symmetry obsessions with ordering, checking, and rereading rituals. Mr. C also had secondary depressive symptoms that included loss of appetite, difficulty falling asleep, anergia, amotivation, and increased withdrawal. He denied lethality. His initial YBOCS score was 29.

Due to a demanding school schedule and fears regarding initiating behavior therapy, pharmacotherapy was selected as the treatment of choice. As Mr. C was 6'1" and 165 pounds, it was felt that he might be able to tolerate maximal doses, up to 80 mg of fluoxetine; however, he was started at a lower dose of 40 mg to minimize side effects and cost. Initially, some worsening of his sleep disturbance was reported, but schedule changes (i.e., taking the whole dose in the morning) alleviated this side effect. After 12 weeks of therapy, Mr. C came in for an office visit smiling and reporting a "70% reduction" in symptoms. In fact, his YBOCS was 13 at this visit.

Clomipramine (Anafranil)

Clomipramine differs from all other antiobsessionals in both the nature of its side effects and its lack of specific action. Although the parent compound clomipramine, like the more specific SSRIs, inhibits serotonin reuptake, the metabolite desmethylclomipramine inhibits noradrenaline reuptake. Initially, it was felt that this lack of specificity might actually make the SSRIs more effective antiobsessional medications than clomipramine, but subsequent data have not born this out. Head-to-head comparisons with fluvoxamine (Freeman et al., 1994; Koran et al., 1996), paroxetine (Zohar et al., 1996) and fluoxetine (Pigott et al., 1990) have found the SSRIs only to be equally efficacious. And meta-analysis (Greist et al., 1995b) has shown clomipramine to have a significantly larger effect size than sertraline, fluoxetine, and fluvoxamine in similar multicenter trials; although this effect size, which was two to four times larger, may well have been affected by certain biases such as the treatment naivet, of the patients (see section on sertraline). Clomipramine is viewed by clinicians as one of the primary agents in the treatment of OCD (March et al., 1997). Based on cross-responsivity data with fluoxetine by Pigott (1996) (also see Chapter 13 in this volume), it would appear that clomipramine response is a good harbinger for response to other agents. In their study, patients who responded to clomipramine had a 65%

chance of responding to fluoxetine, but patients who responded to fluoxetine had an 80% chance of responding to clomipramine.

Probably the biggest disincentive to using clomipramine as the first agent in treating OCD is its side-effects profile. Structured as a typical tricyclic antidepressant, its side effects include constipation, dry mouth, tremor, weight gain, sedation, and blurry–double vision. More serious side effects, such as lowering the seizure threshold, especially in doses over 250 mg, and heart block, which can make it problematic in older cardiac patients and lethal in overdose, often make the SSRIs a better option. In addition, along with the SSRIs, clomipramine causes significant sexual dysfunction. Nonetheless, these side effects can be used to advantage in patients who cannot deal with the agitation of the SSRIs, and who have significant difficulty falling asleep, especially if given at bedtime.

CASE EXAMPLE: RESPONSE WITH BUSPIRONE AND ERP AUGMENTATION

Mr. D was a 44-year-old male who presented to the clinic after a recent hospitalization for depression. Upon exploration, Mr. D confessed that he was depressed because sexual obscenities and images would "blurt" into his thoughts. He worried that he would become a "Dr. Jekyll and Mr. Hyde" and frantically tried to undo these thoughts with repeating rituals (e.g., retouching an object if a thought came while he had his hand on it) or mental compulsions such as thinking "I'm sorry." He dated the onset of his symptoms to age 10, when he recalled a need to confess "about everything." He had multiple treatments over the years including electroconvulsive therapy, anxiolytics (benzodiazepines), and psychotherapy, but he had never been treated with antiobsessionals until this recent hospitalization. Mr. D reported some of his OCD symptoms in his most recent hospitalization, and he had been started on clomipramine, up to 150 mg. Although his depressive symptoms improved, he was still plagued by sexual obsessions, repeating, and mental compulsions; as well as other OCD symptoms such as perfectionism, obsessions involving saving, compulsions involving rereading, and rituals around recycling garbage. His YBOCS score on this initial visit to the OCD program posthospitalization was 28, indicating severe symptoms.

Immediate treatment consisted of maximizing his dose of clomipramine to 250 mg/day. In 10 weeks, his score dropped to 24. Subsequent behavioral treatment dropped his YBOCS further to 20. Augmentation with buspirone (up to 60 mg/day) did not bring any further improvement in his symptoms.

Sertraline (Zoloft)

Sertraline has generally shown significant improvement in OCD symptoms when compared to placebo (Greist et al., 1995a). However, to date, unlike fluoxetine (Pigott et al., 1990), fluvoxamine (Freeman et al., 1994; Koran et al., 1996), and paroxetine (Zohar et al., 1996), there are no head-to-head trials comparing it to other antiobsessionals. In addition, in the meta-analysis by Greist et al. (1995b), sertraline had the smallest effect size, though not significantly different from fluoxetine and fluvoxamine. Clomipramine's effect size was significantly larger than these three. (See Chapter 13 in this volume for a review of the pitfalls of these meta-analyses.) Most recently, a reanalysis of the sertraline data was done, including only those patients who were SRI-naive (Rasmussen, Baer, & Shera, 1997). This reanalysis showed comparable effect sizes for clomipramine and sertraline. This matches the conditions seen with most of the data collected for the original clomipramine trials, since at the time that these studies were conducted (the mid 1980s), no antiobsessionals were available in the United States.

The sertraline efficacy findings are also somewhat complicated by two unusual results in the fixed-dose study (Greist et al., 1995a). The first was that although 50 mg and 200 mg of sertraline, compared to placebo, showed significant improvement on the YBOCS and the NIMH Global Obsessive–Compulsive Scale, the 100 mg dose did not show significant improvement on the YBOCS but only the NIMH global measure. There is no adequate explanation for this finding, though it would seem to imply a trial at 200 mg is warranted if 50 mg does not work. The second unusual finding from the fixed-dose study was that, unlike some other antiobsessional drug trials, the placebo response rate was rather high: 30% for the placebo group (25/84) compared to 38.9% of the sertraline treated group (93/240). This in part could be explained by the inclusion of less severely ill patients in the study, who were more likely to respond to placebo.

With regard to side effects, sertraline is well tolerated, somewhere between fluoxetine and clomipramine. It causes less weight gain and sedation than clomipramine but is not as agitating as fluoxetine. Like other SSRIs, it can cause sexual dysfunction, headache, and nausea, and may be a bit more prone to causing diarrhea (March et al., 1997). However, in one patient we treated, simply taking it on an empty stomach resolved all the diarrhea. In the recent consensus report (March et al., 1997), fluvoxamine and fluoxetine showed a statistically significant preference over sertraline and paroxetine. Meta-analytic findings that showed a low effect size for sertraline would seem to support this preference (Greist et al., 1995b). However, the recent findings by Rasmussen et al. (1997) would seem to imply more equivalent efficacy.

CASE EXAMPLE: WITH ERP AUGMENTATION

Ms. E was a 14-year-old female referred by an eating disorder clinic after aggressive obsessions and compulsive note taking became apparent in her therapy for anorexia nervosa. Ms. E presented with her parent, who reported she became agitated unless she was allowed to bring her notebook with her wherever she went. When asked to explain this behavior, Ms. E stated that she so feared harming others that whenever she did something that could result in perceived harm, she wrote it down to log it, so she would not forget to avoid such behavior in the future. Examples included walking too close to other students on stairwells for fear of pushing them down, and giving anorexia nervosa to others. On her first visit, Ms. E's YBOCS score was 26. She had already been started on 150 mg of sertraline for her anorexia nervosa, so this was increased to 200 mg. After 3 months on 200 mg of Zoloft, her YBOCS score dropped to 20. During the 8-month course of treatment, which included augmentation with behavioral therapy, Ms. E was able to leave her notebook home and, eventually, she threw it away. After 8 months of combined treatment, Ms. E's YBOCS score dropped to 12.

Paroxetine (Paxil)

Reports of efficacy of paroxetine in OCD date back to Wheadon et al. (1993). This study was a fixed-dose trial in which 40 mg and 60 mg of paroxetine were each more effective than placebo, and 20 mg did not differ from placebo. A more recent study (Zohar et al., 1996) reported that in a 12-week acute trial comparing patients on paroxetine ($n = 198$), clomipramine ($n = 94$) and placebo ($n = 99$), patients in the paroxetine and clomipramine groups had similar therapeutic efficacy and were superior to placebo. In addition, 28% of patients had drug-related adverse experiences on clomipramine, but only 16% of patients had drug-related adverse experiences on paroxetine.

Like the other SSRIs, paroxetine causes sexual dysfunction, some diarrhea, and nausea. However, it may be slightly less agitating and a bit more sedating than some of the other SSRIs (March et al., 1997). Although generally well tolerated, there have been some anecdotal reports of a severe withdrawal syndrome even with a gradual taper. Symptoms have included severe vertigo, emesis, nausea, diarrhea, and myalgia (Barr, Goodman, & Price, 1994). And finally, as noted earlier in the recent consensus report (March et al., 1997), fluvoxamine and fluoxetine showed a statistically significant preference over sertraline and paroxetine. Though this withdrawal phenomena can be problematic, paroxetine, as noted in the case example below, can be an effective agent even when other antiobsessionals have failed. Some of this preference may well be related to the fact that paroxetine is one of the newer FDA-approved agents for OCD, and there have not been as many published findings of its efficacy compared to the other agents available.

CASE EXAMPLE: RESPONSE WITH FEWER SIDE EFFECTS AND BUSPIRONE AUGMENTATION

Mr. F was a 31-year-old, single male who presented to the clinic requesting help for previously diagnosed OCD and a compulsion to mentally "overanalyze everything." He reported odd or bizarre, random, intrusive thoughts, which he then felt compelled to analyze, even if "they made no sense or had no obvious connection." An example would be that the words "cat," "buttocks," and "itch" would enter his mind, and then he would spend an hour trying to determine how these words came together. Mr. F also had obsessions involving saving and perfectionism that resulted in hoarding, checking, and avoidance. He dated his symptom onset to age 15, when he became excessively "careful." After 3 years of psychotherapy, he was diagnosed with OCD and prescribed clomipramine. He said he received good relief on clomipramine, but excessive sweating ("I'd be soaked!") led to trials of fluoxetine and fluvoxamine, with the same problematic side effect. At the time of his presentation, his YBOCS score was 24, and he was on paroxetine (40 mg), which he was tolerating well except for some "mild jitteriness."

Initial treatment included maximizing the paroxetine to 60 mg/day. Mr. F tolerated this increase with no additional side effects. At 3 months, his YBOCS score came down to 20 from 24 on 60 mg of paroxetine, and Mr. F reported that his ability to engage in activities and focus had improved. He enrolled in a vocational program with the hope of eventually securing work and completing college. Buspirone augmentation was tried 2 months later to see if further improvement could be achieved. After 8 weeks on 40 mg of buspirone, Mr. F reported more gains and had a YBOCS score of 14. He was able to participate in part-time and temporary employment, and began to plan long-term goals for his future.

CONCLUSIONS

In closing, although there are some differences between these medications, especially with respect to chemical structure and side effects, they may have comparable efficacy in improving OCD symptoms. Thus, there are several general principles to guide pharmacological treatment:

1. Give an adequate dose for at least 10–12 weeks before abandoning any treatment trial.
2. Although fixed-dose studies with fluoxetine, sertraline, and paroxetine have shown some efficacy at lower than maximal doses, further improvement was noted in many patients when the dose was increased toward the maximum tolerated. Thus, it is probably advisable not to abandon the trial of a particular antiobsessional until the maximum tolerated dose has been given for between 4–7 weeks (March et al., 1997).
3. In considering augmentation strategies, especially in the case of the first medication tried, it is probably not worth adding an augmentor after 10 weeks if there has not already been some response with monotherapy.
4. Behavioral therapy, specifically ERP, may be an essential augmentation component for most patients, especially in light of the data, though sparse, that shows that the majority of patients relapse with the discontinuation of pharmacotherapy when behavioral therapy has not been pursued.

Recently, a consensus panel of 69 experts in OCD treatment were surveyed. Their findings were compiled by March et al. (1997). These findings represent the most up-to-date compendium of clinical knowledge by those who regularly treat patients with OCD, and they include the integration of the combined literature in the field. This publication provides a detailed extension of the recommendations presented above.

REFERENCES

American Psychiatric Association. (1994). *Diagnostic and statistical manual of mental disorders* (4th ed.). Washington, DC: Author.

Barr, L. C., Goodman, W. K., & Price, L. H. (1994). Physical symptoms associated with paroxetine discontinuation. *American Journal of Psychiatry, 151,* 289.

Black, D. W., Monahan, P. O., Clancy, G. P., Baker, P. B., & Gabel, J. M. (1997, May). *Hoarding predicts poor response in OCD.* Paper presented at the annual meeting of the American Psychiatric Association, San Diego, CA.

Clomipramine Collaborative Study Group. (1991). Efficacy of clomipramine in OCD: Results of a multicenter double-blind trial. *Archives of General Psychiatry, 48,* 730–738.

Devane, C. L. (1994). Pharmacogenetics and drug metabolism of newer antidepressant agents. *Journal of Clinical Psychiatry, 55*(Suppl. 12), 38–45.

DeVeaugh-Geiss, J., Landau, P., & Katz, R. (1989). Treatment of obsessive–compulsive disorder with clomipramine. *Psychiatric Annals, 19,* 97–101.

Eisen, J. L., & Rasmussen, S. A. (1993). Obsessive–compulsive disorder with psychotic features. *Journal of Clinical Psychiatry, 54,* 373–379.

Fernandez, C. E., & Lopex-Ibor, J. J. (1967). Monoclorimipramine in the treatment of psychiatric patients resistant to other therapies. *Actas Luso-Españolas de Neurologia, Psiquiatria y Ciencias Afines, 26,* 119–147.

Foa, E. B. (1979). Failure in treating obsessive–compulsives. *Behaviour Research and Therapy, 17,* 169–176.

Foa, E. B., & Kozak, M. J. (1995). DSM-IV field trial: Obsessive–compulsive disorder. *American Journal of Psychiatry, 152,* 90–96.

Freeman, C. P. L, Trimble, M. R., Deakin, J. F. W., Stokes, T. M., & Ashford, J. J. (1994). Fluvoxamine versus clomipramine in the treatment of obsessive–compulsive disorder: A multicenter randomized, double-blind, parallel group comparison. *Journal of Clinical Psychiatry, 55,* 301–305.

Goodman, W. K., McDougle, C. J., Barr, L. C., Aronson, S. C., & Price, L. H. (1993). Biological approaches to treatment-resistant obsessive–compulsive disorder. *Journal of Clinical Psychiatry, 54*(Suppl. 6), 16–26.

Goodman, W. K., Price, L. H., Rasmussen, S. A., Masure, C., Fleishmann, C., Hill, C., Heninger, G., & Charney, D. (1989). The Yale–Brown Obsessive–Compulsive Scale: I. Development, use, and reliability. *Archives of General Psychiatry, 46,* 1006–1011.

Greist, J. H., Chouinard, G., Duboff, E., Halaris, A., Kim, S. K., Koran, L., Liebowitz, M., Lydiard, R.B., Rasmussen, S., White, K., & Sikes, C. (1995a). Double-blind parallel comparison of three dosages of sertraline and placebo in outpatients with obsessive–compulsive disorder. *Archives of General Psychiatry, 52,* 289–295.

Greist, J. H., Jefferson, J. W., Kobak, K. A., Katzelnick, D. J., & Serlin, R. C. (1995b). Efficacy and tolerability of serotonin transport inhibitors in obsessive–compulsive disorder. *Archives of General Psychiatry, 52,* 53–60.

Greist, J. H., Jenike, M. A., Robinson, D., & Rasmussen, S. A. (1995c). Efficacy of fluvoxamine in obsessive–compulsive disorder: Results of a multicentre, double-blind placebo-controlled trial. *European Journal of Clinical Research, 7,* 195–204.

Insel, T. R., & Akiskal, H. S. (1986). Obsessive–compulsive disorder with psychotic features: A phenomenological analysis. *American Journal of Psychiatry, 143*, 1527–1533.

Jacobsen, F. M. (1995). Risperidone in the treatment of affective illness and obsessive–compulsive disorder. *Journal of Clinical Psychiatry, 56*, 423–429.

Jefferson, J. Q., & Greist, J. H. (1996). The pharmacotherapy of obsessive–compulsive disorder. *Psychiatric Annals, 26*, 202–209.

Jenike, M. A. (1992). Pharmacologic treatment of obsessive compulsive disorders. In M. A. Jenike (Ed.), *Psychiatric clinics of North America* (Vol. 15, pp. 895–919). Philadelphia: Saunders.

Jenike, M. A. (1993). Augmentation strategies for treatment-resistant obsessive compulsive disorder. *Harvard Review of Psychiatry, 1*, 17–26.

Jenike, M. A., Baer, L., & Buttolph, L. (1991). Buspirone augmentation of fluoxetine in patients with obsessive–compulsive disorder. *Journal of Clinical Psychiatry, 1*, 13–14.

Jenike, M. A., Baer, L., & Greist, J. H. (1990a). Clomipramine versus fluoxetine in obsessive compulsive disorder: A retrospective comparison of side effects and efficacy. *Journal of Clinical Psychopharmacology, 10*, 122–124.

Jenike, M. A., Baer, L., Minichiello, W. E., Schwartz, C. E., & Carey, R. J. (1986). Concomitant obsessive–compulsive disorder and schizotypal personality disorder. *American Journal of Psychiatry, 143*, 530–532.

Jenike, M. A., Hyman, S. E., Baer, L., Holland, A., Minichiello, W. E., Buttolph, L., Summergrad, P., Seymour, R., & Ricciardi, J. (1990b). A controlled trial of fluvoxamine for obsessive–compulsive disorder: Implications for a serotonergic theory. *American Journal of Psychiatry, 147*, 1209–1215.

Jenike, M. A., & Pato, C. N. (1986). Disabling "fear of AIDS" responsive to imipramine. *Psychosomatics, 27*, 143–144.

Koran, L. M., McElroy, S. L., Davidson, J. R. T., et al. (1996). Fluvoxamine vs. clomipramine for obsessive–compulsive disorder: A double-blind comparison. *Journal of Clinical Psychopharmacology, 16*, 121–129.

Kozak, M. J., & Foa, E. B. (1994). Obsessions, overvalued ideas, and delusions in obsessive–compulsive disorder. *Behaviour Research and Therapy, 32*, 343–353.

Lelliott, P. T., Noshirvani, H. F., Basoglu, M., Marks, I. M., & Monteiro, W. O. (1988). Obsessive–compulsive beliefs and treatment outcome. *Psychological Medicine, 18*, 697–702.

Leonard, H. L., Swedo, S. E., Lenane, M. D., Rettew, D. C., Cheslow, D. L., Hamburger, S. D., & Rapoport, J. L. (1991). A double-blind desipramine substitution during long-term clomipramine treatment in children and adolescents with obsessive–compulsive disorder. *Archives of General Psychiatry, 48*, 922–927.

Leonard, H. L., Swedo, S. E., Rapoport, J. E., et al. (1989). Treatment of childhood obsessive–compulsive disorder with clomipramine and desmethylimipramine in children and adolescents: A double-blind crossover comparison. *Archives of General Psychiatry, 46*, 1088–1092.

Levine, R., Hoffman, J. S., Knepple, E. D., & Kenin, M. (1989). Long-term fluoxetine treatment of a large number of obsessive compulsive patients. *Journal of Clinical Psychopharmacology, 9*, 281–283.

March, J. S., Frances, A., Carpenter, D., & Kahn, D. A. (1997). Expert Consensus Guideline series on treatment of obsessive–compulsive disorder. *Journal of Clinical Psychiatry, 58*(Suppl. 4).

Markovitz, P. J., Stagnos, J., & Calabresa, J. R. (1990). Buspirone augmentation of fluoxetine on obsessive compulsive disorder. *American Journal of Psychiatry, 147*, 798–800.

McDougle, C. J., Goodman, W. K., Leckman, J. F., Holzer, J. C., Barr, L. C., McCance-Katz, E., Heninger, G. R., & Price, L. H. (1993). Limited therapeutic effect of addition of buspirone in fluvoxamine refractory obsessive–compulsive disorder. *American Journal of Psychiatry, 150,* 647–649.

McDougle, C. J., Goodman, W. K., Price, L. H., Delgado, P. L., Krystal, J. H., Charney, D. S., & Heninger, G. R. (1990). Neuroleptic addition in fluvoxamine refractory obsessive compulsive disorder. *American Journal of Psychiatry, 147,* 652–654.

McDougle, C. J., Price, L. H., Goodman, W. K., Charney, D. S., & Heninger, G. R. (1991). A controlled trial of lithium augmentation in fluvoxamine refractory obsessive compulsive disorder: Lack of efficacy. *Journal of Clinical Psychopharmacology, 11,* 175–184.

Pato, M. T., Eisen, J. L., & Pato, C. N. (1994). Rating scales for obsessive–compulsive disorder. In E. Hollander, J. Zohar, D. Marazziti, & B. Olivier (Eds.), *Current insights in obsessive compulsive disorder* (pp. 77–92). West Sussex, UK: Wiley.

Pato, M. T., Hill, J. L., & Murphy, D. L. (1990). What is the lowest therapeutically effective dose in obsessive compulsive disorder patients? *Psychopharmacology Bulletin, 26,* 211–214.

Pato, M. T., Murphy, D. L., & DeVane, C. L. (1991). Sustained plasma concentrations of fluoxetine and/or norfluoxetine four and eight weeks after fluoxetine discontinuation. *Journal of Clinical Psychopharmacology, 11,* 224–225.

Pato, M. T., Zohar-Kadouch, R., Zohar, J., & Murphy, D. (1988). Return of symptoms after discontinuation of clomipramine in patients with obsessive compulsive disorder. *American Journal of Psychiatry, 145,* 1521–1525.

Pigott, T. A. (1996). OCD: Where the serotonin selective story begins. *Journal of Clinical Psychiatry, 57*(Suppl. 6), 11–20.

Pigott, T. A., L'Hereux, F., Hill, J. L., Bihari, K., Bernstein, S. E., & Murphy, D. L. (1992a). A double-blind study of adjuvant buspirone hydrochloride in clomipramine-treated patients with obsessive compulsive disorder. *Journal of Clinical Psychopharmacology, 12,* 11–18.

Pigott, T. A., L'Heureax, F., Rubenstein, C. S., Bernstein, S. E., Hill, J. I., & Murphy, D. L. (1992b). A double-blind, placebo-controlled study of trazodone in patients with obsessive compulsive disorder. *Journal of Clinical Psychopharmacology, 12,* 156–162.

Pigott, T. A., Pato, M. T., Bernstein, S. E., Grover, G., Hill, J., Tolliver, T., & Murphy, D. (1990). Controlled comparison of clomipramine and fluoxetine in the treatment of obsessive–compulsive disorder. *Archives of General Psychiatry, 47,* 926–932.

Price, L. H., Goodman, W. K., Charney, D. S., Rasmussen, S. A., & Heninger, G. R. (1987). Treatment of severe obsessive–compulsive disorder with fluvoxamine. *American Journal of Psychiatry, 144,* 1059–1061.

Rasmussen, S. A., Baer, L., & Shera, D. (1997, May). *Previous SSRI treatment and efficacy of sertraline for OCD: Combined analysis of four multicenter trials.* Paper presented at the annual meeting of the American Psychiatric Association, San Diego, CA.

Rasmussen, S. A., & Eisen, J. L. (1991). Phenomenology of obsessive–compulsive disorder. In J. Zohar, T. Insel, & S. Rasmussen (Eds.), *Psychobiology of obsessive compulsive disorder* (pp. 743–758). New York: Springer-Verlag.

Rasmussen, S. A., Eisen, J. L., & Pato, M. T. (1993). Current issues in the pharmacologic management of obsessive–compulsive disorder. *Journal of Clinical Psychiatry, 54*(Suppl. 6), 4–9.

Ricciardi, J. N., Baer, L., Jenike, M. A., Fischer, S. C., Sholtz, D., & Buttolph, M. L. (1992). Changes in DSM-III-R Axis II diagnoses following treatment of obsessive–compulsive disorder. *American Journal of Psychiatry, 149,* 829–831.

Swedo, S. E., Rapoport, J. L., Leonard, H., Lenane, M., & Cheslow, D. (1989a). Obsessive–compulsive disorder in children and adolescents: Clinical phenomenology of 70 consecutive cases. *Archives of General Psychiatry, 46,* 335–341.

Swedo, S. E., Schapiro, M. B., Grady, C. L., Cheslow, D. L., Leonard, H. L., Kumar, A., Friedland, R., Rapoport, S. I., & Rapoport, J. L. (1989b). Cerebral glucose metabolism in childhood-onset obsessive–compulsive disorder. *Archives of General Psychiatry, 46,* 518–523.

Tollefson, G. D., Birkett, M., Koran, L., & Genduso, L. A. (1994a). Continuation treatment of OCD: Double-blind and open-label experience with fluoxetine. *Journal of Clinical Psychiatry, 55*(Suppl. 10), 69–76.

Tollefson, G. D., Rampey, A. H., Potvin, J. H., Jenike, M. A., Rush, A. J., Dominguez, R. A., Koran, L. M., Shear, M. K., Goodman, W., & Genduso, L. A. (1994b). A multicenter investigation of fixed dose fluoxetine in the treatment of obsessive–compulsive disorder. *Archives of General Psychiatry, 51,* 559–567.

Wheadon, D., Bushnell, W., & Steiner, M. (1993). *A fixed dose comparison of 20, 40, or 60 mg paroxetine to placebo in the treatment of obsessive–compulsive disorder.* Paper presented at the annual meeting of the American College of Neuropsychopharmacology, Honolulu, Hawaii.

Wood, A., Tollefson, G. D., & Birkett, M. (1993). Pharmacotherapy of obsessive–compulsive disorder—experience with fluoxetine. *International Clinical Psychopharmacology, 8,* 301–306.

Yayura-Tobias, J. A., Neziroglu, F., & Bergman, L. (1976). Clorimipramine for obsessive–compulsive neurosis: An organic approach. *Current Therapeutic Research, 20,* 541–547.

Zohar, J., Judge, R., & the OCD Paroxetine Study Investigators. (1996). Paroxetine versus in the treatment of OCD. *British Journal of Psychiatry, 169,* 468–474.

Chapter 15

COMBINATION TREATMENTS FOR OBSESSIVE–COMPULSIVE DISORDER

Anton J. L. M. van Balkom
Richard van Dyck

As already discussed in the preceding chapters, effective treatments for obsessive–compulsive disorder (OCD) consist mainly of cognitive-behavioral therapy (CBT) and antidepressants. However, certain patients react less favorably to these treatment strategies than do others, and some patients improve only slightly. In order to maximize the effects of treatment, antidepressants and CBT are frequently combined in clinical practice, despite the fact that the scientific support for this practice is surprisingly thin. Up until now, five studies have been carried out in which combination treatments for OCD were compared with CBT or antidepressants alone.

In this chapter, we review the literature on (1) the relative efficacy of antidepressants and CBT, (2) the short- and long-term effects of combination treatments compared to their separate elements, and (3) predictors of outcome following treatment with antidepressants, CBT, or a combination of the two. In addition, this chapter includes a discussion of the practical aspects of providing combination treatments as well as a decision tree for selecting the appropriate treatment strategy for a given patient.

RELATIVE EFFICACY OF ANTIDEPRESSANTS AND CBT

From an extensive body of research, we know that antidepressants and CBT are effective in the treatment of OCD (see Chapters 11 and 12 of this volume). The differential effect of these treatments remains obscure, as comparisons in randomized, controlled trials are scarce. Until now, only one study with a small study has been published (not including several studies that also had a combined treatment condition—reviewed in a later section). This study compared clomipramine to flooding and thought stopping, respectively (Solyom & Sookman, 1977). Although the three treatments appeared to lead to decreased OCD severity, findings were based on clinical judgment, and therefore their validity is questionable.

Because direct comparisons of CBT and antidepressants have been scarce, several investigators have conducted quantitative comparisons between studies by means of meta-analytic techniques. In a "between-study" comparison, literature is searched for outcome studies on the efficacy of either antidepressants or cognitive-behavioral treatments. In order to compare these treatments between studies, treatment efficacy must first be expressed in a standardized way—using a measure of effect size, d. One of the methods to calculate d is to subtract the mean pretest from the mean posttest score, and then divide the remainder by the pooled standard deviation. The effect size for one treatment condition (e.g., antidepressants) is calculated by averaging all effect sizes for this treatment, derived from the literature search. Subsequently, the magnitude of the effect sizes for the various treatment conditions can be compared using statistical methods (e.g., d for antidepressants vs. the d for CBT).

Three meta-analyses comparing antidepressants and CBT in OCD have been published. Two earlier meta-analyses (Christensen, Hadzi-Pavlovic, Andrews, & Mattick, 1987; Cox, Swinson, Morrison, & Lee, 1993) led to the conclusion that both kinds of treatment have an equally positive effect on obsessive–compulsive symptoms. In an update, van Balkom et al. (1994) published a meta-analytic review, including relevant treatment studies published before the end of 1993. Eighty-six treatment studies were reviewed, including 2,954 patients at pretest, 385 (13%) dropouts, and 2,569 patients at posttest. In these 86 studies, placebo treatment was studied 18 times, antidepressants 49 times, and CBT 46 times. For each of these treatment conditions, a mean d was calculated as described earlier. These effect sizes are presented in Table 15.1.

Antidepressant treatment conditions included treatment with clomipramine, fluoxetine, or fluvoxamine. Although paroxetine and sertraline were recently found to be effective in OCD, these drugs were not included. Up to 1993, no data on the efficacy of paroxetine in OCD were published, and the use of sertraline in this disorder was still in an experimental stage. The CBT included in the meta-analysis comprised various formats of exposure *in vivo* with response prevention. Most exposure *in vivo* exercises studied were given on an outpatient basis, using self- or therapist-assisted gradual exposure *in vivo* or flooding.

In Table 15.1, the effect sizes for obsessive–compulsive symptoms are presented for self- and assessor-ratings separately. This important distinction was made because the magnitude of the effect sizes for self-ratings was significantly smaller than for assessor ratings, especially in studies of antidepressants. The statistical analysis was therefore carried out separately for each type of rating. Table 15.1 shows that serotonergic antidepressants and behavior therapy are effective treatments in OCD, since they are associated with large effect sizes (magnitude higher than 0.8). The effect sizes associated with placebo treatment are small on

TABLE 15.1. Mean Effect Size (Cohen's *d*), Standard Deviation (*SD*), and Sample Size (*n*) per Treatment Condition on Self-Rated and Assessor-Rated Obsessive–Compulsive Symptoms

	Antidepressants	Placebo	CBT
Self-rating			
d	0.95	0.20	1.46
SD	0.70	0.27	0.75
n	21	8	45
Assessor rating			
d	1.63	0.59	1.47
SD	0.91	0.69	0.70
n	38	17	29

Note. CBT, cognitive-behavioral therapy.

self-ratings (effect sizes smaller than 0.2) and moderately large on assessor ratings (effect sizes of about 0.5).

On self- and assessor ratings, serotonergic antidepressants and behavior therapy were significantly superior to placebo. On self-ratings, the magnitude of the effect size for behavior therapy was significantly higher when compared with antidepressants. On assessor ratings, however, no differences were found between the two treatments.

Also, the effect sizes for assessor ratings exceeded those for self-ratings significantly in studies on antidepressants, whereas this difference was not found in studies with CBT. This unexpected result appeared to be related to the use of different measurement instruments in drug and nondrug studies. In studies on CBT, related self- and assessor ratings were frequently used. Examples of these related ratings are the patient and assessor ratings derived from the same Anxiety Discomfort Scales. In contrast, self- and assessor ratings used in studies on antidepressants usually have not been related. In these studies, we find among others the self-rated Leyton Obsessional Inventory, together with the assessor-rated Yale–Brown Obsessive–Compulsive Scale (YBOCS).

From these results, the following conclusions can be distilled. First, outcome measurement in OCD is significantly influenced by the format and type of instruments used. Second, both CBT and antidepressants are effective treatments. Third, CBT is superior to antidepressants when measured on self-ratings, but not on assessor ratings.

COMBINING ANTIDEPRESSANTS WITH CBT: SHORT- AND LONG-TERM OUTCOME

In total, five studies have been published on the efficacy of combined treatments for OCD. The first comparison (Marks, Stern, Mawson, Cobb, & McDonald,

1980; Rachman et al. 1979) included 48 patients with OCD, of which 40 were completers. Patients with covert compulsions only were excluded. During the first 7 weeks, this study used a 2 × 2 factorial design to investigate the effects of four treatment conditions: (1) clomipramine plus exposure *in vivo* and response prevention, (2) clomipramine plus relaxation, (3) placebo plus exposure *in vivo* and response prevention, and (4) placebo plus relaxation. In the first 4 weeks, the patients received treatment with a maximum of 225 mg of clomipramine or placebo on an outpatient basis. Because of disturbing side effects, the actual mean daily clomipramine dose was 183 mg. From weeks 4–10, the patients were admitted to hospital. During the first 3 weeks of hospitalization, they received 15 sessions of either exposure or relaxation. After week 7, relaxation was terminated. At this point, the patients treated with relaxation received 15 sessions of exposure *in vivo*, whereas patients formerly treated with exposure received another 15 sessions of exposure. After week 10, the patients were discharged from hospital. The medication (either clomipramine or placebo) was continued until week 36 and then tapered off over a period of 4 weeks (Marks et al., 1980). The patients were followed up naturalistically for 6 years (O'Sullivan, Noshirvani, Marks, Monteiro, & Lelliott, 1991). In Table 15.2, the design of the study is shown.

At several times, assessments took place investigating the presence and severity of obsessive–compulsive symptoms, depression, and social functioning. Included in the statistical analyses were 40 patients who completed the first year of the study. These patients were evenly divided over the four conditions. No intent to treat analyses were performed.

The results of the 2 × 2 factorial design were analyzed after 7 weeks of treatment. At that point, the specific treatments (clomipramine and exposure *in vivo*) yielded more improvement than the control treatments (placebo and relaxation). Although the combination of clomipramine with exposure *in vivo* yielded slightly superior results relative to the three other conditions on most ratings, there was no statistically significant interaction between exposure *in vivo* and clomipramine.

Because patients in all four conditions received exposure *in vivo* treatment after week 7, comparisons were only possible between the 20 patients treated with clomipramine versus those treated with placebo. Until week 36, clomipramine was significantly superior to placebo on most ratings of OCD symptoms, mood, and

TABLE 15.2. Design of the Rachman et al. (1979) Study

Pretreatment (Week 0)	Midtreatment 1 (Week 4)	Midtreatment 2 (Week 7)	Midtreatment 3 (Week 10)	Posttreatment (Week 36)	Follow-up (Week 348)
CLM	CLM + EXP	CLM + EXP	CLM	Not controlled for treatments received	
CLM	CLM + REL	CLM + EXP	CLM		
PLA	PLA + EXP	PLA + EXP	PLA		
PLA	PLA + REL	PLA + EXP	PLA		

Note. CLM, clomipramine; PLA, placebo; EXP, exposure *in vivo*; REL, relaxation.

social adjustment. Post hoc analyses revealed that these clomipramine–placebo differences were mainly caused by the superior effect of clomipramine in the subgroup consisting of the most depressed patients. The authors therefore concluded that in OCD, treatment with clomipramine should be reserved for depressed patients.

Of the 40 patients who completed the outcome study, 34 individuals were followed up 6 years later (O'Sullivan, Noshirvani, Marks, Monteiro, & Lelliott, 1991). At follow-up, there was no longer a difference between the patients who originally received treatment with placebo versus clomipramine. In spite of supplementary therapies for both groups, the outcome of patients who had originally received 30 inpatient sessions of exposure *in vivo* was superior to that of those who had received only 15 sessions of exposure.

The second study (Marks et al., 1988) investigated 27 weeks of treatment in four different conditions (see Table 15.3). All 55 patients included received outpatient treatment, except for 11 patients (randomized over the four conditions) who were admitted to hospital during the trial because of the distance to their home or the severity of their problems. Patients with covert compulsions only were excluded.

In the first condition, clomipramine was combined with 23 weeks of "antiexposure" instructions involving encouragement to avoid fearful situations and to perform compulsions as much as desired. In the second condition, clomipramine was combined with 23 weeks of self-controlled exposure *in vivo* with response prevention. In this condition, patients conducted daily homework exercises for a maximum of 3 hours, progress was monitored weekly, and new exposure homework was assigned. In the third and fourth condition, either clomipramine or placebo was given in a double-blind fashion and combined with self-controlled exposure *in vivo* during weeks 1 to 8, and therapist-controlled exposure from weeks 8 to 23. During the 15 therapist-aided exposure sessions, the therapist encouraged patients to confront anxiety-provoking situations in real life. Most of these sessions took place at the psychiatric outpatient department, but one-third were carried out at home. The patients taking clomipramine received a maximum of 200 mg/day. The mean clomipramine dosage was 157 mg ($SD = 49$ mg) at week 4, and 127 mg ($SD = 67$ mg) at week 17. From weeks 23 to 27, either placebo or clomipramine was continued without any behavior therapy, and from

TABLE 15.3. Design of the Marks et al. (1988) Study

Pretreatment (Week 0)	Midtreatment 1 (Week 8)	Midtreatment 2 (Week 17)	Midtreatment 3 (Week 23)	Posttreatment (Week 27)	Follow-up (Week 131)
CLM	CLM + Anti-EXP	CLM + Anti-EXP	CLM	Not controlled for	
CLM	CLM + Self-Exp	CLM + Self-EXP	CLM	treatments received	
CLM	CLM + Self-Exp	CLM + Ther-EXP	CLM		
PLA	PLA + Self-Exp	PLA + Ther-EXP	PLA		

Note. CLM, clomipramine; PLA, placebo; Anti-EXP, antiexposure; Self-EXP, self-controlled exposure; Ther-EXP, therapist-controlled exposure.

week 27 to 31, the medication was tapered. The patients were naturalistically followed up after 2 years (Kasvikis & Marks, 1988).

Of the 55 patients who were included, 49 completed the trial. The assessment strategy used was the same as in the previous study. No intent to treat analyses was performed. Patients in the antiexposure condition stayed intact for the first 12 weeks only. Because most of them did not improve substantially, exposure *in vivo* treatment was offered to them for ethical reasons.

During the first 8 weeks, clomipramine plus exposure was more effective than placebo plus exposure. At week 17, however, this difference disappeared, suggesting that clomipramine accelerates the effects of exposure *in vivo*. Clomipramine with antiexposure was inferior to clomipramine plus exposure, indicating that exposure *in vivo* enhances the efficacy of clomipramine. No differences were found between the patients treated with therapist-aided exposure *in vivo* and self-directed exposure exercises. In other words, the efficacy of self-controlled exposure *in vivo* was not enhanced by involving therapists in the exposure exercises. After 23 weeks of treatment, no differences remained between the four conditions.

After 2 years, Kasvikis & Marks (1988) reassessed 39 patients (80%) from the completer sample. For the purposes of data analysis, the four initial conditions were combined into one group, because of the lack of significant differences across groups after 23 weeks of treatment. At follow-up (relative to posttreatment), no significant further improvement was observed overall. Few patients had relapsed, and others had improved further. The authors did not provide any information about the number of patients receiving treatment elsewhere, nor about the modality of these possible treatments. But since the results of the outcome study were maintained at follow-up, they conclude that "[despite] inevitable extraneous influences after cessation of the experimental manipulations, . . . the sample as a whole remained significantly improved compared to their initial profile" (pp. 296–297).

A third study (Cottraux et al., 1990) compared (1) fluvoxamine with antiexposure, (2) fluvoxamine with ERP, and (3) placebo with ERP in a 24 week study (see Table 15.4). Of the 60 participants (20 per condition), 2 suffered from obsessions only. The patients received fluvoxamine or placebo up to 300 mg/day. The authors did not provide data about the actual daily fluvoxamine dosage. After 24 weeks, medication was tapered over 4 weeks. The antiexposure instructions in the fluvoxamine plus antiexposure condition were similar to those used by Marks

TABLE 15.4. Design of the Cottraux et al. (1990) Study

Pretreatment (Week 0)	Midtreatment (Week 8)	Posttreatment (Week 24)	Follow-up (Week 102)
Fluvoxamine plus antiexposure		Not controlled for treatments received	
Fluvoxamine plus exposure *in vivo*			
Placebo plus exposure *in vivo*			

et al. (1988). In the conditions involving ERP, patients completed exposure homework for entire 24 weeks of the study, although the exact format of the exposure *in vivo* treatment is not clear. In addition to the exposure *in vivo* exercises, patients also received cognitive therapy, marital therapy, and assertiveness training when necessary. After one and a half years, a naturalistic follow-up assessment was conducted (Cottraux, Mollard, Bouvard, & Marks, 1993b).

Measurements took place at pretreatment, midtreatment (after 8 weeks), posttreatment, and 18-month follow-up, using self- and assessor ratings of OCD symptoms and depressed mood. A behavioral avoidance test was administered as well. At posttest, 16 patients had dropped out prematurely, leaving 44 completers (13 patients in fluvoxamine plus antiexposure, 16 in fluvoxamine plus exposure, 15 in placebo plus exposure). Only completer analyses were presented. The proportion of dropouts did not differ significantly in the three conditions.

At midtreatment, significant improvement was observed on most outcome variables in the three conditions. This improvement continued during the subsequent 16 weeks of treatment. At posttest, both the fluvoxamine conditions were superior to the placebo condition in ameliorating depressed mood. The patients receiving the combination treatment of fluvoxamine plus exposure *in vivo* improved most, although comparisons with the other conditions did not yield significant differences.

These results do not indicate the superiority of the combining fluvoxamine and exposure *in vivo* compared to the combination of placebo and exposure. Nor was the combination with fluvoxamine superior to treatment with fluvoxamine alone. The lack of differences between the conditions may have been caused by confounding factors. In contrast to the Marks et al. (1988) study, patients in this study were not compliant with the antiexposure instructions due to low credibility for this condition. Most patients knew about the efficacy of exposure *in vivo* of OCD. Therefore, the authors state retrospectively that this condition could better be considered as "neutral" with respect to exposure. Another confounding factor might be the relatively high dropout rate (35%) in the fluvoxamine plus antiexposure condition (7 of 20 patients) compared with the 20% dropout rate in the fluvoxamine plus exposure *in vivo* condition (4 of 20 patients). Given the fact that responders are more likely to complete a trial than nonresponders, intent to treat analyses might have shown group differences.

Follow-up data after 18 months were available for 33 patients, 55% of the original sample (Cottraux et al., 1993b). On clinical ratings, the patients of this sample did not differ significantly from the patients who were lost at follow-up. After 18 months, no between-group differences were found. In general, between posttreatment and follow-up, improvement was maintained, and few patients had received booster sessions of exposure *in vivo*. After tapering off the medication (week 24 to 28), 6 patients relapsed in the fluvoxamine plus antiexposure condition. All of these patients were treated again with antidepressants at follow-up. Of the patients who received the combination of fluvoxamine or placebo with exposure *in vivo*, over 80% were without medication, as opposed to 40% of the patients who had received fluvoxamine alone. It appears that exposure *in vivo* may reduce the likelihood of relapsing after stopping medication in OCD patients.

The fourth combination study was designed to investigate earlier impressions that depressed patients with OCD might not benefit from CBT as much as nondepressed patients (Foa, Kozak, Steketee, & McCarthy, 1992). This hypothesis was tested in a 2 × 2 factorial design, comparing imipramine versus placebo for OCD patients with either severe or mild levels of depression. All patients received exposure *in vivo* with response prevention. The study used a sequential combination of medication with exposure *in vivo* (see Table 15.5).

Treatment took place at an outpatient department, except in the case of 18 patients, from across the four conditions, who were hospitalized. Forty-eight patients, all suffering from overt compulsions, entered this 22-week study. On the basis of their initial score on the Beck Depression Inventory (BDI), they were subdivided into highly and mildly depressed subgroups. The scores on the BDI were approximately 36 for the former and 15 for the latter group. Subsequently, both groups were given either placebo or imipramine, in a double-blind fashion.

In the first 6 weeks, patients were treated either with imipramine or placebo alone. The maximum dosage of imipramine was 250 mg/day, with a mean of 229 mg, ranging from 150–250 mg. During the next 3 weeks (weeks 7 to 10), all patients received 15 daily, 2-hour sessions of exposure *in vivo* and *in vitro*, followed by response prevention. From week 10 onwards, all patients were seen weekly for "supportive behavioral therapy," mainly consisting of motivating the patients to keep applying the behavioral techniques they had learned in initial 3 weeks of behavior therapy. Medications were tapered after 22 weeks. Ten patients dropped out prematurely, leaving 38 completers. A 2-year follow-up assessment was carried out with less than half the number of completers.

Severity of OCD symptoms and depressed mood was assessed at pretreatment, after 6 and 10 weeks of treatment, at posttreatment, and at follow-up. After 6 weeks of treatment, imipramine had significantly alleviated the depressed mood in the conditions with highly depressed patients, although patients were still in the depressed range on the BDI. Placebo had no effect on depression. In

TABLE 15.5. Design of the Foa et al. (1992) Study

Pretreatment (Week 0)	Midtreatment 1 (Week 6)	Midtreatment 2 (Week 10)	Posttreatment (Week 22)	Follow-up (Week 146)
Imipramine in highly depressed patients	Imipramine plus exposure *in vivo*		Not controlled for treatments received	
Imipramine in mildly depressed patients	Imipramine plus exposure *in vivo*			
Placebo in highly depressed patients	Placebo plus exposure *in vivo*			
Placebo in mildly depressed patients	Placebo plus exposure *in vivo*			

none of the conditions had imipramine or placebo ameliorated OCD symptoms. After the 3-week period of intensive behavioral therapy, OCD symptoms had improved in all four conditions, and no between-group differences emerged. Findings were similar at the posttreatment and follow-up assessments. These results are difficult to interpret because of the limited effect of imipramine on depression.

The purpose of the fifth comparative treatment study (van Balkom et al., in press) was to investigate whether the effects of cognitive therapy or exposure *in vivo* with response prevention for obsessive–compulsive ritualizers could be enhanced by adding fluvoxamine before the start of these cognitive-behavioral treatments. Five conditions were compared in this 16-week study: (1) cognitive therapy, (2) exposure *in vivo* with response prevention, (3) fluvoxamine combined with cognitive therapy after 8 weeks, (4) fluvoxamine combined with exposure *in vivo* after 8 weeks and (5) an 8-week waiting-list control condition. A naturalistic follow-up assessment was completed after 6 months (de Haan et al., 1997) (see Table 15.6).

In the first 8 weeks, six treatment sessions were delivered, followed by another 10 sessions during the second 8-week period. In cognitive therapy, patients learned to identify anxiety-evoking automatic thoughts. By means of a Socratic dialogue, these automatic thoughts were challenged and replaced by alternative, rational, and nondistressing thoughts. The format of exposure *in vivo* was gradual, self-controlled exposure with gradual, self-imposed response prevention. In the first 8 weeks of the fluvoxamine conditions, no cognitive therapy or exposure *in vivo* was provided. In the absence of disturbing side effects, the fluvoxamine dosage was increased over 3 weeks to a maximum of 300 mg/day. The mean daily dosage of fluvoxamine was 235 mg ($SD = 73$ mg) after 8 weeks, and 197 mg ($SD = 82$ mg) after 16 weeks of treatment. During the second 8-week period, the fluvoxamine dosage was kept stable. In addition to fluvoxamine, patients received 10 sessions of either cognitive therapy or exposure *in vivo*. After the posttreatment assessment, patients were allowed to continue fluvoxamine if they wished to do so.

Outcome was assessed by several OCD-rating scales and the BDI before treatment, after 8 weeks (midtreatment), and after 16 weeks (posttreatment). A total of 117 patients were randomized over the five conditions. Thirty-one pa-

TABLE 15.6. Design of the van Balkom et al. (in press) Study

Pretreatment (Week 0)	Midtreatment (Week 8)	Posttreatment (Week 16)	Follow-up (Week 42)
Cognitive therapy	Cognitive therapy	Not controlled for treatments received	
Exposure *in vivo*	Exposure *in vivo*		
Fluvoxamine	Fluvoxamine plus cognitive therapy		
Fluvoxamine	Fluvoxamine plus exposure *in vivo*		
Waiting list			

tients dropped out prematurely, 70 completed the 16 weeks of treatment, and 16 completed the eight-week waiting-list condition. The dropout rates among patients in the fluvoxamine plus cognitive therapy and the exposure *in vivo* conditions were 41% and 36%, respectively. The dropout rates in the fluvoxamine conditions exceeded those in the cognitive therapy (24%) and exposure *in vivo* (15%) conditions. Thus, in addition to completer analyses, intent-to-treat analyses were performed.

In contrast to the four treatments, the waiting-list control condition did not result in a significant decrease in symptoms. At midtreatment, cognitive therapy, exposure *in vivo*, and fluvoxamine had significantly reduced the OCD symptoms. No differences between these treatments were found. At posttest, all four treatment packages led to decreases in OCD symptoms and ratings of depression, but they did not differ in effectiveness. The results of the intent-to-treat analyses were identical to those of the completer analyses, suggesting that the effect of cognitive therapy or exposure *in vivo* with response prevention in OCD was not enhanced by adding fluvoxamine before the start of these treatments.

Sixty-one of the 70 completers were followed up after 6 months (de Haan et al., 1997). This period was not controlled for the treatments received. Compared with posttreatment, patients had improved significantly on OCD symptoms and depressed mood at follow-up. Again, no differences were found between the four conditions. Patients were classified into responders or nonresponders on the basis of their improvement and posttest rating on the YBOCS. Responders were patients who had improved more than 6 points on the YBOCS, and had a posttreatment score of less than 12. Seventeen patients, regarded as nonresponders at posttreatment, had become responders after 6 months of further treatment. These results indicate that short-term treatment failures can become successful when treatments are continued.

Together, two studies suggest a superior effect of combination therapy. One study suggests that the combination of exposure *in vivo* with serotonergic antidepressants could lead to earlier improvement for OCD symptoms than exposure *in vivo* and response prevention alone (Marks et al., 1988). Another study shows a superior effect for OCD patients with concomitant depression (Marks et al., 1980; Rachman et al., 1979). However, a superior effect of the combination over exposure *in vivo* alone in the long term has not been demonstrated. Furthermore, it is worth treating patients for longer periods, even when they do not react favorably to short-term treatments. It appears that long-term treatment can turn short-term treatment failures into successes (de Haan et al., 1997).

The short-term treatment effect of antidepressants can be enhanced by the addition of exposure *in vivo* with response prevention. The effect of exposure *in vivo*, however, is not augmented by the addition of antidepressants. Relapses after stopping pharmacological treatment can be prevented by the addition of exposure exercises to antidepressants before tapering the medication. It should be noted that most research on combination treatment has been performed with patients suffering from compulsions. No data are available for patients with obsessions alone.

ANTIDEPRESSANTS, CBT, OR THE COMBINATION

Confronted with a patient suffering from OCD, it is important for the clinician to choose a treatment approach that will maximize the likelihood of success. Of the five combination studies, two have examined clinical characteristics that predict the optimal treatment for a given patient (Cottraux, Messy, Marks, Mollard, & Bouvard, 1993a; de Haan et al., 1997). Findings from these studies as well as other outcome studies can aid in selecting an appropriate treatment.

Cottraux et al. (1993a) carried out a discriminant analysis to identify outcome predictors in their sample of 60 patients (Cottraux et al., 1990). They investigated which of 10 clinical baseline variables correctly classified the patients as treatment successes or failures after 24 weeks of therapy. Treatment success was defined as a reduction of more than 30% in the duration of the compulsions measured at pretreatment. Dropouts were considered as treatment failures. Under this definition, 54% of the patients treated with fluvoxamine with antiexposure were classified as "successes," versus 69% of the fluvoxamine plus exposure *in vivo* condition, and 40% of the group receiving the combination of placebo plus exposure *in vivo*. The strongest predictor of outcome was severity of OCD symptoms. Independent of the treatment condition, the higher the pretreatment OCD severity, the less likely it was treatment would be successful. Other variables found to correctly classify patients into the success or failure subgroups were (1) the expectation of improvement following treatment with fluvoxamine or exposure *in vivo* and (2) depression. For none of these predictors was a treatment-specific relationship found.

De Haan et al. (1997) did not find treatment-specific predictors either. They investigated the association between several clinical variables and improvement following CBT alone and CBT combined with fluvoxamine. In a sample of 99 patients treated with either cognitive therapy, exposure *in vivo*, or these treatments combined with fluvoxamine (van Balkom et al., in press), correlational analyses were performed at posttreatment and 6-month follow-up in order to identify clinical variables that predict outcome. In all four treatments, better outcome was associated with less severe OCD symptoms and better motivation at pretreatment. The presence of a Cluster A personality disorder, as measured by the self-rated Personality Disorders Questionnaire—Revised, was associated with poorer outcome in the four conditions. This association disappeared after correction for the severity of associated psychopathology, as measured on the Symptom Checklist 90.

The other studies investigating combined treatments for OCD have tended not to show statistical differences between the various conditions at posttest and follow-up. As a consequence, in the statistical analyses, the various conditions have been considered as one large sample. Therefore, these analyses have not examined treatment-specific predictors.

An important question to be resolved is whether patients with OCD and concomitant depression should be treated with the combination of antidepressants with CBT. As already discussed, Rachman et al. (1979) found a depressed subgroup of patients to benefit more from the combination of clomipramine with exposure *in vivo* than nondepressed patients with OCD. In the sample from the Marks et al. (1988) study, Basoglu, Lax, Kasvikis, and Marks (1988) found that higher OCD severity, greater social disability, being male, the presence of checking rituals and the presence of uncontrollable obsessions were all associated with poorer treatment outcome. In this study, depression did not predict outcome. Nor did Cottraux et al. (1993a) or de Haan et al. (1997) find treatment-specific associations between depression and outcome.

Taken together, there is only little evidence that depressed patients with OCD respond better to the combination of antidepressants and CBT than to CBT alone. Limitations in the interpretation of the data are the small sample sizes of the respective studies and the study criteria, which often exclude severely depressed patients. Until the availability of more appropriate studies, these negative results should not be taken as a definitive judgment. Given these limitations, we think that the combination treatment for OCD patients who are also depressed is still worth trying in clinical practice.

The research on predictors is not the only source for the clinician who must decide which treatment should be offered to a particular patient. An important element in the decision should be the relative efficacy. A recent meta-analysis (van Balkom et al., 1994) showed that CBT was superior to antidepressants on self-ratings for obsessive–compulsive complaints. Compared with CBT, antidepressants have a higher dropout rate and a higher relapse rate after stopping treatment. Thus, when given alone, CBT is more effective than antidepressants.

From the outcome studies, we can deduce that the combination treatment is equally effective as CBT alone. Since more patients drop out prematurely from the combination treatment than from CBT alone, the combination offers no advantages over cognitive-behavioral treatment. The combination treatment, however, is superior to antidepressants alone. Moreover, compared with the combination, antidepressants alone give a higher relapse rate after discontinuation of medications. Thus, the combination treatment enhances the efficacy of antidepressants in OCD.

On the basis of these conclusions, a decision tree has been constructed for clinical practice (Figure 15.1). This decision tree is especially intended for patients with overt compulsions. Little is known about which would be the most effective treatments for patients with obsessions and covert compulsions only. For these patients, antidepressants and/or cognitive therapy seem indicated, since exposure *in vivo* to covert compulsions is difficult to carry out. In other cases of OCD, the decision tree can be applied. It is our impression that the choice of a combination therapy is made more often for patients with severe OCD symptoms, despite the lack of scientific evidence supporting this practice, even for patients with severe impairment. We suggest the application of the decision tree even for these patients.

Initially, treatment is provided on an outpatient basis. For patients with OCD, the clinician diagnoses the presence and severity of a comorbid depressive disorder. In case of a severe comorbid mood disorder, especially when there is

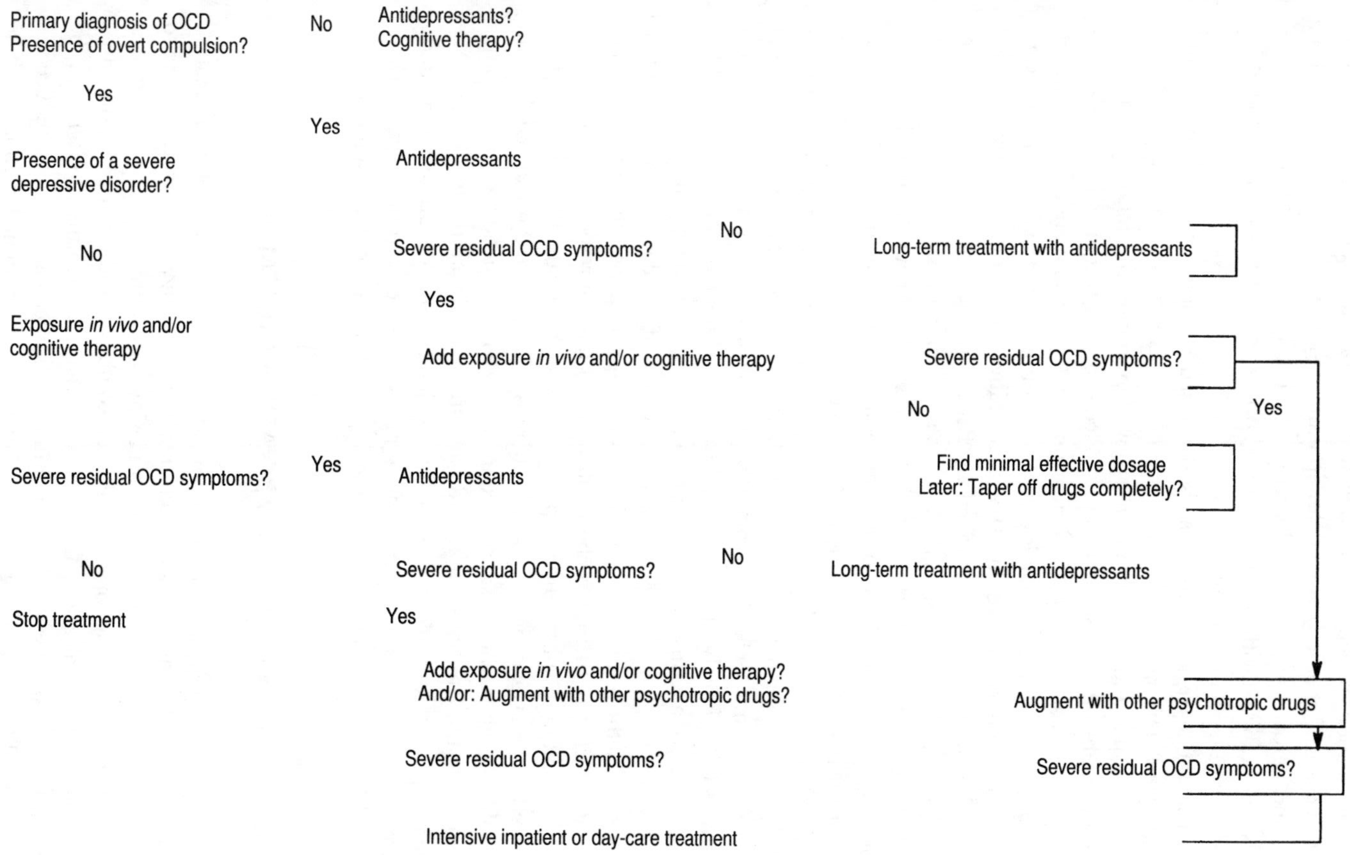

FIGURE 15.1. Decision tree on the selection of treatments in OCD.

suicidal ideation, patients are treated with one of the serotonergic antidepressants. One can choose between clomipramine, fluoxetine, fluvoxamine, sertraline, and paroxetine (Jenike, 1990). After minimally 8 weeks, these antidepressants are combined with either exposure *in vivo* or cognitive therapy (combination treatment in sequential format).

For nondepressed or moderately depressed patients with OCD, we would recommend starting with CBT because of its superior efficacy compared with antidepressants. Either exposure *in vivo* with response prevention or cognitive therapy can be offered. Since therapist-aided exposure is equally effective as self-controlled exposure *in vivo*, the latter treatment is recommended. To enhance compliance, the format chosen is gradual exposure and gradual response prevention (Hoogduin & Hoogduin, 1984). Cognitive or rational–emotive therapy should be similar to that described by Beck and colleagues (Beck, Emery, & Greenberg, 1985), Salkovskis (1985), or van Oppen and Arntz (1994). Most patients improve to some degree within 4 months of treatment. Even in the case of little response, it is advisable to continue treatment, since a considerable proportion of the patients are late responders. When CBT is unsuccessful, the treatment plan is changed, and antidepressants are prescribed. When, again, no improvement occurs, augmentation can be tried with, for example, haloperidol (McDougle et al., 1994), buspirone (Pigott et al., 1992), or the aforementioned forms of CBT. Finally, an intensive treatment can be offered on an inpatient basis or in a day-care hospital (van Dyck, van Balkom, & van Oppen, 1996).

Some factors may necessitate a modification of the decision tree presented. One such factor is the treatment history of the patient. Usually, in clinical practice, an alternative therapy is chosen if a patient has not responded to a particular treatment in the past. Another practical factor that might affect the treatment selected is the availability of CBT. If there is a long waiting list for CBT or no available therapist who is experienced in CBT, we recommend starting with antidepressants and later introducing CBT in combination with the medication. Another important variable is the patient's preference for a particular treatment. Given the fact that increased motivation predicts greater improvement (de Haan et al., 1997), it is advisable to follow the patient's preference to a certain extent.

ORGANIZATION OF THE COMBINATION TREATMENT

Below, practical suggestions are presented for the application of combination therapy in OCD. For details of each treatment element, we refer the reader to Chapters 11–14 of this volume. Considering that administering medication is less time consuming than providing CBT, a combination therapy can more easily be started with medication. In the second phase of treatment, CBT may be added. In the third phase, while continuing CBT, medication can be reduced to the minimal effective dosage and eventually be discontinued completely. The combination treatment can be delivered on an inpatient or outpatient basis.

For the combination therapy, the availability of a psychiatrist or a physician, as well as a behavioral therapist, is necessary. Depending on the therapist's specialization, the whole combination treatment can be carried out by the same person. When two therapists are involved, it is important to make a responsibility protocol in which the tasks of each therapist are specified. The treatment package should be offered to the patient step-by-step, with both therapists evaluating the patient together to determine the effectiveness of each therapy element. The patient should be informed in advance of the probable components of treatment. The evaluations should be planned at points in time when changes occur in the treatment, such as starting the exposure *in vivo* or tapering medication. It is advisable to use validated measures of OCD symptomatology to establish changes in OCD severity.

In the first phase of the treatment, only the physician needs to meet with the patient. The efficacy of the combination treatment in OCD has been documented with clomipramine and fluvoxamine, but the other antidepressants known to be effective in OCD can be used as well. The medication should be increased slowly, with attention to side effects. The treatment is started with daily dosages of 50 mg of clomipramine, fluvoxamine, or sertraline, or 20 mg of fluoxetine or paroxetine. If disturbing side effects do not occur, in 3 weeks, the dose can be increased to a maximum of 300 mg of clomipramine or fluvoxamine, 200 mg of sertraline, or 60 mg of fluoxetine or paroxetine, subdivided over two or three administrations (Greist, Jefferson, Kobak, Katzelnick, & Serlin, 1995; Jenike, 1990). Although clomipramine is sometimes administered at higher dosages, the threshold for seizures appears to be lower as dosage increases beyond 250 mg. DeVeaugh-Geiss, Landau, and Katz (1989) reported that the rate of seizures was 2.1% at dosages of 300 mg or more, but only 0.48% at dosages of 250 mg or less.

It is recommended that the patient be seen frequently during this phase and to schedule telephone consultations if disturbing side effects occur. After 8 weeks of treatment, the effect of the antidepressant can be evaluated. In the case of any residual OCD symptoms, CBT may be added. Since nonresponse to one of these antidepressants does not predict nonresponse to the others, all the antidepressants mentioned can be tried in succession, which will extend the duration of this phase.

In the following phase, the medication should be kept at a constant level, and CBT should be started. If there are two therapists, the patient should see the physician less frequently for prescriptions and checkups. The frequency of the CBT sessions may be weekly, for example. If the therapist and patient agree that the treatment goals have been met, the frequency of the sessions may be reduced. This is usually the case after several months of CBT. It is important that the patient is able to contact the physician if problems with the medication arise. The cognitive-behavioral therapist should have a basic knowledge of the use and side effects of the antidepressants given.

A commonly used form of behavior therapy is gradual, self-controlled exposure *in vivo* with response prevention. The patient is encouraged to conduct exposure to fearful situations and to endure the anxiety that is evoked by these exercises. It is agreed with the patient that he or she will attempt to refrain from carrying out compulsions. Once a fear hierarchy has been established, the first homework exercise is chosen. Each day, the patient should register the frequency and severity of the obsessive–compulsive symptoms. Homework should be discussed in each session, and new homework should be assigned (Emmelkamp, Bouman, & Scholing, 1992; Hoogduin & Hoogduin, 1984; Steketee, 1993).

In cognitive therapy, irrational cognitions that cause anxiety and discomfort are identified by means of a diary. During treatment, the irrational cognitions are challenged through a "Socratic dialogue" and modified in such a way that associated negative feelings occur less frequently. As a consequence, compulsive rituals used to reduce anxiety and discomfort provoked by these irrational thoughts are no longer necessary and improve as well (Emmelkamp et al., 1992; van Oppen & Arntz, 1994).

If the clinical status of the patient has remained stable for some time, and no important changes are expected in the life circumstances, the daily dose of the antidepressant may be reduced in order to find the minimal effective dose. During this time, the patient may need to visit the psychiatrist more often, and CBT can be temporarily terminated. If the symptoms recur, a remission of the symptoms can be accomplished by booster sessions of CBT. In this situation, the dose of the medication may be temporarily kept at the earlier level until the patient has recovered. Only after recovery should medication reduction start again. The duration of this reduction phase differs greatly from patient to patient but often is in the range of 6 months.

When the patient has been stable on the minimal effective dosage of the antidepressant for 4–6 months, further use of medication has to be decided upon. Some patients will ask for a continuation of the medication. Ultimately, these patients can be referred back to the general practitioner for prescriptions. Other patients will ask for termination of the medication. It is important to clarify the patient's motives for this. Patients can be concerned about possible negative effects of long-term use of antidepressants, such as becoming dependent on the drug or developing physical problems. Patients may also believe that once the symptoms have disappeared, the OCD has been cured. Appropriate arguments to terminate medication are unacceptable side effects, pregnancy, or the desire to have children.

If psychiatrist, behavior therapist, and patient agree that the medication should be stopped, the patient may visit the therapists regularly to check for relapse. It is important to point out to the patient that he or she should keep applying the cognitive-behavioral techniques that led to an improvement in the OCD symptoms. When the patient is without medication, and the complaints do not recur, a therapy-free follow-up period should be agreed upon. After a successful follow-up period, contact may be discontinued.

CONCLUSION

In this chapter we discussed the efficacy of combination treatment in OCD. Five studies were reviewed, each suggesting that combination treatment is not superior to treatment with CBT alone. Patients treated with a combination of antidepressants and CBT improve more quickly, but after 4 months of treatment, the differences disappear. Based on this limited evidence, we presented a decision tree for choosing between the three treatment options for OCD now available: antidepressants, CBT, or a combination of the two. Little is known about clinical variables that are likely to predict success in one treatment modality over another. More research is also needed to determine the optimal order in which combination-treatment components should be administered. In addition, more research is needed to determine the optimal duration of treatment with antidepressants in the combination treatment, the speed with which medications should be discontinued, and appropriate interventions in the case of relapse. Such research would identify logical steps in the order of treatments so as to assure an optimal treatment for patients with OCD.

REFERENCES

Basoglu, M., Lax, T., Kasvikis, Y., & Marks, I. M. (1988). Predictors of improvement in obsessive–compulsive disorder. *Journal of Anxiety Disorders, 2*, 299–317.

Beck, A. T., Emery, G., & Greenberg, R. L. (1985). *Anxiety disorders and phobias: A cognitive perspective.* New York: Basic Books

Christensen, H., Hadzi-Pavlovic, D., Andrews, G., & Mattick, R. (1987). Behavior therapy and tricyclic medication in the treatment of obsessive–compulsive disorder: A quantitative review. *Journal of Consulting and Clinical Psychology, 55*, 701–711.

Cottraux, J., Messy, P., Marks, I. M., Mollard, E., & Bouvard, M. (1993a). Predictive factors in the treatment of obsessive–compulsive disorders with fluvoxamine and/or behaviour therapy. *Behavioural Psychotherapy, 21*, 45–50.

Cottraux, J., Mollard, E., Bouvard, M., & Marks, I. (1993b). Exposure therapy, fluvoxamine, or combination treatment in obsessive–compulsive disorder: One year follow-up. *Psychiatry Research, 49*, 63–75.

Cottraux, J., Mollard, E., Bouvard, M., Marks, I., Sluys, M., Nury, A. M., Douge, R., & Ciadella, P. (1990). A controlled study of fluvoxamine and exposure in obsessive–compulsive disorder. *International Clinical Psychopharmacology, 5*, 17–30.

Cox, B. J., Swinson, R. P., Morrison, B., & Lee, P. S. (1993). Clomipramine, fluoxetine and behavior therapy in the treatment of obsessive compulsive disorder. *International Clinical Psychopharmacology, 5*, 17–30.

de Haan, E., van Oppen, P., van Balkom, A. J. L. M., Spinhoven, P., Hoogduin, C. A. L., & van Dyck, R. (1997). Prediction of outcome and early versus late improvement in OCD patients treated with cognitive behaviour therapy and pharmacotherapy. *Acta Psychiatrica Scandinavica, 96*, 354–362.

DeVeaugh-Geiss, J., Landau, P., & Katz, R. (1989). Treatment of obsessive compulsive disorder with clomipramine. *Psychiatric Annals, 19*, 97–101.

Emmelkamp, P. M. G., Bouman, T. K., & Scholing, A. (1992). *Anxiety disorders: A practitioner's guide.* Chichester, UK: Wiley.

Foa, E. B., Kozak, M. J., Steketee, G. S., & McCarthy, P. R. (1992). Treatment of depressive and obsessive–compulsive symptoms in OCD by imipramine and behaviour therapy. *British Journal of Clinical Psychology, 31*, 279–292.

Greist, J. H., Jefferson, J. W., Kobak, K. A., Katzelnick, D. J., & Serlin, R. C. (1995). Efficacy and tolerability of serotonin transport inhibitors in obsessive–compulsive disorder. *Archives of General Psychiatry, 52,* 53–60.

Hoogduin, C. A. L., & Hoogduin, W. A. (1984). The out-patient treatment of patients with an obsessive–compulsive disorder. *Behaviour Research and Therapy, 22,* 455–460.

Jenike, M. A. (1990). Drug treatment of obsessive–compulsive disorder. In M. A. Jenike, L. Baer, & W. E. Minichiello (Eds.), *Obsessive–compulsive disorders: Theory and practice* (pp. 249–282). Chicago: Year Book Publishers.

Kasvikis, Y., & Marks, I. M. (1988). Clomipramine, self-exposure, and therapist-accompanied exposure in obsessive–compulsive ritualizers: Two-year follow-up. *Journal of Anxiety Disorders, 2,* 291–298.

Marks, I. M., Lelliott, P., Basoglu, M., Noshirvani, H., Monteiro, W., Cohen, D., & Kasvikis, Y. (1988). Clomipramine, self-exposure and therapist-aided exposure for obsessive–compulsive rituals. *British Journal of Psychiatry, 152,* 522–534.

Marks, I. M., Stern, R. S., Mawson, D., Cobb, J., & McDonald, R. (1980). Clomipramine and exposure for obsessive–compulsive rituals. *British Journal of Psychiatry, 136,* 1–25.

McDougle, C. J., Goodman, W. K., Leckman, J. F., Lee, N. C., Heninger, G. R., & Price, L. H. (1994). Haloperidol addition in fluvoxamine-refractory obsessive–compulsive disorder. *Archives of General Psychiatry, 51,* 302–308.

O'Sullivan, G., Noshirvani, H., Marks, I., Monteiro, W., & Lelliott, P. (1991). Six-year follow-up after exposure and clomipramine therapy for obsessive–compulsive disorder. *Journal of Clinical Psychiatry, 52,* 150–155.

Pigott, T. A., L'Heureux, F., Hill, J. L., Bihari, K., Bernstein, S. E., & Murphy, D. L. (1992). A double-blind study of adjuvant buspirone hydrochloride in clomipramine-treated patients with obsessive–compulsive disorder. *Journal of Clinical Psychopharmacology, 12,* 11–18.

Rachman, S., Cobb, J., Grey, S., McDonald, B., Mawson, D., Sartory, G., & Stern, R. (1979). The behavioural treatment of obsessional–compulsive disorders with and without clomipramine. *Behaviour Research and Therapy, 17,* 467–478.

Salkovskis, P. M. (1985). Obsessional–compulsive problems: A cognitive-behavioural analysis. *Behaviour Research and Therapy, 23,* 571–583.

Solyom, L., & Sookman, D. (1977). A comparison of clomipramine hydrochloride (Anafranil) and behaviour therapy in the treatment of obsessive neurosis. *Journal of International Medical Research, 5*(Suppl. 5), 49–61.

Steketee, G. (1993). *Treatment of obsessive–compulsive disorder.* New York: Guilford Press.

van Balkom, A. J. L. M., de Haan, E., van Oppen, P., Spinhoven, Ph., Hoogduin, C. A. L., & van Dyck, R. (in press). Cognitive-behavioural therapy versus the combination with fluvoxamine in the treatment of obsessive–compulsive disorder. *Journal of Nervous and Mental Disease.*

van Balkom, A. J. L. M., van Oppen, P., Vermeulen, A. W. A., van Dyck, R., Nauta, M. C. E., & Vorst, H. C. M. (1994). A meta-analysis on the treatment of obsessive compulsive disorder. *Clinical Psychology Review, 14,* 359–381.

van Dyck, R., van Balkom, A. J. L. M., & van Oppen, P. (1996). *Behandelingsstrategiën bij angststoornissen* [Treatment strategies in the anxiety disorders]. Houten/Diegem, The Netherlands/Belgium: Bohn Stafleu van Loghum.

van Oppen, P., & Arntz, A. (1994). Cognitive therapy for obsessive compulsive disorder. *Behaviour Research and Therapy, 32,* 79–87.

Chapter 16

OBSESSIVE–COMPULSIVE DISORDER IN CHILDREN AND ADOLESCENTS

John S. March
Henrietta L. Leonard

One of the more common neuropsychiatric disorders in children and adolescents (Flament, 1990), obsessive–compulsive disorder (OCD) often comes to the attention of mental health providers because of its propensity to severely disrupt academic, social, and family functioning (Leonard, Swedo, et al., 1993b). Nonetheless, despite the substantial prevalence and morbidity associated with pediatric OCD, relatively few affected young persons receive a correct diagnosis, and fewer still receive appropriate treatment (Flament, Whitaker, et al., 1988) even though demonstrably effective cognitive-behavioral (March, Mulle, et al., 1994) and pharmacological (March, Leonard, et al., 1995) treatments have become available over the past 10 years (March & Leonard, 1996).

Taking these recent improvements in our understanding of the diagnosis and treatment of pediatric OCD as our text, this chapter reviews the epidemiology, diagnostic criteria, phenomenology and natural history, neurobiology, and treatment of young persons with OCD. The interested reader may wish to peruse a more in-depth treatment of assessment issues (Goodman & Price, 1992; March & Albano, 1996), diagnosis and comorbidity (Swedo, Rapoport, et al., 1989; Cohen & Leckman, 1994), OCD in the school setting (Adams, Waas, et al., 1994), spectrum disorders (Leonard, Lenane, et al., 1991a; Rapoport, 1991; Swedo, 1993), natural history (Leonard, Swedo, et al., 1993b); neuropsychiatry (March, Leonard, et al., in press), general treatment (Leonard, Lenane, et al., 1993a), cognitive-behavioral psychotherapy (March, Mulle, et al., 1994; March, 1995; March & Mulle, 1996), and pharmacotherapy (Leonard & Rapoport, 1989).

EPIDEMIOLOGY

As with adults (Rasmussen & Eisen, 1994), OCD is substantially more common in children and adolescents than once thought, with a 6-month prevalence of approximately 1 in 200 children and adolescents (Rutter, Tizard, et al., 1970). Among adults with OCD, one-third to one-half develop the disorder during childhood (Rasmussen & Eisen, 1990), implying that the childhood-onset form of OCD foreshadows considerable adult morbidity. Unfortunately, children and adolescents with the disorder often go unrecognized. In Flament's epidemiological survey, only 4 of the 18 children found to have OCD were under professional care (Flament et al., 1988). Not one of the 18 had been correctly identified as suffering from OCD, including the 4 children in mental health treatment, perhaps confirming Jenike's characterization of OCD as a "hidden epidemic" (Jenike, 1989). Reasons that have been advanced for underdiagnosis and undertreatment include OCD-specific factors (secretiveness and lack of insight), health care provider factors (such as incorrect diagnosis and either lack of familiarity or unwillingness to use proven treatments), and general factors (such as lack of access to treatment resources).

DIAGNOSIS

As described in DSM-IV, OCD is characterized by recurrent obsessions and/or compulsions that cause marked distress and/or interference in one's life (American Psychiatric Association, 1994). Key features of the DSM-IV diagnosis of OCD include the following:

• To merit a diagnosis of OCD, an affected youngster must have either obsessions or compulsions, although the great majority have both. *Obsessions* are recurrent and persistent thoughts, images, or impulses that are ego–dystonic, intrusive, and, for the most part, acknowledged as senseless. Obsessions are generally accompanied by dysphoric affects, such as fear, disgust, doubt, or a feeling of incompleteness, and so are distressing to the affected individual.

• Like adults, young persons with OCD typically attempt to ignore, suppress, or neutralize obsessive thoughts and associated feelings by performing *compulsions*, which are repetitive, purposeful behaviors performed in response to an obsession, often according to certain rules or in a stereotyped fashion. Compulsions, which can be observable repetitive behaviors, such as washing, or covert mental acts, such as counting, exist at least in part because they serve to neutralize or alleviate obsessions and accompanying dysphoric affects over the short run.

• Since there are many normal obsessive–compulsive-behaviors, DSM-IV specifies that OCD symptoms be distressing, time consuming (more than an hour a day), or significantly interfere with school, social activities, or important relationships.

- DSM-IV specifies that affected individuals recognize at some point in the illness that obsessions originate within the mind and are not simply excessive worries about real problems; similarly, compulsions must be seen as excessive or unreasonable. Persons of all ages who lack insight receive the designation "poor insight type." Most children and adolescents recognize the senselessness of OCD; however, the requirement that insight be preserved is waived for children because of the general (but not necessarily correct) perception that children and adolescents more frequently see OCD symptoms as reasonable.

- Finally, to be clear about the origin of the symptoms, DSM-IV also requires that the specific content of the obsessions cannot be related to another Axis I diagnosis, such as thoughts about food resulting from an eating disorder, or guilty thoughts (ruminations) originating with depression.

PHENOMENOLOGY

Symptoms

Common obsessions and compulsions seen in pediatric OCD are presented in Table 16.1. In the pediatric population, the most common obsessions are fear of contamination, harm to self, harm to a familiar person, and symmetry/exactness urges. Corresponding compulsions in children are washing and cleaning, followed by checking, counting, repeating, touching, and straightening (Swedo, Rapoport, et al., 1989). In almost every case, these symptoms can be driven by one or more dysphoric affects, including fear, doubt, disgust, rudimentary urges, and "just so" feelings, which some have labeled "sensory incompleteness" (Rasmussen & Eisen, 1994). For example, washing rituals may be a reaction to contamination fears or a response to feeling "sticky." The former is cognitive–phobic in origin; the latter may occur in response to a sensorimotor dysesthesia or without an obvious trigger. Whatever their origin, most children experience washing and checking rituals at some time during the course of the illness.

OCD symptoms frequently change over time, often with no clear progression pattern. Many, if not most, children have more than one OCD symptom at

TABLE 16.1. Common OCD Symptoms

Common obsessions	Common compulsions
• Contamination	• Washing
• Harm to self or others	• Repeating
• Aggressive themes	• Checking
• Sexual ideas/urges	• Touching
• Scrupulosity/religiosity	• Counting
• Symmetry urges	• Ordering/arranging
• Need to tell, ask, confess	• Hoarding
	• Praying

any one time, and many will have experienced almost all the classic OCD symptoms by the end of adolescence (Rettew, Swedo, et al., 1992). Those with only obsessions or compulsions are very rare (Swedo, Rapoport, et al., 1989). This is especially so now that DSM-IV makes a clear distinction between mental rituals and mental compulsions, thereby reducing the number of patients misclassified as pure obsessionals but who, in fact, have mental rituals.

A clinically useful detailed Symptom Checklist accompanies the Yale–Brown Obsessive–Compulsive Scale (YBOCS; Goodman, Price, et al., 1989b, 1989c), and should be a regular part of the initial assessment and maintenance care of every patient with OCD.

Comorbidity

Children with a variety of psychiatric disorders may exhibit obsessions or ritualistic behaviors, confounding the diagnosis of OCD in some patients. In addition, more than one disorder may be diagnosed in a single patient, since the diagnosis of OCD is not exclusionary. Tic disorders, anxiety disorders, disruptive behavior disorders, and learning disorders are common in clinical (Swedo, Rapoport, et al., 1989; Riddle, Scahill, et al., 1990) and epidemiological (Flament et al., 1988) samples of children with OCD. For unknown reasons, comorbid major depression, although not uncommon in clinical and epidemiological samples of youth with OCD (Swedo, Rapoport, et al., 1989; Valleni-Basile, Garrison, et al., 1994), may be less common as a comorbid condition than in adult OCD (Rasmussen & Eisen, 1994). Clinically, comorbid obsessive–compulsive spectrum disorders, such as trichotillomania, body dysmorphic disorder, and habit disorders, such as nail biting, are not uncommon in patients with OCD. A surprisingly small number of children exhibit obsessive–compulsive personality disorder (OCPD), implying that obsessive–compulsive personality traits, while overrepresented among children with OCD, are neither necessary nor sufficient for the diagnosis, although the relationship between OCD and OCPD merits further study (Swedo, Rapoport, et al., 1989).

Age, Gender, and Ethnicity

In a clinical sample, the modal age of onset of OCD was 7 and the mean age at onset was 10 in clinical samples (Swedo, Rapoport, et al., 1989). Boys appear more likely to have a prepubertal onset and to have a family member with OCD or Tourette's syndrome (TS), whereas girls are more likely to have OCD start during adolescence. In the Flament et al. (1988) epidemiological study, the ratio of males to females was 1:1, implying (1) that the male:female ratio equalizes in adolescence or (2) that there is an ascertainment bias in the clinical samples, or both. In general, comorbid internalizing and externalizing symptoms are more common in boys (earlier onset) than in girls (later onset) as well (Swedo, Rapoport, et al., 1989; Valleni-Basile et al., 1994). For unclear reasons, OCD is more common in Caucasian than African American children in clinical samples, although epidemiological data in adults suggest no differences in prevalence as a function of ethnicity or geographic region (Rasmussen & Eisen, 1994).

Developmental Considerations

Most, if not all, children exhibit normal age-dependent obsessive–compulsive behaviors. For example, young children frequently like things done "just so," or insist on elaborate bedtime rituals (Gesell, Ames, et al., 1974). Such behaviors often can be understood in terms of developmental issues involving mastery and control, and are usually gone by middle childhood, to be replaced by collecting, hobbies, and "focused interests." Clinically, normative obsessive–compulsive behaviors can be reliably discriminated from OCD on the basis of timing, content, and severity (Leonard, Goldberger, et al., 1990). Developmentally sanctioned obsessive–compulsive behaviors occur early in childhood, are rare during adolescence, are common to large numbers of children, and are associated with mastery of important developmental transitions. In contrast, OCD occurs somewhat later, appears "bizarre" to adults and to other children, if not to the affected child, and always produces dysfunction rather than mastery. Parenthetically, the common belief that children and adolescents with OCD often lack insight into the senseless nature may in part represent an artifact of (1) difficulty maintaining insight during acute "attacks" of OCD or (2) confounding of insight and secretiveness due to fear of punishment or simple embarrassment.

Natural History

Before the arrival of modern pharmacotherapy and cognitive-behavioral therapy (CBT), the outcome of treatment was dismal. Currently, although OCD often remains a chronic mental illness in adult (Rasmussen & Eisen, 1990) and pediatric patients (Leonard, Swedo, et al., 1993b), most patients achieve meaningful symptom relief with well-delivered, comprehensive treatment. Interestingly, young boys with OCD and no tics are at clear risk for later development of tic disorders (Leonard, Lenane, et al., 1992). Those developing tics evidence greater anxiety, a younger age at onset of OCD, and a higher likelihood of a family member with a tic disorder than those without tics, suggesting that OCD and TS may be alternative manifestations of the same underlying illness. Finally, successful treatment, by definition, interrupts even if only temporarily the natural history of OCD. Though the relative merits of pharmacotherapy and CBT have not been resolved, CBT seems the more durable treatment (March, Mulle, et al., 1994; March & Mulle, 1995). Since relapse commonly follows medication discontinuation (Leonard, Swedo, et al., 1991b), adding CBT may limit relapse when medications are discontinued (March et al., 1994). Of even greater potential interest is the association between onset of OCD/TS and upper respiratory tract infection (see below), which promises early identification of risk (the biological marker for rheumatic fever) and intervention (prophylactic antibiotics).

PEDIATRIC OCD AS A NEUROPSYCHIATRIC DISORDER

Successful treatment of OCD with serotonin reuptake inhibitors initially leads to a neurobehavioral explanation for OCD in the form of the "serotonin hypothesis" (reviewed in Barr, Goodman, et al., 1992). Later, phenomenological similarities between obsessive–compulsive symptoms (washing, picking, and licking) coupled with studies of trichotillomania lead to the hypothesis that OCD is (in some patients) a "grooming behavior gone awry" (Swedo, 1989). Taken in this context, Esman (1989), reviewing the psychoanalytic understanding of OCD, noted that insight-oriented psychotherapy has proven disappointing at best in ameliorating OCD symptoms. Although some argue that some OCD symptoms have underlying dynamic meaning, it is doubtful whether specific OCD symptoms really represent derivatives of intrapsychic conflicts since there is a finite number of OCD symptoms that are universally experienced in typical patterned fashion. Moreover, there is no reason to suggest that OCD patients are any more conflicted about sexual matters than other psychiatric patients (Staebler, Pollard, et al., 1993).

On the contrary, OCD is often cited as an example of the quintessential neuropsychiatric disorder (March et al., in press). Evidence favoring a neuropsychiatric model of the etiopathogenesis of OCD includes (1) family genetic studies suggesting that OCD and TS may in some, but not all, cases represent alternate expressions of the same gene(s), may represent different genes, or may arise spontaneously (Pauls, Alsobrook, et al., 1995; Pauls, Towbin, et al., 1986); (2) neuroimaging studies implicating abnormalities in circuits linking basal ganglia to cortex (Rauch, Jenike, et al., 1994; Swedo, Schapiro, et al., 1989), with these circuits "responding" to either cognitive-behavioral or pharmacological treatment with a serotonin reuptake inhibitor (Baxter, Schwartz, et al., 1992); and (3) neurotransmitter and neuroendocrine abnormalities in childhood-onset OCD (Hamburger, Swedo, et al., 1989; Swedo & Rapoport, 1990).

Of these lines of evidence, the relationship between OCD and TS is particularly relevant (Cohen & Leckman, 1994). It is now well documented that there is an increased rate of tic disorders in individuals with OCD; the converse is also true (Pauls et al., 1995). Additionally, in systematic family genetic studies of probands with TS or other tic disorders, first-degree relatives show an increased rate of both tic disorders and OCD (Pauls et al., 1986). Similar findings are present in first-degree relatives of OCD probands (Leonard et al., 1992). Interestingly, Pauls and colleagues (1995) note that early onset may indicate a greater degree of genetic vulnerability.

As with adults, children and adolescents with OCD frequently exhibit subtle neurological (Denckla, 1989) and neuropsychiatric (Cox, Fedio, et al., 1989) abnormalities, often involving nonverbal reasoning skills, which may place them at risk for specific learning problems such as dysgraphia, dyscalculia, poor expressive written language, and slow processing speed and efficiency. Although some have speculated that these neurocognitive impairments may adversely affect the outcome of pharmacotherapy for OCD (Hollander, Schiffman, et al., 1990;

March, Johnston, et al., 1990), others have found no such association (Leonard & Rapoport, 1989; Swedo, Leonard, et al., 1990). Clinically, the overlap between OCD and learning disorders should prompt a careful neurospychological evaluation in OCD patients having trouble with academic tasks rather than a reflexive acceptance that school problems are due to OCD alone.

OCD symptoms arising or exacerbating in the context of Group A beta-hemolytic streptococcal infection (GABHS) may define a singular subgroup of children with OCD (Allen, Leonard, et al., 1995). Obsessive–compulsive symptoms are not uncommon in pediatric patients with Sydenham's chorea, which represents a neurological variant of rheumatic fever (RF). Moreover, when compared with nonchoreic RF patients, OCD is far more common when chorea is present than when absent (Swedo, Rapoport, et al., 1989). Resembling rheumatic carditis, Sydenham's is believed to represent an autoimmune inflammation of the basal ganglia triggered by antistreptococcal antibodies (Kiessling, Marcotte, et al., 1994). Thus, Swedo and colleagues have theorized that OCD in the context of Sydenham's chorea may provide a medical model for the etiopathogenesis of OCD and tic disorders (Swedo, Leonard, et al., 1993). In this model, antineuronal antibodies formed against GABHS cell wall antigens are seen to cross-react with caudate neural tissue, with consequent initiation of obsessive–compulsive symptom. In turn, this would suggest that acute onset or dramatic exacerbation of OCD or tic symptoms should prompt investigation of GABHS infection, especially since immunomodulatory treatments, including antibiotic therapies, may be of benefit some patients (Swedo, Leonard, et al., 1994).

The interested reader is referred to recent reviews for a more detailed discussion of these and related topics (Cohen & Leckman, 1994; Giedd, Rapoport, et al., 1996; Rapoport, 1989; Swedo & Rapoport, 1990).

CLINICAL ASSESSMENT

Children and adolescents with OCD vary widely regarding the nature and impact of the disorder. Some children are embarrassed and secretive, despite full awareness that their obsessions are senseless and their rituals excessive. In some cases, comorbidities, such as social phobia, attention-deficit/hyperactivity disorder, and the tic disorders present complex problems in differential therapeutics. Thus, an accurate assessment of the pediatric patient with OCD, including a careful search for complicating comorbidities, is essential to skillful diagnosis and treatment (Thyer, 1991; Wolff & Wolff, 1991).

Semistructured interviews, such as the Anxiety Disorders Interview for Children (Kearney & Silverman, 1990), and scalar measures, such as the Leyton Obsessional Inventory (Berg, Rapoport, et al., 1985), are sometimes helpful when evaluating OCD in the context of an overall diagnostic assessment. Although psychometric studies of instruments for assessing the full range of pediatric anxiety disorders are scarce at best, progress on this front is increasing a focus of active research (March, Parker, et al., 1997b; March & Albano, in press). As with adults, the YBOCS is currently considered the instrument of choice for identifying and rating OCD symptoms (Goodman, Price, et al., 1992). In addition to comprehensively inquiring into the nature of the child's OCD symptoms, the YBOCS provides an index of symptom frequency, intensity, interference, and the child's inclination and ability to resist OCD. Recent studies suggest that the child and adolescent version of the YBOCS shows reasonable psychometric properties (Scahill, Riddle, et al., 1997). Family members, peers, and teachers also may provide important information about a child's OCD, with teachers being especially important if the child is having OCD-related problems at school (Adams et al., 1994).

Interestingly, in the RF literature, a simple upper respiratory tract illness (URI) was often the precipitant for exacerbated rheumatic carditis in a vulnerable child. Thus, an abrupt onset of OCD (and/or tic) symptoms or a dramatic exacerbation of preexisting symptoms, especially in the presence of hay fever, other upper respiratory allergies, an upper respiratory infection, or family or personal history of RF necessitates a careful search for pediatric autoimmune neuropsychiatric disorder associated with strep. In addition to a careful history, this may include nose and throat strep cultures and an antistreptolysin O titer or an anti-DNAse (strep) b test. Positive findings suggest that immunomodulatory treatments, such as oral antibiotics, may be indicated.

Once a comprehensive multimethod, multi-informant evaluation has been completed, it is preferable to monitor the process and outcome of treatment using measures that sample specific symptom domains, such as washing versus avoidance, functional domains, such as home or school, and symptomatic distress during exposure, such as subjective units of discomfort (SUDS) (March, 1995). Additionally, since many patients improve considerably but far fewer become symptom free, global measures of impairment, such as the Clinical Global Impairment and NIMH global scales, and improvement, such as the Clinical Global Improvement scale, may help understand the need for ongoing or additional treatment(s). Further details regarding the systematic assessment of patients with OCD and complicating comorbidities within a subspecialty clinic approach to pediatric anxiety disorders can be found in March, Mulle, et al. (1995) and March and Albano (1996).

TREATMENT

OCD Expert Consensus Practice Guidelines

Clinicians need answers to practical questions: When do you use behavior therapy in children and adolescents with OCD? When do you use drug therapy? Is there an advantage to combined CBT and drug therapy? How should these treatments be combined? What do you do when patients respond partially? When they do not respond at all, even to aggressive combination treatment?

What are reasonable times to wait before modifying or switching treatments? How should treatment be discontinued?

Expert consensus guidelines may help answer the questions clinicians face in moving toward "best practice" treatments that are compatible with managed care network objectives of cost-effective quality care (March, Frances, et al., 1997a). Expert consensus guidelines have several advantages over practice guidelines developed under the auspices of processional organizations or chapters (such as this one) penned by experts with a narrow basis for deciding clinical strategies. Most research studies are difficult to generalize to clinical practice, because rigorous patient selection criteria and experimental controls limit the real-world representativeness of the sample. We need practice guidelines for help with precisely those patients who would not meet the narrow selection criteria used in most research studies. Moreover, clinical practice is so complicated that it inherently generates far too many questions for the clinical research literature to ever answer comprehensively through systematic studies. Finally, changes in the accepted best clinical practice often occur at a much faster rate than the necessarily slower paced research efforts that would provide scientific documentation for the change. As new treatments become available, clinicians often find them to be superior for many indications that go far beyond narrower indications supported by the available controlled research. For all these reasons, the aggregation of expert opinion is a crucial bridge between the clinical research literature and clinical practice in developing practice guidelines.

With a team from the departments of psychiatry of Columbia University, Cornell University, and Duke University, one of us (J.S.M.) recently developed expert treatment guidelines for pediatric OCD (March et al., 1997a). In the OCD Expert Consensus Guidelines, CBT, or CBT plus medication, is recommended as the initial treatment of choice, with CBT alone preferred in younger patients and those with milder symptoms. The guidelines also include recommendations for how best to manage the patient who responds poorly to initial treatment, treatment-refractory patients, selecting among medications and CBT techniques, maintenance therapy and discontinuation of medications, and how best to manage medical and psychiatric comorbidity. Additionally, the OCD Expert Consensus Guidelines includes a patient handout developed in association with the Obsessive–Compulsive Foundation. Figures 16.1 and 16.2 present the executive summary and treatment algorithms from the Expert Consensus Guidelines for OCD (March et al., 1997a), which are readily applicable to pediatric patients.

Cognitive-Behavioral Therapy

Cognitive-behavioral psychotherapy is routinely described as the psychotherapeutic treatment of choice for children, adolescents, and adults with OCD (Berg, Rapoport, et al., 1989; March & Mulle, 1996; Wolff & Wolff, 1991). Unlike other psychotherapies that have been applied to OCD, CBT presents a logically consistent and compelling relationship between the disorder, the treatment, and

Obsessive–Compulsive Disorder Executive Summary

A. Consensus Recommendations for First-Line Treatments by Clinical Situation

Selecting the initial treatment strategy and the sequence of treatments

Age-specific
considerations
- Prepubescent children: CBT first for milder or more severe OCD
- Adolescents: CBT first for milder OCD; CBT + SRI for more severe OCD
- Adults: CBT first for milder OCD; CBT + SRI or SRI alone first for more severe OCD

Considerations based on overall efficacy, speed, and durability of treatment
- Milder OCD: CBT alone; or CBT + SRI
- More severe OCD: CBT + SRI

Considerations based on tolerability and patient acceptability
- Milder OCD: CBT alone; or CBT + SRI
- More severe OCD: CBT + SRI; or SRI alone

Selecting CBT strategy

Obsessions and compulsions ⟶ ERP (exposure/response prevention)
ERP + CT (cognitive therapy)

Tailoring treatment for specific symptoms
Contamination fears, symmetry rituals,
counting/repeating, hoarding, aggressive urges   ERP
Scupulosity and moral guilt, pathological doubt ⟶ CT

Intensity of CBT ⟶

- Gradual (i.e., weekly); recommended for most patients (usually 13–20 sessions)
- Intensive (i.e., daily): recommended when speed is of the essence; or for patients who have not responded to gradual CBT or who have extremely severe symptoms

Selecting a specific medication: use serotonin reuptake inhibitors (SRIs)

- Fluvoxamine   Recommendations for timing
- Fluoxetine   • Inadequate response to average SRI dose: push to maximum
- Clomipramine   dose in 4–9 weeks from start of treatment
- Sertraline   • Inadequate response after 4–6 additional weeks at maximum
- Paroxetine   dose: switch to another SRI

Treatment resistance

If no response or partial response to CBT alone ⟶ Add an SRI; add more CBT with changes in approach
If no response or partial response to SRI alone ⟶ Add CBT or switch to another SRI
If no response to combined CBT and SRI ⟶ Switch to another SRI
If partial response to combined CBT and SRI ⟶ Switch to another SRI
Add more CBT with changes in approach
Augment with another medication
After failing trials of 2–3 SSRIs + CBT ⟶ Try clomipramine
If no response or partial response to
combined CBT and 3 SRI trials ⟶ Augment with another medication (select agent based
(one of which was clomipramine)   on associated features)
Add more CBT with changes in approach

Maintenance treatment

When to use long-term medication ⟶ After 3–4 mild/moderate relapses or 2–4 severe relapses despite
adequate CBT
How to stop medication ⟶ Gradually taper meds after 1–2 years while continuing monthly CBT
(decrease meds by 25% and wait 2 months before next
decrease)
Frequency of office visits
Full recovery with CBT alone ⟶ Monthly for the next 3–6 months
Partial recovery with CBT alone ⟶ Weekly to monthly for next 3–6 months
Full or partial recovery with
medications ⟶ Monthly for the next 3–6 months

Note: CBT, cognitive-behavioral therapy; SRI (serotonin reuptake inhibitor) refers to the five compounds clomipramine, fluoxetine, fluvoxamine, paroxetine, and sertraline; SSRI (selective SRI) refers to all but clomipramine.

FIGURE 16.1. Executive summary (from OCD Expert Consensus Guidelines).

B. Consensus Recommendations for First-Line Psychosocial Treatments

Cognitive-behavioral therapy
For OCD, CBT involves exposure plus response prevention (ERP) combined with cognitive therapy (CT)

- When available, CBT is likely to be used for every patient with OCD except those who have very severe symptoms or who are unwilling to participate in CBT
- Add when patient has been a nonresponder or partial responder to SRI alone
- Use alone if patient is intolerant to side effects of medication or is pregnant or has a medical condition that contraindicates medication
- Comorbidity with other psychiatric disorders for which CBT may be helpful, especially if modified for the comorbid disorder

Exposure plus response prevention (ERP)

- Especially helpful for contamination or other fears, symmetry rituals, counting/repeating, hoarding, aggressive urges

Cognitive therapy

- Especially helpful for scrupulosity, moral guilt, and pathological doubt

Treatment format and intensity
Format:

- Individual weekly therapy sessions combined with homework or therapist-assisted out-of-office (*in vivo*) techniques
Consider adding family therapy when appropriate

Frequency:

- 13–20 sessions typically required to treat an uncomplicated OCD patient

Intensity:

- Gradual, i.e., weekly: recommended for most patients
Intensive, i.e., daily: recommended when speed is of the essence or patients have not responded to gradual CBT or have very severe symptoms

Maintenance schedule:

- Schedule: monthly booster sessions for 3–6 months

C. Consensus Recommendations for First-Line Somatic Treatments

Selective serotonin reuptake inhibitors (SSRIs)
(fluvoxamine, fluoxetine, sertraline, paroxetine)

- Combine with CBT or use alone in adults with moderate to severe symptoms
- Add when no response or partial response to CBT alone
- Rather than clomipramine when anticholinergic, cardiovascular, sexual, sedative, or weight-gain side effects are a concern
- Comorbidity with other psychiatric disorders for which an SSRI may be helpful

Clomipramine

- After 2–3 failed SSRI trials
- Augment SSRI in partially responsive or nonresponsive patient
- Less likely than SSRIs to cause insomnia, akathisia, nausea, or diarrhea
- Comorbidity with other psychiatric disorders for which a TCA may be helpful

Note: SRI (serotonin reuptake inhibitor) refers to the five compounds clomipramine, fluoxetine, fluvoxamine, paroxetine, and sertraline; SSRI (selective SRI) refers to all but clomipramine.

D. Consensus Recommendations for OCD Complicated by Comorbid Illness

Comorbidity
Pregnancy   CBT alone
Heart disease   CBT alone; or CBT + SSRI
Renal disease   CBT alone; or CBT + SSRI
Tourette's disorder   CBT + conventional antipsychotic + SRI
Attention-deficit/hyperactivity disorder   CBT + SSRI + psychostimulant
Panic disorder or social phobia   CBT + SSRI
Major depressive disorder   CBT + SSR (start SRI first for severe symptoms)
Bipolar disorder (I or II)   CBT + mood stabilizer alone; or CBT + mood stabilizer + SRI
Oppositional/conduct/antisocial   CBT + family therapy + SRI
Schizophrenia   SRI + neuroleptic

FIGURE 16.1. (*continued*).

Overall Strategies for Acute Phase Treatment of OCD

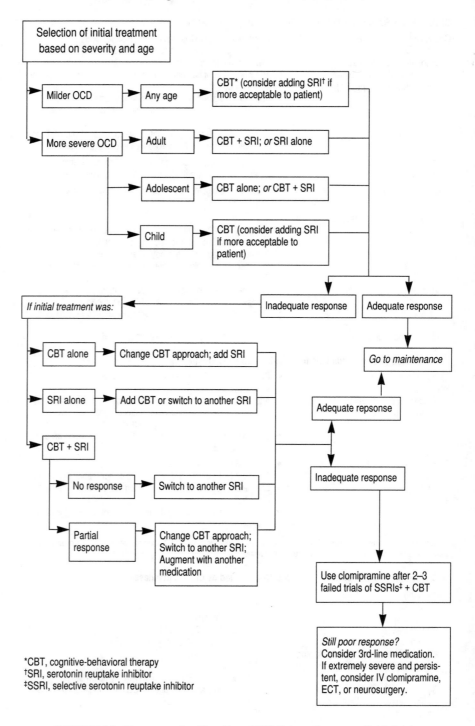

FIGURE 16.2. Treatment algorithm (from OCD Expert Consensus Guidelines).

Tactics for Duration and Intensity of Treatment During Acute and Maintenance Phases

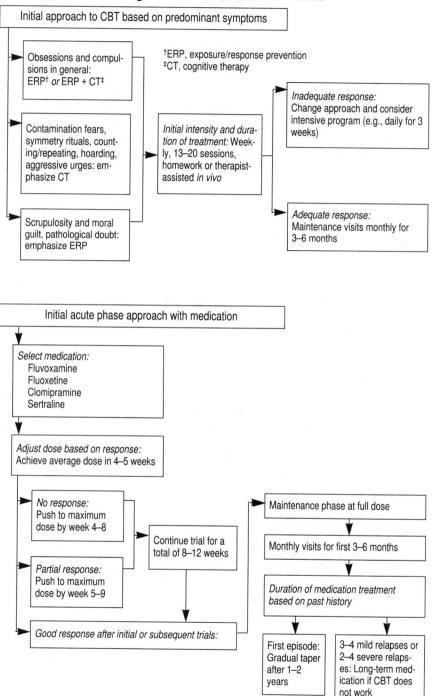

FIGURE 16.2. *(continued).*

the specified outcome (Foa & Kozak, 1985). As in adults, where CBT has long been demonstrated to be a remarkably effective and durable treatment for OCD (Dar & Greist, 1992), CBT helps the child to internalize a strategy for resisting OCD, which depends on a clear understanding of the disorder within a medical framework.

Treatment relies primarily on exposure and response prevention (ERP), with cognitive therapy and anxiety management training filling adjunctive roles. As applied to OCD, the exposure principle relies upon the fact that anxiety usually attenuates after sufficient duration of contact with a feared stimulus (March, 1995). Thus, a child with phobic symptoms regarding germs must come into and remain in contact with "germy" objects until his or her anxiety extinguishes. Repeated exposure is associated with decreased anxiety across exposure trials until the child no longer fears contact with specifically targeted phobic stimuli (March & Mulle, 1995). Adequate exposure depends on blocking rituals or avoidance behaviors, a process termed "response prevention" (March, 1995). For example, a child with germ worries must not only touch "germy things," but also must refrain from ritualized washing until after his or her anxiety diminishes substantially.

In pediatric patients, ERP is typically implemented in a gradual fashion (sometimes termed "graded exposure"), with exposure targets under patient or, less desirably, therapist control (March, 1995; March et al., 1994). For the most part, reduction in anxiety is target specific, although generalization across symptomatic baselines does occur (March & Mulle, 1995). Not surprisingly, a detailed understanding of the child's OCD symptoms is necessary to guide treatment. Finally, although periodic "booster" session may be required, those who are successfully treated with CBT alone tend to stay well (March, 1995). Moreover, since relapse commonly follows medication discontinuation, the finding of March et al. (1994) that improvement persisted in 6 of 9 responders following the withdrawal of medication provides limited support for the hypothesis that behavior therapy inhibits relapse when medications are discontinued.

Summary of Our CBT Protocol

Table 16.2 summarizes the treatment protocol, which is presented in detail in *OCD in Children and Adolescents: A Cognitive-Behavioral Treatment Manual* (March & Mulle, 1998). Treatment takes place in four steps, usually distributed over 12–20 sessions. Each session includes a statement of goals, a careful review of the preceding week, introduction of new information, therapist-assisted "nuts-and-bolts" practice, homework for the coming week, and monitoring procedures. Information sheets describing the goals and homework for that week are given at the end of each session. Step 1 focuses on psychoeducation during two sessions in the first week. Step 2, cognitive training, overlaps with Step 1 in the first and second weeks, whereas Step 3, mapping OCD, is completed during two sessions in the second week. These first three steps form the basis for Step 4. Step 4 initiates intensive, graded ERP over weeks 3–20, though many children require far fewer sessions.

TABLE 16.2. CBT Treatment Protocol

Visit No.	Goals
Session 1	Psychoeducation
Session 2	"Tool kit"
Session 3	Mapping OCD "Tool kit"
Session 4	Further mapping Trial exposure
Weeks 3–20	Exposure and response prevention
Weeks 18–19	Relapse prevention
Weeks 1, 7, and 11	Parent sessions

Step 1 places OCD firmly within a neurobehavioral model by linking OCD with a specific set of behavioral treatments and a desired outcome (i.e., symptom reduction). To cement the neurobehavioral framework, the therapist makes use of analogies to medical illnesses such as asthma or diabetes. Metaphors for obsessions are also introduced, such as brain hiccups or problems with the volume-control knob for use with younger children.

The analogy to medical illness is not as far-fetched as it might at first seem. Because OCD has its roots in disordered information processing in the brain, changes in symptoms with CBT ought to reflect changes in brain function, which is just what Baxter and Schwartz discovered when they looked at images of the brain at work in OCD patients before and after drug or behavior therapy. In those patients who responded to treatment, the PET images returned to normal in patients treated with drugs *and* patients treated with CBT (Schwartz, 1996; Schwartz, Stoessel, et al., 1996). Looked at this way, patients with OCD can be approached in the same way as patients with diabetes—only the target organ, and thus the symptom picture, differs. Each disorder involves medications, which in diabetes might be insulin and in OCD a serotonin reuptake inhibitor. Each involves psychosocial interventions that change the somatic substrate toward more normal function. In diabetes, the psychosocial treatments of choice are diet and exercise; in OCD, they involve CBT. And finally, not everyone recovers completely, so some interventions need to target coping with residual symptoms, such as diabetic foot care in diabetes. In OCD, family support groups also may help patients and their families cope skillfully with OCD (Black & Blum, 1992; Tynes, Salins, et al., 1992).

In addition to an extensive discussion of OCD as a medical illness, Step 1 also presents the risks and benefits of behavioral treatment for OCD and reviews specific details of the treatment protocol. Step 1 also begins the process of externalizing OCD, with younger children giving OCD a nasty nickname, and older children often simply calling the problem OCD. In this way, the child and his or her family can ally with the therapist against OCD in order to "boss back" the obsessions and compulsions. Adolescents and parents ordinarily appreciate a more detailed discussion of OCD as a neurobehavioral disorder.

Step 2 introduces cognitive training, defined as training in cognitive tactics for resisting OCD as distinct from response prevention for mental rituals. Goals of cognitive training include increasing a sense of personal efficacy, predictability, controllability, and self-attributed likelihood of a positive outcome for ERP tasks. Targets for cognitive training include reinforcing accurate information regarding OCD and its treatment, cognitive resistance ("bossing OCD"), and self-administered positive reinforcement and encouragement. To increase the patient's sense of predictability and controllability, we explicitly frame ERP as the strategy and the therapist and parents (and sometimes teacher or friends) as the allies in the child's "battle" against OCD. To further emphasize the child's responsibility for resisting OCD without inviting further "blaming" by family members, teachers, and friends, cognitive training includes a very simple but effective intervention: We ask the child to give OCD a nasty nickname. By always using a disparaging name to refer to OCD, the therapist "externalizes" OCD (White & Epston, 1991), so that OCD becomes a discrete "enemy" and not a "bad habit" that may have been associated with previous punishment experiences. Adolescents frequently find this procedure silly and prefer to refer to OCD by its medical name, but the principle of externalizing the disorder remains the same. Approaching OCD in this way allows everyone to ally with the child in order to "boss back" OCD, and thereby provides a narrative scaffolding on which to hang family interventions. We also use three techniques, each well validated in the CBT literature, to meet these goals: (1) constructive self-talk (Kendall, Howard, et al., 1988), (2) cognitive restructuring (March et al., 1994; van Oppen & Arntz, 1994), and (3) cultivating detachment (Schwartz, 1996). Each must be individualized to match the specific OCD symptoms that afflict the child, and must mesh with the child's cognitive abilities, developmental stages, and individual differences in preference among the three techniques. It also is generally best to develop a tailored "short form" that the child can use on a regular basis during ERP. Used in this fashion, cognitive training provides the child with a cognitive "tool kit" to use during ERP tasks, which in turn facilitates ERP compliance.

Step 3 maps the child's experience with OCD, including specific obsessions and compulsions and triggers, avoidance behaviors, and consequences. In behavioral terms, these steps generate a *stimulus hierarchy* within a narrative context. We use cartographic metaphors, diagrammed in Figure 16.3, to understand where the child is free from OCD, where OCD and the child each "win" some of the time, and where the child feels helpless against OCD. We call the central region, where the child already has some success in resisting OCD, the transition zone. Continuing the map metaphor, "standing" with the child on territory free from OCD allows us to strengthen the twin beliefs that we are, first, on his or her side in the struggle against OCD, and second, interested in him or her as a person who wants desperately to author OCD out of the story. In one of the clinical pearls that drives the treatment forward, the therapist teaches the child to recognize and utilize the transition zone, thereby providing a reliable guide to graded

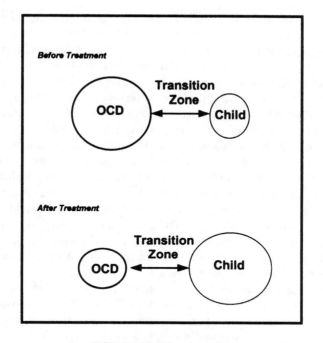

FIGURE 16.3. Mapping OCD.

exposure throughout the treatment program. In practice, the lower end of the stimulus hierarchy usually defines the transition zone.

Steps 2 and 3 include easy trial exposure-based interventions (see below) to gauge the patient's tolerance of anxiety, level of understanding, and willingness or ability to comply with treatment, and at the same time instill the idea that it is possible to successfully resist and then "win" against OCD. Trial ERP tasks also demonstrate whether the transition zone has been accurately located, thereby avoiding disruptive "surprises" due to mistargeted goals for exposure or response prevention.

Step 4 fully implements the core of CBT for the anxiety disorders, namely, intensive graded ERP, including therapist-assisted imaginal and *in vivo* ERP practice coupled to weekly homework assignments. *Exposure* occurs when the child exposes him- or herself to the feared object, action, or thought. *Response prevention* is the process of blocking rituals and/or minimizing the avoidance behaviors. Take, for example, the child with a "contamination" fear about touching doorknobs. In this case, since doorknobs trigger the obsession, the exposure task would require the child to touch the "contaminated" doorknob until his or her anxiety disappears. Response prevention takes place when the child refuses to perform the usual anxiety-driven compulsion, such as washing hands or using a tissue to grasp the doorknob.

As in a contest, OCD is framed as the adversary, and all parties remain intransigent against OCD. This attitude explicitly requires that the child use his or her allies (therapist, and then parents or friends) and new strategies (cognitive training and ERP) to resist OCD, thereby preventing the therapy from becoming an excuse to avoid exposure. However, since only the child can do the actual combat (read ERP), he or she necessarily remains in charge of choosing targets from the transition zone. We update the transition zone at the beginning of each session as the child becomes more competent and successful at resisting OCD.

Beginning with Step 1, which emphasizes psychoeducation, parents are an important part of the treatment process. Parents are included explicitly in sessions 1, 7, 9, 13, and 14. At the end of Step 1, parents receive an information booklet (*Tips for Parents*, included in March & Mulle, 1998) that includes tips for handling OCD. Parents check in with the therapist at the beginning and/or end of each session, and we invite parents to comment on how the child is progressing in his or her struggle against OCD. Parent sessions 7 and 9 focus on incorporating targets for parental response prevention or extinction, with the child again selecting targets from the transition zone. Parent sessions 13 and 14 focus on generalization training and relapse prevention.

Homework assignments are presented each week with individualized clues to help the child successfully "boss back" OCD. We liberally use positive reinforcers, such as within-session praise and small goodies, such as pencils or gum, and larger between-session rewards, such as a trip for pizza with friends. In order to facilitate positive reinforcement and to extinguish punishment by adults and peers, we also make a special effort to help the youngster tell other people (such as friends, teachers, or grandparents) how he or she has successfully reduced OCD's influence over his or her life.

Treatment ends with a graduation ceremony, followed by a booster session 6 weeks later.

Pharmacotherapy

Medication trials in adults with OCD clearly demonstrate efficacy for the serotonin reuptake inhibitors (SRIs) (Greist, Jefferson, et al., 1990; Jenike, 1992). Studies in pediatric OCD patients suggest that these compounds yield a similar benefit (for reviews, see March, 1995; Piacentini, Jaffer, et al., 1992; Rapoport, Swedo, et al., 1992).

Of the SRIs, clomipramine is the best-studied medication in the pediatric population. Initial studies reported that clomipramine was significantly superior to placebo (Flament, Rapoport, et al., 1985) and to desipramine. In 1989, an 8-week multicenter double-blind parallel comparison of clomipramine versus placebo led to FDA approval of clomipramine for the treatment of OCD in children and adolescents age 10 and above (DeVeaugh-Geiss, Moroz, et al., 1992). Notable findings from this study included (1) little or no placebo effect; (2) on average, clinical effects beginning at 3 weeks and reaching a plateau at 10 weeks; and (3) a 37% reduction in OCD symptoms as measured on the YBOCS. This degree of improvement corresponded to markedly to moderately improved on a measure of global improvement; conversely, less than 20% of the sample fell below the threshold for clinical disorder at the end of treatment, suggesting that medication is helpful but not a panacea for most children.

Side effects for clomipramine—primarily anticholinergic, antihistaminic, and alpha-blocking effects—were comparable to (but typically milder than) those seen in the adult multicenter clomipramine trial (Katz, DeVeaugh, et al., 1990; Leonard, Swedo, et al., 1989). Although long-term clomipramine maintenance has not revealed any unexpected adverse reactions (DeVeaugh-Geiss et al., 1992; Leonard, Swedo, et al., 1991b), tachycardia and slightly increased PR-, QRS-, and QT-corrected intervals on the electrocardiogram are common in children treated with both desipramine and clomipramine (Leonard, Meyer, et al., 1995b). Given the potential for tricyclic antidepressant-related cardiotoxic effects, pretreatment and periodic electrocardiographic and therapeutic drug monitoring is warranted (Elliott & Popper, 1991; Schroeder, Mullin, et al., 1989).

All of the selective serotonin reuptake inhibitors (SSRIs) are likely effective treatments for OCD in youth (March et al., 1995; Rapoport, Leonard, et al., 1993), but systematic trials are just now reaching publication. Fluoxetine has shown benefit in a one controlled trial (Riddle et al., 1992); sertraline and fluvoxamine have shown benefit in open studies (Apter, Ratzioni, et al., 1994; Cook, Charak, et al., 1994). Large multicenter registration trials of fluvoxamine and sertraline in children and adolescents have been completed; both drugs appear effective, with the magnitude of improvement approximating that of clomipramine (Riddle, Claghorn, et al., 1996; March, Biederman, Wolkow, & Safferman, 1997). Younger and older patients seem to respond equally well (Geller, Biederman, et al., 1995).

Although comparisons are limited by the differences between studies in design and dosing regimen, the side effects for the SSRIs in these pediatric multicenter trials are generally comparable to the safety findings in previous placebo-controlled studies of SSRIs in adults with OCD (Greist, Chouinard, et al., 1995a; Greist, Jefferson, et al., 1995b). The most frequently occurring adverse events are nausea–diarrhea, insomnia–somnolence, hyperstimulation, headache, and sexual side effects. Importantly, side-effects data from the as yet unpublished fluvoxamine and sertraline multicenter trials (Solvay Pharmaceuticals, 1996, and Pfizer Pharmaceuticals, 1997, personal communication) do not support the need for a lower SSRI starting dose in children as compared to adolescents, irrespective of body weight, age, or gender.

Furthermore, the magnitude of improvement seen in pediatric OCD is at least as large than that seen in a recent meta-analysis of data from the adult multicenter registration trials for clomipramine, fluoxetine, fluvoxamine, and sertraline (Greist et al., 1995b). In this study, the SSRIs as a group were clearly better than placebo but perhaps not as effective as clomipramine (Greist et al., 1995b). However, this conclusion is undermined by (1) sequential sampling (e.g., 40% of patients in the sertraline trial already had received two SRI trials, and (2) findings from recent multicenter head-to-head comparisons of clomipramine versus fluvoxamine, which showed equivalent efficacy (Freeman, Trimble, et al., 1994; Koran, McElroy, et al., 1996). Thus, it would seem likely that the SRIs as a group are effective treatments for OCD, with no clear indication for superiority of a particular compound in children, adolescents, or adults. Conversely, because of greater potential for side effects, most expert psychiatrists begin with an SSRI, proceeding to a clomipramine trial after two or three failed SSRI trials (March et al., 1997a).

Approximately one-third of patients may fail to respond to monotherapy with a given SRI (DeVeaugh-Geiss et al., 1992), and the likelihood of responding drops considerably after a third SRI trial. Since a substantial minority of patients will not respond until after 8 or even 12 weeks of treatment (DeVeaugh-Geiss, Katz, et al., 1992; Goodman, Price, et al., 1989a; March et al., 1995), it is important to wait at least 8 weeks, and preferably 10 weeks, before changing agents, adopting high dosage strategies, or undertaking augmentation regimens.

In the nonresponsive or partially responsive patient, augmentation of the SRI with a second medication is sometimes useful (Jenike & Rauch, 1994; Leonard & Rapoport, 1989). However, only neuroleptics have shown benefit in controlled studies (McDougle, Goodman, et al., 1994); clonazepam has proven helpful in one controlled study in adults (Pigott, L'Heureux, et al., 1992) and an open study in pediatric OCD (Leonard, Topol, et al., 1995a). Given concerns about physiological dependence with clonazepam and extrapyramidal side effects with neuroleptics, these agents should probably be restricted to patients with high levels of anxiety (clonazepam) and tics or thought disorder symptoms (a neuroleptic), respectively. Many experts recommend low-dose clomipramine augmentation of an SRI, especially in partial responders (March et al., 1997a), but the potential for drug–drug interactions leading to clomipramine-mediated cardiotoxicity (DeVane & Sallee, 1996) suggests caution in using this combination. Furthermore, since concomitant CBT may be the most powerful augmenting treatment in medication-unresponsive patients (March et al., 1994), complex medication strategies for OCD should only be offered to those patients who have not done well with high-quality combined treatment with an SRI and CBT.

Combined Treatment

Clinically, pharmacotherapy and CBT work well together. Many clinicians believe that children with OCD require, or likely would benefit more from, combined treatment (Johnston & March, 1993; Piacentini et al., 1992). However, there are as yet no published controlled studies comparing CBT, medication, or their combination in children and adolescents with OCD. In one study of protocol-driven CBT added to partial responders medication, the average magnitude of improvement on the YBOCS (50%) was noticeably greater than that usually seen with medications alone (30–40%) (March et al., 1994). Although these findings may suggest an advantage for combination treatment over monotherapy with medication, additional research will clearly be necessary to discover the relative meritis of CBT and SRIs alone or in combination for specific patient subgroupings.

Predictors of Outcome

Whereas comorbid schizotypy (Baer, Jenike, et al., 1992) and tic disorders (McDougle et al., 1994), have been identified as treatment impediments (and indications for neuroleptic augmentation) in adults, no specific predictors of treatment outcome have been identified for pediatric OCD. Patient age, sex, and socioeconomic status failed to predict response to treatment in the NIMH (Leonard et al., 1989) and CIBA studies (DeVeaugh-Geiss et al., 1992) or to predict relapse on desipramine substitution (Leonard et al., 1991b). Among OCD-specific factors, neither initial severity, duration of symptoms, or symptom pattern predicted response to treatment (Leonard et al., 1989). Children who acknowledge that their obsessions are senseless and rituals are distressing may be better candidates for CBT than those who do not (Leonard, Swedo, et al., 1996), although lack of insight does not necessarily render CBT ineffective (Kettl & Marks, 1986). Clinically, comorbidity, especially with the oppositional disorders, appears to predict treatment resistance to both pharmacotherapy and CBT, but the hypothesis remains untested in child patients. Similarly, while family dysfunction is neither necessary nor sufficient for the onset of OCD (Lenane, 1989), families affect and are affected by OCD, as illustrated by the finding that high "expressed emotion" may exacerbate OCD; a calm, supportive family may improve outcome (Hibbs, Hamburger, et al., 1991).

FUTURE DIRECTIONS

Empirical evidence favoring CBT as a treatment for OCD in young persons remains weak relative to the ample evidence favoring pharmacotherapy in child patients (March & Leonard, 1996) or CBT in adults (Dar & Greist, 1992). Little is known regarding what predicts treatment success or, in children who respond to treatment, relapse. Similarly, considerable effort needs to be placed on evaluating research-based treatments to real-world clinical practice. In this context, future research will of necessity focus on seven areas: (1) controlled trials comparing medications, behavior therapy, and combination treatment to controls to determine whether medications and behavior therapy are synergistic or additive in their effects on symptom reduction; (2) follow-up studies to evaluate relapse rates, including examining the utility of booster CBT in reducing relapse rates in patients treated with medications, alone or in combination with CBT; (3) component analyses, such as a comparison of ERP, anxiety management training, and their combination, to evaluate the relative contributions of specific treatment components to symptom reduction and treatment acceptability; (4) comparisons of individual- and family-based treatments to determine which is more effective in which children; (5) development of innovative treatments for OCD subtypes, such as obsessional slowness, primary obsessional OCD, and tic-like OCD, that do not respond as well to CBT or pharmacotherapy; (6) targeting treatment innovations to factors, such as family dysfunction, that constrain the application of

CBT to patients with OCD; and (7), exporting research treatments to divergent clinical settings and patient populations in order to judge the acceptability and effectiveness of different treatments for child and adolescent OCD in clinical settings.

Along with Edna Foa at Allegheny University in Philadelphia, we are currently beginning an NIMH-funded comparative treatment outcome study to answer questions about relative treatment efficacy and durability and predictors of response and relapse. Using a volunteer sample of 120 (60/site) youth aged 8–16 with a DSM-IV diagnosis of OCD, this 5-year treatment outcome study contrasts the degree and durability of improvement obtained across three active treatment conditions: OCD-specific CBT, medication with sertraline (MED), both MED and CBT (COMB), and two control conditions, pill placebo (PBO) and Educational Support (ES). The experimental design covers two phases. Phase I compares the outcome of MED, CBT, COMB, and their corresponding control conditions. In Phase II, responders advance to a 16-week discontinuation study to assess treatment durability. The primary outcome measure is the YBOCS. Assessments blind to treatment status take place at week 0 (pretreatment); weeks 1, 4, 8, and 12 (Phase I treatment); and weeks 16, 20, 24, and 28 (Phase II discontinuation). Besides addressing comparative efficacy and durability of the specified treatments, this study also examines time–action effects; differential effects of treatment on specific aspects of OCD, including functional impairment; and predictors of response to treatment and relapse risk. When completed, this study should considerably advance our understanding of the developmental psychopathology and multimodality treatment of OCD in children and adolescents.

SUMMARY

It is increasingly clear that pediatric-onset OCD is a relatively common neurobehavioral disorder characterized by dysregulation in circuits linking frontal cortex to striatum and thalamus. In turn, sertonergic and perhaps dopaminergic neurotransmission substantially conditions the pathophysiology of OCD and points to effective pharmacotherapy for the disorder. As with pharmacotherapy, CBT also may be conceptualized as acting directly on the somatic substrate of the disorder, in addition to helping patients and families cope with what yet cannot be cured. As with other neuropsychiatric disorders, comorbidity with other psychiatric conditions complicates both the diagnostic and treatment picture, and must be, first, skillfully assessed, and second, factored into treatment planning. Ideally, all young persons should receive treatment with CBT, with or without pharmacotherapy with a serotonin reuptake inhibitor. Quite a few children and adolescents with OCD exhibit GABHS infection-related OCD and/or tic symptoms; immunomodulatory therapies, alone or in combination with CBT and an SRI, may prove useful in these patients. Although current treatments are not generally curative, given a correct diagnosis and the skillful combination of OCD-specific treatments, most children and adolescents with OCD can be helped to resume a more normal developmental trajectory.

REFERENCES

Adams, G. B., Waas, G. A., et al. (1994). Obsessive compulsive disorder in children and adolescents: The role of the school psychologist in identification, assessment, and treatment. *School Psychology Quarterly, 9*(4), 274–294.

Allen, A. J., Leonard, H. L., et al. (1995). Case study: A new infection-triggered, autoimmune subtype of pediatric OCD and Tourette's syndrome. *Journal of the American Academy of Child and Adolescent Psychiatry, 34*(3), 307–311.

American Psychiatric Association. (1994). *Diagnostic and statistical manual of mental disorders* (4th ed.). Washington, DC: Author.

Apter, A., Ratzioni, G., et al. (1994). Fluxoxamine open-label treatment of adolescent inpatients with obsessive–compulsive disorder or depression. *Journal of the American Academy of Child and Adolescent Psychiatry, 33*, 342–348.

Baer, L., Jenike, M. A., et al. (1992). Effect of Axis II diagnoses on treatment outcome with clomipramine in 55 patients with obsessive–compulsive disorder. *Archives of General Psychiatry, 49*(11), 862–866.

Barr, L. C., Goodman, W. K., et al. (1992). The serotonin hypothesis of obsessive compulsive disorder: Implications of pharmacologic challenge studies. *Journal of Clinical Psychiatry, 53*, 17–28.

Baxter, L. J., Schwartz, J. M., et al. (1992). Caudate glucose metabolic rate changes with both drug and behavior therapy for obsessive–compulsive disorder. *Archives of General Psychiatry, 49*(9), 681–689.

Berg, C., Rapoport, J., et al. (1989). Behavioral treatment for obsessive–compulsive disorder in childhood. In J. Rapoport (Ed.), *Obsessive–compulsive disorder in children and adolescents* (pp. 169–185). Washington, DC: American Psychiatric Press.

Berg, C. J., Rapoport, J. L., et al. (1985). The Leyton Obsessional Inventory—Child Version. *Psychopharmacology Bulletin, 21*(4), 1057–1059.

Black, D. W., & Blum, N. S. (1992). Obsessive–compulsive disorder support groups: The Iowa model. *Comprehensive Psychiatry, 33*(1), 65–71.

Cohen, D. J., & Leckman, J. F. (1994). Developmental psychopathology and neurobiology of Tourette's syndrome [review]. *Journal of the American Academy of Child and Adolescent Psychiatry, 33*(1), 2–15.

Cook, E., Charak, D., et al. (1994, October). Sertraline treatment of obsessive–compulsive disorder in children and adolescents: Preliminary findings. *Scientific Proceedings of the American Academy of Child and Adolescent Psychiatry Annual Meeting,* New York, 57–58.

Cox, C., Fedio, P., et al. (1989). Neuropsychological testing of obsessive–compulsive adolescents. In J. Rapoport (Ed.), *Obsessive–compulsive disorder in children and adolescents* (pp. 73–86). Washington, DC: American Psychiatric Press.

Dar, R., & Greist, J. (1992). Behavior therapy for obsessive–compulsive disorder. *Psychiatric Clinics of North America, 15*(4), 885–894.

Denckla, M. (1989). Neurological examination. In J. Rapoport (Ed.), *Obsessive–compulsive disorder in children and adolescents* (pp. 107–118). Washington, DC: American Psychiatric Press.

DeVane, C., & Sallee, F. (1996). Serotonin selective reuptake inhibitors in child and adolescent psychiatry: A review of published experience. *Journal of Clinical Psychiatry, 57,* 55–66.

DeVeaugh-Geiss, J., Moroz, G., et al. (1992). Clomipramine hydrochloride in childhood and adolescent obsessive–compulsive disorder—a multicenter trial. *Journal of the American Academy of Child and Adolescent Psychiatry, 31*(1), 45–49.

Elliott, G., & Popper, C. (1991). Tricyclic antidepressants: The QT interval and other cardiovascular parameters. *Journal of Child and Adolescent Psychopharmacology, 1,* 187–191.

Esman, A. (1989). Psychoanalysis in general psychiatry: Obsessive–compulsive disorder as a paradigm. *American Psychoanalytic Association Journal, 37,* 319–336.

Flament, M. F. (1990). Epidemiology of obsessive–compulsive disorder in children and adolescents [French]. *Encéphale, 311,* 311–316.

Flament, M. F., Rapoport, J. L., et al. (1985). Clomipramine treatment of childhood obsessive–compulsive disorder: A double-blind controlled study. *Archives of General Psychiatry, 42* (10), 977–983.

Flament, M. F., Whitaker, A., et al. (1988). Obsessive compulsive disorder in adolescence: An epidemiological study. *Journal of the American Academy of Child and Adolescent Psychiatry, 27*(6), 764–771.

Foa, E., & Kozak, M. (1985). Emotional processing of fear: Exposure to corrective information. *Psychological Bulletin, 90,* 20–35.

Freeman, C. P., Trimble, M. R., et al. (1994). Fluvoxamine versus clomipramine in the treatment of obsessive compulsive disorder: A multicenter, randomized, double-blind, parallel group comparison. *Journal of Clinical Psychiatry, 55* (7), 301–305.

Geller, D. A., Biederman, J., et al. (1995). Similarities in response to fluoxetine in the treatment of children and adolescents with obsessive–compulsive disorder. *Journal of the American Academy of Child and Adolescent Psychiatry, 34*(1), 36–44.

Gesell, A., Ames, L., et al. (1974). *Infant and child in the culture today.* New York: Harper & Row.

Giedd, J. N., Rapoport, J. L., et al. (1996). Case study: Acute basal ganglia enlargement and obsessive–compulsive symptoms in an adolescent boy. *Journal of the American Academy of Child and Adolescent Psychiatry, 35*(7), 913–915.

Goodman, W. K., & Price, L. H. (1992). Assessment of severity and change in obsessive compulsive disorder [review]. *Psychiatric Clinics of North America, 15*(4), 861–869.

Goodman, W. K., & Price, L. H., et al. (1989a). Efficacy of fluvoxamine in obsessive–compulsive disorder. A double-blind comparison with placebo. *Archives of General Psychiatry, 46*(1), 36–44.

Goodman, W. K., & Price, L. H., et al. (1989b). The Yale–Brown Obsessive–Compulsive Scale: I. Development, use, and reliability. *Archives of General Psychiatry, 46*(11), 1006–1011.

Goodman, W. K., Price, L. H., et al. (1989c). The Yale–Brown Obsessive–Compulsive Scale: II. Validity. *Archives of General Psychiatry, 46*(11), 1012–1016.

Greist, J. H., Chouinard, G., et al. (1995a). Double-blind parallel comparison of three dosages of sertraline and placebo in outpatients with obsessive–compulsive disorder. *Archives of General Psychiatry, 52*(4), 289–295.

Greist, J. H., Jefferson, J. W., et al. (1995b). Efficacy and tolerability of serotonin transport inhibitors in obsessive–compulsive disorder: A meta-analysis. *Archives of General Psychiatry, 52*(1), 53–60.

Greist, J. H., Jefferson, J. W., et al. (1990). Clomipramine and obsessive compulsive disorder: A placebo-controlled double-blind study of 32 patients [see comments]. *Journal of Clinical Psychiatry, 51*(7), 292–297.

Hamburger, S. D., Swedo, S., et al. (1989). Growth rate in adolescents with obsessive–compulsive disorder. *American Journal of Psychiatry, 146*(5), 652–655.

Hibbs, E. D., Hamburger, S. D., et al. (1991). Determinants of expressed emotion in families of disturbed and normal children. *Journal of Child Psychology and Psychiatry and Allied Disciplines, 32*(5), 757–770.

Hollander, E., Schiffman, E., et al. (1990). Signs of central nervous system dysfunction in obsessive–compulsive disorder [see comments]. *Archives of General Psychiatry, 47*(1), 27–32.

Jenike, M. A., & Rauch, S. (1994). Managing the patient with treatment resistant obsessive compulsive disorder: Current strategies. *Journal of Clinical Psychiatry, 55*(Suppl. 3), 11–17.

Jenike, M. A. (1989). Obsessive–compulsive and related disorders: A hidden epidemic [editorial; comment]. *New England Journal of Medicine, 321*(8), 539–541.

Jenike, M. A. (1992). Pharmacologic treatment of obsessive compulsive disorders. *Psychiatric Clinics of North America, 15*(4), 895–919.

Johnston, H. & March, J. (1993). Obsessive–compulsive disorder in children and adolescents. In W. Reynolds (Ed.), *Internalizing disorders in children and adolescents* (pp. 107–148). New York: Wiley.

Katz, R. J., DeVeaugh, G. J., et al. (1990). Clomipramine in obsessive–compulsive disorder [see comments]. *Biological Psychiatry, 28*(5), 401–414.

Kearney, C. A. & Silverman, W. K. (1990). Treatment of an adolescent with obsessive–compulsive disorder by alternating response prevention and cognitive therapy: An empirical analysis. *Journal of Behavior Therapy and Experimental Psychiatry, 21*(1), 39–47.

Kendall, P. C., Howard, B. L., et al. (1988). The anxious child: Cognitive–behavioral treatment strategies. *Behavior Modification, 12*(2), 281–310.

Kettl, P., & Marks, I. (1986). Neurological factors in obsessive–compulsive disorder. *British Journal of Psychiatry, 149*, 315–319.

Kiessling, L. S., Marcotte, A. C., et al. (1994). Antineuronal antibodies: tics and obsessive–compulsive symptoms. *Journal of Developmental Behavioral Pediatrics, 15*(6), 421–425.

Koran, L. M., McElroy, S. L., et al. (1996). Fluvoxamine versus clomipramine for obsessive–compulsive disorder: A double-blind comparison. *Journal of Clinical Psychopharmacology, 16*(2), 121–129.

Lenane, M. (1989). Families in obsessive–compulsive disorder. In J. Rapoport (Ed.), *Obsessive–compulsive disorder in children and adolescents* (pp. 237–249). Washington, DC: American Psychiatric Press.

Leonard, H. L., Goldberger, E. L., et al. (1990). Childhood rituals: Normal development or obsessive–compulsive symptoms? *Journal of the American Academy of Child and Adolescent Psychiatry, 29*(1), 17–23.

Leonard, H. L., Lenane, M. C., et al. (1991a). A double-blind comparison of clomipramine and desipramine treatment of severe onychophagia (nail biting). *Archives of General Psychiatry, 48*(9), 821–827.

Leonard, H. L., Lenane, M. C., et al. (1992). Tics and Tourette's disorder: A 2- to 7-year follow-up of 54 obsessive–compulsive children. *American Journal of Psychiatry, 149*(9), 1244–1251.

Leonard, H. L., Lenane, M., et al. (1993a). Obsessive–compulsive disorder. In H. L. Leonard (Ed.), *Child psychiatric clinics of North America: Anxiety disorders* (Vol. 2, pp. 655–666). New York: Saunders.

Leonard, H. L., Meyer, M. C., et al. (1995b). Electrocardiographic changes during desipramine and clomipramine treatment in children and adolescents [see comments]. *Journal of the American Academy of Child and Adolescent Psychiatry, 34*(11), 1460–1468.

Leonard, H. L., & Rapoport, J. L. (1989). Pharmacotherapy of childhood obsessive–compulsive disorder. *Psychiatric Clinics of North America, 12*(4), 963–970.

Leonard, H. L., Swedo, S. E., et al. (1989). Treatment of obsessive–compulsive disorder with clomipramine and desipramine in children and adolescents: A double-blind crossover comparison. *Archives of General Psychiatry, 46*(12), 1088–1092.

Leonard, H. L., Swedo, S. E., et al. (1991b). A double-blind desipramine substitution during long-term clomipramine treatment in children and adolescents with obsessive–compulsive disorder. *Archives of General Psychiatry, 48*(10), 922–927.

Leonard, H. L., Swedo, S. E., et al. (1993b). A 2- to 7-year follow-up study of 54 obsessive–compulsive children and adolescents. *Archives of General Psychiatry, 50*(6), 429–439.

Leonard, H. L., Swedo, S., et al. (1996). Obsessive–compulsive disorder. In G. Gabbard (Ed.), *Synopsis of treatments of psychiatric disorders* (pp. 143–148). Washington, DC: American Psychiatric Press.

Leonard, H. L., Topol, D., et al. (1995a). Clonazepam as an augmenting agent in the treatment of childhood-onset obsessive–compulsive disorder. *Journal of the American Academy of Child and Adolescent Psychiatry, 33*(6), 792–794.

March, J. S. (1995). Cognitive-behavioral psychotherapy for children and adolescents with OCD: A review and recommendations for treatment. *Journal of the American Academy of Child and Adolescent Psychiatry, 34*(1), 7–18.

March, J. S. & Albano, A. (1996). Assessment of anxiety in children and adolescents. In L. Dickstein, M. Riba, & M. Oldham (Eds.), *Review of psychiatry* (Vol. 15, pp. 405–427). Washington, DC: American Psychiatric Press.

March, J. S. & Albano, A. (in press). New developments in assessing pediatric anxiety disorders. In T. Olendick (Ed.), *Advances in clinical child psychology.* Washington, DC: American Psychological Association Press.

March, J., Biederman, J., Wolkow, R., & Safferman, A. (1997, May). *Sertraline in children and adolescents with obsessive–compulsive disorder: A placebo-controlled multicenter, double-blind study.* Paper presented at the annual meeting of the American Psychiatric Association, San Diego, CA.

March, J. S., Frances, A., et al. (1997a). Expert consensus guidelines: Treatment of obsessive–compulsive disorder. *Journal of Clinical Psychiatry, 58*(Suppl. 4), 1–72.

March, J. S., Johnston, H., et al. (1990). Do subtle neurological impairments predict treatment resistance in children and adolescents with obsessive–compulsive disorder. *Journal of Child and Adolescent Psychopharmacology, 1,* 133–140.

March, J. S., Leonard, H., et al. (1995). Pharmacotherapy of obsessive–compulsive disorder. In M. Riddle (Ed.), *Child psychiatric clinics of North America: Pharmacotherapy* (pp. 217–236). Philadelphia: Saunders.

March, J. S. & Leonard, H. (1996). Obsessive–compulsive disorder: A review of the past ten years. *Journal of the American Academy of Child and Adolescent Psychiatry, 35*(10), 1265–1273.

March, J. S., Leonard, H., et al. (in press). Neuropsychiatry of pediatric obsessive compulsive disorder. In E. Coffey & R. Brumback (Eds.), *Textbook of pediatric neuropsychiatry.* Washington, DC: American Psychiatric Press.

March, J. S., & Mulle, K. (1995). Manualized cognitive-behavioral psychotherapy for obsessive–compulsive disorder in childhood: A preliminary single case study. *Journal of Anxiety Disorders, 9*(2), 175–184.

March, J. S. & Mulle, K. (1996). Banishing obsessive–compulsive disorder. In E. Hibbs &

P. Jensen (Eds.), *Psychosocial treatments for child and adolescent disorders* (pp. 82–103). Washington, DC: American Psychological Association Press.

March, J. S., & Mulle, K. (1998). *OCD in children and adolescents: A cognitive-behavioral treatment manual*. New York: Guilford Press.

March, J. S., Mulle, K., et al. (1994). Behavioral psychotherapy for children and adolescents with obsessive–compulsive disorder: An open trial of a new protocol-driven treatment package. *Journal of the American Academy of Child and Adolescent Psychiatry, 33*(3), 333–341.

March, J. S., Mulle, K., et al. (1995). Organizing an anxiety disorders clinic. In J. March (Ed.), *Anxiety disorders in children and adolescents* (pp. 420–435). New York: Guilford Press.

March, J. S., Parker, J., et al. (1997b). The Multidimensional Anxiety Scale for Children (MASC), Factor structure, reliability and validity. *Journal of the American Academy of Child and Adolescent Psychiatry, 36*(4), 554–565.

McDougle, C., Goodman, W., et al. (1994). Haloperidol addition in fluvoxamine-refractory obsessive–compulsive disorder. *Archives of General Psychiatry, 51*, 302–308.

Pauls, D., Towbin, K., et al. (1986). Gilles de la Tourette syndrome and obsessive compulsive disorder: Evidence supporting a genetic relationship. *Archives of General Psychiatry, 43*, 1180–1182.

Pauls, D. L., Alsobrook, J. P., et al. (1995). A family study of obsessive–compulsive disorder. *American Journal of Psychiatry, 152*(1), 76–84.

Piacentini, J., Jaffer, M., et al. (1992). Psychopharmacologic treatment of child and adolescent obsessive compulsive disorder. *Psychiatric Clinics of North America, 15*(1), 87–107.

Pigott, T., L'Heureux, F., et al. (1992). *A controlled trial of clonazepam augmentation in OCD patients treated with clomipramine or fluoxetine.* Paper presented at the 145th annual meeting of the American Psychiatric Association, Washington, DC.

Rapoport, J. L. (1989). The biology of obsessions and compulsions. *Scientific American, 260*(3), 82–89.

Rapoport, J. L. (1991). Recent advances in obsessive–compulsive disorder [see comments]. *Neuropsychopharmacology, 5*(1), 1–10.

Rapoport, J. L., Leonard, H. L., et al. (1993). Obsessive compulsive disorder in children and adolescents: Issues in management. *Journal of Clinical Psychiatry, 54*, 27–29.

Rapoport, J. L., Swedo, S. E., et al. (1992). Childhood obsessive compulsive disorder. *Journal of Clinical Psychiatry, 56*, 11–16.

Rasmussen, S. A., & Eisen, J. L. (1990). Epidemiology of obsessive compulsive disorder. *Journal of Clinical Psychiatry, 53*, 10–13.

Rasmussen, S. A., & Eisen, J. L. (1994). The epidemiology and differential diagnosis of obsessive compulsive disorder. *Journal of Clinical Psychiatry, 55*, 5–10.

Rauch, S. L., Jenike, M. A., et al. (1994). Regional cerebral blood flow measured during symptom provocation in obsessive–compulsive disorder using oxygen 15–labeled carbon dioxide and positron emission tomography. *Archives of General Psychiatry, 51*(1), 62–70.

Rettew, D. C., Swedo, S. E., et al. (1992). Obsessions and compulsions across time in 79 children and adolescents with obsessive–compulsive disorder. *Journal of the American Academy of Child and Adolescent Psychiatry, 31*(6), 1050–1056.

Riddle, M., Claghorn, J., et al. (1996, June). *A controlled trial of fluvoxamine for OCD in children and adolescents.* Paper presented at the NCDEU, Boca Raton, FL.

Riddle, M. A., Scahill, L., et al. (1990). Obsessive compulsive disorder in children and adolescents: Phenomenology and family history. *Journal of the American Academy of Child and Adolescent Psychiatry, 29*(5), 766–772.

Rutter, M., Tizard, J., et al. (1970). *Education, health, and behavior.* London: Longman.

Scahill, L., Riddle, M., et al. (1997). Children's Yale–Brown Obsessive–Compulsive Scale: Reliability and validity. *Journal of the American Academy of Child and Adolescent Psychiatry, 36*(6), 844–852.

Schroeder, J. S., Mullin, A. V., et al. (1989). Cardiovascular effects of desipramine in children. *Journal of the American Academy of Child and Adolescent Psychiatry, 28*(3), 376–379.

Schwartz, J. (1996). *Brain lock.* New York: HarperCollins.

Schwartz, J. M., Stoessel, P. W., et al. (1996). Systematic changes in cerebral glucose metabolic rate after successful behavior modification treatment of obsessive–compulsive disorder. *Archives of General Psychiatry, 53*(2), 109–113.

Staebler, C. R., Pollard, C. A., et al. (1993). Sexual history and quality of current relationships in patients with obsessive compulsive disorder: A comparison with two other psychiatric samples. *Journal of Sex and Marital Therapy, 19*(2), 147–153.

Swedo, S. E. (1989). Rituals and releasers: An ethological model of obsessive–compulsive disorder. In J. Rapoport (Ed.), *Obsessive–compulsive disorder in children and adolescents* (pp. 269–288). Washington, DC: American Psychiatric Press.

Swedo, S. E. (1993). Trichotillomania. *Psychiatric Annals, 23*(7), 402–407.

Swedo, S. E., Leonard, H., et al. (1990). Childhood-onset obsessive–compulsive disorder. In M. Jenike, L. Baer, & W. M. Minichello (Ed.), *Obsessive–compulsive disorder.* Littleton, MA: PSG.

Swedo, S. E., Leonard, H. L., et al. (1993). Sydenham's chorea: Physical and psychological symptoms of St Vitus dance. *Pediatrics, 91*(4), 706–713.

Swedo, S. E., Leonard, H., et al. (1994). Speculations on anti-neuronal antibody-mediated neuropsychiatric disorders of childhood. *Pediatrics, 93*(2), 323–326.

Swedo, S. E., & Rapoport, J. (1990). Neurochemical and neuroendocrine considerations of obsessive–compulsive disorder in childhood. In W. Deutsch, A. Weizman, & R. Weizman (Eds.), *Application of basic neuroscience to child psychiatry* (pp. 275–284). New York: Plenum.

Swedo, S. E., Rapoport, J. L., et al. (1989). High prevalence of obsessive–compulsive symptoms in patients with Sydenham's chorea. *American Journal of Psychiatry, 146*(2), 246–249.

Swedo, S. E., Schapiro, M. B., et al. (1989). Cerebral glucose metabolism in childhood-onset obsessive–compulsive disorder. *Archives of General Psychiatry, 46*(6), 518–523.

Thyer, B. A. (1991). Diagnosis and treatment of child and adolescent anxiety disorders. *Behavior Modification, 15*(3), 310–325.

Tynes, L. L., Salins, C., et al. (1992). A psychoeducational and support group for obsessive–compulsive disorder patients and their significant others. *Comprehensive Psychiatry, 33*(3), 197–201.

Valleni-Basile, L. A., Garrison, C. Z., et al. (1994). Frequency of obsessive–compulsive disorder in a community sample of young adolescents [published erratum appears in *Journal of the American Academy of Child and Adolescent Psychiatry,* 1995, *34*(2), 128–129]. *Journal of the American Academy of Child and Adolescent Psychiatry, 33*(6), 782–791.

van Oppen, P., Arntz, A. (1994). Cognitive therapy for obsessive–compulsive disorder. *Behaviour Research and Therapy, 32*(1), 79–87.

White, M., & Epston, D. (1991). *Narrative means to therapeutic ends.* New York: Norton.

Wolff, R. P., & Wolff, L. S. (1991). Assessment and treatment of obsessive–compulsive disorder in children. *Behavior Modification, 15*(3), 372–393.

Part III

OBSESSIVE–COMPULSIVE SPECTRUM DISORDERS

Chapter 17

CONCEPTUAL FOUNDATIONS OF OBSESSIVE–COMPULSIVE SPECTRUM DISORDERS

Toby Goldsmith
Nathan A. Shapira
Katharine A. Phillips
Susan L. McElroy

Over the past 15 years, it has been increasingly recognized that a wide range of psychiatric and neuropsychiatric disorders might be related to obsessive–compulsive disorder (OCD), and thus, together, may form a family of related disorders often referred to as obsessive–compulsive (or OCD) spectrum disorders (Hollander, 1993; McElroy, Phillips, & Keck, 1994b; Rasmussen, 1994). The grouping of these conditions is based largely on clinical observations that they share phenomenological features with OCD; that is, they are characterized by obsessive thinking and/or compulsive behaviors. Further evidence that these conditions are related is provided by their having courses of illness, psychiatric comorbidity and family history patterns, neurobiological abnormalities, and responses to psychopharmacological and psychological treatments similar to that of OCD and one another. Disorders frequently proposed to be OCD spectrum disorders include the somatoform disorders, body dysmorphic disorder (BDD), and hypochondriasis; the eating disorders, particularly anorexia nervosa, but also bulimia nervosa and binge-eating disorder (BED); the impulse control disorders (ICDs) and possible ICDs, such as compulsive buying, repetitive self-mutilation (RSM), onychophagia (severe nail biting), and psychogenic excoriation (compulsive skin picking); the paraphilias and nonparaphilic sexual addictions (NPSAs) (also called sexual compulsions); and Tourette's syndrome and other movement disorders.

In this chapter, we review the evidence supporting the grouping of these conditions into a family of OCD-related disorders and discuss the theoretical and clinical implications of such a grouping. Of note, evaluating the OCD spectrum hypothesis is limited by the lack of established operational criteria for what constitutes an OCD spectrum disorder (Rasmussen, 1993). Moreover, relatively few studies have directly compared persons with proposed OCD spectrum disorders and persons with OCD. In addition, some aspects of the putative OCD spectrum disorders have received little or no investigation, limiting their comparison with OCD.

BODY DYSMORPHIC DISORDER

DSM-IV defines BDD as a preoccupation with an imagined or slight defect in physical appearance (e.g., a big or crooked nose, an egg-shaped head, redness or paleness of the complexion, an asymmetrical beard, or a small penis) that causes significant distress or impairment in functioning (American Psychiatric Association, 1994; Phillips, McElroy, Keck, Pope, & Hudson, 1993; Phillips, McElroy, Keck, Hudson, & Pope, 1994).

BDD and OCD have many phenomenological similarities. First, BDD preoccupations are "structurally" similar to OCD obsessions in that they are repetitive, intrusive thoughts that are associated with anxiety or distress, and that are usually difficult to resist or control. Also, the "content" of some BDD preoccupations is similar to that of some OCD obsessions (e.g., asymmetry or the sense that something "isn't right"). Second, most individuals with BDD (approximately 90%) perform time-consuming, repetitive, and sometimes ritualistic behaviors related to their BDD preoccupations that resemble OCD compulsions. These behaviors include checking the supposed defect in mirrors or other reflecting surfaces (sometimes with magnifying glasses), comparing the defect with the same body part on others, camouflaging or hiding the defect, excessive grooming behaviors, frequent requests for reassurance about the defect, and compulsive skin picking (McElroy, Hudson, Phillips, Keck, & Pope, 1993; Phillips et al., 1993; Phillips, McElroy, Keck, Hudson, & Pope, 1994). Indeed, use of a slightly modified version of the Yale–Brown Obsessive–Compulsive Scale (BDD-YBOCS) (Phillips et al., 1997) to assess BDD preoccupations and behaviors indicates that patients with BDD obtain total scores similar to those obtained by OCD patients on the YBOCS: 53 BDD patients evaluated by our group displayed a mean ± standard deviation for BDD-YBOCS score (10-item) of 23.7 ± 6.6 compared to 23.1 ± 7.4, respectively, for 53 OCD patients on the YBOCS.

A third phenomenological similarity with OCD is that BDD can be associated with impaired insight and delusional thinking (McElroy et al., 1993; Phillips et al., 1994; Phillips, McElroy, Hudson, & Pope, 1995). In other words, like OCD obsessions, BDD preoccupations appear to span a dimension from good to poor to absent insight. Finally, just as OCD patients typically have multiple obsessions and compulsions, BDD patients usually have concerns with multiple body parts and several associated ritualistic behaviors. The first 100 BDD patients evaluated by our group, for example, displayed a mean number of three preoccupations per patient (Phillips et al., 1994).

Like OCD, BDD appears to be approximately equally common in men and women. Also similar to OCD, BDD typically begins in adolescence and has a chronic, often waxing and waning, course. In addition, just as OCD symptoms may remain the same or change over time, BDD bodily concerns may remain the same or change (Phillips et al., 1993, 1994).

Comorbidity data also support a relationship between BDD and OCD. First, high rates of OCD have been found in patients with BDD (Hollander, Co-hen, & Simean, 1993). For example, of 188 individuals meeting the DSM-IV criteria for BDD evaluated by our group, 56 (30%) had a lifetime history of OCD (Phillips & Diaz, 1997). Second, there appear to be relatively high rates of BDD in patients with OCD (Brawman-Mintzer et al.,1995). In the DSM-IV OCD field trial, for example, Hollander et al.(1993) found that 37% of the OCD patients at their site also met DSM-III-R criteria for BDD. And our group has found that 15% of 62 patients with OCD had comorbid BDD (Phillips et al., 1995). Third, similar to OCD, BDD is associated with elevated rates of mood, anxiety, and psychoactive substance-use disorders. Of the 188 BDD patients evaluated by our group, for example, 154 (82%) met DSM-III-R criteria for a lifetime mood disorder, 113 (60%) for an anxiety disorder, and 67 (36%) for a psychoactive substance use disorder (Phillips & Diaz, 1997). A fourth similarity is that BDD, like OCD, may be associated with high rates of certain personality disorders, especially avoidant, paranoid, and obsessive–compulsive (Phillips & McElroy, 1997; Veale et al., 1996).

Family-history data provide further support for a BDD–OCD link. Hollan-der et al. (1993) found that 17% of the family members of 50 patients with BDD (78% of whom had comorbid OCD) had OCD. By contrast, of the first 50 BDD patients evaluated by our group, only 4% of the first-degree relatives had OCD. However, the family-history method probably underestimates the prevalence of this often-secret disorder in family members.

Although ongoing double-blind, placebo-controlled trials have not yet been completed for BDD, open data suggest that, like OCD, BDD may respond to SRIs (Phillips et al., 1993, 1994, 1995). In a recently completed 16-week, open-label trial of fluvoxamine in 30 subjects with DSM-IV BDD, 19 (63%) were classified as responders (Phillips, Dwight, & McElroy, in press). Available clinical data further suggest that BDD may respond preferentially to serotonin reuptake inhibitors (SRIs). Of 76 SRI trials conducted in 100 BDD patients evaluated by our group, 43 (57%) were associated with moderate or marked (i.e., 30–100%) reduction in BDD symptoms, whereas only 4 (10%) of 41 trials with non-SRI tricyclics resulted in similar improvement (Phillips et al., 1994).

Controlled psychotherapy trials have not yet been done in BDD. Nonetheless, data from open trials suggest that BDD, like OCD, may respond to behavior therapy (in particular, exposure and response prevention) (Josephson & Brondolo, 1993; Neziroglu & Yaryura-Tobias, 1993; Rosen, Reiter, & Orosan, 1995), but not to insight-oriented psychotherapy (McElroy et al., 1993). Of note, medical and surgical treatments rarely relieve BDD preoccupations (Veale et al., 1996). Of the 188 patients evaluated by our group, for example, 86% of surgical, dermatological, or other nonpsychiatric medical treatments resulted in either no change or a worsening of the concern with the perceived defect (Phillips & Diaz, 1997).

There are, however, some differences between OCD and BDD, suggesting that they are not identical disorders. BDD preoccupations revolve around appearance and acceptability of the self, whereas OCD symptoms generally involve overestimation of harm and danger (Hollander, et al., 1993). Furthermore, BDD preoccupations appear less likely than OCD symptoms to be associated with good insight and to more often involve overvalued ideation or delusional thinking (Eisen, Phillips, Rasmussen, & Luce, 1997). Also, preliminary data from a comparison study of 53 subjects with OCD and 53 subjects with BDD found that BDD subjects were less likely to be married, had more comorbid major depression and social phobia, had made more suicide attempts because of their disorder, and had a higher rate of substance-use disorders in first-degree relatives (Phillips et al., 1995).

HYPOCHONDRIASIS

In DSM-IV, the essential feature of hypochondriasis is preoccupation with the fear of having, or the idea that one has, a serious disease based on the person's misinterpretation of bodily signs or symptoms (American Psychiatric Association, 1994). The preoccupation may be with bodily functions (e.g., heartbeat or sweating); with minor physical abnormalities (e.g., a small sore or an occasional cough); with vague and ambiguous physical sensations (e.g., a "tired heart" or "aching veins"); or with a specific organ or a single disease (e.g., fear of having cardiac disease or a brain tumor).

Like BDD, hypochondriasis has many phenomenological similarities with OCD (Fallon, Rasmussen, & Liebowitz, 1993c). Most notably, in both disorders, the patient is fearful. (In OCD, the person often fears being harmed or causing harm; in hypochondriasis, the person fears illness, disability, and death). Also, somatic obsessions are common in OCD. Rasmussen and Tsuang (1986), for example, reported that 34% of 100 patients with OCD had somatic obsessions that compelled them to undergo repeated medical evaluations. Moreover, hypochondriacal preoccupations resemble OCD obsessions in that they are often experienced as intrusive and persistent, are often resisted, and often produce anxiety or distress. In fact, it may be difficult to distinguish between a somatic or contamination obsession of OCD (e.g., fear of contamination with the human immunodeficiency virus [HIV]) and a hypochondriacal fear (e.g., fear of being infected with HIV).

Another phenomenological similarity is that hypochondriacal patients often display repetitive checking behaviors similar to OCD compulsions, including bodily checking and checking whether one is ill, repeatedly requesting medical treatment, and repeatedly requesting reassurance that one is not ill. Fallon et al. (1993c) have stated that hypochondriasis is characterized by "obsessions about being ill and compulsions to check with others for either diagnosis and treatment or reassurance that one is not ill" (p. 71). Finally, like BDD preoccupations and OCD obsessions, hypochondriacal fears may be associated with poor insight and resemble overvalued ideas or delusions. Indeed, in the early 20th century, Kraepelin (1919) associated hypochondriasis with psychosis.

Psychiatric comorbidity studies provide further support for a link between hypochondriasis and OCD. First, OCD appears to be more common in patients with hypochondriasis than in the general population. Comparing 42 patients with DSM-III-R hypochondriasis (American Psychiatric Association, 1987) from a general medical clinic with a random sample of 76 outpatients from the same setting, Barsky, Wyshak, and Klerman (1986) found that the lifetime rate of DSM-III (American Psychiatric Association, 1980) OCD was significantly higher in the hypochondriacal patients (9.5%) than in the control subjects (2.6%). Of 21 patients with DSM-III-R hypochondriasis evaluated by Fallon et al. (1993c), 33% had a lifetime history of OCD. Second, hypochondriasis may be relatively common in patients with OCD. As mentioned earlier, 34% of 100 patients with OCD evaluated by Rasmussen and Tsuang (1986) had somatic obsessions that compelled them to seek medical treatment. Third, hypochondriasis, like BDD and OCD, is associated with high rates of mood and anxiety disorders. Barsky (1992) reported that their 42 patients with DSM-III-R hypochondriasis were 8.1 times more likely to have dysthymia, 7.1 times more likely to have major depression, and 10.1 times more likely to have generalized anxiety disorder than were control patients. Moreover, in an earlier study, this group found that the strongest correlate of hypochondriacal symptoms in patients with DSM-III hypochondriasis was severity of depressive symptoms. Indeed, some authors have concluded that hypochondriasis without an associated psychiatric disorder (so-called "primary" hypochondriasis) is uncommon (Fallon, Klein, & Liebowitz, 1993a; Fallon, Rasmussen, & Liebowitz, 1993c).

Although controlled trials have not yet been completed, preliminary evidence suggests that, like OCD, hypochondriasis—with or without comorbid depression—may respond to SRIs. In a 12-week, open-label trial of fluoxetine (mean dose 53 ± 24 mg/day) in 16 patients with DSM-III-R hypochondriasis without major depression conducted by Fallon et al. (1993b), 10 of the 14 completers were rated as "much" improved at 12 weeks. Moreover, open data suggest that hypochondriasis responds poorly to insight-oriented psychotherapy (Ladee, 1966) but may respond acutely and over the long term to behavior therapy (Fallon et al., 1993a; Josephson & Brondolo, 1993; Visser & Bouman, 1992; Warwick & Marks, 1988).

There are some differences, however, between hypochondriasis and OCD. Hypochondriacal fears are, by definition, fueled by bodily sensations. In OCD, bodily perceptions rarely precede obsessions or compulsions (Barsky, 1992). Hypochondriacal patients in the Barsky et al. (1986) study, unlike patients with

OCD, did not display elevated rates of eating or psychoactive substance-use disorders. Also, patients with hypochondriasis (including those without major depression) have been reported to respond to non-SRI antidepressants (Wesner & Noyes, 1991). Since controlled comparison trials have not yet been conducted, it is presently unknown whether hypochondriasis, like OCD, responds preferentially to SRIs.

Indeed, it has been hypothesized that hypochondriasis may have several distinct subtypes, one of which is more similar to OCD, and another more similar to somatization disorder (Barsky, 1992). Further research on these proposed subtypes is needed to confirm their existence and to evaluate their relationship with OCD.

EATING DISORDERS

DSM-IV states that the eating disorders are characterized by "severe disturbances in eating behavior," and provides two specific diagnoses (anorexia nervosa and bulimia nervosa) as well as a residual category, eating disorder not otherwise specified (NOS). DSM-IV defines anorexia nervosa as (1) refusal to maintain a minimally normal body weight; (2) intense fear of gaining weight or becoming fat, even though underweight; (3) significant disturbance in perception of body shape or size, undue influence of body weight or shape on self-evaluation, or denial of the seriousness of the current low body weight; and (4) in females, amenorrhea. DSM-IV further specifies two subtypes of anorexia nervosa: (1) restricting type, in which the person has not regularly engaged in binge eating or purging behavior (i.e., self-induced vomiting, misuse of laxatives or diuretics, or enemas), and (2) binge eating/purging type, in which the person has regularly engaged in binge eating and/or purging behaviors.

DSM-IV defines bulimia nervosa as recurrent episodes of binge eating followed by inappropriate compensatory behaviors designed to prevent weight gain, such as self-induced vomiting, misuse of laxatives or diuretics, fasting, or excessive exercise. Two subtypes of the disorder are specified: purging and nonpurging. Given as an example of eating disorder NOS and included in the DSM-IV appendix, BED is characterized by recurrent episodes of binge eating in the absence of regular use of inappropriate compensatory behaviors characteristic of bulimia nervosa (American Psychiatric Association, 1994; de Zwaan, Mitchell, Raymond, & Spitzer, 1994). Of note, an episode of binge eating is defined similarly for all eating disorders as (1) eating, in a discrete period of time, an amount of food that is definitely larger than most people would eat during a similar period of time; and (2) a sense of lack of control over eating during the episode.

There is considerable overlap among anorexia nervosa, bulimia nervosa, and BED. All three disorders are characterized by a core preoccupation with food and body weight. Patients with anorexia nervosa often have periods of bulimia nervosa, and patients with bulimia nervosa frequently display periods of anorexia nervosa or BED. Also, some individuals with BED engage in inappropriate compensatory behaviors. Finally, compared with obese subjects without BED, obese subjects with BED may have higher lifetime rates of bulimia nervosa (de Zwaan et al., 1994).

It has long been recognized that eating disorders and OCD have many phenomenological similarities (Formea & Burns, 1995; Jarry & Vaccarino, 1996; Kaye, Weltzin, & Hsu, 1993a, 1993b; Rothenberg, 1986; Rubenstein, Pigott, L'Hereux, Hill, & Murphy, 1992; Rubenstein, Pigott, Altemus, L'Heureux, & Murphy, 1993; Rubenstein, Altemus, Pigott, Hess, & Murphy, 1995). The core abnormal thoughts and behaviors about food and eating characteristic of the eating disorders have obsessional and compulsive features. The excessive fear of gaining weight (often called a "weight phobia") of anorexia nervosa and the preoccupation with food and weight of all three disorders resemble OCD obsessions. The urge to binge eat is often experienced as senseless, repugnant, intrusive, persistent, distress-producing, and difficult to resist or control. The relentless dieting of anorexia nervosa, the purging behavior of anorexia nervosa and bulimia nervosa, and the binge eating of all three disorders resemble OCD compulsions. Indeed, binges are often associated with a sense of loss of control over eating and relief of distress (Beglin & Fairburn, 1992). In addition, patients with eating disorders often perform specific rituals in their pursuit of weight loss, binge eating, and purging (Rubenstein et al., 1993; Rothenberg, 1986).

Eating disorders and OCD also appear to have similar courses of illness. Like OCD, anorexia nervosa, bulimia nervosa, and BED all often begin in adolescence or early adulthood and may be chronic.

Substantial comorbidity data provide further support for a relationship between eating disorders and OCD. First, numerous studies have consistently found high rates of OCD in persons with eating disorders. For example, in 1988, Rothenberg compiled data from 11 studies of comorbidity in anorexia nervosa and concluded that obsessive–compulsive symptoms were the second most frequent associated symptoms (after those of depression; see below). More recently, Rubenstein et al. (1993) evaluated 25 women with a primary diagnosis of bulimia nervosa and found that 32% displayed a lifetime history of OCD, with an additional 24% meeting subthreshold criteria for OCD at some point in their lives. Similarly, in a study of 93 female inpatients who met DSM-III-R criteria for anorexia nervosa or bulimia nervosa, Thiel, Broocks, Ohlmeier, Jacoby, and Schussler (1995) reported that 34 (37%) also met DSM-III-R criteria for OCD. And in their study of 51 women with anorexia nervosa, Råstam, Gillberg, and Gillberg (1995) found that 31% of the patients displayed a lifetime history of OCD.

Indeed, several studies using the YBOCS to assess obsessive–compulsive symptoms in eating disorder patients have found relatively high frequencies of obsessions and compulsions, as well as relatively high severity scores for these symptoms (Kaye et al., 1993b; Rubenstein et al., 1993, 1995). For example, comparing the obsessions and compulsions in 18 patients with anorexia nervosa and 16 patients with OCD with the YBOCS, Bastiani et al. (1996) reported that both groups displayed similar scores on the YBOCS (19 ± 9 vs. 22 ± 6, respectively), and concluded that both disorders had similar magnitudes of impairment from these symptoms.

Conversely, patients with OCD consistently display high rates of eating disorders (Rubenstein et al., 1992). For example, Tamburrino, Kaufman, and Hertzer (1994) found that 13 (42%) of 31 women with OCD had a past or current history of anorexia nervosa alone (26%), bulimia nervosa alone (3%), or both anorexia and bulimia (13%). Similarly, in a survey study of the snacking patterns and rates of previous eating disorder diagnoses in 170 patients with OCD and 920 controls, O'Rourke et al. (1994) found that both male and female OCD patients reported significantly higher frequencies of binge eating and of a previous diagnosis of anorexia nervosa or bulimia nervosa than did control subjects.

A third comorbidity similarity is that controlled phenomenological studies have consistently found increased rates of lifetime mood, anxiety, and psychoactive substance-use disorders in women with anorexia nervosa and bulimia nervosa (Hudson & Pope, 1990). Comparison studies have found similar degrees of depressive symptoms in patients with bulimia nervosa and those with OCD (Bulik, Beidel, Duchmann, Weltzin, & Kaye, 1992; Rubenstein et al., 1995). Open studies have found high rates of associated mood and anxiety disorders in patients with "nonpurging bulimia nervosa" and BED (McCann & Agras, 1990). Compared with nonbingeing obese persons, obese persons who binge eat generally have higher depression scores on various measures of depression, report a higher frequency of depression, and have an increased prevalence of psychiatric disorders, especially mood disorders (de Zwaan et al., 1994). Moreover, epidemiological data support an association between binge eating and mood disorder. In their Zurich cohort study, Vollrath, Koch, and Angst (1992) found that female binge eaters had received the diagnosis of depression significantly more often than similarly aged controls without bingeing.

Similar to some family studies of OCD, controlled family studies of women with anorexia or bulimia nervosa have consistently found elevated rates of mood and anxiety disorders in their first-degree relatives (Hudson & Pope, 1990). Also similar to OCD, neurobiological studies suggest that abnormalities in central serotonergic and possibly catecholaminergic neurotransmission play a role in the pathophysiology of anorexia nervosa and binge eating. Indeed, Jarry and Vaccarino (1996) have hypothesized that eating disorders and OCD both exist on a serotonergically mediated behavioral continuum. At one end of this continuum, the authors speculate, eating disorders and OCD are each characterized by avoidant behaviors (e.g., avoidance of food and germs, respectively). This pole, the authors suggest, would be characterized by high levels of serotonin markers (e.g., increased cerebrospinal fluid [CSF] 5-hydroxyindolacetic acid [5-HIAA] concentrations). At the other end of the continuum, both disorders are characterized by disinhibited approach behaviors (e.g., binge eating without resistance and impulsive handwashing, respectively), which would be associated with low levels of serotonin markers (e.g., reduced CSF 5-HIAA concentrations). Indeed, such a hypothesis would account for the inconsistencies in the specific serotonergic abnormalities found in studies of persons with eating disorders and OCD.

Treatment studies further support a relationship between eating disorders and OCD. First, substantial data suggest that anorexia nervosa, bulimia nervosa, and BED all respond to SRIs. Although, to our knowledge, there are no published controlled studies of SRIs in anorexia nervosa, Kaye, Weltzin, Hsu, and Bulik (1991) reported an open-label trial of fluoxetine administered to 31 patients with DSM-III-R anorexia nervosa after inpatient weight restoration. In this study, 29 (94%) patients had maintained their weight at or above 85% average body weight after a mean of 11 months of fluoxetine treatment. Interestingly, restrictor anorectics responded significantly better than bulimic or purging-type anorectics.

Double-blind, placebo-controlled trials have found fluoxetine to be effective in reducing binge eating and purging in bulimia nervosa (Hudson & Pope, 1990; Fluoxetine Bulimia Nervosa Collaborative Study Group, 1992) and fluvoxamine to be effective in reducing binge eating in BED (Hudson et al., 1994). Also, possibly similar to OCD (which may respond better to higher SRI doses than generally needed to treat depression), the only controlled study that compared two doses of fluoxetine with placebo in patients with bulimia nervosa found that fluoxetine 60 mg/day was superior to both fluoxetine 20 mg/day and placebo in decreasing the frequency of weekly binge eating and vomiting (Fluoxetine Bulimia Nervosa Collaborative Study Group, 1992).

Controlled trials comparing SRIs with non-SRI antidepressants have not yet been conducted in anorexia nervosa, bulimia nervosa, or BED. However, the response of anorexia nervosa to open-label fluoxetine reported by Kaye et al., 1991, coupled with negative studies of other non-SRI antidepressants, suggest that anorexia nervosa might respond preferentially to SRIs. Also, one controlled study found that the serotonin-releasing agent fenfluramine was significantly superior to desipramine in suppressing binge eating in women with bulimia (Blouin, Blouin, Perez, et al., 1988).

Moreover, controlled studies indicate that behavior therapy—including exposure and response prevention and CBT—may be effective in reducing bulimic symptoms (Agras, 1991; Broekmate, Heymans, & Jansen, 1992; Fairburn, Jones, Peveler, Hope, & O'Connor, 1993; Telch et al., 1990).

There are, however, differences between OCD and the eating disorders. First, several comparison studies suggest that there may be differences in the types or severity of obsessions and compulsions. Bastiani et al. (1996) found that, compared with OCD patients, who endorsed a greater variety and quantity of obsessions and compulsions, patients with anorexia nervosa were more likely to endorse symptoms that were related to symmetry and order. In the comparison study by Rubenstein et al. (1995), although patients with bulimia nervosa had more obsessive–compulsive symptoms than normal controls, they had fewer than patients with OCD. Second, bulimia nervosa appears to more often be associated with impulsive behaviors, including self-destructive behaviors, stealing, and alcohol and psychoactive-substance abuse (Yanovski, Nelson, Dubbert, & Spitzer, 1993). Third, anorexia nervosa and bulimia nervosa (though possibly not BED) are far more common in women than men. Fourth, bulimia nervosa has been shown to respond to a wide range of antidepressants from different chemical classes with different putative mechanisms of action, including tricyclics, monoamine oxidase inhibitors (MAOIs), and atypical antidepressants (e.g., bupropion, trazodone, and nomifensine) in addition to SRIs (Hudson & Pope, 1990). Also, nonpurging bulimia nervosa (which is probably closely related to BED) has been shown in a double-blind, placebo-controlled study to respond to desipramine (McCann & Agras, 1990).

Finally, there may be important differences in the responses of eating disorders and OCD to psychological treatments. First, behavior therapy has not been shown to be superior to general supportive treatment in restoring or maintaining weight in anorexia nervosa. Second, preliminary data suggest that interpersonal therapy may be more effective than behavior therapy in bulimia nervosa (Fairburn et al. 1993). Indeed, there are reports of the successful use of insight-oriented psychotherapeutic techniques in patients with bulimia nervosa. Third, conflicting evidence exists as to whether the behavioral procedure of exposure (to binge eating food) and response (bingeing or purging) prevention is superior to, adds to, or subtracts from the efficacy of cognitive-behavioral therapy (American Psychiatric Association, 1993).

IMPULSE CONTROL DISORDERS

DSM-IV defines an impulse control disorder (ICD) as the failure to resist an impulse, drive, or temptation to perform some act that is harmful to the person or others. DSM-IV specifies that for most ICDs, the individual experiences an increasing sense of tension or arousal before committing the act, and then pleasure, gratification, or relief at the time of committing the act. DSM-IV does not have a formal category for ICDs. Rather, ICDs are either listed in a residual category—the ICDs not elsewhere classified, which includes intermittent explosive disorder (IED), kleptomania, pathological gambling, pyromania, trichotillomania, and ICD NOS—or given as examples of ICDs but classified under other diagnostic categories (e.g., psychoactive substance-use disorders and paraphilias). Disorders possibly meeting criteria for ICD NOS are compulsive buying or shopping (also called buying mania or oniomania), repetitive self-mutilation (RSM), onychophagia (nail biting), some forms of psychogenic excoriation (compulsive skin picking), and nonparaphilic sexual addictions (NPSAs; also called sexual compulsions) (McElroy et al., 1994a,b, 1995).

The ICDs and OCD have generally been considered separate diagnostic entities, with ICD impulses and actions distinguished from OCD obsessions and compulsions by the former being considered more harmful, less senseless, more spontaneous, more likely to be associated with pleasure, and, hence, more ego–syntonic (Frosch & Wortis, 1954). In actuality, however, both OCD and ICD symptoms vary considerably with respect to these variables (McElroy et al., 1993). Like OCD obsessions, ICD impulses are often experienced as senseless or repugnant, intrusive, persistent, irresistible, and associated with anxiety or tension. Like OCD compulsions, ICD acts are often experienced as uncontrollable, compelling, and anxiety or tension relieving; are repetitive and sometimes performed in a ritualized manner; may be resisted; are often followed by self-reproach or guilt; and are often concealed or denied.

Conversely, OCD symptoms may be impulsively enacted and associated with poor insight (McElroy et al., 1993). Indeed, DSM-IV uses the term "impulse" to define an obsession. We have also seen OCD patients who claim to experience pleasurable feelings with their obsessions or compulsions. Also, compulsive forms of ICDs, individuals with OCD and high degrees of impulsivity, and impulsive individuals with compulsive behaviors have all been reported (Coid, 1991; Hollander, 1993; McElroy et al., 1993). Finally, just as persons with OCD often display multiple obsessions and compulsions, patients with an ICD often display multiple ICDs (Specker, Carlson, Christenson, & Marcotte, 1995).

Little is known about the course of most ICDs. However, like OCD, most begin in adolescence or early adulthood, and many may have a chronic, often waxing and waning course.

Comorbidity data provide further support for a relationship between ICDs and OCD. High rates of OCD have been reported in some, but not all, studies of patients with various ICDs. Of 27 subjects with DSM-IV IED evaluated by our group, 6 (22%) displayed a lifetime history of OCD (McElroy, Soutullo, Beckman, et al., in press). Of 20 patients with DSM-III-R kleptomania evaluated by our group, 10 (50%) met criteria for past or present OCD (McElroy, Pope, Hudson, Keck, & White, 1991). In a study of 25 pathological gamblers, Linden, Jonas, and Pope (1986) reported that 5 (20%) displayed a lifetime history of OCD. Of 60 adult chronic hair pullers, 50 (83%) of whom met DSM-III-R criteria for trichotillomania, 33% reported obsessions and/or compulsions, and 9 (15%) met DSM-III-R criteria for past or present OCD (Christenson, Mackenzie, & Mitchell, 1991). Of 20 compulsive buyers evaluated by our group, 7 (35%) displayed a lifetime history of DSM-III-R OCD. And of 30 dermatologically referred patients with psychogenic excoriation evaluated by our group, 7 (25%) met DSM-III-R criteria for lifetime OCD (Arnold et al., in press).

To our knowledge, no studies have assessed the rates of ICDs in persons with OCD. However, many studies suggest that, similar to OCD, ICDs, including IED, kleptomania, pathological gambling, pyromania, trichotillomania, compulsive buying, and psychogenic excoriation, may have high comorbidity with mood, anxiety, psychoactive substance use, and eating disorders (McElroy et al., 1993, 1995, 1996).

Studies of family history and serotonergic function offer additional, though limited, support for an ICD–OCD relationship. Relatively high rates of OCD have been found in first-degree relatives of patients with kleptomania and trichotillomania; and high rates of mood disorder and alcohol abuse have been described in the families of probands with impulsive aggression, kleptomania, and pathological gambling (McElroy et al., 1995). Individuals with impulsive aggression (some meeting DSM-III criteria for IED), impulsive fire setting, and RSM have been shown to have abnormalities in central serotonergic neurotransmission (e.g., reduced CSF concentrations of 5-HIAA) (Linnoila et al., 1983; Simeon et al., 1992; Stein et al., 1993). Moreover, as is the case for OCD, preliminary studies suggest that ICDs may also involve abnormalities in noradrenergic and dopaminergic systems (Roy et al., 1988).

Further supporting an ICD–OCD relationship are preliminary clinical data suggesting that many ICDs, including IED, kleptomania, pathological gambling, trichotillomania, compulsive shopping, onychophagia, and psychogenic excoriation may respond to SRIs (Arnold et al., in press; Black, 1996; Black, Monahan, & Gabel, 1997; De Caria et al. 1996; Hollander, 1993; Leonard, Lenane, Swedo, Rettew, & Rapoport, 1991; McElroy et al., 1993, 1994a, 1995, 1996, in press; Swedo et al., 1989). Moreover, two controlled comparison trials suggest that some ICDs may respond better to SRIs than to non-SRI antidepressants. In the first, a 10-week, double-blind, crossover trial of clomipramine and desipramine in the treatment of 13 women with severe DSM-III-R trichotillomania, clomipramine was significantly more effective than desipramine in reducing the frequency and intensity of hair-pulling urges and hair pulling, and in increasing the ability to resist hair pulling (Swedo et al., 1989). In the second, a similarly designed 10-week, double-blind, crossover trial in 14 patients with severe onychophagia, clomipramine was superior to desipramine in decreasing nail biting (Leonard et al., 1991). Also similar to OCD, available clinical data suggest that many ICDs may respond to various forms of behavior therapy but not to psychodynamic psychotherapy (Josephson & Brondolo, 1993).

However, there are important differences between ICDs and OCD. First, ICD symptoms are probably more likely than OCD symptoms to involve harmful or exciting behaviors, poor insight into the dangerousness or consequences of the behaviors, lack of resistance, disinhibited thinking or behaviors, and pleasurable feelings, and thus, to be more impulsive and ego–syntonic (McElroy et al., 1993, 1996). For example, in a comparison of the clinical features in 8 patients with trichotillomania and 13 patients with OCD, trichotillomania patients reported a significantly greater degree of pleasure during hair pulling than did OCD patients did during ritualizing (Stanley, Swann, Bowers, Davis, & Taylor, 1992). Also, compared with OCD patients, trichotillomania patients displayed significantly fewer obsessive–compulsive symptoms, less anxiety and depression, and more extraversion. Similarly, in a recent comparison of 12 patients with trichotillomania and 17 patients with OCD, trichotillomania patients displayed significantly lower scores on the YBOCS and on measures of resistance, and higher scores on measures of impulsiveness (Stein et al., 1995a).

Second, different ICDs have different prevalence rates in men and women, with kleptomania, trichotillomania, compulsive buying, and psychogenic excoriation being more common in women, and IED, pathological gambling, and pyromania being more common in men. Third, although not yet systematically studied, ICDs may be more likely than OCD to be associated with other conditions characterized by impulsive symptoms, such as bipolar disorder, psychoactive substance-use disorders, attention-deficit/hyperactivity disorder (ADHD), and borderline and antisocial personality disorders (McElroy et al., 1996). Fourth, ICDs and OCD may have some biological differences. In their review of the relationship between trichotillomania and OCD, for example, Stein, Simeon, Cohen, and Hollander (1995b) concluded that the findings of serotonergic abnormalities in trichotillomania have been inconclusive and recommended investigation of other neurotransmitter systems, especially the dopamine system. Also, when compared with OCD patients, patients with trichotillomania do not display increased neurological soft signs or differential brain glucose metabolic rates as determined by position emission tomography (Stein et al., 1995b). Fifth, some ICDs may respond to a broad range of thymoleptic agents rather than preferentially to SRIs. Although controlled comparison studies have not been done for ICDs other than trichotillomania and onychophagia, non-SRI antidepressants (e.g., tricyclics, MAOIs) and mood stabilizers (e.g., lithium, carbamazepine, and valproate) from a wide variety of classes and with different putative mechanisms of action have been reported to be effective in many different ICDs (primarily in case reports and small, open-label studies) (McElroy et al., 1996). Also, one controlled trial suggests that the antiepileptic phenytoin (which has been reported to have mood-stabilizing effects) may reduce rage episodes in IED (Barratt, Kent, Bryant, & Felthouse, 1991). Finally, data on the efficacy of SRIs for trichotillomania are inconclusive. Two double-blind, placebo-controlled, crossover trials showed that fluoxetine was not more effective than placebo as an acute treatment for trichotillomania (Christenson et al., 1991; Streichenwein & Thornby, 1995). Clinical experience further suggests that acute response of trichotillomania to an SRI is often not maintained over extended periods of time (Pollard et al., 1991).

SEXUAL DISORDERS

In DSM-IV, paraphilias are defined as sexual disorders characterized by recurrent, intense, sexually arousing fantasies, sexual urges, or behaviors generally involving nonhuman objects, the suffering or humiliation of oneself or one's partner, or children, or other nonconsenting persons. Paraphilias listed in DSM-IV are exhibitionism, fetishism, frotteurism, pedophilia, sexual masochism, sexual sadism, transvestic fetishism, voyeurism, and paraphilia NOS. Examples of the NOS category include telephone scatologia, necrophilia, partialism, zoophilia, coprophilia, klismaphilia, urophilia, and autoerotic asphyxiation.

NPSAs are not included in DSM-IV as formal mental disorders but are possible examples of sexual disorders NOS. They have been defined as repetitive sexual acts involving "conventional," "normative," or nondeviant sexual behaviors that the person feels compelled or driven to perform, which may or may not cause distress (Anthony & Hollander, 1993; Hollander & Wong, 1995; Kafka, 1995). Examples include compulsive promiscuity, compulsive use of pornography, ego–dystonic dependence on sexual "accessories" to maintain sexual arousal, or severe incompatibility between partners because of differing degrees of sexual desire. Of note, although paraphilias and sexual compulsions are distinguished from each other by the "deviance" of the sexual fantasies or behaviors, there is considerable overlap between these two conditions (Kafka, 1995). Many patients with paraphilias also have sexual compulsions.

These sexual disorders and OCD share many phenomenological features. First, sexual obsessions are common in OCD, occurring in 32% of the 100 patients with OCD studied by Rasmussen and Tsuang (1986). Second, the sexual fantasies and impulses of both paraphilias and NPSAs may be intrusive, repugnant, recurrent, resisted, and associated with anxiety or tension, and thus similar to OCD obsessions. Indeed, it is sometimes difficult to distinguish the sexual impulses of paraphilias and NPSAs from the sexual obsessions of OCD when the former are ego–dystonic and not enacted. Third, the sexual acts of both paraphilias and NPSAs are often performed compulsively and associated with relief, and viewed with shame or disgust. Hollander and Wong (1995) have observed that these disorders are similar to OCD in that afflicted persons feel the urge to both avoid and complete sexual behaviors in order to minimize anxiety. Finally, similar to the multiple obsessions and compulsions seen in most patients with OCD, most paraphilic individuals have multiple abnormal sexual impulses and behaviors (Abel, Becker, Cunningham-Rathner, Mittelman, & Rouleau, 1988).

Although less is known about the course of illness of paraphilias and NPSAs, clinical data indicate that, similar to OCD, those disorders often begin in adolescence and early adulthood, sometimes begin in childhood, and often have a chronic, waxing and waning course.

Comorbidity studies provide further support for a relationship between these sexual disorders and OCD. Although rates of sexual disorders, to our knowledge, have not been assessed in persons with OCD, preliminary clinical data suggest that patients with paraphilias and NPSAs may have high rates of OCD. For example, of 10 patients with paraphilias and/or NPSAs evaluated by Stein et al. (1992), 7 (70%) had comorbid OCD. Of 22 adolescent male sex offenders evaluated by our group, all of whom met DSM-III-R diagnostic criteria for pedophilia (except the age requirement), 6 (27%) met lifetime DSM-III-R criteria for OCD (Galli, Raute, Kizer, McConville, & McElroy, 1995). Furthermore, similar to OCD, paraphilias and NPSAs may have high comorbidity with mood, anxiety, and substance-use disorders. Of 15 men with DSM-III-R paraphilias evaluated by Kruesi, Fine, Valladares, Phillips, and Rapoport (1992), 9 (60%) had a lifetime mood disorder, 6 (40%) an anxiety disorder, and 8 (53%) a substance-use disorder. Evaluating 20 men with sexual compulsions recruited by newspaper advertisement (10 of whom also had at least one DSM-III-R paraphilia), Kafka and Prentky (1992a) found that 19 (95%) met DSM-III-R criteria for a history of dysthymia, and 11 (55%) met criteria for current major depression. And of the 22 adolescents with pedophilia evaluated by our group, 18 (82%) met DSM-III-R criteria for a mood disorder, 12 (55%) for an anxiety disorder, and 11 (50%) for a substance-use disorder (Galli et al., 1995).

To our knowledge, there are no family-history studies of mental disorders in the relatives of probands with paraphilias or sexual compulsions. However, Cryan, Butcher, and Webb (1992) described a case of monozygotic twins in which both had OCD and a paraphilia.

Preliminary data suggest that patients with paraphilias and NPSAs, like those with OCD, may respond to various SRIs (Kafka, 1994, 1995; Kafka & Prentky, 1992b). Moreover, a recent controlled case study of a male patient with exhibitionism treated with fluvoxamine, desipramine, and placebo in a crossover design suggests that some paraphilic patients may respond preferentially to SRIs (Zohar, Kaplan, & Benjamin, 1994). In this patient, fluvoxamine eliminated "abnormal" sexual impulses and behavior without affecting "normal" sexual desire, whereas desipramine and placebo were both associated with relapse.

However, there are important differences between these sexual disorders and OCD. First, paraphilias and NPSAs are probably more common in men. Second, although systematic, phenomenological comparison studies have not yet been conducted, paraphilic and NPSA symptoms are probably more often associated with pleasure (especially sexual pleasure) and are more likely to be enacted, and thus, are more likely to be ego–syntonic than are OCD symptoms. Paraphilias may also be associated with higher rates of psychoactive substance use and antisocial personality disorders than is OCD (Kruesi et al., 1992). Finally, individuals with paraphilias have been reported to respond to thymoleptic agents other than SRIs, including non-SRI antidepressants and lithium (Cesnik & Coleman, 1989; Ward, 1975). Indeed, in the only controlled antidepressant trial published to date in a group of patients with paraphilias, desipramine and clomipramine were equally effective in reducing the severity of paraphilic symptoms relative to treatment with single-blind placebo (Kruesi et al., 1992).

TOURETTE'S DISORDER

Tourette's disorder is a chronic neuropsychiatric disorder characterized by motor tics and one or more vocal tics beginning before the age of 18 years (American Psychiatric Association, 1994). Of note, DSM-IV defines a tic as a sudden, rapid, recurrent, nonrhythmic, stereotyped motor movement or vocalization.

Tourette's tics share phenomenological similarities with OCD compulsions (Como, 1995; Leckman, 1993; Leckman, Walker, Goodman, Pauls, & Cohen, 1994). Although patients may be able to suppress their tics for varying lengths of time, they eventually experience them as irresistible and perform them, during which they often experience relief. Also, Tourette's patients often state that they need to perform tics until they are felt to be "just right" (Leckman et al., 1994). In addition, Tourette's patients often experience sensory phenomena preceding or accompanying their tics that resemble OCD obsessions, including uncomfortable premonitory urges that are relieved with performance of the tic. Finally, like OCD symptoms, tics are often exacerbated by stress (Como, 1995).

Comorbidity studies have consistently found elevated rates of obsessive–compulsive symptoms and OCD in patients with Tourette's disorder, with rates ranging from 12% to 90% (Como, 1995; Leckman, 1993; Leckman et al., 1994; Pitman, Green, Jenike, & Mesulam, 1987; Robertson, Trimble, & Lees, 1988). Conversely, relatively high rates of tics or tic disorders have been found in persons with OCD (Como, 1995). For example, Pitman et al. (1987) reported that 6 (37%) of 16 patients with OCD met criteria for a tic disorder. Also, in a 2- to 7-year follow-up study, 54 children with OCD without Tourette's disorder, Leonard et al. (1992) reported that 32 (59%) had lifetime histories of tics. More recently, Zohar et al. (1997) evaluated 40 nonreferred adolescents with "obsessive–compulsive spectrum disorders" and found that adolescents with tics were more prone to aggressive and sexual images and obsessions than were adolescents without tics.

Family-history studies have found elevated rates of OCD and depression in first-degree relatives of probands with Tourette's disorder (Cohen, Shaywitz, Caparulo, Young, & Bowers, 1978; Leckman, 1993; Pauls, 1992; Robertson et al., 1988). Preliminary neurobiological studies suggest that Tourette's disorder, like OCD, may involve disordered central serotonergic, dopaminergic, and noradrenergic neurotransmission (Leckman et al., 1995a). Moreover, neuroimaging techniques have found hypermetabolic changes in the orbito-frontal cortex and basal ganglia in Tourette's patients similar to those found in OCD patients (Baxter & Guze, 1992; Chase et al., 1984).

Tourette's disorder and OCD display some similarities in treatment response. Open studies suggest that the obsessions and compulsions of Tourette's patients, and occasionally the tics, may respond to SRIs (Como, 1995). Also, tics, along with the premonitory urges to perform them, may respond to a variety of behavior therapy techniques, such as habit reversal, self-monitoring, and contingency management (Como, 1995; Josephson & Brondolo, 1993; Peterson & Azrin, 1992).

There are, however, important differences between Tourette's disorder and OCD. First, Tourette's disorder is much more common in males. Second, more cognitions and autonomic anxiety and fewer sensory phenomena have been reported to precede OCD compulsions than Tourette's disorder tics (Miguel, et al., 1995, 1997). Third, Tourette's disorder is frequently accompanied by impulsive behaviors, including rage outbursts, ADHD symptoms, self-injury, and inappropriate sexual behavior (Robertson et al., 1988). Fourth, there are differences in the course of illness. Tourette's disorder generally has an earlier age of onset than does OCD (the median age of onset of motor tics is seven years, with tics often first apparent by five years of age). Also, although Tourette's disorder is often a lifelong condition, symptoms frequently diminish during adolescence and adulthood, remissions may occur, and, in some patients, symptoms may disappear entirely by early adulthood (Como, 1995). Fifth, family and twin studies indicate that Tourette's disorder is genetically transmitted via an autosomal dominant pattern (Pauls, 1992). There are also important differences in treatment response. The tics of Tourette's disorder, and to a lesser extent the associated OCD symptoms, have been shown in controlled studies to respond to neuroleptics (Shapiro et al., 1989) and clonidine (Leckman et al., 1991)—drugs that are ineffective as single agents for OCD obsessions and compulsions. And although Tourette's patients with comorbid OCD may display decreased OCD symptoms in response to SRIs, the tics themselves often do not respond or may even increase in response to these agents (Caine, Polinsky, Ebert, Rapaport, & Mikkelsen, 1979; Delgado, Goodman, Price, Heninger, & Charney, 1990). Furthermore, obsessions and compulsions with associated tics may respond less favorably to SRIs alone than those not associated with tics. In a retrospective, case-controlled analysis of fluvoxamine, McDougle et al. (1993) found that patients with pure OCD displayed a higher response rate (52%) than OCD patients with comorbid chronic tics (21%). To account for these important differences between Tourette's disorder and OCD, it has been suggested that OCD related to Tourette's disorder may be distinct from OCD without tics (Leckman, 1993; Leckman et al., 1995a,b; McDougle et al., 1993).

DISCUSSION

Considerable preliminary evidence suggests that the disorders reviewed in this chapter may be related to OCD, and thus, together, may form a family of OCD spectrum disorders. Perhaps the strongest evidence linking these conditions are their phenomenological similarities with OCD and one another. Regardless of the "content" of the core mental or behavioral symptoms, the "structure" of these symptoms is characterized by obsessive thinking or compulsive behaviors and, thus, is similar to OCD obsessions or compulsions. Indeed, even the "content" of some OCD spectrum disorders overlaps with that of classic OCD. Thus, for example, the preoccupation with symmetry in physical appearance of some BDD patients is similar to the obsessive need for symmetry of some OCD patients. The illness fears of hypochondriasis resemble the germ contamination obsessions of OCD. The sexual impulses of paraphilias are sometimes indistinguishable from OCD sexual obsessions, and the aggressive impulses of IED are similar to OCD violent obsessions. Moreover, repeated requests for reassurance are characteristic of BDD and hypochondriasis, and frequent checking is characteristic of BDD, hypochondriasis, anorexia nervosa, and psychogenic excoriation.

Further supporting a relationship among these syndromes and OCD are their similarities in course of illness, psychiatric comorbidity, family history, biology, and treatment response. Many of the disorders reviewed in this chapter begin in adolescence or adulthood and display a chronic course with waxing and waning symptom severity. Most disorders are associated with a high rate of classic OCD symptoms and/or syndromal OCD, as well as mood, anxiety, and psychoactive substance-use disorders. Kleptomania, trichotillomania, and Tourette's disorder may be associated with high familial rates of OCD; BDD, eating disorders, and many ICDs are associated with elevated rates of familial mood disorder. Available data indicate that eating disorders, IED, pyromania, repetitive self-mutilation, and Tourette's disorder may be associated with central nervous system serotonergic abnormalities. Many of these disorders have been shown to respond to thymoleptic agents and behavior therapy. Moreover, preliminary data suggest that some of these conditions may respond preferentially to SRIs (e.g., BDD, anorexia nervosa, onychophagia, and possibly trichotillomania), or may require higher SRI doses (e.g., bulimia nervosa) or longer durations of treatment (e.g., BDD) with these agents than is needed for major depression.

Indeed, some authors have argued that the OCD spectrum disorder family should be broadened to include all conditions characterized by obsessive thinking or compulsive or repetitive behaviors (Hollander, 1993). Other potential OCD spectrum disorders might therefore include (1) other Axis I disorders (e.g., depersonalization disorder, somatoform disorders other than BDD and hypochondriasis, the anxiety disorders, panic disorder, agoraphobia, social phobia, specific phobia, and posttraumatic stress disorder, and schizophrenia with associated obsessions or compulsions); (2) Axis II disorders with compulsive features (e.g., avoidant and obsessive–compulsive personality disorders); and (3) other neuropsychiatric disorders (e.g., Sydenham's chorea, autistic disorder, Prader–Willi syndrome, and stuttering). More broadly, because OCD itself may be associated with impulsivity (lack of insight, automatic enactment of behaviors, and possibly pleasure in addition to anxiety relief), because some of the proposed OCD spectrum disorders have prominent impulsive features (e.g., ICDs, bulimia nervosa and BED, paraphilias and sexual compulsions, and Tourette's syndrome), and because impulsivity and compulsivity may be related, the OCD spectrum disorder family might also include other disorders with impulsive behaviors, such as psychoactive substance-use disorders, ADHD, borderline and antisocial personality disorders, and various organic syndromes. Indeed, it has been hypothesized that the OCD spectrum disorders are related by sharing a core disturbance in compulsivity and/or impulsivity (Hollander, 1993), and that they therefore may constitute a family of conditions more accurately termed compulsive–impulsive spectrum disorder (McElroy et al., 1996).

However, it is important that the OCD spectrum disorder concept not be excessively broad, especially given the relative lack of empirical data on the disorders that have been hypothesized to belong to this family (Rasmussen, 1994). It is presently unclear how similar a putative OCD spectrum disorder must be to OCD and what these similarities should consist of. Even at this preliminary stage of knowledge, some disorders, such as BDD and anorexia nervosa, seem more closely related to OCD than do some of the other putative OCD spectrum disorders, such as bulimia nervosa, binge-eating disorder, ICDs, and paraphilias. Moreover, as discussed in this chapter, even those OCD spectrum disorders that may be more closely related to OCD still have important differences with OCD. Further complicating this issue is the likelihood that OCD, as well as some (if not all) of the putative OCD spectrum disorders, are each heterogeneous disorders (Rasmussen, 1994). Thus, some of the putative OCD spectrum disorders may have subtypes that are more or less related to OCD.

Indeed, various models have been proposed to explain the similarities and differences among the putative OCD spectrum disorders, including the possibility that these conditions vary along a single dimension of compulsivity versus impulsivity (Hollander, 1993; McElroy et al., 1993, 1994b, 1995, 1996). According to this model, all OCD spectrum disorders and, more broadly, compulsivity and impulsivity would be characterized by intrusive, persistent thoughts associated with anxiety or tension, and/or by repetitive behaviors aimed at reducing discomfort. However, one extreme of this proposed dimension would consist of purely compulsive or ego–dystonic disorders, characterized by performance of harm-avoidant behaviors, good insight into the senselessness of the behaviors, resistance to performing the behaviors, and absence of pleasure when the behaviors are performed. The other end of this hypothesized dimension would consist of purely impulsive or ego–syntonic disorders, characterized by performance of harmful or exciting behaviors, little insight into the dangerousness or consequences of the behaviors, little resistance to the behaviors, and pleasure when the behavior is performed. Various mixed compulsive–impulsive forms would be situated in between, such as OCD with poor insight or impulsive features, ICDs with good insight or compulsive features, and the co-occurrence of OCD and an ICD in the same individual.

Such a compulsivity–impulsivity dimension might explain the relationship among apparently related clusters of OCD spectrum disorders. For example, anorexia nervosa, restricting type, might represent the more compulsive eating disorder, bulimia nervosa, purging type, the more impulsive eating disorder, with mixed compulsive–impulsive conditions (e.g., binge eating/purging anorexia nervosa and nonpurging bulimia nervosa) situated in between. The sexual disorders might also span a dimension from compulsivity to impulsivity, with OCD with sexual obsessions at the compulsive extreme, paraphilias at the impulsive extreme, and NPSAs and various mixed forms (e.g., OCD and a paraphilia occurring in the same individual) situated in between.

However, the above model does not explain the extensive overlap of OCD and most putative OCD spectrum disorders with mood disorders. To account for this overlap, we have hypothesized that OCD, most putative OCD spectrum disorders, and more broadly, all disorders characterized by a core disturbance in compulsivity and/or impulsivity might belong to the larger family of affective spectrum disorder (McElroy et al., 1993, 1995, 1996; Phillips et al., 1995). Affective spectrum disorder is a hypothesized family of disorders related to mood disorders, characterized by high comorbidity with mood disorder, high familial rates of mood disorder, and response to thymoleptic agents, and thus, possibly a common pathophysiological abnormality with mood disorder (Hudson & Pope, 1990).

We have hypothesized further that compulsivity and impulsivity may be related to mood dysregulation, with depression (or unipolarity) sharing features with compulsivity, mania (or bipolarity) sharing features with impulsivity, and mixed affective states similar to mixtures of compulsivity and impulsivity (McElroy et al., 1996). Specifically, compulsivity and depression are each characterized by inhibited or ruminative thinking and behavior, maintenance of insight or ego–dystonicity, and less marked fluctuations in mood state, with dysphoria usually alternating with relief rather than with euphoria or pleasurable feelings. Similarly, impulsivity and mania (or bipolarity) are each characterized by disinhibited or facilitated thinking and behavior, poor insight or ego–syntonicity, and marked changes in mood state between dysphoric and pleasurable affects.

If these speculations are correct, the OCD spectrum disorders might be arranged along an axis (or related axes) of compulsivity/unipolarity versus impulsivity/bipolarity, where disorders characterized by maximum compulsivity and unipolarity (e.g., OCD and BDD with a comorbid depressive disorder) are at one end of this hypothesized axis, and those with maximum impulsivity and bipolarity (e.g., ICDs and paraphilias with a comorbid bipolar disorder) are at the other. This hypothesis is supported by findings that most of the putative OCD spectrum disorders reviewed in this chapter have high rates of associated mood disorders, and by preliminary data suggesting that more impulsive OCD spectrum disorders (e.g., ICDs, paraphilias) may be associated with higher rates of bipolar disorder relative to depressive disorders (McElroy et al., 1996). Indeed, further preliminary support for such a dimension are the possible differences in thymoleptic responsiveness of various OCD spectrum disorders, with more compulsive forms (e.g., BDD, anorexia nervosa) possibly responding preferentially to SRIs, and more impulsive forms (e.g., bulimia nervosa, BED, ICDs, and paraphilias) responding to a larger range of thymoleptics (e.g., non-SRI antidepressants and mood stabilizers, as well as SRIs).

Although highly speculative, this model of the OCD spectrum disorders may have important clinical implications. First, awareness of the high comorbidity of these disorders with one another and with other psychiatric disorders, especially mood disorder, should increase recognition of the related disorders when a patient presents with OCD or an OCD spectrum disorder. Second, if pharmacological responsiveness also varies along a compulsivity–impulsivity dimension (with more compulsive forms responding preferentially to SRIs, and more impulsive forms responding to a wider range of thymoleptic agents), pharmacological responsiveness might be predicted based upon presenting phenomenology and mood disorder comorbidity. In other words, the degree of presenting compulsive versus impulsive features of an OCD spectrum disorder, along with the type of comorbid mood disorder (e.g., depressive vs. bipolar), might help guide the choice of both psychopharmacological and psychological treatments. Third, consideration of an OCD spectrum disorder in patients inadequately responsive to standard treatment might lead to consideration of other, possibly more effective interventions (e.g., delusional disorder poorly responsive to antipsychotics might in fact be a delusional OCD spectrum disorder preferentially responsive to SRIs).

Confirmation or disconfirmation of our hypothesis awaits further investigation of the OCD spectrum disorders. More data are needed on their phenomenology, course of illness, comorbidity, family history, neurobiology, and response to psychological and psychopharmacological treatments. Importantly, direct comparison studies of the OCD spectrum disorders with OCD, mood disorder, and one another are needed to elucidate the interrelationships among this proposed family of disorders.

REFERENCES

Abel, G. G., Becker, J. V., Cunningham-Rathner, J., Mittelman, M., & Rouleau, J. (1988). Multiple paraphilic diagnosis among sex offenders. *Bulletin of the American Academy of Psychiatry and the Law, 16*(2), 153–168.

Agras, W. S. (1991). Nonpharmacologic treatments of bulimia nervosa. *Journal of Clinical Psychiatry, 52*(Suppl. 10), 29–33.

American Psychiatric Association. (1980). *Diagnostic and statistical manual of mental disorders* (3rd ed.). Washington, DC: Author.

American Psychiatric Association. (1987). *Diagnostic and statistical manual of mental disorders* (3rd ed., rev.). Washington, DC: Author.

American Psychiatric Association. (1993). Practice guidelines for eating disorders. *American Journal of Psychiatry, 150,* 212–228.

American Psychiatric Association. (1994). *Diagnostic and statistical manual of mental disorders.* (4th ed.). Washington, DC: Author.

Anthony D. T., & Hollander, E. (1993). Sexual compulsions. In E. Hollander (Ed.), *Obsessive–compulsive related disorder* (pp. 139–150). Washington, DC: American Psychiatric Press.

Arnold, L. M., McElroy, S. L., Mutasim, D. F., Dwight, M. M., Lamerson, C. L., & Morris, E. M. (in press). Characteristics of 34 adults with psychogenic excoriation. *Journal of Clinical Psychiatry.*

Barratt, E. S., Kent, T. A., Bryant, S. G., & Felthous, A. R. (1991). A controlled trial of phenytoin in impulsive aggression [letter]. *Journal of Clinical Psychopharmacology, 11,* 388–389.

Barsky, A. J. (1992). Hypochondriasis and obsessive compulsive disorder. *Psychiatric Clinics of North America, 15,* 791–801.

Barsky, A. J., Wyshak, G., & Klerman, G. L. (1986). Hypochondriasis: An evaluation of the DSM-III criteria in medical outpatients. *Archives of General Psychiatry, 43,* 493–500.

Bastiani, A. M., Altemus, M., Pigott, T. A., Rubenstein, C. S., Weltzin, T., & Kaye, W. (1996). Comparison of obsessions and compulsions in patients with anorexia nervosa and obsessive compulsive disorder. *Biological Psychiatry, 39,* 966–969.

Baxter, L. R., & Guze, B. A. (1992). Neuroimaging. In R. Kurlan (Ed.), *Handbook of Tourette's syndrome and related tic and behavioral disorders* (pp. 289–304). New York: Dekker.

Beglin, S. J., & Fairburn, C. G. (1992). What is meant by the term "binge"? *American Journal of Psychiatry, 149,* 123–124.

Black, D. W. (1996). Compulsive buying: A review. *Journal of Clinical Psychiatry, 57*(Suppl. 8), 50–55.

Black, D. W., Monahan, P., & Gabel, J. (1997). Fluvoxamine in the treatment of compulsive buying. *Journal of Clinical Psychiatry, 58,* 159–163.

Blouin, A. G., Blouin, J. H., Perez, E. L., et al. (1988). Treatment of bulimia with fenfluramine and desipramine. *Journal of Clinical Psychopharmacology, 8,* 261–269.

Brawman-Mintzer, O., Lydiard, R. B., Phillips, K. A., Morton, A., Czepowicz, V., Emmanuel, N., Villareal, G., Johnson, M., & Ballenger, J. C. (1995). Body dysmorphic disorder in patients with anxiety disorders and major depression: A comorbidity study. *American Journal of Psychiatry, 152*(11), 1665–1667.

Brewerton, T. D. (1995). Toward a unified theory of serotonin dysregulation in eating and related disorders. *Psychoneuroendocrinology, 20,* 561–590.

Bulik, C. M., Beidel, D. C., Duchmann, E., Weltzin, T. E., & Kaye, W. H. (1992). Comparative psychopathology of women with bulimia nervosa and obsessive–compulsive disorder. *Comprehensive Psychiatry, 33,* 262–268.

Caine, E. D., Polinsky, R. J., Ebert, M. H., Rapoport, J. L., & Mikkelsen, E. J. (1979). Trial of chlorimipramine and desipramine for Gilles de la Tourette's syndrome. *Annals of Neurology, 5,* 305–306.

Cesnik, J. A., & Coleman, E. (1989). Use of lithium carbonate in the treatment of autoerotic asphyxia. *American Journal of Psychotherapy, 43,* 277–286.

Chase, T. N., Foster, N. L., Fenio, P., Brooks, R., Monsi, L., Kessler, R., & Di Chiro, G. (1984). Gilles de la Tourette syndrome: Studies with fluorine 18 labeled fluorodeopyglucose positron emission tomographic methods. *Annals of Neurology, 15*(Suppl.), S175.

Christenson, G. A., Faber, R. J., de Zwaan, M., Raymond, N. C., Specker, S. M., Ekern, M. D., Mackenzie, T. B., Crosby, R. D., Crow, S. J., Eckert, E. D., Mussell, M. P., & Mitchell, J. E. (1994). Compulsive buying: Descriptive characteristics and psychiatric comorbidity. *Journal of Clinical Psychiatry, 55*(1), 5–11.

Christenson, G. A., MacKenzie, T. B., & Mitchell, J. E. (1991). Characteristics of 60 adult chronic hair pullers. *American Journal of Psychiatry, 148,* 365–370.

Christenson, G. A., MacKenzie, T. B., Mitchell, J. E., & Callies, A. L. (1991). A placebo-controlled, double-blind crossover study of fluoxetine in trichotillomania. *American Journal of Psychiatry, 148,* 1566–1571.

Cohen, D. J., Shaywitz, B. A., Caparulo, B., Young, J. G., & Bowers M. B. Jr. (1978). Chronic, multiple tics of Gilles de la Tourette's disorder: CSP acid monoamine metabolites after probenecid administration. *Archives of General Psychiatry, 35*(2), 245–250.

Cohen, L. J., Stein, D. J., Simeon, D., Spadaccini, E., Rosen, J., Aronowitz, B., & Hollander, E. (1995). Clinical profile, comorbidity, and treatment history in 123 hair-pullers: A survey study. *Journal of Clinical Psychiatry, 56,* 319–326.

Coid, J. W. (1991). An affective syndrome in psychopaths with borderline personality disorder? *British Journal of Psychiatry, 162,* 641–650.

Como, P. (1995). Obsessive–compulsive disorder in Tourette's syndrome. In W. J. Weiner & A. E. Lang (Eds.), *Behavioral neurology of movement disorders* (pp. 281–291). New York: Raven Press.

Cryan, E. M. J., Butcher, G. J., & Webb, M. G. T. (1992). Obsessive–compulsive disorder and paraphilia in a monozygotic twin pair. *British Journal of Psychiatry, 161,* 694–698.

De Caria, C., Hollander, E., Grossman, R., Wong, C. M., Mosovich, S. A., & Cherkosky, S. (1996). Diagnosis, neurobiology, and treatment of pathological gambling. *Journal of Clinical Psychiatry, 57*(Suppl. 8), 80–84.

Delgado, P. L., Goodman, W. K., Price, L. H., Heninger, G. R., & Charney, D. S. (1990). Fluvoxamine/pimozide treatment of concurrent Tourette's and obsessive–compulsive disorder. *British Journal of Psychiatry, 157,* 762–765.

de Zwann, M., Mitchell, J. E., Raymond, N. C., et al. (1994). Binge eating disorder: Clinical features and treatment of a new diagnosis. *Harvard Review of Psychiatry, 1,* 310–325.

Eisen, J. L., Phillips, K. A., Rasmussen, S. A., & Luce, D. (1997, May 21). *Insight in body dysmorphic disorder versus OCD.* Paper presented at the 150th Annual Meeting of the American Psychiatric Association, San Diego, CA.

Fahy, T. A., Osacar, A., & Marks, I. (1993). History of eating disorders in female patients with obsessive compulsive disorder. *International Journal of Eating Disorders, 14*(4), 439–443.

Fairburn, C. G., Jones, R., Peveler, R. C., Hope, R. A., & O'Connor, M. (1993). Psychotherapy and bulimia therapy, and cognitive behavior therapy. *Archives of General Psychiatry, 50*, 419–428.

Fallon, B. A., Klein, B. W., & Liebowitz, M. R. (1993a). Hypochondriasis: Treatment strategies. *Psychiatric Annals, 7*, 374–381.

Fallon, B. A., Liebowitz, M. R., Salman, E., Schneier, F. R., Jusino, C., Hollander, E., & Klein, D. F. (1993b). Fluoxetine for hypochondriacal patients without major depression. *Journal of Clinical Psychopharmacology, 13*, 438–441.

Fallon, B. A., Rasmussen, S. A., & Liebowitz, M. R. (1993c). Hypochondriasis. In E. Hollander (Ed.), *Obsessive–compulsive related disorders* (pp. 71–92). Washington, DC: American Psychiatric Press.

Fallon, B. A., Schneier, F. R., Marchall, R., Campeas, R., Vermes, D., Goetz, D., & Liebowitz, M. R. (1996). The pharmacotherapy of hypochondriasis. *Psychopharmacology Bulletin, 32*, 607–611.

Fluoxetine Bulimia Nervosa Collaborative Study Group. (1992). Fluoxetine in the treatment of bulimia nervosa. *Archives of General Psychiatry, 49*, 139–147.

Formea, G., & Burns, G. (1995). Relation between the syndromes of bulimia nervosa and obsessive compulsive disorder. *Journal of Psychopathology and Behavioral Assessment, 17*(2), 167–176.

Frosch, J., & Wortis, S. B. (1954). A contribution to the nosology of the impulse disorders. *American Journal of Psychiatry, 111*, 132–138.

Galli, V. J., Raute, N. J., Kizer, D. L., McConville, B. J., & McElroy, S. L. (1995, May 31–June 3). *A study of the phenomenology, comorbidity, and preliminary treatment response of pedophiles and adolescent sex offenders.* New Clinical Drug Evaluation Unit (NCDEU) 35th Annual Meeting, Orlando, FL (abstract).

George, M. S., Trimble, M. R., Ring, H. A., Sallee, F. R., & Robertson, M. M. (1993). Obsessions in obsessive–compulsive disorder with and without Gilles de la Tourette's syndrome. *American Journal Psychiatry, 150*, 93–97.

Goodman W. K., Price, L. H., Rasmussen, S. A., Mazure, C., Fleischmann, R. C., Hill, C. L., Heninger, G. R., & Charney, D. S. (1989). The Yale–Brown Obsessive–Compulsive Scale: I. Development, use, and reliability. *Archives of General Psychiatry, 46*, 1006–1011.

Hollander, E. (Ed.). (1993). *Obsessive–compulsive-related disorders.* Washington, DC: American Psychiatric Press.

Hollander, E., Cohen, L., & Simean, D. (1993). Body dysmorphic disorder. *Psychiatric Annals, 23*(7), 359–373.

Hollander, E., Frenkel, M., DeCaria, C. M., Trungold, S., & Stein, D. J. (1992). Treatment of pathological gambling with clomipramine [letter]. *American Journal of Psychiatry, 149*, 710–711.

Hollander, E., & Wong, C. M. (1995). Body dysmorphic disorder, pathologic gambling, and sexual compulsions. *Journal of Clinical Psychiatry, 56*(4), 7–12.

Holzer, J. C., Goodman, W. K., McDougle, C. J., Baer, L., Boyarsky, B. K., Leckman, J. F., & Price, L. H. (1994). Obsessive compulsive disorder with and without a chronic tic disorder: A comparison of symptoms in 70 patients. *British Journal of Psychiatry, 164*, 469–473.

Hudson, J. I., McElroy, S. L., Raymond, N. C., Crow, S., Keck, P. E. Jr., Carter, W. P.,

Mitchell, J. E., Strakowski, S. M., Pope, H. G. Jr., Coleman, B., & Jonas, J. M. (1994, May 26). Fluvoxamine treatment of binge eating disorder: A multicenter, placebo-controlled trial. *New Research Program and Abstracts of the 1994 Annual Meeting of the American Psychiatric Association*, Philadelphia, PA, Abstract No. 620, p. 218.

Hudson, J. I., & Pope, H. G. Jr. (1990). Affective spectrum disorder: Dose antidepressant response identify a family of disorders with a common pathophysiology? *American Journal of Psychiatry, 147*, 552–564.

Jarry, J. L., & Vaccarino, F. J. (1996). Eating disorder and obsessive compulsive disorder: Neurochemical and phenomenological commonalities. *Journal of Psychiatry and Neuroscience, 21*, 36–48.

Josephson, S. C., & Brondolo, E. (1993). Cognitive-behavioral approaches to obsessive–compulsive-related disorders. In E. Hollander (Ed.), *Obsessive–compulsive-related disorders* (pp. 215–240). Washington, DC: American Psychiatric Press.

Kafka, M. P. (1994). Sertraline pharmacotherapy for paraphilias and paraphilia-related disorders. *Annals of Clinical Psychiatry, 6*, 189–195.

Kafka, M. P. (1995). Sexual impulsivity. In E. Hollander & D. Stein (Eds.), *Impulsivity and aggression* (pp 201–228). New York: Wiley.

Kafka, M.P., & Prentky, R. (1992a). A comparative study of nonparaphilic sexual addictions and paraphilias in men. *Journal of Clinical Psychiatry, 53*, 345–350.

Kafka, M. P., & Prentky, R. (1992b). Fluoxetine treatment of nonparaphilic sexual addictions and paraphilias in men. *Journal of Clinical Psychiatry, 53*, 351–358.

Kaye, W. H., Weltzin, T. E., & Hsu, L. K. G. (1993a). Relationship between anorexia nervosa and obsessive and compulsive behaviors. *Psychiatric Annals, 23*(7), 365–373.

Kaye, W. H., Weltzin, T. E., & Hsu, L. K. G. (1993b). Anorexia nervosa. In E. Hollander (Ed.), *Obsessive–compulsive-related disorders* (pp. 49–70). Washington, DC: American Psychiatric Press.

Kaye, W. H., Weltzin, T. E., Hsu, L. K. G., & Bulik, C. M. (1991). An open trial of fluoxetine in patients with anorexia nervosa. *Journal of Clinical Psychiatry, 52*(11), 464–471.

King, R., Scahill, L., Vitulano, L., Schwab-Stone, M., Tercyak, K., & Riddle, M. (1995). Childhood trichotillomania: Clinical phenomenology, comorbidity and family genetics. *Journal of the American Academy of Child and Adolescent Psychiatry, 34*(11), 1451–1459.

Kraepelin, E. (1919). *Dementia praecox and paraphrenia*. Chicago: Chicago Medical Books.

Kruesi, J. P., Fine, S., Valladares, L., Phillips, R. A. Jr., & Rapoport, J. L. (1992). Paraphilias: A double-blind crossover comparison of clomipramine versus desipramine. *Archives of Sexual Behavior, 21*(6), 587–593.

Ladee, G. H. (1966). *Hypochondriacal syndromes*. New York: Elsevier.

Leckman, J. F. (1993). Tourette's syndrome. In E. Hollander (Ed.), *Obsessive–compulsive-related disorders* (pp. 113–137). Washington, DC: American Psychiatric Press.

Leckman, J. F., Goodman, W. K., Anderson, G. M., Riddle, M. A., Chappell, P. B., & McSwiggan-Hardin, M. T. (1995a). Cerebrospinal fluid biogenic amines in obsessive–compulsive disorder, Tourette's syndrome, and healthy controls. *Neuropsychopharmacology, 12*, 73–86.

Leckman, J. F., Goodman, W. K., Riddle, M. A., Hardin, M. T., & Anderson, G. M. (1990). Low CSF 5HIAA and obsessions of violence: Report of two cases. *Psychiatry Research, 33*, 95–99.

Leckman, J. L., Grice, D. E., Barr, L. C., de Vries, A. L. C., Martin, C., Cohen, D. J., Goodman, W. K., & Rasmussen, S. A. (1995b). Tic-related vs. non tic-related obsessive compulsive disorder. *Anxiety, 1*, 208–215.

Leckman, J. F., Hardin, M. T., Riddle, M. A., Stevenson, J., Ort, S. I., & Cohen, D. J. (1991). Clonidine treatment of Tourette's syndrome. *Archives of General Psychiatry, 48,* 324–328.

Leckman, J. F., Walker, D. E., Goodman, W. K., Pauls, D. L., & Cohen, D. J. (1994). "Just right" perceptions associated with compulsive behavior in Tourette's syndrome. *American Journal of Psychiatry, 155,* 675–680.

Leonard, H. L., Lenane, M. C., Swedo, S. E., Rehew, D. C., Gershon, E. S., & Rapoport, J. L. (1992). Tics and Tourette's disorder: A 2- to 7-year follow-up of 54 obsessive–compulsive children. *American Journal of Psychiatry, 149,* 1244–1251.

Leonard, H. L., Lenane, M. C., Swedo, S. E., Rettew, D. C., & Rapoport, J. L. (1991). A double-blind comparison of clomipramine and desipramine treatment of severe onychophagia (nail biting). *Archives of General Psychiatry, 48,* 821–827.

Lesieur, H. R., & Rosenthall, R. J. (1991). Pathological gambling: A review of the literature. *Journal of Gambling Studies, 7,* 5–39.

Linden, R. D., Jonas, J. M., & Pope, H. G. (1986). Pathological gambling and major affective disorder: Preliminary findings. *Journal of Clinical Psychiatry, 47,* 201–203.

Linnoila, M., Virkkunen, M., Scheinin, M., Nuutila, A., Rimon, R., & Goodwin, F. K. (1983). Low cerebrospinal fluid 5-hydroxyindoleacetic acid concentration differentiates impulsive from nonimpulsive violent behavior. *Life Sciences, 33,* 2609–2614.

Mattes, J. A. (1990). Comparative effectiveness of carbamazepine and propranolol for rage outbursts. *Journal of Neuropsychiatry and Clinical Neuroscience, 21,* 249–255.

McCann, V. D., & Agras, W. S. (1990). Successful treatment of nonpurging bulimia nervosa with desipramine: A double-blind, placebo-controlled study. *American Journal of Psychiatry, 147,* 1509–1513.

McConaghy, N., Armstrong, M. S., Blaszczyniski, A., & Allcock, C. (1983). Controlled comparison of aversive therapy and imaginal desensitization in compulsive gambling. *British Journal of Psychiatry, 142,* 366–372.

McDougle, C., Goodman, W., Leckman, J., Barr, L., Heninger, G., & Price, L. (1993). The efficacy of fluvoxamine on obsessive–compulsive disorder: Effects of comorbid tic disorder. *Journal of Clinical Psychopharmacology, 13*(5), 354–358.

McElroy, S. L., Hudson, J. I., Phillips, K. A., Keck, P. E. Jr., & Pope, H. G. Jr. (1993). Clinical and theoretical implications of a possible link between obsessive–compulsive and impulse control disorders. *Depression, 1,* 121–132.

McElroy, S. L., Keck, P. E. Jr., Pope, H. G., Smith, J., & Strakowski, S. M. (1994a). Compulsive buying: A report of 20 cases. *Journal of Clinical Psychiatry, 55*(6), 242–248.

McElroy, S. L., Pope, H. G., Hudson, J. I., Keck, P. E. Jr., & White, K. (1991). Kleptomania: A report of 20 cases. *American Journal of Psychiatry, 148,* 652–657.

McElroy, S. L., Pope, H. G. Jr., Keck, P. E. Jr., & Hudson, J. I. (1995). Disorders of impulse control. In E. Hollander & D. J. Stein (Eds.), *Impulsivity and aggression* (pp. 109–136). Chichester, UK: Wiley.

McElroy, S. L., Pope, H. G. Jr., Keck, P. E. Jr., Hudson, J. I., Phillips, K. A., & Strakowski, S. M. (1996). Are impulse control disorders related to bipolar disorder? *Comprehensive Psychiatry, 37,* 229–240.

McElroy, S. L., Phillips, K. A., Keck, P. E. Jr. (1994b). Obsessive–compulsive spectrum disorder. *Journal of Clinical Psychiatry, 55*(Suppl. 10), 33–51.

McElroy, S. L., Soutullo, C. A., Beckman, D. A., Taylor, P. Jr., & Keck, P. E. Jr. (in press). DSM-IV Intermittent explosive disorder: A report of 27 cases. *Journal of Clinical Psychiatry.*

Miguel, E. C., Baer, L., Coffey, B. J., Rauch, S. L., Savage, C. R., O'Sullivan, R. L.,

Phillips, K. A., Moretti, C., Leckman, J. F., & Jenike, M. A. (1997). Phenomenological differences appearing with repetitive behaviours in obsessive–compulsive disorder and Gilles de la Tourette's syndrome. *British Journal of Psychiatry, 170,*
140–145.

Miguel, E. C., Coffey, B. J., Baer, L., Savage, C. R., Rauch, S. L., & Jenike, M. A. (1995).
Phenomenology of intentional repetitive behaviors in obsessive–compulsive disorder
and Tourette's disorder. *Journal of Clinical Psychiatry, 56,* 246–255.

Moskowitz, J. A. (1980). Lithium and lady luck: Use of lithium carbonate in compulsive
gambling. *New York State Journal of Medicine, 80,* 785–788.

Neziroglu, F. A., & Yaryura-Tobias, J. A. (1993). Exposure, response prevention, and cognitive therapy in the treatment of body dysmorphic disorder. *Behavior Therapy, 24,*
431–438.

O'Rourke, D. A., Wurtman, J. J., Wurtman, R. J., Tsay, R. J., Gleason, R., Baer, L., &
Jenike, M. A. (1994). Aberrant snacking patterns and eating disorders in patients
with obsessive–compulsive disorder. *Journal of Clinical Psychiatry, 55*(10), 445–447.

Pauls, D. L. (1992). The genetics of obsessive–compulsive disorder and Gilles de la
Tourette's syndrome. *Psychiatric Clinics of North America, 15*(4),759–766.

Pauls, D. L., Towbin, K. E., Leckman, J., Zahner, G. E. P., & Cohen, D. J. (1986). Gilles de
la Tourette's syndrome and obsessive–compulsive disorder. *Archives of General Psychiatry, 43,* 1180–1182.

Peterson, A. L., & Azrin, N. H. (1992). An evaluation of behavioral treatments for
Tourette syndrome. *Behavioural Research and Therapy, 30,* 167–174.

Phillips, K. A., & Diaz, S. F. (1997). Gender differences in body dysmorphic disorder. *Journal of Nervous and Mental Disease, 185,* 570–577.

Phillips, K. A., Dwight, M., & McElroy. S. L. (in press). Efficacy and safety of fluoxamine
in body dysmorphic disorder. *Journal of Clinical Psychiatry.*

Phillips, K. A., Hollander, E., Rasmussen, S. A., Aronowitz, B. R., De Caria, C., & Goodman, W. K. (1997). A severity rating scale for body dysmorphic disorder: Development of reliability and validity of a modified version of the Yale–Brown Obsessive–Compulsive Scale. *Psychopharmacology Bulletin, 33,* 17–22.

Phillips, K. A., Kim, J., & Hudson, J. I. (1995). Body image disturbance in body dysmorphic disorder and eating disorders: Obsessions or delusions? *Psychiatric Clinics of North
America, 18,* 317–334.

Phillips, K. A., & McElroy, S. L. (1996, May). *Fluvoxamine in body dysmorphic disorder.* Paper
presented at the 149th annual meeting of the American Psychiatric Association, New
York, NY.

Phillips, K. A., & McElroy, S. L. (1997, May). *Personality traits and disorders in body dysmorphic
disorder.* Paper presented at the 150th annual meeting of the American Psychiatric Association, San Diego, CA.

Phillips, K. A., McElroy, S. L., Hudson, J. I., & Pope, H. G. Jr. (1995). Body dysmorphic
disorder: An obsessive–compulsive spectrum disorder, a form of affective disorder, or
both? *Journal of Clinical Psychiatry, 56*(Suppl. 4), 41–51.

Phillips, K. A., McElroy, S. L., Keck, P. E., Hudson, J. I., & Pope, H. G. Jr. (1994). A comparison of delusional and non-delusional body dysmorphic disorder in 100 cases.
Psychopharmacology Bulletin, 30, 179–186.

Phillips, K. A., McElroy, S. L., Keck, P. E., Pope, H. G., & Hudson, J. I. (1993). Body dysmorphic disorder: Thirty cases of imagined ugliness. *American Journal of Psychiatry,
150,* 302–3028.

Pitman, R. K., Green, R. C., Jenike, M. A., & Mesulam, M. M. (1987). Clinical comparison of Tourette's disorder and obsessive–compulsive disorder. *American Journal of Psychiatry, 144,* 1166–1171.

Pollard, C. A., Ibe, I. O., Krojanker, D. N., Kitchen, A. D., Bronson, S. S., & Flynn, T. M. (1991). Clomipramine treatment of trichotillomania: A follow-up report on four cases. *Journal of Clinical Psychiatry, 52,* 128–130.

Rasmussen, S. A. (1993). Genetic studies of obsessive compulsive disorder. *Annals of Clinical Psychiatry, 5,* 241–247.

Rasmussen, S. A. (1994). Obsessive compulsive spectrum disorders [commentary]. *Journal of Clinical Psychiatry, 55,* 89–91.

Rasmussen, S. A., & Tsuang, M.T. (1986). Clinical characteristics and family history in DSM-III-obsessive–compulsive disorder. *American Journal of Psychiatry, 143*(3), 317–322.

Råstam, M., Gillberg, I., & Gillberg, C. (1995). Anorexia nervosa 6 years after onset: Part II. Comorbid psychiatric problems. *Comprehensive Psychiatry, 36*(1), 70–76.

Robertson, M. M., Trimble, M. R., & Lees, A. J. (1988). The psychopathology of Gilles de la Tourette syndrome: A phenomenological analysis. *British Journal of Psychiatry, 152,* 383–390.

Rosen J. C., Reiter, J., & Orosan, P. (1995). Cognitive-behavioral body image therapy for body dysmorphic disorder. *Journal of Consulting and Clinical Psychology, 63,* 263–269.

Rothenberg, A. (1986). Eating disorder as a modern obsessive–compulsive syndrome. *Psychiatry, 49*(1), 45–53.

Rothenberg, A. (1988). Differential diagnosis of anorexia nervosa and depressive illness: A review of 11 studies. *Comprehensive Psychiatry, 29,* 427–432.

Roy, A., Adinoff, B., Roehrick, L., Lamparski, D., Custer, R., Lorenz, V., Barbaccia, M., Guidotti, A., Costa, E., & Linnoila, M. (1988). Pathological gambling: A psychobiological study. *Archives of General Psychiatry, 45,* 369–373.

Rubenstein, C. S., Altemus, M., Pigott, T. A., Hess, A., & Murphy, D. L. (1995). Symptom overlap between OCD and bulimia nervosa. *Journal of Anxiety Disorders, 9,* 1–9.

Rubenstein C. S., Pigott T. A., Altemus, M., L'Heureux, F., & Murphy, D. L. (1993). High rates of comorbid OCD in patients with bulimia nervosa. *Eating Disorders, The Journal of Treatment and Prevention, 1*(2), 147–155.

Rubenstein, C. S., Pigott, T. A., L'Heureux, F., Hill, J., & Murphy, D. L. (1992). A preliminary investigation of the lifetime prevalence of anorexia and bulimia nervosa in patients with obsessive compulsive disorder. *Journal of Clinical Psychiatry, 53,* 309–314.

Salkovskis, P. M., & Warwick, H. M. (1986). Morbid preoccupations, health anxiety, and reassurance: A cognitive-behavioral approach in hypochondriasis. *Behaviour Research and Therapy, 24,* 597–602.

Schlosser, S., Black, D. W., Blum, N., & Goldstein, R. B. (1994a). The demography, phenomenology, and family history of 22 persons with compulsive hair-pulling. *Annals of Clinical Psychiatry, 6,* 147–152.

Schlosser, S., Black, D. W., Repertinger, S., & Freet, D. (1994b). Compulsive buying: Demography, phenomenology, and comorbidity in 46 subjects. *General Hospital Psychiatry, 16,* 205–212.

Shapiro, E. S., Shapiro, A. K., Fulop, G., Hubbard, M., Mandeli, J., Nordlie, J., & Phillips, R. A. (1989). Controlled study of haloperidol, pimozide, and placebo for the treatment of Gilles de la Tourette's syndrome. *Archives of General Psychiatry, 46,* 722–730.

Simeon, D., Stanley, B., Frances, A., Mann, J. J., Winchel, R., & Stanley, M. (1992). Self-mutilation in personality disorder: Psychological and biological correlates. *American Journal of Psychiatry, 149,* 221–226.

Specker, S. M., Carlson, G. A., Christenson, G. A., & Marcotte, M. (1995). Impulse control disorders and attention deficit in pathological gamblers. *Annals of Clinical Psychiatry, 7,* 175–179.

Stanley, M., Swann, A. C., Bowers, T. C., Davis, M. L., & Taylor, D. J. (1992). A comparison of clinical features in trichotillomania and obsessive–compulsive disorder. *Behaviour Research and Therapy, 30*(1), 39–44.

Stein, D. J., Hollander, E., Anthony, D., Schneier, F., Fallon, B., Liebowitz, M., & Klein, D. (1992). Serotonergic medications for sexual obsessions, sexual addictions and paraphilias. *Journal of Clinical Psychiatry, 53*(8), 267–271.

Stein, D. J., Hollander, E., & Liebowitz, M. R. (1993). Neurobiology of impulsivity and the impulse control disorders. *Journal of Neuropsychiatry Clinical Neuroscience, 5,* 9–17.

Stein, D. J., Mullen, L., Islam, M., Cohen, L., De Caria, C., & Hollander, E. (1995a). Compulsive and impulsive symptomatology in trichotillomania. *Psychopathology, 28*(4), 208–221.

Stein, D. J., Simeon, D., Cohen, L. J., & Hollander, E. (1995b). Trichotillomania and obsessive compulsive disorder. *Journal of Clinical Psychiatry, 56*(4), 28–34.

Streichenwein, S. M., & Thornby, J. I. (1995). A long-term, double-blind, placebo-controlled, crossover trial of the efficacy of fluoxetine for trichotillomania. *American Journal of Psychiatry, 152,* 1192–1196.

Swedo, S. E., Leonard, H. L., Rapoport, J. L., Lenane, M. C., Goldberger, E. L., & Cheslow, D. L. (1989). A double-blind comparison of clomipramine and desipramine in the treatment trichotillomania (hair-pulling). *New England Journal of Medicine, 321,* 497–501.

Tamburrino, M. B., Kaufman, R., & Hertzer, J. (1994). Eating disorder history in women with obsessive compulsive disorder. *Journal of the American Medical Women's Association, 49*(1), 24–26.

Thiel, A., Broocks, A., Ohlmeier, M., Jacoby, G., & Schussler, G. E. (1995). Obsessive–compulsive disorder among patients with anorexia nervosa and bulimia nervosa. *American Journal of Psychiatry, 152,* 72–75.

Veale, D., Boocock, A., Gournay, K., Dryden, W., Shah, F., Willson, R., & Walburn, J. (1996) Body Dysmorphic Disorder: A Survey of Fifty Cases. *British Journal of Psychiatry, 169*(2), 196–201.

Visser, S., & Bouman, T. K. (1992). Cognitive-behavioral treatment of illness phobia and hypochondriasis: Six single-case crossover studies. *Behaviour Research and Therapy, 30,* 301–306.

Vollrath, M., Koch, R., & Angst, J. (1992). Binge eating and weight concerns among young adults: Results from the Zurich Cohort Study. *British Journal of Psychiatry, 160,* 498–503.

Warwick, H. M. C., & Marks, I. M. (1988). Behavioral treatment of illness phobia and hypochondriasis: A pilot study of 17 cases. *British Journal of Psychiatry, 152,* 239–241.

Ward, N. G. (1975). Successful lithium treatment of transvestism associated with manic depression. *Journal of Nervous and Mental Disease, 161,* 204–206.

Wesner, R. B., & Noyes, R. B. (1991). Imipramine, an effective treatment for illness phobia. *Journal of Affective Disorders, 22,* 43–48.

Yanovski S. Z., Nelson, J. E., Dubbert, B. K., & Spitzer, R. L. (1993). Association of binge eating disorder and psychiatric comorbidity in obese subjects. *American Journal of Psychiatry, 150,* 1472–1479.

Zohar, J., Kaplan, Z., & Benjamin, J. (1994). Compulsive exhibitionism successfully treated with fluvoxamine: A controlled case study. *Journal of Clinical Psychiatry, 55*(1), 86–88.

Zohar, A. H., Pauls, D. L., Ratzoni, G., Apter, A., Dycian, A., Binder, M., King, R., Leckman, J. F., Kron, S., & Cohen, D. J. (1997). Obsessive–compulsive disorder with and without tics in an epidemiological sample of adolescents. *American Journal of Psychiatry, 154,* 274–276.

Chapter 18

RECOGNITION AND TREATMENT OF OBSESSIVE–COMPULSIVE SPECTRUM DISORDERS

Donald W. Black

The conceptual basis supporting a spectrum of disorders hypothetically related to obsessive–compulsive disorder (OCD) was outlined in the previous chapter, but there is little agreement about its breadth. Depending on the views of the investigator, the obsessive–compulsive spectrum includes the impulse control disorders (e.g., pathological gambling, trichotillomania), body experience disorders (e.g., body dysmorphic disorder, hypochondriasis), tic disorders, eating disorders, and obsessive–compulsive personality disorder (Hollander, 1993). Some researchers have even included the paraphilias, addictive disorders, and impulsive personality disorders (e.g., borderline personality) within the spectrum, probably because these conditions each involve unrestrained, excessive, or poorly regulated behaviors that superficially resemble OCD. Nonetheless, the evidence both for and against a relationship of these various disorders to OCD varies considerably, ranging from relatively robust, as with the family data supporting a connection between OCD and Tourette's disorder, to relatively weak, such as the data supporting a connection between OCD and borderline personality disorder.

While the breadth of the obsessive–compulsive spectrum is still being debated, the concept has considerable value in bettering our understanding of a wide range of patients (Hollander, 1993). Looking beyond the strict definition of OCD and drawing comparisons with other disorders has reinvigorated research and has led to new treatment approaches for many persons who may have been previously ignored or thought to be treatment refractory. This, perhaps, is the value of studying these conditions, for whether or not an obsessive–compulsive spectrum holds up under scientific scrutiny, we are clearly developing a better understanding of these difficult patients and their varied problems.

Although many disorders have been linked to the obsessive–compulsive spectrum, this chapter focuses only on the following conditions, and involves discussion of their definition, differential diagnosis, epidemiology, symptoms, and clinical management (both psychological and somatic): Tourette's disorder, body experience disorders (including eating disorders, body dysmorphic disorder, hypochondriasis, and depersonalization), impulse control disorders (including trichotillomania, pathological gambling, kleptomania, compulsive buying), and compulsive sexual behavior. Etiology and pathophysiology were explored in the previous chapter, and will not be discussed here. Although subclinical OCD is undoubtedly within the spectrum (Black, Noyes, Goldstein, & Blum, 1992; Pauls, Alsobrook, Goodman, Rasmussen, & Leckman 1995), it will not be discussed further, because its recognition and management is similar to that given for OCD. Subclinical OCD represents a mild, or subsyndromal, form of OCD, generally involving the presence of obsessions or compulsions that are either viewed as desirable and/or cause no impairment.

RECOGNITION OF OBSESSIVE–COMPULSIVE SPECTRUM DISORDERS

Clinicians are often unaware of these common, widespread, and problematic disorders, and to recognize them requires one to consider the possibility of their presence. Psychiatric patients should always be screened for the presence or absence of obsessional thinking and ritualistic behavior, but relatively nonintrusive inquiries can also be made about the existence of motor and vocal tics, hair-pulling behavior, distorted body images or experiences, inappropriate spending and gaming behaviors, as well as sexual preoccupations and excess.

Clinicians should recognize that obsessive–compulsive spectrum disorders often overlap or coexist. A patient with one obsessive–compulsive spectrum disorder will often have another disorder within the spectrum. For example, research has shown that patients with body dysmorphic disorder or trichotillomania often have OCD (Christensen, Mackenzie, and Mitchell, 1991; Phillips, 1996a). On the other hand, persons with compulsive buying or pathological gambling frequently develop other impulse control disorders (Black, 1996; Specker, Carlson, Christensen, & Marcotte, 1995), perhaps indicating a more general problem with impulsivity.

Table 18.1 includes examples of questions that can be used to screen for these varied conditions. A positive response to any of the inquiries should generally be followed up with specific examples. If a problem with imagined ugliness is indicated, for instance, a person might be asked to describe which body part is thought to be misshapen or malformed and what the person has done about it. If a problem with compulsive sexual behavior is indicated, a person might be asked to describe the cognitions or excessive behavior. Distress or impairment related to these problems should also be explored (e.g., social withdrawal, debts due to excessive use of "900" numbers).

TABLE 18.1. Screening Questions for the Assessment of Obsessive–Compulsive Spectrum Disorders

Condition	Screening questions
Tic disorders (e.g., Tourette's disorder)	Have you ever had twitches, jerks, tics, or other unusual body movements that you could not control?
	Have you ever found yourself involuntarily making noises such as grunts or throat clearing, or saying words that you cannot seem to stop or control?
Body experience disorders	
Anorexia nervosa	Have you ever weighed less than you ought to, or felt fat when others said you were too thin?
Bulimia nervosa	Have you ever eaten a large amount of food in a short period of time, or ever tried to counteract the effects of a binge?
Body dysmorphic disorder	Do you worry that a part of your face or body is misshapen or malformed, or feel ugly, even though friends and family members have tried to reassure you?
Hypochondriasis	Do you worry excessively about having an illness the doctor cannot confirm?
Depersonalization	Have you ever felt separated from your mind or body, or had feelings of unreality?
Impulse control disorders	
Trichotillomania	Have you ever repetitively pulled your scalp or body hair, or felt that you could not control your hair-pulling behavior?
Compulsive buying or pathological gambling	Have you ever spent more, or gambled more than you wanted to, or felt that your spending or gambling behavior was out of control?
Kleptomania	Have you ever stolen or shoplifted items even though you could afford them?
Compulsive sexual behavior	Do you have any persistent or repetitive sexual thoughts or behaviors that have made you feel out of control?

There are other clues to the diagnosis of an obsessive–compulsive spectrum disorder. A clinician may notice twitches, jerking movements, grunting noises, or coprolalia indicative of Tourette's disorder and other tic disorders. A patient with trichotillomania may have obvious hair loss, as indicated by bald spots or patches, or even generalized balding in women, which can resemble male-pattern hair loss. The use of wigs, hair-extenders, or hats may also provide clues to the diagnosis. Persons with body dysmorphic disorder or hypochondriasis may be somatically preoccupied and spontaneously report their symptoms or, for example, point to the affected organ or describe the illness of concern. Persons with pathological gambling, compulsive buying, or kleptomania may present at the behest of a concerned spouse, the recommendation of a creditor, or sometimes an attorney or law enforcement officer. Compulsive sexual behavior may also lead to intervention, particularly if the behavior involves illegal activity (e.g., voyeurism, exhibitionism). The patient with anorexia nervosa will be excessively thin or malnourished, and display telltale signs such as the presence of lanugo hair or poor dentition (due to emesis-related dental erosion). Patients with an obsessive–compulsive spectrum disorder may be anxious and embarrassed about their symptoms, and may need considerable reassurance before disclosing their thoughts and behaviors. Clinicians should reassure them about the confidential nature of the doctor–patient relationship.

With the possible exceptions of subclinical OCD and body dysmorphic disorder, obsessive–compulsive spectrum disorders seldom involve obsessional thinking or compulsive rituals in the strict sense. Because obsessive–compulsive spectrum patients generally view their thoughts as rational and appropriate, and seldom resist them, the thoughts are best considered *preoccupations* or *ruminations*. Likewise, the rituals of OCD are inherently distressing, interfere with functioning, and lead to efforts to resist them. Behaviors of excess involving sex, gambling, spending, and even hair pulling are generally experienced as pleasurable and are resisted only when they cause secondary, deleterious consequences. A pathological gambler loves to bet but may not like his considerable debts; the compulsive buyer loves to shop and spend, and stops only when his or her credit has been canceled.

ASSESSMENT OF OBSESSIVE–COMPULSIVE SPECTRUM DISORDERS

Because of the resurgence of interest in disorders possibly related to OCD, several researchers have developed structured interviews and assessments to help identify, diagnose, and rate these conditions (see Table 18.2). Christenson and coworkers (1994) have developed the Minnesota Impulsive Disorders Interview (MIDI), which is used to assess the presence of impulse control disorders including compulsive buying, kleptomania, trichotillomania, intermittent explosive disorder, pathological gambling, compulsive sexual behavior, and compulsive exercise. Expanded modules have been created for trichotillomania, compulsive buying, and compulsive sexual behavior, and involve detailed questions about various aspects of these conditions. A similar instrument has been developed by McElroy, Keck, Pope, Smith, and Strakowski (1994).

Tourette's and tic disorders can be assessed using the Yale Tourette Syndrome Questionnaire developed by Pauls, Raymond, Stevenson, and Leckman (1991), or a similar instrument developed by Robertson and Gourdie (1990). The Movement Disorder Questionnaire may also be used to comprehensively assess Tourette's and other tic disorders, whereas severity of, and change in, symptoms of Tourette's can be rated using the Tourette's Syndrome Severity Scale (Shapiro, Shapiro, Young, & Feinberg, 1987), or the Motor Tic, Obsession and Compulsion, and Vocal Tic Evaluation Survey (MOVES; Gaffney, Sieg, & Hellings, 1994). Eating disorders can be assessed with the Eating Disorders In-

TABLE 18.2. Selected Instruments Used to Assess or Rate Obsessive–Compulsive Spectrum Disorders

Instrument	Classification	Description	Scoring features
General instruments			
Minnesota Impulsive Disorders Interview (MIDI)	Semistructured, modular design	Items pertinent to DSM-III-R impulse control disorders	Has expanded modules for trichotillomania, compulsive buying, and compulsive sexual behavior
Yale–Brown Obsessive–Compulsive Scale (YBOCS) modified for body dysmorphic disorder, compulsive buying, pathological gambling, trichotillomania	Clinician-rated	10 items; assesses time involved, impairment, and resistance for both cognitive and behavioral components of disorder	Scale is sensitive to change
Tourette's disorder			
Yale Tourette Syndrome Questionnaire	Structured	Items pertinent to assessing Tourette's and related disorders	Also assesses obsessive–compulsive disorders
Movement Disorder Questionnaire	Self-report	Comprehensively assesses medical, social, and tic history	May be filled in by patient or parent
Tourette's Syndrome Severity Scale	Clinician-rated	4 subscales; assesses important aspects of Tourette's	Scale is sensitive to change
Motor Tic, Obsession and Compulsion, and Vocal Tic Evaluation Survey (MOVES)	Self-rated	5 subscales; subscales can be combined to yield a tic or obsessive–compulsive subscale	Scale is sensitive to change
Eating disorders			
Eating Disorders Inventory (EDI)	Self-report	91 items; 6-point frequency scale	8 subscales + 3 provisional scales to rate eating disorders
Eating Attitudes Test (EAT)	Self-report	40 items; 6-point frequency scale	Scale is sensitive to change
Eating Disorders Inventory	Semistructured	Items pertinent to DSM-III-R eating disorders	Clinical judgment; application of DSM-III-R decision rules
Depersonalization			
Structured Clinical Interview for DSM-III-R Dissociative Disorders	Structured	Items pertinent to DSM-III-R dissociative disorders	Clinical judgment; application of DSM-III-R decision rules
Dissociative Disorders Interview Schedule	Structured	Items pertinent to DSM-III-R dissociative disorders	Clinical judgment; application of DSM-III-R decision rules

(continued)

TABLE 18.2. *Continued*

Instrument	Classification	Description	Scoring features
Depersonalization (*cont.*)			
Dissociative Experiences Scale	Self-report	28 items; assesses typical dissociative experiences	Scores range to 100, with scores over 30 indicating dissociation
Pathological gambling			
Addiction Severity Index (ASI)	Clinician-rated	Assess 8 dimensions, including gambling	Scale is sensitive to change
South Oaks Gambling Screen (SOGS)	Clinician-rated	Items pertinent to DSM-III-R pathological gambling	Scale is sensitive to change
Hypochondriasis			
Whiteley Index	Self-report	14 items; assesses bodily preoccupation, disease phobia, and disease conviction	Items taken from Illness Behavior Questionnaire
Somatosensory Amplification Scale	Self-report	Assess sensitivity to unpleasant but non-pathological bodily and environmental sensations	5-point ordinal scales
Illness Attitudes Scale	Self-report	Measures hypochondriasis, illness, attitudes, and behavior	5-point ordinal scale
Compulsive sexual behavior			
Sexual Outlet Inventory	Clinician-rated	Has categories for conventional and unconventional sexual behavior	Assesses weekly incidence of fantasies, urges, and behavior
Trichotillomania			
Psychiatric Institute Trichotillomania Scale	Clinician-rated	5 items; assesses sites, duration of pulling, severity, and resistance	Scale is sensitive to change
Trichotillomania Symptom Severity Scale	Clinician-rated	Assesses time involved, strength of urge, subjective discomfort, and interference	Scale is sensitive to change
Trichotillomania Severity Scale	Clinician-rated	Assesses overall impairment	Scale is sensitive to change

ventory (Garner, 1992) or the Eating Disorders Examination (Cooper & Fairburn, 1987), and can be rated for severity using the Eating Attitudes Test (Garner & Garfinkel, 1979). Dissociative disorders, including depersonalization disorder, can be assessed with the Structured Clinical Interview for DSM-III-R Dissociative Disorders (Steinberg, Rounsaville, & Cicchetti, 1990) or the Dissociative Disorders Interview Schedule (Ross et al., 1989). Severity of dissociation can be measured with the Dissociative Experiences Scale (Bernstein & Putnam, 1986). The Sexual Outlet Inventory (Kafka & Prentky, 1992a) can be used to assess sexual fantasies, urges, and activities during a designated week.

The Yale–Brown Obsessive–Compulsive Scale (YBOCS), used to rate severity of OCD and change in clinical trials (Goodman et al., 1989), has been successfully modified for use in research on body dysmorphic disorder (Phillips et al., 1997), compulsive buying (Monahan, Black, & Gabel, 1996), pathological gambling (C. DeCaria, personal communication, May 1997), and trichotillomania (Stanley, Prather, Wagner, Davis, & Swann, 1993). The South Oaks Gambling Screen is used to assess and rate overall severity of pathological gambling (Lesieur & Blume, 1987). The Addiction Severity Index (Lesieur & Blume, 1991) may be used to evaluate outcome in alcohol- and drug-abuse treatment, but also assesses gambling behavior.

The Trichotillomania Symptom Severity Scale (TSS) and the Trichotillomania Impairment Scale (TIS) can be used together both to assess and rate hair-pulling behavior (Swedo et al., 1989). Severity of trichotillomania can also be assessed with the Psychiatric Institute Trichotillomania Scale (Winchel et al., 1992). Hypochondriasis can be assessed and rated with the Whiteley Index, a subscale of the Illness Behavior Questionnaire (Pilowsky & Spence, 1983), the Illness Attitude Scales (Kellner 1981; 1986), and the Somatosensory Amplification Scale (Barsky, Wyshak, & Klerman, 1990c).

TOURETTE'S DISORDER

Tourette's disorder is a chronic, lifelong disorder characterized by the presence of multiple motor and vocal tics, and at least one form of vocal tic must have been present for at least 1 year (American Psychiatric Association, 1994). Vocal tics typically consist of loud grunts or barks, but may involve shouting words such as obscenities (coprolalia). The patient is aware of saying these words or phrases and can exert some control over them but ultimately has to submit to expressing them as an uncontrollable urge overwhelms him or her. Tics often occur in bursts, ranging in frequency from rare to nearly nonstop. Their forcefulness can vary tremendously and may be soft and barely noticeable or loud and frightening. Tourette's disorder tends to improve in late adolescence and early adulthood, and vocal tics may cease altogether, with motor tics becoming reduced in number (Leckman, 1993). Many patients also develop frank obsessions and compulsions. Sensorimotor symptoms may accompany tics and OCD behavior, such as premonitory feelings and urges that are relieved by performance of the act and a need to perform tics and compulsions "just right" (Leckman, Walker, Goodman, Pauls, & Cohen, 1994).

The disorder is relatively rare, affecting from 0.1% to 0.6% of boys. The prevalence among girls is substantially lower (Comings, Himes, & Comings, 1990). Tourette's disorder is familial, as confirmed by both twin and family studies. In some instances, OCD may arise from the same underlying diathesis as Tourette's (Pauls, Towbin, Leckman, Zahner, & Cohen, 1986).

Tourette's disorder typically begins in early childhood with transitory bouts of simple motor tics. They eventually become more persistent and increase in number and variety (Leckman, 1993). Although the course is not predictable, a "rostral–caudal" progression has been described. Complex motor tics are often disguised by patients profoundly embarrassed by their symptoms, for example, by pretending to scratch the back of the head. Vocal tics begin 1–2 years after the onset of motor tics and are generally simple in character, such as throat clearing.

A patient presenting with Tourette's disorder should undergo a comprehensive neurological evaluation to rule out other causes for the tics. The patient should be examined for stigmata of Wilson's disease, and a family history should be obtained to assess the possibility of Huntington's disease. An electroencephalograph may be helpful in ruling out seizure disorders, and the patient should be evaluated for other psychiatric conditions, because comorbidity with attention deficit disorder and symptoms of mood and anxiety disorders is relatively common. Many persons with Tourette's disorder meet criteria for OCD (Leckman, 1993).

Haloperidol has been used as the first-line treatment for Tourette's disorder at doses typically lower than those used to treat psychoses, generally ranging from 1 to 5 mg/day (Peterson, 1996). Pimozide is also effective at doses generally ranging from 8 to 10 mg per day. Nearly 70% of Tourette's disorder patients improve with these agents, and the mean symptom reduction ranges from 70% to 80% (Shapiro et al., 1989). Tics continue to fluctuate in intensity and severity, although at a reduced level. The use of neuroleptics can produce unwanted consequences including dystonias, akathisia, akinesia, cognitive slowing, or weight gain; pimozide may affect cardiac conduction at doses above 10 mg/day. Clonidine, a selective alpha-2 adrenergic receptor agonist, has been used at does ranging from 0.15 to 0.5 mg/day, but is probably less effective (Leckman, Hardin, Riddle, Stevenson, Ort, & Cohen, 1991). Risperidone, an atypical antipsychotic, has been used at doses between 0.5 and 4 mg/day, but its effect appears moderate (Peterson, 1996). Serotonin reuptake inhibitors (SRIs) may help to reduce OCD symptoms associated with Tourette's disorder but probably have little effect on vocal or motor tics.

Apart from medication, families need to be educated about the disorder, and patients will need psychological support (Cohen, Ort, Leckman, Riddle, & Hardin, 1988). Because of the considerable social embarrassment it causes, Tourette's disorder has the potential for serious long-term social complications, and supportive psychotherapy for the patient or family may help to minimize these problems.

BODY EXPERIENCE DISORDERS

Many patients have a disturbance in the way that they view their body or body parts, in their interpretation of bodily symptoms, or in the way they experience themselves. For these reasons, I have grouped these disturbances together as *body experience disorders.*

Eating Disorders

Anorexia nervosa is characterized by a refusal to maintain body weight and weight loss leading to maintenance of body weight less than 85% of that expected; intense fear of gaining weight or becoming fat even though underweight; a disturbance in the way in which one's body shape is experienced; and, in women, absence of at least three consecutive menstrual cycles (American Psychiatric Association, 1994). *Bulimia nervosa,* on the other hand, consists of recurrent episodes of binge eating; a feeling of a lack of control over the binge episodes; inappropriate compensatory behaviors designed to counteract the effect of the binges, such as vomiting or vigorous exercise; at least two binge episodes per week for 3 months; and persistent overconcern for body shape and weight. There is clearly overlap between the disorders, as many bulimics will have a history of anorexia nervosa, and many anorexics exhibit binge/purge behavior.

Estimates from high school and college age populations yield a prevalence rate among women of approximately 1% for anorexia nervosa and 4% for bulimia nervosa, but isolated symptoms, such as bingeing, purging, or fasting, are even more common (Striegel-Moore, Sibertsein, Frensch, & Rodin, 1991). For both disorders, the frequency for men is about one-tenth that for women. There has been some concern that eating disorders are increasing in prevalence, and several investigators have suggested that anorexia nervosa is more common than it was just 20 years ago (Lucas, Beard, O'Fallon, & Kurlan, 1991). It is likely, however, that increasing public awareness has simply led to the recognition of the disorder, and because treatments have become available, patients may be more likely to seek help. Anorexia nervosa typically has an earlier age of onset (early teens) than bulimia nervosa (late teens, early 20s). The disorders are found in all socioeconomic groups (Gard & Freeman, 1996). The course of anorexia nervosa is variable, although it is severe and chronic for many. In a recent 10-year follow-up (Eckert, Halmi, Marchi, Grove, & Crosby, 1995) of 76 anorectics, although nearly 25% were recovered, the remainder were still symptomatic, and 7% had died, substantially more than expected. Although less follow-up data are available for bulimics, it is likely that bulimia has a waxing and waning course, with a tendency toward improvement with increasing age (Yager, Landsverk, & Edelstein, 1987).

The anorexic person quickly develops a repertoire of behaviors in the pursuit of weight loss (Andreasen & Black, 1995). These behaviors often include extreme dieting, adoption of special diets or vegetarianism, and developing an intense interest in physical exercise. Anorexic persons often show an unusual interest in food that belies their fear of gaining weight (e.g., collecting and clipping recipes, preparing elaborate meals). Many anorexic patients begin to abuse laxatives, diuretics, or stimulants in an effort to enhance their weight loss. With the bulimic, vomiting, vigorous exercise, and laxative, diuretic, or stimulant abuse serves to counteract the effects of binge eating.

Research on anorexia nervosa shows substantial overlap with other disorders. In a study of 62 women with anorexia nervosa, Halmi et al. (1991) reported that 84% had a history of a mood disorder, 65% had a history of an anxiety disorder (including 26% with OCD), and 8% had a history of an alcohol-use disorder. Axis II disorders are also common in patients with anorexia nervosa, who tend to be rigid, perfectionistic, risk avoidant, and show restraint in expressing emotion (Casper, 1990; Strober, 1980). Bulimics, similarly, have high lifetime rates of mood, anxiety, and substance-use disorders (Hudson, Pope, Yurgelun-Todd, Jonas, & Frankenburg, 1988). As with anorexia nervosa, patients with bulimia also show abnormal personality traits, such as those from the "dramatic" and "anxious" clusters (Yates, Sieleni, Reich, & Brass, 1989).

Physical symptoms of anorexia nervosa tend to center around the eating behaviors manifested by the patient. Anorexic persons can appear emaciated or cadaverous, develop hypothermia, dependent edema, bradycardia, hypotension, or show growth of lanugo hair. Hormonal abnormalities can include elevated growth hormone levels, increased plasma cortisol, and reduced gonadotropin levels. Although thyroxin and thyroid-stimulating hormone are usually normal, triiodothyronine (T_3) may be reduced (Fava, Copeland, Schweizer, & Herzog, 1989). Medical complications may be found, such as hypocalcemia or hypokalemic alkalosis in persons who engage in self-induced vomiting or abuse laxatives and diuretics. Electrolyte disturbances can result in weakness, lethargy, or cardiac arrhythmias. Serum transaminases are sometimes elevated, reflecting fatty degeneration of the liver. Elevated serum cholesterol and carotenemia can develop, both a reflection of malnutrition (Sharp & Freeman, 1993). Bulimics may develop calluses on the dorsal surface of the hands, dental erosion and caries and, in extreme cases, esophageal tears—all complications of frequent vomiting.

Treatment efforts with eating-disordered patients generally involve restoring weight to within a normal range and modifying the patients' distorted eating behavior. Treatment is usually conducted on an outpatient basis, although hospitalization is necessary for patients with severe weight loss or evidence of hypotension, hypothermia, or electrolyte imbalance. Behavioral modification to restore normal eating behavior involves the use of protocols in which specific weight goals for anorexic patients are set and abnormal behaviors are targeted for correction (e.g., reducing the number of vomiting episodes). Positive reinforcement is used to help patients achieve the specific goals outlined in a treatment contract that is agreed to by the patient (American Psychiatric Association, 1993). Individual psychotherapy is used to educate patients about their illness, to improve morale, and to help patients solve day-to-day problems. Cognitive therapy, in particular, is an effective treatment for bulimia nervosa in helping to modify disturbed attitudes, as well as decreasing self-induced vomiting (Fairburn et al.,

1991). Psychodynamic approaches are sometimes recommended to help patients resolve conflicts that may have contributed to (or reinforced) the abnormal eating behavior. Family therapy may be helpful, particularly when the patient is living at home and the eating behavior has been perpetuated by disturbed family interactions (American Psychiatric Association, 1993).

Medication may be helpful in selected patients. Tricyclic antidepressants, monoamine oxidase inhibitors, trazodone, and fluoxetine have been shown to decrease both bingeing and purging behaviors, and can be helpful in treating the bulimic patient, although they have no specific role in treating anorexia nervosa (American Psychiatric Association, 1993; Fluoxetine Bulimia Nervosa Collaborative Study Group, 1992). Antidepressants may be particularly useful in anorexic or bulimic patients with a superimposed major depression, although the role of antidepressants in treating depressed eating-disorder patients has not specifically been studied. Some success has been demonstrated with cyproheptadine (Periactin) in helping anorexic patients to gain weight, particularly those without a history of bulimia (Halmi, Eckert, La Du, & Cohen, 1986). Anxiolytics and antipsychotics have also been used to reduce anticipatory anxiety before meals. There is some evidence that SRIs may be of benefit in weight restoration and weight maintenance (Gwirtsman, Guze, Yager, & Gainsley, 1990; Kaye, Weltzin, Hsu, & Bulik, 1991), but they have not been subjected to controlled trials.

Body Dysmorphic Disorder

A patient with *body dysmorphic disorder* (BDD) is usually preoccupied with an imagined defect in appearance rather than having more diffuse complaints, and for this reason, BDD is sometimes referred to as a disorder of imagined ugliness (American Psychiatric Association, 1994). If a slight defect is present, the person's concern is markedly excessive. In addition, the disorder causes clinically significant distress, or impairment in social, occupational, or other areas of functioning. In DSM-IV, BDD is grouped with the somatoform disorders.

Patients with BDD tend to focus on imagined defects involving their face and head, but any body part may be a focus of concern, including the genitals. Mirror checking, comparing oneself to others, camouflaging the affected body part, ritualized grooming, and repeated requests for reassurance are typical (Phillips, 1995). Patients with BDD often have poor insight into their disorder and fail to see their view of themselves as distorted (Phillips, 1996a).

Although there are no data on community prevalence, about 4% of patients surveyed in a medical outpatient setting had BDD, as did 8% of patients with major depression, and 12% of psychiatric outpatients (Phillips, 1996c). BDD shows a slight male preponderance, although symptoms in both men and women are similar. A large proportion (up to three-fourths) of persons with BDD are unmarried. BDD usually begins in adolescence but can occur in children. The disorder is generally chronic, with waxing and waning symptom severity (Phillips, 1991; Phillips, Atala, & Albertini, 1995). Nearly 80% of patients with BDD suffer recurrent major depression. Other frequent comorbid disorders include OCD (in about one-third), social phobia, and substance-use disorders.

The condition needs to be differentiated from monohypochondriacal paranoia (delusional disorder, somatic type), in which the patient has a fixed belief that a body part is grossly deformed and distorted. In BDD, the patient is not delusional and will generally acknowledge the possibility that his or her concerns are excessive and unreal.

A patient with BDD was seen in our clinic and illustrates many of its typical symptoms.

CASE 1

Arthur first began to think of his face as a problem when he was a senior in high school. He noticed that when his face was in repose, his brows would droop over his eyes and give him a "devious look." He also noticed that his jawline seemed weak and receding. He tried to camouflage these "defects" by keeping his lower jaw jutted forward and his eyebrows raised. His attempts at camouflage became almost habitual, but he consulted a surgeon to obtain a jaw augmentation and to have his eyebrows raised, because he felt that the camouflaging made him self-conscious and decreased his spontaneity. He did not feel the cosmetic surgery would materially affect his work or social life.

Arthur was an excellent student, but participated in few activities and dated only occasionally. He had not had a close relationship with a woman, nor had he had sexual intercourse. He experienced a brief "bad period" in high school, during which he rebelled against family standards, quit studying, and smoked marijuana. After several months of this behavior, he began to feel depressed, apathetic, guilt ridden, and paranoid. He did not have a full set of depressive symptoms, nor did he have any delusions or hallucinations, and the episode gradually passed, and he returned to his usual lifestyle. He completed 1 year of college but then dropped out to work so he could obtain money for cosmetic surgery. After the surgery was completed, he planned to return to college and perhaps go to medical school and pursue a career in psychiatry.

The patient was actually a rather handsome young man with heavy dark eyebrows, but a perfectly normal, and perhaps even prominent jawline. He related his motivation for seeking surgery to his general pattern of pursuing perfection in all aspects of life. He considered himself well adjusted and normal, in fact, superior to most people. He saw no need for psychiatric treatment and refused a recommendation for a trial of medication (adapted from Andreasen & Bardach, 1977).

Treatment efforts are complicated by the fact that most BDD patients seek treatment from nonpsychiatric physicians, including plastic surgeons, dermatologists, or family practitioners, before eventually seeing a psychiatrist (Phillips, McElroy, Keck, Hudson, & Pope, 1994). Although many physicians refuse to provide medical or surgical treatment to patients with BDD, or advise them it is unnecessary, some patients will persist in seeking a physician who will treat them, and even undergo plastic surgery.

Although there are no controlled treatment studies of BDD, preliminary data point to a preferential response of BDD to SRIs. In one series, 43 (70%) of 61 patients showed improvement on SRIs (Phillips, 1995). In patients with delusional BDD, adding an antipsychotic (such as pimozide) to the SRI may be helpful. In 9 (60%) of 15 cases, neuroleptic augmentation resulted in improved insight or decreased delusions of reference (Phillips, 1996a). A positive response leads to decreased distress, less time spent preoccupied with the "defect," and improved social and occupational functioning.

Cognitive-behavioral therapy can also be helpful. Patients are instructed to stay away from mirrors, remove their makeup, or take off their hats (Neziroglu & Yaryura-Tobias, 1993). Although supportive and psychodynamic psychotherapy may help to boost morale, provide hope, or offer insight to the behavior, these techniques probably do not decrease BDD symptoms (Phillips, McElroy, Keck, Pope, & Hudson, 1993). *The Broken Mirror*, a book for persons with BDD, is now available (Phillips, 1996b).

Hypochondriasis

Hypochondriasis involves a preoccupation with the fear of having a serious illness based on a person's misinterpretation of bodily symptoms (American Psychiatric Association, 1994). This preoccupation persists even though appropriate medical evaluation has ruled out the presence of a physical disorder that could account for the symptoms, and other mental disorders (e.g., major depression) have been excluded. In DSM-IV, hypochondriasis is grouped with the somatoform disorders. When the illness belief reaches delusional proportions, the diagnosis becomes delusional disorder, somatic type.

Hypochondriacal patients display an abnormal concern with their health and amplify normal physiological sensations, misinterpreting them as indicators of disease. They often fear a particular disease such as cancer or the acquired immunodeficiency syndrome and cannot be adequately reassured despite careful and repeated examinations. According to Noyes et al. (1993), hypochondriacal patients view their health as worse, have more health worries, and have more severe psychiatric symptoms than control subjects. Additionally, they have poorer physical functioning, work performance, and have greater health care utilization, even though they tend to be dissatisfied with the results. The following patient was evaluated in our hospital and shows the disease conviction typical with this disorder.

CASE 2

Mabel, an 80-year-old, retired schoolteacher, was admitted for evaluation of an 8-month preoccupation with having colon cancer. The patient had a history of a single-vessel coronary artery disease and diabetes mellitus controlled by oral hypoglycemic agents, but was otherwise well. There was no history of mental ill-ness.

On admission to the hospital, Mabel reported her concern about having colon cancer "just like my two brothers." As evidence of possible cancer, she reported having mild, diffuse abdominal pain, and cited an abnormal barium enema examination she had had a year earlier (the examination revealed diverticulosis). Because of her excessive concern about having cancer, Mabel had seen 11 physicians, but each in turn had been unable to reassure her that she did not have cancer.

Despite her complaints, Mabel denied depressed mood, displayed a full affect, and appeared to enjoy life. She reported sleeping less than usual, but she attributed this to her abdominal discomfort. At the hospital, Mabel was pleasant and cooperative but chose not to socialize with other patients, whom she characterized as "crazy." She continued to be preoccupied with the possibility that she had cancer despite our reassurance. A benzodiazepine was prescribed for her sleep disturbance, but she refused any other form of psychiatric treatment (adapted from Andreasen & Black, 1995).

Despite the frequency with which the term "hypochondriasis" is used, little is known about the disorder or its prevalence in the general population. A survey by Barsky, Wyshak, and Klerman (1990a) of general medical clinic patients found that nearly 9% were rated as hypochondriacal using a screening questionnaire, whereas Kellner, Abbott, Pathak, Winslow, and Umland, (1983–1984) reported that 9% of a sample of family practice patients and 2% of clinic employees were hypochondriacal. In another survey, Barsky, Wyshak, and Klerman (1990b) estimated the 6-month prevalence of hypochondriasis among patients in a medical clinic to fall between 4.2% and 6.3%. A recent family study (Noyes, Holt, Happel, Kathol, & Yagla, 1997) showed no increase in the frequency of hypochondriasis among the relatives of hypochondriasis probands.

Studies of hypochondriacal patients usually show a female preponderance, and most subjects are middle-aged. Comorbidity is the rule, and many patients with hypochondriasis meet lifetime criteria for major depression, panic disorder, phobias, somatization disorder, psychotic disorders, or personality disorders (Fallon, Rasmussen, & Liebowitz, 1993). For example, Barsky, Wyshak, and Klerman (1992) reported in a study of 42 patients with hypochondriasis that 33% had major depression, 45% had dysthymia, 33% had phobias, and 21% each had somatization disorder or generalized anxiety disorder. In evaluating hypochondriacal patients, it is important to understand that hypochondriacal concerns can occur in the context of another disorder, including major depression, panic disorder, phobias, generalized anxiety, somatization disorder, OCD, personality disorders, and the psychoses. All must be excluded as a potential cause of the hypochondriacal complaint. When hypochondriacal complaints occur in the course of another illness, treatment of the primary disorder will often lead to reduction of hypochondriacal symptoms, as was demonstrated by Noyes, Reich, Clancy, and O'Gorman (1986) in the case of panic disorder.

The treatment of hypochondriasis has traditionally been considered unsatisfactory. Recent work suggests that hypochondriasis may respond to antidepressant medication. In an open trial of fluoxetine, 5 of 6 patients completing the trial had responded at 6 weeks (Fallon et al., 1991). One particular form of hypochondriasis, illness phobia, may respond to tricyclics. Patients with illness phobia have an unreasonable fear that they have a specific or serious illness. A study of 14 such patients showed that imipramine was an effective treatment (Wesner & Noyes, 1991) and helped to reduce abnormal illness behavior.

Patients with hypochondriasis may additionally benefit from individual psychotherapy that involves education about illness and selective perception of symptoms. Cognitive restructuring techniques that help to correct misinterpretations of internal stimuli are reported to be helpful (Josephson & Brandolo, 1993; Salkovskis & Warwick, 1986). Exposure and response prevention techniques have also been used to treat hypochondriasis, similar to that used to treat OCD. Warwick and Marks (1988) employed standard behavior techniques of *in vivo* exposure (e.g., to hospitals), response prevention (patients received no reassurance), satiation (patients were instructed to write down concerns), and paradoxical intention (e.g., trying to have a heart attack while exercising). More than one-third of the patients showed significant improvement on measures of fear and social functioning.

Depersonalization Disorder

Depersonalization disorder is characterized by periods in which persons may feel detached from their own mental processes or body and feel they are outside observers; or, they may describe a dream-like state (American Psychiatric Association, 1994). The experience often makes persons feel mechanical and separated from their thoughts, emotions, or identity. Some people with depersonalization disorder, for instance, describe themselves as feeling like robots or automatons. Depersonalization may be accompanied by derealization, which involves a sense of detachment, unreality, and altered relationship to the outside world. It is important to rule out other disorders that may be associated with depersonalization, such as schizophrenia, major depression, specific phobias, panic disorder, OCD, drug abuse, sleep deprivation, partial complex seizures, and migraine (Simeon & Hollander, 1993). In DSM-IV, depersonalization disorder is grouped with the dissociative disorders.

The prevalence of depersonalization disorder is unknown, but it is apparently common in mild forms, and many psychiatrically normal persons have transiently experienced this phenomenon. Transient depersonalization may occur under conditions such as sleep deprivation, travel to unfamiliar places, or acute intoxication with hallucinogens, marijuana, or alcohol (Simeon & Hollander, 1993). In a study of college-age students, from one-third to one-half have reported experiencing depersonalization (Dixon, 1963). A high frequency of depersonalization has been reported in persons exposed to life-threatening situations such as serious accidents (Noyes, Hoenk, Kuperman, & Slymen, 1977).

The disorder usually begins in adolescence or early adult life but rarely after age 40 (Simeon & Hollander, 1993). Many persons with depersonalization will vividly recall their first episode, which was typically abrupt and without a precipitating stressor. Others report a precipitating event, such as smoking marijuana. The duration of the episodes varies from person to person, and range from hours to days to weeks. The course of depersonalization disorder is probably chronic; some persons will experience remissions and exacerbations, and others will have an unremitting course with nearly continuous depersonalization. Exacerbations may follow psychologically stressful situations, such as a death in the family.

There are no proven treatments for the condition, but both desipramine and clonazepam are reported to be beneficial (Noyes, Kuperman, & Olsen, 1987; Stein & Uhde, 1989). Like other benzodiazepines, clonazepam may be particularly helpful in managing the anxiety that accompanies depersonalization. Several cases have been reported showing benefit from fluoxetine (Fichtner, Horevitz, & Brown, 1992; Ratliff & Kerski, 1995), and a report that 6 of 8 patients responded to various SRIs suggests these medications may hold promise for treating this condition (Hollander et al., 1990).

Both behavioral and psychodynamic therapies have also been used to treat depersonalization. Behavioral approaches emphasize *in vivo* exposure, imaginal flooding, paradoxical suggestion, negative reinforcement, or reward contingency, but their effectiveness is unknown (Simeon & Hollander, 1993). Psychodynamic treatment for depersonalization has focused on examining its defensive functions and its relationship to underlying conflicts and traumata. Most patients will benefit from education about the disorder and learning to accept its often chronic symptoms (Steinberg, 1991).

IMPULSE CONTROL DISORDERS

Disorders of impulse control are frequently underdiagnosed and underappreciated despite the fact that some, such as pathological gambling, are quite common in the general population. All can cause considerable emotional distress, as well as social, occupational, or legal consequences. Impulse control disorders are unified by the presence of irresistible urges or impulses to carry out potentially harmful or self-destructive behaviors, and all are grouped together in DSM-IV. The following disorders are described in this chapter: kleptomania, pathological gambling, trichotillomania, and compulsive buying.

Kleptomania

Kleptomania involves the recurrent failure to resist impulses to steal objects not needed for personal use or for their monetary value; an increasing sense of tension immediately before committing the theft; and pleasure, gratification, or relief at the time of the theft. The stealing is not committed to express anger or vengeance and is not in response to hallucinations or delusions, and the stealing is not better accounted for by antisocial personality disorder, a conduct disorder, or a manic episode (American Psychiatric Association, 1994).

The prevalence of kleptomania has been estimated at 6 per 1000, which may be an underestimate, since most persons with this disorder are ashamed of their behavior and probably do not report it to physicians (McElroy, Pope, Hudson, Keck, & White, 1991a). McElroy, Hudson, Pope, and Keck (1991b) reviewed 56 case reports in the literature and found that 77% were female; in their own work, 15 of 20 patients with kleptomania evaluated were women (McElroy et al., 1991a). The disorder probably begins in adolescence or early adulthood and tends to be chronic. The author currently follows an 80-year-old woman with a history of impulsive stealing since age 16. Only the humiliation of an arrest at age 78, and the resultant publicity, has kept her from stealing again, despite her nearly continuous urges and temptations.

Mood and anxiety disorders are frequently comorbid with kleptomania. McElroy et al. (1991b) reported that of 56 kleptomania patients described in the literature, 57% had affective symptoms, and 36% would probably have met lifetime criteria for major depression or bipolar disorder. Stealing impulses and behaviors often change in frequency or intensity consistent with the patient's mood alteration. Anxiety disorders, including OCD, panic disorder, and social phobia, were common in the sample of McElroy et al. (1991a), as were substance use and eating disorders; 40% had at least one other impulse control disorder.

Antidepressant medication has been used to reduce stealing behavior (McElroy, Keck, Pope, & Hudson, 1989). In a case series of 20 patients with kleptomania, 10 of 18 receiving treatment with various antidepressants and/or mood stabilizers had improvement after several weeks of treatment with dosages typical of those used to treat mood disorders. In 2 of the patients, stealing behavior resumed when the medication was discontinued (McElroy et al., 1991a).

Various forms of behavioral treatment for kleptomania, including aversive therapy and covert sensitization, have been described. In covert sensitization, the patient was instructed to pair images of nausea and vomiting with the urge to steal. Psychodynamic psychotherapy has also been used, in which kleptomania is conceptualized as a symptom of an underlying conflict (Goldman, 1991).

Because kleptomania is relatively common, it seems clear that few persons actually request treatment. Many kleptomaniacs are arrested for shoplifting and are handled through the courts. Embarrassment and shame may keep some persons from acting on their urges, like the 80-year-old woman described earlier. Probation may be helpful by providing a regular reminder of what might occur if violated. According to Goldman (1991), perhaps the most common treatment method is the self-imposed banning of all shopping in an attempt to head off potential thefts.

Pathological Gambling

Pathological gambling is characterized by a continuous or periodic loss of control over gambling. The diagnostic criteria are patterned after those used for substance dependencies, because there are many superficial similarities (e.g., preoccupation with gambling, repeated efforts to stop gambling) (American Psychiatric Association, 1994). For this reason, many persons consider gambling an *addiction*. The disorder is easily diagnosed, particularly in advanced cases, despite the patient's denial, which is also typical of the substance abuser.

Pathological gambling affects between 2% and 3% of the general population (DeCaria et al., 1996). The prevalence is less in locations with limited gaming opportunities. About one-third of gamblers are women, who generally start gambling later in life than men. In men, disorder typically begins in adolescence, and a few people become hooked almost from their first bet (Lesieur & Rosenthal, 1991). More men who present for help will have had the problem for decades, whereas women usually have been ill for only a few years. Others may have a more insidious onset following years of social gambling. Pathological gambling is associated with significant psychiatric comorbidity, particularly mood and substance-use disorders (Linden, Jonas, & Pope, 1986).

Although many different treatments have been described, few have been carefully studied. For many, the treatment of pathological gambling will involve total abstinence. Referral to Gamblers Anonymous, a 12-step program similar to Alcoholics Anonymous, may be helpful, although between 75% and 90% drop out in the first year, and reported success rates at 1- and 2-year follow-up are low (8% and 7%, respectively) (Brown, 1985). Inpatient treatment and rehabilitation programs similar to those for substance-use disorders may be helpful to selected patients (Russo, Taber, McCormick, & Ramirez, 1984; Taber, McCormick, Russo, Adkins, & Ramirez, 1987).

Other patients will benefit from individual psychotherapy geared toward helping them understand why they gamble and assisting them in dealing with feelings of hopelessness, depression, and guilt. Cognitive restructuring techniques can be used to address the irrational perceptions associated with locus of control (Josephson & Brandolo, 1993). Relapse prevention needs to focus on knowledge of specific triggers that lead to gambling and teaching patients how better to deal with these triggers. Family therapy is often crucial and offers the gambler an opportunity to make amends, to learn better communication skills, and to repair the rifts that gambling inevitably creates in families (Rosenthal, 1992).

There has been almost no research on the use of medication to treat pathological gambling. In an early report, Moskowitz (1980) reported improvement in three gamblers given lithium carbonate. More recently, 7 of 10 pathological gamblers treated with the SRI fluvoxamine improved during an 8-week trial (C. DeCaria, personal communication, June 26, 1997), and in a single case report, clomipramine was better than placebo (Hollander, Frenkel, DeCaria, Trungold, & Stein, 1992). Haller and Hinterhuber (1994) reported the experience of a gambler who improved with carbamazepine.

Trichotillomania

Trichotillomania is characterized by recurrent pulling out of one's hair, resulting in noticeable hair loss (American Psychiatric Association, 1994). This is usually associated with an increasing sense of tension before pulling out the hair, and pleasure, gratification, or relief when pulling out the hair. Persons with trichotillomania usually report substantial subjective distress or develop other evidence of impairment (Christenson et al., 1991).

The disorder is generally chronic, although it tends to wax and wane in symptom severity. It can affect any site where hair grows, including the scalp, eyelids, eyebrows, body, axillary, and pubic regions. In clinical samples, 70–90% of hair pullers are female, and most report a childhood onset (Christenson et al., 1991; Schlosser, Black, Repertinger, & Freet, 1994). Surveys show that it affects up to 1% of adolescents and college students (Christenson et al., 1991; King et al., 1995). Compulsive hair pullers frequently suffer comorbid mood and anxiety disorders (including OCD), other impulse control disorders, or personality disorders. In one study (Schlosser et al., 1994), 41% of 22 subjects had a lifetime history of a mood disorder, 55% had anxiety disorder, and 18% had a substance-use disorder. Over 50% met criteria for a personality disorder, mainly from the "anxious" cluster.

The diagnosis is easily made once alternate diagnoses and medical conditions have been ruled out. Most patients have no obvious balding, but have small, easily disguised bald spots or patches, or missing eyebrows and eyelashes. A typical patient seen in our clinic is described below.

CASE 3

Shirley, a 42-year-old married homemaker, presented for evaluation of compulsive hair pulling. She had recently learned of a new medication (clomipramine) that might be helpful and wished to try it.

Shirley grew up in a small Midwestern farming community. Her childhood was relatively happy, and her family life was harmonious. As a young girl, she began to twist and twirl her hair and later, before age 10, began to pull out scalp, eyebrow, and eyelash hair.

The amount of hair-pulling has fluctuated over the years, but she has never been free of it. The pulling is sometimes automatic, as when she is reading or watching television, but at other times, it is more deliberate. Shirley reported that she had tried to stop pulling her hair, but her many attempts had all failed.

At her interview, Shirley mentioned that she was wearing a wig. She removed it, revealing an essentially bald scalp except for a fringe around the top. She had no eyebrows or eyelashes, which she disguised with makeup and eyeglasses. She admitted to feeling embarrassed and ashamed by her problem, and tearfully remembered how classmates had made fun of her as a child. Over the years, she had received many medical and dermatological evaluations. Ointments and solutions had been prescribed, all without benefit.

She was given clomipramine up to 150 mg/day, which appeared to reduce her urge to pull, but it was not helpful cosmetically. A trial of fluoxetine was unhelpful, and she declined referral for behavior therapy. Supportive psychotherapy was helpful in assisting her to accept her disorder and to develop improved self-esteem (adapted from Andreasen & Black, 1995).

Treatment generally involves both behavior therapy and medication. Nevertheless, a recent survey of 123 hair pullers found that the majority had never been treated; of those who sought treatment, most reported minimal benefit (Cohen et al., 1995). With behavior therapy, patients are taught to identify when their hair pulling occurs (it is often automatic) and to substitute other, more benign behaviors. These techniques are often referred to as *habit reversal*. In a controlled trial of habit reversal versus negative practice (in which a patient is taught to go through the motions of hair pulling but stopping short of pulling it), patients receiving habit reversal experienced a 91% reduction in hair pulling at 4 months and 87% at 22 months (Azrin, Nunn, & Frantz, 1980). Stanley and Mouton (1996) have recently described this treatment, and have provided a useful manual.

Medication has also been shown helpful to some patients. In an early study, Swedo et al. (1989) showed that clomipramine was more effective than desipramine in reducing hair-pulling behavior. This early report contributed to a surge in interest in using SRIs to treat trichotillomania, although results have been mixed (Christenson & O'Sullivan, 1996). For example, open, but not controlled, trials of fluoxetine in patients with trichotillomania have shown benefit (Christenson et al., 1991; Streichenwein & Thornby, 1995). Some patients will benefit from cognitive psychotherapy that aims at upgrading their often low self-esteem, addressing relationship and family issues, and helping to correct faulty cognitions (e.g., "No one likes me because my eyebrows are missing"). Black and Blum (1992) have reported that a topical steroid may be helpful to patients who describe localized itching that prompts hair pulling, and they describe a successfully treated case. Hypnosis has also been used and is reported to benefit some persons (Christenson & Crow, 1996).

Compulsive Buying

Compulsive buying is characterized by inappropriate, excessive, or unnecessary shopping or buying that leads to social or occupational impairment, or legal/financial problems (Black, 1996; McElroy et al., 1994). The buying is generally prompted by a preoccupation with spending, or impulses to spend that are experienced as irresistible. There is no category for compulsive buying in DSM-IV, and it is best considered a disorder of impulse control, not otherwise specified.

The prevalence of compulsive buying has been estimated at between 2% and 8% (Faber & O'Guinn, 1992). In clinical samples, as well as community surveys, the disorder shows a female preponderance ranging from 80% to 92% (Black, 1996). Age of onset has been reported to range from 18 to 30 years, and the disorder has a chronic but waxing and waning course (Christenson et al., 1994; McElroy et al., 1994; Schlosser et al., 1994).

Compulsive buyers typically show substantial psychiatric comorbidity, particularly mood, anxiety, substance-use, eating, and personality disorders (Christenson et al., 1994; Schlosser et al., 1994). Other impulse control disorders, such as pathological gambling, are also found at rates higher than expected (McElroy et al., 1994). In one study of 46 subjects (Schlosser et al., 1994), nearly 60% of the sample met criteria for at least one personality disorder, most commonly obsessive–compulsive, borderline, and avoidant types.

Compulsive buyers typically buy for themselves and shop alone. They tend to buy small, inexpensive items such as clothing, shoes, jewelry, and makeup, and rely more on credit cards than normal buyers (O'Guinn & Faber, 1989). Most subjects try unsuccessfully to control their behavior using willpower (Black, 1996).

Although no controlled treatment studies have been reported, many patients will probably benefit from a combination of psychotherapy and medication. Psychotherapy should focus on exploring triggers that tend to prompt the behavior, and assisting the patient in developing strategies to resist the temptation that follows. Cognitive restructuring techniques may also be helpful in assisting patients to develop more appropriate responses to their excessive urges and impulses. Exposure and response prevention techniques have been successful in two cases (Bernik, Akerman, Amaral, & Braun, 1996).

Like the kleptomaniac, persons with compulsive buying should be encouraged to reduce access to credit (e.g., cutting up credit cards), adopt a self-imposed ban on shopping, or shop while accompanied to reduce the impulse to spend. Patients should be encouraged to develop new pasttimes that are meaningful and satisfying to replace the shopping behavior. Patients with severe financial problems or those facing bankruptcy will benefit from a referral to a credit counselor or financial advisor. Some will need legal help.

Antidepressant medication may help some compulsive buyers. In a series of 20 cases, McElroy et al. (1994) reported that 10 of 13 compulsive buyers receiving various psychotropic medications, including antidepressants, anxiolytics, mood stabilizers, or antipsychotics, improved. (In contrast, 2 of 9 patients receiving psychotherapy improved.) Black, Monahan, and Gabel (1997a) reported that 9 of 10 nondepressed compulsive buyers responded to fluvoxamine. Subjects reported fewer cognitions and preoccupations with shopping and had fewer shopping behaviors. One of the patients enrolled in the trial is described below.

CASE 4

Heather was an attractive but slightly overweight 35-year-old woman who had been compulsively shopping and spending since receiving her first credit card at age 18. She knew her behavior was excessive and irrational, but her efforts to change had always failed.

Heather's life revolved around shopping and spending, even though she worked full time and had two small children. She often took them shopping with her, and they, too, expressed keen interest in shopping. Heather typically bought new clothing for herself or her children, paperback books, cosmetics and hair-care products, and numerous small items. Her grocery store purchases not only included the new food products, but also nonfood items such as books, greeting cards, and tabloid magazines. Heather's closets and storage spaces were filled with clothing that she did not need and rarely wore, and her kitchen cabinets were packed as well.

Heather loved shopping and was distressed only by its consequences. She admitted she had sought help mainly because her husband was fed up with her behavior. They were beginning to have financial problems, even though both had adequate incomes.

Heather suffered from recurrent major depression, although she was not clinically depressed at the time of her intake into the study. She also had a history of infrequent panic attacks but did not meet criteria for panic disorder.

After giving informed consent, Heather was enrolled in the 9-week study. She was started on a low dosage of fluvoxamine (50 mg/day) after a 1-week placebo washout. The dose was gradually increased as tolerated to a maximum of 300 mg/day. During the regularly scheduled sessions, Heather was interviewed about her shopping behaviors, adverse events, and other questions she had about the study or the medication.

Heather responded well to fluvoxamine and, upon completing the treatment, reported that she thought less frequently about shopping and was less compelled to shop. She still enjoyed shopping but said it was no longer interfering with her life. She had started to repay some of her loans taken out earlier to pay off shopping debts, had a renewed interest in hobbies, and was spending more time with her family. Her husband was very pleased with the results of the treatment. After she was withdrawn from the fluvoxamine, her symptoms began to recur. At the end of the 4-week observation, she asked to be remedicated (Black, 1996).

Twelve-step programs such as Debtors' Anonymous, patterned after Alcoholics Anonymous, have also been developed and may be helpful. Many compulsive buyers accumulate substantial debts and benefit from the help and support of those who are similarly afflicted. Several self-help books are also available, such as *Women Who Shop Too Much* (Wesson, 1990) or *Born to Spend* (Arenson, 1991).

COMPULSIVE SEXUAL BEHAVIOR

Compulsive sexual behavior (CSB) involves excessive or uncontrolled sexual thoughts or behaviors that lead to subjective distress, social or occupational impairment, or legal or financial consequences (Black, Kehrberg, Flumerfelt, & Schlosser, 1997b; Coleman, 1992; Goodman, 1992).

It has been estimated that perhaps 5% of the general population have CSB, although this could be an underestimate because of the embarrassment and shame associated with the condition (Coleman, 1992). More men than women are identified with the problem, but this difference could be culturally based, since, at least in the United States, sexuality is often defined from a masculine perspective. Age of onset is in the late teens or early 20s, and the disorder is chronic or recurrent for most (Black et al., 1997b).

CSB involves a broad range of symptoms that have been categorized as *paraphilic* or *nonparaphilic* (Coleman, 1992; Kafka & Prentky, 1992a). Paraphilic CSB involves unconventional sexual behaviors in which there is a disturbance in the object of sexual gratification or in the expression of sexual gratification (e.g., exhibitionism, pedophilia). Nonparaphilic CSB involves conventional sexual behaviors that have become excessive or uncontrolled. Coleman (1992) delineated five subtypes of nonparaphilic CSB, including compulsive cruising and multiple partners, compulsive fixation on an unobtainable partner, compulsive masturbation, compulsive multiple love relationships, and compulsive sexuality within a relationship. There is no DSM-IV equivalent for nonparaphilic types of compulsive sexual behavior.

Frequent comorbidity with anxiety disorders, depression, and alcohol and drug abuse has been reported (Black et al., 1997b; Kafka & Prentky, 1994). Associated symptoms include sexually transmitted diseases, unwanted pregnancies, somatic complaints, relationship discord, sexual dysfunction, and child abuse. In a recent study of 36 subjects (Black et al., 1997b), sexual behavior was both excessive and poorly controlled, caused subjective distress, was overly time consuming, or led to impairment in interpersonal or occupational functioning. Sixty-four percent had a lifetime history of a substance-use disorder, more than 33% a lifetime history of major depression or dysthymia, and more than 40% a lifetime history of a phobic disorder. Personality disorders were present in nearly one-half, particularly the paranoid, histrionic, obsessive–compulsive and passive–aggressive types.

Most subjects reported the disorder to be episodic, and nearly all acknowledged being overly preoccupied with sexual fantasies or being overly sexually active. Most had tried to resist the behavior, making pacts or New Year's resolutions that generally failed. Although many felt the behavior distracted them from other concerns or problems, or relieved anxiety, they reported feeling out of control or experiencing remorse. Additionally, most reported that substance abuse frequently accompanied their uncontrolled sexual behavior, perhaps disinhibiting them sufficiently to allow the activity, to enhance their pleasure, or to numb their sense of shame.

The clinical management of these disorders has never been satisfactory, probably due in part to the fact that these patients rarely step forward for treatment. Embarrassment, shame, concern with legal consequences, and perhaps the guilty pleasure they derive from the CSB may prevent them from seeking help. For most patients, treatment will involve a combination of medication and psychotherapy. Antiandrogens including medroxyprogesterone and cyproterone have been prescribed to help control deviant or dangerous sexual behaviors, but they have also been used with nonparaphilic forms of CSB. Both agents affect testosterone, with medroxyprogesterone lowering serum levels by reducing testosterone production, and cyproterone inhibiting androgenic receptor sites. The effect of these agents is to decrease sexual drive, sexual fantasies, and erectile function. For example, Berlin and Meinecke (1981) reported that only 3 of 20 subjects with paraphilias relapsed while taking medication. Low-dose oral medroxyprogesterone (60 mg/day) may be as effective as high-dosage injectable depot forms (i.e., 500–800 mg intramuscularly weekly) (Gottlesman & Schubert, 1993). The dosage of the antiandrogenic agent can usually be adjusted to preserve conventional sexual arousal, which may help to enhance compliance. An example of their use occurred in the following patient treated in our hospital.

CASE 5

Frank, a 38-year-old mechanic, presented requesting help for compulsive masturbation. He learned to masturbate at age 12 and was soon masturbating up to five times daily while fantasizing about women he had seen during the day. Frank reported that his masturbation was irresistible, and that he was powerless to stop. He frequently masturbated in his car, which led to several arrests for indecent exposure. Feeling guilty and wanting to make amends, Frank sought psychotherapy following each arrest but would soon drop out. One psychiatrist prescribed thioridazine to dampen his sex drive, but it only caused retrograde ejaculation. Another physician recommended that he read pornography and masturbate in private.

Although socially awkward with women and not dating until age 21, Frank married at age 23 and had a stable marriage and a satisfying sexual relationship. He admitted, however, that he preferred masturbation to sexual intercourse with his wife.

Physical examination showed the absence of the right testicle, but results of the examination were otherwise normal. Serum testosterone was 288 ng/dl (normal serum levels, 200–800 ng/dl). Treatment was started with oral medroxyprogesterone acetate. At a follow-up visit 1 month later, his serum testosterone had fallen to 41 ng/dl. He had been able to resist masturbating and no longer had spontaneous erections. He felt he could control his sexual behavior better. Six months later, he chose to discontinue the medication and within one month had returned to his baseline. A follow-up 10 years later showed that his CSB had persisted unchanged (adapted from Andreasen & Black, 1995).

SRIs have been used more recently and may be more acceptable to patients. When effective, they can help to regulate sexual impulses in a fashion similar to their effect on obsessive–compulsive symptoms. In an open trial of fluoxetine, Kafka and Prentky (1992b) reported that 13 of 16 men completing a 12-week trial had reduced their abnormal sexual behavior to less than 30 minutes per day. In a subsequent study, Kafka (1994) reported that 17 of 24 men treated for at least 4 weeks with sertraline or fluoxetine improved. There are no controlled data on the use of these agents or the antiandrogens in treating persons with CSB.

Several psychotherapeutic techniques have been developed to treat disorders of sexual excess, including behavioral therapy, group therapy, twelve-step programs (e.g., Sex Addicts Anonymous), and individual therapy using psychodynamic or cognitive-behavioral techniques. With behavior therapy, satiation has been used to reduce deviant arousal patterns, while covert sensitization has been used to generate arousal in response to nondeviant themes (Marshall & Barbaree, 1978; McConaghy, Armstrong, & Blaszczynski, 1985). Through individual psychotherapy, persons can learn better ways to manage anxiety and to express their sexuality in more appropriate ways. Patients may also learn to understand factors that may have contributed to or maintained inappropriate sexual arousal or behavior. Family therapy and couples therapy are often necessary to help overcome the damaging effects of CSB on a patient's marriage and family life (Coleman, 1992).

ACKNOWLEDGMENT

Portions of this chapter are based in part on chapters in Andreasen and Black (1995). Copyright 1995 by American Psychiatric Press. Adapted by permission.

REFERENCES

American Psychiatric Association. (1994). *Diagnostic and statistical manual of mental disorders* (4th ed.). Washington, DC: Author.

American Psychiatric Association. (1993). Practice guidelines for eating disorders. *American Journal of Psychiatry, 150,* 212–228.

Andreasen, N. C., & Bardach, J. (1977). Dysmorphophobia: Symptom or disease? *American Journal of Psychiatry, 134,* 673–676.

Andreasen, N. C., & Black, D. W. (1995). *Introductory textbook of psychiatry* (2nd ed.). Washington, DC: American Psychiatric Press.

Arenson, G. (1991). *Born to spend.* Blue Ridge Summit, PA: Tab Books.

Azrin, N. H., Nunn, R. G., & Frantz, S. E. (1980). Treatment of hair-pulling (trichotillomania): A comparative study of habit reversal and negative practice training. *Journal of Behavior Therapy and Experimental Psychiatry, 11,* 13–20.

Barsky, A. J., Wyshak, G., & Klerman, G. L. (1990a). Transient hypochondriasis. *Archives of General Psychiatry, 47,* 746–752.

Barsky, A. J., Wyshak, G., & Klerman, G. L. (1990b). The prevalence of hypochondriasis in medical outpatients. *Social Psychiatry and Psychiatric Epidemiology, 25,* 89–94.

Barsky, A. J., Wyshak, G., & Klerman, G. L. (1990c). The somatosensory amplification scale and its relationship to hypochondriasis. *Journal of Psychiatric Research, 24,* 323–334.

Barsky, A. J., Wyshak, G., & Klerman, G. L. (1992). Psychiatric comorbidity in DSM-III-R hypochondriasis. *Archives of General Psychiatry, 49,* 101–108.

Berlin, F. S., & Meinecke, C. F. (1981). Treatment of sex offenders with antiandrogenic medication: Conceptualization, review of treatment modalities, and preliminary findings. *American Journal of Psychiatry, 138,* 601–607.

Bernik, M. A., Akerman, D., Amaral, J. A. M. S., & Braun, R. C. D. N. (1996). Cue exposure in compulsive buying [letter]. *Journal of Clinical Psychiatry, 57,* 90.

Bernstein, E. M., & Putnam, F. W. (1986). Development, reliability, and validity of a dissociation scale. *Journal of Nervous and Mental Disease, 144,* 727–735.

Black, D. W. (1996). Compulsive buying: A review. *Journal of Clinical Psychiatry, 57*(Suppl. 8), 50–55.

Black, D. W., & Blum, N. (1992). Trichotillomania treated with clomipramine and a topical steroid [letter]. *American Journal of Psychiatry, 149,* 842–843.

Black, D. W., Kehrberg, L. L. D., Flumerfelt, D. L., & Schlosser, S. S. (1997b). Characteristics of 36 subjects reporting compulsive sexual behavior. *American Journal of Psychiatry, 154,* 243–249.

Black, D. W., Monahan, P., & Gabel, J. (1997a). Fluvoxamine in the treatment of compulsive buying. *Journal of Clinical Psychiatry, 58,* 159–163.

Black, D. W., Noyes, R., Goldstein, R. B., & Blum, N. (1992). A family study of obsessive–compulsive disorder. *Archives of General Psychiatry, 49,* 362–368.

Brown, R. I. F. (1985). The effectiveness of Gambler's Anonymous. In W. Eadington (Ed.), *The gambling studies.* Reno: University of Nevada Bureau of Business and Economic Research.

Casper, R. C. (1990). Personality features of women with good outcome from restricting anorexia nervosa. *Psychosomatic Medicine, 52,* 156–170.

Christenson, G. A., & Crow, S. J. (1996). The characterization and treatment of trichotillomania. *Journal of Clinical Psychiatry, 57*(Suppl. 8), 42–49.

Christenson, G. A., Faber, R. J., de Zwaan, M., Raymond, N. C., Specker, S. M., Ekern, M. D., Mackenzie, T. B., Crosby, R. D., Crow, S. J., Eckert, E. D., Mussell, M. P., & Mitchell, J. E. (1994). Compulsive buying: Descriptive characteristics and psychiatric comorbidity. *Journal of Clinical Psychiatry, 55,* 5–11.

Christenson, G. A., MacKenzie, T. B., & Mitchell, J. E. (1991). Characteristics of 60 adult chronic hair-pullers. *American Journal of Psychiatry, 148,* 365–370.

Christenson, G. A., MacKenzie, T. B., Mitchell, J. E., & Callies, A. L. (1991). A placebo-controlled, double-blind crossover study of fluoxetine in trichotillomania. *American Journal of Psychiatry, 148,* 1566–1571.

Christenson, G. A., & O'Sullivan, R. (1996). Trichotillomania: Rational treatment options. *CNS Drugs, 6,* 23–34.

Christenson, G. A., Pyle, R. L., & Mitchell, J. E. (1991). Estimated lifetime prevalence of trichotillomania in college students. *Journal of Clinical Psychiatry, 52,* 415–417.

Cohen, D. J., Ort, S. I., Leckman, J. F., Riddle, M. A., & Hardin, M. T. (1988). Family functioning and Tourette's syndrome. In D. J. Cohen, R. D. Brown, & J. F. Leckman (Eds.), *Tourette's syndrome and tic disorders: Clinical understanding and treatment* (pp. 179–196). New York: Wiley.

Cohen, L. J., Stein, D. J., Simeon, D., Spadaccini, E., Rosen, J., Aronowitz, B., & Hollander, E. (1995). Clinical profile, comorbidity, and treatment history in 123 hair-pullers: A survey study. *Journal of Clinical Psychiatry, 56,* 319–326.

Coleman, E. (1992). Is your patient suffering from compulsive sexual behavior? *Psychiatric Annals, 22,* 320–325.

Comings, D. E., Himes, J. A., & Comings, B. G. (1990). An epidemiological study of Tourette's syndrome in a single school district. *Journal of Clinical Psychiatry, 51,* 463–469.

Cooper, Z., & Fairburn, C. G. (1987). The Eating Disorders Examination: A semi-structured interview for the assessment of the specific psychopathology of eating disorders. *International Journal of Eating Disorders, 6,* 1–8.

DeCaria, C., Hollander, E., Grossman, R., Wong, C. M., Mosovich, S. A., & Cherkasky,

S. (1996). Diagnosis, neurobiology, and treatment of pathological gambling. *Journal of Clinical Psychiatry, 57*(Suppl. 8), 80–84.

Dixon, J. C. (1963). Depersonalization phenomena in a sample of college students. *British Journal of Psychiatry, 109,* 371–375.

Eckert, E. D., Halmi, K. A., Marchi, P., Grove, W., & Crosby, R. (1995). Ten-year follow-up of anorexia nervosa: Clinical course and outcome. *Psychological Medicine, 25,* 143–156.

Faber, R. J., & O'Guinn, R. J. (1992). A clinical screener for compulsive buying. *Journal of Consumer Research, 19,* 459–469.

Fairburn C. G., Jones, R., Peveler, R. C., Carr, S. J., Solomon, R. A., O'Connor, M. E., Burton, J., & Hope, R. A. (1991). Three psychological treatments for bulimia nervosa. *Archives of General Psychiatry, 48,* 463–469.

Fallon, B. A., Liebowitz, M. R., Schneier, F., Campeas, R., Salmon, E., & Davies, S. O. (1991). An open-trial of fluoxetine for hypochondriasis. *New Research Program and Abstracts, 188,* 93. 144th Annual Meeting of the American Psychiatric Association. New Orleans, LA.

Fallon, B. A., Rasmussen, S. A., & Liebowitz, M. R. (1993). Hypochondriasis. In E. Hollander (Ed.), *Obsessive–compulsive-related disorders* (pp. 71–92). Washington, DC: American Psychiatric Press.

Fava, M., Copeland, P. M., Schweiger, U., & Herzog, D. B. (1989). Neurochemical abnormalities of anorexia nervosa and bulimia nervosa. *American Journal of Psychiatry, 146,* 963–971.

Fichtner, C. G., Horevitz, R. P., & Brown, B. G. (1992). Fluoxetine in depersonalization disorder [letter]. *American Journal of Psychiatry, 149,* 1750–1751.

Fluoxetine Bulimia Nervosa Collaborative Study Group. (1992). Fluoxetine in the treatment of bulimia nervosa: A multicenter, placebo-controlled, double-blind trial. *Archives of General Psychiatry, 49,* 139–147.

Gaffney, G. R., Sieg, K., & Hellings, J. (1994). The MOVES: A self-rating scale for Tourette's syndrome. *Journal of Child and Adolescent Psychopharmacology, 4,* 269–280.

Gard, M. C. E., & Freeman, C. P. (1996). The dismantling of a myth: A review of eating disorders and socio-economic status. *International Journal of Eating Disorders, 20,* 1–12.

Garner, D. M. (1992). *Eating Disorder Inventory 2: Professional manual.* Odessa, FL: Psychological Assessment Resources.

Garner, D. M., & Garfinkel, P. E. (1979). The Eating Attitudes Test: An index of the symptoms of anorexia nervosa. *Psychological Medicine, 9,* 273–279.

Goldman, M. J. (1991). Kleptomania: Making sense of the nonsensical. *American Journal of Psychiatry, 148,* 986–996.

Goodman, A. (1992). Sexual addiction: Designation and treatment. *Journal of Sex and Marital Therapy, 18,* 303–314.

Goodman, W. K., Price, L. H., Rasmussen, S. A., Mazure, C., Fleischmann, R. C., Hill, C. L., Heninger, G. R., & Charney, D. S. (1989). The Yale–Brown Obsessive–Compulsive Scale: I. Development, use, and reliability. *Archives of General Psychiatry, 46,* 1006–1011.

Gottesman, H. G., & Schubert, D. S. P. (1993). Low-dose oral medroxyprogesterone acetate in the management of the paraphilias. *Journal of Clinical Psychiatry, 54,* 182–188.

Gwirtsman, H. E., Guze, B. H., Yager, J., & Gainsley, B. (1990). Fluoxetine treatment of anorexia nervosa: An open clinical trial. *Journal of Clinical Psychiatry, 51,* 378–382.

Haller, R., & Hinterhuber, H. (1994). Treatment of pathological gambling with carbamazepine. *Pharmacopsychiatry, 27,* 129.

Halmi, K. A., Eckert, E., LaDu, T. J., & Cohen, J. (1986). Anorexia nervosa: Treatment efficacy of cyproheptadine and amitriptyline. *Archives of General Psychiatry, 43,* 177–181.

Halmi, K. A., Eckert, E., Marchi, P., Sampugnaro, V., Apple, R., & Cohen, J. (1991). Comorbidity of psychiatric diagnoses in anorexia nervosa. *Archives of General Psychiatry, 48,* 712–718.

Hollander, E. (Ed.). (1993). *Obsessive–compulsive-related disorders.* Washington, DC: American Psychiatric Press.

Hollander, E., Frenkel, M., DeCaria, C. M., Trungold, S., & Stein, D. J. (1992). Treatment of pathological gambling with clomipramine [letter]. *American Journal of Psychiatry, 149,* 710–711.

Hollander, E., Liebowitz, M. R., DeCaria, C., Fairbanks, J., Fallon, B., & Klein, D. F. (1990). Treatment of depersonalization with serotonin-reuptake blockers. *Journal of Clinical Psychopharmacology, 10,* 200–203.

Hudson, J. I., Pope, H. G., Yurgelun-Todd, D., Jonas, J. M., & Frankenburg, F. R. (1987). A controlled study of lifetime prevalence of affective and other psychiatric diseases in bulimic outpatients. *American Journal of Psychiatry, 144,* 1283–1287.

Josephson, S. C., & Brandolo, E. (1993). Cognitive-behavioral approaches to obsessive–compulsive-related disorders. In E. Hollander (Ed.), *Obsessive–compulsive-related disorders* (pp. 215–240). Washington, DC: American Psychiatric Press.

Kafka, M. P. (1994). Sertraline pharmacotherapy for paraphilias and paraphilia-related disorders. *Annals of Clinical Psychiatry, 6,* 189–195.

Kafka, M. P., & Prentky, R. (1992a). A comparative study of nonparaphilic sexual addictions and paraphilias in men. *Journal of Clinical Psychiatry, 53,* 345–350.

Kafka, M. P., & Prentky, R. (1992b). Fluoxetine treatment of nonparaphilic sexual addictions and paraphilias in men. *Journal of Clinical Psychiatry, 53,* 351–358.

Kafka, M. P., & Prentky, R. (1994). Preliminary observations of DSM-III-R Axis I comorbidity in men with paraphilias and paraphilia-related disorders. *Journal of Clinical Psychiatry, 55,* 481–487.

Kaye, W. H., Weltzin, T. E., Hsu, L. K., & Bulik, C. M. (1991). An open trial of fluoxetine in patients with anorexia nervosa. *Journal of Clinical Psychiatry, 52,* 464–471.

Kellner, R. (1981). *Abridged manual for the Illness Attitude Scales.* Albuquerque: University of New Mexico.

Kellner, R. (1986). *Somatization and hypochondriasis.* New York: Praeger.

Kellner, R., Abbott, P., Pathak, D., Winslow, W. W., & Umland, B. E. (1983–1984). Hypochondriacal beliefs and attitudes in family practice and psychiatric patients. *International Journal of Psychiatry and Medicine, 13,* 127–139.

King, R. A., Zohar, A. H., Ratzoni, G., Binder, M., Kron, S., Dycian A., Cohen, D. J., Pauls, D. L., & Apter, A. (1995). An epidemiologic study of trichotillomania in Israeli adolescents. *Journal of the American Academy of Child and Adolescent Psychiatry, 34,* 1212–1215.

Leckman, J. F. (1993). Tourette's syndrome. In E. Hollander (Ed.), *Obsessive–compulsive-related disorders* (pp. 113–137). Washington, DC: American Psychiatric Press.

Leckman, J. F., Hardin, M. T., Riddle, M. A., Stevenson, J., Ort, S. I., & Cohen, D. J. (1991). Clonidine treatment of Tourette's syndrome. *Archives of General Psychiatry, 48,* 324–328.

Leckman, J. F., Walker, D. E., Goodman, W. K., Pauls, D. L., & Cohen, D. J. (1994). "Just right" perceptions associated with compulsive behavior in Tourette's syndrome. *American Journal of Psychiatry, 151,* 675–680.

Lesieur, H. R., & Blume, S. B. (1991). Evaluation of patients treated for pathological gambling in a combined alcohol, substance abuse, and pathological gambling treatment unit using the addiction severity index. *British Journal of Addiction, 86,* 1017–1028.

Lesieur, H. R., & Blume, S. B. (1987). The South Oaks Gambling Screen (SOGS): A new instrument for the identification of pathologic gamblers. *American Journal of Psychiatry, 144,* 1184–1188.

Lesieur, H. R., & Rosenthal, R. J. (1991). Pathological gambling: A review of the literature. *Journal of Gambling Studies, 7,* 5–39.

Linden, R. D., Jonas, J. M., & Pope, H. G. (1986). Pathological gambling and major affective disorder: Preliminary findings. *Journal of Clinical Psychiatry, 47,* 201–203.

Lucas, A. R., Beard, C. M., O'Fallon, W. M., & Kurlan, L. T. (1991). Fifty-year trends in the incidence of anorexia nervosa in Rochester, Minnesota: A population-based study. *American Journal of Psychiatry, 148,* 917–922.

Marshall, W. L., & Barbaree, H. E. (1978). The reduction of deviant arousal: Satiation treatment for sexual aggressiveness. *Criminal Justice and Behavior, 5,* 294–303.

McConaghy, N., Armstrong, M. S., & Blaszczynski, A. (1985). Expectancy, covert sensitization, and imaginal desensitization in compulsive sexuality. *Acta Psychiatrica Scandinavica, 72,* 176–187.

McElroy, S. L., Hudson, J. I., Pope, H. G., & Keck, P. E. (1991b). Kleptomania: Clinical characteristics and associated psychopathology. *Psychological Medicine, 21,* 93–108.

McElroy, S. L., Keck, P. E., Pope, H. G., & Hudson, J. I. (1989). Pharmacological treatment of kleptomania and bulimia nervosa. *Journal of Clinical Psychopharmacology, 9,* 358–360.

McElroy, S. L., Keck, P. E., Pope, H. G., Smith, J. M. R., & Strakowski, S. M. (1994). Compulsive buying: A report of 20 cases. *Journal of Clinical Psychiatry, 55,* 242–248.

McElroy, S. L., Pope, H. G., Hudson, J. I., Keck, P. E., & White, K. L. (1991a). Kleptomania: A report of 20 cases. *American Journal of Psychiatry, 148,* 652–657.

Monahan, P., Black, D. W., & Gabel, J. (1996). Reliability and validity of a scale to measure change in persons with compulsive buying. *Psychiatry Research, 64,* 59–67.

Moskowitz, J. (1980). Lithium and lady luck: Use of lithium carbonate in compulsive gambling. *New York State Journal of Medicine, 80,* 785–788.

Neziroglu, F. A., & Yaryura-Tobias, J. A. (1993). Exposure, response prevention, and cognitive therapy in the treatment of body dysmorphic disorder. *Behavior Therapy, 24,* 431–438.

Noyes, R., Hoenk, P. R., Kuperman, S., & Slymen, D. J. (1977). Depersonalization in accident victims and psychiatric patients. *Journal of Nervous and Mental Disease, 164,* 401–407.

Noyes, R. Jr., Holt, C. S., Happel, R. L., Kathol, R. G., & Yagla, S. J. (1997). A family study of hypochondriasis. *Journal of Nervous and Mental Disease, 185,* 223–232.

Noyes, R., Kathol, R. G., Fisher, M. M., Phillips, B. M., Suelzer, M. T., & Holt, C. S. (1993). The validity of DSM-III-R hypochondriasis. *Archives of General Psychiatry, 50,* 961–970.

Noyes, R., Kuperman, S., & Olsen, S. B. (1987). Desipramine: A possible treatment for depersonalization disorder. *Canadian Journal of Psychiatry, 32,* 782–784.

Noyes, R., Reich, J., Clancy, J., & O'Gorman, T. W. (1986). Reduction in hypochondriasis with treatment of panic disorder. *British Journal of Psychiatry, 149,* 631–635.

O'Guinn, T. C., & Faber, R. J. (1989). Compulsive buying: A phenomenological exploration. *Journal of Consumer Research, 16,* 147–157.

Pauls, D. L., Alsobrook, J. P., Goodman, W., Rasmussen, S., & Leckman, J. F. (1995). Family study of obsessive–compulsive disorder. *American Journal of Psychiatry, 142,* 76–84.

Pauls, D. L., Raymond, C. L., Stevenson, J. M., & Leckman, J. F. (1991). A family study of Gilles de la Tourette syndrome. *American Journal of Human Genetics, 48,* 154–163.

Pauls, D. L., Towbin, K. E., Leckman, J., Zahner, G. E. P., & Cohen, D. J. (1986). Gilles de la Tourette's syndrome and obsessive–compulsive disorder. *Archives of General Psychiatry, 43,* 1180–1182.

Peterson, B. S. (1996). Considerations of individual history and pathophysiology in the psychopharmacology of Tourette's syndrome. *Journal of Clinical Psychiatry, 57*(Suppl. 9), 23–34.

Phillips, K. A. (1991). Body dysmorphic disorder: The distress of imagined ugliness. *American Journal of Psychiatry, 148,* 1138–1149.

Phillips, K. A. (1995). Body dysmorphic disorder: Clinical features and drug treatment. *CNS Drugs, 3,* 30–40.

Phillips, K. A. (1996a). Body dysmorphic disorder: Diagnosis and treatment of imagined ugliness. *Journal of Clinical Psychiatry, 57*(Suppl. 8), 61–65.

Phillips, K. A. (1996b). *The broken mirror: Understanding and treating body dysmorphic disorder.* New York: Oxford University Press.

Phillips, K. A. (1996c, April 29). *Body dysmorphic disorder and OCD: Similarities and differences.* Paper presented at symposium, Anxiety Disorders in Women: Focus on OCD, Denver, CO.

Phillips, K. A., Atala, K. D., & Albertini, R. S. (1995). Case study of body dysmorphic disorder in adolescents. *Journal of the American Academy of Child and Adolescent Psychiatry, 34,* 1216–1220.

Phillips, K. A., Hollander, E., Rasmussen, S. A., Aronowitz, B. R., DeCaria, C., & Goodman, W. K. (1997). A severity rating scale for body dysmorphic disorder. *Psychopharmacology Bulletin, 33,* 17–22.

Phillips, K. A., McElroy, L., Keck, P. E., Hudson, J. I., & Pope, H. G. (1994). A comparison of delusional and non-delusional body dysmorphic disorder in 100 cases. *Psychopharmacology Bulletin, 30,* 179–186.

Phillips, K. A., McElroy, L., Keck, P. E., Pope, H. G., & Hudson, J. I. (1993). Body dysmorphic disorder: Thirty cases of imagined ugliness. *American Journal of Psychiatry, 150,* 302–308.

Pilowsky, I., & Spence, N. D. (1983). *Manual for the Illness Behavior Questionnaire* (2nd ed.). Adelaide, Australia: Department of Psychiatry, University of Adelaide.

Ratliff, N. B., & Kerski, D. (1995). Depersonalization treated with fluoxetine [letter]. *American Journal of Psychiatry, 152,* 1689–1690.

Robertson, M. M., & Gourdie, A. (1990). Familial Tourette's syndrome in a large British pedigree-associated psychopathology, severity, and potential for linkage analysis. *British Journal of Psychiatry, 156,* 515–521.

Rosenthal, R. T. (1992). Pathological gambling. *Psychiatric Annals, 22,* 72–78.

Ross, C. A., Heber, S., Norton, G. R., Anderson, D., Anderson, G., & Burchet, P. (1989). The Dissociative Disorder Interview Schedule: A structured interview. *Dissociation, 2,* 169–189.

Russo, A. M., Taber, J. I., McCormick, R. A., & Ramirez, L. F. (1984). An outcome study of an inpatient treatment program for pathological gamblers. *Hospital and Community Psychiatry, 35,* 323–327.

Salkovskis, P. M., & Warwick, H. M. (1986). Morbid preoccupations, health anxiety, and reassurance: A cognitive-behavioral approach in hypochondriasis. *Behaviour Research and Therapy, 24,* 597–602.

Schlosser, S., Black, D. W., Blum, N., & Goldstein, R. B. (1994). The demography, phenomenology, and family history of 22 persons with compulsive hair-pulling. *Annals of Clinical Psychiatry, 6,* 147–152.

Schlosser, S., Black, D. W., Repertinger, S., & Freet, D. (1994). Compulsive buying: Demography, phenomenology, and comorbidity in 46 subjects. *General Hospital Psychiatry, 16,* 205–212.

Shapiro, A. K., & Shapiro, E. S. (1988). Treatment of tic disorders with haloperidol. In D. J. Cohen, R. D. Brown, & J. F. Leckman (Eds.), *Tourette's syndrome and tic disorders: Clinical understanding and treatment* (pp. 267–280). New York: Wiley.

Shapiro, A. K., Shapiro, E., Young, J. G., & Feinberg, T. E. (1987). *Gilles de la Tourette's syndrome* (2nd ed.). New York: Raven Press.

Shapiro, E. S., Shapiro, A. K., Fulop, G., Hubbard, M., Mandeli, J., Nordlie, J., & Phillips, R. A. (1989). Controlled study of haloperidol, pimozide, and placebo for the treatment of Gilles de la Tourette's syndrome. *Archives of General Psychiatry, 46,* 722–730.

Sharp, C. W., & Freeman, C. P. L. (1993). The medical complications of anorexia nervosa. *British Journal of Psychiatry, 162,* 452–462.

Simeon, D., & Hollander, E. (1993). Depersonalization disorder. *Psychiatric Annals, 23,* 382–388.

Specker, S. M., Carlson, G. A., Christenson, G. A., & Marcotte, M. (1995). Impulse control disorders and attention deficit in pathological gamblers. *Annals of Clinical Psychiatry, 7,* 175–179.

Stanley, M. A., & Mouton, S. G. (1996). Trichotillomania treatment manual. In V. B. Van Hasselt & M. Hersen (Eds.), *Psychological treatment manuals for adult disorders* (pp. 657–687). New York: Plenum.

Stanley, M. A., Prather, R. C., Wagner, A. L., Davis, M. L., & Swann, A. (1993). Can the Yale–Brown Obsessive–Compulsive Scale be used to assess trichotillomania? A preliminary report. *Behaviour Research and Therapy, 31,* 171–178.

Stein, B. J., Hollander, E. Anthony, D. T., Schneier, F. R., Fallon, B. A., Liebowitz, M. R., & Klein, D. F. (1992). Serotonergic medications for sexual obsessions, sexual addictions, and paraphilias. *Journal of Clinical Psychiatry, 53,* 267–271.

Stein, M. B., & Uhde, T. W. (1989). Depersonalization disorder: Effects of caffeine and response to pharmacotherapy. *Biological Psychiatry, 26,* 315–320.

Steinberg, M. (1991). The spectrum of depersonalization: Assessment and treatment. In A. Tasman & S. M. Goldfinger (Eds.), *Review of psychiatry* (Vol. 10, pp. 223–247). Washington, DC: American Psychiatric Press.

Steinberg, M., Rounsaville, B., & Cicchetti, D. V. (1990). The Structured Clinical Interview for DSM-III-R Dissociative Disorders: Preliminary report on a new diagnostic instrument. *American Journal of Psychiatry, 147,* 76–82.

Streichenwein, S. M., & Thornby, J. I. (1995). A long-term, double-blind, placebo-controlled crossover trial of the efficacy of fluoxetine for trichotillomania. *American Journal of Psychiatry, 152,* 1192–1196.

Striegel-Moore, R. H., Sibertsein, L. R., Frensch, P., & Rodin, J. (1991). A prospective study of disordered eating among college students. *International Journal of Eating Disorders, 8,* 499–509.

Strober, M. (1980). Personality and symptomatological features in young, non-chronic anorexia nervosa patients. *Journal of Psychosomatic Research, 24,* 353–359.

Swedo, S. E., Leonard, H. L., Rapoport, J. L., Lenane, M. C., Goldberger, E. L., & Cheslow, D. L. (1989). A double-blind comparison of clomipramine and desipramine in the treatment of trichotillomania (hair-pulling). *New England Journal of Medicine, 321,* 497–501.

Taber, J. I., McCormick, R. A., Russo, A. M., Adkins, B. J., & Ramirez, L. F. (1987). Follow-up of pathological gamblers after treatment. *American Journal of Psychiatry, 144,* 757–761.

Warwick, H. M. C., & Marks, I. M. (1988). Behavioral treatment of illness phobia and hypochondriasis: A pilot study of 17 cases. *British Journal of Psychiatry, 152,* 239–241.

Wesner, R. B., & Noyes, R. B. (1991). Imipramine, an effective treatment for illness phobia. *Journal of Affective Disorders, 22,* 43–48.

Wesson, C. (1990). *Women who shop too much: Overcoming the urge to splurge.* New York: St. Martin's Press.

Winchel, R. M., Jones, J. S., Molcho, A., Parsons, B., Stanley, B., & Stanley, M. (1992). The Psychiatric Institute Trichotillomania Scale. *Psychopharmacology Bulletin, 28,* 463–476.

Yager, J., Landsverk, J., & Edelstein, C. K. (1987). A 20-month follow-up study of 628 women with eating disorders: I. Course and severity. *American Journal of Psychiatry, 144,* 1172–1177.

Yates, W. R., Sieleni, B., Reich, J., & Brass, C. (1989). Comorbidity of bulimia nervosa and personality disorder. *Journal of Clinical Psychiatry, 50,* 57–59.

Appendix

LIST OF RESOURCES FOR OBSESSIVE–COMPULSIVE DISORDER AND OBSESSIVE–COMPULSIVE SPECTRUM DISORDERS

Karen Rowa
Martin M. Antony

NATIONAL ORGANIZATIONS: NORTH AMERICA

Obsessive–Compulsive Disorder

Obsessive–Compulsive Foundation
P.O. Box 70
Milford, CT 06460-0070
Tel: (203) 878–5669
Fax: (203) 874–2826
E-mail: jphs28a@prodigy.com
Web Page: http://pages.prodigy.com/alwillen/ocf.html
- Newsletter
- Information on self-help groups
- Book catalog

Obsessive–Compulsive Information Center
Dean Foundation for Health, Research, and Education
2711 Allen Boulevard
Middleton, WI 53562
Tel: (608) 827–2390
Fax: (608) 827–2399
Web Page: http://www.deancare.com/info/infoll.htm
- Information for sufferers and professionals

Obsessive–Compulsive Anonymous
P.O. Box 215
New Hyde Park, NY 11040
Tel: (516) 741–4901
Web Page: http://members.aol.com/west24th/index.html
• 12-Step self-help recovery program
• Information on meetings in the United States and Canada
• Help for those who want to start a meeting

Anxiety Disorders

Anxiety Disorders Association of America
11900 Parklawn Drive, Suite 100
Rockville, MD 20852
Tel: (301) 231–9350
Fax: (301) 231–7392
E-mail: anxdis@aol.com
Web Page: www.adaa.org
• Newsletter
• Information on support groups in the United States
• Names of professionals who treat anxiety disorders in the United States and elsewhere
• Book catalog

Anxiety Disorders Network
1848 Liverpool Road, Suite 199
Pickering, Ontario, Canada L1V 6M3
Tel: (905) 831–3877
• Newsletter
• Names of professionals who treat anxiety disorders in Canada, the United States, and the United Kingdom

Obsessive–Compulsive Spectrum Disorders

Trichotillomania Learning Center
1215 Mission Street, Suite 2
Santa Cruz, CA 95060
Tel: (408) 457–1004
Fax: (408) 457–1004
Web Page: http://www.trich.org
• Newsletter
• Information on support groups in the United States
• Names of professionals who treat trichotillomania in the United States

- Information package
- Video

Tourette Syndrome Foundation of Canada
194 Jarvis Street, Suite 206
Toronto, Ontario, Canada M5B 2B7
Tel: (416) 861–8398 or (800) 361–3120
- Information on support groups and professionals who treat Tourette's Syndrome
- Newsletter
- Information, education, video library

ORGANIZATIONS OUTSIDE NORTH AMERICA

Australia

Mental Health Info.
62 Victoria Road
Gladsville, New South Wales, Australia 2111
Tel: (02) 9816–5688
Fax: (02) 9816–4056
E-mail nswamh@gpo.com.au
- Support group

United Kingdom

British Psychological Society
St. Andrews House
48 Princess Road East
Leicester LE1 7DR, United Kingdom
Tel: 0116 254 9658
E-mail enquiry@bps.org.uk

Obsessive Action
P.O. Box 6097
London W2 1WZ, United Kingdom

First Steps to Freedom
22 Randall Road
Kenilworth, Warwickshire CV8 1JY, United Kingdom
Warwick line: (01926) 851608
- Help for those who suffer with OCD

No Panic
92 Brands Farm Way
Randlay, Telford, Shropshire TF3 2JQ, United Kingdom
Tel: (01952) 590005
Fax: (01952) 270962
Helpline: (01952) 590545
• Support group information
• Individual therapy

France

Association Française des Troubles Obsessionnels Compulsifs et du Syndrome de Gilles de la Tourette (AFTOC-Tourette)
Cedex 15
14610 Villons les Buissons, France
Tel/Fax: 02 31 44 03 81
E-mail: aftoc@mail.cpod.fr
Web Page: http://www.lifl.fr/~descamps/aftoc.html
                http://infobiogen.fr/agora/associations/AFTOC/AFTOC.html
• Information and newsletter

Association Francophone de Formation et de Recherche en Thérapie Comportementale et Cognitive (AFFORTHECC)
10 Avenue Gantin
74150 Rumilly, France
Tel: 04.50.01.49.80
Fax: 04.50.64.58.46
E-mail: afforthecc@aol.com

Association Française de Thérapie Comportementale et Cognitive
100 Rue de la Santé
75674 Paris Cedex, France
Tel: 01.45.88.35.28
Fax: 01.45.89.55.66

South Africa

OCD Association of South Africa
P.O. Box 87127
Houghton, Johannesburg, South Africa 2041
Tel: 887–3678
Fax: 887–6617
• Information evenings
• Referrals
• Support groups
• Support groups for families

CONSUMER-ORIENTED READING MATERIALS

Obsessive–Compulsive Disorder

Baer, L. (1991). *Getting control: Overcoming your obsessions and compulsions.* Boston: Little, Brown.

Ciarrocchi, J. W. (1995). *The doubting disease: Help for scrupulosity and religious compulsions.* New York: Integration Books.

de Silva, P., & Rachman, S. (1998). *Obsessive compulsive disorders* (2nd ed.). Oxford, UK: Oxford University Press.

Foa, E. B., & Wilson, R. (1991). *Stop obsessing!: How to overcome your obsessions and compulsions.* New York: Bantam Books.

Greist, J. (1991). *Obsessive compulsive disorder: A guide.* Madison, WI: University of Wisconsin, Anxiety Disorders Center.

Neziroglu, F., & Yaryura-Tobias, J. A. (1991). *Over and over again.* Lexington, MA: Heath.

Schwartz, J. M. (1996). *Brainlock: Free yourself from obsessive–compulsive behavior.* New York: Regan Books.

Steketee, G., & White, K. (1990). *When once is not enough: Help for obsessive compulsives.* Oakland, CA: New Harbinger.

Obsessive–Compulsive Disorder Spectrum Disorders

Anders, J. L., & Jefferson, J. W. (1994). *Trichotillomania: A guide.* Madison, WI: Dean Foundation.

Phillips, K. A. (1996). *The broken mirror: Understanding and treating body dysmorphic disorder.* New York: Oxford University Press.

RECENT ACADEMICALLY ORIENTED BOOKS

Hollander, E. (1993). *Obsessive–compulsive related disorders.* Washington, DC: American Psychiatric Press.

Hollander, E., & Stein, D. J. (Eds.). (1997). *Obsessive–compulsive disorders: Diagnosis, etiology, and treatment.* New York: Dekker.

Jenike, M. A., Baer, L., & Minichiello, W. E. (1990). *Obsessive–compulsive disorders: Theory and management.* Chicago: Year Book Medical Publishers.

March, J., Frances, A., Carpenter, D., & Kahn, D. (Eds.). (1997). Treatment of obsessive compulsive disorder—Expert consensus series. *Journal of Clinical Psychiatry, 58*(Suppl. 4).

Rapoport, J. L. (1989). *Obsessive–compulsive disorder in children and adolescents.* Washington, DC: American Psychiatric Press.

Tortora Pato, M., & Zohar, J. (1991). *Current treatments of obsessive–compulsive disorder.* Washington, DC: American Psychiatric Press.

Yaryura, J. A., & Neziroglu, F. A. (1997). *Obsessive–compulsive disorder spectrum: Pathogenesis, diagnosis, and treatment.* Washington, DC: American Psychiatric Press.

Zohar, J., Insel, T. R., & Rasmussen, S. A. (1991). *The psychobiology of obsessive–compulsive disorder.* New York: Springer.

RECENT COGNITIVE-BEHAVIORAL TREATMENT GUIDES FOR PROFESSIONALS

Kozak, M. J., & Foa, E. B. (1997). *Mastery of your obsessive–compulsive disorder.* San Antonio, TX: Psychological Corporation. Therapist guide and client workbook available.

Kozak, M. J., & Foa, E. B. (1996). Obsessive–compulsive disorder. In V. B. Van Hasselt & M. Hersen (Eds.), *Sourcebook of psychological treatment manuals for adult disorders* (pp. 65–122). New York: Plenum.

March, J. S., & Mulle, K. (1998). *OCD in children and adolescents: A cognitive-behavioral treatment manual.* New York: Guilford Press.

Riggs, D. S., & Foa, E. B. (1993). Obsessive compulsive disorder. In D. H. Barlow (Ed.), *Clinical handbook of psychological disorders* (2nd ed., pp. 189–239). New York: Guilford Press.

Steketee, G. S. (1993). *Treatment of obsessive compulsive disorder.* New York: Guilford Press.

Turner, S. M., & Beidel, D. C. (1988). *Treating obsessive compulsive disorder.* New York: Pergamon Press.

RESOURCES ON THE INTERNET

Anxiety Disorders Association of America
www.adaa.org

Expert Consensus Treatment Guidelines for OCD
www.psychguides.com/eks_ocgl.htm

Guide to Diagnosis and Treatment of Tourette's Syndrome
www.mentalhealth.com/book/p40-gtor.html

Internet Mental Health: Obsessive–Compulsive Disorder
www.mentalhealth.com/dis/p20-an05.html

National Anxiety Foundation
www.lexington-on-line.com/naf.html

Obsessive–Compulsive Anonymous
members.aol.com/west24th/index.html

Obsessive–Compulsive Disorder
www.fairlite.com/ocd/

Obsessive–Compulsive Disorder
www.kidsource.com/kidsource/content/obsess.html#top

Obsessive–Compulsive Disorder Central
www.geocities.com/HotSprings/5403/index.html

The Obsessive–Compulsive Disorder Resource Center
www.ocdresource.com

Obsessive–Compulsive Foundation
pages.prodigy.com/alwillen/ocf.html

Poetry Written by Individuals with OCD
neuro-chief-e.mgh.harvard.edu/MIND/Poetry/OCDMenu.html

Scientific Papers
www.fairlite.com/ocd/abstracts/

OCD Newsgroup
alt.support.ocd

Tourette's Newsgroup
alt.support.tourette

Mailing List on OCD
Listserv@vm.marist.edu
Type "subscribe OCD-L <your name here>" in the body of your message
for example. . . . subscribe OCD-L John Smith

INDEX